FIFTH EDITION

Strategies for Teaching Students with Learning and Behavior Problems

Candace S. Bos
University of Texas–Austin

Sharon Vaughn
University of Texas–Austin

Allyn and Bacon

Boston   London   Toronto   Sydney   Tokyo   Singapore

To Bob and Jim and Jon

Executive Editor: *Virginia Lanigan*
Series Editorial Assistant: *Erin Liedel*
Marketing Manager: *Amy Cronin*
Editorial-Production Service: *Omegatype Typography, Inc.*
Composition Buyer: *Linda Cox*
Manufacturing Buyer: *Julie McNeill*
Cover Administrator: *Linda Knowles*
Photo Research: *Katharine S. Cook*

Library of Congress Cataloging-in-Publication Data

Bos, Candace S.
   Strategies for teaching students with learning and behavior problems / Candace S. Bos,
Sharon Vaughn.—5th ed.
      p.   cm.
   Includes bibliographical references and index.
   ISBN 0-205-34195-0 (alk. paper)
   1. Learning disabled children—Education—United States.   2. Problem
children—Education—United States.   3. Remedial teaching—United States.   I. Vaughn,
Sharon, 1952–   II. Title.

LC4705 .B67 2002
371.9–dc21

                                                                    2001022109

Printed in the United States of America
10   9   8   7   6   5   06   05   04   03

Photo credits: p. 1: Stone/Andy Sachs; p. 28, 68, 113, 169, 228, 279, 332, 458: Will Hart; p. 381: Robert
Harbison; p. 431: Bob Daemmrich/Stock, Boston; p. 499: Will Faller; p. 515: Robin Buckson/The Detroit News.

Contents

CHAPTER 5
Reading: Fluency and Comprehension   169

CHAPTER 6
Written Expression   228

CHAPTER 9
Socialization and Classroom Management   381

CHAPTER 10
Transition Planning and Life Skills/ Transition Education   431

Preface

While traveling by car on a typical Arizona scorcher between Phoenix and Tucson following a state Association for Children and Adults with Learning Disabilities meeting, we were discussing the content and assignments to the methods courses we teach at our respective universities. The topic inevitably drifted to what we would like to do better. Since both of us are responsible for preparing teachers and potential teachers to work effectively with students who have learning and behavior problems, we spend a considerable amount of time considering the content of our classes. We concluded that we would like the class and the textbook for the class to provide adequate background in procedures for teaching skill and content areas such as reading, math, oral and written expression, and social and study skills. We also would like our students to understand which methods are most effective with what types of students and why.

The first edition of this book was the result of that initial lengthy discussion, which focused on the ideal content that would prepare teachers to meet the needs of elementary and secondary students with learning and behavior problems. With each new edition, we continue to present fresh ideas and information, but always while keeping sight of our original purpose.

AUDIENCE AND PURPOSE

We have written this book for graduate and undergraduate students who are developing expertise in teaching students with learning and behavior problems. This book is also intended for professionals in the field, including special and general education teachers, school psychologists, speech/language specialists, and school administrators who are interested in learning more about working successfully with students who have learning and behavior problems.

The purpose of this book is to provide:

1. Information about general approaches to learning and teaching so the foundation for the methods and procedures for teaching all learners can be better understood.
2. Descriptions of methods and procedures that include sufficient detail so that teachers and other professionals can read about them and know how to use them.
3. Information regarding classroom and behavior management, consultation, and working with parents and professionals so that beginning teachers can develop a plan of action for the school year and experienced teachers can refine these skills.

ORGANIZATIONAL OVERVIEW

First we deal with foundational concepts. Chapter One describes the characteristics of the target population a range of alternative learning environments, the teaching–learning process. Features of effective instruction and strategies for evaluating and monitoring progress, including individual educational programs as reflected in the 1997 reauthorized Individuals with Disabilities Education Act (IDEA). Chapter Two presents approaches to learning and teaching: operant learning and applied behavior analysis, cognitive strategy instruction, sociocultural theory of cognitive development, and information processing and schema theories. These learning models provide the basis for the methods and strategies presented later in the book.

We then focus on learning and teaching in specific skill and content areas. The emphasis in Chapters Three through Ten is on methods and procedures for effectively teaching skills, strategies, and content to students with learning and behavior problems. Information is presented not only on how to teach but also on why and when to use different instructional approaches. Careful attention has been paid to emphasizing instructional approaches that have research-based evidence of their effectiveness with students who have learning and behavior problems.

Because of the extensive problems experienced in the area of literacy by special learners, Chapters Three through Six deal specifically with oral language, reading, and writing. These chapters are organized to provide background in the content areas and detailed descriptions of strategies for teaching specific skills and processes. Due to the increasing focus on study skills and content area learning (e.g., social studies, science, career/vocational education) at the upper-elementary and secondary levels, Chapter Seven deals with teaching content area subjects and teaching study skills, including time and notebook management, memorization and test-taking skills, listening and notetaking skills, and textbook usage skills. Chapter Eight deals with mathematics, covering such areas as measurement, time, verbal math problem solving, and computational skill development. Chapter Nine focuses on teaching social skills and behavior management as well as information related to social competence and difficulties including social alienation, suicide, eating disorders, and drug-related problems. Chapter Ten focuses on transition planning and life skills education, which is so important for students with learning and behavior problems.

Next, we focus on coordinating instruction, communicating with parents, and collaborating and co-

teaching with general education teachers and other professionals. Chapter Eleven discusses such issues as how to get started and scheduling. Strategies for effective inclusion and collaborating and coteaching with general classroom teachers are also discussed, since the majority of these students spend most of their school day in general education classes. Chapter Twelve focuses on effective communication and making and maintaining professional relationships with general classroom teachers, special education teachers, and specialists such as school psychologists, speech/language and occupational therapists, and school administrators. Parents, the most effective agents for change, and their special needs are also presented.

This edition reflects a major revision of the book with an emphasis on effective instruction, progress monitoring, technology, and diversity. For example, we have added a section on effective instruction in Chapter One and revised Chapter Two to highlight the use of explicit instruction and cognitive strategy instruction, two orientations to instruction that research has shown to be critical for the educational success of students with learning and behavior problems. Besides addressing progress monitoring in Chapter One, we have provided examples of how to use progress monitoring in each of the content chapters. We have incorporated technology into each chapter and feature a Tech Talk that demonstrates how technology can be integrated into instruction and management. Finally, we have emphasized information on second language acquisition in Chapter Three and added information and examples about students from culturally and linguistically diverse backgrounds throughout the book. We have also increased the emphasis on secondary-level students with learning and behavior problems by incorporating more information on how to teach higher-order thinking skills throughout the content chapters and by adding a new chapter on transition planning and life skill/transition education authored by Dr. James Patton. All chapters reflect the current guidelines from IDEA 1997.

Some of the greatest changes are reflected in the chapters on teaching reading. Chapter Four has been renamed Reading: Phonological Awareness, Alphabetic Principle, and Word Recognition. Sections have been added and the use of explicit instruction to teach early reading skills is emphasized based on the recent research syntheses in reading and with students who have learning/reading difficulties. In Chapter Five the section on fluency has been expanded as well as the use of cognitive strategy instruction to teach reading comprehension. Other significant revisions include:

— Chapter Three provides additional information and strategies for teaching English language learners.
— Chapter Six reflects the research on how students with learning and behavior problems can use writing to enhance learning across the curriculum.
— Chapter Seven reflects increased emphasis on using content enhancement tools to teach content information.
— Chapter Eight includes the revised National Council for Teaching Mathematics (NCTM) standards and an interpretation for students with disabilities.
— Chapter Nine incorporates the current research and practice on implementing positive behavior supports school-wide and within classrooms.
— Chapter Ten is entirely new and focuses on transition planning, including individualized transition plans (ITPs) and life skills/transition education for secondary-level students.
— Chapter Eleven provides many more practical ideas for collaborating and coteaching with general classroom teachers.
— Chapter Twelve provides strategies for how teachers can facilitate genuine and continued involvement of parents in their children's educational programs.

For you, the readers, we continue to use and add to the instructional features that assist in using this text, including:

— Chapter Outline
— Key Topics for Mastery
— Apply the Concepts
— Tech Talk
— Instructional Activities
— Summary
— Websites
— Think and Apply

We also have a new companion Website for this book at www.ablongman.com/bos5e that features chapter learning objectives, activities, Weblinks, and practice tests. We hope you find these features and the Website beneficial for your learning.

ACKNOWLEDGMENTS

Many people deserve a great deal more acknowledgment than their names appearing here will provide. We wish to acknowledge and thank the teachers whom we have written about in this book. The time we have spent in their classrooms–observing, discussing, and teaching–has afforded us the ability to write a book that is grounded in classroom experiences and practices. These teachers include Juan Caberra, Judy Cohen, Joan Downing, Mary Lou Duffy, Joyce Duryea, Jane Eddy, Louise Fournia, Joan Gervasi, Sally Gotch, Linda Jones, Sharon Kutok, Tom Lebasseur, Tiffany Royal, Marynell Schlegel, Mary Thalgott, and Nina Zaragoza.

We wish to acknowledge those individuals who reviewed the manuscripts of previous editions for Allyn and Bacon: Judy Englehard, Radford University; Anthony DeFeo, University of Arizona; Susan Munson, Duquesne University; Linda Patriarcha, Michigan State University; Sharon Raimondi, Buffalo State College; Katherine Sacca, Buffalo State College; Sandra Squires, University of Nebraska; Elizabeth Whitten, University of Illinois–Champaign; and Cynthia Wilson, University of Miami. Special thanks go to Carol Sue Englert, Michigan State University, and to Corrine Roth Smith, Syracuse University, for their expert comments.

We especially wish to acknowledge Lee Cross, University of Central Florida; Lynn M. Gelzheiser, University at Albany; Evie Gleckel, Keene State College; David Katims, University of Texas at San Antonio; and Esther Minskoff, James Madison University for their reviews of the fifth edition for Allyn and Bacon.

We also want to thank the students in our methods classes who field-tested the book and provided us with valuable ideas. Our appreciation and thanks go to Mary Alibrandi and Kwang Sun Blair, and special appreciation is extended to Alison Gould Boardman, Ae-hwa Kim, Kathy Haagenson, Pauline Havens, Carolyn Lee, and Kathy Madsen for their assistance in reviewing and synthesizing the literature. Special thanks to Deborah Rhein, Rhia Roberts, Lorri Johnson Santamaria, Jane Sinagub, Dheepa Sridhar, and Sandra Stroud, whose suggestions, editing, and revisions are included throughout the book. A special thanks to Krista Breyfogle, Patricia Foreman, Brenda Jacobson, Mary Kord, Tara Newell, Sandy Richards, and Tajel Shah for their assistance in preparing the manuscripts.

Special thanks also to our husbands, Bob and Jim, who wondered if we would ever come out from behind our word processors.

Most important of all, we would like to thank the teacher whose observations, research, and thinking has done more to guide our development and the field of special education than any other, Samuel A. Kirk.

Last, we want to thank each other. Many people start off coauthoring a book as friends—we still are. For this, we are grateful.

1

The Teaching– Learning Process

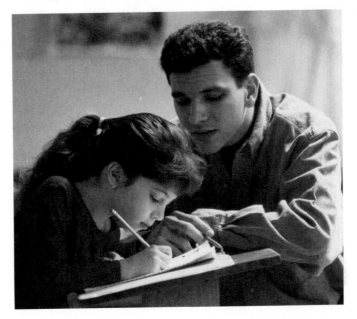

OUTLINE

KEY TOPICS FOR MASTERY

- *How to identify students with learning and behavior problems*
- *How to determine the severity of a student's learning and/or behavior problem*
- *How to distinguish between these concepts—"least-restrictive environment" and "mainstreaming"*
- *The teaching-learning process—the model for understanding and helping students with special needs upon which these authors' philosophy is based*
- *The importance of knowing your student—his/her knowledge, attitudes, academic levels, and learning strategies—in determining how to help him/her*
- *The importance of a teacher's self-knowledge; our beliefs and attitudes determine how we teach and profoundly affect how our students learn*
- *The instructional cycle—an effective model for developing, implementing, and evaluating a plan for instruction*
- *The IEP—Individualized Educational Program—a procedure, mandated by law, for setting annual goals and planning instruction for students receiving specific education services*
- *The features of effective instruction—assessing progress and designing instruction*
- *How to effectively evaluate student progress*

 BRIGHT IDEA

Turn to page 27 and read Think and Apply.

This book is about children and adolescents who have difficulty learning and interacting appropriately in school. If you saw these children in school you would not be able to identify them by how they look. You would, however, be able to identify them by what they do. What are these students like? Teachers describe them this way:

Servio has a very poor self-concept. He is extremely sensitive and gets upset at the least little thing. For example, yesterday he noticed that his red crayon was broken and he started to cry. When I told him he could have another red crayon, he continued to cry, saying that he wanted this red crayon fixed. He often says he can't do things, that he doesn't care, and that he

is bad. When he has problems at home he says he's going to be bad. He often says that he was punished at home for being bad and he's going to be bad today at school. He used to throw things at school but he doesn't do that anymore. He doesn't have any friends in the class and most of the other students don't want him around them.

Dana has a great deal of difficulty with her work. She appears to have trouble remembering. Well, not always. Sometimes she remembers how to read a word; other days she looks at the same word and it's like she has to scan all of the information in her head to try to locate the name of the word. I know she is trying, but it is very frustrating because her progress is so slow. She is also very easily distracted. Even when the instructional assistant is working with her alone she will look up and stop working at the littlest things. Something like the air conditioning going on and off will distract her from her work. I know she is bright enough, but she seems to have serious problems learning.

Tina is more work for me than the rest of my class put together. She has both academic problems and behavior problems. For example, after I have explained an assignment to the class, Tina always asks me several questions about the assignment. It's like I have to do everything twice, once for the class and then again for Tina. She has a terrible time with reading. She reads so slowly and she often reads the wrong word. For example, she will say carrot *for* circus *and* monster *for* mister. *She often doesn't know what she's read after she's finished reading it. Also, she can never sit still. She is always moving around the room, sharpening her pencil, getting a book, looking out the window. It is hard for her to do the same thing for more than a few minutes. She's always "bugging" the other students. She's not really a bad kid, it's just that she is always doing something she's not supposed to be doing, and she takes a lot of my time.*

The purpose of this book is to acquaint you with the teaching skills and strategies necessary to understand and teach students like Servio, Dana, and Tina. This chapter provides background information on students with learning and behavior problems and an overview of the teaching-learning process.

WHAT ARE THE CHARACTERISTICS OF STUDENTS WITH LEARNING AND BEHAVIOR PROBLEMS?

Most professionals are able to recognize with little difficulty those students with learning and behavior problems. They are students who call attention to themselves in the classroom because they have difficulty learning and interacting appropriately. Students with learning and/or behavior problems manifest one or more of the following behaviors:

— *Poor academic performance.* Students often display significant problems in one or more academic areas such as spelling, reading, and mathematics.
— *Attention problems.* Many students seem to have difficulty working for extended periods of time on a task. They may have trouble focusing on the teacher's directions. These students are often described by teachers as being easily distracted.
— *Hyperactivity.* Some students are overactive and have a difficult time staying in their seats and completing assigned tasks. They move from task to task, often from location to location in the classroom. They can be working on an assignment and the least little noise will distract them.
— *Memory.* Many students have a hard time remembering what they were taught. Often their difficulty remembering is associated with symbols such as letters and numbers. These students may remember something one day but not the next.
— *Poor language abilities.* Many students have language difficulties that are manifested in a number of ways. As toddlers, these students may have taken longer in learning to talk. Often these language problems can be corrected through speech therapy. Many also have difficulty developing phonological awareness skills (Torgesen, Wagner, and Rashotte, 1997). Students may have difficulty with vocabulary, understanding the concept, using language to adequately express themselves, or producing correct sounds.
— *Aggressive behavior.* Some students are physically or verbally assaultive. They may hit, kick, get into fights, and/or verbally threaten or insult others. These children are easily upset and cope with being upset by acting out.
— *Withdrawn behavior.* Some students seldom interact with others. Unlike shy students, who may have one or two friends, these students are real loners who avoid involvement with others.

— *Bizarre behavior.* Some students display very unusual patterns of behavior. They may stare for long periods of time at objects they hold in the light, they may sit and rock, or they may display aggressive behaviors at times and withdrawn behaviors at other times.

Students with learning and/or behavior problems often exhibit more than one of these behaviors. Yet some students exhibit these behaviors and are not identified as having learning and behavior problems. There are other factors teachers consider when determining how serious a learning and behavior problem is.

WHAT FACTORS SHOULD BE CONSIDERED WHEN DETERMINING HOW SERIOUS A LEARNING OR BEHAVIOR PROBLEM IS?

Fifteen to 25 percent of all students have some type of learning or behavior problem. Students with learning disabilities are five times more prevalent than those with behavior disorders. There are several factors to consider when you are determining how serious the problem is.

1. *Persistence of the problem.* Sometimes a student has a learning or behavior problem for a short period of time, perhaps while there is some type of crisis in the family, and then it disappears. These behaviors and feeling states are not considered problems if they occur occasionally. Other students display persistent learning and behavior problems throughout their schooling experience. These persistent learning and behavior problems have more serious consequences for the student.

2. *Severity of the problem.* Is the student's learning or behavior problem mild, moderate, or severe? Is the student performing slightly below or significantly below what would be expected of him or her? Is the behavior slightly different or substantially different from the student's peers?

3. *Speed of progress.* Does the student appear to be making steady progress in the classroom despite the learning and behavior problem? We do not expect all students to learn at the same rate. In fact, in an average fourth-grade classroom the range of performance varies from second-grade level to seventh-grade level.

4. *Motivation.* Is the student interested in learning? Does the student persist at tasks and attempt to learn? Does the student initiate and complete tasks without continual praise and encouragement?

5. *Parental response.* How do the parents feel about their child's academic and/or behavioral progress? How do they think it compares with the child's progress in the past? Are they concerned about how their child's abilities compare with other children the same age? How have siblings performed in school?

6. *Other teachers' responses.* How did the student perform in previous classes? What do previous or other teachers say about learning style, academic abilities, and behavior?

7. *Relationship with the teacher.* What type of relationship does the student have with his or her present teacher? Sometimes there is a poor interpersonal match between the student and the teacher that may interfere with the student's academic performance and/or behavior.

8. *Instructional modifications and style.* What attempts has the present teacher made to modify the student's academic and/or behavioral program? Does the student seem responsive to attempts at intervention? If the student is not performing well in a traditional reading program, has the teacher tried other instructional approaches to reading? Has the student had opportunities to work with different students in the class? If the problem is behavior, what type of behavior change programs have been implemented? Are any successful?

   What kind of match is there between the student and the classroom setting? Some children function best in a highly structured classroom where the rules, expectations, and assignments are very clearly stated. Other children function better in a learning environment where there is more flexibility.

9. *Adequate instruction.* Has the student had adequate exposure to the material and time to learn? Some students have little experience with school learning situations before coming to school. Other students have multiple experiences, including preschool programs that teach letters and letter sounds. Students who have less exposure to school learning situations, or whose parents provide few schoollike learning experiences, may need more time and exposure to the learning environment before gains are made. Determine what prerequisite skills are missing and how they can be acquired.

10. *Behavior-age discrepancy.* Does the student display problems that are unusual or deviant for the student's age? For example, whining and withdrawing to another room is demonstrated by many preschoolers, but few children over grade 2.

11. *Other factors.* Are there other factors that may be contributing to the student's learning and/or behavior problems? For example, how closely do the student's background experiences, culture, and language match those of the teacher and other students in the class?

Are there any health-related factors that may be interfering with the student's learning or behavior?

Have the student's vision and hearing been adequately assessed to determine whether they may be affecting the student's learning or behavior?

Considering these factors should help you identify how serious the problem is.

WHAT LEARNING AND EDUCATIONAL ENVIRONMENTS ARE AVAILABLE FOR STUDENTS WITH LEARNING AND BEHAVIOR PROBLEMS?

Most students with learning and behavior problems receive their educational program in the regular classroom. Students whose learning and behavior problems are so severe that they warrant special assistance may be involved in a range of support services. These support services include reading or math support, counseling, individualized instruction with a teaching assistant, and special education.

PL 94–142, reauthorized as the Individuals with Disabilities Education Act (IDEA), assures that a continuum of placements is available for students. This continuum is conceptualized from the least to the most restrictive. *Restrictive,* in an educational sense, refers to the extent to which the student is educated with nondisabled peers. A more restrictive setting is one in which the student spends no part of his or her educational program with nondisabled peers. In a less restrictive setting, the student may spend part of his or her educational day with nondisabled peers. PL 94–142 mandates that all students should be educated in the least-restrictive educational system possible.

INCLUDING SPECIAL EDUCATION STUDENTS

When special education students are included in the general education classroom their specialized services are provided to them either within the general education class or through pull-out for special services.

The decision to include a special education student is made by an Individual Educational Planning (IEP) and placement committee. This committee is typically made up of one or both of the child's parents, the special education teacher, relevant professionals such as the school psychologist, and the administrator who supervises the special education program in which the student participates. At the recommendation of the special education and general education teachers and the professionals who evaluate the student's progress, the committee collectively decides whether the student's social and educational needs would best be met in the regular classroom.

Most students with emotional and learning disabilities spend at least some of their school day in regular classrooms with their nondisabled peers.

Almost 2.5 million students with disabilities, or 45 percent of the special education population, received instruction in general education settings during the 1994–1995 school year (Special Education Report, 1997).

Although the concept of mainstreaming was not specifically mandated in IDEA a related concept, *least-restrictive environment* (LRE), was embraced by the law. With the emphasis on moving even more students with special needs into full-time placement in the regular classroom with the special education teacher serving as a consultant/collaborator to the classroom teacher, the emphasis on mainstreaming and consultation/collaborative models has grown (e.g., January 1988 issue of *Journal of Learning Disabilities,* Fall 1988 issue of *Learning Disabilities Focus,* April 1990 issue of *Exceptional Children,* and November/December issue of *Remedial and Special Education*).

The language used in the latest reauthorization of IDEA (1997) is even stronger in its mandate to provide greater access to the general education curriculum for students with disabilities.

There are several reasons why inclusion is important for students with learning and behavior problems. First, the research has not clearly demonstrated either the academic or social benefits of placing students in segregated special education classrooms in comparison to regular classrooms. Second, students are likely to be viewed as more socially and academically acceptable when they remain in the regular classroom. Third, court decisions have encouraged placement of students with learning disabilities in the regular classroom to the extent possible (Gottlieb, Alter, and Gottlieb, 1983; Hallahan, Keller, McKinney, Lloyd, and Bryan, 1988; McKinney and Hocutt, 1988; Prillaman, 1981; Schultz and Turnbull, 1984).

The Realities of Inclusion

A series of research studies conducted in a large Southeastern school district suggests that inclusion may not always work as well as was intended by the law, or as was envisioned by the families of special education students and by the schools that serve them (McIntosh et al., 1993; Schumm and Vaughn, 1991; Schumm and Vaughn, 1992; Schumm et al., 1995; Vaughn and Schumm, 1994).

These studies suggest that the problem is many-faceted. First, collaboration between the special education and regular education teachers is insufficient to ensure that the student with special needs receives appropriate services. Second, classroom teachers do not specifically plan for students with special needs; the heterogeneous makeup of the student population in most classrooms makes specific planning for students with special needs an unrealistic expectation. The typical and persistent focus of the general education teacher is on the needs of the class, not on those of the individual (Fuchs et al., 1995).

Communication Gap Between Special and Regular Education Teachers

Lawmakers intended for special education students who are mainstreamed to receive accommodations for their learning and/or emotional needs within the regular classroom. The special education teacher, as consultant/collaborator to the regular classroom teacher, is to help the regular education teacher become familiar with the mainstreamed student's IEP, and then to help that teacher plan and, in some cases, deliver appropriate instruction. The regular classroom teacher has responsibility for planning and delivering the instruction or intervention the student needs.

Most secondary level (middle and high school) classroom teachers who participated in these research studies stated that they had not used IEPs or psychological reports to guide their planning for mainstreamed special education students. They had, however, gathered information from the parents and former teachers of students with special needs. Some teachers said they had very little contact with the special education teacher who monitored their students with special needs and that they were not aware the student had an IEP. A few teachers had no contact with a special education teacher and were unaware that they had a student with special needs in their class. In such cases, there was clearly a lack of communication between the special education teacher responsible for monitoring the progress of the students with special needs and the regular classroom teacher.

MAINSTREAMING
AND INCLUSION

The least restrictive environment (LRE) is required by law; however, LRE does not mean that every student must be mainstreamed. LRE refers to the level of services that is most appropriate for the student while providing the most integration with nondisabled students. Sometimes, placement in a self-contained classroom for students with disabilities is the LRE. Mainstreaming, the placement of students with disabilities from part-time to full-time in general education classes, is not required by law but can provide one way for achieving the LRE. Mainstreaming includes accommodations and support as part of a shared responsibility on the part of all educators in the school toward providing an appropriate education for the student with disabilities. Mainstreaming is a means for providing students with disabilities educational services in the general education classroom to the extent it is appropriate to meet their needs.

What is inclusion and how does it differ from mainstreaming? *Inclusion* refers to the full-time integration of students with disabilities in general education classrooms and often in their neighborhood schools. *Inclusion* and *mainstreaming* are often used interchangeably; however, there are differences. Advocates of full-inclusion support the notion that all students with disabilities, regardless of their special needs, should be placed full-time in general education settings all of the time (Stainback and Stainback, 1992.) Mainstreaming allows the opportunity for students with special needs to receive part of their services from a special educator in a setting other than the regular classroom. Inclusion advocates provide no options for pull-out services, because students with disabilities would not then be educated entirely in the same setting as students without disabilities.

At issue is the extent to which a continuum of services is provided. Advocates of full-inclusion are concerned that by maintaining a continuum of services we provide too easy an option for students with disabilities to be placed outside the general education classroom. Debate continues over the extent to which full-inclusion should be required for all students with disabilities (Fuchs and Fuchs, 1994). Of particular concern for students with learning disabilities is the extent to which their educational and social needs can be adequately met in the general education classroom (Vaughn and Schumm, 1995). Parents and advocates for individuals with learning disabilities are aware that before passage of IDEA there were few supports for their children/students and that the general education classroom did not adequately meet their needs. They are concerned that full-inclusion may be a return to the conditions that existed prior to IDEA.

There are many areas of agreement. All advocates want students with disabilities to be educated in general education classrooms to the extent possible. The issues relate to the type and placement of support services and the extent to which students with disabilities make adequate progress in general education settings without pull-out support. Figure 1.1 provides a description of the issues related to inclusion.

DEVELOPING AN
INDIVIDUALIZED
EDUCATION PROGRAM

For students who have been identified as requiring special education services (including students with learning or emotional disabilities), procedures for setting goals and planning instruction have been designated by law. IDEA requires that an individualized education program (IEP) be developed for each student with special educational needs. The multidisciplinary team develops and implements the IEP. The multidisciplinary team provides two major functions: (a) to determine whether a student has a disability and meets the eligibility criteria for special education, and (b) to develop the IEP, which provides the foundation for establishing the student's specialized program.

Who are the members of the multidisciplinary team? Members include a representative of the local education agency, the student's parents or guardians, the special education teacher, and at least one general education teacher if the student is participating or is likely to participate in the general education environment.

■ **FIGURE 1.1** *Arguments for Full-Inclusion and Mainstreaming the Continuum of Services*

Arguments for Full-Inclusion

- Students with disabilities should be educated in general education classes all of the time.
- Students with disabilities should not be pulled out of the general education classroom to receive specialized education.
- Benefits of placing students with disabilities in specialized classes, either for their academic or social growth, have not been demonstrated.
- Comprehensive, professional development that prepares teachers to meet the educational and social needs of all students is required.
- All students with disabilities have the right to education in the most normalized setting, the general education classroom.

Arguments for Maintaining the Continuum of Services

- Students with disabilities should be educated in general education classes to the extent it meets their educational and behavioral needs.
- Some students with disabilities need to have their educational needs met outside of the general education classroom for part or all of the school day. A continuum of services to meet the needs of students with disabilities is required.
- Benefits and pitfalls of full-inclusion models for all students with disabilities have not been empirically documented.
- General education teachers are inadequately prepared to meet the specialized needs of all students with disabilities.
- Inclusion is a philosophy, not a place; students have the right to receive the appropriate educational services to meet their learning needs in the site that is most suitable to do so.

Source: S. Vaughn, C. Bos, and J. S. Schumm, *Teaching Mainstreamed, Diverse, and At-Risk Students in the General Education Classroom* (Boston: Allyn and Bacon, 1997), p. 30. Reprinted with permission of the publisher.

What should be included in the IEP? According to Section 300.347 of the law, as of July 1, 1998, the IEP must include:

1. The student's current levels of educational performance, including how the student's disability affects the student's involvement and progress in general education settings.
2. Measurable annual goals, including benchmarks or short-term objectives to enable the student to participate in and progress in the general education classroom, and meet the student's educational needs resulting from the disability.
3. Special education and related services and supplementary aids and services to be provided to the student, and a statement of the program modifications or supports for school personnel that will be provided for the student.
4. The extent to which the student will not participate in general education classes.
5. A statement indicating whether the student will participate in state or district-wide assessments, and outlining any modifications and accommodations to be provided during testing. If student will not participate in state or district assessments, an explanation of why the student will not participate in these assessments and how the student will be assessed.
6. When will services begin, frequency, location, and duration of services and modifications.
7. How will progress toward annual goals be measured and how will the parents be regularly informed regarding progress toward annual goals and whether progress is sufficient to enable the student to meet the goals by the end of the year.
8. At least by the age of 14, a transition plan, and by age 16 transition services needed.
9. A list of the committee members present.
10. Signatures of appropriate persons, including parents and teachers.

A major part of the IEP includes the annual goals and short-term objectives or benchmarks. The goals of an IEP usually cover the entire school year; short-term objectives usually cover a six- to nine-week period. Completion of a related set of the short-term objectives or benchmarks should lead to the accomplishment of the annual goals developed by the multidisciplinary team. The written statements of annual goals must meet certain requirements. These include (Gibb and Dyches, 2000):

1. It must be measurable.
2. It must tell what the student can reasonably achieve in a year.
3. It must relate to helping the student be successful in general education settings and/or address other educational needs ensuing from the disability.
4. It must include benchmarks or short-term objectives.

Short-term objectives or benchmarks must also meet three conditions (Gibb and Dyches, 2000):

1. It describes the behavior in an observable, measurable way. (Luis will add two-digit numbers).
2. It describes the circumstances under which the behavior will take place. (given manipulatives and peer-assistance).
3. It describes the criterion for mastery. (with 85% accuracy).

In addition to the areas mentioned above, other relevant factors such as student motivation, prior knowledge, previous learning experiences, the student's strategies for learning, and the teacher's attitudes and teaching style are generally taken into consideration when developing an individualized education program. The IEP must be reviewed at least on an annual basis. Furthermore, the IEP must be revised to address any lack of expected progress toward the annual goals and in general education settings, the results of any re-evaluations, and relevant information provided by the parents. Figure 1.2 presents a sample IEP completed for John, a fifth grader with learning disabilities.

Parent Involvement

The people who formulated IDEA considered that parents need to be actively involved in their child's education. The IEP serves as a safeguard not only for students but for parents, families, and the education team. All reasonable attempts to assure the participation of parents in the IEP should be taken. This includes:

1. Schedule the meetings at times that are convenient for parents by checking with them in advance to determine a suitable date, time, and location.
2. Notify parents well in advance of the meeting. The purpose, time, and location of the meeting and the persons who will be in attendance should be included in the notice. Parents should be involved in the decision about whether the student will attend.
3. If neither parent chooses to attend after reasonable efforts to accommodate their schedules have been attempted, the school should use other methods to involve parents, including telephone calls or home visits.
4. If meeting is held without a parent in attendance, the school must document its attempts to involve the parent.
5. Parent involvement in the development of the IEP should be documented, and parents should receive a copy of the IEP.

Remember, often too much emphasis is placed on compliance rather than on genuine communication (Harry, Allen, and McLaughlin, 1995). Consider the following (Dettmer et al., 1993):

— Educators and parents are working as a team for a common goal, the student's success.
— Pay attention to when and why defensive behavior arises. Put your feelings aside and help others, including the parents, build positive relationships. If the team is unable to act positively, postpone interactions until the defensiveness can be handled.
— Remember that the values of parents are not what is being addressed, only the needs and interests of parents and their child. Consider what the problem is, not who the person is.

■ **FIGURE 1.2** *Individualized Education Program Form*

Individualized Education Program

I. Demographic Information

Last First M.I.			Date
Smith, John E.			May 12, 2001

Student I.D.	Address	Home Phone	Work Phone
2211100	23 Lakeview St. Collier, MN 32346	(459)555–5555	(459)555–5000

Date of Birth	Grade Level Home School	Program Eligibility
03/02/87	5 Lakeview Elementary	Learning Disabilities

Reason for Conference: ❑ Staffing   ☑ Review

II. Conference

Parent Notification

Attempt #1:	Attempt #2:	Attempt #3:
Letter: 3–02–01	Phone call: 3–13–01	Notice sent home with student: 3–22–01

Parent Response: *Will attend as per phone call on 3–13–01*

III. Present Levels of Educational Performance

John is a 5th grade students whose disability inhibits his ability to read required material. John can read 35/100 in two minutes from a 4.0 grade level paragraph and 45/100 in two minutes from a 3.0 grade level paragraph. John can answer 8/10 literal questions and 4/10 inference questions from a 4.0 grade level passage read to him.

IV. Annual Goals and Short-Term Benchmarks

1. *John will increase reading fluency at the 4.0 grade level.*
   John will read orally a passage at the 4.0 grade level in 2 minutes with 50 or more words correct.
   John will use correct intonation and prosody when reading orally a passage at the 4.0 grade level 50% of the time.
2. *John will improve the percentage of accuracy when responding to literal and inferential questions.*
   John will answer literal questions from a 4.0 grade level passage read to him with 75% accuracy.
   John will answer inferential questions from a 4.0 grade level passage read to him with 90–100% accuracy.

Describe the extent to which the student will not participate in general education settings and explain why the student cannot be placed in general education settings.

John will not participate in general education settings for language arts, science, and social studies instruction. John requires close supervision when completing tasks, high levels of assistance, and intensive, systematic instruction.

V. Related Services

Type of Service, Aid or Modification			Location	Time per day/week
Assistive Technology:	❑ Yes	☑ No		
Adaptive PE:	❑ Yes	☑ No		
Audiology Services:	❑ Yes	☑ No		
Counseling:	❑ Yes	☑ No		
Interpreter:	❑ Yes	☑ No		
Medical Services:	❑ Yes	☑ No		
Occupational Therapy:	❑ Yes	☑ No		
Orientation/Mobility:	❑ Yes	☑ No		
Physical Therapy:	❑ Yes	☑ No		
Psychological Services:	❑ Yes	☑ No		
Special Transportation:	❑ Yes	☑ No		
Speech/lang. Therapy:	☑ Yes	❑ No	*Self-contained class, 30 min./wk*	

VI. Assessment Participation

Will the student participate in state and district assessments: ☑ Yes   ❑ No
If yes, what accommodations or modifications will be provided?
❑ None   ☑ Flexible Setting   ❑ Flexible Presentation   ☑ Flexible Scheduling
❑ Flexible Responding

If no, indicate why state and district assessments are inappropriate:

VII. Transition Planning/Statement

☑ Under 14: Transition planning not needed.

❑ 14–15 years old: Statement of transition services needed that focuses on student's course of study.

❑ 16 years old: Outcome statement that describes a direction and plan for the student's post-high school years from the perspective of student, parent, and team members.

_____

_____

_____

_____

_____

(continued)

FIGURE 1.2 *Continued*

VIII. Scheduled Report to Parents/Guardians
John's parents will be informed of progress toward his annual goals via parent/teacher conferences and interim report cards (4 times per year). Parents will be notified of goals that have been met and the rate of progress toward meeting all of the annual goals.

IX. Initiation/Duration Dates
Special education and related services will initiate <u>*September 2001*</u>, through <u>*June 2002*</u>.
(MM/YY)   (MM/YY)

IX. Persons Attending Conference

Signature	Position	Date
Mary Smith	*Parent*	*May 12, 2001*
Jonathan Smith	*Parent*	*May 12, 2001*
Laura Jones	*Special Education Teacher*	*May 12, 2001*
Rafael González	*General Education Teacher*	*May 12, 2001*
Larry Brick	*LEA Representative*	*May 12, 2001*
Harrison Washington	*School Psychologist*	*May 12, 2001*
John Smith	*Student*	*May 12, 2001*

- Do not waste time wishing that the people would be different. Accept people as they are. Respect parents' rights to have their own values and opinions.
- Tell yourself that most parents are doing the best that they can under the circumstances of their life. People do not decide to be poor parents.

Chapter Twelve describes strategies you can use for actively involving parents in their child's education, including planning and implementing programs.

Student Involvement

By law, students need to attend the IEP meetings only if appropriate. In practice many students with learning and emotional disabilities do not attend these meetings, even when the students are in secondary-level settings. Yet involving students in this decision-making process helps them develop a commitment to learning and a sense of responsibility and control over the decisions made regarding their learning.

Why do many students not attend the conference? In interviewing junior high students with learning disabilities and their parents, two major reasons are evident (Van Reusen and Bos, 1990). First, frequently parents are not aware that students can attend. Second, even when students are invited to attend, they choose not to because they feel that they do not know what to say or do, and they are afraid that the major topic of discussion will be "how bad they are doing."

To alleviate these two concerns, Van Reusen and his colleagues developed a self-advocacy strategy (I PLAN) that is designed to inform students and

TECH TALK 1.1 ▬▬▬▬▬▬▬▬▬▬▬▬▬▬▬▬▬▬▬▬▬▬▬▬▬▬▬

USING COMPUTERS TO ASSIST IN IEP MANAGEMENT

Individualized Education Programs (IEPs) can be developed and tracked by multidisciplinary teams (MT) as they determine the best methods of treatment for an individual child. But this process can be repetitive, time-consuming, and tedious if the MT is using a traditional paper document system. The process of developing an IEP can be facilitated by the use of computer software such as *InfoHandler* or *IEP Track 2 version 2.6* (information available online at http://www.ieptrack.com/), which can also produce IEP

reports and transition plans. Some programs, such as *InfoHandler* and *Class Plus* (information available online at http://www.classplus.com/classplus), are supported by both Macintosh and IBM-compatible computers. An IEP can even be written and maintained on the Internet through, for example, a service provided by Software Solutions Inc. (information available online at http://www.softwaresolutions. com/), enabling ease of access by parents, teachers, and administrators via the Internet.

Source: InfoHandler Software by InfoHandler.com.

prepare them to participate in educational planning or transition planning conferences (Van Reusen, Bos, Deshler, and Schumaker, 1994). Teachers can teach students this strategy in about five to six hours over a one- to two-week period. We have found that junior high and high school students with learning disabilities who learn this strategy provide more information during IEP conferences than students who are only told about the IEP conference but not taught the strategy (Bos and Van Reusen, 1986; Van

Reusen and Bos, 1990). Apply the Concept 1.1 describes this strategy and how to teach it.

▬▬▬▬▬▬▬▬▬▬▬▬▬▬▬▬

HOW DO TEACHERS TEACH STUDENTS WITH LEARNING AND BEHAVIOR PROBLEMS?

Instruction for students like Servio, Dana, and Tina needs to be carefully orchestrated to take into account

APPLY THE CONCEPT 1.1

I PLAN: AN EDUCATIONAL PLANNING STRATEGY

Purpose: To provide students with the skills and knowledge to participate effectively in an educational planning or transition planning conference.

Target Audience: The strategy can be taught to students in upper elementary, secondary, or post-secondary settings who will be participating in an educational planning or transition planning conference. This could include an IEP conference as well as other educational planning conferences.

Type of Instruction: Small group to large group instruction, usually three to ten students.

Time: Five to six hours of instruction.

Description of Strategy: The strategy the students learn consists of five steps. They complete the first step prior to the conference and use the remaining steps during the conference. The steps are:

Step 1:   Inventory your
                  learning strengths
                  learning weaknesses
                  goals and interests
                  choices for learning
Step 2:   Provide your inventory information
Step 3:   Listen and respond
Step 4:   Ask questions
Step 5:   Name your goals

To help the students remember the steps in the strategy, the acronym *I PLAN* can be made from the first letter in each step.

The teacher and students participate in activities that assist the students in creating an Inventory Sheet. This sheet lists their learning strengths, learning weaknesses to improve, learning and career goals and interests, and ways they learn best (e.g., size of group, type of activity, type of test).

The students are also taught to use *SHARE* behaviors to help with effective communication during the conference. They are:

Sit up straight
Have a pleasant tone of voice
Activate your thinking
       Tell yourself to pay attention
       Tell yourself to participate
       Tell yourself to compare ideas
Relax
       Don't look uptight
       Tell yourself to stay calm
Engage in eye communication

Teaching the Strategy: The strategy is taught by using the acquisition and generalization steps used to teach motivation strategies. Motivation strategies are techniques and procedures that involve the learner in the learning process, and they are used to increase the students' commitment to learn. They represent processes that learners can acquire and use to increase their interest and efforts in learning and to gain greater control over their own learning progress (Van Reusen, Bos, Deshler, and Schumaker, 1987). The strategies are based on research in motivation and are adapted from the learning strategies model (Deshler, Ellis, and Lenz, 1996).

The teacher uses seven steps to teach the strategy:

Step 1:   Orient and Obtain Commitment
Step 2:   Describe
Step 3:   Model and Prepare
Step 4:   Verbal Rehearsal
Step 5:   Group Practice and Feedback
Step 6:   Individual Practice and Feedback
Step 7:   Generalization

During the first step, the teacher and students discuss how involvement in education planning conferences will empower students by giving them more control over what they are learning and their plans for the future. The importance and purpose of these conferences are discussed and the teacher obtains the students' commitment to learn the I PLAN strategy.

During the second step, *Describe,* the strategy is described to the students and the students begin to memorize the steps in the strategy and the SHARE behaviors.

During the third step, *Model and Prepare,* the students work with the teacher to prepare their Inventory Sheets. Through modeling and discussion, they systematically develop lists of learning strengths and weaknesses in the areas of reading, math, writing, study skills, social skills, and vocational skills. For transition planning conferences the students develop inventories that also focus on independent living skills, career and employment skills, and community involvement. Based on these same areas and their current classes, they also identify weaknesses to improve. They also inventory their learning and career goals and interests and their preference for learning. In addition to preparing the Inventory Sheet, the teacher models the rest of the steps in the strategy (PLAN) and the SHARE behaviors.

During the fourth step, *Verbal Rehearsal,* students learn the steps in the I PLAN strategy and the SHARE behavior to an automatic level.

During the fifth step, *Group Practice and Feedback,* students review the steps in the strategy and practice using the strategy by providing feedback to each other during a simulated planning conference.

During the sixth step, *Individual Practice and Feedback,* students practice the strategy with the teacher during a simulated conference.

During the seventh step, *Generalization,* students use the steps in the strategy during the scheduled educational planning or transition planning conference. Once the strategy has been taught, it can be reviewed for each additional educational planning conference scheduled and the Inventory Sheet can be updated or redeveloped.

A teaching manual has been developed that explicitly describes how to teach the I PLAN strategy (Van Reusen, Bos, Deshler, and Schumaker, 1994).

---

the interactive nature of the *teaching–learning process.* The teaching–learning process is a model of teaching and learning that takes into account the complexity of the learning environment or context, the beliefs and characteristics of the learner and teacher, and the instructional cycle the teacher orchestrates to facilitate learning. It is based on notions of *individual programming.* Although students may be instructed in groups, the teacher studies and plans for each student's needs, realizing that students have both common and unique needs. The teaching-learning process is represented in Figure 1.3. It is the foundation upon which the rest of this book rests in that it presents a reflective, problem-solving approach to teaching students with learning and behavior problems. Let us look first at the key players in this process—the learner and the teacher.

The Learner

The learner brings to school beliefs and attitudes about learning and the world in which he or she lives, a variety of skills and knowledge on which to build,

and strategies to assist in the learning process. In a way, we are speaking of the *characteristics of the learner.* As teachers, we often seem most concerned about the *skill level* of students. Our assessment process focuses on determining at what level the student is functioning and what skills the student can and cannot perform. However, *knowledge, attitudes,* and *strategic learning* can also provide us with a wealth of information concerning the learner and may prove to be the critical features when determining how to facilitate learning.

If the learner has little knowledge of the topic being studied, then you, the teacher, can assist the student by providing activities that build background knowledge and help the student link this new knowledge to current knowledge.

Skills and knowledge not only play an important role in learning, but they also influence the learner's attitudes about learning and the world. Randy and Tamara illustrate this point. In fifth grade, Randy was determined to learn how to read, although at the time he was struggling with beginning reading books. He worked all year on his reading and at the end of the

■ **FIGURE 1.3** *The Teaching–Learning Process*

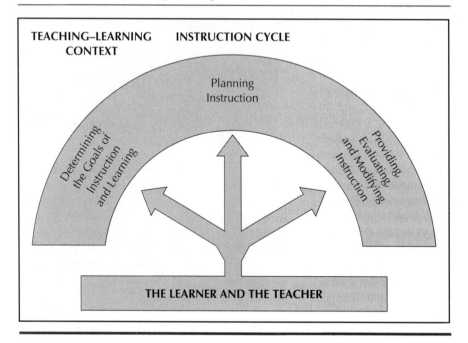

year he had grown in his reading skill by about one grade level. Still, he carried with him the attitude that reading was important and that he should continue to struggle with a process that for him was quite difficult. Tamara, on the other hand, was a sixth grader who was reading at about the third-grade level. For her, learning to read was a much easier process, yet she finished the year making only marginal gains. Why? She believed that reading simply was not necessary for her life and that her future goal, being a mother, just didn't require her to be a good reader. These students' attitudes influenced their rate of learning.

A student's strategies for learning also affect the teaching–learning process. When you are told to read a chapter in a textbook and study for a test, what strategies do you employ? Do you preview the chapter before reading? Do you ask questions as you read to check your comprehension? Do you underline or take notes? Do you review your notes before the test, rehearsing the important points? These are all strategies that make you a more effective student.

The Teacher

The second player in the teaching–learning process is you, the teacher. Just like the student, you bring to the learning situation your teaching knowledge and skills, your beliefs and attitudes about teaching, learning, and the world, and your strategies for teaching. One purpose of this chapter is to heighten your awareness of your beliefs and attitudes about teaching.

As you read this section, reflect on your beliefs and attitudes about teaching, learning, and students who experience learning and behavior problems. What is the nature of learning and what is your role as a teacher?

Learning can be perceived as changes in behavior that result in a student demonstrating new knowledge and skills. The role of the teacher is that of an educational technician who engineers or arranges the environment so that the probability of learning is increased. This is accomplished by providing the student with the cues to trigger learning and the rewards for learning. The student is the receiver of the new knowledge and skills, whereas the teacher imparts them or arranges the context so that they are imparted by others. An effective teacher is one who conveys knowledge and skills in a systematic, explicit manner. This perception of learning and teaching is probably best reflected in behavior theory and cognitive behavior modification, both of which are discussed in Chapter Two. It is also reflected in instructional strategies and materials that are based on systematic ordering and teaching of skills. You will find that some of the strategies and materials presented in the content chapters reflect this perspective on learning and teaching.

Learning can also be perceived as a dynamic process in which the student plays an active role, constantly interacting with the environment and people around him or her. Not only do the student's notions, ideas, and skills change in the learning process but so does the environment in which the learning takes place. Thus, learning is not merely the accumulation of knowledge and skills but it is the active construction and transformation of ideas based on observations and experiences. This perception of learning is represented in information processing and schema theories, which are presented in Chapter Two. The teacher, serving as a facilitator for learning, creates an environment in which the students can take risks and develop flexible learning and thinking strategies as they acquire skills and knowledge. You will also find this perspective represented in the content chapters, Chapters Three through Ten.

Just as the *characteristics of the learner* affect the teaching–learning process, so will your *beliefs and attitudes* as a teacher. And since the teaching–learning process is dynamic and interactive in nature, your beliefs and attitudes will change, depending on the needs of the learner. For example, Ms. Kranowski, a special education teacher who works with students who have learning and behavior problems, has eleven students, fourth through sixth grade, in her self-contained class. Each day after lunch they practice writing. Ms. Kranowski uses a process approach to teaching writing in which students select their own topics and write about them, sometimes taking several weeks to complete a piece. Students usually write multiple drafts, sharing their work with other students and the teacher.

At first, the learners in Ms. Kranowski's class needed to develop a process for writing. They needed to develop purposes for their writing other than to please the teacher or to complete the worksheets. As the students became more confident of their drafts, they needed to learn such skills as how to organize a descriptive paragraph and a story, and how to use dialogue and quotation marks. Although Ms. Kranowski continues with this process approach to writing, she now also spends some time teaching skills to small groups. She uses systematic skill lessons whereby she models a skill, then has the students practice it in their own writing and in published and teacher-made materials. Whereas the first approach to teaching represents an interactive model of teaching and learning, during skill lessons Ms. Kranowski serves as the conveyor of knowledge by explicitly teaching systematic skill sequences. Ms. Kranowski's instruction shifts to reflect the needs of the students in her class.

How does Ms. Kranowski explain her simultaneous use of these different approaches to the teaching-learning process?

Well, when I first began using a process approach to teaching writing, I found that the students really learned to like writing. For me, that was a big accomplishment, since most of these kids had previously hated writing. But I also found that because these students have so many learning problems and take so much practice to learn a new skill, they just weren't getting enough opportunities to practice intensely a new writing skill when they were first trying to learn it. Consequently, they never learned the skills very well. Now, two days a week we take about twenty minutes for a skill lesson. I select the skill based on the needs of the students as a group. Right now we are working on dialogue and quotation marks. I introduce the skill and show how I use it in my writing. Then several of the students demonstrate how they can use it in their writing. We use an overhead projector, and they project their writing on the screen. We talk about how to add quotation marks, and they add them right then. For the next several weeks when they are writing their pieces, I encourage them to use dialogue, and we make an effort to compliment each other when the quotation marks are right. If the students need additional practice, I provide them with stories where they have to add quotation marks to the writing. We also take turns reading stories and books that have lots of dialogue and the students identify the dialogue and tell where the quotes go. I realize that this is really mixing two philosophies of teaching and learning, but for me it's the best way to get the job done.

The Instructional Cycle

Within the teaching–learning process, the *instructional cycle* helps to shape and sequence teaching and learning (refer to Figure 1.1 again). Ms. Kranowski uses this cycle in her teaching as she sets instructional goals, plans instruction, and provides, evaluates, and modifies instruction based on evaluation. She uses this cycle in a flexible way, taking into account the *characteristics of the learner,* her *teaching beliefs and attitudes,* and the *context* in which the teaching and learning are happening. Sometimes she changes her instructional goals based on input from the students or on feedback regarding rate of learning. Sometimes she modifies her plans and the way in which she instructs to reach her instructional goals more effectively. When Ms. Kranowski added skill lessons to the writing curriculum, she changed her plans, which resulted in changes in instruction. The features of effective instruction should be considered when developing and implementing each part of the instructional cycle.

FEATURES OF EFFECTIVE INSTRUCTION

Effective instruction is tantamount to a balancing act. Some teachers appear to be magicians because they seem to balance the various features of effective instruction effortlessly. However, keeping this balance requires a clear understanding of each feature as well as knowledge about how and when to implement

them. Following are some of the features of effective instruction that should be present in all teaching:

— Assessing progress
— Designing instruction
  • Determining goals of instruction
  • Flexible grouping
  • Adaptations
  • Scaffolding
  • Careful use of instructional time

These features will benefit all the students in your classroom, but they are particularly helpful for students with learning and behavior problems.

Assessing Progress

Assessment is an essential component of instruction for students with learning and behavior difficulties. Assessing progress means continually examining student data from both formal and informal assessments to determine students' knowledge and skills. When assessing students, it is recommended that a variety of assessment tools be used. You can obtain information from reading inventories, standardized tests, observations, and student work samples to assist you in monitoring students' progress and to guide your planning. Monitoring students' learning will help you determine when students require extra assistance and you will be able to adjust instruction accordingly. Monitoring of student progress should be frequent (one to three times per week) and ongoing.

According to the instructional cycle (Figure 1.3), once learning and instructional goals have been established and instruction has been planned, instruction is implemented. However, instruction is more effective and efficient if, at the same time the instruction is being implemented, it is also being evaluated and—from the evaluation—modified.

As we evaluate, it is crucial to keep a written record of student progress. The written record provides a means for objectively reflecting on the data to determine if progress is evident (e.g., Deno, 1985; Fuchs and Deno, 1991; Fuchs, Deno, and Mirkin, 1984; Isaacson, 1988; Utley, Zigmond, and Strain, 1987). This written record also provides a means for communicating with others regarding student progress. Sharing progress with parents, principals, other teachers—and, most importantly, the student—provides a sense of accomplishment and satisfaction for all involved. Having students monitor their own progress can increase their motivation toward learning and give them a sense of pride in learning. Self-monitoring procedures have been used with students who have learning and behavior problems (e.g., Frith and Armstrong, 1986; Hallahan, Lloyd, Kosiewicz, Kauffman, and Graves, 1979; Jackson and Boag, 1981; Swanson, 1985).

Types of Evaluation Measures

Although a teacher or student can use many methods to evaluate progress, generally he or she will use one or more of three basic types: progress graphs and charts, performance records, and process records. The first type is frequently used for measuring daily progress on individual skills or knowledge. Performance records are usually used for measuring progress across time (e.g., grading period, semester, and year). Curriculum-based measurement (Fuchs and Deno, 1991) is an example of a performance record that is closely tied to the curriculum being taught. Process records focus not only on the progress evident in the products but also document progress in the learning process. Portfolios, learning logs, and dialogue journals can be used for this purpose.

Progress Graphs and Charts

Progress graphs and charts are generally used to measure progress on one behavior or skill. Graphs seem particularly suited for self-monitoring because the results are displayed in such a manner that they are easy to interpret (see Figures 1.4 and 1.5). To use a progress graph, the behavior, skill, or knowledge must be quantifiable, either by time or by occurrence. For example, Ms. Shiller, the junior high teacher for a self-contained classroom of emotionally handicapped students, uses progress graphs for the following activities:

1. Silent reading rate
2. Speed in completing math facts
3. Percent of questions answered correctly for the social studies assignment

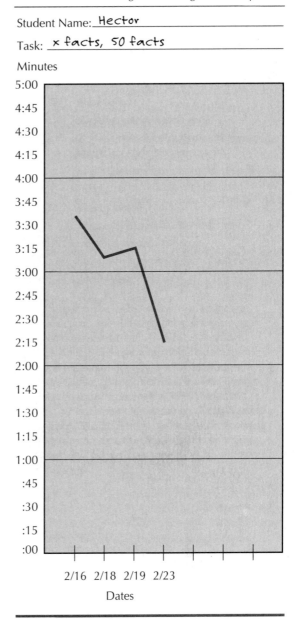

■ **FIGURE 1.4** *Timing Chart Using a Line Graph*

Student Name: Hector

Task: x facts, 50 facts

4. Number of times student disrupted other students during the morning independent learning activity
5. Student and teacher rating of written pieces based on interest and readability

■ **FIGURE 1.5**   *Timing Chart Using a Bar Graph*

Student Name:__Hector_____

Task: __×facts, 50 facts_____

Minutes

Dates

With a progress graph the measurement unit is marked on the vertical axis. For example, *time* would be marked on the vertical axis for graphing silent reading rate, and *speed* for graphing math facts completed. *Percent* would be marked on the vertical axis for graphing the percent of social studies questions answered correctly. On the horizontal axis, the occurrence unit is marked (e.g., date, teaching session, social studies assignment number). It is relatively easy to plot progress data on either a line graph, as depicted in Figure 1.4 or a bar graph (Figure 1.5).

Progress charts are usually used in the same manner as progress graphs, to measure progress on one skill or behavior. The difference between a progress chart and graph is that with a chart you report the score but do not present it in a relational manner (see Figure 1.6). Although progress charts are generally more efficient in the use of space, they do not provide the clear visual representation of the student performance; therefore, student progress or lack of it is not so automatically apparent. Consequently, graphing is generally recommended over charting for student self-monitoring.

Performance Records

Performance records are often used to record student progress across a set of skills or knowledge and for a significant length of time. An IEP is a performance record in that annual goals and short-term objectives are written, and evaluation of the goals and objectives is recorded on the IEP (see Figure 1.2). Many school districts have developed skill and knowledge competencies or objectives that students need to attain at various grade levels. These are often arranged on an individual student performance record so that as a student becomes proficient in a listed competency, it can be noted (see Figure 1.7). Many commercial reading, math, writing, and other content area programs publish performance records so student progress can be recorded. One caution in using such performance records is that, although most of them measure proficiency, they do not measure maintenance, generalization, or application. Consequently, a teacher may receive a performance record on a student and find that the student cannot perform some of the skills listed as mastered.

In addition to collecting permanent products, the teacher and/or the students may want to keep progress journals. Usually this journal accompanies the performance record or progress graphs and charts and provides the student or teacher a space where each can write comments concerning progress. Ms. Shiller

■ **FIGURE 1.6**   *Progress Chart for Sight Words*

Name: Lisa

	3/12	3/14	3/15	3/18
sometimes	+ + +	+ + +	+ + +	+ + +
everyone	– – o	– o +	o + +	+ + +
when	– – –	o o +	– o +	o + +
themselves	– o +	o + +	o + +	+ + +
mystery	– o o	o o +	+ o +	+ o +
hurry	o o +	+ + +	+ + +	+ + +
their	– o –	o + o	+ o +	+ + +
friend	+ o +	+ + +	+ + +	+ + +
mountain	– o o	o o +	+ + o	+ + +
trail	– + –	– o –	– + +	+ o +
route	– – o	o + o	o + o	o o +

+   Correct and Automatic

o   Correct but Not Automatic

–   Incorrect

found that progress journals were particularly helpful for documenting progress regarding students' behavior. She used this in combination with graphs to
evaluate several students' progress. She found that
her dated journal entries provided insights into how
she might modify the instructional context and the
instruction.

Curriculum-based measurement (CBM) is one
system of performance records that highlights the
close tie between curriculum and student performance, using frequent samplings from the curriculum
materials to assess the student's academic performance (e.g., Fuchs and Deno, 1991; Tindal and Mar-

ston, 1990). CBM has been used successfully in
mainstreamed and special-education classrooms with
students who have learning and behavior problems
to increase reading fluency, reading comprehension,
spelling, and arithmetic computation (e.g., Deno,
1998; Deno, 1985; Fuchs et al., 1984; Fuchs, Fuchs,
and Hamlett, 1989; Fuchs, Fuchs, Hamlett, and
Allinder, 1991; Fuchs, Fuchs, Hamlett, Phillips, and
Karns, 1995). For example, reading fluency in a third-
grade class can be measured each week by having
each student read 100-word passages from the reading curriculum and by graphing fluency rates across
time. This type of measurement provides ongoing

■ **FIGURE 1.7**   *Competency-Based Performance Record*

Student: Karen

Competency Area and Skill	Mastery
Early Reading	
Identifies letters of alphabet	10/00
Names letters of alphabet	12/00
Holds book, turns pages one at a time	9/00
Looks first at left page, then at right	9/00
Distinguishes print from pictures	9/00
Scans left to right, top to bottom	9/00
Reads along listening to a familiar book	9/00
Rhymes words	11/00
Identifies words in a familiar book	10/00
Beginning Reading	
Reads simple stories (preprimer/primer)	3/01
Identifies consonant sounds	2/01
Identifies short vowel sounds	2/01
Identifies long vowel sounds	4/01
Identifies simple sight words in isolation	2/01
Recognizes that "s" makes words plural etc.	4/01

data for making instructional decisions. Mercer and Mercer (1993) suggest that you can assess changes in student performance over time by considering: (a) level of performance as affected by instructional change; (b) rate of learning (as reflected by changes in the slope of the trend line) compared to the goal or aim rate; and (c) variability in the consistency of the performance.

Process Records: Portfolios, Learning Logs, and Dialogue Journals

Portfolios, dialogue journals, and learning logs not only highlight product performance across time but document progress in the learning process. In a portfolio, samples are collected across the semester or year (e.g., Paulson, Paulson, and Meyer, 1991; Tierney, Carter, and Desai, 1991). Not only are the final products collected, but also rough drafts, planning or brainstorming sheets, and practice sheets. For example, a student's writing portfolio might contain five stories and essays as well as the brainstorm sheets, research notes, rough drafts, revisions and edited drafts associated with each piece of writing. Whereas reading samples (including oral reading and discussions) can be collected on audiotape, written products can be collected for writing and math. Photographs of projects in subject areas as well as the associated written work can be collected for content area work such as social studies and science. You may want to set up a portfolio for each student in the class. Have students help select which pieces to place in the portfolio, and then review the portfolios with them to identify areas of progress and assist in targeting other areas on which to work.

In addition to collecting portfolios, you may want to use learning logs or dialogue journals (e.g., Atwell, 1987; Harste, Shorte, and Burke, 1988) to share thoughts about projects on which the students are working. Learning logs allow the students to reflect on their learning and the processes they have used in learning. Learning logs provide not only another source of information and evaluation, but in the context of reading and writing Harste and his colleagues note, "When learners reflect, they come to value the strategies they are developing through engaging in reading and writing and through observing the demonstrations of other readers and writers around them" (p. 286). Because learning logs focus on communicating ideas or problems with how and what the students are learning, the focus is not on correct spelling or grammar. The entry of Jose (see Figure 1.8), a fifth grade student with written-expression difficulties, reflects what he is learning as a reader and author after reading the chapter entitled "Harassing Miss Harris" in the book *The Great Gilly Hopkins* (Paterson, 1978).

Dialogue journals also provide a means of evaluation and allow the students the opportunity to carry on a written conversation with the teacher. Ms. Shiller regularly uses a dialogue journal to communicate with Tamara, a sixth-grade student with conduct disorders, about the literature Tamara is reading. Tamara's journal entry about the same chapter in *The Great Gilly Hopkins* reflects how she uses the journal to communicate both her learning processes and her sense of identification with Gilly (see Figure 1.8).

■ **FIGURE 1.8**   *Learning Log Entry for Jose and Dialogue Journal Entry for Tamara on "Harassing Miss Harris" from* The Great Gilly Hopkins *(not corrected for spelling)*

Jose

> I like this chaptr of the book. Even thow it was hari to read, I liked it. I think that is becuase the auther lets you know just how terrible Gilly feels in her new school. I think that letting you know feelings makes writing more interesting.

Tamara

> I just read the chapter on Harassing Miss Harris. I liked it a lot because sometimes I feel like Gilly. I feel so mad that I just wont to get mad and not do the work. I really like the way the author lets you know just how Gilly feels. I guess that is why I liked it so much. You know Gilly's feelings.

One of the major obstacles in evaluating student progress is planning and organizing an evaluation system. Early in the school year:

1. Determine what you want to evaluate.
2. Determine how you will evaluate it (e.g., progress graphs, charts, permanent product records, portfolios).
3. Determine if and when you will use student self-monitoring (e.g., learning logs and dialogue journals).
4. Develop the forms you need for evaluation.
5. Set up the system so that it is easy to collect, file, and retrieve progress data.

Coordinate your evaluation system with the school system, and then collect and use the data to make instructional decisions.

Even though you approach instruction with a plan of action, it is important to remember that your plan will need to be modified. Effective instruction is obtained when the instructional procedures and content match the overall teaching-learning process. Since the teaching–learning process is dynamic and flexible, the instructional process must also be dynamic and flexible.

DESIGNING INSTRUCTION

Once objectives have been set and students' skills assessed, you can begin designing instruction. Designing instruction refers to using student data to plan for effective instruction (Chard, Elliott, Morris, Smith, and Vaughn, 2000). When teachers systematically adjust instruction in response to assessment information, students' rate of learning increases (Fuchs et al., 1995).

How can you design instruction so that the needs of all the students in your classroom are met? Many teachers find it difficult to teach the wide range of skills their students are lacking. Because these deficits are so many and varied in level, it seems impossible to cover them all. The steps to designing instruction as follows:

1. Use the information gathered from various assessment tools. Curriculum-based measurements are particularly suited for this purpose because they are ongoing and closely aligned with curricular goals (Chard et al., 2000).
2. Group students with similar instructional needs.
3. Set specific instructional targets that focus on particular concepts using curricular objectives and annual goals as a guideline.
4. Prepare a schedule and choose and sequence appropriate activities and tasks.
5. Put in place a group management system specifically designed to provide instruction in a variety of grouping patterns.
6. Identify students who need additional, more intensive instruction.

Determining Goals of Instruction

Setting goals for instruction helps you know where you are going. Several questions you may want to ask when you are setting goals for instruction and learning are:

- Have I used the information I have about the characteristics of the learner?

- Have I taken into account my beliefs and attitudes?
- Have I involved the students in setting the goals?
- Have I set goals that are realistic yet challenging to both the learner and myself?
- How do these goals fit with the larger teaching-learning context (e.g., goals of the school, curriculum, long-range career goals of the student)?

When Ms. Kranowski set her instructional goals for writing she decided that she had two major objectives: (1) to have the students enjoy writing and feel good about themselves as authors, and (2) to have the students develop writing skills that would help them in school and later in life. She wanted very much to involve the students in setting goals, believing that if they set shared goals then the students would have a greater commitment to reaching those goals. She began the year by telling the students about "the way that writing works" in the classroom. She shared the importance of supporting each other, for she wanted students to set a goal of working together. As they worked together, shared their writing, and got to know each other better, Ms. Kranowski would sit down with each one of them and help them select skills for improvement. By analyzing the students' written products, observing the students as they wrote, talking with the students about their writing, and using her knowledge about the scope and sequence of writing skills, she felt comfortable working with students in selecting goals. In this way, Ms. Kranowski's instructional goals were interwoven with the students' learning goals.

Flexible Grouping

Deciding on what type of grouping pattern to use is also part of designing instruction. Because of the large range of abilities, interests, and background knowledge in most classrooms, it is best to use flexible grouping. Flexible grouping is another component of effective instruction, and it refers to the use of a variety of grouping practices that change depending on the goals and objectives for the lesson. Mixed-ability groups, same-ability groups, whole-group, pairs, and individualized instruction can be used to meet different student needs. Groups should be flexible, and students should be regrouped on a regular basis.

Adaptations

"The goal of adaptations is to provide all students with the opportunity to participate to the maximum extent possible in typical activities of the classroom" (Deschenes, Ebeling, and Sprague, 1994, p. 13). The use of adaptations enhance learning in all students, not only those with learning and behavior problems. Adaptations can be divided into three categories:

— Instructional design (e.g., accessing resources, collaborating with other professionals, having a plan for adaptations, and integrating technology).
— Instructional and curricular (e.g., making learning visible and explicit, using clear, simple language, breaking a task or activity into steps, and providing multiple ways of demonstrating learning).
— Behavioral support (e.g., teaching alternative behaviors, being consistent, providing structure, and being proactive).

The use of adaptations is one way to demonstrate acceptance, respect, and interest for individual learning differences (Deschenes et al., 1994).

Scaffolding

An essential element of effective instruction for students with learning and behavior problems is the use of scaffolding. *Scaffolding* means adjusting and extending instruction so that the student is challenged and able to develop new skills. You can scaffold instruction to meet the needs of your students by manipulating the task, materials, group size, pace, presentation, etc. You will learn more about scaffolding in Chapter Two.

Time Management

One of the most powerful tools for improving learning is *careful use of instructional time.* For teachers who are working with students who are functioning below grade level, effective time management becomes an essential part of designing and providing instruction. In addition to avoiding wasting time, teachers must decide how much time to give to each activity or concept. Good and Brophy (1997) found that as much as 70 percent of the school day is spent doing seatwork. When deciding how to sequence activities and how much time to spend on each, think about the learner, the materials, and the task (Kameenui and Carnine, 1998; Rosenshine, 1997). As discussed earlier, the features of effective instruction must be balanced carefully and their implementation must be ongoing. Assessment is a necessary step in designing instruction, and, similarly, instruction is an integral part of assessment and student monitoring.

Ms. Kranowski watched and listened to the students and analyzed their written products over time. She used curriculum-based measures to gauge skills in capitalization, punctuation, spelling, and grammar. All these evaluative measures led her to the same conclusion: her students' writing skills were not improving at a rate she considered adequate. Ms. Kranowski decided to compile all the data using a class summary sheet. She then examined the data to find similar needs among her students. Estrella, Aileen, José, Jacqueline, and Sally were having difficulty capitalizing proper nouns. While the rest of the class completed a first draft of a story, Ms. Kranowski spent 10 minutes with them and provided them with direct and explicit instruction on the rules of capitalization. She had prepared several examples of proper nouns and she used them to monitor her students' understanding by asking them to think aloud as to why the nouns were or were not capitalized.

In determining how to modify her instruction, Ms. Kranowski thought about the ideas presented in Figure 1.9. She felt she had adequately addressed the first four questions. Student motivation, attention, encouragement, and modeling had been good. She did not feel as comfortable about her answers to the next three questions: prior knowledge, manner of presentation, and practice. Sometimes she thought she wasn't focused enough on one or two writing skills. She tended to present too much and not allow for enough practice and feedback. Ms. Kranowski decided her modifications had to alleviate the problems with presentation, practice, and feedback. Her

■ **FIGURE 1.9** *Questions for Evaluating the Instructional Process*

- *Student motivation* Am I creating a context in which learning is valued?
- *Student attention* Am I creating an environment in which students can and are encouraged to attend to the learning task?
- *Encouragement* Am I creating a setting in which students are encouraged to take risks and be challenged by learning?
- *Modeling* Are the students given the opportunity to watch, listen, and talk to others so that they can see how the knowledge or skill is learned?
- *Activating prior knowledge* Am I getting the students to think about what they already know about a skill or topic, and are they given the opportunity to build upon that information in an organized fashion?
- *Rate, amount, and manner of presentation* Are the new skills and knowledge being presented at a rate and amount that allows the students time to learn, and in a manner that gives them enough information yet does not overload them?

- *Practice* Are the students given ample opportunity to practice?
- *Feedback* Are the students given feedback on their work so they know how and what they are learning?
- *Acquisition* Are the students given the opportunity to learn skills and knowledge until they feel comfortable with them and to the point they do or know something almost automatically?
- *Maintenance* Are the students given the opportunity to continue to use their skills and knowledge so that they can serve as tools for further learning?
- *Generalization* Are the students generalizing the skills and knowledge to other tasks, settings, and situations? Are the students, other teachers, or parents seeing the learning?
- *Application* Are the students given the opportunity to apply their skills and knowledge in new and novel situations, thereby adapting their skills to meet the new learning experiences?

---

solution was the skill lessons that focused on teaching specific writing skills twice a week. For Ms. Kranowski and her students, this solution was successful. Her students began acquiring and maintaining the targeted writing skills. Now she is asking questions and planning for generalization and application.

WEBSITES AS RESOURCES TO ASSIST IN THE TEACHING–LEARNING PROCESS

http://www.ldonline.org/ld_indepth/iep/iep_process.html
  This Website provides an overview of the IEP process.

http://www.ldonline.org/ld_indepth/iep/iep_guidance.html
  This Website provides information on practical and legal guidance for parents.

http://www.ncld.org/ld/legal6.html
  This Website contains information on evaluation of students with learning disabilities (LD).

http://specialed.about.com/education/specialed/msub13.htm
  This Website contains various resources related to IEP (i.e., development of IEP, Q&A on IEP, etc.)

http://specialed.about.com/education/specialed/msub06.htm
  This Website contains various resources related to behavior issues.

http://specialed.about.com/education/specialed/msub27.htm
  This Website contains various resources related to evaluation.

http://www.quasar.ualberta.ca/ddc/incl/b1a.htm
> This Website contains information of IEP (i.e., definition, components, evaluation, etc.)

http://circleofinclusion.org
> This Website contains various resources related to inclusion (articles, guideline, other links related to inclusion, etc.)

http://www.usoe.k12.ut.us/sars/Upi/inclusion_basics.htm
> This Website contains various links related to inclusion (definition, inclusion strategies, etc.)

http://www.usoe.k12.ut.us.sars/Upi/dan_10_99.htm
> This Website provides brief tips for evaluation.

http://specialed.about.com/education/specialed/gi/dynamic/ffsite.htm?site=http:www.closingthegap.com/cgi%2Dbin/liblibDsply.pl%3Fa=1143%26amp%3B1=1%26amp%3Bc=2
> This Website introduces a software program to facilitate inclusion.

INVITATION FOR LEARNING

As you read this book, we encourage you to reflect on how the information presented can be interwoven into your beliefs and thoughts about the teaching–learning process. We also encourage you to use the reflective, problem-solving orientation to teaching that Ms. Kranowski did in her classroom. A reflective, problem-solving model of teaching and learning is critical for success with students who have learning and behavior problems.

THINK AND APPLY

— What are some of the characteristics of students with learning and behavior problems?
— What factors should be considered when you are determining how serious a learning or behavior problem is?
— What is the teaching-learning process and how can you apply it to students with learning and behavior problems?
— How do the individualized educational program (IEP) and student and teacher involvement relate to the instructional cycle?
— What measures can be used to evaluate student progress?
— What are some of the features of effective instruction?
— What adaptations can be made to promote learning for students with learning or behavior problems?

2

Approaches to Learning and Teaching

KEY TOPICS FOR MASTERY

— *The principles of operant learning theory and the key concepts of reinforcement, shaping, modeling, Premack principle, contingencies, extinction, punishment, and time-out and their implications for teaching*

— *Strategies for increasing and decreasing behaviors and their implications for teaching*

— *The levels of mastery or learning including entry, acquisition, proficiency, maintenance, generalization, and application*

— *The principles of cognitive strategy instruction including the key features of strategy steps, modeling, self-regulation, verbalization, and reflective thinking*

— *The application of cognitive strategy instruction through instructional programs such as the Learning Strategies Curriculum*

— *The principles of a sociocultural theory of cognitive development including the key features of zone of proximal development, scaffolded instruction, modeling, thinking aloud, interactive dialogues, and the social nature of learning*

— *Information processing theory including the processes of attention, perception, memory, and executive functioning*

— *The interactive nature of these information processes, the important role that context and motivation play in learning, and their implications for teaching*

 BRIGHT IDEA

Turn to page 67 and read Think and Apply.

Models and theories for learning can assist us in understanding and explaining how students learn. They also guide us in modifying our teaching thus promoting effective and efficient learning. This chapter overviews four theories or approaches to learning and teaching: operant learning and applied behavior analysis, cognitive strategy instruction, sociocultural theory of learning, and information processing and schema theory. The models are sequenced in the chapter from less to more cognitively oriented. Many of the general principles presented in this chapter will be applied to specific content areas in subsequent chapters. As you read this chapter, we encourage you to think about students who you know are not succeeding in school and who have learning and behavior problems.

How are their learning patterns and habits explained by the various approaches to learning described in this chapter? What general teaching principles do the different approaches suggest to help such students? How can technology assist in the teaching–learning process (see Tech Talk)?

OPERANT LEARNING AND APPLIED BEHAVIOR ANALYSIS

Operant learning theorists, teachers, and other professionals who employ applied behavior analysis believe that behavior is learned and, for this reason, it

TECH TALK 2.1

USING THE INTERNET, MULTIMEDIA, EDUCATIONAL SOFTWARE, AND ASSISTIVE TECHNOLOGY TO SUPPORT LEARNING

Technology is changing the way we teach and learn. It provides a wide array of instructional options that were not available to teachers less than a decade ago.

Students now use the Internet as a major source for obtaining information about the subjects they are studying in school. At the end of each chapter is a selected list of relevant Websites that provide resources for you as a teacher and for your students.

Students are also using multimedia to creatively demonstrate what they are learning. *Multimedia* software provides students with opportunities to study complex relationships in more dynamic ways. Multimedia refers to the use of computers for presenting information in the form of text, images, graphics, sound, animation, and motion video linked together in a creative, nonlinear format. In a multimedia context, the user can move from one source and media of information to another without having to move linearly through the information.

Educational software is one of the most popular means of supporting learning for students with learning and behavior problems. Biter and Pierson (1999) suggest the following categories of educational software:

- *Drill-and-Practice.* Allows the learners to practice facts, relationships, problems, vocabulary, and skills that have been previously learned until the material is automatic.
- *Instructional Game.* Provides the same type of practice as drill-and-practice but uses a game format.

- *Tutorial.* Provides for acquisition of new knowledge through explanations, descriptions, questions, and graphic illustrations.
- *Problem Solving.* Requires students to apply higher-order strategies and synthesize knowledge from multiple areas to solve problems.
- *Simulation.* Allows students to interact during events or phenomena that they are not able to experience in personal.
- *Reference.* Are computerized resources and references.
- *Tool.* Helps teachers and students become efficient and productive managers of textual, numerical, and graphical information. Includes word processors, spreadsheets, databases, graphics, and presentation programs.

Assistive technology is "any item, piece of equipment, or product system, whether acquired commercially off the shelf, modified, or customized, that is used to increase, maintain, or improve functional capabilities of individuals with disabilities" (PL 100–407, the Technology-Related Assistance Act, Section 3.1). For students with learning disabilities this can include a wide array of high- and low-tech devices such as pencil grips, laptop computers for taking notes, tape recorders for listening to recorded lectures or books, and spell checkers, to name a few.

Throughout this book are more ideas for integrating technology into your instruction for students with learning and behavior problems. It is important that you continue to learn about technology to support these students, for technology has done much to improve their success in school and later life.

---

can be unlearned or the student can be taught new behaviors. Operant learning and applied behavior analysis focus on identifying observable behaviors and manipulating the antecedents and consequences of these behaviors to change behavior. Operant learning theory, for the most part, is not concerned with

what you think or tell yourself during the learning process.

In this section on operant learning and applied behavior analysis, we will discuss how to manipulate antecedents and use consequences to increase behaviors we want to see continued, and how to eliminate undesirable behaviors. We also discuss how to teach to different levels of learning.

Manipulating Antecedents

An antecedent is an environmental event or stimulus that precedes a behavior and influences the probability that it will recur in the future. Antecedents influence desirable and undesirable behaviors. It is relatively easy for teachers to manipulate antecedents to change student behaviors. Teachers can analyze the environment and identify factors that contribute to desirable and undesirable behaviors. By identifying and changing these factors, teachers can increase student learning and minimize or eliminate antecedents that interfere. In observing antecedent behaviors the teacher usually considers instructional content, classroom schedule, classroom rules, classroom arrangement, and peer interactions.

Instructional Content

The teacher can consider a number of ways to manipulate instructional content to control behavior: make activities more interesting, incorporate student preferences, reduce task difficulties or length, provide choices, and develop functional or age-appropriate activities. By modifying educational programs, teachers can prevent students' inappropriate or undesirable behavior, and establish a pleasant classroom environment. For example, Blair (1996) found that incorporating the students' activity preferences into circle time and academic activities in a preschool/kindergarten essentially eliminated the undesirable behavior of young students with significant behavior problems.

Classroom Schedule

A well designed schedule allows everyone to predict what will occur during the school day and assist with the allocation of instructional time. For students with learning and behavior problems, teachers can involve students in planning the daily schedule. It is important to avoid revising a schedule because this can be disruptive, undermining students' ability to predict what will happen during the day.

Classroom Rules

Carefully selected rules, when properly developed and stated, can contribute to a positive classroom atmosphere. They help students understand what will and will not be accepted in the classroom. It is important to select a limited number of rules to make it easier for students to remember them. Seek student input on the rules to increase their commitment to following them. State rules positively to help students identify the acceptable behavior and post the rules so students can refer to them.

Room Arrangement

Noises and crowding in the classroom sometimes increase undesirable behaviors. Arranging the furniture in the classroom to partition some areas can reduce the noise level, and limiting the number of students in one area can reduce crowding.

Peer Interactions

The classroom and the school are important social communities and peer interactions play an important role in determining the levels of desirable and undesirable behaviors. Teachers can facilitate peer interaction by: (a) pairing students who have good social skills with students who have more difficulty in prosocial skills, (b) encouraging interaction between students with and without disabilities, and (c) teaching prosocial skills to decrease inappropriate behaviors and to increase appropriate behaviors.

Increasing Desirable Behaviors Through Consequences

During the past few weeks, Ms. Glenn has focused on teaching Marjorie, Sheila, and Jose subtraction with regrouping. During this time she demonstrated many of the principles by using "ten packs" of sticks. The students recently practiced applying the principles on the chalkboard. Ms. Glenn then asked the students to practice the skills independently by completing a math paper with twelve subtraction-with-regrouping problems. She watched them complete the first problem correctly. She then needed to teach another group, yet she wanted to be sure that these three students would continue the desirable behavior of working on their math while she was working with her other group.

According to operant learning principles, behavior is controlled by the consequences that follow it. Ms. Glenn needed to decide what consequences would follow appropriate math performance to maintain or increase its occurrence. She told Marjorie, Sheila, and Jose, "If you complete this math sheet with 80 percent or better accuracy, I will let you have five minutes of free time in the Fun Corner." Free time in the Fun Corner was very reinforcing to all three students, and they accurately completed the math sheet while she worked with other students.

There are several principles to apply when attempting to maintain or increase behavior:

1. The behavior must already be in the student's repertoire. In the preceding example, Ms. Glenn's students knew how to perform the math task. If you want to maintain or increase social or academic behaviors, you must first be sure the student knows how to perform the target behaviors.
2. A consequence must follow the precise behavior you want to change or be linked to it through language. For example, "Because you completed all of your math assignments this week, I'll let you select a movie to watch on the VCR."
3. A reinforcer is whatever follows a behavior and maintains or increases the rate of the behavior.
4. To be most powerful, reinforcement should occur immediately following the behavior.

Thus, to increase behavior we can manipulate the consequence that follows the behavior. Consequences that increase behavior, such as reinforcement and the Premack Principle, will be discussed next.

Reinforcement

Reinforcement is the most significant means of increasing desirable behavior. There are two types of reinforcement, positive and negative; both increase responding. How do they differ? The major difference between positive and negative reinforcement is that *positive reinforcement* is the presentation of a stimulus to increase responding, whereas *negative reinforcement* is the removal of a stimulus to increase responding.

Positive reinforcement increases responding by following the target behavior with activities, objects, food, and social rewards that are associated with increasing the target behavior. Toys, clothes, and privileges such as helping the teacher or having an extra recess are examples of positive reinforcers.

The effectiveness of a reinforcement program depends on the selection of reinforcers that are actually reinforcing. The use of a reinforcer preference checklist is recommended when identifying a reinforcer. Activities and events that a student selected when given a wide choice are more likely to be strongly reinforcing. To prevent students from being satiated with the reinforcer, reinforcement menus are recommended. Instead of providing one reinforcer over time, giving a choice of reinforcers increases their value and prevents the satiation.

When using reinforcers it is important to start with more *intrinsic reinforcers* such as using activities that are reinforcing to the student (e.g., listening to records, coloring) and move to more *tangible reinforcers* such as tokens and food only as necessary. For example, Christian (1983) suggests a seven-level hierarchy of reinforcers, ranging from food and hugs to internal self-reinforcement ("I did a good job"). This hierarchy is presented in Table 2.1.

The practice of negative reinforcement is often misused because the term *negative* is misinterpreted to mean harmful or bad and, therefore, the implication is that positive reinforcement is good and negative reinforcement is bad. Negative reinforcement means taking away something unpleasant contingent on the performance of a specific behavior. If a teacher scowls at a student until the student works, removing the scowl is negative reinforcement. The learning that takes place through negative reinforcement is avoidance learning. A common use in schools is the completion of work assignments to avoid staying after school. Students often use negative reinforcement with adults. An example is a child who throws a temper tantrum until he or she gets what he or she wants.

■ **TABLE 2.1** *Practical Reinforcement Hierarchy for Classroom Behavior Modification*

Consequence Level	Examples
Positive physical contact	Hugs, pats, proximity
Food	Milk, raisins, crackers, gum
Toys	Balloon, marbles, kite, clay
School implements	Eraser, ruler, notepad, pencil
Privilege	Free time, errands, computers, eat lunch with teacher
Praise	Positive comments, grades, certificate
Internal self-reinforcement	"I did well." "My work is complete."

(Left margin: Concrete, Tangible ← → Abstract, Intrinsic)

Source: Adapted from B. T. Christian, "A Practical Reinforcement Hierarchy for Classroom Behavior Modification," *Psychology in the Schools, 20* (1983): 83–84. Used with permission.

How we select reinforcers has considerable influence on the extent to which they are effective. Hall and Hall (1998) provide the following suggestions for selecting reinforcers:

— Consider the age and interests of the person whose behavior you want to improve.
— Specify the behavior you want to improve through reinforcement.
— After you consider what you know about the person, their age, interests and what they like and dislike, identify a list of potential reinforcers.
— Use the behaviors that the person likes to engage in as reinforcers for the behaviors that they like less.
— Interview the person about the things that they like and would be reinforcing to them.
— Try something new as a reinforcer.
— Consider using reinforcers that occur naturally in the environment.

— Be sure to keep a record of the target behavior and the extent to which it is influenced by the reinforcers.

In their book on reinforcement, Hall and Hall (1998) provide lists of reinforcers that are associated with age ranges of infancy to adulthood.

Secondary Reinforcers

A *secondary reinforcer* is a previously neutral behavior that is paired with a reinforcer and therefore takes on reinforcing properties of its own. Thus if the teacher always calls a student up to the teacher's desk prior to rewarding him or her, then being called to the teacher's desk becomes reinforcing—a secondary reinforcer.

Sincere praise and attention are the most frequently used secondary reinforcers. Teachers are often quite skillful at using such subtle but effective secondary reinforcers as a hand on the shoulder, a pat on the head, a smile, or a wink. Many teachers position themselves carefully in the room to be near students whose behavior they want to reinforce with their attention. Figure 2.1 provides options for letting students know you value their good work and behavior.

Token reinforcement systems are frequently used by special education teachers. A *token system* is an economy in which a symbol (e.g., points, chips, or stars) is given contingent on designated behaviors. Tokens are symbols in that they usually have little inherent value themselves but can be exchanged for valuable things or privileges. Token systems can be very simple (e.g., receiving stars for completing writing assignments, with each star worth three minutes of extra recess). Figure 2.2 presents several cards that could be used with younger students to record points. Token economies can also be very complicated and may even involve a level system with rewards and privileges varying according to the level the student is on. Students are assigned to levels contingent on their behavior. Being raised or lowered to a different level occurs as points are accumulated. Points are awarded and deducted for a full range of behaviors. More complicated token systems are typically used to

■ **FIGURE 2.1**   *33 Ways to Say "Very Good"*

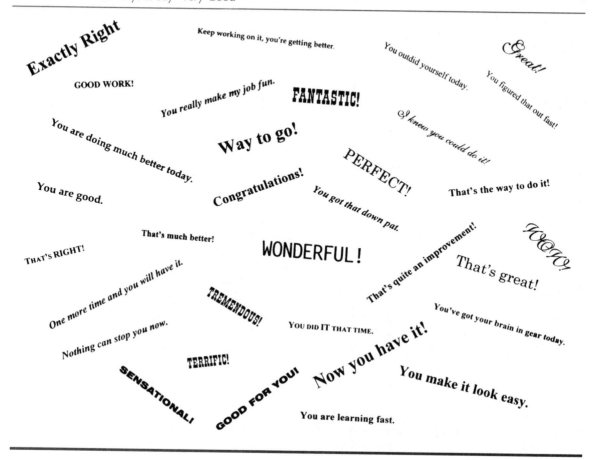

manage aggressive behaviors displayed by severely disturbed students.

Shaping

If reinforcement maintains or increases the rate of behavior already occurring, what does the teacher do if the behavior is occurring at a very low rate or not at all?

For example, Mr. Kladder's goal is to shape Rhonda's behavior so that she is performing multiplication facts quickly and automatically. During the initial teaching phase Mr. Kladder rewards her for computing 3 × 5 by adding five threes. After Rhonda demonstrates she can perform this behavior with high accuracy, Mr. Kladder no longer reinforces her for adding the numbers but only for skip counting 5, 10, 15, and then writing the answer. After Rhonda is successfully able to skip count she is reinforced for computing the answer in her head and writing it down. Now Mr. Kladder begins to give Rhonda timed tests in which she is reinforced only for beating her best time. Mr. Kladder is *shaping* Rhonda's behavior by reinforcing responses that more and more closely approximate the target response.

Premack Principle

If one activity occurs more frequently than another, the more frequently occurring activity can be used

■ **FIGURE 2.2** *Forms for Recording Points Earned in a Token Economy*

Source: From *It's Positively Fun: Techniques for Managing the Learning Environment,* by Kaplan, Kohfeldt, and Sturla, 1975, pp. 15–16. Reproduced by permission of Love Publishing Company.

as a reinforcer to increase the rate of the less frequently occurring activity (Premack, 1959). For example, Adam more frequently participates in outdoor play than in writing stories. His teacher can make outdoor play contingent on completing the writing assignment. The advantage of the Premack Principle is that a teacher can use events that are already occurring in the classroom. One possibility is to inventory the student and rank behaviors from most liked to least liked, for example, (1) reading, (2) math, (3) spelling. Thus reading could be contingent on completing spelling. A more appropriate list for most students with learning and behavior problems might include five minutes of free time contingent on completing spelling. Reinforcing activities such as talking quietly with friends or listening to music can be used to increase the rate of less desirable activities such as completing a book report.

Group Contingencies

Group contingencies can be used to increase desirable behavior or decrease undesirable behavior. When using *group contingencies,* a group of students, or an individual student, is either reinforced or loses reinforcement, contingent on the behavior of the entire group or a target student in the group. For example, the teacher could establish a twenty-minute block of free time at the end of the school day. Every time the noise level of the classroom exceeds the teacher's limits she subtracts one minute from the allocated free time. In addition to changing group behavior, group contingencies can be used to change the behavior of one student in the class. For instance, Carla is a twelve-year-old child who has been mainstreamed into a sixth-grade class. During Carla's first couple of weeks in the class she continually got into fights with her classmates during recess. The teacher told the class that she would extend their recess by ten minutes if Carla did not get into any fights during recess. The class included Carla in their group play and fighting was eliminated. However, there are dangers in group contingencies being dependent on the behavior of an individual. It is possible the individual will use his or her position to manipulate the behavior of others in the class. It is also possible that the individual will view himself or herself negatively because of this position.

Axelrod (1998) defines group contingencies by identifying a 10-step program for their use:

— Select only one behavior to change.
— Carefully specify in a written format the behavior that you want to change.
— Determine through careful observation how often and when the behavior occurs.
— Think about what might be reinforcing to all members of the group.
— Decide what the group contingency will be for the reinforcer.
— Be sure to identify a behavior that everyone in the group is capable of performing.
— Provide the reinforcer contingent upon a reasonable improvement in the target behavior.
— Let each member of the group as well as the group as a whole know when they are behaving appropriately.
— Monitor the progress of the group and each member of the group.
— Revise the program as needed.

Contingency Contracting

Contingency contracting is an agreement between two or more persons that specifies their behaviors and consequences. A common example of a contingency contract is the agreement between parent and child regarding an allowance. The child agrees to perform certain behaviors in return for a specified amount of money each week. The contingency contract should specify who is doing what, when, under what conditions, and for what consequences (see Figure 2.3).

■ **FIGURE 2.3**   *Sample Contingency Contract Form*

I've Got An Offer You Can't Refuse

If_____
_____
_____ by _____

Then _____
_____
_____

date   student   witness   Teacher

Source: From *It's Positively Fun: Techniques for Managing the Learning Environment,* by Kaplan, Kohfeldt, and Sturla, 1975, p. 21. Reproduced by permission of Love Publishing Company.

Decreasing Undesirable Behaviors Through Consequences

Unfortunately, students manifest behaviors that interfere with their learning or the learning of others. Techniques for decreasing these undesirable behaviors include: extinction, differential reinforcement, punishment, and time-out.

Extinction

Extinction is the removal of reinforcement following the behavior. For example, a teacher wants to extinguish a student's behavior of shouting out and determines that telling the student to raise his hand is reinforcing the shouting out. To extinguish shouting out, the teacher removes the reinforcer ("Raise your hand") and ignores the student's shouting out.

Extinction can be an effective means of decreasing undesirable behaviors, but it is often slow and can be impractical for many behaviors that occur within the classroom because the reinforcers for the undesirable behavior are often difficult for the teacher to control. For example, let's return to the student who continually shouted out in class. In this situation the student was being reinforced not only by the classroom teacher's attention ("Raise your hand") but also by other students who looked and attended to him when he shouted out. A teacher attempting to reduce this behavior through extinction would have to eliminate both the teacher's reinforcement and the reinforcement of others in the class. To compound the difficulty, slip-ups by the teacher or students would intermittently reinforce the behavior and maintain it for a long time.

Another characteristic of extinction is its effect on the rate at which the target behavior continues to occur. During extinction the target behavior will increase in rate or intensity before decreasing. Thus a teacher attempting to eliminate tantrums through extinction will observe the tantrums occurring more frequently, lasting longer, and perhaps even being louder and more intense than before extinction. As long as the teacher continues to withhold reinforcement, usually attention, the rate and intensity will decrease and tantrums can be eliminated. For this reason it is extremely important to chart behavior when using extinction. To document behavior change, take *baseline data,* a record of the frequency and/or duration of the behavior before implementing the intervention, and continue to take data after intervention is implemented.

Although extinction can be an effective means of decreasing undesirable behaviors, it requires patience and the ability to control all of the reinforcers. Ignoring, the most frequently applied form of extinction in the classroom, is an important skill for teachers to learn. A summary of points to remember about using ignoring as a means of decreasing undesirable behavior follows:

1. Ignoring can be effective when the behavior is being reinforced by teachers or students who are willing to discontinue reinforcement.
2. If the teacher attempts to eliminate a behavior through ignoring, the behavior must be ignored every time it occurs.
3. Ignoring will not be effective if the behavior is being maintained by other reinforcers, such as the attention of selected classmates.

Differential Reinforcement
Differential reinforcement involves strengthening one set of responses in contrast to another. It is an effective procedure for developing a positive behavior management plan. The main advantage of differen-

tial reinforcement is that positive consequences are used to reduce the strength of undesirable behavior. Therefore, negative side effects associated with punishment procedures are avoided. There are several forms of differential reinforcement. The definitions and examples are as follows:

Differential Reinforcement of Incompatible Behaviors (DRI) and Alternative Behaviors (DRA). Differential reinforcement of incompatible behaviors involves identifying desirable behaviors. Reinforcement is then provided contingent on the occurrences of the targeted desirable behaviors. For example, while ignoring the out-of-seat behavior of a student, the teacher targets and reinforces the desirable behavior that is incompatible, in this case, in-seat behavior. Therefore, when Scott is sitting in his seat the teacher is quick to catch his appropriate behavior and reinforce. In addition, the teacher would intermittently reinforce Scott for being in his seat. In the case of DRI, the new response (incompatible behavior) is selected because it represents an incompatible alternative to the disruptive behavior; the two behaviors cannot occur simultaneously. The alternative behavior selected in DRA is not necessarily incompatible with the disruptive response, and the alternative response can occur at the same time as the undesirable behavior. The goal of using DRA is to strengthen a range of appropriate behaviors that teachers will attend to naturally, thereby reinforcing a broad repertoire of appropriate behavior. Careful planning should ensure that the reinforcers selected are sufficiently attractive and delivered with sufficient frequency to motivate student performance while removing reinforcers from the undesirable behavior. Both DRI and DRA ensure that new behaviors are fostered at the same time that undesirable behaviors are being diminished.

Differential Reinforcement of Other Behaviors (DRO). Differential reinforcement of other behaviors (DRO) is the reinforcement of the nonoccurrence of target behavior during a specified time period; reinforcers are delivered following time intervals in which the target behavior did not occur. For example, a teacher may allow the student free time at the end of each 30-minute scheduled period in which no target behavior occurred. Therefore, determining the length of the reinforcement period prior to using DRO is important. Brief intervals of one to ten minutes may be selected for high rate behaviors, and intervals up to a day in length may be used for low rate behaviors. DRO may be most effective when used in combination with a DRA procedure by reinforcing occurrences of alternative behavior as well as providing reinforcement for intervals in which a zero rate of the target behavior occurred. When combined with other methods, DRO can be one of the most powerful procedures (Sulzer-Azaroff and Mayer, 1991).

Regardless of the type of differential reinforcement, reinforcing behavior through consequences requires you, the teacher, to do four things:

1. Identify the behavior you want to change (interfering behavior).
2. Identify the incompatible behavior.
3. Stop reinforcing the interfering behavior.
4. Reinforce the desirable behavior.

Response Cost

Response cost is a procedure in which a specified amount of a reinforcer is removed following each occurrence of the target behavior. Withdrawal of favored activities and tangible reinforcers are common response strategies for young children. For example, a student is not allowed to play during free choice session because of his or her aggression toward peers. One of the most common response-cost strategies for older students is the use of withdrawal of tokens following a target behavior. For example, students may earn 20 points for completing each assignment throughout the day. Points can be exchanged for primary reinforcers at the end of the day. Engaging in a target behavior may result in a response cost of 30 points. Response cost is an aversive procedure which should be used carefully. It can inadvertently be used to punish positive behaviors. For example, teachers may be tempted to ask students to complete additional work if assignments are completed prior to the end of the class period. Additional work requirements may act as a response cost for early assignment completion.

Thibadeau (1998) provides the following suggestions when implementing response cost:

— Provide a description of the behavior that will allow you to determine if there has been any change.
— Collect measures of student's current level of performance.
— Identify which reinforcers will be removed following the target undesirable behavior.
— Specify the amount of the reinforcer that will be removed.
— Be sure the student(s) understands the rules of response cost.
— Implement the response cost strategy with limited attention.
— When appropriate behaviors occur be certain to reinforce them.
— Monitor the progress of the response cost on an ongoing fashion.
— Make appropriate changes to the response cost system when needed.

Punishment

Punishment, the opposite of reinforcement, is following a behavior with a consequence that decreases the strength of the behavior or reduces the likelihood the behavior will continue to occur. Unfortunately, punishment does not assure the desired behavior will occur. For example, a student who is punished for talking in class may stop talking, but may not attend to his or her studies for the remainder of the day.

There are many significant arguments against the use of punishment:

1. Punishment is ineffective in the long run.
2. Punishment often causes undesirable emotional side effects such as fear, aggression, and resentment.
3. Punishment provides little information to the person as to what to do, *teaching the individual* only what not to do.
4. The person who administers the punishment is often associated with it and also becomes aversive.

5. Punishment frequently does not generalize across settings, thus it needs to be readministered.
6. Fear of punishment often leads to escape behavior.

If there are so many arguments for not using punishment, why is it so frequently used as a means for changing behavior? There are many explanations, including lack of familiarity with the consequences of punishment and the inability to effectively use a more positive approach. Also, punishment is often reinforcing to the punisher, reducing the occurrence of the undesirable behavior, therefore reinforcing its use.

Punishment should be used only when behaviors are harmful to the child or others. In this case, the student should be told ahead of time what the consequence (punishment) for exhibiting the behavior will be. When the undesirable behavior occurs, the punishment should be delivered quickly and as soon as the inappropriate behavior is initiated. Punishment should be applied consistently every time the designated behavior occurs. If you choose to use punishment you should identify several other behaviors you would like to see maintained and give extensive reinforcement for their occurrence.

Time-Out

Time-out occurs when the student is removed from the opportunity to receive any reinforcement. Time-out is when the teacher asks a student to sit in the hall during the remainder of a lesson, when a young child is asked to leave the group, or when a student is asked to sit in a quiet chair until he or she is ready to join the group.

Unfortunately, time-out is frequently used inappropriately. The underlying principle behind the successful use of time-out is that the environment the student is leaving must be reinforcing and the time-out environment must be without reinforcement. This may not be as easy to achieve as you might think. For example, when Elizabeth was talking and interfering with others during the science lesson, her teacher thought she would "decrease" Elizabeth's behavior by sending her to time-out, which was a chair in the back of the room away from the group. The teacher became discouraged when Elizabeth's inappropriate behavior during science class increased in subsequent lessons rather than decreased. A likely explanation for the ineffectiveness of time-out in this situation is that Elizabeth did not enjoy science class and she found sitting in a chair in the back of the room looking at books reinforcing. The efficacy of time-out is strongly influenced by environmental factors. If the environment the student is leaving is unrewarding, then time-out is not an effective means of changing the student's behavior.

Teachers who use secluded time-out areas or contingent restraint (holding the student down plus withdrawal, exclusion, and seclusion) should be aware of the legal implications of such intervention, and should obtain the necessary authorization from within the school setting and from parents or guardians. A position paper on the use of behavior reduction strategies has been issued by the Council for Children with Behavior Disorders, Council for Exceptional Children (CCBD, 1990) and policies developed for physical intervention by the Council for Exceptional Children (1995). Recommended procedures for successfully implementing time-out are listed in Apply the Concept 2.1.

Peer Confrontation System

Peers as well as the teacher can serve as behavior controllers for students. In a procedure referred to as the peer confrontation system (Salend, Jantzen, and Giek, 1992), the teacher and students identify behavior problems in the group. The teacher informs the students in the group to respond to students that are having a behavioral problem in the following way:

— Teacher says, "Mark seems to be having some difficulty. Who can tell Mark what the problem is?"
— Selecting a student from the group, the teacher says, "Can you tell Mark what the problem is?"
— The teacher follows with, "What does Mark need to do to solve the problem?"

In the Salend et al. (1992) study, 12 of the 13 students indicated that they would like to continue using the peer confrontation system.

APPLY THE CONCEPT 2.1

GUIDELINES FOR IMPLEMENTING TIME-OUT

Time-out, like punishment, should be used as a last resort. Teachers should discuss this intervention with school administrators and parents before implementing it.

1. The student should be told in advance which behaviors will result in time-out.
2. The amount of time the student will be in time-out should be specified ahead of time.
3. The amount of time the student is in time-out should be brief (one to five minutes).
4. The student should be told once to go to time-out. If the student does not comply, the teacher should unemotionally place the student in time-out.
5. Time-out must occur every time the undesirable behavior occurs.
6. Contingencies should be set in advance for the student who fails to comply with time-out rules.
7. Do not leave the time-out area unmonitored.
8. When time-out is over, the student should return to the group.
9. Reinforce positive behaviors that occur after time-out.

Hall and Hall (1998) provide very helpful suggestions about how to handle the potential problems that occur with time-out. Several of their suggestions follow:

- Add time to the student's time-out for refusing to go to time-out or displaying other inappropriate behaviors such as screaming, yelling, and kicking.
- Students should be required to clean up any mess made during time-out before they return from time-out.
- Be sure to have a back-up consequence if a student refuses to go to time-out and the amount of time added reaches 30 minutes (usually considered the maximum amount).
- Do not argue with individuals when they either try to talk you out of time-out or indicate that you have no right to put them in time-out. Ignore their comments.
- If the inappropriate behavior involves two persons and it is not possible to determine the source of the problem, do not argue; put both students in time-out.
- If the student displays the behavior in a place where it is not possible to use time-out, indicate that time-out will be provided when you return to the classroom.
- Be sure to chart the effects of time-out so you can determine whether or not it is working.

Stages of Learning

One way the principles of operant learning can be applied is through *stages of learning.* The stages of learning (see Figure 2.4) are the levels a student moves through in acquiring proficiency in learning (Rivera and Smith, 1997). For example, the first stage of learning, *entry,* is the level of performance the student is presently exhibiting. During the second stage, *acquisition,* the components of the target behavior are sequenced into teachable elements. Each teachable element is taught to mastery through a high rate of reinforcement, shaping, and consistent use of cues. When the behavior is occurring at a high level of ac-

curacy, the focus of the learning is on *proficiency.* During this stage the teacher's goal is to increase the student's accuracy and fluency in performing the behavior. At the next stage, *maintenance,* the goal is for the behavior to be maintained at the target level of accuracy and proficiency with intermittent reinforcement and a reduction in teacher assistance and cues. The next stage is *generalization,* in which the target behavior transfers across settings, persons, and materials. Stokes and Baer (1977) suggest that generalization may be a separate skill that needs to be taught. Apply the Concept 2.2 provides further information on how to teach for generalization. At the final stage, *application,* the learner is required to extend and uti-

■ **FIGURE 2.4** *Stages of Learning*

Source: Adapted from D. P. Rivera, and D. D. Smith, 1997. *Teaching Students with Learning and Behavior Problems,* (3rd ed.) (Boston: Allyn and Bacon, 1997).

lize the learning in new situations. Application is a difficult skill for special learners, and the teacher's role is to demonstrate and provide a range of opportunities for applying the newly acquired skill.

In summary, the principles of operant learning and applied behavior analysis are applicable within the classroom for both instructional and classroom management purposes. In a classroom based on operant learning theory, the teacher has behavioral objectives that specify the behavior the students need to perform to be judged successful. If the target response does not occur naturally, then it is important for the teacher to develop a method of shaping the be-

havior. The behaviors are sequenced from the simple to the more difficult. A full range of reinforcers is used, such as verbal praise, smiles from the teacher, gold stars, tokens, free time, and other specialized reinforcers that are effective with students. Students are dealt with individually, with target behaviors reflecting the needs of the student. Behaviors are initially taught through continuous reinforcement; after acquisition of these behaviors, they are maintained through intermittent reinforcement. Teachers reduce inappropriate behavior by ignoring it and reinforcing incompatible behavior. Teachers avoid the use of punishment. Behaviors are discussed in observable terms, and learning is measured by the acquisition of new behaviors.

COGNITIVE STRATEGY INSTRUCTION

Cognitive strategy instruction integrates notions from operant, social, and cognitive learning theories, and assumes that cognitive behavior (thinking processes), like observable behaviors, can be changed. This model of instruction is based on the earlier work from social learning theory (Bandura, 1977, 1986) and cognitive behavior modification (Harris, 1985; Michenbaum, 1977). It incorporates principles of operant learning, but it adds principles from social learning theory and cognitive theory that are important to consider when the goal of instruction is to change the way one thinks. Cognitive strategy instruction has been shown through numerous research studies to be particularly effective with students who have learning and behavior problems (Swanson, 1999).

Let's look at how Mrs. Neal uses cognitive strategy instruction to help Marlow and his classmates better understand the science concepts and textbook she is using in her seventh-grade resource science class.

Even though Marlow, a student with behavior disorders, can identify most of the words in the text, he only remembers a few details from what he reads. Mrs. Neal wants to teach Marlow and his classmates

APPLY THE CONCEPT 2.2 ▬▬▬▬▬▬

GENERALIZATION STRATEGIES

Change Reinforcement

Description/Methods

Vary amount, power, and type of reinforcers.

- Fade amount of reinforcement.

- Decrease power of reinforcer from tangible reinforcers to verbal praise.

- Increase power of reinforcer when changing to mainstreamed setting.
- Use same reinforcers in different settings.

Examples

- Reduce frequency of reinforcement from completion of each assignment to completion of day's assignment
- Limit use of stars/stickers and add more specific statements, e.g., "Hey, you did a really good job in your math book today."
- Give points in regular classroom although not needed in resource room.
- Encourage all teachers working with student to use the same reinforcement program.

Change Cues

Description/Methods

Vary instructions systematically.

- Use alternate/parallel directions.

- Change directions.

- Use photograph.
- Use picture to represent object.

- Use line drawing or symbol representation.

- Use varying print forms.

Examples

- Use variations of cue, e.g., "Find the . . ."; "Give me the . . ."; "Point to the. . . ."
- Change length and vocabulary of directions to better represent the directions given in the regular classroom, e.g., "Open your book to page 42 and do the problems in set A."
- Move from real objects to miniature objects.
- Use actual photograph of object or situation.
- Move from object/photograph to picture of object or situation.
- Use drawings from workbooks to represent objects or situations.
- Vary lower and upper case letters; vary print by using manuscript, boldface, primary type.
- Move from manuscript to cursive.

Change Materials

Description/Methods

Vary materials within task.

- Change medium.

- Change media.

Examples

- Use unlined paper, lined paper; change size of lines; change color of paper.
- Use various writing instruments such as markers, pencil, pen, typewriter.
- Use materials such as films, microcomputers, filmstrips to present skills/concepts.
- Provide opportunity for student to phase into mainstream.

Change Response Set

Description/Methods	Examples
Vary mode of responding.	
• Change how student is to respond.	• Ask child to write answers rather than always responding orally. • Teach student to respond to a variety of question types such as multiple choice, true/false, short answer.
• Change time allowed for responding.	• Decrease time allowed to complete math facts.

Change Some Dimension(s) of the Stimulus

Description/Methods	Examples
Vary the stimulus systematically.	
• Use single stimulus and change size, color, shape. • Add to number of distractors. • Use concrete (real) object. • Use toy or miniature representation.	• Teach colors by changing the size, shape, and shade of "orange" objects. • Teach sight words by increasing number of words from which child is to choose. • Introduce rhyming words by using real objects. • Use miniature objects when real objects are impractical.

Change Setting(s)

Description/Methods	Examples
Vary instructional work space.	
• Move from structured to less structured work arrangements.	• Move one-to-one teaching to different areas within classroom. • Provide opportunity for independent work. • Move from one-to-one instruction to small-group format. • Provide opportunity for student to interact in large group.

Change Teachers

Description/Methods	Examples
Vary instructors.	
• Assign child to work with different teacher.	• Select tasks so that child has opportunities to work with instructional aide, peer tutor, volunteer, regular classroom teacher, and parents.

Source: From S. Vaughn, C. S. Bos, and K. A. Lund, *Teaching Exceptional Children,* Spring, 1986, pp. 177–178. Copyright 1986 by The Council for Exceptional Children. Reprinted with permission.

how to understand and remember the major points. She decided that if she wants to teach the students this cognitive behavior, she will have to give them a consistent set of steps to use in completing the process, much in the same way we use a consistent set of steps to tie shoes. She also knows that for the students to learn what to do, they need to observe someone else. But how can she do this?

Mrs. Neal uses cognitive strategy instruction. First, she selects the steps she wants to teach Marlow and the other students to use when they read their science text. Next, she and the students discuss the strategies the students currently use and their effectiveness. They also discuss the importance of improving this skill and the payoff for improvement. Mrs. Neal then tells the students about the steps she uses when she reads. To model these steps, she reads and explains what she is thinking (i.e., cognitive modeling). Then she talks them through the steps as the students try them. Finally, Mrs. Neal gives the students lots of opportunities to practice the steps when reading their textbooks, encouraging them at first to say the steps aloud as they work through them. She provides feedback on how they are doing and she also teaches them how to evaluate their own performance.

Using these systematic techniques, Mrs. Neal finds that in several weeks Marlow and his classmates are improving in their ability to remember the important information from their science text. In addition, they are beginning not to rely so much on the strategy she taught them. It is almost as if they are using it automatically, without having to consciously remember to use it. Mrs. Neal feels that she has taught her students a good strategy for thinking about what they are reading and that she has changed their cognitive behavior (thinking processes). To promote generalization, Mrs. Neal discusses with Marlow and his classmates other opportunities they have for using the strategy. The students begin keeping a list on the board of all occasions when the strategy can be used. They also begin using the strategy on these different occasions (e.g., reading the newspaper during current events, reading other textbooks, editing each others' stories and essays) and discussing how useful the strategy was in helping them.

Mrs. Neal used *cognitive strategy instruction* (CSI). This approach includes an analysis of the task as well as an analysis of the thinking processes involved in performing the task. It also includes teaching routines that utilize cognitive modeling, self-instructional techniques, and evaluation of performance (Meichenbaum, 1977; Meichenbaum and Biemiller, 1998).

Several key learning and teaching principles are associated with cognitive strategy instruction. One principle is *cognitive modeling* or "thinking aloud." When Mrs. Neal explained what she was thinking as she read, she was using cognitive modeling. Another principle is *guided instruction*. Mrs. Neal used this principle when she guided the students through the reading task by telling them the steps in the process as they read. *Self-instruction* is another principle. When learners use language to guide their performance, they are using self-instruction. For instance, if you talk or think through the steps in solving a complex algebra problem while completing it, you are using self-instruction.

Self-evaluation and self-regulation are two more principles. *Self-evaluation* refers to making judgments concerning the quality or quantity of performance. Mrs. Neal had Marlow and his classmates judge the quality of their performance by having them pause at the end of each section of the science text and comment on how they were doing. *Self-regulation* refers to the learner monitoring his or her own thinking strategies through language mediation. Self-regulation also occurs when the learner corrects or uses fix-up strategies when he or she detects a problem. For example, Mrs. Neal taught Marlow and his classmates to say to themselves what the main idea was when they finished reading each paragraph or section of the text. If the students could not give the main idea, then she demonstrated and encouraged them to use a fix-up strategy. In this case, she showed them how to go back and reread the first sentence in the paragraph to see if that helped them to remember the main idea. If this did not work, she demonstrated how to review the paragraph quickly.

Common Features of Cognitive Strategy Instruction

Cognitive strategy instruction has been used to develop a range of academic and social skills. Common features of CSI include: strategy steps,

modeling, self-regulation, verbalization, and reflective thinking.

Strategy Steps

A series of steps is usually identified for the student to work through when solving a problem or completing a task. These steps are based on a task analysis of the cognitive and observable behaviors needed to complete the task. Before Mrs. Neal began teaching, she determined the steps in the reading strategy she wanted to teach Marlow and his classmates.

Graham and Harris and their colleagues have developed a series of writing strategies to assist students in writing stories and other pieces (Graham and Harris, 1993; Graham, MacArthur, and Schwartz, 1995; MacArthur, Graham, Schwartz, Schafer, 1995; MacArthur, Schwartz, Graham, Molloy, and Harris, 1996). Each strategy has steps that the students learn to assist them with specific aspects of writing. For example, to help students write a story Graham and Harris (1989a) used the following strategy steps:

1. Look at the picture (picture prompts were used).
2. Let your mind be free.
3. Write down the story part reminder (W-W-W; What = 2; How = 2). The questions for the story part reminder were:
   - Who is the main character? Who else is in the story?
   - When does the story take place?
   - Where does the story take place?
   - What does the main character want to do?
   - What happens when he or she tries to do it?
   - How does the story end?
   - How does the main character feel?
4. Write down the story part ideas for each part.
5. Write your own story; use good parts and make sense.

Modeling

In CSI, modeling is used as a primary means of instruction. Research in social learning theory as well as in cognitive behavior modification supports the notion that modeling is a very effective teaching technique. With CSI, students are asked not only to watch observable behaviors as the instructor performs the task, but also to listen to the instructor's self-talk. In this way the instructor is modeling both observable behaviors and the unobservable thinking processes associated with those behaviors. Being able to model unobservable thinking processes is an important component for teaching such cognitive skills as verbal math problem solving, finding the main idea in a paragraph, editing written work, and solving social problems. In most instances the person modeling is the teacher or a peer, but video and puppets have also been used. Vaughn, Ridley, and Bullock (1984) used puppets as models for teaching interpersonal social skills to young, aggressive children. The puppets were used to demonstrate appropriate social behaviors and strategies for solving interpersonal problems.

Self-Regulation

Self-regulation refers to the learner monitoring his or her thinking and actions through language mediation. Students first use language to mediate their actions by overtly engaging in self-instruction and self-monitoring. Later, this language mediation becomes covert.

Using self-regulation, students act as their own teachers. Students are expected to take active roles in the learning process and to be responsible for their own learning (Harris and Pressley, 1991; Michenbaum and Biemiller, 1998; Pressley, Brown, El-Dinary, and Afflerbauch, 1995). Although they work under the guidance of a teacher, students are expected to monitor their learning, change or modify strategies when difficulties arise, evaluate their performance, and in some cases provide self-reinforcement.

Peers have also been used to promote student regulation and monitoring. For example, MacArthur, Graham, and their colleagues (MacArthur, Schwartz, and Graham, 1991a) used a peer editing strategy to increase students' knowledge about writing and revising and to increase their revising activity. The strategy was taught by special education teachers who were using a process approach to teaching writing (see Chapter Six) and word processing. The steps in the Student Editor Strategy were:

1. LISTEN and read along as the author reads.
2. TELL what it was about and what you like best.
3. READ and make NOTES about: CLEAR? Is there anything that is difficult to understand? DETAILS? Where could more information be added?

4. DISCUSS your suggestions with the author.
5. The author makes revisions on the computer. (MacArthur et al., 1991a, p. 234)

The procedure involved peers in that steps 1 and 2 were completed for both students. Then the two students worked independently to complete step 3 and again met together for step 4 to discuss each paper and the suggested revisions. For step 5 each author worked at the computer to make the revisions that he or she thought were useful.

Class-wide peer tutoring (Greenwood, Delquardri, and Hall, 1989) and peer-assisted learning (Fuchs, Fuchs, Mathes, and Simmons, 1997) have been used extensively with students who are low achievers and/or have learning and behavior problems. These procedures allow students to support each other in practicing skills such as solving math word problems or building reading fluency, and to assist each other in setting goals and monitoring progress.

For students with behavior disorders, particularly those with conduct disorders, aggression replacement theory (Goldstein and Glick, 1987) uses self-regulation as an effective procedure for assisting students in controlling their anger. Through aggression replacement theory students learn to identify anger-producing situations (triggers) and to recognize their responses to these situations (cues). They then learn a number of techniques designed to assist them in relaxing and cognitively handling the situation. In reviewing self-regulation outcome research conducted with students with behavior disorders, Nelson, Smith, Young, and Dodd (1991) found numerous studies indicating that self-regulation procedures can be extremely effective in enhancing both the academic and social behavior of these students.

Verbalization

Verbalization is typically a component of self-instruction and self-monitoring with overt verbalization being faded to covert verbalization. Many CSI programs rely on a "talk aloud" or "think aloud" technique (e.g., Deshler, Ellis, and Lenz, 1996; Harris and Graham, 1992; Montague and Bos, 1986b; Swanson, 1999b). After listening to the teacher think aloud as

he or she performs the targeted processes and task, students are encouraged to talk aloud as they initially learn the strategy. For example, Ramon might say the following as he completes a two-digit subtraction problem without regrouping, "Start at the one's place and take the bottom number away from the top. Write the answer in the one's place. Now go to the ten's place. Do the same thing." Usually these overt verbalizations occur only during the initial stages of learning. As the strategy becomes more automatic, students are encouraged to "think to themselves" instead of "aloud."

In addition to verbalization concerning the learning processes, students are also encouraged to make self-statements about their performance. For example, "That part is done. Now go to the next part." or "I'm getting much faster at this." or "I need to think about all my choices before I decide."

Meichenbaum (1977) has suggested several ways to encourage students to use self-talk:

1. The teacher can model self-talk and self-statements as he or she performs the task.
2. The teacher can begin with tasks at which the students are already somewhat proficient. Later, as the students are comfortable with self-talk, the teacher can switch to the targeted tasks.
3. Students can develop and use cue cards to help them remember the steps they are to talk through. For example, Camp, Blom, Herbert, and Van Doorninck (1977) used the pictures in Figure 2.5 as cue cards when teaching self-control to twelve aggressive second-grade boys. The cue cards were used as reminders to self-verbalize as the boys applied these questions first to cognitive and then to interpersonal tasks.

Reflective Thinking

Reflective thinking requires students to take the time to think about what they are doing. Teaching students who have learning and behavior problems to "stop and think" is an important skill to include in instruction (Troia, Graham, and Harris, 1999). Many of these students are impulsive in their actions, seeming to act without thinking (Lerner, 2000; Kauffman, 2001). These students have limited and ineffective

■ **FIGURE 2.5** *Cue Cards Used for Teaching Self-Control*

1 What is my problem?

2 How can I do it?

3 Am I using my plan?

4 How did I do?

Source: Reprinted with permission from B. W. Camp and M. A. S. Bash (1985). *Think Aloud: Increasing Social and Cognitive Skills—A Problem-Solving Program for Children. Classroom Program: Grades 1–2* (pp. 48–51). Champaign, IL: Research Press.

strategies for approaching academic tasks or social situations. They approach these tasks and situations in a disorganized, haphazard way, and often without thinking about the consequence of the actions. In using cognitive strategy instruction, teachers assist students in using reflective thinking.

Let's look at how Wong, Wong, Perry, and Sawatsky (1986) encouraged reflective thinking when they taught seventh-grade students to use self-questioning when summarizing social studies texts. After teaching the students how to identify the main idea of

paragraphs and how to summarize paragraphs, Wong and colleagues taught the students a summarization strategy. The questions the students asked themselves were:

1. In this paragraph, is there anything I don't understand?
2. In this paragraph, what's the most important sentence (main-idea sentence)? Let me underline it.
3. Let me summarize the paragraph. To summarize, I rewrite the main-idea sentence, and add important details.
4. Now, does my summary statement link up with the subheading?
5. When I have written summary statements for a whole subsection:
   a. Let me review my summary statements for the whole subsection. (A subsection is one with several paragraphs under the same subheading.)
   b. Do my summary statements link up with one another?
6. At the end of an assigned reading section: Can I see all the themes here? If yes, let me predict the teacher's test question on this section. If no, let me go back to step 4 (Wong et al., 1986, pp. 25–26).

The specificity of the questions and cues can be important for success. For example, Graham, MacArthur, and Schwartz (1995) found that cueing students to revise in order to add specific information resulted in better-quality writing than telling students to revise to make the paper better.

Teaching Implications of Cognitive Strategy Instruction

Cognitive strategy instruction is designed to actively involve students in learning. Meichenbaum and Biemiller (1998) characterize the student as a collaborator in learning. General guidelines to consider include:

1. Analyze the target behavior carefully.
2. Determine if and what strategies the student is already using.

3. Select strategy steps that are as similar as possible to the strategy steps used by good problem solvers.
4. Work with the student in developing the strategy steps.
5. Teach the prerequisite skills.
6. Teach the strategy steps using modeling, self-instruction, and self-regulation.
7. Give explicit feedback.
8. Teach strategy generalization.
9. Help the student maintain the strategy.

Guidelines for monitoring the effects of training (see Table 2.2) have also been suggested (Rooney and Hallahan, 1985). A growing body of research supports the use of cognitive strategy instruction for developing academic, cognitive, and social skills (Deshler, Ellis, and Lenz, 1996; Graham, Harris, and Troia, 1998; Pressley, 1998), and recent reviews of research on students with learning and behavior problems consistently identify CSI as one of the most effective instructional strategies for teachers to use (Gersten, Schiller, and Vaughn, 2000; Mastropieri and Scruggs, 1997; Swanson, 1999b;). As discussed in Apply the Concept 2.3, researchers at Center for Research on Learning at the University of Kansas have developed a learning strategy curriculum as well as a number of task-specific strategies (e.g., finding the main idea, word identification, test taking, listening and taking notes) that employ cognitive strategy instruction.

SOCIOCULTURAL THEORY OF COGNITIVE DEVELOPMENT

The sociocultural theory of cognitive development (Vygotsky, 1978) is similar to cognitive strategy instruction in that it highlights the importance of modeling and the use of language to facilitate learning. However, the theory assumes that learning is socially constructed, and as a social activity is highly influenced by the funds of knowledge that learners bring to the situation. Knowledge is meaningfully constructed in these social activities (Englert, Rozendal, and Mariage, 1994; Moll, 1990; Rogoff, 1990; Tharp,

Estrada, Dolton, and Yamauchi, 1999; Trent, Artilles, and Englert, 1998).

Vygotsky was a Russian psychologist who conducted his most important work during the 1920s and 1930s. However, due to the popularity of behavioral theories, Piaget's theory, and information processing theory, his work did not attract great interest until the last 20 years (Byrnes, 1996). The *Cognitive Strategy Instruction in Writing* (CSIW) (Englert, Raphael, Anderson, Anthony, and Stevens, 1991), the *Early Literacy Project* (ELP) (Englert, Garmon, Mariage, Rozendal, Tarrant, and Urba, 1995), and the *Optimal Learning Environment* (OLÉ) (Ruiz, Garcia, and Figueroa, 1996) are three examples that we highlight in this section because they focus directly on students with disabilities or young children who are at risk for developing academic learning disabilities. Although Vygotsky's theory of cognitive development embraces many concepts, we have highlighted three that are particularly important in using this theory for teaching students who may have special needs or are from diverse cultural and linguistic backgrounds. These overarching concepts include the use of resources, the social nature of learning (including the use of interactive dialogue), and the use of scaffolded instruction.

Use of Resources

One key concept associated with this theory is that the teacher needs to consider and use the resources that the students bring to learning (Diaz, Moll, and Mehan, 1986). These include such aspects as culture and language as well as background knowledge the learners can apply to the problem being solved or the knowledge being constructed. For example, in assisting Mexican-American elementary students to develop literacy, Moll and Greenberg (1990) began by first exploring the *funds of knowledge* that could be gained from the community and the Hispanic and southwestern cultures. They also examined how literacy functioned as a part of community and home life. They brought this information into the schools and used it to build a literacy program. In this way, culturally diverse students were given the opportunity to use sources of knowledge that are not often highlighted in traditional school curriculums.

■ **TABLE 2.2**   *Guidelines for Assessing Strategy Effectiveness*

Behavior	*Assessment Questions*
Independence	Can the student use the strategy without cues or assistance?
	Can the student match the appropriate strategy to the task?
	Can the student adapt the strategy if necessary?
Spontaneity	Does the student use the strategy without being asked or cued to do so?
Flexibility	Can the student modify and adapt the strategy to match the situation?
	Can the student pick out the cues in the situation to guide strategy use?
Generalization	Does the student use the strategy appropriately in various situations?
	Does the student use the strategy across different class periods?
Maintenance	Does the student continue to use the strategy after direct instruction of the strategy has stopped?
Reflective Thinking	Does the student stop and think about how to do a task before beginning?
	Does the student think about which strategy to use before beginning?
	Does the student reflect on his or her performance and adjust the strategy if necessary?
Improved Performance	Has the student's performance on the targeted task improved?
	Is there improvement in the student's productivity, accuracy, and task completion?
Improved Self-Concept	Does the student see himself or herself as an active participant in learning?
	Does the student see himself or herself in control of his or her learning?
	Does the student regard himself or herself as more successful?

Source: Adapted from K. J. Rooney and D. P. Hallahan, "Future Direction for Cognitive Behavior Modification Research: The Quest for Cognitive Change," *Remedial and Special Education* 6(2) (1985): 49. Copyright © 1985 by PRO-ED. Used with permission.

Social Nature of Learning and Interactive Dialogue

Another important theoretical concept is the premise that learning occurs during social interactions; that is, learning is a social event in which language plays an important role. Using this concept, teachers and students discuss what they are learning and how they are going about learning. Such interactive dialogue or instructional conversations between teachers and learners provides language models and tools for guiding one's inner talk about learning (Bos and Reyes, 1996; Englert et al., 1995; Mariage, 2000; Moll, 1990). Initially, a more expert person may model the self-talk and vocabulary related to the cognitive processes. However, this gives way to a collaborative or interactive dialogue in which the learner assumes increasing responsibility. This type of teaching allows for the instruction of cognitive and metacognitive strategies within purposeful, meaningful discussions and also provides a means for selecting, organizing, and relating the content matter being discussed. For example, in reciprocal teaching (Palincsar and Brown, 1984), a technique

APPLY THE CONCEPT 2.3

*APPLICATION OF COGNITIVE STRATEGY INSTRUCTION:
THE LEARNING STRATEGIES CURRICULUM*

Can the principles of cognitive strategy instruction be applied to academic tasks in such a way that adolescents with learning disabilities can be successful in performing the skills required for secondary school settings? This is one of the major questions that was addressed by Don Deshler, Jean Schumaker, and their colleagues at the Kansas University Center for Research on Learning. The Strategies Intervention Model (Deshler, et al., 1996; Lenz, Ellis, and Scanlon, 1996) is a comprehensive example of an intervention model based on cognitive strategy instruction.

The goal of the Strategies Intervention Model is "to teach learning disabled adolescents strategies that will facilitate their acquisition, organization, storage, and retrieval of information, thus allowing them to cope with the demands of social interaction" (Alley and Deshler, 1979, p. 8). Learning strategies are techniques, principles, or routines that enable students to learn to solve problems and complete tasks independently. Strategies include how a person thinks and acts when planning, executing, and evaluating performance on a task and its outcomes. Broadly, a learning strategy (a) includes a general approach to solving a set of problems; (b) promotes goal-directed behavior, (c) teaches selection of appropriate procedures; (d) guides implementation of a procedure; (e) shows how to monitor progress; (f) can be controlled; and (g) provides and focuses on cues to take action. Learning strategies instruction focuses on how to learn and how to use what has been learned.

The Learning Strategies Curriculum contains three strands of academic, task-specific strategies. The Acquisition Strand enables students to gain information from written materials and includes such strategies as the Word Identification Strategy (Lenz, Schumaker, Deshler, and Beals, 1993) and the Paraphrasing Strategy (Schumaker, Denton, and Deshler, 1993). The Storage Strand consists of strategies to assist students in organizing, storing, and retrieving information. The First-Letter Mnemonic Strategy (Nagel, Schumaker, and Deshler, 1994) is an example of a storage strategy. The Expression and Demonstration of Competence Strand contains strategies that

enable students to complete assignments, express themselves, and take tests. The Test Taking Strategy (Hughes, Schumaker, Deshler, and Mercer, 1993), the Paragraph Writing Strategy (Lyerla, Schumaker, and Deshler, 1994), and the Error Monitoring Strategy (Schumaker, Nolan, and Deshler, 1994) are examples of strategies that assist students in taking tests, writing cohesive paragraphs, and editing written work.

Each strategy uses a teaching model that incorporates principles of cognitive behavior modification. The stages in the model are:

Acquisition

Stage 1	**Pretest and Make Commitments**
	Obtain measure(s) of current functioning
	Make students aware of inefficient/ineffective habits
	Obtain students' commitments to learn
Stage 2	**Describe the Strategy**
	Insure that students have rationales for strategy use
	Ensure that students know characteristics of situations for when and where to use the strategy
	Describe results that can be expected
	Supervise goal setting
	Describe and explain the strategy steps
	Present the remembering system
Stage 3	**Model the Strategy**
	Demonstrate the entire strategy "Thinking Aloud"
	Involve the students in a demonstration
Stage 4	**Elaboration and Verbal Rehearsal**
	Assist students to verbally rehearse the strategy steps and what each step means
	Require students to memorize the strategy

Stage 5	**Controlled Practice and Feedback**	Phase II	**Activation**

Stage 5   **Controlled Practice and Feedback**

Supervise practice in "easy" materials

Provide positive and corrective feedback

Move from guided practice to independent practice

Require mastery

Stage 6   **Advanced Practice and Feedback**

Supervise practice in materials from regular coursework

Provide positive and corrective feedback

Fade prompts and cues for strategy use and evaluation

Move from guided practice to independent practice

Require mastery

Stage 7   **Confirm Acquisition and Make Generalization Commitments**

Obtain measure(s) of progress

Make students aware of progress

Obtain the students' commitment to generalize

Phase I   **Orientation**

Discuss situations, settings, and materials in which the strategy can be used

Evaluate appropriateness of strategy in various settings and materials

Identify helpful aspects of the strategy and adjustments

Make students aware of cues for using the strategy

Phase II   **Activation**

Program the students' use of the strategy in a variety of situations

Provide feedback

Reinforce progress and success

Phase III   **Adaptation**

Identify cognitive processes

Discuss how the strategy can be modified to meet differing demands

Assist students in applying the modifications

Phase IV   **Maintenance**

Set goals related to long-term use

Conduct periodic reviews

Identify self-reinforcers and self-rewards

Provide feedback

This teaching model relies heavily on modeling, self-instruction, and self-regulation. It encourages students to assume an active and collaborative role in learning. The teaching model has been validated with a number of specific learning strategies (e.g., Bulgren, Hock, Schumaker, and Deshler, 1995; Hughes and Schumaker, 1991; Lenz and Hughes, 1990; Schumaker, Deshler, Alley, Warner, and Denton, 1982). Several of the specific learning strategies are presented in the chapters on reading, written expression, and content areas learning and study skills.

Note: The University of Kansas University Center for Research on Learning requires that persons planning to implement the Learning Strategies Model obtain training available through the Center for Research on Learning, 1122 West Campus Road, University of Kansas, Lawrence, KA 66045; 785-864-4780, http://www.ku-crl.org.

designed to foster comprehension and comprehension monitoring, the teacher and students take turns leading dialogues which focus on their knowledge of the information they are studying and on the processes they are using for understanding and for checking their understanding (see Chapter Five).

Englert, Raphael, Anderson, and their colleagues have designed an instructional writing program based on a sociocultural theory of cognitive development entitled *Cognitive Strategy Instruction in Writing* (CSIW). The program (see Chapter Six) fosters interactive dialogue among teachers and students about the writing process and problem-solving strategies (Englert, Raphael, Anderson, Anthony, and Stevens 1991; Englert, Raphael, and Anderson 1992). In the program, think sheets help the teacher and students see, discuss, and think about the questions, text structures, and problem-solving strategies that good writers use when planning, drafting, editing, redrafting and final drafting a written piece. In this program, interactive dialogue plays a critical role in successful instruction. For example, Ms. Patrick and her students discuss editing a piece of her writing on how to plant bulbs. Ms. Patrick's goal is to demonstrate and guide students in how to reread their texts for meaning and organization from the perspective of a reader, and examine their texts to see if they accomplished their goals related to purpose and text structure (Englert, 1992). During this discussion, Ms. Patrick has put her writing on the overhead for students to comment on and edit.

T: Okay, as I read my paper…listen for several things. Listen for key words. [Check for] clear steps. Ask, "Does it make sense?" *She reads her own story.*

Jim: It has five key words. First, next, then, then, next. *Two students reread her paper aloud and another goes up spontaneously and circles her key words on the overhead. As students begin to circle her key words, she responds.*

T: Go ahead and circle my key words, that's just a draft; I'll be revising it anyway. *The students count five key words.*

T: Was it clear?

Ss: Yes.

T: What was clear about it?

Meg: You said how to put it in the pot and then how to do it . . . [You said] put soil in the pot.

T: Was anything unclear?

Roy: If you added more, it would be awful. I think it was perfect.

T: Even my writing isn't perfect all the time. I never said what kind of soil to put in there. And when I said pour half the soil in the pot, I wonder if they know to buy a bag.

Roy: You need to say, "First, you need to tell them to go to the store and buy pot, soil, and

bulbs." They are going to say, "Where do I get this stuff?"

T: You are right . . . I think I'll write in the margins. (Englert, 1992, p. 159)

In this example, Ms. Patrick guides the students to demonstrate and discuss editing strategies. She creates a context where students come to understand and negotiate the meaning of text and to share their understandings about writing. She thinks aloud, e.g., "I think I'll write [notes] in the margin," and then demonstrates on her draft.

Scaffolded Instruction

Another concept of the sociocultural theory of learning relates to the role of the teacher or the expert, who encourages learners by providing temporary and adjustable support as they develop new skills, strategies, and knowledge. The instruction is referred to as *scaffolded instruction* (Tharp and Gallimore, 1988) or *mediated learning* (Kozulin and Presseisen, 1995). The metaphor of a scaffold captures the idea of an adjustable and temporary support that can be removed when no longer necessary. Vygotsky (1978) describes learning as occurring in the *zone of proximal development* or "the distance between the actual developmental level as described by independent problem solving and the level of potential development as determined through problem solving under adult guidance or in collaboration with more capable peers" (p. 86). Important to promoting development within the students' zones of proximal development is the teacher's ability to relinquish control of the strategies to the students (Johnson Santamaria, Fletcher, and Bos, in press). In the example of Ms. Patrick, Englert (1992) discusses how Ms. Patrick relinquishes control of her paper by letting the students circle the key words. Englert (1992) notes that this "transfer of control was prompted in earlier lessons when Ms. Patrick instructed her students to take the overhead marker and mark up texts" (p. 163). In fact, research on the CSIW program in fourth- and fifth-grade general education classrooms with students who have learning disabilities demonstrated that teachers who were most effective in promoting the student gains and transfer in writing (a) modeled the writing strategies, (b) involved students in classroom dialogues about writing, (c) promoted strategy flexibility, and (d) relinquished control of strategies to students (Anderson, Raphael, Englert, and Stevens, 1991).

In the *Early Literacy Project* (ELP) (Englert et al., 1994; 1995; Mariage, 2000), the literacy curriculum is structured to include activities that provide opportunities for scaffolded instruction and the teaching of strategies. Figure 2.6 provides an overview of these activities and the principles of the ELP. Important to promoting development within the students' zones of proximal development is the teacher's ability to relinquish control of the strategies to the students. To illustrate the dialogue that works within the zone of proximal development, Englert and her colleagues (1994) describe the interactive dialogues among the teacher and students, including students at risk for learning disabilities, during the morning news. "In this lesson, the class constructed a morning news about the information from their thematic unit on dinosaurs. Each student took responsibility for drafting a section of the story, and the class reread and edited the various sections. The teacher (T) used this opportunity to model specific writing and editing conventions and to highlight the multiple sources and classroom resources that can be employed in the literacy process.

T: Lauren, you wrote this part. Would you like to read this part for us?

L: I need help with it.

T: Okay, would you like to pick somebody to read that part with you? *Lauren picks a student to help her pronounce unfamiliar words that she can't read.*

T: Does anyone have a question for Lauren about cavemen? *When no one responds, the teacher proceeds to illustrate.* Where did you get the idea about cavemen? When we were talking [referring to the time when she interacted with Lauren as she wrote this section], did we say that dinosaurs ate cavemen?

Ss: No.

T: You know what Lauren told me as she wrote that idea? She got it out of her imagination.

But this paper is kind of telling true things, so I'm wondering if we should leave it in or take it out. SH, what do you think?

SH: There was cavemen. See that book right there? *Points to book.*

T: You can get it. I guess what I'm wondering is if we know for sure if they [dinosaurs] ate cavemen?

A: I saw it in a movie.

T: Was it a real movie or a cartoon movie? *Ss talks about movie and book.* All right. Do we want to leave that [part] in?

Ss: U-huh!

B: Didn't dinosaurs eat other dinosaurs?

T: We have to ask Meg because she was the writer. *B turns to Meg and repeats comment. Meg agrees that B's idea can go in the story. Then the teacher turns to ask the opinion of the class.* What do you think about adding that idea [to our story], boys and girls? 'Dinosaurs eat other dinosaurs.' I want you to put your thumb up if you think that is a good idea. *Surveys students.* So I'm going to put a caret here and I'm going to say, 'Dinosaurs eat other dinosaurs.' (Englert et al., 1994, p. 198)

This dialogue illustrates the way the teacher uses interactive dialogue and classroom resources to support scaffolded instruction. "For example, she encouraged Lauren to select a peer to help her read and asked students to turn to each other in making final decisions about the text. She also acknowledged the contribution of movies, texts, and students' own imagination in the writing process" (Englert et al., 1994, p. 198).

Instructional Implications

There are many instructional implications from the sociocultural theory of cognitive development. Four that seem particularly important are:

1. Instruction is designed to facilitate scaffolding and cooperative knowledge sharing among students and teachers within a context of mutual respect and critical acceptance of others' knowledge and experiences.

Choral and Partner Reading/Writing

Description
Choral reading & taped story reading
Partner reading & partner writing

Purpose: To provide opportunities for students to fluently read & write connected texts; to provide opportunities for students to use literacy language and knowledge; to develop reading/ writing vocabulary and enjoyment of reading

Thematic Unit

Description
Teacher and students brainstorm, organize, write drafts, read texts or interview people to get additional information about a topic or theme from multiple sources, and use reading/writing strategies flexibly to develop and communicate their knowledge
Oral/written literacy connections are made apparent

Purpose: Model learning processes; introduce literacy language, genre and strategies; model reading/writing processes and connections; provide interrelated and meaningful contexts for acquisition and application of literacy knowledge; conventionalize and develop shared knowledge about the purpose, meaning and self-regulation of literacy acts

Silent Reading

Description
Independent reading
Reading to an adult
Listening to new story at listening center

Purpose: Work on fluency for author's chair; provide experience with varied genres

Morning News

Description
Students dictate personal experience stories
Teacher acts as a scribe in recording ideas and as a coach in modeling, guiding, and prompting literacy strategies

Purpose: To model and conventionalize writing and self-monitoring strategies; demonstrate writing conventions; provide additional reading and comprehension experiences; promote sense of community; empower students; provide meaningful and purposeful contexts for literacy strategies

Principles of the Early Literacy Project

Using Meaningful Activities

Teaching to Self-Regulate

Apprenticing Students in the Dialogue

Empowering Students in the Community

Sharing Chair

Description
Read books, poems, personal writing
Students control discourse and support each other
Students ask questions; answer questions, and act as informants to peers and teacher

Purpose: Promote reading/writing connection; empower students as members of the community; allow students to make public their literacy knowledge and performance; develop shared knowledge

Author's Center

Description
Process Writing Approach (students plan, organize, draft, edit texts)
Students partner-write and work collaboratively to brainstorm ideas, gather additional information, write drafts, share drafts, receive questions, and write final draft
Students use literacy strategies modeled in thematic units

Purpose: To develop a sense of community; develop shared knowledge; provide opportunities for students to rehearse literacy strategies; empower students in appropriating and transforming strategies

Literature/Story Response

Description
Students read stories and respond to them in various ways (e.g., sequence stories, illustrate story events, map story events or story structure, summarize story, etc.)
Students make a personal affective response to stories
Students work with partners or small groups to develop response

Purpose: To promote students' application of literacy strategies; present varied genres to students; promote students' ownership of the discourse about texts; futher students' enjoyment of texts; make text structure visible to students

Source: C. S. Englert, M. S. Roszendal, and M. Mariage (1994). Fostering the search for understanding: A teacher's strategies for leading cognitive development in "zones of proximal development." *Learning Disability Quarterly, 17,* p. 191. Reprinted by permission of Council for Learning Disabilities.

2. Learning and teaching should be a meaningful, socially embedded activity.
3. Instruction should provide opportunities for mediated learning, with the teacher or expert guiding instruction within the students' zones of proximal development.
4. Students' sociocultural backgrounds should provide the basis upon which learning is built.

This last implication is highlighted in the *Optimal Learning Environment* (OLÉ) (Ruiz, Garcia, and Figueroa, 1996). It was designed for students with disabilities who are from culturally and linguistically diverse backgrounds. Apply the Concept 2.4 describes this curriculum.

Research suggests that this approach is particularly effective for students with disabilities who are from culturally and linguistically diverse backgrounds (e.g., Ruiz and Figueroa, 1995; Ruiz, Figueroa, and Boothroyd, 1995). Many of the strategies incorporated into the curriculum are further described in Chapters 4–6.

INFORMATION PROCESSING AND SCHEMA THEORIES

Whereas the operant learning and applied behavior analysis model focuses on observable behaviors and views learning as the establishing of functional relationships between a student's behavior and the stimuli in the environment, cognitive learning theory focuses on what happens in the mind, and views learning as changes in the learner's cognitive structure.

Information processing theory, one of the dominant cognitive theories since the 1970s attempts to describe how sensory input is perceived, transformed, reduced, elaborated, stored, retrieved, and used (Anderson, 1990; Atkinson and Shiffrin, 1968; Ericsson and Kintsch, 1995; Massaro and Cowan, 1993). Psychologists and educators studying information processing attempt to understand how thinking processes operate to allow humans to complete such complex cognitive tasks as summarizing a chapter in a text-

book, solving complex math problems, writing a mystery novel, and comparing and contrasting theories of learning.

A simplified model depicting the sequence of stages in which information is processed or learned is presented in Figure 2.7. Although the figure implies that each activity is relatively separate, these processes are highly interactive with a gradual increase in the amount of integrative and higher order processing used. This processing system is controlled by *executive functioning* or *metacognition,* which assists the learner in coordinating, monitoring, and determining which strategies the learner should employ for effective learning (Brown, 1980).

We can use this model to explain how Greg, a high-school student with learning disabilities, might acquire and remember some new information about "seizure" as it relates to the Fourth Amendment of the United States Constitution. Mr. Gomez is explaining the concepts of "search and seizure" to Greg and the rest of the students in government class. He writes the word *seizure* on the board and says, "Seizure is when the police take your possessions away from you because those possessions are illegal. Sometimes the police need a search warrant to seize your possessions and sometimes they do not. As you read this chapter see if you can determine the rules for when the police need a search warrant."

According to the model presented in Figure 2.7, the first step in learning and remembering the information on the concept of "seizure" is to receive the information through the senses. Mr. Gomez exposed Greg to both visual and auditory information by writing the word on the board and by talking about it.

Next, the information is transported to the sensory register. Here, both the visual representation of "seizure" and the auditory information is stored. At this point Greg has neither attended to the information nor connected meaning to it.

Now Greg can attend to the information, but since he cannot attend to all sensory information, he must screen out some in order to attend to specific parts. If Greg is attending to the hum of the air conditioner or thinking about a Friday night date rather than purposefully listening to the teacher, the information Mr.

APPLY THE CONCEPT 2.4

OPTIMAL LEARNING ENVIRONMENT (OLÉ)

Optimal Learning Environment (OLÉ) is built on Vygotsky's sociocultural theory (1978) and Krashen's (1985) concept of *comprehensible input.* These suggest that for culturally and linguistically diverse students who may or may not have learning disabilities, it is important for teachers to provide learning environments that enable students to go beyond their actual levels of performance with deliberate "scaffolding." Krashen's concept of *comprehensible input* (e.g., visual cues, regalia, total physical response) acts as a scaffold for students who are learning English as a second language.

The *Optimal Learning Environment* is a flexible literature-based language arts curriculum that integrates reading, listening, speaking, and writing. Using OLÉ, teachers create a learning situation that is highly contextualized under optimal conditions where teachers employ instructional strategies to promote the 12 optimal learning conditions:

- Student choice
- Student-centered
- Whole-part-whole approach
- Active student participation
- Focus on ideas before mechanics
- Authentic purposes for learning
- Immersion in language and print
- Teacher and peer demonstrations
- Approximation
- Immediate response
- Classrooms as learning communities
- High expectations

The optimal conditions are based on the work of Cambourne and Turnbull (1987) and classroom research with culturally and linguistically diverse students in general or special educational environments (e.g., Echevarria and McDough, 1996; Ruiz and Figueroa, 1995).

The OLÉ curriculum integrates the teaching and use of nine strategies or activities that are often used in process-oriented, learning strategies classrooms. They include:

- Interactive journals
- ABC wall chart or class book
- Shared reading with decodable and predictable texts
- Pocket chart reading with decodable and predictable texts
- Patterned writing with decodable and predictable texts
- DEAR (Drop Everything and Read) time
- Literature study
- Creating texts from wordless books
- Writers' workshop

Each strategy is a collaborative undertaking. Students as well as teachers write in *interactive journals* on a daily basis, independently choosing topics. These journals function as a record of their writing development, and students receive a response each time they write. Emergent readers and writers "read" their entries to the teacher so that the teacher can respond with a vocalized written question for students to answer.

ABC wall charts or *class books* ensure that students are learning the letters that will enable them to decode with better accuracy. Creating their own pictures and key words for each letter gives students the opportunity to relate the letters to their own knowledge and thus remember them more easily. Posting these personal letter representations in place of a conventional letter chart gives students ownership of the alphabet and boosts their self concept.

In *shared reading,* students read alone or in a small group with an expert who assists them in unlocking the alphabetic code. Fluency, automaticity, and strategic reading are the goals of shared reading, especially when decodable texts are used. Reading the text using various methods (i.e., echo reading, choral reading, Reader's Theatre, see Chapter 5) allows for automaticity and opportunities for readers to develop strategies such as predicting a word's meaning from the context or detecting the mood of the story.

Pocket chart reading supports students in developing word recognition skills. With words written on sentence strips or tag board cards, students work with the text without depending on pictures to decode.

To develop writing skills, predictable texts are used to assist in *patterned writing.* New books can be created by taking students directly through the writing process in a safe environment that is teacher-assisted. Patterned writing involves taking a piece of the predictable text and allowing students to complete the sentence or phrase with their own words.

During the 10 to 15 minutes of *DEAR (Drop Everything and Read) time,* students and teachers alike act as avid readers, either alone or sharing a favorite story with a friend. Students are encouraged to discuss story elements, illustrations, or interesting vocabulary words.

Literature studies are a natural progression from shared reading and DEAR time. In small groups, students are encouraged to construct meanings, interpret text, and respond to literature in many other ways. Teachers act as facilitators during these literature discussions.

Creating texts for wordless books, and *writers' workshop,* go side by side in providing teachers opportunities to demonstrate and scaffold the writing process. The Optimal Learning Environment (OLÉ) encourages students to use their funds of knowledge about literacy and life to develop knowledge and skills in reading and writing. Within the OLÉ framework it is important to provide learning opportunities that are sequentially ordered so that students are continually stretched to learn within their zones of proximal development but not unduly frustrated (Johnson Santamaria, Fletcher, and Bos, in press).

Gomez shared with Greg cannot be learned because Greg has not selectively attended to it.

Next, Greg can recognize or perceive the information by detecting the salient features in the information and using the context and his prior knowledge to assist in perception. For example, Greg can use salient visual features in the word *seizure,* his sight word recognition for the word (prior knowledge), and Mr. Gomez's discussion of seizure (context) to perceive the word written on the board as *seizure* rather than the word *leisure* or *search.*

Once the information is perceived, it can be held for a short period of time in working or short-term memory. However, if Greg wants to learn the information, he can either transfer and store the information in long-term memory or use a strategy to keep the information active in short-term memory. Unless some effort is made to remember the information, it will fade in about fifteen seconds. We can use a variety of memory strategies to keep information active. We can rehearse it (repeat it aloud and to ourselves), chunk it (group it together to make fewer pieces of information to remember), elaborate on it (expand on it by using information we already know), and so on. Greg rehearses the word and its definition by saying it several times to himself.

Greg is aware that the information related to "seizure" needs to be remembered for a long time or at least until the test next week. Therefore, the information must be meaningfully stored in long-term memory to become part of his cognitive structure. This way, he should be able to retrieve the information next week for the test. One efficient means of storing new information is to relate the new information to old information. Greg retrieves from his memory a story about a senior who tried to raise marijuana in his backyard. The police found it, arrested him, and seized the marijuana. When he hears or reads the word *seizure,* he can think of the senior having the marijuana seized. Greg also retrieves from his memory that search and seizure are discussed in the Fourth Amendment. Greg can relate the new information to old information almost as if he were filing it in an organized filing system.

When the exam is given next week, and Mr. Gomez asks for the definition of seizure, Greg should be able to retrieve the information from long-term memory into working memory and then write the definition because he filed it in a meaningful way.

Throughout the process, learning is orchestrated by executive functioning or metacognition. For example, when Greg decided to rehearse the word and

■ **FIGURE 2.7** *An Information Processing Model of Learning* its definition rather than write them down, he was using his executive functioning to coordinate the learning process.

Although we process information in a logical sequence (see Figure 2.7), we generally process information very quickly and don't think consciously about what we are doing. We do not necessarily say to ourselves, "Now I need to rehearse this so I won't forget it," or "I have to relate this information to what I already know so that I can remember it." Information processing is also very interactive. Feedback is possible both from observable responses we make and unobservable thinking responses. These interactions are depicted by the bi-directional arrows in Figure 2.7. Let's explore information processing further by looking at each component and at the overall coordinating processes of executive functioning and metacognition.

Sensing

Sensing involves the use of one or more of our senses to obtain information. It refers to our system's capacity to use the sensory processes to obtain information, not our system's ability to attend or discriminate. Stimuli from the environment are received through all our senses. However, much of the information we learn in school-related tasks is received through visual and auditory senses.

Sensory Register

The *sensory register* holds all incoming information for approximately a second, just long enough for us to attend to and perceive it (Loftus and Loftus, 1976). Although we have the ability to retain large amounts of information in the sensory register, the information quickly fades unless we actively attend to and perceive it (Sperling, 1960).

Attention

Most of us use the term *attention* to refer to a wide range of behaviors. We speak of attending to details when we are concerned about the quality of a job, we ask people if they are attending to us when we want them to hear what we are about to say, and we

measure students on the amount of time they attend to tasks. *Selective attention* is the capacity to focus awareness on selected incoming stimuli. As depicted in Figure 2.7., we attend only to some of the information, depending on the task demands.

The importance of selective attention can be demonstrated in relation to the reading process. You have probably experienced reading a text by going through the mechanical motions (identifying the words) only to realize suddenly that you are not attending and cannot remember what you were reading. Instead, your mind has drifted to thoughts about a friend's problems, the music playing in the background, or how good the apple pie baking in the oven smells. An effective learner must selectively attend to the relevant stimuli.

Attention is a limited resource and can only be allocated to a few cognitive processes at a time. However, the more proficient you are at a process, the less attention it will require. Well-practiced processes require little attention and are said to be *automatic,* whereas processes requiring considerable attention have been referred to as *deliberate* or purposive (Hasselbring, Goin, and Bransford, 1987; Swanson, 1996). LaBerge and Samuels (1974; Samuels, 1987) have applied these principles to the reading process. Poor readers, including many students with learning and behavior problems, must allocate so much of their attention to identifying the words in the text that little is left to allocate toward comprehension. Good readers, however, have word recognition at an "automatic" level, and therefore have more attentional capacity to allocate to understanding what they read (Adams, 1990).

Not only do students with learning disabilities have to allocate more attention to some tasks than nondisabled students, they also have difficulty selectively attending to the relevant stimuli and attending for sustained periods of time (Hynd, Obrzut, and Bowen, 1987; Richards, Samuels, Turnure, and Ysseldyke, 1990; Swanson, 1996). Because information will quickly fade from the sensory register, lessons, particularly for students with learning and behavior problems, should be planned to gain the attention of students and direct their attention toward the relevant information (Lerner, 2000).

Perception

Once we allocate our attention to incoming stimuli, the next step in processing is to recognize or perceive the information. *Perception* can be defined as "the process of 'recognizing' a raw, physical pattern in sensory store as representing something meaningful" (Loftus and Loftus, 1976, p. 23). Students who have perceptual disabilities usually have trouble interpreting and obtaining meaning from the stimuli in the environment.

One explanation of how perception works entails the perceiver using feature analysis and the context in which the stimulus is presented to give the stimulus meaning. In *feature analysis,* the perceiver uses the critical features to recognize the stimuli. For example, the critical feature between *n* and *u* and *p* and *b* is orientation. We process more slowly and are prone to confuse letters that have minimal feature differences such as *C* and *G* or *b* and *d* (Kinney, Marsetta, and Showman, 1966). Similar findings have been shown with speech sounds (phonemes). Feature analysis is used across a variety of contexts. For instance, a listener might use the salient clue "Once upon a time" to recognize that she is listening to a story.

The perceiver also uses the *context* in which the stimulus is presented to assist in perception. Read the two words presented in Figure 2.8. Did you have any difficulty reading *THE CAT?* Now look closely at the *H* and the *A*. They are the exact same visual image. The context provided by the words facilitates the appropriate interpretation (Neisser, 1967). Context also plays an important role in perceiving auditory stimuli. Our store of background information, as represented in long-term memory (see Figure 2.7), interacts with the incoming stimuli to assist us in the perception process.

■ **FIGURE 2.8**   *Effect of Context on Letter Recognition*

THE CAT

Short-Term or Working Memory

Once information is perceived it can move into working or short-term memory. *Short-term,* or *working, memory* can be thought of as activated memory since it represents the information that is easily accessible. Working memory has a limited capacity in that we have the ability to store only a small amount of information in working memory at any one time (i.e., seven bits of information plus or minus two bits) (Anderson, 1995; Miller, 1956).

Working memory can be contrasted with long-term memory. Long-term memory represents the information stored outside the attentional spotlight (Ericsson and Kintsch, 1995; Rumelhart, 1977). Working memory is similar to the material on a computer screen in that it will be lost when the power is turned off unless the information has been saved (Anderson, 1995). An example can clarify the difference between short-term and long-term memory.

Study the following numbers so that you can remember them: 9–6–5–8–2–4–1–7. Now cover the numbers, wait for at least fifteen seconds, and then write them. After you attended and perceived the numbers, you probably studied them to keep them active in your working memory and then you wrote them. To keep the numbers active you may have rehearsed the numbers, closed your eyes and tried to visualize them, or used some other memory strategy.

Now write the phone numbers of your two best friends. This information is stored in long-term memory. You had to search your long-term memory for your two best friends. You probably used their names in searching, although you could have used their appearances or an idiosyncratic characteristic. Then you retrieved their phone numbers and transferred them to working memory. Once the information was in working memory you were ready to use the information, so you wrote their phone numbers.

Now, without looking back, write the numbers you were asked to remember earlier. You will probably have difficulty with this task. Since information fades from working memory if you do not work with it, and since you filled your working memory with the phone numbers of your two best friends, you probably cannot write the original numbers. If you had stored the original numbers in long-term memory, you might be able to retrieve them, but the task did not require you to do this. Consequently, they are lost forever.

A number of concepts were demonstrated by this example:

1. Working or short-term memory is activated memory.
2. Working memory has a limited capacity. We can keep a limited amount of information in working memory (i.e., seven pieces of information plus or minus two pieces). These pieces may vary in scope or size. For example, they may be seven single digits, seven phone numbers, or seven major concepts.
3. The more we cluster or group information into larger related concepts, the more information we can keep in working memory. For example, we can cluster information for a shopping list by meats: chicken, hamburger, pork chops; bread: wheat, white, rye; and fruit: apple, orange, banana.
4. If we do not actively work with the information in working memory, it will fade rapidly (up to about 30 seconds).
5. We can use various strategies to keep information active in working memory. For example, we can rehearse the information, elaborate on it, create visual images of it, and so on.
6. Information in working memory is easily replaced by new incoming information (e.g., recalling your friends' phone numbers).
7. Information not transferred to long-term memory cannot be retrieved.
8. Information that is stored in long-term memory is sometimes retrievable. How the information is organized in long-term memory affects how easily it can be retrieved.
9. Information from long-term memory is transferred to working memory. Then you can use that information (e.g., writing the phone numbers of your best friends).

Some students with learning and behavior problems have difficulties with tasks requiring them to listen to or look at numbers, pictures, letters, words, or sentences, hold them in working memory, and then recall them (e.g., Brainerd and Reyna, 1991; Howe, Brainerd, and Kingma, 1985; Swanson, 1991; 1996; Torgesen, Rashotte, Greenstein, Houck, and Portes, 1987). Students with significant reading disabilities have smaller working memory spans than average readers (Swanson and Trahan, 1992). However, the more a person knows about something, the better able the person is to organize and absorb it, and students with learning and behavior problems can be taught strategies to make more efficient use of their working memory (Mastropieri and Scruggs, 1998; Pressley, 1998; Slavin, 2000).

Long-Term Memory and Schemas

We have already discussed the role that long-term memory plays in learning. Using Figure 2.7 as a reference, we see that *long-term memory* aids us in perceiving incoming stimuli. It provides the context that allows us to use top-down processing when perceiving information (e.g., to perceive the stimuli *THE CAT* even though the visual images of the *H* and the *A* are the same). It helps us fill in the words or speech sounds of a conversation that we do not fully hear because we are at a noisy party. Information is retrieved from long-term memory and transferred to working memory before it can be used to make responses.

If long-term memory plays such an important part in the information processing system, how is it organized? If it has to hold all the information we know, including our store of knowledge about the world, procedural information on how to do numerous skills such as tie shoes and play basketball, and information about our goals and values, how does long-term memory keep all this information straight? Cognitive psychologists do not know just how this vast array of information is organized, but they do have some logical hunches.

According to one theory, schema theory, our knowledge is organized into schemas. *Schemas* can be defined as organized structures of stereotypic knowledge (Schank and Abelson, 1977). They are higher-order cognitive structures that assist in understanding and recalling events and information.

It is hypothesized that we have innumerable schemas or scripts for events and procedures and it is our schemas that allow us to make inferences about the events that happen around us (Anderson, 1995; Rumelhart, 1980).

Read the following short passage about an event John experienced.

> John had been waiting all week for Friday evening. He skipped lunch just to get ready for the occasion. At 6:30 P.M. he got in his car and drove to the restaurant. He planned to meet several friends. When he arrived, he got out of his car and waited outside for his friends.

At this point you are probably using a general schema for restaurants. You could answer such questions as "Is John going to eat dinner?" "Will John eat dinner with his friends?" However, you have not been given enough information to utilize a more specific restaurant schema. Now read on to see how your schema is sharpened.

> After a few minutes, John's friends arrived. They entered the restaurant and walked up to the counter. John placed his order first. After everyone ordered, they carried the trays of food to a booth.

How has your schema changed? You should be using a more specific schema, one for fast-food restaurants. Now you can probably answer more specific questions such as "What kind of food did John and his friends probably eat?" "Did John leave a tip?" Utilizing schemas (e.g., our prior knowledge about stereotypic events) allows us to make inferences, thereby filling in the gaps and giving meaning to incoming information. Schemas serve a crucial role in providing an account of how old or prior knowledge interacts with new or incoming information (Anderson, 1990, 1995; Rumelhart, 1985).

Within and across schemas, concepts or ideas are organized so as to promote understanding and retrieval. Information can be stored in semantic networks composed of concepts and relationships between concepts (Ericsson and Kintsch, 1995; Rumelhart, 1980). Figure 2.9 presents a representation of the concept of *bird.* (Your network for *bird* is prob-

ably more extensive than the one presented in this figure.) The closer together the concepts are in the network, the better they serve as cues for each other's recall (Anderson, 1995; Swanson and Cooney, 1996). For example, *wings* should serve as a better recall cue for *bird* than should *two.* A concept does not exist in isolation in semantic memory but is related to other concepts at higher, lower, or the same levels. In the case of *birds,* it could be filed along with *reptiles* and *mammals,* under the superordinate concept of *animals.*

Schemas and semantic networks allow us to organize our knowledge in such a way that we can retrieve information and effectively add new information to long-term memory. They also assist us in determining the relationships among ideas. However, students with learning and behavior problems may not spontaneously use their prior knowledge, and teachers must link new knowledge to existing knowledge.

Memory that deals with concepts and semantic networks like the ones just described is referred to as *semantic memory* (Tulving, 1993). In contrast, visual and other sensory images of events in one's life are referred to as *episodic memory* (Tulving, 1993). Students with memory difficulties may have good episodic memory, but more difficulty storing and accessing semantic memory. Hence, while they can remember the event, they may struggle to remember the concepts.

Executive Functioning or Metacognition

The specific processes in the information processing system (i.e., attention, perception, working memory, and long-term memory) are controlled or coordinated by what has been referred to as *executive functioning* (see Figure 2.7). In the same way that a business executive has many departments that he or she has to coordinate and many decisions to make regarding how best to use those various departments, the learner has to coordinate his or her various learning processes and strategies and make decisions regarding learning. For example, as learners, we must decide (1) which stimuli to attend to (e.g., the book

■ **FIGURE 2.9** *A Semantic Network for the Concept of "Bird"*

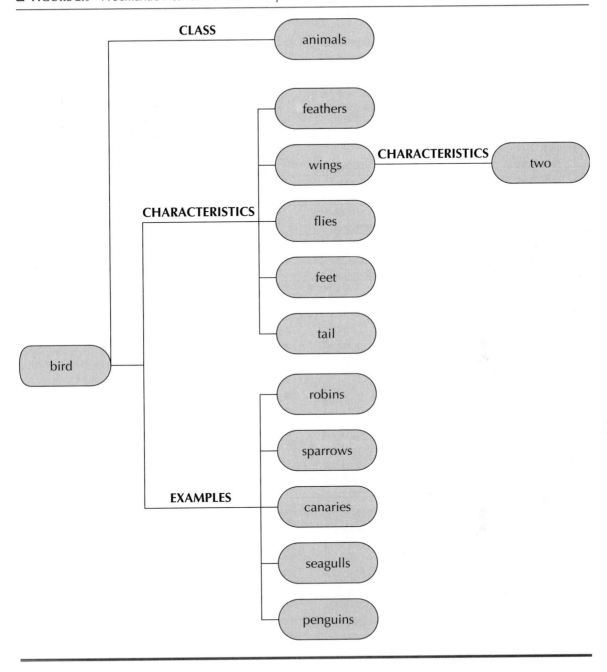

we are reading and/or the smell of the apple pie baking); (2) whether to rely more on feature analysis or context and prior knowledge when perceiving information; (3) what memory strategies are most effective for keeping the information active in working memory; and (4) what is an effective and efficient way to store the information so we can retrieve it later. Making decisions allows us to control the learning process.

This executive functioning has also been referred to as metacognition (Brown, 1980; Flavell, 1976). *Metacognition* is generally considered to have two components (Brown, 1980):

1. An awareness of what skills, strategies, and resources are needed to perform a cognitive task
2. The ability to use self-regulatory strategies to monitor the thinking processes and to undertake fix-up strategies when processing is not going smoothly

In many ways, metacognition and executive functioning are similar to the concepts of self-evaluation and self-regulation presented in the section on cognitive strategy insruction (Hacker, Dunlosky, and Graesser, 1998).

Metacognition and executive functioning require the learner to monitor the effectiveness of his or her learning and, based on feedback, regulate learning by activating task-appropriate strategies. Read the short essay in Apply the Concept 2.5 and see how you use your metacognition.

Students with learning and behavior problems certainly have potential for difficulties with executive functioning or metacognition. For example, the essay you read in Apply the Concept 2.5 was also read by groups of seventh graders, some of whom had reading disabilities and others who were average achievers. They were asked to read the essay to see if it made sense. Although most of the average-achieving students recognized the inconsistency, most of the students with learning disabilities reported that there was nothing wrong with the essay (Bos and Filip, 1984). Wong suggests that, because most students with reading disabilities have difficulty with decoding, many of their cognitive resources are allocated to this task, leaving limited resources for comprehension. Others have found similar metacognitive deficits for these students on reading, writing, and math tasks (Cherkes-Julkowski, 1985; Montague and Bos, 1986b; Torgesen, 1985; Swanson, 1996; Swanson and Trahan, 1992; Welch, 1992).

APPLY THE CONCEPT 2.5

COMPREHENSION MONITORING

Read the following short essay:

There are some things that almost all ants have in common. For example, they are all very strong and can carry objects many times their own weight. Sometimes they go very, very far from their nest to find food. They go so far away that they cannot remember how to go home. So, to help them find their way home, ants have a special way of leaving an invisible trail. Everywhere they go, they put out an invisible chemical from their bodies. This chemical has a special odor. Another thing about ants is they do not have noses to smell with. Ants never get lost (Bos and Filip, 1984, p. 230).

As you read the first part of this essay, you probably read along smoothly and quickly, comprehending the information and confirming that in fact what you are reading makes sense. However, when you read the last couple of lines of the essay, you probably slowed your reading rate, possibly went back and reread, and/or stopped and thought about what you were reading. If these are the types of cognitive strategies in which you engaged, then you were using your executive functioning or metacognition to monitor your information processing system.

Teaching Implications of Information Processing and Schema Theories

Information processing and schema theories have definite educational implications for students with learning and behavior problems. As you read the content chapters in this book, think about how information processing theory helped to shape the instructional techniques. When teaching, think about how you can modify your teaching and the learning environment to facilitate directing a student's attention to the relevant stimuli and his or her perception of the incoming information. For example, teachers who frequently made suggestions about students using metamemory strategies and gave cues for their use found that the students showed better maintenance and more deliberate use of the strategies than students whose teachers rarely made such suggestions (Lucangeli, Galderisi, and Cornoldi, 1995). What strategies can you teach students so that information can stay active in working memory, and how can you present information to facilitate its storage and organization of long-term memory? How can you teach students to use executive functioning to coordinate the various learning and memory strategies?

Several general implications are:

1. *Provide cues to students so they might be guided to the relevant task(s) or salient features of the task.* For instance, when giving a lecture, provide cues to assist the students in attending to the key points by giving an overview of the lecture, writing important concepts on the board, provide the students with a written outline of the lecture, or teaching the students how to listen and look for behaviors that signal important information (e.g., raised voice, repetition).

2. *Have students study the critical feature differences between stimuli when trying to perceive differences.* For example, highlight the "stick" part of the letters *b* and *d;* provide instances and noninstances when discussing a concept.

3. *Have the students use the context to aid in perception.* Students are not likely to substitute *bog* for *dog* if they are reading a story or sentence about a dog.

4. *Facilitate the activation of schemas and provide labeled experiences.* In this way students can develop adequate schemas and modify their current schemas for better understanding of the concepts being presented in both skill and content area subjects.

5. *Teach students to use specific memory strategies.* These could include association, visualization, chunking, and rehearsal.

6. *Use organization techniques to assist students in organizing their long-term memories.* using such content enhancements as semantic maps, relationship charts, and concept diagrams.

7. *Teach students how to be flexible thinkers and to solve problems, thereby encouraging them to use executive functioning.*

SUMMARY

This chapter presents approaches to learning and teaching for guiding the teaching–learning process. The models provide principles that influence the way you, as a teacher, observe, record, interact, and evaluate the teaching–learning process with students.

The first model, operant learning theory and applied behavior analysis, focuses on observed behavior and the antecedents and consequences that control the behavior. In this model the teacher is able to modify the antecedents, by adjusting such variables as the class climate and schedule. The teacher can also increase or maintain desirable behaviors through positive and negative reinforcement, secondary reinforcers, the Premack Principle, shaping, and group contingencies. Through operant learning the teacher is also able to decrease undesirable behaviors by using extinction, differential reinforcement, punishment, and time-out. Teachers can use the principles from operant learning to enhance students' progress through the stages of learning. These include entry, acquisition, proficiency, maintenance, generalization, and application. The teaching–learning process in the operant learning model is highly teacher-directed.

The second model, cognitive strategy instruction, uses principles from both operant learning theories and cognitive-oriented theories. Key features of cognitive strategy instruction are that they include strategy steps, modeling, self-regulation, verbalization, and reflective thinking. Through cognitive strategy insruction the student and the teacher have a more interactive role in the teaching-learning process.

The third model, a sociocultural theory of learning, emphasizes the social nature of learning and encourages interactive discussions between students and teachers. In these discussions the teacher is encouraged to use the students' funds of knowledge and to provide the needed support for the student to acquire new strategies, skills, and knowledge.

The fourth model, information processing and schema theories, explains how information is received, transformed, retrieved, and expressed. Key features of information processing are sensing, sensory register, attention, perception, memory, and executive functioning or metacognition. The information processing model focuses on an interactive role between the teacher and the student, with the concentration on activating prior background knowledge in the student, relating new learning to information the learner has already learned, and maintaining the student as an active learner who thinks about how he or she thinks, studies, and learns.

Throughout the remaining chapters you will see many examples of the principles for teaching and learning that were presented in this chapter. These examples will assist you in understanding how the different approaches to learning and teaching can be applied when interacting with students. In a sense, this chapter provides the theoretical underpinnings for the strategies presented in the subsequent chapters. As you read the subsequent chapters, think about how theory guides the instructional practices and how it will guide your teaching as you work with students experiencing learning and behavior problems.

WEBSITES AS RESOURCES FOR APPROACHES TO TEACHING AND LEARNING

http://specialed.about.com/education/specialed/gi/dynamic/offsite.htm?site=
http://www.lsi.ukans.edu/beach/pbs/html/7s.htm
   This Website introduces Functional Behavior Assessment (FBA).

http://specialed.about.com/education/specialed/gi/dynamic/offsite.htm?site=
http://www.geocities.com/Athens/Styx/7315/subjects/behavior.html
   This Website provides an overview of behavior management and also provides various links containing related issues.

http://education.indiana.edu/~p540/webcourse/web.html
   This Website presents different kinds of theories related to learning.

http://www.analytictech.com/mb870/schema.htm
    The Website provides an overview of schema theory.

http://pitts.rhon.itam.mx/English/Areas/Schema.htm
    This Website provides some features of schema theory.

http://snow.utoronto.ca/Learn2/introll.html
    This Website teaches about the importance of self-awareness and self-regulated learning.

http://psych.hanover.edu/vygotsky/bacalar.html
    This Website provides an overview of soical constructivism.

http://129.7.160.115/inst5931/Behaviorism.html
    This Website provides an overview of history and behaviorism.

http://www.biozentrum.uni-wuerzburg.de/genetics/behavior/learning/behaviorism.html
    This Website provides an overview of operant conditioning and behaviorism.

http://faculty.washington.edu/chudler/chmemory.html
    This Website provides short-term memory games, tricks, and techniques.

http://www.gwo.edu/~tip/vygotsky.html
    This Website provides information on Vygotsky and his theory of cognitive development.

THINK AND APPLY

— Within the operant learning model, what procedures can be used to increase desirable behavior? Decrease undesirable behavior?

— What are the stages of learning and how can they be applied using the operant learning model?

— What are the common characteristics of cognitive strategy instruction?

— Using principles associated with cognitive strategy instruction, design a strategy that one could use to solve subtraction problems with regrouping.

— What implications does a sociocultural perspective have on teaching and learning?

— Why does a sociocultural theory provide particularly relevant support and scaffolds for students who are culturally and linguistically diverse?

— How does long-term memory relate to working memory and perception?

— Using implications from information processing and schema theories, what could you do to assist a student who is having difficulties remembering the information needed to pass an objective social studies test?

3

Oral Language

OUTLINE

KEY TOPICS FOR MASTERY

— *The concept that language is a vehicle or tool for communication and that it includes oral and written language as well as sign and gestures*

— *The differences and interrelationships between language comprehension (receptive language) and production (expressive language)*

— *The components of language including content (semantics), form (phonology, morphology, and syntax), and use (pragmatics) and the interrelationships among these components*

— *The development of oral language during the school-age years and the difficulties that students with learning, language, and behavior problems experience with oral language during the school-age years*

— *The 12 general principles for teaching oral language and examples of how to teach each principle*

— *Strategies for teaching content including word-finding ability and using more elaborative language; strategies for teaching form; and strategies for teaching use*

— *The integral relationship between language and culture and strategies for enhancing language development by using the students' cultural backgrounds*

— *The acquisition of basic interpersonal communicative skills and cognitive/academic language proficiency in second-language and dialect learners and its implications for teaching language to students with learning and behavior problems*

 BRIGHT IDEA

Turn to page 109 and read Think and Apply.

Jerry is a handsome second grader who is good at sports. He seems bright until you hear him talk. Whether he is having a conversation with you or trying to read, he has difficulty thinking of the right words. Yesterday he was trying to describe the work that he and his dad had done on his go-cart. He could not think of the words *screwdriver, hammer, sandpaper, wheels, axle, steering wheel,* and *engine.* Sometimes he attempted to describe what he was trying to say; for example, when he could not think of *screwdriver,* he said, "It's the thing you use to put in things that are kind of like nails." Sometimes he can only think of a word that is similar to the word he is trying to say; for example, "I was using the hitter to hit some nails." Jerry also has trouble remembering words when he reads. He does not remember simple sight words and consequently has to resort to attempting to sound out the words. Often the words he cannot remember are not phonetic (e.g., *come, are, was, very*), so his strategy is only somewhat useful. Jerry is currently in a second grade classroom but he receives speech and language therapy for his language problems and services from the special education teacher for his reading difficulties.

Carmen is in eighth grade. If you just listen to Carmen, you would not necessarily recognize that she has a language problem. Her vocabulary is adequate for a student her age, and she uses fairly sophisticated sentences. But Carmen's language frequently seems to get her in trouble. Carmen is growing up in a tough neighborhood, and she is bused across town. She has difficulty switching her language style to match this new context. She continues to use her "street language," resulting in the interpretation that she is both arrogant and disrespectful to teachers. Carmen also has other problems using language effectively. She has difficulty determining when the listener is not understanding what she is trying to explain. Instead of reexplaining her point, she continues with her description or explanation. When the listener asks her to clarify a point, Carmen implies the listener is stupid. She also fails to take turns easily during conversations. She either monopolizes the conversation or expects the other person to do all the talking while she gives little feedback to let the other person know that she is listening. Consequently, Carmen is perceived as a student with behavior problems, although there is no indication of any serious emotional problems. She sees her counselor once a week and has a special education English class. In the last several months, the speech/language pathologist has been consulting with the special education teacher and counselor concerning Carmen. They are working with Carmen to help her use language more effectively and to vary it across contexts. It will be interesting to see if this will help to eliminate some of the social and behavior problems Carmen is currently experiencing.

Teddy is a child with language delays. He started talking at age three and a half, and now, as a third grader, his language seems more like that of a first grader. He began receiving speech and language therapy at age four. Although he is currently placed in a class for students with mild to moderate disabilities, he receives speech and language therapy for thirty minutes, four days a week. Teddy is delayed in all aspects of language. His vocabulary is limited, he uses simple sentence patterns, and he uses language primarily to obtain information and attention and to inform others of his needs. He rarely initiates a

conversation, but he will carry on a conversation if the other person takes the lead. Mrs. Borman, his special education teacher, is working closely with the speech/language pathologist to help ensure that Teddy is receiving the structured language programming he needs throughout the school day. One of Mrs. Borman's roles in this programming is to provide Teddy with many opportunities to practice and receive feedback on the skills he is learning in speech/language therapy.

As special education teachers, we will undoubtedly work with students like Jerry, Carmen, and Teddy. To assist these students in developing effective language and communication skills, we need to understand the *content of language instruction* and *strategies for teaching language.*

CONTENT OF LANGUAGE INSTRUCTION

Language is a vehicle for communicating our ideas, beliefs, and needs. It is "a code whereby ideas about the world are represented through a conventional system of arbitrary signals for communication" (Bloom and Lahey, 1978, p. 4). Language allows us to share our knowledge with others and, as discussed in Chapter Two, organize the knowledge in our long-term memory so that we can retrieve it and use it to communicate.

The major purpose for language is communication. Both in school and in our society language is a powerful resource. We use language to:

- Maintain contact with others
- Gain information
- Give information
- Persuade
- Accomplish goals
- Monitor our own behavior when we talk to ourselves

Language functions as an integral part of the communication process because it allows us to represent ideas by using a conventional code.

A person's ability to understand what is being communicated is referred to as *comprehension* or *receptive language,* whereas a person's ability to convey the intended message is referred to as *production* or *expressive language.* A basic assumption for the communication process to be effective is that both the speaker and the listener use the same code and know the same rules of language. You have probably had the experience of trying to explain a need to someone who speaks a different language. You probably found yourself using many more gestures than usual. This is because although your listener could not understand your verbal communication code, he or she could understand your nonverbal code (gestures).

Some students with learning and behavior problems experience developmental delays in *comprehension* or receptive language. They frequently ask for information to be repeated or clarified. In school these students have difficulties with:

— Following directions
— Understanding the meaning of concepts (particularly temporal and spatial concepts and technical or abstract concepts)
— Seeing relationships among concepts
— Understanding humor and figurative language
— Understanding multiple meanings
— Understanding less common and irregular verb tenses
— Understanding compound and complex sentences
— Realizing they are not understanding what is being said

Students with learning and behavior problems also have delays in *production* or expressive language. Sometimes these students choose not to communicate as frequently as other students. Students with delays in expressive language have difficulty:

— Using correct grammar
— Using compound and complex sentences
— Thinking of the right word to convey the concept (*word finding*)
— Discussing abstract, temporal, or spatial concepts

— Changing the communication style to fit various social contexts
— Providing enough information to the listener (e.g., starting a conversation with, "He took it to the fair," when *he* and *it* have not been previously identified)
— Maintaining the topic during a conversation
— Repairing communication breakdowns

Although some students with learning and behavior problems have difficulty with both receptive and expressive language, other students experience difficulty primarily with expressive language. Students who have only expressive language difficulties generally understand much more than they are able to communicate.

Relationship of Oral and Written Communication

We use language when we read and write and when we communicate orally. In written communication, the writer is similar to the speaker in that the person is responsible for sending the message. The reader is similar to the listener, whose job it is to interpret or construct the message. The relationship of speaking and listening to writing and reading is presented in Figure 3.1. Since both oral and written communication are language based, if a student is having difficulty in oral communication (e.g., understanding figurative language), he or she will also have difficulty in written communication. For example, research consistently tells us that vocabulary knowledge is one of the best predictors of reading achievement (Catts and Kamhi, 1999). However, there are important differences between oral and written communication (Bunce, 1993). For example, in oral language there is a dynamic shifting between roles of the speaker and listener. A speaker can obtain immediate feedback from a listener. Consequently, the speaker can adjust the way in which the message is expressed (e.g., lower the vocabulary level, reexplain, or restate) more easily than the author. This chapter presents methods for teaching students who have difficulty with oral communication; the next three chapters describe ways for teaching students who have

■ **FIGURE 3.1** *Relationship of Oral and Written Communication*

A Model of the Communication Process

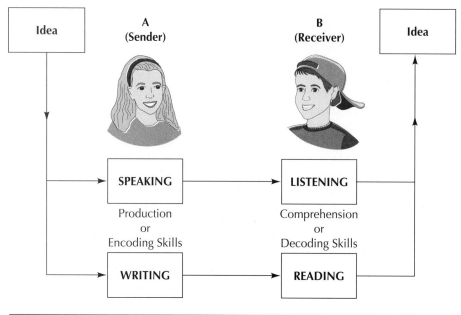

Source: Adapted from J. Lerner, *Learning Disabilities: Theories, Diagnosis, and Teaching Strategies,* 8th ed. (Boston: Houghton Mifflin, 2000), p. 344.

difficulty with written communication (reading and writing). Some of the instructional ideas will be similar because of the underlying language base of both oral and written communication. In some instances an instructional strategy that is suggested as a reading comprehension strategy can also be used as a listening or writing strategy (e.g., teaching students to ask themselves the questions of Who, What, When, Where, Why, and How as they read, write, speak, or listen). We encourage you to keep in mind the close relationship of oral and written communication as you read the next four chapters.

Components of Language

The content of language instruction for students with learning and behavior problems focuses on teaching the language code, the rules of the code, and how to use the code to communicate. To help us understand language so that we can more effectively plan the content of language instruction, we will consider several components of language.

Content

Content, also called *semantics,* refers to the ideas or concepts we are communicating. Elsa can communicate her desire for two chocolate chip cookies in numerous ways. For example, she can say, "I want two chocolate chip cookies," or "Me want choc-chip cookies" (while pointing to the cookie jar and then holding up two fingers). In both cases, the content or ideas are the same.

When we teach content, we are teaching concepts and helping students learn the labels (vocabulary) for those concepts. When a young child asks such questions as "What's that?" or "What are you doing?" we often respond by giving the label for the object (e.g., spoon, blanket, shirt) or the action (i.e., stirring, making the bed, ironing). In this way we are teaching the labels for the ideas or concepts.

We are also teaching content when we help students see the relationships among the ideas or concepts. The diagram or semantic network of the concept of "bird," as depicted in Figure 2.9, is one way to demonstrate how ideas are related. In this case, we used a network that represented the concept of "bird" in terms of its class, properties, and examples. Much of education, whether teaching about fruits and vegetables in primary grades or the characteristics of capitalism and communism in high school, centers on teaching about ideas, the relationships among the ideas, and the vocabulary that labels the ideas (Anders and Bos, 1986; Bunce, 1993; Lenz and Bulgren, 1995; Reyes and Bos, 1997).

Form

Form refers to the structure and sound of language. In the example of Elsa wanting two chocolate chip cookies, two different forms were presented for the underlying meaning of the message. Form is usually further divided into phonology, morphology, and syntax.

Phonology.   *Phones* are the actual sounds produced by speakers. *Phonemes* are the smallest linguistic units of sound that can signal a meaning difference. In the English language there are approximately forty-five phonemes or speech sounds that are classified as either vowels or consonants. Learning the speech sounds and their relationships to the written letters can help students identify unknown words when they read and spell (Blachman, 2000; Catts and Kamhi, 1999; Wagner, Torgensen, and Rashotte, 1994). More information about speech sounds and letter-sound correspondence is provided in Chapter Four. *Phonology* refers to the rules for combining and patterning phonemes within the language. Phonology also includes the control of vocal features (timing, frequency, duration) that influence the meaning we express when talking. Without changing any words, we can vary the underlying meaning of a sentence simply by the way we change our voice (e.g., intonation, pitch, and stress). For example, try saying, "I like *that?*" and "I *like* that." Depending on the intonation, stress, and pitch, the first statement can mean "I don't like that" and the second one can mean "I do like that."

Morphology.   While phonology focuses on sounds, *morphology* focuses on the rule system that governs the structure of words and word forms. While phonemes are the smallest sound units, *morphemes* are the smallest unit of language that convey meaning. There are two different kinds of morphemes: root words or words that can stand alone (e.g., cat, run, pretty, small, form), and affixes (prefixes, suffixes, and inflectional endings) that are added to words that change the meaning of the words (e.g., cat*s*, *re*run, small*est*, *trans*form*ation*).

Helping elementary and secondary students learn the various affixes and their meanings can assist them in decoding words, determining the meaning of words, and spelling. For example, students who do not recognize or know the meaning of the word *predetermination* can break it into the root word *determine* (to decide), the prefix *pre-* (before), and the suffix *tion* (denoting action in a noun). Then the students can decode or spell the word and generate the meaning of *predetermination* as a decision made in advance.

Developmentally, inflectional endings are the easiest to learn, followed by suffixes, and then prefixes (Owens, 1999; Rubin, 1988). While inflectional endings can be taught through conversational milieu, suffix and prefixes usually require more formal instruction in both oral and written form (Moats, 1995). The most frequently used prefixes in American English are *un-, in-, dis-,* and *non-*. Table 3.1 presents some common prefixes, suffixes, and inflectional endings with their meanings and several examples. As you can see from the table, definitions of prefixes and suffixes are sometimes vague. Although only one or two definitions are provided, some affixes have four or more definitions (Gunning, 2001). Teaching this information (or a simplified list for elementary-aged students) can assist students in understanding and learning new vocabulary and in decoding unknown words. To give students a sense of the meanings, provide experiences with several examples. More ideas for teaching affixes is provided in "Teaching Word Recognition and Word Study" in Chapter Four.

■ **TABLE 3.1**   *Common Inflectional Endings, Prefixes, and Suffixes*

Common Forms	*Meanings*	*Examples*
	Inflectional Endings	
-ed	notes past tense on verbs	helped, studied
-ing	notes present progressive on verbs	helping, studying
-s/-es	notes third person singular on verbs	he helps, she studies
-s/-es	notes plurals on nouns	cats, parties
-'s	notes possessive	Jon's, cat's
	Prefixes	
ante-	before, front	antecedent, anterior
anti-	against	antifreeze, antitoxin
bi-	two	bicycle, bisect
co-	with, together	coworker, cooperate
de-	down, remove, reduce	decent, dethrone, devalue,
	do the opposite	deactivate
dis-	opposite	distrust, distaste
en-	to cover, to cause to be	encompass, enslave
ex-	former, from	expatriate, explain
hyper-	above, more, excessive	hyperactive, hyperventilate
hypo-	below, less	hypoactive, hypodermic
il-	not	illogical
im-	not, in, into	impatient, incomplete
in-	not, in, into	incomplete, inclusion
inter-	between, together	interact, intervene
ir-	not, into	irreversible
mis-	wrong	miscalculate
non-	not	nonstop
out-	beyond, exceeds	outlast, outside
pre-	before, in front of	preface, precaution
pro-	before, in front of, in favor of	proceed, proactive
re-	again, backward motion	repeat, rewind
semi-	half	semifinalist
sub-	under, less than	subordinate, subtitle
super-	above, superior	superordinate
trans-	across, beyond	transportation
un-	not	unlucky, unclear
	Suffixes	
-able	capable of, tendency to	dependable
-age	result of action or place	breakage, orphanage
-al	pertaining to	personal
-ance	changing an action to a state	hindrance
-ation	changing an action to a state	determination
-ant	one who (occupation)	accountant, attendant
-en	noting action from an adjective	harden, loosen
-ence	changing an action to a state	dependence, reference

Common Forms	Meanings	Examples

Suffixes

Common Forms	Meanings	Examples
-er/or	notes occupation or type of person	lawyer, writer, sculptor
-er	notes comparative (between two)	larger, younger
-est	notes superlative (among more than two)	largest, youngest
-ful	full of	bountiful, joyful
-fy	to make	magnify, identify
-ible	capable of, tendency to	credible, collectible
-ion/-tion	changing an action to a state	confusion, transformation
-ish	belonging to, characteristic of	Finnish, greenish
-ist	one who (occupation)	artist, biologist
-ive	changes action to characteristic or tendency	creative, active
-less	unable to, without	harmless, thoughtless
-ly	denotes adverbs	loudly, friendly
-ment	result of an action (noun)	entertainment, excitement
-ness	quality, state of being	happiness, deafness
-ous	full of, having	victorious, harmonious
-some	quality or state	handsome, bothersome
-ward	turning to	homeward, wayward
-y	characterized by, inclined to	dirty, sleepy

Syntax.   *Syntax* refers to the order of words in sentences and the rules for determining the order. Just as phonemes combine to form words, words combine to form phrases and sentences. In the same way that rules determine how phonemes can be combined, rules also determine how words can be combined. The basic syntactical structure for English is subject + verb + object (e.g., Mike eats cereal).

The rules for combining words vary across languages. For example, in English, adjectives almost always precede the noun they modify (e.g., a delicious apple), whereas in Spanish, adjectives generally follow the noun they modify (e.g., *una manzana deliciosa*—an apple delicious).

Use

Language use or pragmatics grows significantly during the school-age years (Owens, 1999; Reed, 1994). *Pragmatics* refers to the purposes or functions of communication or how we use language to communicate (Roberts and Crais, 1989). During the school years students become quite adept in using communication for a variety of functions. During later school years students use language proficiently in figurative language, sarcasm, jokes, and multiple meanings (Schultz, 1974). Students also learn to vary their communication style or *register* based on the listener's characteristics and knowledge concerning the topic. By the age of thirteen, students can switch from peer register to adult register depending on the person with whom they are talking, and from formal register to an informal register depending on the setting and circumstances (McKinley and Larson, 1991; Owens, 1999). Pragmatics for students in middle school is an important aspect of functioning within the classroom, because pragmatic skills are critical to academic progress and in building peer relationships (Brice and Montgomery, 1996).

The way a speaker uses language will also be influenced by the knowledge the speaker thinks the listener has about the topic being discussed. If you are describing how to hang a picture on a wall, your language is quite different if the listener is familiar with a plastic anchor and screw. The manner in which a topic is introduced, maintained, and changes, as well as how we reference topics, is governed by pragmatic rules. Students learning English as a second language and bilingual students with communication disorders may need explicit instruction in pragmatics.

Formalist views of language have assumed that language is a composite of various rule systems consisting of semantics, phonology, morphology, syntax, and pragmatics. However, more recent views of language and language intervention have highlighted language as a social tool; and as such, pragmatics is viewed as the overall organizing aspect of language (Owens, 1999; Prutting 1982). This model (see Figure 3.2) has direct implications for language intervention both in terms of targets for intervention and methods of intervention. An approach in which pragmatics is the overall organizing aspect calls for an interactive, conversational approach to teaching and one that mirrors the environment in which the language is to be used (Owens, 2001). This has been referred to as a *functional* or *holistic approach* to language intervention (Muma, 1986).

■ **FIGURE 3.2** *Components of Language from a Functionalist Perspective*

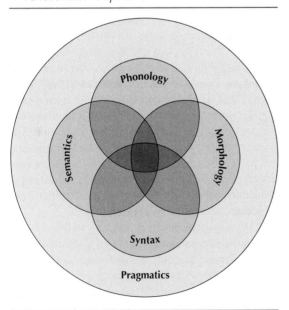

School-Age Language Development and Difficulties

Knowing how language develops during the school-age years and what difficulties students with learning and behavior problems demonstrate during these years will further help us make decisions concerning the content and focus of language instruction.

Much of the research in language development has focused on the preschool child. Between the ages of zero to five, most children become amazingly facile with their language and communication (Brown, 1973; deVilliers and deVilliers, 1978; Owens, 1999). Due to the quantity and quality of development that occurs during this period, the preschool child has been the center of focus for most language researchers. However, during the last twenty years there has been a growing interest in the language development that takes place during the school years (Merritt and Culatta, 1998; Nippold, 1998; Wallach and Miller, 1988) and in the difficulties that students encounter with language in school settings (Bashir and Scavuzzo, 1992; Bunce, 1993; Johnson et al., 1999; Wiig, 1992). Bashir and Scavuzzo (1992) summarized the longitudinal research that has studied school-aged children who have language disorders in the preschool years and noted: (1) these children show changes in the type and severity of their language problems during the school-age years; (2) the acquisition of language forms is the same as for non-disordered children but occurs more slowly; (3) language problems persist for many of these children throughout childhood and adolescence; and (4) additional language problems may develop in middle school when children are required to understand or produce more complex language, develop and understand narratives and expository text structures, and use language for higher-order thinking skills such as persuasion and interpretation.

Although not enough research is available to support a comprehensive scope and sequence for school-age language development, there is enough information to assist us in planning the content of language instruction.

Knowing about school-age language development is particularly important for teachers of students who have learning and behavior problems. There is growing evidence to suggest that these students have mild to moderate language problems (Gerber, 1993; Johnson et al., 1999; Nelson, 1998; Rubin, Patterson, and Kantor, 1991; Sanger, Maag, and Shapera, 1994; Wiig and Wilson, 1994). The largest subgroup of students with learning disabilities are those who experience language difficulties (Simon, 1985; Wiig and Secord, 1994).

Let's examine the development of content, form, and use at the school-age level and the difficulties that students with learning and behavior problems demonstrate.

Content

During the school-age period, children increase the size of their vocabularies and their ability to understand and talk about abstract concepts.

Vocabulary Growth.   During the school years, one of the areas in which students demonstrate the greatest amount of growth is vocabulary. When students enter school their estimated speaking vocabulary is about 2,500 words (Owens, 1999). In comparison, when technical words are discounted, average adult speakers converse in everyday conversation using about 10,000 words, and an estimated 60,000 to 80,000 words are known and used by the average high-school graduate (Carroll, 1964). School provides students with the opportunities to listen, read, and learn, thus increasing their vocabularies. Even math, which is often considered less language-based than social studies and science, contains a significant number of concepts and words to learn (e.g., subtract, estimate, rational number, trapezoid).

There is also an increase in the breadth and specificity of meanings. For example, the word *bird* to a preschooler may refer to animals that fly. However, most children later learn a whole set of specific vocabulary that defines different types of birds and their characteristics. The semantic network that was depicted in Figure 2.9 (page 63) grows more and more complex and more interrelated as a student's knowledge of birds increases.

During school-age years, students' ability to understand and organize abstract concepts increases

significantly (Anglin, 1970; Nippold, 1998). This results in the ability to group words by such abstract features as animate or inanimate, spatial (location) or temporal (time) relationships, and so on. For example, in learning about fossils, students learn to simultaneously classify different types of fossils (e.g., trilobites, crinoids, brachiopods) according to plant/animal, extinct/not extinct, and location (e.g., sea, lake, or land).

Multiple meanings of many common words are acquired during the school-age years (Menyuk, 1971; Nippold, 1998). For example, *bank* has several meanings and can function as both a noun and verb:

> Lou sat on the *bank* fishing.
> You can *bank* on him to be there.
> Put your money in the *bank* for now.

Students with learning and behavior problems generally have vocabularies that are more limited, and their word meanings are generally more concrete and less flexible (Gerber, 1993; Wiig and Secord, 1994). For example, in teaching a group of seventh-grade students with learning disabilities about fossils, we found the students sometimes had difficulty considering three different characteristics of fossils simultaneously (Bos and Anders, 1990a). Questions such as "Which fossils are extinct sea animals?" required them to juggle too much information. In comparison, the students could easily answer questions in which they had to deal with only one characteristic at a time, for example, "Which fossils live in the sea?" "Which fossils are animals?" and "Which fossils are extinct?"

These students also have greater difficulty understanding that words can have multiple meanings and knowing which meaning to apply. In the question, "Was the *fare* that you paid for your taxi ride to the *fair* a *fair* price?" students are required to have and use three different meanings for the word *fair/fare*.

Figurative Language.   Students also develop greater understanding and ability to use figurative language. *Figurative language* represents abstract concepts and usually requires an inferential rather than literal interpretation. Figurative language allows students to use language in truly creative ways (Owens, 1999). The primary types of figurative language include:

— *Idioms* (It is raining cats and dogs.)
— *Metaphors* (She had her eagle-eye watching for him.)
— *Similes* (He ran like a frightened rabbit.)
— *Proverbs* (The early bird catches the worm.)

Students with language disorders and other disabilities, and students who are from other cultures or who have English as their second language, tend to have difficulty with figurative language. Yet figurative language, particularly idioms, is used frequently in the classroom. Classroom research has shown that teachers use idioms in approximately 11 percent of their utterances, while third- to eighth-grade reading programs contain idioms in approximately 6.7 percent of their sentences (Lazar, Warr-Leeper, Nicholson, and Johnson, 1989). Table 3.2 presents some common American English idioms. For students with language disorders and for second language learners, discussing and using these idioms and adding to the

■ **TABLE 3.2** *Common American English Idioms*

Animals	red-letter day	***Tools and Work***
a bull in a china shop	true blue	bury the hatchet
as stubborn as a mule		has an axe to grind
going to the dogs	***Games and Sports***	hit the nail on the head
playing possum	ace up my sleeve	jockey for position
a fly in the ointment	cards are stacked against me	throw a monkey wrench into it
clinging like a leech	got lost in the shuffle	doctor the books
grinning like a Cheshire cat	keep your head above water	has a screw loose
	paddle your own canoe	hit the roof
Body Parts	ballpark figure	nursing his wounds
on the tip of my tongue	get to first base	sober as a judge
raised eyebrows	keep the ball rolling	
turn the other cheek	on the rebound	***Vehicles***
put your best foot forward		fix your wagon
turn heads	***Foods***	like ships passing in the night
	eat crow	on the wagon
Clothing	humble pie	don't rock the boat
dressed to kill	that takes the cake	missed the boat
hot under the collar	a finger in every pie	take a back seat
wear the pants in the family	in a jam	
fit like a glove		***Weather***
strait laced	***Plants***	calm before the storm
	heard it through the grapevine	haven't the foggiest
Colors	resting on his laurels	steal her thunder
grey area	shrinking violet	come rain or shine
once in a blue moon	no bed of roses	right as rain
tickled pink	shaking like a leaf	throw caution to the wind
has a yellow streak	withered on the vine	

Source: From R. E. Owens, Jr., *Language Disorders: A Functional Approach to Assessment and Intervention,* 2nd ed. (Boston: Allyn and Bacon, 1995), p. 347. Copyright © 1995 by Allyn and Bacon. Reprinted with permission. Compiled from Boatner, Gates, and Makkai (1975); Clark (1990); Gibbs (1987); Gullard and Hinds-Howell (1986); Kirkpatrick and Schwarz (1982); Palmatier and Ray (1989).

list can assist them in improving their understanding and use of the English language.

Word Retrieval.   Some students with learning and behavior problems also experience difficulties with *word retrieval* or *word finding* (German, 1987, 1992; McGregor and Leonard, 1989; Nippold, 1998). A word retrieval problem is like having the word on the tip of your tongue but not being able to think of it. The following dialogue presents a conversation between two third-grade students—one with normal language and the other with word retrieval problems.

Setting: Third-grade classroom
  Topic: Discussion about how to make an Easter basket

Susan: Are you going to make, uh, make, uh . . . one of these things (pointing to the Easter basket on the bookshelf)?
  Cori: Oh, you mean an Easter basket?
Susan: Yeah, an Easter basket.
  Cori: Sure, I'd like to but I'm not sure how to do it. Can you help me?
Susan: Yeah, first you'll need some, uh, some, uh, the things you cut with, you know . . . .
  Cori: Scissors.
Susan: Yeah, and some paper and the thing you use to stick things together with.
  Cori: Tape?
Susan: No, uh, uh, sticky stuff.
  Cori: Oh, well let's get the stuff we need.
Susan: Let's go to, uh, uh, the shelf, uh, where you get, you know, the stuff to cut up.
  Cori: Yeah, the paper, and let's also get the glue.

It is obvious from the conversation that both students were frustrated by the communication process. Susan's language is filled with indefinite words (*thing*) (*stuff*), circumlocutions ("The things you cut with"), and fillers ("Let's go to, uh, the shelf, um, where you get, you know, the stuff to cut up"). At first, students like Susan may seem very talkative because of their overuse of descriptions, circumlocutions, and fillers (Swafford and Reed, 1986); how-

ever, after listening for a while, their language seems empty of information.

Word retrieval or word finding problems can result from two possible sources (Kail and Leonard, 1986). One source is with the storage, in that the student's understanding is not elaborate. In other words, the semantic network is not well developed and the meaning is shallow (German, 1992). For example, when a student's semantic network for the concept *bird* (see Figure 2.9, page 63) is well developed it will be easier to retrieve the word than if the semantic network is limited and the word has been learned in isolation. Therefore, in assisting students it will be important to help them develop more elaborated understandings of concepts. A second source of word finding problems is with the retrieval or search and recovery of the word. In this case, teaching and providing cues (it's what you ride; bread and _____ ; it's a type of bird) can assist in retrieval (Nippold, 1992, 1998; Wiig and Semel, 1984). Students with learning and behavior problems may have difficulty with word storage problems, word retrieval problems, or both (German, 1992; Johnson et al., 1999).

Form
During the school-age years, students continue to grow in the ability to use more complex sentence structures (Nippold, 1993, 1998; Scott and Stokes, 1995). Although by age five most students understand and generate basic sentences, first graders produce sentences that are neither completely grammatical (*He'll might go to jail*) nor reflect the syntactical complexities of the English language. Table 3.3 presents the sequence for selected syntactical structures (Carrow, 1973). Some of the most difficult structures require the use of complex sentences and cohesive devices such as causals (*because*), conditionals (*if*), and enabling relationships (*so that*).

Another later-developing sentence structure involves passive construction (*The boy is chased by the dog*), which is usually not established until ages five to seven (Chomsky, 1969; Owens, 2001). What makes older students' language different from younger students in terms of form is the new arrangements and increasingly complex combinations of basic forms (Scott and Stokes, 1995).

■ **TABLE 3.3**   *Developmental Sequence for Comprehension of Sentence Types*

Syntactic Structure	Sentence	Age of Comprehension By 75%		By 90%
Simple imperative	Go!	4–6*	to	6–0 years
Negative imperative	Don't cross!	5–6	to	7–0+ years
Active declarative				
Regular noun and present progressive	The girl is jumping.	3–0	to	3–0 years
Irregular noun and present progressive	The sheep is eating.	6–6	to	7–0 years
Past tense	The man painted the house.	5–6	to	7–0+ years
Past participle	The lion has eaten.	6–0	to	7–0+ years
Future	He will hit the ball.	7–0	to	7–0+ years
Reversible	The car bumps the train.	6–6	to	7–0+ years
Perfective	The man has been cutting trees.	7–0+	to	7–0+ years
Interrogative				
Who . . .	Who is by the table?	3–0	to	3–0 years
What . . .	What do we eat?	3–6	to	5–0 years
When . . .	When do you sleep?	3–6	to	5–6 years
Negation				
Explicit	The girl isn't running.	5–6	to	7–0+ years
Inherent	These two are different.	6–6	to	7–0+ years
Reversible passive	The boy is chased by the dog.	5–6	to	6–0 years
Conjunction				
If . . .	If you're the teacher, point to the dog; if not, point to the bear.	7–0+	to	7–0+ years
. . . then	Look at the third picture; then point to the baby of his animal.	7–0+	to	7–0+ years
neither . . . nor	Find the one that is neither the ball nor the table.	7–0+	to	7–0+ years

*4–6 = 4 years, 6 months

Source: E. H. Wiig and E. Semel, *Language Assessment & Intervention for the Learning Disabled,* 2nd ed. (Columbus, OH: C. E. Merrill, 1984). Reprinted with permission of the senior author, Elizabeth H. Wiig, Ph.D., Knowledge Research Institute, Inc.

As sentence complexity increases, so does the average length of sentences. Yet it is important to know that mature language still has some grammatical errors, false starts, hesitations, and revisions. Table 3.4 demonstrates the growth in the number of words per sentence or communication unit. As evident in Table 3.4, spoken sentence length matches chronological age (i.e., an eight-year-old student's sentences are, on the average, eight words long) until the age of approximately nine years, when the growth curve begins to slow. By high school, adolescents' conversational utterances average ten to twelve words (Nelson, 1998; Scott and Stokes, 1995). Average sentence length, however, is consistently shorter in

■ **TABLE 3.4** *Average Number of Words per Communication Unit (mean)*

Grade	High Group	Random Group	Low Group
1	7.91	6.88	5.91
2	8.10	7.56	6.65
3	8.38	7.62	7.08
4	9.28	9.00	7.55
5	9.59	8.82	7.90
6	10.32	9.82	8.57
7	11.14	9.75	9.01
8	11.59	10.71	9.52
9	11.73	10.96	9.26
10	12.34	10.68	9.41
11	13.00	11.17	10.18
12	12.84	11.70	10.65

Source: W. Loban, *Language Development: Kindergarten through Grade Twelve,* Res. Report #18 (Urbana, IL: National Council of Teachers of English, 1976), p. 27. Reprinted by permission of the publisher.

conversational discourse than in narrative discourse (Leadholm and Miller, 1992).

Children also continue to increase in their ability to use inflectional endings, suffixes, prefixes, and irregular verbs. Table 3.5 presents the order of and age ranges for the acquisition of selected features. Students with language problems are slower to develop advanced syntactic structures, and these delays are most evident in the elementary grades (Owens, 1999).

Use

The area of most important linguistic growth during the school-age years is language use or pragmatics (Nippold, 1998; Owens, 1999). During the school years the child becomes quite adept in using communication for a variety of functions. During later school years students become proficient in using language in sarcasm, jokes, and double meanings (Schultz, 1974). Throughout the schooling years students become more empathetic toward the listener and able to understand a variety of perspectives. Older children can vary their communication style or *register* in that they are much more aware of and take into account the listener's knowledge concerning a topic and the communication context (Eckert, 1990; Nippold, 1998).

According to White (1975), young school-age children use language to:

— Gain and hold adult attention in a socially acceptable manner.
— Use others, when appropriate, as resources for assistance or information.
— Express affection or hostility and anger appropriately.
— Direct and follow peers.
— Compete with peers in storytelling and boasts.
— Express pride in himself or herself and in personal accomplishments.
— Role play.

By adolescence, students reflect communicative competence (Fujiki, Brinton, and Todd, 1996; Owens, 2001; Wiig and Semel, 1984) in that they can:

— Express positive and negative feelings and reactions to others.
— Present, understand, and respond to information in spoken messages related to persons, objects, events, or processes that are not immediately visible.
— Take the role of another person.
— Understand and present complex messages.
— Adapt messages to the needs of others.
— Based on prior experience, approach verbal interactions with expectations of what to say and how to say it.
— Select different forms for their messages based on the age, status, and reactions of the listeners.
— Use sarcasm and double meanings.
— Make deliberate use of metaphors.

Some students with learning and behavior disorders also experience difficulties with language *use* or pragmatics (Brinton, Fujiki, and McKee, 1999; Owens, 1999). The following dialogue demonstrates how Brice, an adolescent with behavior disorders and subsequent learning problems, has difficulty using language effectively in a conversation with a peer. He tends to switch topics (lack of topic maintenance), does not provide enough context for his listener, does not provide adequate referents for his pronouns, and does not respond to his listener's requests for clarification.

■ **TABLE 3.5** *Development of Word Formation Rules and Irregular Verbs*

Word Formation Rules and Irregular Verbs	Age Range (in Years–Months)
Regular noun plurals (balls, chairs)	3–6 to 7–0+
Present progressive tense (running)	3–0 to 3–6
Present progressive tense (going)	3–6 to 5–6
Adjective forms	
Comparative (smaller, taller)	4–0 to 5–0
Superlative (shortest, tallest)	3–0 to 3–6
Noun derivation	
-er (hitter, painter, farmer)	3–6 to 6–6
-man (fisherman)	5–6 to 6–0
-ist (artist, bicyclist)	6–6 to 7–0+
Adverbial derivation (easily, gently)	7–0+
Irregular verbs	
went	4–6 to 5–0
broke, fell, took, came, made, sat, threw	5–0 to 6–0
bit, cut, drive, fed, ran, wrote, read, rode	6–0 to 7–0
drank, drew, hid, rang, slept, swam	7–0 to 8–0
caught, hung, left, built, sent, shook	8–0 to 9–0

Source: Adapted from E. Carrow, *Test of Auditory Comprehension of Language* (Austin, TX: Urban Research Group, 1973); K. Shipley, M. Maddox, and J. Driver, "Children's Development of Irregular Past Tense Verb Forms," *Language, Speech, and Hearing Services in Schools, 22* (1991), pp. 115–112; E. H. Wiig and E. Semel, *Language Assessment and Intervention for the Learning Disabled,* 2nd ed. (Columbus, OH: C. E. Merrill, 1984).

Setting: Computer Lab
Topic: Brice is explaining to Reid how to play a computer game

Brice: Did you get in trouble for last night?
Reid: What do you mean for last night?
Brice: You know, for what you did.
Reid: I'm not sure what you are talking about.
Brice: Want to learn how to play Chopperlifter?
Reid: Yeah, I guess, but what about last night?
Brice: Well, one thing you do is put it in the slot and turn on the computer.
Reid: What thing? Do you mean the CD?
Brice: Sure I do. Now watch. (Brice boots the CD and selects Chopperlifter from a game menu.) You got to take it and go pick up the men.
Reid: You mean the helicopter?
Brice: Yeah, aren't you listening?
Reid: Yeah, but you're not telling me enough about the game.

Brice: Yes I am. You're just like my brother, you don't listen.
Reid: I'm not going to put up with this. I'll see you around.

Although not reflected in his language sample, Brice also has difficulty varying his language for different audiences. Like other students with pragmatic language problems (Kuder, 1997; Nelson, 1998; Sanger, Maag, and Shapera, 1994), he sometimes sounds disrespectful to adults because he does not vary his language to suit different speakers or speaking environments. Finally, Brice and other students with pragmatic language difficulties, including students with behavior disorders, tend to misinterpret emotions or meanings indicated by nonverbal communication, including facial expressions and body language, more frequently than their normal peers (Brinton and Fujiki, 1999; Fujiki, et al., 1996; Giddan, Bade, Rickenberg, and Ryley, 1995; McDonough, 1989).

However, it is important to remember that content, form, and use are related. Sometimes students who appear to have difficulties with language use have these difficulties because of limited content and form. For these students, it would be important to focus instruction in the areas of content and form and see if language use automatically improves.

Conclusion

Even though students enter school with many language skills already mastered, there are still many skills that develop during the school years. Students' vocabulary grows significantly in breadth, size, and abstractness. They learn to use and control more difficult sentence structures such as compound, complex, and passive sentences, and they learn to use more complex figurative language, prefixes, suffixes, and inflectional endings. Students' uses for language expand and their ability to communicate increases as they become more aware of the listener and his or her needs in the communication process. In short, language development in the areas of content, form, and use increases measurably during the school-age years. Whereas this process happens almost automatically for most students because of the opportunities that school and expanding environments afford for learning language, students with learning and behavior problems are often delayed in this development and require more explicit instruction. We will now focus on the procedures for language instruction.

GUIDELINES FOR TEACHING LANGUAGE

In educating students with learning and behavior problems, we have traditionally focused on teaching academic skills and have placed less emphasis on the development of oral language skills. However, it is clear that language continues to develop during the school-age years and that students with learning and behavior problems evidence difficulties in oral language that affect oral as well as written communication. Let's look at some general principles and procedures for teaching oral language skills to these students.

General Guidelines for Teaching Oral Language

Opportunities for teaching oral language abound in the school setting. When we teach students new concepts and vocabulary in content area subjects we are teaching oral language. When students learn how to give oral reports or retell a story, how to introduce themselves, or how to use irregular verbs, they are learning language. A list of general procedures or guidelines for teaching language to students with learning and behavior problems is presented in Figure 3.3 and discussed in this section. The principles can serve as guidelines for teaching. You will also find that the speech/language pathologist is a good source for additional guidelines, techniques, and teaching ideas.

Teach language in purposeful contexts. Whether you are teaching a student to use causal relationships (form), to categorize fossils (content), or how to use the telephone to request information

■ **FIGURE 3.3** *General Principles for Teaching Language*

- Teach language in purposeful contexts.
- In most cases, follow the sequence of normal language development.
- Teach comprehension and production.
- Use conversations to promote language development.
- Adjust pacing, chunk information, and check for understanding to promote comprehension.
- Increase wait time to promote production.
- Use effective teaching strategies when presenting a new concept or skill.
- Use self-talk and parallel talk to describe what you and others are doing or thinking.
- Use modeling to demonstrate language.
- Use expansion and elaboration.
- Use structured language programs to provide intensive practice and feedback.
- Use language as an intrinsic motivator.
- Systematically plan and instruct for generalization.

(use), it is important to teach language in context. It is difficult to imagine teaching someone how to use a hammer, drill, or saw unless we had nails, boards, and probably the goal of making a simple wood project in mind. The same should apply when teaching students to use language. Rote practice of sentence structures or rehearsal of word definitions will teach the student little unless paired with how to use language.

To foster teaching language in context, plan activities that highlight the language skill you are teaching. For example, Mr. Cardoni used the contexts of following a recipe for chocolate-chip cookies and of building bird feeders to teach the vocabulary related to fractions (e.g., half, one-quarter, two-thirds, part, whole, fraction). During the activities the students measured and compared the different fractional parts (e.g., determining what fraction one teaspoon is of one tablespoon). This allowed Mr. Cardoni and his students to talk about the concepts of fractions in a situation where they played an important role in the project and to demonstrate with concrete examples the differences between fractions.

In most cases, follow the sequence of normal language development. Determining the content of instruction is a major part of the teaching-learning process, whether it be in language, academics, content areas, or social areas. Although the developmental sequence of language skills for students with learning and behavior problems is not well-documented, there is some evidence to suggest that these students develop language knowledge and skills in the same sequence as students who are normal-achieving, but at a slower rate (Kahmhi, 1999; Nelson, 1998; Nippold, 1998; Wiig and Semel, 1984). They may also have more difficulty in one component of language: content, form, or use. For example, Susan, the third grader with word-finding problems (see page 79) has difficulty primarily in the area of content. On the other hand, Brice (see page 82) appears to have adequate content and form in his language, but has difficulty with use. Therefore, in planning a language program, begin by determining what knowledge and skills the student has already acquired in the areas of content, form, and use, and then target the subsequent areas in the development process. For instance, if a student is already using past tense (*The boy ate the cake*), then

you might next focus on past participle (*The boy has eaten the cake*) (see Table 3.3). A speech/ language pathologist should be an excellent resource for helping to determine what to teach next.

Teach comprehension and production. Be sure to give the students opportunities to develop both their understanding (comprehension) and their ability to express (production) the new knowledge or skill you are teaching. For example, when teaching students to comprehend the past participle, you will want to label examples of events that have already happened (e.g., *Juan has sharpened his pencil. Kim has finished her math assignment.*). When providing intensive practice and feedback, you could show the students picture-sequence cards (see Figure 3.4) and have the students identify the picture that demonstrates that something "has happened." To teach production, have the students explain what has happened by using the past participle form. For example, you could ask students, "What *have* you just done?" When teaching the concepts and vocabulary associated with a new unit or piece of literature, provide students with opportunities not only to listen to explanations but to discuss their knowledge of the concepts. Using the pause procedure (Di Vesta and Smith, 1979; Ruhl, Hughes, and Gajar, 1990) provides such opportunities. The teacher pauses at logical breaks in the lecture or discussion and lets students discuss what they are learning with a partner or in a small group.

■ **FIGURE 3.4** *Sequence Cards to Help Students Comprehend and Produce Tenses*

APPLY THE CONCEPT 3.1

PROMOTING LANGUAGE THROUGH CONVERSATIONS

- Talk about things in which the child is interested.
- Follow the child's lead. Reply to the child's initiations and comments. Share his/her excitement.
- Don't ask too many questions. If you must, use questions such as *how did/do . . . , why did/do . . . ,* and *what happened . . .* that result in longer explanatory answers.
- Encourage the child to ask questions. Respond openly and honestly.
- Use a pleasant tone of voice. You can be light and humorous. Children love it when adults are a little silly.

- Don't be judgmental or make fun of a child's language. If you try to catch and correct all errors, he/she will stop talking to you.
- Allow enough time for the child to respond.
- Treat the child with courtesy by not interrupting when he/she is talking.
- Include the child in family and classroom discussions. Encourage participation and listen to his/her ideas.
- Be accepting of the child and of the child's language. Hugs and acceptance can go a long way.
- Provide opportunities for the child to use language and to have that language work to accomplish his or her goals.

Source: Adapted from R. E. Owens, Jr., *Language Disorders: A Functional Approach to Assessment and Intervention,* 2nd ed. (Boston: Allyn and Bacon, 1995), p. 416.

Use conversations to promote language development. Students with language problems need opportunities to engage in conversations. Observational research has shown that teachers, in general, are not as responsive to students with language problems as they are to average- and high-achieving students (Pecyna-Rhyner, Lehr, and Pudlas, 1990). Plan opportunities for students to engage in conversations with you and other students as they work, think, and play. Using discussion groups rather than a question/answer format for reviewing a book or current event is an example of how conversations can be integrated into the classroom. During conversations, let the students direct the topics of the conversations. These conversations need not be long, and in secondary settings can be accomplished as students enter the room. Apply the Concept 3.1 provides more ideas that you can use and share with parents about how to promote language through the use of conversations.

Adjust pacing, chunk information, and check for understanding to promote comprehension. Students with learning and behavior problems, and second language learners, often have difficulty comprehending what is being said during class, particularly in content area classes. To promote language comprehension, adjust your pacing so these students have time to process the language input. The flow of instruction need not suffer, but when you are discussing new or difficult concepts or ideas, slow the pace and highlight the key ideas by writing them demonstrating their meaning and/or repeating them. When teaching, it is not unusual for teachers to identify several students that they use to gauge the pacing of their instruction and to determine when to move on. In this group be sure to include the students with language and learning problems.

It is also helpful if the amount of information that is provided in each segment is reduced. Consequently, information can be chunked or segmented into smaller amounts. For example, when Mr. Fong observed his students in Mr. Hunt's fifth grade science class, he noticed that his students usually listened to Mr. Hunt present the first five of fifteen vocabulary words for a new chapter and they recorded about three of the words in their science notebooks. After Mr. Fong shared this information with Mr. Hunt, Mr. Hunt decided that he would chunk the vocabulary into groups of three to five and introduce each group only when they were needed rather than all of them at the beginning of a new chapter.

Checking for understanding is also important for facilitating language comprehension. Having students repeat directions or tell another student what was just discussed are ways to check for understanding other than asking questions.

Increase wait time to promote production. When Sharon Kutok, a speech/language pathologist, talks about the most important principles for teachers to use when teaching students with language and learning problems, the first one she mentions is wait time. Some students need time to understand what has just been said and to construct a response. These students may have particular difficulty with form (e.g., syntax) and need the extra time to think about the form they should use in constructing their response. For students with difficulty in the area of content, they may have difficulty with word retrieval or word finding (German, 1992).

Use effective teaching strategies when presenting a new concept or skill. Critical to new content or concepts is the use of effective teaching strategies. Student's knowledge of concepts grow exponentially during the school age years as discussed in the section on vocabulary development. Your use of effective teaching strategies will assist students with language difficulties gain the concepts and content that are necessary for success in content area classes. Based on the teaching-learning process, there are a number of effective teaching strategies that should be incorporated into language instruction. Figure 3.5 lists key strategies you can use when teaching a new concept.

Use self-talk and parallel talk to describe what you and others are doing or thinking. Using self-talk and parallel talk demonstrates how language is connected to activities. Self-talk describes what you are doing or thinking, while parallel talk describes what the student(s) are doing or thinking. Ms. DeLong, a special education teacher who is co-teaching in a first grade classroom, uses parallel and self-talk when she joins the students at the different learning centers. She explains, "When I join a center, I try to sit down and join in the activities rather than asking students questions. I describe what I am doing

■ **FIGURE 3.5** *Effective Teaching Strategies for Presenting a New Concept or Skill*

When teaching new language concepts or patterns, keep the following strategies in mind:

- Gear the activities to the students' interests and cognitive level.
- Get the students' attention before engaging in communication activities.
- Bombard the student with the concept or skill frequently throughout the day in a functional manner.
- When speaking, place stress on the target concept or language pattern.
- Pause between phrases or sentences so that the student has time to process the new concept or language pattern.
- Decrease the rate of presentation when first introducing the concept or language pattern.
- When introducing a new concept or language pattern, use familiar, concrete vocabulary and simple sentence patterns.
- If possible, present the new concept or language pattern by using more than one input mode (e.g., auditory, visual, kinesthetic). Gestures and facial expressions that are paired with a specific language pattern often assist students in understanding the form. For example, giving a look of puzzlement or wonder when asking a question can serve as a cue to the students.
- Pair written symbols with oral language. For instance, demonstrating morphological endings such as *s* (plurals) and *ed* (past tense) can be done in writing. The students can then be cued to listen for what they see.

and what other students in the group are doing. For example, I might say, 'José is making a clay animal. It's blue and right now he is putting a ferocious snarl on the animal's face. I wonder what kind of animal it is? I think I'll ask José.'" In this way, the students get to hear how words can describe what someone is doing and thinking, and it focuses the attention on José and the on-going activities.

Use modeling to demonstrate language. Modeling plays an important role in learning language. Whether for learning a new sentence structure, new vocabulary, or a new function or use for language,

TECH TALK 3.1

USING SYNTHETIC SPEECH AND SPEECH RECOGNITION TO SUPPORT LANGUAGE AND LITERACY LEARNING

One of the fastest growing areas of educational technology is in synthetic speech and speech recognition. Synthetic speech is the speech that is generated by the computer and speech recognition refers to the computer's ability to recognize and interpret human speech. For students with learning and related language disabilities, the quality of the speech produced by the computer and the ability of the computer to recognize speech and produce text from it are important considerations in planning instructional interventions.

In a recent study, Reynolds and Fucci (1998) compared the use of natural speech with synthetic speech on the language comprehension of students with specific language impairment. The results indicated that *DECtalk,* which produces synthetic speech,

was more difficult to comprehend than natural speech, but that over time students became proficient at comprehending the synthetic speech although not at the level of natural speech. Furthermore, practicing phonological awareness skills using synthetic speech has led to increases in natural speech production (Blischak, 1999) and improved performance on phonological skills and word recognition (Olson and Wise, 1992; Wise and Olson, 1998).

Speech recognition technology has been used as assistive technology for students with learning disabilities to help compensate for writing difficulties. Such programs as *Dragon Dictate* and *Naturally Speaking* (Dragon Systems) and *ViaVoice* (IBM) have also been used to enhance reading and spelling (Raskind and Higgins, 1999).

---

modeling is a powerful tool. For example, Ms. Simons and her eighth-grade students in resource English class were working on improving discussion skills during literature discussion groups. Ms. Simon was concerned about the number of students who did not clarify what they were saying when it was obvious that other students were not understanding.

To teach clarification skills, Ms. Simons initiated a discussion about clarifying ideas and then modelled how not clarifying ideas and not asking for clarification leads to confusion. She exaggerated the examples, and the students seemed to enjoy this. Next, Ms. Simons modelled clarification skills as she participated with the students in their literature discussions. As individual students used effective clarifying skills, she commented on this, so that peers were also serving as models. Use of computers with speech recognition and synthetic speech also provides for language models and systematic practice (see Tech Talk).

Use expansion and elaboration. Language expansion is a technique used to facilitate the development of more complex language form and content.

By repeating what students say in a slightly more complex manner, the teacher demonstrates how their thoughts can be more fully expressed. For example, Ms. Lee, an elementary special education resource teacher, is working to get Rob to connect his ideas and to use adverbs to describe his actions. As he finished several math problems, Rob reported, "I got the first one easy. The second one was hard." Ms. Lee replied, "Oh, you got the first one *easily, but* the second one was hard." You do not want to imply that you are correcting the student, but simply showing him or her a more complex way of expressing the thought. Also, you should expand only one or two elements at once or the expansion will be too complex for the student to profit from it.

Language elaboration is used to build on the content of the student's language and provide additional information on the topic. For example, Chris, a fourth-grade student with language disabilities, was explaining that snakes have smooth skin. Peggy Anderson elaborated on Chris's idea by commenting, "Snakes have smooth skin and so do lizards. Are there other animals in the desert that have smooth skin?"

Use structured language programs to provide intensive practice and feedback. Teaching in context is critical for learning and generalization. However, sometimes by teaching in context we do not provide the students with adequate opportunities to practice a new skill. Students who have learning problems need the practice and feedback provided in many language programs and activities to gain mastery of the skill. For example, *Language for Learning* (Engleman and Osborn, 1999), *DISTAR Language* (Engelmann and Osborn, 1987), and *Figurative Language: A Comprehensive Program* (Gorman-Gard, 1992) provide intensive practice in different language content and forms. However, these programs should not serve as the students' entire language program. Although they provide practice and feedback, they generally do not teach the skill within the relevant contexts that are needed for purposeful learning and generalization.

Use language as an intrinsic motivator. Because language is such an enabling tool, it carries a great deal of intrinsic reinforcement for most children. Rather than using praise ("I like the way you said that" or "Good talking"), we can capitalize on the naturally reinforcing nature of language. For example, during a cooking activity Mr. Warren asks the students, "How can we figure out how much two-thirds of a cup plus three-fourths of a cup of flour is?" After Lydia explained, Mr. Warren comments, "Now we know how to figure that out. Shall we give it a try?" Later, the teacher asks how to sift flour. After Rona explained, he says, "I've got it. Do you think we can sift it just the way Rona explained to us?" Rather than commenting on how "good" their language was and disrupting the flow of communication, Mr. Warren complimented Lydia and Rona by letting them know how useful the information was. When a student's purposes and intents are fulfilled because of the language he or she uses, those language behaviors are naturally reinforced. The student learns that appropriate language use is a powerful tool in controlling the environment (Nelson, 1998; Owens, 1999).

Systematically plan and instruct for generalization. As is the case when teaching other skills, language instruction must incorporate into the instructional sequence a variety of contexts, settings, and persons with which the student interacts if he or she is to generalize the language skills.

Because language is a tool that is used across so many contexts, it is relatively easy to incorporate generalization into language instruction. Mrs. McDonald, the special education resource teacher; Mrs. Kim, the second grade teacher; and Ms. Cortez, the speech/language pathologist, are working with Julie, a second-grade child with learning disabilities, on sequencing events and using sequence markers (e.g., first, second, next, last). When Julie goes to language and resource classes, Mrs. Kim sends a note that lists, in order, the activities Julie participated in thus far during the day. When Julie returns from language and resource, Ms. Cortez sends back a note that lists her language activities. Each teacher then converses with Julie about what she did in the other teachers' classes, emphasizing sequence and sequence markers. Other activities also build generalization for Julie. Whenever the teachers or Julie's mom reads Julie a story, Julie retells the story and is asked sequence questions. During the weekly cooking activity, Julie and the other students tell the steps in making the food for the day, and these steps are written on large chart paper with numbers listed beside them. Julie also arranges picture sequence cards and is then asked to describe them. In this way Julie is receiving numerous opportunities to generalize this language skill to a variety of contexts, persons, and settings.

Teaching Content

We teach language content throughout the day. For example, one of the major goals in teaching a new unit in social studies and science is for the students to understand and use the new vocabulary. What are some of the basic vocabulary categories that we may want to teach? Table 3.6 lists some general categories of words and word relationships. Let us look at some strategies for teaching content or vocabulary, whether it be the more general vocabulary listed in Table 3.6, or the specific vocabulary found in content area instruction.

■ **TABLE 3.6**   *Categories of Words and Word Relationships*

Categories	*School-Related Examples*
Existence/Nouns	science, math, reading, vowels, consonants, sentences, paragraphs
Actions/Verbs	verbs often used in instruction—draw, write, circle, underline, discuss, compare, critique, defend
Attributes/Adjectives	words that describe such attributes as size, shape, texture, weight, position (high/low, first/last), color, age, speed, affect, attractiveness
Attributes/Adverbs	words that describe actions, such as easily, hurriedly, busily, willingly
Prepositions	locative (in, on, under, beside, in front of, ahead of, behind), directional (off, out of, away from, toward, around, through), temporal (before, after, between), for, from, at, of, to, with, without

Personal pronouns	*Subjective*	*Objective*	*Possessive*
	I	me	my, mine
	you	you	your
	she, he, it	her, him, it	her, his, its
	we	us	our
	they	them	their

Demonstrative pronouns	this, that, these, those
Indefinite and negative pronouns	a/an, someone, somebody, something, somewhere, anyone, anybody, anything, anywhere, no one, nobody, nothing, nowhere, the
Antonyms	full/empty, boiling/freezing, easy/hard, soft/hard
Synonyms	pants/slacks/trousers/britches laugh/giggle/chuckle happy/glad/pleased/elated/tickled pink
Homonyms	sail/sale, bear/bare
Multiple-meaning words	run fast, run in your stocking, go for a run, in the long run
Comparative relationships	taller than, shorter than
Spatial relationships	*see* Prepositions
Temporal-sequential relationships	words connoting measurement, time (days of the week, minutes, seasons), temporal prepositions (first, last, next, then)
Conditional relationships	if . . . then
Causal relationships	because, therefore, since
Conjunctive relationships	and
Disjunctive relationships	either . . . or
Contrastive relationships	but, although
Enabling relationships	in order that, so that
Figurative language	*Idioms:* catch a plane; hit the road *Metaphors:* her eagle-eye *Similes:* her eyes twinkled like stars; busy as a beaver *Proverbs:* The early bird catches the worm

Emphasize the distinguishing and critical features of the concepts being taught. When teaching new concepts, emphasize the features that are important to the meaning. For example, when teaching the concepts of "mountains" and "hills" the distinguishing or critical features to emphasize are "size" and "height." In comparison, the "texture of the land" is not important since it is not a feature that usually helps us distinguish between hills and mountains. Comparing and contrasting two concepts using a Venn diagram can help students see the important characteristics (see Figure 3.6). Students remember vocabulary better if they think about how they can use it. Figure 3.7 presents one way students can think about a concept in multiple ways.

Concepts should be introduced in a number of different ways. When teaching the concept of "precipitation," for instance, present pictures of different types of precipitation (e.g., snow, rain, sleet, hail, and mist). Have the students tell about a time when they remember each type of precipitation. Discuss what is happening to the water in the atmosphere when it is precipitating and discuss what the weather is like when precipitation is present.

Present examples and nonexamples of the concept. For example, when learning about cactus, have the students generate two lists of plants, one that represents examples of cacti and one that represents nonexamples. Then talk about and list the features that make the cacti different from the nonexamples.

Categorize new concepts so that students understand how the concept relates to other concepts. If the concept of "melancholy" is being taught, the students should learn that this is an example of a feeling or emotion. Other feelings are "gladness," "relief," and "hurt." Characteristics of people who are melancholy are "not happy," "quiet," "not talkative," and "somber." These ideas can be positioned in a visual diagram, such as a *semantic map,* which shows how the different concepts relate to one another (see Figure 3.8).

Present new vocabulary in simple sentences or phrases. It is harder to learn a new concept or idea if the teacher is using difficult language to explain what it means. The rule of thumb is to use simple sentences or phrases to introduce new concepts (i.e., four- to seven-word sentences and two- to four-word phrases.)

Use games and other activities to reinforce newly introduced concepts. For example, Twenty Questions is a good game to use to get students to think about the characteristics of a concept and the categories in which the concept falls.

Name That Category is a game that can be played similarly to Name That Tune, except the object of the game is to earn points by naming the category when examples of a category are given. The sooner the category is named, the more points the player(s) receives.

Oral or written *cloze* passages as shown in Figure 3.9 can be used to highlight a particular set of concepts being taught.

Idioms, metaphors, similes, and proverbs can be used when playing Charades, with the students acting out the literal meanings of the phrases (e.g., catch a plane, blow your stack).

Additional ideas for teaching new concepts and the relationships among those concepts, particularly as they relate to teaching content area subjects (i.e., science, social studies, vocational areas), are discussed in Chapter Seven. A number of language materials and programs are available for teaching concepts to school-age students. Chapter Appendix 3.1 on page 110 presents the names and short descriptions for several of these programs and materials.

■ **FIGURE 3.6**   *Venn Diagram for Comparing Concepts*

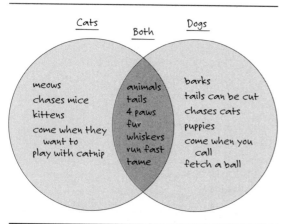

■ **FIGURE 3.7**   *Thinking about a Concept in Multiple Ways*

Definition	Sentence	Illustration
an oven or furnace for hardening or drying something	a kiln is for rapid drying of lumber.	
Synonym	**Word**	**Antonym**
Microwave	Kiln	Freezer
Create an original sentence using the vocabulary word.	Create an analogy using the vocabulary word.	Where might you hear this word used?
I used a kiln to dry my lumber for a house.	Kiln is to microwave as icebox is to freezer.	You might find this in a glass blower's shop.

■ **FIGURE 3.8**   *Semantic Map of the Concept of "Melancholy"*

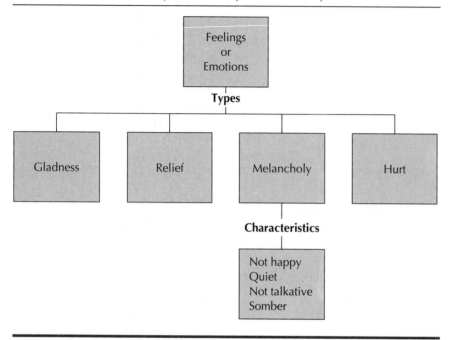

■ **FIGURE 3.9**   *Sample Cloze Emphasizing Prepositions*

Cloze passages can be used either as an oral or written activity or combined with the oral activity reinforcing the written.

> More than anything else, Robert wanted _____ climb _____ the top _____ the mountain. Every day _____ his way home _____ school he looked up _____ the mountain. It was so high that the few trees _____ the top looked very small. He had heard that it would take a day _____ climb _____ the summit, and a day to get back _____ the mountain. One evening when he was looking _____ his window, he saw a campfire burning _____ the top of the mountain. He knew _____ only he practiced hiking, he could make it.
>
> Well, this spring he would start practicing. He and his friend, Jim, could join the Young Hikers' Club and _____ early summer they would be ready _____ the climb. Robert could hardly wait _____ spring _____ come.

Increasing Word-Finding Ability

Another difficulty that some students with learning and behavior problems encounter is word finding. These students know the word but are unable to recall it automatically. Most frequently, these words are nouns. Several techniques can be used to assist students in increasing their ability to recall words, thereby increasing the accuracy and fluency of their expressive language (Casby, 1992; Clark and Klecan-Aker, 1992; German, 1992; Lahey and Edwards, 1999; Nippold, 1998).

Teach students to classify and categorize words. Teaching students to classify and categorize words should improve their long-term memory and thus help them recall and retrieve specific words. When learning new concepts, students should be encouraged to name the category and then rapidly name the vocabulary in the category. Pictures, written words, and graphic representations such as a semantic map (see Figure 3.8) may help with this activity. When students are having difficulty retrieving a word, providing the category helps them to retrieve the word (Halperin, 1974).

Teach students to use visual imagery. Getting students to "see" in their minds the objects they are trying to retrieve can sometimes help them think of the word. To help students develop these mental images, encourage them to picture new words in their minds. For example, when students are trying to learn the parts of a flower, have them picture a flower in their minds, with the labels for the parts written on the different parts. Have them talk about the kind of flower they pictured, discussing the parts as they describe the flower.

Teach students to use word association clues to help in retrieving words. Activities in which students learn and practice word associations (e.g., bread and _____; red, white, and _____) can facilitate word retrieval. These activities may be as broad as asking students to name as many things as they can think of in a given amount of time. But generally the teacher will want to focus the associations. Figure 3.10 presents a variety of association tasks that are more focused. In using these focused activities, keep the pace rapid and the total time for the activity short (1 to 3 minutes). If students have established strong word associations, then when they cannot think of the correct word, providing an associative clue may assist them in retrieving the correct word.

Teach students to use synonyms and antonyms. When students cannot recall the precise word they want, an alternate word can be used. Students may be taught to state that the desired word "is the opposite of _____" or "is almost like _____." For example, when struggling to find the word "joyful," a student can be encouraged to say, "It's when you're really happy," or "It's the opposite of feeling sad."

Use sound, semantic, or multiple choice cues to assist students in recalling words. Providing students with cues can assist them in retrieving words. For example, you might cue, "It starts with a /k/" (sound cue), It's not a peach, it's a _____" (semantic cue), or "It's either a banana, a cat, or a bowl" (multiple choice cue).

Increasing Elaboration in Language

Some students with learning and behavior problems use language that is not very elaborated. When asked to retell stories or events, or to give descriptions, these students provide only the most basic information.

To teach language elaboration, Wiig and Semel (1984) suggest that the teacher use a sequence of three steps for, first, an object or pictured object; then for an event or pictured event; and finally for an event sequence or pictured event sequence. Their three steps for an object or pictured object are:

1. *Model elaboration by introducing familiar objects or pictured objects and by demonstrating verbal descriptions of their attributes and functions.* In this step you are describing the object, noting its attributes and functions. In some instances you may want to contrast it to similar or related objects. For example, describe a cactus and compare it to a rosebush.

2. *Have students elaborate in response to direct questions.* After modeling, ask the students direct questions about the object that require the student to focus on its attributes and functions. For example: What kind of stem does a cactus have? Why does it have such a chunky stem?

3. *Have students spontaneously describe the object or pictured object.* Ask the student to describe the object, using such cues as: Tell me about the cactus. What else can you tell me about it? Are there any other things about it that are important? In what way is a cactus like a rosebush?

The sequence for teaching events and event sequences would be the same.

Teaching Form

Form refers to the structure of language. Tables 3.3 and 3.5 (pages 80 and 82) present syntactical and morphological forms that are relevant when teaching school-age students with language and learning problems. Some procedures and activities for teaching these language forms are:

Teach new sentence structures or prefixes, suffixes, and inflectional endings according to developmental sequences or the order of difficulty. Tables 3.3 and 3.5, as well as language programs and activities designed to teach form (see Chapter

■ **FIGURE 3.10**   *Associative Tasks for Improving Word Retrieval and Developing Vocabulary*

Free Association Tasks

Name as many things as you can in a specified amount of time (usually one to three minutes).

Controlled Association Tasks

Name as many foods, animals, things you take hiking, kinds of fish, etc., as you can think of in a specified amount of time (usually one to three minutes).

Antonym Association Tasks

Listen to each word and tell me the word that means the exact opposite.

> girl
> man
> hot
> inside
> happy

Synonym Association Tasks

Listen to each word and tell me the word that means about the same thing.

> small
> giggle
> mad
> rapid

Categorization Tasks

Listen to these words and tell me what they are.

> dog, cat, fish, alligator
> bread, fruit, vegetables, chicken
> robin, sparrow, eagle

Temporal Relationship Tasks

Listen to each word and tell me what you think of.

> winter   (ice skating, skiing, sledding)
> evening   (watching TV, supper, homework)
> Christmas   (gifts, Santa Claus, carols)

Agent-Action Relationship Tasks

Listen to the names of these animals and objects. Each of them goes with a special action. Tell me what special thing each one of these does.

> plane   (flies)
> lion   (roars)
> doorbell   (rings)

Action-Object Relationship Tasks

Listen to these actions. Each one goes with special objects. Tell me what the objects are.

> fly   (planes, helicopters, kites)
> run   (animals, insects)
> button   (shirts, jackets)

Source: E. H. Wiig and E. Semel, *Language Assessment & Intervention for the Learning Disabled,* 2nd. ed. (Columbus, OH: C. E. Merrill, 1984). Reprinted with permission of the senior author, Elizabeth H. Wiig, Ph.D., Knowledge Research Institute, Inc.

Appendix 3.1), can assist you in deciding the order in which to teach the various sentence and morphological forms.

When teaching a new structure or form, use familiar, concrete examples and vocabulary. For example, Mrs. Ogle wants to have her students work on passive sentences. She begins by having her students act out simple events (e.g., Julio tagged Maria during a relay race). Then she asks the students to tell her a sentence about the event. She writes it on the board (*Julio tagged Maria*). Next she shows the students how she can say what had happened in a different way (*Maria was tagged by Julio*). Then the students act out other events and give passive sentences. In this way, Mrs. Ogle starts with concrete experiences and uses familiar, simple vocabulary to teach the new sentence structure.

Use simple sentences when teaching a new sentence or morphological form. When Mrs. Ogle initially taught her students passive sentences, she used very simple sentences. She could have said, "Julio chased Maria while playing tag," but this sentence would have been much more difficult for the students to put in the passive form.

Once the students have learned the new form have the students extend it to situations that need

more elaborated and complex sentences and less familiar vocabulary. For example, when teaching the morphological ending -*er*, move from familiar vocabulary such as *teacher, reader,* and *writer,* to less familiar vocabulary such as *painter, plumber, framer,* and *landscaper* in the context of house construction, and to the exceptions in this area, such as *mason* and *electrician.*

Use actual objects and events or pictures of them when initially teaching a new structure or form. Also, pair oral communication with written communication. Mrs. Ogle uses the event of playing tag in order to teach passive sentences. She also pairs the oral sentences with the written sentences by writing them on the board. Word and sentence boundaries are clarified by written language, and pictures or actual experiences can assist the students in focusing on the target language pattern. Figure 3.11 demonstrates how pictures and written words demonstrate possessives.

New sentence or word forms should be introduced in a variety of ways. For example, when teaching comparative and superlative forms of adjectives during a measuring activity, Ms. Kamulu has the students determine who has the "long/longer/longest" pencils, pens, scissors, shoelaces, hair, and

■ **TABLE 3.7** *Comparison Chart*

Item	Long	Longer	Longest
red pencils	Susan	Kim	Danny
blue pencils	Susan	Cori	Ken
yellow pencils	Kim	Danny	Ken
white shoelaces	Kim	Danny	Ken
black shoelaces	Cori	Susan	Kim
brown hair	Cori	Kim	Susan
blond hair	Danny	Ken	Steve

so on. Numerous comparisons can be made by using items found in a classroom, and the various comparisons may be depicted on a chart such as the one shown in Table 3.7. Students can then use the examples and the chart to discuss the comparisons and to practice the targeted language skills.

Teaching Use

Instruction in language use is often one of the most important areas for students with learning and behavior problems. One way to organize pragmatic language instruction is based on five ways in which language is used (Wells, 1973). These include ritualizing, informing, controlling, feeling, and imagining. Examples of ritualizing include greeting and farewells, introductions, requests to repeat and requests to clarify, and initiating and responding to telephone calls. Informing examples include asking for and telling information, asking for and telling about objects and events, asking for and telling about conditions and states, and asking for telling about preferences. Some examples of controlling are asking for and telling about wants and needs; asking for and offering favors, help, or assistance; giving and responding to warnings; asking for and giving permission; asking for and telling about intentions; and making and responding to complaint. Examples in the area of feeling include expressing and responding to affection, expressing and responding to expressions of appreciation and approval, asking for and telling about feelings, apologizing and responding to apologies, and expressing and responding to agreements and disagreements. Imagining includes understanding and

■ **FIGURE 3.11** *Visual Representation Depicting Possessive Marker*

Jon's   fishing pole

telling a story, and understanding and telling a joke. These skills are drawn from *Let's Talk for Children* (Wiig and Bray, 1983), a language program designed to assist preschool and early elementary-level children to acquire, use, maintain, and generalize communication functions, and *Let's Talk: Developing Prosocial Communication Skills* (Wiig, 1982a), a language program designed for preadolescents, adolescents, and young adults.

Other pragmatic skills that can be taught include:

- Vary language to match the person to whom one is talking (e.g., speak differently to a young child, a peer, and an adult).
- Vary language to match the context in which the language is occurring (e.g., school, playground).
- Maintain a topic during a conversation.
- Take turns during a conversation.
- Recognize when the listener is not understanding and take clarifying actions to assist the listener.
- Be a considerate speaker and listener (i.e., attend to the cognitive, affective, and language needs of the other person).

Several guidelines can be used when teaching the various skills associated with language use.

Use role playing to simulate different situations in which the targeted pragmatic skills are required. Ms. Peterson uses role playing in her class so students will have some idea what it will feel like when they are put in a situation that requires them to communicate in a certain way or for a specific purpose. Last week the students had to ask each other for directions to their houses during "pretend" telephone conversations. This week students are practicing how to ask questions during a simulated science lesson.

Use pictures or simulations to represent feelings. Some students have difficulty discriminating different nonverbal and verbal communication that accompanies various feelings. By using pantomime or pictures, students can determine what feelings are being expressed and can discuss the cues that helped them determine the feelings. Encourage students to attend to other students' feelings by using such statements as, "You look like you're feeling. . . ." or "I bet you feel really. . . ." or "I can't tell how you're feeling."

Use conversations as a framework for teaching functional language. Conversations about topics familiar to the students or about common experiences can serve as ideal situations for building students' pragmatic skills (Hoskins, 1990; Merritt and Culatta, 1998). The teacher can serve as a facilitator by assisting the students in using the following conversational skills (Hoskins, 1987):

- Introducing a topic
- Maintaining a topic
- Introducing a topic in an elaborated form
- Extending a topic
- Changing a topic
- Requesting clarification
- Responding to requests for clarification

PLANNING INSTRUCTION FOR STUDENTS WHO ARE CULTURALLY AND LINGUISTICALLY DIVERSE (CLD)

As a teacher, you will have students from many different cultures and students who are in the process of acquiring English as a second language or second dialect. You may or may not be familiar with the culture and language of these students. Still, it will be important for these students to feel comfortable in your class and to learn.

Francisco is a good example of such a student. He immigrated from Costa Rica to New Mexico at the age of four with his parents and siblings. Moving from a rural community in Costa Rica, his parents spoke only Spanish when they arrived. Francisco and his family now live in a Spanish-speaking community within an urban setting. While he has some exposure to English and his father is taking a night course to learn English, Francisco entered school at age five with Spanish as his first language and only limited knowledge of his second language, English. This same scenario is true of children who immigrate from many countries including Central and South American countries, Asian and Pacific Island countries, and Eastern European countries. The U.S. Department of Education estimates that of the 40 million students in public and private schools, over 2 million have limited proficiency in English (Diaz-Rico and Weed, 1995). The growth rate has been more than 50 percent in the last five years (Pompa, 1998).

The implications of this are that a growing number of students who enter school in the United States are learning English as a second language while in school. As a special education teacher, your knowledge of second language acquisition and general instructional guidelines can help make school a success for students like Francisco. Students must know that their home language and culture are viewed as assets rather than obstacles to learning (Altwerger and Ivener, 1994; Echevarria and Graves, 1998).

To promote learning, you should incorporate their first language and culture into the curriculum, demonstrate that you value their culture and language, have high expectations for these students, and make accommodations so that they can learn successfully. Research on the characteristics of effective teachers of students with cultural and linguistic diversities (Garcia, 1991; Ladson-Billings, 1995; O'Shea, Williams, and Sattler, 1999; Tikunoff, 1983) indicates that effective teachers:

— Have high expectations of their students and believe that all students are capable of academic success

— See themselves as members of the community and see teaching as a way to give back to the community

— Believe in diversity, meeting individual student needs, and interacting with other teachers to support shared decision-making

— Display a sense of confidence in their ability to be successful with students who are culturally and linguistically diverse

— Communicate directions clearly, pace lessons appropriately, involve the students in decisions, monitor students' progress, and provide feedback

Second Language Aquisition

When students are acquiring a second language, an important variable is the degree of acquisition or proficiency in the first language. Cummins (1991) in a review of research concluded that the better developed the students' first language proficiency and conceptual foundation, the more likely they were to develop similarly high levels of proficiency and conceptual ability in the second language. He has referred to this as the *common underlying proficiency* and has used the analogy of an iceberg (see Figure 3.12) to explain the relationship between first and second language acquisition, and why proficiency in the first language compliments proficiency in the second language (Cummins, 1981).

As can be seen from Figure 3.12, both languages have separate surface features, represented by two different icebergs. However, less visible below the surface is the underlying proficiency that is common to both languages. For example, Table 3.8 compares the phonological, morphological, and syntactical features in Spanish and English, and Table 3.9 highlights some of the grammatical contrasts in African American Vernacular English and Standard American English. Regardless of the language a person is using, the thoughts that accompany the talking, reading, writing, and listening come from the same language core. One implication of this analogy is that individuals who are *balanced bilinguals* have an advantage over monolingual individuals in that they have greater cognitive flexibility and a greater understanding of language (Galambos and Goldin-Meadow, 1990; Skutnabb-Kanagas, 1981).

Important to the learning process is the developmental nature of the second language. Cummins (1984) suggested that, in general, students acquire competency with the *basic interpersonal communication skills* (BICS) prior to competency with *cognitive academic language proficiency* (CALP). The BICS refer to the conversational competencies that

■ **FIGURE 3.12**   *Iceberg Analogy of Language Proficiency*

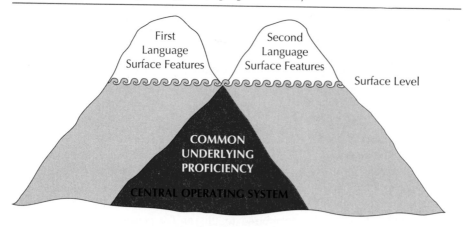

Source: Adapted from J. Cummins, *Bilingualism and Minority Language Children,* (Ontario: Ontario Institute for Studies in Education, 1980). Reprinted with permission of University of Toronoto Press.

■ **TABLE 3.8**   *Comparison of Spanish and English Languages*

Phonological	Morphological	Syntactical
Fewer vowel sounds: no short *a* (hat), short *i* (fish), short *u* (up), short double *o* (took), or schwa (sofa)	*de* (of) used to show posses-sion: *Joe's pen* becomes *the pen of Joe*	use of *no* for *not:* He no do his homework.
Fewer consonant sounds: no /j/ (jump), /v/ (vase), /z/ (zipper), /sh/ (shoe), /ŋ/ (sing), /hw/ (when), /zh/ (beige)	*más* (more) used to show comparison: *faster* becomes *more fast*	no auxiliary verbs: She no play soccer.
Some possible confusions:		adjectives after nouns: the car blue
/b/ pronounced /p/: *cab* becomes *cap*		agreement of adjectives: the elephants bigs
/j/ pronounced /y/: *jet* becomes *yet*		
/ŋ/ pronounced as /n/: *thing* becomes *thin*		no inversion of question: Anna is here?
/ch/ pronounced as /sh/: *chin* becomes *shin*		
/v/ pronounced as /b/: *vote* becomes *boat*		articles with professional titles: I went to the Dr. Rodriguez.
/y/ pronounced as /j/: *yes* becomes *jes*		
/sk/, /sp/, /st/ pronounced as /esk/, /esp/, /est/: *speak* becomes *espeak*		
/a/ pronounced as /e/: *bat* becomes *bet*		
/i/ pronounced as /ē/: *hit* becomes *heat*		
/ē/ pronounced as /i/: *heal* becomes *hill*		
/u/ pronounced as /o/: *hut* becomes *hot*		
/o͝o/ pronounced as /o͞o/: *look* becomes *Luke*		

Source: Adapted from C. A. O'Brien, *Teaching the Language-Different Child to Read* (Columbus, OH: C. E. Merrill, 1973).

■ **TABLE 3.9** *Grammatical Contrasts between African American English and Standard American English*

African American English Grammatical Structure	SAE Grammatical Structure
Possessive -'s	
Nonobligatory word where word position expresses possession	Obligatory regardless of position
Get *mother* coat.	Get *mother's* coat
It be mother's.	It's mother's.
Plural -s	
Nonobligatory with numerical quantifier	Obligatory regardless of numerical quantifier
He got ten *dollar*.	He has ten *dollars*.
Look at the cat.	Look at the cats.
Regular past -ed	
Nonobligatory; reduced as consonant cluster	Obligatory
Yesterday, I *walk* to school.	Yesterday, I *walked* to school.
Irregular past	
Case by case, some verbs inflected, others not	All irregular verbs inflected
I *see* him last week.	I *saw* him last week.
Regular present tense third person singular -s	
Nonobligatory	Obligatory
She *eat* too much.	She *eats* too much.
Irregular present tense third person singular -s	
Nonobligatory	Obligatory
He *do* my job.	He *does* my job.
Indefinite an	
Use of indefinite *a*	Use of *an* before nouns beginning with a vowel
He ride in a airplane.	He rode in *an* airplane.
Pronouns	
Pronominal apposition: pronoun immediately follows noun	Pronoun used elsewhere in sentence or in other sentence; not in apposition
Momma *she* mad. She . . .	Momma is mad. *She* . . .
Future tense	
More frequent use of *be going to* (gonna)	More frequent use of *will*
I *be going to* dance tonight.	I *will* dance tonight.
I *gonna* dance tonight.	I *am going to* dance tonight.
Omit *will* preceding *be*	Obligatory use of *will*
I *be* home later.	I *will* (I'll) *be* home later.

(continued)

TABLE 3.9   *Continued*

African American English Grammatical Structure	*SAE Grammatical Structure*

Negation

Triple negative	Absence of triple negative

| *Nobody don't never* like me. | *No* one ever likes me. |

| Use of *ain't*. | *Ain't* is unacceptable form |

| I *ain't* going. | *I'm not* going. |

Modals

Double modals for such forms as *might, could,* and *should*	Single modal use

| I *might could* go. | I *might be able to* go. |

Questions

Same form for direct and indirect	Different forms for direct and indirect

| What *it is*? | What *is it*? |

| Do you know what *it is*? | *Do you* know what *it is*? |

Relative pronouns

Nonobligatory in most cases	Nonobligatory with *that* only

| He the one stole it. | He's the one *who* stole it. |

| It the one you like. | It's the one (that) you like. |

Conditional if

Use of *do* for conditional *if*	Use of *if*

| I ask *did* she go. | I asked *if* she went. |

Perfect construction

Been used for action in the distant past	*Been* not used

| He *been* gone. | He left a long time ago. |

Copula

Nonobligatory when contractible	Obligatory in contractible and noncontractible forms

| He sick. | He's sick. |

Habitual or general state

Marked with uninflected *be*	Nonuse of *be;* verb inflected

| She *be* workin'. | She's *working* now. |

Source: From R. E. Owens, Jr., *Language Disorders: A Functional Approach to Assessment and Intervention,* 3rd ed. (Boston: Allyn and Bacon, 1999), pp. 412–413. Copyright © 1999 by Allyn and Bacon. Reprinted with permission. Data drawn from Baratz (1968); Fasold and Wolfram (1970); R. Williams and Wolfram (1977).

we develop with a second language. They are the greetings and the "small talk" between peers that do not require much cognitive effort or social problem solving. The CALP, on the other hand, refers to the more cognitively demanding language skills that are required for new learning that is characteristic of school settings. In general, BICS develop in a second language prior to CALP. Cummins (1981) suggested that it takes from one to two years to develop BICS, while it takes five to seven years to develop CALP.

While these generalizations are influenced by situational factors, linguistic input, and the learner characteristics, they do have implications for teaching. You might assume that students who can converse easily in their second language are ready to learn new concepts, strategies, and skills in that language, but this is not necessarily the case. The process of second language acquisition varies substantially with each individual (Ovander and Collier, 1998). This is related to the interactions among sociocultural processes, language development, academic development, and cognitive development.

For example, when Jong Hoon entered Ms. Miles's third-grade class, she immediately noticed that he conversed easily with the other students in the class and with her. Jong Hoon immigrated from Korea two years ago and began learning English through the school's ESL program. His parents are also studying English in a night course and feel that learning English is important for their economic and personal success in America. Still, Korean is the language spoken primarily in the home. Jong Hoon's language acquisition experiences illustrate the four components described by Ovander and Collier (1998).

These components have strong implications for the classroom teacher. As Ms. Miles became familiar with Jong Hoon she realized that while his conversational skills made him a comfortable member of the classroom community (*language development*), he was not proficient in academic tasks such as reading and writing in English (*academic development*). She also found that in social studies and science, it was important for her to provide lots of context for teaching new concepts (*cognitive development*).

When Ms. Miles referred Jong Hoon for possible special education services because of his difficulty with academics, she was not aware of typical patterns of second language acquisition difficulties. But in problem-solving discussions with the bilingual speech/language pathologist and ESL teacher, she learned that different timelines for developing academic knowledge and skills are to be expected and not confused with learning disabilities (*sociocultural processes*) (Duran, 1989; Hamayan and Damico, 1991; Langdon, 1992; Ovander and Collier, 1998; Willig and Ortiz, 1991).

Strategies for Teaching Culturally and Linguistically Diverse Learners

When planning for second language learners who may or may not also have learning and behavior problems, it is important to incorporate the first language and culture. Culturally and linguistically responsive teaching results in lesson modifications and adaptations that are culturally relevant for students (Graves, 1995). For example, in preparing for a thematic unit on California, Ms. Miles worked with the ESL teacher and incorporated an extended segment on farming communities in the unit because Jong Hoon and other students came from Asian and Mexican farming communities. For Jong Hoon and the other students she checked out books and magazines from the school and public libraries about farming and rural life in China, Vietnam, Korea, Mexico, and Central America. The students also had the opportunity to visit not only a California market, but also Asian and Mexican food markets. They compared the foods from the three markets and learned how the foods were grown. For Jong Hoon and the other students who came from other cultures and who were in the process of acquiring English as a second language, providing the link to their cultures helped to give them a context in which the students could build both their language and cognitive skills. This is an example of the context embedded communication and instruction that Cummins (1981) and others (Chamot and O'Malley, 1994; Echevarria and Graves, 1998) recommend to facilitate second language learning.

Other teaching strategies and accommodations include:

- Simplify your language.
- Repeat important phrases and emphasize key vocabulary.
- Demonstrate concepts; use manipulatives.
- Make use of all senses.
- Adapt the materials, don't "water down" the content.
- Include both language development and content vocabulary development and learning.
- Brainstorm with the whole group.
- Provide direct experiences (e.g., read sources, watch videos).
- Increase wait time.
- Respond to the *message,* not to the correctness of the pronunciation or grammar.
- Don't force reluctant students to speak.
- Pair or group native speakers together.
- Use cooperative learning and peer group strategies.
- Learn as much as you can about the language and culture of your students.
- Build on the students' prior knowledge.
- Bring the students' home language and culture into the classroom and curriculum. (Bos and Reyes, 1996; Echevarria and Graves, 1998; Gersten and Baker, 2000; Sullivan, 1992; Towell and Wink, 1993).

Second language acquisition can be facilitated by using a good English-language development program (Gersten and Baker, 2000). Components of such a program that could complement second language acquisition are a focus on development and proficiency in English, teaching phonological, morphological, and grammatical aspects of the use of English, and learning new academic content in English.

Many educators suggest that students should be encouraged to continue to develop proficiency in their first language even if it is not formally supported through bilingual education (e.g., Baker, 1993; Cummins, 1989; Tharp, Estrada, Dalton, and Yamauchi, 1999). To promote this, teachers can:

- Encourage students to use the first language around the school.
- Provide opportunities for students from the same language group to communicate with one another in their first language where possible (e.g., in cooperative learning groups, during informal conversations throughout the school).
- Learn some common words and phrases in the student's native language.
- Recruit people who can tutor students in the first language.
- Provide books written in the various languages in both the classrooms and school library.
- Incorporate greetings and information in the various languages in newsletters and other official school communications (Cummins, 1989).

As a special education teacher, you will undoubtedly work with students who are culturally and linguistically diverse. Making accommodations and using strategies that promote second language acquisition while fostering an understanding of the students' first languages and cultures will assist your students in becoming successful learners.

METALINGUISTICS

When students use metalinguistics, they think about, analyze, and reflect on language as an object in much the same way one describes a table or friend (Wallach and Miller, 1988). *Metalinguistics* refers to the awareness that learners develop about language, and it requires that the learner shift attention from the meaning of language to its form, thereby seeing language as an entity separate from its function (Nelson, 1998; Reed, 1994).

Young children learn to use language without really understanding how it operates and functions. They use the linguistic rules that govern language, but if you asked them to tell you about or explain the rules, they would have great difficulty. As children mature, however, they become more sophisticated language learners. For example, when preschool children begin telling you that "care" and "bear" rhyme, that "little" and "lucky" start with the same sound, or they can clap the number of words in a sentence, they are using metalinguistics. Starting about age two children begin to develop metalinguistic knowledge and skills. Wallach and Miller (1988) have arranged information on the development of metalinguistic skills to correspond in rough approximations to Piaget's stages of cognitive de-

velopment (see Figure 3.13). It is evident from this table that during the second stage, children develop metalinguistic knowledge and skills that are important for the development of early literacy. These are discussed in more detail in Chapter 4.

Teaching students with learning and behavior problems to understand how language operates is important for their success as language users. For example, understanding that words can have multiple meanings, that figurative language does not use literal meanings, and that you can manipulate language style or register to fit the audience and context allows

---

■ **FIGURE 3.13** *Stages of Children's Metalinguistic Development*

Stage One (Ages 1½ to 2)

- Distinguishes print from nonprint
- Knows how to interact with books: right side up, page turning from left to right
- Recognizes some printed symbols, e.g., TV character's name, brand names, signs

Stage Two (Ages 2 to 5½ or 6)

- Ascertains word boundaries in spoken sentences
- Ascertains word boundaries in printed sequences
- Engages in word substitution play
- Plays with the sounds of language
- Begins to talk about language parts and about talking (speech acts)
- Corrects own speech/language to help the listener understand the message (spontaneously or in response to listener request)
- Self-monitors own speech and makes changes to more closely approximate the adult model; phonological first; lexical and semantic speech style last
- Believes that a word is an integral part of the object to which it refers (word realism)
- Able to separate words into syllables
- Unable to consider that one word could have two different meanings

Stage Three (Ages 6 to 10)

- Begins to take listener perspective and use language form to match

- Understands verbal humor involving linguistic ambiguity, e.g., riddles
- Able to resolve ambiguity: lexical first, as in homophones; deep structures next, as in ambiguous phrases ("Will you join me in a bowl of soup?"); phonological or morphemic next (Q: "What do you have if you put three ducks in a box?" A: "A box of quackers.")
- Able to understand that words can have two meanings, one literal and the other nonconventional or idiomatic, e.g., adjectives used to describe personality characteristics such as *hard, sweet, bitter*
- Able to resequence language elements, as in pig Latin
- Able to segment syllables into phonemes
- Finds it difficult to appreciate figurative forms other than idioms

Stage Four (Ages 10+)

- Able to extend language meaning into hypothetical realms, e.g., to understand figurative language such as metaphors, similes, parodies, analogies, etc.
- Able to manipulate various speech styles to fit a variety of contexts and listeners

---

Source: G. P. Wallach and L. Miller, *Language Intervention and Academic Success* (San Diego: College Hill, 1998), p. 33. Reprinted with permission.

students to become highly sophisticated users of language. Labeling and explaining such language concepts is critical to the development of metalinguistic knowledge and skills. Examples of language concepts that can be taught include:

- Phoneme, syllable, and word boundaries
- Figurative language and multiple meanings
- The structure of stories (e.g., setting, problem, episodes with attempts to solve the problem and outcomes from the attempts, final resolution, and ending)
- How to manipulate speech style to fit the audience and context

As you read the next three chapters on teaching reading and written expression, think about how written language and print support the development of metalinguistic knowledge and skills.

INSTRUCTIONAL ACTIVITIES

This section provides instructional activities that are related to oral language. Some of the activities teach new skills; others are best suited for practice and reinforcement of already acquired skills. For each activity, the objective, materials, and teaching procedures are described.

■ Find the Way

Objective: To provide students with practice in giving and interpreting directions.

Grades: All grades

Materials: (1) Maps of different areas. For example, use a map of the school for younger students, and use a map of the local area, the state, or the area you are studying in social studies for older students. The map should be labeled. (2) Put the names of places on the map and on small cards so the cards can be drawn during the game.

Teaching Procedures: One student is designated as "It." This student is given a map and draws a card that gives the name of the place he or she is to find. The student draws the route on his or her map. The other students are given the same map, but they do not know the destination or the route. Without showing the map to the other students, the student who is "It" must describe, by using words only, how to get to the destination. The other students are allowed to ask three questions to help clarify the directions.

To modify this exercise into a game format, each student can receive a point for each time he or she is successful in directing the other students to the location. After a student has finished, discuss how he or she was effective in giving directions and make recommendations to improve his or her language abilities.

Adaptations: A similar format can be used with one student directing the other students on a treasure hunt.

■ Many Meanings

Objective: To give students practice using homonyms and multiple meaning words.

Grades: Intermediate and secondary

Materials: (1) Any generic gameboard with a die or spinner and pieces to serve as players. (2) A variety of meaning cards and homonyms or words that have multiple meanings (e.g., *heal-heel, meet-meat*) written on one side.

Teaching Procedures: Have the students set up the game and clarify the rules. For each turn a student rolls the die or spins the spinner. The student then picks a card and uses each homonym in a separate sentence to show the difference between the meanings of the words or the multiple meanings. If the student's sentences reflect correct meanings, he or she moves the marker the number of spaces shown on the die or spinner. If the student is unable to make a sentence, other students may help him or her, but the student cannot move the marker. The student to reach the finish line first wins.

Adaptations: Have the students work in teams or have the students give definitions of the words rather than using them in sentences.

■ Surprise Pouches

Objective: To give students practice in describing objects.

Grades: Primary

Materials: (1) Cloth pouch with a drawstring. (2) Small objects that will fit in the pouch.

Teaching Procedures: Place a small object in the pouch and have one student in the group feel the object without looking in the pouch. The student cannot give the name of the object, but must describe it. The student describes what he or she feels while the rest of the students in the group try to guess what is in the pouch. When the student feeling the object thinks the other students have guessed correctly, he or she takes the object out to see if the students are right. Have the students discuss how the descriptive words helped them guess the object. For example, "Smooth and round made me think it was a ball."

Put a new object in the pouch and have another student describe the object. Each student should get several turns at describing the objects.

■ I Spy

By Deborah Rhein

Objective: To provide students opportunities to develop descriptive vocabulary.

Grades: Elementary

Materials: Objects in classroom, playground, or any surrounding environment.

Teaching Procedure: Locate an object in the environment. Provide the students with clues that describe the object using the stem "I spy . . ." For example, "I spy something that has green, narrow leaves." "I spy something that has rough bark." After each clue the students try to guess what you are spying. The first person to identify the object becomes the next person to select an object.

Adaptations: For some students you may need to assist in picking an object and giving "I spy" clues.

■ The Add-On Game

Objective: To provide students practice in remembering and recalling lists of ideas.

Grades: Primary

Materials: Starter phrases that allow students to develop a list. For example:

> I am going on a trip to Disneyland and in my suitcase I will pack . . .
> I am going to a restaurant and I am going to eat . . .
> I went to Old McDonald's farm and saw . . .

Teaching Procedures: The students and teacher sit in a circle. A student begins the game by saying, "I am going on a trip to Disneyland and in my suitcase I will pack . . ." This student names one article appropriate to take on the trip. The next person in the circle then repeats the sentence, listing the first item and adds another item. The next person repeats both items and adds a third, and so on. This game can be played in two ways. To play competitively, the person is eliminated from the game when he or she cannot list all the items. The last person to be "out" wins the game. To play cooperatively, the object of the game is for the group to beat the number of items remembered in previous games. In order to keep all students in the game, each student may be allowed two assists from a friend during the game (students are not "out" when incorrect). If a student has already used the two assists, then the number of items the group has correctly remembered is determined and compared to see if the group beat previous scores.

Adaptations: This can be adapted to current events or holidays (e.g., gifts for Christmas or treats you got for Halloween).

■ Round Robin Stories

By Deborah Rhein

Objective: To provide students opportunities to develop story grammar.

Grades: Elementary

Materials: None required although a picture of a scene or setting may help the students start the story.

Procedures: To get the students ready to start Round Robin Stories tell them that they are going to be telling a story as a group and that each student is to build onto the story. Using a picture (if available and needed), tell what the story is going to be about. For example, "This story is about a group of friends who want to earn money to buy something." Then begin telling the story and include the students as characters in the story. After several sentences, start a sentence and have one student in the group finish the sentence. Based on their ending, start another sentence and have another student finish it. As students become accustomed to this story telling process, students should be able to build directly on each other's sentences without your starting each sentence.

Adaptations: Use the same procedure but use wordless picture books to guide students in telling the story.

■ Barrier Game

Objective: To provide pairs of students practice in describing how to make something and to provide practice in listening to directions.

Grades: Elementary

Materials: (1) Colored blocks for building objects or crayons for drawing objects. (2) Some type of barrier to block the view between the two students or the student and the teacher.

Teaching Procedures: Divide class into pairs and explain the directions to the students. Have the stu-

dents sit so that the barrier is between them. One student draws a simple picture or builds a simple block design. During or after the building or drawing, he or she describes to the other student how to make the design. The other student attempts to duplicate the work, and can ask questions to get help. When the other student has finished, remove the barrier and have the students compare their work.

Adaptations: After the students become successful at the activity, the number of questions that can be asked can be limited.

■ Category Sort

Objective: To provide students practice in sorting objects or word cards by categories.

Grades: Primary

Materials: (1) Objects or word cards that can be sorted by one or more categories (e.g., colored bears, colored blocks, colored buttons, colored marbles, types of animals, types of food). (2) Word cards that represent categories. (3) Sorting boxes (i.e., small boxes into which the students can sort).

Teaching Procedure: Put a category word card next to each box. Demonstrate how to name each object or word card and then put all the like objects or cards in the same box. Once the student has sorted the objects or cards, he or she names each category and the objects or cards in each category. The student then talks about what is alike about all the objects or cards in one category.

■ **Create a Comic**

Objective: To provide students practice in using dialogue and telling stories.

Grades: Intermediate and junior high

Materials: (1) Familiar comic strips or sequences in comic books. Blank out the words in the balloons.

Teaching Procedures: Present the comic strip to the students and discuss with them what they know about the comic strip characters, what is happening, and what could be written in each of the balloons. Have the students write in the different balloons. Take turns reading the comic strip with different students reading what different characters say. The different comic strips can be put into a comic book that can be shared with other students.

Adaptations: After students are comfortable with this activity they can illustrate and dictate their own comic strips.

■ **Play the Part**

Objective: To provide students practice in using language during simulations of typical interactions.

Grades: Intermediate and secondary

Materials: Simulation cards. Each card should describe the situation, the characters, and the goal of the language interaction. Several examples are given below.

━ **SITUATION 1:** Two friends meet a third person who is an old friend and known to only one of them. Characters: new friend, old friend, person making the introductions.

Goal: introduce new friend to old friend and get a conversation started between the three of you.

━ **SITUATION 2:** One person approaches another asking how to find a store about ten blocks away. Characters: stranger, person giving directions. Goal: give directions that will allow the stranger to find the store.

━ **SITUATION 3:** Two friends are in a store. One tells the other that he or she intends to steal a small item from the store.

Characters: friend, person persuading. Goal: convince the friend not to shoplift.

Teaching Procedures: Explain that each person is to assume the described role and participate as if this were a real situation.

Have the students assume the various characters and discuss what they are going to say in their roles. The students then carry out the role play. Have the students discuss how effective each person was in using his or her language to accomplish the goal.

SUMMARY

Language is a vehicle for communicating our ideas, beliefs, and needs. We use language to gain and give information, accomplish goals, support interpersonal relationships, and monitor our own behavior and thinking. Although most children enter school with many language skills already mastered, language continues to develop throughout the school years. Students realize significant growths in vocabulary, the ability to represent abstract concepts in language, and the ability to use figurative language, sarcasm, and humor. They communicate easily, using complex sentences and other more advanced sentence and word forms. They increase in the ability to use language to accomplish goals. They also learn how language operates and are able to talk about the characteristics of language (metalinguistics).

Some students with learning and behavior problems experience considerable difficulty in the development of language skills during the school-age years. Some of these students may have problems primarily focused in one of the three components of language (content, form, and use), but because of the interactive nature of these components such students generally have difficulty in all three areas.

In planning instruction for students with language difficulties, we should take into consideration what language skills the students have already developed, what skills developmentally come next, and whether the child is from a culturally or linguistically diverse background. In this way we can target skills that will build directly on the students' current skills. When implementing instruction, we should present new skills in context, using intensive practice to reinforce the skills being taught. This means that we have to plan activities in which the language will be a functional and useful tool for communication.

Given the complexity of language at the school-age level and the need to teach language in context, providing language instruction for students with learning and behavior problems is a challenge. As you work on this challenge we encourage you to work with a speech/language pathologist. You should find this specialist willing to participate in collaborative language programs for students. Such efforts will help to make your instruction consistent and integrative. Finally, we encourage you to accept the challenge of teaching language. Providing students with the language skills to be effective communicators in school and other life settings may be one of the most important tasks we undertake as special education teachers.

WEBSITES AS RESOURCES TO ASSIST IN TEACHING ORAL LANGUAGE AND ENGLISH AS A SECOND LANGUAGE

http://www.asha.org
> This Website is from the American Speech-Language-Hearing Association and provides a wide variety of resources for assessing and teaching oral language.

http://teach.virginia.edu/go/cise/ose/categories/cd.html#top
> This Website is from the U.S. Department of Education, Office of Special Education. It provides resources on communication disorders.

http://www.nidcd.nih.gov/
> This Website is for the National Institute on Deafness and Other Communication Disorders at the National Institutes of Health.

http://www.ldanatl.org/factsheets/fact3.shtml
> This Website provides a brief overview of oral/spoken language difficulties and strategies.

http://www.aaiep.org/links3.html
> This Website is from the American Association of Intensive English Programs.

http://www.catesol.org/
> This Website is from the California Teachers of English to Speakers of Other Languages (CATESOL). It supports English as a second language teachers throughout California and Nevada.

http://www.iatefl.org/
> The Website is from the International Association of Teachers of English as a Foreign Language and supports the English language teaching professionals worldwide.

4

Reading: Phonological Awareness, Alphabetic Principle, and Word Recognition

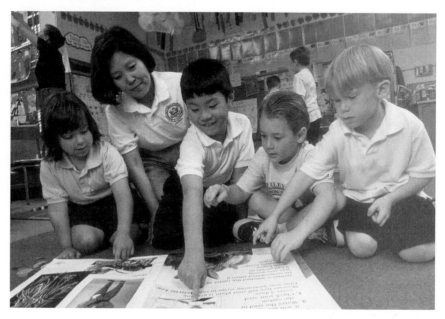

KEY TOPICS FOR MASTERY

- *The interrelationships among oral language, reading, and writing and the need to integrate activities across oral language and literacy*
- *Reading as a skilled and strategic process in which learning to decode and read words accurately and rapidly is essential*
- *Reading as understanding the text and dependent upon active engagement and interpretation by the reader*
- *Reading instruction being composed of phonological awareness, letter–sound correspondences, the alphabetic principle, word recognition and word study, fluency, vocabulary, and comprehension*
- *Reading as including the effortless decoding of words and reading fluently so that attention can focus on meaning and comprehension*
- *Readers as using a variety of strategies for decoding words including phonic analysis, onset-rime, structural analysis, syllabication, automatic word recognition, and syntax and semantics*
- *Students with learning/reading disabilities often have difficulty with phonological awareness, the alphabetic principle, and learning to effectively use phonic and structural analysis and syllabication; struggling readers often overrely on syntax and semantics*
- *Students with learning/reading disabilities need direct, explicit instruction in phonological awareness, letter–sound correspondence, and the alphabetic principle*
- *Teaching word recognition and word study can include approaches that use more explicit code instruction or more implicit code instruction*
- *Instruction in word recognition as including techniques for building sight words to promote fluency*

 BRIGHT IDEA

Turn to page 165 and read Think and Apply.

As a special education teacher, you teach many students who have difficulties in learning to read. Whether working as a coteacher with a kindergarten or first grade teacher, working with a group of students and providing intensive, small group instruction in an elementary school, or teaching English/reading in a middle or high school, you will spend a great deal of your effort teaching reading. Why is this the case?

First, reading is considered by many to be the most important area of education (National Reading Panel, 2000; Snow, Griffin, and Burns, 1998). Skill at reading is a prerequisite for many of the learning activities in content-area classes such as social studies, science, and vocational education and for successful employment. Second, students with learning and behavior disabilities have reading targeted as an area of need and have IEP goals related to reading more than any other academic area. Third, longitudinal research indicates that if students with learning and behavior problems do not learn to read by the end of third grade, their chances of having reading difficulties throughout their schooling and into adulthood are about 50 percent (Lyon, 1998). Therefore, it is critical that students learn to read and accomplish this task early in their schooling.

Students with whom you work undoubtedly will have a variety of strengths and needs in the area of reading. Let's look at two students and see what effective instruction might be for these students. Charles is a second grader receiving special education services for his learning disability in the area of reading. He reads at a beginning level and is able to recognize only about 30 words. When he comes to a word he does not recognize, he sometimes attempts to sound out the word. However, he has difficulty remembering common letter–sound correspondences. This means that when he sees letters, he does not know automatically the sound that letter makes. He also struggles with blending the sounds so he can generate a word that is close enough to the correct word that he can figure it out. For Charles, reading instruction will focus primarily on building phonological awareness, letter–sound correspondences, decoding strategies, and fluent word identification. Methods for teaching these components of reading are presented in this chapter and will assist in providing him the automatic word recognition that will allow him to focus more of his attention on understanding what he reads. However, while the emphasis is placed on these more basic skills, his instructional program should also include repeated reading of independent and instructional-level decodable books (i.e., books that primarily use words that reflect the phonic and word patterns he has already learned) to build fluency. It should also include the listening, supported reading, and discussion of a wide variety of literature and content area materials to support his development of vocabulary and comprehension. Strategies for teaching these components (fluency, vocabulary development, and reading comprehension) are discussed in Chapters Five and Seven. Finally, it will be

important for Charles to pair reading and writing activities so that as he builds reading decoding skills, he can work simultaneously on spelling. Similarly, as he develops his understanding of different types of text and genres (e.g., narratives such as folktales, adventure stories, and mysteries; expositions such as descriptions, comparisons/contrasts, persuasions), he can build skills at writing (see Chapter Six).

Manuel, the other student, is an eighth grader who is reading at approximately the fourth grade level. He entered school speaking both Spanish and English. He struggled with learning to read in Spanish because of his limited vocabulary knowledge and comprehension skills (e.g., getting the main idea, comprehension monitoring). He began reading in English during second grade and continued to struggle with vocabulary knowledge and comprehension and also had difficulty with decoding in English, because its letter–sound relationships are not as regular as those in Spanish. As an eighth grader he is taking English/language arts from Ms. Gonzalez, the special education teacher. Ms. Gonzalez described Manuel's instructional reading program as follows:

> *Manuel and the other students in his group are working on building their vocabulary, comprehension, and advanced decoding skills. Currently, they are learning to decode multi-syllabic words (e.g.,* construction, renovation, reconsider) *in which they learn to identify and separate the prefixes, suffixes, and endings. Then if they don't recognize the root word, they use the information they know about open and closed syllables to decode the root word. One of the benefits of this strategy is that the students learn the meanings of the prefixes and suffixes so that it really helps them in learning what the word means. They also use the context by rereading the sentence or the surrounding sentences. For Manuel, this helps him build both his decoding skills and vocabulary knowledge at the same time. We also take the time to learn related words. For example, if the word is* construction, *we make a "struct" web with words such as* destruction, construct, reconstruction,

deconstruct, etc. For teaching comprehension, Manuel and his classmates are learning to use collaborative strategic reading. It teaches the comprehension strategies previewing, questioning, summarizing, clarifying, and comprehension monitoring. The students work in collaborative learning groups and we have been focusing on the eighth grade social studies content since Manuel and his fellow students are in general education social studies classes. Next semester the social studies teacher and I are planning to coteach and we'll use collaborative strategic reading two to three days a week to build comprehension skills while learning social studies content knowledge.

Like Charles, Manuel's reading program contains various components of reading depending on his needs: word identification (Chapter Four), vocabulary development (Chapter Seven), and comprehension (Chapter Five).

In this chapter we will present specific methods, techniques, and approaches for teaching phonological awareness, letter–sound relationships, and the alphabetic principle as well as strategies for teaching word identification and word study. In Chapter Five we will discuss instructional strategies for assisting students to become fluent readers and active comprehenders. In Chapter Seven we discuss teaching concepts and vocabulary within the context of content area reading.

Although we have divided our discussion of reading and writing instruction into four chapters (Chapters Four through Seven), we stress the importance of the relationships between reading and writing. Critical to successful reading instruction for students with learning and behavior problems are opportunities for them to spell the words they are learning to read, write about what they are reading, and write stories and essays using structures and conventions similar to the ones they are reading. As you read the next four chapters, think about how reading and writing are related, reciprocal processes and how they can be taught in such a way that each complements and supports the other. Also think about how the strategies and instructional techniques that were

discussed in Chapter Three on oral language are related to reading and writing and could be incorporated into your teaching.

READING AND READING INSTRUCTION

The goal of reading instruction is to provide students with the skills, strategies, and knowledge to read fluently and understand the text for purposes of enjoyment and learning, whether reading a book, magazine, sign, pamphlet, e-mail message, or the Internet. To accomplish this goal, it is important to think about two overarching concepts.

1. *Reading is a skilled and strategic process in which learning to decode and read words accurately and rapidly is essential.* Reading entails using the attentional, perceptual, memory, and retrieval processes necessary to automatically identify or decode words. Remember in Chapter Two how you had no difficulty reading *THE CAT* even though the *H* and *A* were exactly the same? You used selective attention, feature analysis, your knowledge of the letter–sound relationships, and context to help you automatically recognize the words. This process of recognizing words is called *decoding* or *word recognition*. As students become proficient readers, they recognize most words with little effort on their part. But as students are learning to read or when readers encounter an unknown word, they use decoding to segment and then blend the word by sounds and patterns (e.g., individual sounds, spelling patterns such as –at, –ight, prefixes, suffixes, syllables) and use syntax and context (e.g., semantics) to assist in decoding. In developing decoding skills, students develop *metalinguistics,* that is, knowledge and skills focused on how language operates.

Knowing and demonstrating how to blend and segment words into sounds or phonemes is a key phonological or metalinguistic skill for decoding and one for which students with learning/reading disabilities have particular difficulty (e.g., Lyon, 1998; Torgesen, 2000). When decoding is fluent, effort can be focused on comprehension. Thus a goal of reading and reading instruction is to decode effortlessly so that attention is on comprehension.

As emergent readers encounter print in their environment, they ask questions and learn about how language is represented in its written form. They engage in the following:

— Pretend to read favorite print (i.e., books, poems, songs, chants)

— Read what they have drawn or written, even when no one else can

— Point to just one word, the first word in a sentence, one letter, the first letter in the word, the longest word, etc.

— Recognize some concrete words (i.e., their names, friend's names, words in the environment such as McDonalds)

— Recognize and generate rhyming words

— Name many letters and tell you words that begin with the common initial sound

(Allington, 1994; Cunningham and Elster, 1994; Sulzby and Teale, 1991)

2. Reading entails understanding the text and is dependent upon active engagement and interpretation by the reader. Understanding is influenced by both the text and the readers' prior knowledge (Anderson and Pearson, 1984). When readers read, the author does not simply convey ideas to the readers but stimulates readers to actively engage in such strategies as *predicting* to make hypotheses about the meaning, *summarizing* to "put in your own words" the major points in the text, *questioning* to promote and check for understanding, and *clarifying* when concepts are not clear. Effective readers regularly monitor their comprehension to see if they understand what they are reading. When they are not sure, they may decide to employ "fix-up" strategies such as rereading, reading on for further clarification, or they may decide not to worry about the confusion based on the purpose for reading. Knowing about these strategies and in which situations to apply different strategies is called *metacognition* (see Chapter Two).

Students who have reading difficulties tend to have difficulty with metacognitive skills, including efficient memory processing for words (Ashbaker and Swanson, 1996; Bauer 1987; Mann 1991) and

comprehension monitoring (Billingsley and Wildman, 1990; Bos and Filip, 1984; Palincsar and Brown, 1987; Wong, 1979, 1987). Research in the area of memory processing indicates that these students do not effectively use elaborative encoding strategies, such as rehearsal, categorization, and association, when trying to remember words or word lists. Studies with good and poor readers suggest that the poor readers do not automatically monitor their comprehension or engage in strategic behavior to restore meaning when there is a comprehension breakdown.

Components of Reading Instruction

These two overarching concepts can assist in organizing reading instruction into components or areas as depicted in Figure 4.1. These components and their integration are important in learning how to read effectively and in using reading as a vehicle for learning and entertainment. Since it is important to emphasize certain components or aspects of reading based on the student's level of development and needs, particularly for students with learning/reading disabilities, instruction should integrate these components. For example, while Charles's reading program emphasized developing phonological awareness, letter–sound correspondences and word recognition skills, he also engaged in activities to promote fluency and listening/reading comprehension. In contrast, Manuel's reading program focused on advanced decoding skills, fluency, and comprehension. In this chapter, we will turn our attention to the first two components of reading and reading instruction.

PHONOLOGICAL AWARENESS, LETTER–SOUND CORRESPONDENCE, AND THE ALPHABETIC PRINCIPLE

What is phonological awareness and the alphabetic principle? Simply stated, *phonological awareness* is knowing and demonstrating that spoken language can be broken down into smaller units (words, syllables, phonemes), which can be manipulated

■ **FIGURE 4.1**   *Components of Reading and Reading Instruction*

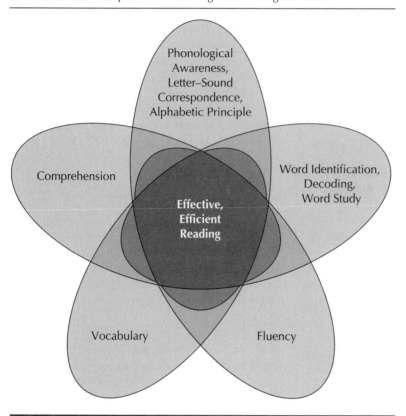

within an alphabetic system or orthography (Pod-hajski, 1999). Phonological awareness encompasses the discrimination, counting, rhyming, alliteration, blending, segmentation, and manipulating of sylla-bles, onset-rimes, and phonemes. Examples of ac-tivities that support these skills are presented in Figure 4.2.

Phonological awareness engages students in oral language activities. However, if students are to apply these skills to reading, they need to understand the alphabetic principle. The *alphabetic principle* is the way in which the sounds of our language (not the letters) map to print. It is knowing how letter names and sounds relate to each other (i.e., *letter–sound cor-respondence*). Let's see how Ms. Hernandez applies these concepts.

Ms. Hernandez, the special education teacher, works for 30 minutes, three times a week in Ms. Har-

ry's kindergarten class. She works with a small group of students who have the most difficulty learning to make letter–sound correspondences and who have difficulty separating words by syllables and blending and segmenting phonemes. With these kindergarten-ers, Ms. Hernandez reinforces the key words that Ms. Harry is teaching with each letter-sound, for example, *b, ball, /b/,* and has students participate in listening activities in which they have to count the number of syllables in words and sounds in simple words (e.g., *me* and *sit*) and create word families (e.g., -it, *sit, mit, bit, fit, hit*). At first she has the students listen when working on these activities. Then she uses letters to demonstrate how the syllables and sounds are related to print.

Ms. Hernandez also works with a small group of six students in Ms. Constable's first grade class who have difficulty learning to read. Ms. Hernandez en-

■ **FIGURE 4.2** *Phonological Skills and Example Activities*

- *Discrimination:* students listen to see if two words begin or end with the same sound
- *Counting:* students clap the number word in a sentence, syllables in a word (e.g., *cowboy, carrot*), sounds in a word (e.g., *me, jump*)
- *Rhyming:* students create word families with rhyming words (e.g., all, call, fall, ball)
- *Alliteration:* students create tongue twisters (e.g., Sally's silly shoe sank slowly in the slime.)
- *Blending:* students say the sounds in a word and then "say them fast" while the teacher pushes blocks or letters together to demonstrate blending
- *Segmenting:* students say the word and then clap and say each syllable or sound (e.g., *running* is /run/ /ing/ is /r/ /u/ /n/ /i/ /ng/)

- *Manipulating:* deleting, adding, substituting, and transposing

  Deleting: students listen to words and say them without the first sound (e.g., *bat* becomes *at*)

  Adding: students listen to words and add syllables (e.g., *run* becomes *running, come* becomes *coming*

  Substituting: students listen and change sounds (e.g., change /r/ in *run* to /b/ and make *bun*

  Transposing: student reverse the sounds (e.g., *nat* becomes *tan*)

gages these students in such activities as listening and clapping the number of sounds in words to help them segment the sounds; saying each sound in a word slowly and then "saying them fast" to practice blending. When writing the sound, she has them say the word, then say the sounds, then say the first sound and write it, then say the first two sounds and write the second sound, and so on until they have written the word. She consistently pairs speech and print with the first graders.

Ms. Hernandez is directly teaching phonological awareness, letter–sound relationships, and the alphabetic principle, all of which are associated with successful reading and spelling. Evidence from research provides consistent support for the important role that phonological awareness and processing play in learning to read (Adams, 1990, Blachman, 2000; National Reading Panel, 2000; Snow, et al., 1998). The skills associated with phonological processing, particularly blending and segmenting individual phonemes, have been one of the most consistent predictors of difficulties in learning to read. Children who lack this metalinguistic insight are likely to be among the poorest readers and because of their poor reading be identified as having a learning or reading disability (e.g., Blachman, 1997; Bradley and Bryant, 1983; Foorman, Fletcher, Francis, and Schatschneider, 1998;

Juel, 1994; Torgesen and Burgess, 1998; Velluntino et al., 1996). Hence, Ms. Hernandez is working with students in kindergarten and first grade to help prevent or lessen later reading disabilities.

Development of Phonological Awareness and the Alphabetic Principle

In general, children's awareness of the phonological structure of the English language develops from larger units of sounds (e.g., words in a sentence, syllables in a word) to smaller units (e.g., onset-rimes, phonemes or individual speech sounds in a word). Skills such as rhyming and alliteration develop earlier, and skills such as sound blending, segmenting, and manipulation develop later. Table 4.1 presents a continuum for the development of phonological awareness with definitions. While phonological awareness encompasses the entire continuum, activities that focus on individual sounds in words describe *phonemic awareness*. It is these more advanced skills of phoneme blending, segmenting, and manipulation that are most related to success in learning to read (Goswami and Bryant, 1990; Stanovich, 1992; Torgesen, Wagner, and Rashotte, 1994).

■ **TABLE 4.1** *Phonological Awareness Continuum*

Later Developing

Skill	Example
Phoneme blending, segmentation, and manipulations	Blending phonemes into words, segmenting words into individual phonemes, and manipulating phonemes (e.g., deleting, adding, substituting, transposing) in spoken words
Onset-rime blending and segmentation	Blending/segmenting the initial consonant or consonant cluster (onset) from the vowel and consonant sounds spoken after it (rime)
Syllable blending and segmentation	Blending syllables to say words or segmenting spoken words into syllables
Sentence segmentation	Segmenting sentences into spoken words
Rhyme/alliteration	Matching the ending sounds of words/producing groups of words that begin with the same initial sound

Early Developing

Source: Adapted from *First Grade Teacher Reading Academy* (Austin: University of Texas, Texas Center for Reading and Language Arts, 2000).

In general, using a developmental sequence is helpful for planning instruction. For example, based on the developmental sequence, you would teach segmenting and blending words and syllables before teaching segmenting and blending onset-rimes and phonemes. However, some children vary in the acquisition of these skills. For example, although some children can learn to blend, segment, and manipulate sounds, they continue to have difficulty with rhyming. Therefore, when older students are struggling with rhyming, do not necessarily wait to include instruction at the phoneme level.

Teaching Phonological Awareness and the Alphabetic Principle

The majority of students at risk for reading difficulties and who are later identified as having a learning or reading disability have poor phonological awareness and can profit from explicit instruction in phonological awareness, particularly blending, segmenting, and manipulating sounds (Foorman et al., 1998; Muter and Snowling, 1998; Torgesen, 1999). As stu-

dents learn the letter–sound correspondences, phonological tasks such as oral blending and segmenting of onset-rimes and phonemes can be paired with graphemes (letters), thereby explicitly teaching the relationship of speech to print (alphabetic principle) (Goswami, 2000; Greaney, Tunmer, and Chapman, 1997).

Teaching phonological awareness includes such activities as:

— Generating rhyming words
— Listening for words that begin with the same sound (e.g., having all the students whose name begins with /b/ line up)
— Clapping the number of words in a sentence, syllables in words, and phonemes in words
— Blending and segmenting words by syllables and sounds

Early developing skills such as rhyming and alliteration may be facilitated by reading books that are based on rhyme and alliteration, such as *There's a Wocket in My Pocket* (Seuss, 1974) and *Each Peach*

Pear Plum (Ahlberg and Ahlberg, 1979) and creating, saying, listening or looking for, and reading rhymes, alliterations, and "silly sayings."

To build blending and segmenting skills, a frequently used technique that assists students in learning to separate and blend sounds is the use of Elkonin procedure (Elkonin, 1973). As a phonological task, students listen to a word and push a marker, block, or other small object into a printed square for each sound they hear (see Figure 4.3). As students gain knowledge about the letter–sound relationships, students can push or write letters in the boxes. It is one way in which an oral language activity can be made more visible and kinesthetic. Other ways are tapping one finger to the thumb for each sound or watching your mouth in a mirror and feeling the facial movements by placing your fingers on your cheeks and concentrating on how your mouth changes when different sounds are made (Lindamood and Lindamood, 1998).

In teaching phonological awareness to students who are having difficulty learning to read, it is important to determine with which tasks they are having difficulty and then focus instruction based on the students' level of development and needs. For example, Emily is a second-semester first grader who can segment and blend syllables and onset-rimes (e.g., s-it, f-at, r-un) but has great difficulty segmenting and blending individual phonemes. She has been using manipulatives and counting on her figures to assist herself, but she is still having difficulty hearing the individual sounds. One activity might be to build on her ability to segment and blend onset-rimes and demonstrate how the rime is further divided into individual sounds. Emily could also watch and feel her mouth as she says each sound to see how it changes when saying the /a/ and then /t/. For Emily, who has learned the letter–sound correspondences for about six consonant sounds and the short vowels /a/, using letters in the boxes can help her understand how speech maps to print.

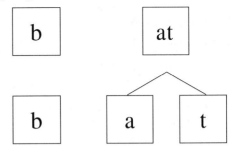

Students may also need assistance in learning how to blend sounds. Figure 4.4 presents a simple procedure for teaching sound blending. The same procedure can be used for teaching how to segment sounds except that you would begin with the sounds separated and then gradually present them closer together until they are blended into a word.

General guidelines for teaching phonological awareness activities include:

— Consider the students' levels of development and tasks that need to be mastered.
— Model each activity.
— Use manipulatives and movement to make these auditory or oral tasks more visible.
— Move from less to more difficult tasks considering:
  • Level of development (syllables, onset-rimes, phonemes)
  • Phoneme position (initial, final, medial)
  • Number of sounds in a word (*cat* is easier than *split*)
  • Phonological features of the words (e.g., continuants consonants /m/, /n/, /s/ are easier then stops or clipped sounds /t/, /b/, /d/)

■ **FIGURE 4.3** *Using the Elkonin Procedure to Support Phonemic Awareness and the Alphabetic Principle*

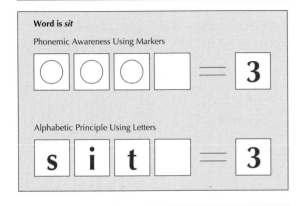

■ **FIGURE 4.4** *Procedure for Teaching Sound Blending*

To train a child in sound blending, use the following procedure.

Teacher: "Say shoe."
Child: "Shoe."
Teacher: "Now, what am I saying? /**sh-sh-sh**/ **oo-oo-oo**/." (Say it with prolonged sounds, but no break between the sounds.) If the child responds correctly, say: "Good. Now what am I saying?" (Give a little break between the sounds.) "/**Sh/oe**/." Then say (with the child), "Shoe. Now what am I saying?" (Give a quarter-second break between the sounds.) "/**Sh/oe**/."
Child: "Shoe."
Teacher: "Shoe. Good. What am I saying now?" (with a half-second break between the sounds) "/**Sh/oe**/."
Child: "Shoe."
Teacher: "Now what am I saying?" (give a one-second break between the sounds) "/**Sh/oe**/."

At each step, if the child does not respond with "shoe," repeat the previous step and then again stretch out the sounds, confirming or prompting at each step. Proceed by increasing the duration until the child can say "shoe" in response to the sounds with approximately one second between them.

Repeat this experience with the word "me."

The main task for the teacher is to give a word with two sounds, increasing the duration of time between them until the child gets the idea of putting the sounds together. Then the child is presented with three-sound words such as /**f/a/t**/, and then with four-sound words such as /**s/a/n/d**/. It is important to recognize that the number of sounds in a word may not correspond to the number of letters in a word. For example, the word "shoe" has four letters, but only two sounds. The teacher must be careful to present the sounds correctly and use the correct timing.

Source: S. A. Kirk, W. D. Kirk, and E. H. Minskoff, *Phonic Remedial Reading Lessons* (Novato, Calif.: Academic Therapy Publications, 1985), pp. 12–13. Reprinted by permission.

— Provide feedback and opportunities for practice and review.
— Make learning fun.

A number of programs and resources are available for teaching phonological awareness and the alphabetic principle (see Figure 4.5 for a selected list) and a number of sources provide lists of children's books focused on different aspects of phonological awareness (Coldwell, 1997; Optiz, 1998; Perfect, 2000; Yopp, 1992). Tech Talk highlights information about using computer software to teach phonological awareness skills.

Teaching Letter–Sound Correspondences

As students learn letter–sound correspondences and move into higher phonological awareness skills such as blending, segmenting, and manipulating sounds, it is important to associate speech with print (Chard and Dickson, 1999; Smith, 1998; Torgesen, 1999), thereby teaching the alphabetic principle or understanding that the sequence of letters in written words represents the sequence of sounds in spoken words. In Figure 4.3, while the first row task involves having the students segment words into sounds by moving a counter into a box for each sounds (phonemic awareness), in the second row the students pair the sounds with letters by writing the letters in the boxes (alphabetic principle). Sometimes a phoneme is represented by more than one letter (e.g., consonant digraphs such as /sh/, /ch/, /ph/). One way to note this is by using a dotted line between the letters in the digraphs.

f	i	s	h

■ **FIGURE 4.5** *Selected Programs and Resources for Teaching Phonological Awareness*

Ladders to Literacy: A Kindergarten Activity Book by O'Connor, R., Notari-Syverson, A., and Vadasy, P. F., 1998, Baltimore, MD: Paul H. Brookes.

Phonemic Awareness in Young Children: A Classroom Curriculum by Adams, M. J., Foorman, B. G., Lundberg, I., and Beeler, T., 1998, Baltimore, MD: Paul H. Brookes

Phonological Awareness and Primary Phonics by Gunning, T. G., 2000, Boston: Allyn and Bacon.

Phonological Awareness Training for Reading by Torgesen, J. K., and Bryant, B. R., 1994, Austin, TX: PRO-ED.

Road to the Code: A Program of Early Literacy Activities to Develop Phonological Awareness by Blachman, B. A., Ball, E. W., Black, R., and Tangel, D. M., 2000, Baltimore, MD: Brookes.

The Phonological Awareness Book by Robertson, C., and Salter, W.,1995, East Moline, IL: LinguiSystems.

Sounds Abound by Catts, H., and Olsen, T., 1993, East Moline: IL: LinguiSystems.

The Lindamood Phoneme Sequencing Program for Reading, Spelling, and Speech by Lindamood, P. A., and Lindamood, P., 1998, Austin, TX: PRO-ED.

The Sounds Abound Program: Teaching Phonological Awareness in the Classroom (formerly *Sound Start*) by Lechner, O., and Podhajski, B., 1998, East Moline, IL: LinguiSystems.

A Basic Guide to Understanding, Assessing, and Teaching Phonological Awareness by Torgesen, J. K., and Mathes, P. G., 2000, Austin, TX: PRO-ED.

Knowledge of individual speech sounds is not particularly important when using oral language to converse. However, in learning to read and write and in developing a second language this knowledge can be quite valuable and is accentuated by these tasks. Expert estimates of the number of speech sounds or phonemes in English vary from 40 to 52. For purposes of teaching students, most estimates are about 44 (Fromkin and Rodman, 1998; Owens, 2001). In learning to read and write, students learn more than 100 spellings (graphemes) for these phonemes.

The largest division of phonemes is consonants (C) or vowels (V). Table 4.2 presents the 25 consonant sounds with their typical spellings and representative words that use these sounds. The sounds are grouped according to the manner in which they are articulated and highlight how the sounds are related. For example, there are eight sound pairs in which the only difference between the two sounds in each pair is whether or not the sounds are produced with a resonance in the throat (voiced) or without resonance (voiceless):

Voiced		Voiceless	
/b/	bat	/p/	pat
/d/	dig	/t/	tack
/g/	gate	/k/	kite
/v/	vase	/f/	fit

/th/	this	/th/	think
/z/	zip	/s/	sat
/zh/	buzz	/sh/	ship
/j/	jump	/ch/	chip

For students who consistently confuse voiced or voiceless sounds, it is helpful to teach whether the sounds are voiced or unvoiced. They can distinguish the difference by feeling the vibrations in their voice boxes by placing their fingers on their throat or by covering both their ears and listening as they say the sound pairs. Having students check to see if they can "feel the sound" can help them to decode or spell a word (Clark and Uhry, 1995).

Consonant sounds can also be distinguished by the flow of air as stops or continuants. *Stops* are aptly named because they are of short duration and the air flow is stopped completely for a short time (Moats, 2000). Stops (or clipped sounds) include: /b/, /d/, /g/, /j/, /k/, /p/, /t/, and /ch/. In contrast, *continuant* sounds can be blended smoothly with the next sound without a break in the air flow (e.g., /f/, /s/, /v/, /w/, /z/, /sh/, /zh/, /th/, /th/). Important information to remember when teaching consonants is:

— CVC words that begin with continuants and end with stops are generally the easiest for blending the sounds (e.g., *fat, sap*).

TECH TALK 4.1

USING COMPUTER TECHNOLOGY TO BUILD PHONOLOGICAL AWARENESS SKILLS AND LETTER–SOUND CORRESPONDENCES

Students with learning/reading disabilities as a group consistently have difficulty with such phonological skills as blending, segmenting, and manipulating phonemes and learning letter–sound correspondences. Oftentimes these students need additional practice to learn these skills to the level that they become automatic and can be applied easily when reading text. A number of programs have been developed to provide practice in these areas. *DaisyQuest* and *CastleQuest* (PRO-ED) are two programs that were developed in the early 1990s to promote skill development in phoneme identification and segmentation. These programs use an adventure game format to provide practice with a wide range of phonological awareness tasks including recognizing rhyming words, matching words on the basis of common first, middle, and last sounds, and counting the number of phonemes in a word. Barker and Torgesen (1995) evaluated the effectiveness of these programs with early elementary grade students who were having significant difficulty decoding. When compared to groups of students who received math practice or *Hint and Hunt,* a software program designed to improve the decoding of medial vowels and vowel combinations, students using *DaisyQuest* and *CastleQuest* made substantially more improvement in phonological awareness. Practice with these programs has also been shown to positively effect the phonological awareness skills of preschool and kindergarten students (K. Foster, Erickson, D. Foster, Brinkman, and Torgesen,1994). *Read, Write & Type* is another program that provides practice in phonological awareness skills and letter–sound identification,

■ *Read, Write & Type*

Source: http://www.readwritetype.com. Copyright © California Neuropsychology Services and Talking Fingers, Inc. Developed by Dr. Jeannine Heiron and Dr. Leslie Grimm.

while students learn keyboarding. When used with the teacher-led instructional activities that accompany the program, this program was effective in improving the phonological awareness skills of struggling readers (Torgesen, 1999). When using these types of programs, it is important to remember that they are only a supplement and need to be part of larger coordinated program to have their greatest impact on students with learning and behavior problems (Okolo, Cavalier, Ferretti, and Mac Arthur, 2000; Wise and Olson, 1998).

— In some programs, it is suggested when blending stops to "bounce the stop sounds," such as /b-b-b-b-a-t-t-t/ is *bat* (Slavin, Madden, Karwit, Dolan, and Wasik, 1992) so that students do not attach a schwa sound to the stop consonants (i.e., /buh/ and /tuh/).

— These nasal sounds are difficult to hear, sound different in the middle of words (e.g., *wet* or *went*), and are often omitted or substituted by emergent readers and writers (Read, 1975). One

strategy students can use to check for a nasal is to hold their nose while saying the word and feel if the nose vibrates.

— Students may have problems hearing the difference between /wh/ and /w/ because many Americans pronounce them in the same manner, for example *witch* and *which* (Moats, 2000).

— The sounds /r/ and /l/ can be difficult for some students because they are some of the last sounds that students learn to articulate and because their

■ **TABLE 4.2**   *Consonant Sounds, Typical Spellings, and Manner of Articulation*

Consonant Sounds	Typical Spellings	Initial	Middle, Final	Manner of Articulation
/p/	p	pot, pick	stop	voiceless stop @ lips
/b/	b	bat, barn	cab, robe	voiced stop @ lips
/t/	t, –ed	time, tap	pot, messed	voiceless stop @ tongue behind teeth
/d/	d, –ed	deer, dinner	bad, ride, cried	voiced stop @ tongue behind teeth
/k/	c, k, ck, qu	kiss, can, quick	back, critique	voiceless stop @ back of mouth
/g/	g	gate, girl	rag	voiced stop @ back of mouth
/f/	f, ph	first, fit	graph, off, rough	voiceless fricative @ lip/teeth
/v/	v	very, vase	love	voiced fricative @ lip/teeth
/th/	th	the, then	mother, either	voiceless fricative @ tongue between teeth
/th/	th	think, thin	both, ether	voiced fricative @ tongue between teeth
/s/	s, c	sap, cent, psychology	less, piece	voiceless fricative @ tongue behind teeth
/z/	z, –es, –s, x	zip, xerox	has, dogs, messes, lazy	voiced fricative @ tongue behind teeth
/sh/	sh	ship, sure, chef	push, mission, ration	voiceless fricative @ roof of mouth
/zh/	z, s		azure, measure, beige	voiced fricative @ roof of mouth
/ch/	ch, tch	chip, chase	much, hatch	voiceless affricate @ roof of mouth
/j/	j, g	jump, gist	judge, soldier	voiced affricate @ roof of mouth
/m/	m	me, mom	him, autumn, comb	nasal @ nose
/n/	n, kn, gn, pn, mn	now, know, gnat, pneumonia, mnemonics	pan, sign	nasal @ nose
/ng/	ng		sing, English	nasal @ nose
/y/	y	you, use	feud	voiced glide @ roof of mouth
/wh/	wh	where, whale		voiceless glide @ back of mouth
/w/	w	we, witch	sewer	voiced glide @ back of mouth
/h/	h	happy, who		voiceless glide @ throat
/l/	l	lady, lion	mail, babble	liquid @ tongue behind teeth
/r/	r	ride, write		liquid @ tongue behind teeth

Source: Adapted from V. Fromkin and R. Rodman, *Introduction to Language,* 4th ed. (Orlando, FL: Harcourt Brace & Co., 1993); and L. C. Moats, *Spelling: Development, Disability and Instruction* (Baltimore: York Press, 1995).

pronunciation varies considerably across languages, (e.g., in Spanish they may be trilled or rolled, in Japanese and Cantonese the two phonemes are said in the same way).

This information about consonant sounds is helpful when you are analyzing a student's oral reading and spelling. Students who know the letter–sound correspondences are more likely to substitute similar sounds. For example, it is more likely that students would substitute /n/ or /m/ for /ng/ than other sounds because they are nasals. Similarly, substitutions of /d/ for /b/ and /p/ for /b/ could well be related to the similar manner in which the sounds are articulated (i.e., /d/ and /b/—similar formation of the mouth, /p/ and /b/—same formation of mouth but voiceless and voiced) rather then to visual processing.

The English language also makes use of consonant digraphs and consonant blends. A *consonant digraph* is two consonants that represent one sound (*ph* for /f/). A *consonant blend* combines the sounds of two or more consonants so that they are clustered together. Table 4.3 provides a listing of the consonant digraphs and blends. When students omit a letter in a cluster such as reading *fog* for *frog,* ask questions that lead them to see that the second sound in the blend is missing (e.g., "Listen, what sound do you hear after the /f/ in *frog,* /f-r-o-g/?" "What two sounds does the word *frog* begin with?"). It may also be helpful to have the students compare the words in written form or use boxes to assist students in seeing the missing letter.

The second category of sounds is vowels. In general, there must be a vowel in every English syllable, and consonants are formed around the vowel. Vowel sounds are open sounds and can be ordered based on the open or closed position of the mouth as shown in the vowel circle in Figure 4.6. Say each of the vowels in the vowel circle and note how your mouth moves from a closed, smiling position (ē) to an open position (o͞o).

Like the consonants, we can analyze students' oral reading and spelling to learn about their knowledge of vowels sounds. For example, substituting an /ĕ/ for /ă/ would be more likely than an /ĕ/ for /ŏ/ because of the closeness of the sounds. It is also obvious why students often confuse /ir/, /er/, and /ur/ in spelling, since these three spellings represent the same sound. Thus, *bird* can be spelled *bird, burd,* and *berd,* and the student must use visual memory to remember that it is *bird.* The vowel sounds have different spelling patterns as demonstrated in Table 4.4. Sometimes the same spelling pattern has different sounds (e.g.,

the "ea" in *beat* and *bread* or the "ou" in *soup, could,* and *shout*). For students with severe difficulties in decoding, it may be helpful to systematically teach the frequency of the sounds for a vowel combination, so that when decoding an unknown word they can try the various sounds in a systematic manner and use syntax and semantics (i.e., context of the text) to determine the word. Vowel combinations with order of frequency for the different sounds (Herzog, 1998) are:

Vowel Combination	Order of Frequency for Different Sounds
ea	/ē/ as in *eat,* /ĕ/ as in *bread,* /ā/ as in *great*
ei	/ē/ as in *ceiling,* /ā/ as in *vein*
ey	/ē/ as in *key,* /ā/ as in *grey*
ie	/ē/ as in *piece,* /ī/ as in *pie*
oo	/o͞o/ as in *moon,* /o͝o/ as in *book,*
ou	/ou/ as in *house,* /o͞o/ as in *soup*
ow	/ou/ as in *owl,* /ō/ as in *snow*

Schwa is the vowel sound often found in unaccented syllables (e.g., suppose, familiar, sofa, mission) and is the most frequently occurring vowel sound (Wilde, 1997). As you can see, schwa has many different spellings.

Students who are acquiring English and speak another language may not have developed fluency in all the English sounds. This is because different languages use different speech sounds and students are most comfortable using the speech sounds of their native language. Table 3.8 on page 98 provides a comparison of the phonological as well as the morphological and syntactical features of Spanish and English. Common phonological confusions include:

/b/ pronounced as /p/
/v/ pronounced as /b/
/ch/ pronounced as /sh/
/j/ pronounced as /h/
/l/ pronounced as /y/
A number of differences in vowel pronunciations

■ **TABLE 4.3**   *Common Consonant Digraphs and Clusters*

Common Consonant Digraphs

Correspondence	Examples
ch = /ch/	chair, church
gh = /f/	rough, tough
kn =/n/	knot, knob
ng = /ŋ/	thing, sing
ph = /f/	phone, photograph
sc = /s/	scissors, scientist
sh = /sh/	shoe, shop
th = /th/	there, them
th = /th/	thumb, thunder
wh = /w/	wheel, where
wr = =/r/	wrench, wrestle

Common Initial Consonant Clusters

With l	Example Words	With s	Example Words
bl	blanket, black	sc	score, scale
cl	clock, clothes	sch	school, schedule
fl	flag, fly	scr	scream, scrub
gl	glove, glue	sk	sky, skin
pl	plum, place	sl	sled, sleep
sl	slide, show	sm	smoke, smile
		sn	snake, sneakers
With r	**Example Words**	sp	spider, spot
br	broom, bread	st	star, stop
cr	crow, crash	str	street, stream
dr	dress, drink	sw	sweater, swim
fr	frog, from		
gr	green, ground		
pr	prince, prepare		

Common Final Consonant Clusters

With n	Example Words	With l	Example Words
nce	prince, chance	ld	field, old
nch	lunch, bunch	lf	wolf, self
nd	hand, wind	lk	milk, silk
nk	tank, wink	lm	film
nt	tent, sent	lp	help
		lt	salt, belt
Other	**Example Words**	lve	twelve, solve
ct	fact, effect		
mp	jump, camp		
sp	wasp, grasp		
st	nest, best		

Source: Adapted from T. G. Gunning, *Creating Reading Instruction for All Children,* 3rd ed. (Boston: Allyn and Bacon, 2000)

Consequently, students may have difficulty not only pronouncing these sounds, but also hearing them. Do not be surprised if *chin* is read and spelled as *shin,* or *vase* is read and spelled as *base.*

Guidelines for Teaching Letter–Sound Correspondence

Students use letter–sound correspondences to decode words. Therefore, for struggling readers, it is impor-

tant to teach these correspondences and how to blend and segment sounds so that they can decode and spell words. A number of programs have been developed to teach letter–sound correspondences and decoding to struggling readers using systematic approaches to introduce the letter–sound relationships and how to decode words (e.g., *Word Detectives: Benchmark Word Identification Program for Beginning Readers* [Gaskins, 1998]; *Corrective Reading* [Engelmann, Meyer, Carnine, Becker, Eisele,

■ **FIGURE 4.6** *Vowel Spellings by Mouth Position Using Phonic Symbols*

Source: L. C. Moats (2000). *Speech to Print: Language Essentials for Teachers* (p. 94). Baltimore: Paul H. Brookes Publishing Co. Reprinted with permission.

and Johnson, 1999]; *Lindamood Phoneme Sequencing Program for Reading, Spelling, and Speech* [Lindamood and Lindamood, 1998]; *Phonic Remedial Reading Lessons* [Kirk, Kirk, and Minskoff, 1985]; *Alphabet Phonics* [Cox, 1992]. These programs have similar features of instruction that include:

— Teach a core set of frequently used consonants and short vowel sounds that represent clear sounds and nonreversible letter forms (e.g., /ă/, /ĭ/, /d/, /f/, /g/, /h/, /l/, /n/, /p/, /s/, /t/). (See Figure 4.7 for a list of 120 words that can be made using these 11 letter–sound correspondences.)

— Begin immediately to blend and segment the sounds to read and spell the words and read the words in decodable text (i.e., text in which most of the words are comprised of letter–sound correspondences that have been taught).

— Separate the introduction of letter–sounds with similar auditory or visual features (e.g., /ĕ/ and /ĭ/, /m/ and /n/, /b and /d/).

— Use a consistent key word to assist students in hearing and remembering the sound (e.g., *a apple* /ă/, *b boy* /b/).

— Teach that some letters can represent more than one sound. For each letter, first teach the most

■ **TABLE 4.4** *Vowel Spellings*

	Vowel Sound	Major Spellings
Short Vowels	/a/	rag, happen
	/e/	get, letter, thread
	/i/	wig, middle, event
	/o/	fox, problem, father
	/u/	bus
Long Vowels	/ā/	name, favor, say, sail
	/ē/	he, even, eat, seed, bean, key, these, either, funny, serious
	/ī/	hide, tiny, high, lie, sky
	/ō/	vote, open, coat, bowl, old, though
	/ū/	use, human, few
Other Vowels	/aw/	daughter, law, walk, off, bought
	/oi/	noise, toy
	/o͝o/	wood, should, push
	/o͞o/	soon, new, prove, group, two, fruit, truth
	/ow/	tower, south
	/ə/	above, operation, similar, opinion, suppose
r Vowels	/ar/	far, large, heart
	/air/	hair, care, where, stair, bear
	/i(ə)r/	dear, steer, here
	/ər/	her, sir, fur, earth
	/or/	horse, door, tour, more

Source: Adapted from T. G. Gunning, *Creating Reading Instruction for All Children,* 3rd ed. (Boston: Allyn and Bacon, 2000).

frequent sound and then teach other sounds (e.g., in English /c/ in *cat* then /s/ in *city* and /g/ in *gate* then /j/ in *Jim;* in Spanish /g/ in *gato* (cat) then /h/ in *gemelo* (twin).

— Teach that different letters can make the same sound, such as the /s/ in *sit* and *city.*

— Teach that sounds can be represented by a single letter or a combination of letters (e.g., /e/ in *me* and *meet*).

— Add a kinesthetic component by having students trace or write the letter as they say the sound.

— Have students use mirrors and feel their mouths to see and feel how sounds are different.

— Color code consonant and vowel so that the two categories of sounds are highlighted.

Teaching letter–sound correspondences is a key element in understanding the alphabetic principle and learning to decode and spell unknown words. How-

ever, programs that focus too much on only teaching letter-sound relationships and not on putting them to use are likely to be ineffective. Through modeling and discussion, students need to understand that the purpose for learning these relationships is to apply them to their reading and writing activities (National Reading Panel, 2000). Hence, it is critical to apply knowledge in phonological awareness, letter–sound relationships, and the alphabetic principle to word identification and decoding as discussed in the next section.

WORD IDENTIFICATION, DECODING, AND WORD STUDY

Word reading quickly and easily is the success to good reading (Ehri, 1998; Gough, 1996). Successful readers identify words fluently and if a word is unknown, have

■ **FIGURE 4.7**   *Words Using 11 Common Letter–Sound Correspondences*

i, t, p, n, s, a, d, l, f, h, g

1. it	16. sin	31. tan	46. tap	61. slat	76. lint	91. pass	106. pits
2. if	17. fin	32. pan	47. nap	62. flat	77. hint	92. lass	107. sits
3. in	18. lid	33. Dan	48. sap	63. flap	78. past	93. glass	108. fits
4. tip	19. did	34. fan	49. lap	64. flag	79. fast	94. pill	109. hits
5. nip	20. hid	35. pad	50. gap	65. span	80. last	95. hill	110. pats
6. sip	21. dig	36. sad	51. gas	66. snap	81. list	96. gill	111. hats
7. pip	22. fig	37. dad	52. snip	67. plan	82. lisp	97. still	112. taps
8. lip	23. pig	38. lad	53. slip	68. glad	83. gasp	98. stiff	113. naps
9. pit	24. gig	39. fad	54. spit	69. snag	84. stand	99. sniff	114. gaps
10. sit	25. at	40. had	55. slit	70. and	85. gland	100. staff	115. slips
11. fit	26. an	41. tag	56. flit	71. sand	86. plant	101. add	116. slits
12. lit	27. pat	42. nag	57. tilt	72. hand	87. slant	102. tips	117. flips
13. hit	28. sat	43. lag	58. flip	73. land	88. split	103. nips	118. flaps
14. tin	29. fat	44. sag	59. spin	74. sift	89. splat	104. sips	119. snaps
15. pin	30. hat	45. pal	60. slid	75. lift	90. splint	105. lips	120. lifts

Source: Neuhas Education Center, Bellaire, Texas. (Based on Cox, A. R. (1992). *Foundations for Literacy: Structures and Techniques for Multisensory Teaching of Written English Skills.* Cambridge, MA: Educators Publishing Services.)

effective decoding strategies to decipher the word. Therefore, it is important that students develop a sight word vocabulary (i.e., words that students recognize without conscious effort) and decoding strategies to support them when they encounter an unknown word (National Reading Panel, 2000; Snow et al., 1998).

What Is a Sight Word?

A *sight word* is a word for which the student can recognize the pronunciation and meaning automatically. When reading words by sight, the words are accessed from information in memory, that is, from your storehouse of words. For emergent readers, visual cues assist in recognizing familiar words when they are highly contextualized (e.g., a child recognizes *Mc-Donalds* when presented with the golden arches but not when it is presented without the context, the arches). As students develop knowledge of letter–sound relationships, this serves as a powerful mnemonic system that ties the written forms of specific words to their pronunciations and allows the child to recognize words (e.g., *McDonalds* as an individual word; Ehri, 1998). In addition, students are able to

more efficiently store words in memory when they group or consolidate words by multiletter units such as onset-rimes, syllables, suffixes, prefixes, and base words. For example, if the reader knows *-tion, in-,* and *-ing* as multiletter units, then learning longer sight words such as *questioning* and *interesting* is easier. Thus, teaching key spelling patterns, prefixes and suffixes, and major syllable types can assist students in learning to automatically recognize words and read more fluently (Juel, 1983).

You can tell when readers are reading words by sight because they read the words as whole units, with no pauses between smaller units (syllables, sounds), and they read the words within one second of seeing them (Ehri and Wilce, 1983). To experience how powerful automatic word recognition is, look at Figure 4.8. Say the name of each picture as quickly as you can and ignore the words printed on the pictures. Was it almost impossible to ignore the words? It is because you are processing the words automatically, in this case, despite your intention to ignore them. It is particularly important that readers have multiple opportunities to practice reading and spelling words until they become automatic and have word identification or decoding strategies to assist them in decoding a word when it is not automatically recognized.

Decoding Strategies for Identifying Words

What decoding or word identification strategies do readers employ to decode words they do not know automatically? Research on teaching struggling readers, including those with specific reading disabilities, would suggest that seven strategies are helpful in teaching these students to decode words (see Figure 4.9).

Phonic Analysis
Identify and Blend Letter–Sound Correspondences into Words. This is referred to as *phonic analysis* or *phonics*. This strategy builds on the alphabetic principle and assumes that the students have basic levels of phonological awareness and knowl-

edge of some letter–sound correspondences. It entails the process of converting letters into sounds, blending the sounds to form a word, and searching memory to find a known word that resembles those blended sounds. Teachers use many cues to assist students in using phonic analysis to decode words:

— Cue the students to say each sound and then say it fast.
— Demonstrate and have the students point to each letter–sound as they say the sound and then have the students sweep their fingers under the word when they say it fast.
— Place letters apart when saying the sounds and then push the letters together when you say it fast.
— Begin with simple familiar VC (*in*) and CVC (*him*) words and then move to more complex sound patterns (e.g., CCVC (*slim*), CVCC (*duck*), CVCE (*make*).

■ **FIGURE 4.8** *Picture-Naming Task Demonstrating How Words Are Processed Automatically*

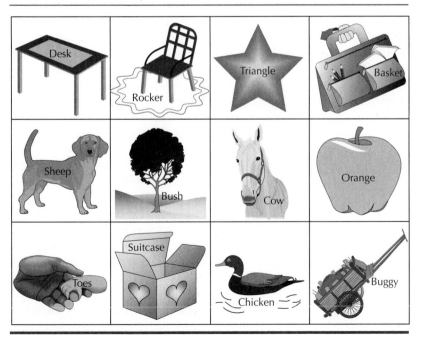

Source: Adapted from L. Ehri, "Learning to Read and Spell Words," *Journal of Reading Behavior, 19,* (1987): 5–11.

■ **FIGURE 4.9** *Strategies for Decoding Unknown Words*

- *Phonic Analysis:* Identify and blend letter–sound correspondences into words
- *Onset-Rime:* Use common spelling patterns (onset-rimes) to decode words by blending the initial sound(s) with the spelling pattern or by using analogy
- *Structural Analysis:* Use knowledge of word structures such as compound word, root words, suffixes, prefixes, and inflectional endings to decode words and assist with meaning
- *Syllabication:* Use common syllable types to decode multisyllabic words
- *Automatic Word Recognition:* Recognize high frequency and less predictable words and practice to automaticity
- *Syntax and Context:* Use knowledge of word order (syntax) and context (semantics) to support the pronunciation and confirm word meaning
- *Use Other Resources:* Use other resources such as asking someone or using a dictionary

---

Appendix 4.1 provides a scope and sequence for teaching phonics.

Onset-Rime

Use Common Spelling Patterns to Decode Words by Blending. One salient feature of the English language is the use of spelling patterns, also referred to as *onset-rimes, phonograms,* or *word families.* When using spelling patterns to decode an unknown word, students can segment the word between the onset (/bl/ in the word *blend)* and the rime (-end) and then blend the onset and rime to make the word (*blend*). Figure 4.10 presents a list of 37 common rimes that make almost 500 words (Wylie and Durrell, 1970) and a more complete list of rimes is presented in Appendix 4.2. Guidelines for teaching onset-rimes follow

■ **FIGURE 4.10** *Thirty-Seven Common Rime Patterns from Primary Grade Texts*

-ack	-ail	-ain	-ake	-ale
-ame	-an	-ank	-ap	-ash
-at	-ate	-aw	-ay	
	-ell	-est		
-eat				
-ice	-ick	-ide	-ight	-ill
-in	-ine	-ing	-ink	-ip
-ir				
-ock	-oke	-op	-ore	-or
-uck	-ug	-ump	-unk	

the same guidelines as those suggested for teaching phonic analysis except that the word is segmented at the level of onset-rime rather than at the phoneme level. In contrast, Spanish does not use onset-rime to the extent that English does, and consequently it is generally not taught. However, words that contain rhyming syllables can form word families such as /sa/ in *masa* (flour), *tasa* (cup), and *casa* (home).

Teaching word analysis by having students learn individual letter–sound correspondences or rime patterns and then blending the sounds together to make the word is referred to as a *synthetic method* for teaching word analysis. For example, if the word is *pan,* then the students would say each sound individually (/p/ /a/ /n/) or the onset- rime (/p/ /an/), and then blend them together to make the word *pan.* Using this method the students are saying the individual sounds or onset-rime and then *synthesizing* or combining them to make the word.

Teachers can also use an *analogy method* for teaching word analysis, thereby providing students with a means of decoding the word other than sounding it out or blending the sounds into a word. When teaching onset-rime, teachers would cue the students to look at the unknown word to determine the spelling pattern (e.g., /an/). Then they think of the key word (e.g., *pan*) or other words with the same spelling pattern (*ran, than, tan*). The students then substitute the initial sound(s) of the unknown word for the initial sound(s) of the key word (*fat*). Cues that students can use to promote decoding by analogy are:

APPLY THE CONCEPT 4.1 ▰▰▰▰▰▰▰

WHICH PREFIXES, SUFFIXES, AND INFLECTIONAL ENDINGS SHOULD YOU TEACH?

How many prefixes do you need to teach? Four prefixes, *un-, re-, in-* (and *im-, ir-, il-* meaning *not*), and *dis-* account for 58 percent of all prefixed words. If you add 14 more prefixes—*en-/em-, non-, in-/im-* (meaning *in*), *mis-, sub-, pre-, inter-, fore-, de-, trans-, super-, semi-, anti-,* and *mid-* you will have accounted for about 95 percent of words with prefixes (White, Sowell, and Yanagihara, 1989). The inflectional endings of *-s/-es, -ed,* and *-ing* account

for about 65 percent of words that have inflectional endings and suffixes. If you add the suffixes *-ly, -er/or, -ion/-tion, -ible/-able, -al, -y, -ness, -ity,* and *-ment* you have accounted for over 85 percent. Other suffixes that are used frequently include *-er/est* (comparative), *-ic, -ous, -en, -ive, -ful,* and *-less* (White et al., 1989). Remember, it is important to teach the meanings along with how to decode them.

"What words do I know that look the same?"
"What words do I know that end (or begin) with the same letters?"

Structural Analysis
Use Knowledge of Word Structures such as Compound Word, Root Words, Suffixes, Prefixes, and Inflectional Endings to Decode Words and Assist with Meaning.   Between third and seventh grades, children learn from 3,000 to 26,000 words. Most of them are encountered through reading, and only a limited number are taught directly (Wysocki and Jenkins, 1987). Teach students to analyze words for compound words, root words, prefixes, suffixes, and inflectional endings because:

— It provides students with ways to segment longer, multisyllabic words into decodable (and meaningful) parts (Henry, 1997).
— It assists students in determining the meaning of words.

For example, the word *unbelievable* can be segmented into three parts, *un-believe-able*. Not only does chunking make this word easier to decode, it also tells us about the meaning. In the case of *unbelievable, un* means "not," and *-able* means "is or can be." Hence, *unbelievable* means something that it not to be believed.

Students can be taught to divide words into meaning parts (morphemes) is oftentimes first begun

by analyzing compound words. Then, high-frequency prefixes (e.g., *dis-, re-, in-, un-*), suffixes (e.g., *-er/or, -ly, -tion/-ion, -ness*), and inflectional endings (e.g., *-s, -es, -ing, -ed*) can be taught. See Apply the Concept 4.1 to learn more about what prefixes and suffixes to teach. Table 3.1 on page 74 provides a list of common prefixes, suffixes and inflectional endings and their meanings.

Ideas and guidelines for teaching and reinforcing structural analysis include:

— Teach the meanings along with recognition of the meaning parts.
— Explain and demonstrate how may "big words" are just "smaller words" with prefixes, suffixes, and endings.
— Write words on word cards and cut them by meaning parts. Have students say each part and then put the word together and blend the parts together to say the word. Discuss the meaning of each part.
— Ask students to sort or generate words by meaning parts. For example

pre- (before)	in (not)	re- (again)	super- (bit)
precaution	incomplete	replace	supermarket
prevent	incompatible	return	superintendent
precede	insignificant	redo	superman

- Present words that have the same prefix or suffix but the prefix or suffix has different meanings. Ask students to sort words by their meanings. For example

People Who Do	Things That Do	More	Words That Have -er
reporter	computer	fatter	cover
geographer	heater	greater	master
runner	dishwasher	shorter	never

If students are sorting, leave space so that they can add more words.

- Ask students to decode words they do not know by covering all but one part of the word and having them identify it, then uncovering the next part and identifying it, and so on. Then blend the parts together to read the word.
- Make a class or student dictionary that has each word part, its meaning, and several example words.
- Develop word webs or maps that demonstrate how one root word can make a cadre of related words (see Figure 4.11).

Syllabication

Use Common Syllable Types.　Many students with reading disabilities have particular difficulty decoding multisyllabic words. This skill becomes critical about third grade. Six basic syllable configurations or types can be identified in English spelling. The syllable types are useful because they encourage students to look for and recognize similar chunks of print across words. The six types are presented in Table 4.5.

In teaching about syllable types, it is important that students learn that each syllable has one vowel sound. However, the vowel sound may be represented by one or more letters (e.g., CVCe, vowel team). Ideas for teaching include dialogues that promote discovering the generalization, word sorts by syllable types, and games to provide practice. For example,

in teaching the CVCe the following dialogue encourages students to induce the generalization:

Teacher:　How many vowel sounds do you hear in each of these words (say *five, rope, cape, cube, kite, these*)?
Students:　One.
Teacher:　(Write *five, rope, cape, cube, kite, these.*) How many vowels do you see?
Students:　Two.
Teacher:　Which vowel sound do you hear? Tell me what is happening with the *e*?
Students:　The first vowel is long and you do not hear the *e*.

Demonstrate how adding the *e* to the end of CVC words makes the short vowel change to a long sound (*cap* becomes *cape, kit* becomes *kite*). For younger students teachers may want to generate a story about how the *e* bosses the vowel and makes it a long vowel sound, hence, "The Bossy E." Books such as *Market Day for Mrs. Wordy* also demonstrate the concept.

Automatic Word Recognition
Automatically Recognize High-Frequency and Less Phonetically Regular Words.　Words, regardless of their letter–sound predictability, need to be taught so that they are automatically recognized. Furthermore, it is not practical to teach students to analyze all words in the English language, because the patterns they follow may not occur frequently enough to teach. Figure 4.12 presents a list of 200 high-frequency words in order of their frequency of appearance. This list is drawn from a compilation of words that appear in books and other materials read by school children and make up about 60 percent of the words found in these texts (Zeno, Ivens, Millard, and Duvvuri, 1995). For example, the most frequently occurring word, *the,* makes up about 2 percent of words.

Two factors should be considered when deciding what words should be taught as high-frequency words: utility and ease of learning (Gunning, 2000). The biggest payoff for students will be learning words that occur most frequently. The words *the, of, and, a, to, in,*

■ **FIGURE 4.11**   *Root Word Map of* Friend

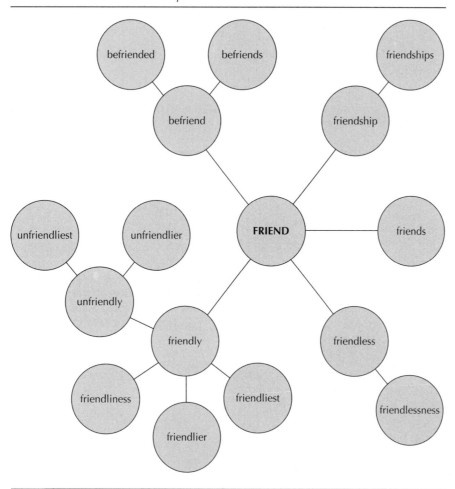

Source: Adapted from C. S. Bos, N. Mather, H. Silver-Pacuilla, and R. Friedmann Narr, "Learning to Teach Early Literacy Skills—Collaboratively," *Teaching Exceptional Children, 32* (5) (2000): 38–45.

is, you, that, and *it* account for more than 20 percent of the words that students will encounter. In considering the ease of learning, nouns and words with a distinctive shape are generally easier to learn. For struggling readers, ultimately you should teach first the words that the students will encounter most frequently.

The following guidelines can be used for teaching less predictable words (Cunningham, 2000; Gunning, 2000):

- Teach the most frequently occurring words.
- Check to see that students understand the meaning, particularly if the students have limited language, a specific language disability, or are English-language learners.
- Introduce these new words before students encounter them in text.
- Limit the number of words introduced in a single lesson.

■ **TABLE 4.5** *Six Syllable Types*

Type	Description/Examples
Closed (CVC)	Ends in at least one consonant; vowel is short. *bed, lost,* and *magnet,* dap- in *dapple,* hos- in *hostel*
Open (CV)	Ends in one vowel; vowel is long. me, mo- in *moment,* ti- in *tiger,* ta- in *table*
Vowel-Consonant-e (CVCe)	Ends in one vowel, one consonant, and a final e. Vowel is long, the final *e* is silent. *name, slope, five,* -pite in *despite,* -pete in *compete*
Vowel Team (CVVC)	Uses two adjacent vowels. Sounds of vowel teams vary. *rain, sweet,* -geal in *congeal,* train- in *trainer,* bea- in *beagle*
R-controlled (CV+r)	Vowel is followed by /r/ and vowel pronunciation is affected by /r/. *fern, burn, car, forge, charter*
Consonant-le (-C+le)	Unaccented final syllable with a consonant plus /l/ and silent *e.* -dle in *candle,* -tle in *little,* -zle in *puzzle*

— Reinforce the association by adding a kinesthetic component such as tracing, copying, and writing from memory.

— Introduce visually similar words (e.g., *where* and *were, was,* and *saw)* in separate lessons to avoid confusion.

— Ask students to compare visually similar words (e.g., *what* for *when)* and highlight the differences between the two words.

— Provide multiple opportunities for the students to read the words in text and as single words until they automatically recognize the words.

— Review words that have been taught previously, particularly if the students miscall them when reading text.

— Provide opportunities for the students to get automatic at recognizing the words such as games that require quick word recognition or power writing (i.e., writing the words multiple times in a short length of time).

Syntax and Semantics
Use Knowledge of Word Order (Syntax) and Context (Semantics) to Support the Pronunciation and Confirm Word Meaning. Although students with reading difficulties often overly on syntax and context to decode unknown words (Briggs, Austin, and Underwood, 1984), good readers use syntax and context to cross-check their pronunciation and monitor comprehension (Share and Stanovich, 1995; Torgesen, 1999). Key questions that students can ask are:

"Does that sound right here?"
"Does that make sense?"

Students should first be taught to decode the unknown word using phonics, structural analysis, and syllabication. Then teach them to cross–check the pronunciation by asking if the word "makes sense." This is evident when students reread a word, phrase, or sentence because "it doesn't make sense."

In looking at these six word identification strategies, it is clear that instruction for students who are having difficulty learning to read should include systematic instruction in letter–sound correspondences, phonic and structural analysis, and syllabication because they are the powerful strategies for reading text in alphabetic writing systems. In addition, reading instruction should provide many and varied opportunities to read and write so that students can employ semantic and syntactic clues and so that the recognition of words becomes automatic. This frees most of the reader's attention to focus on comprehension.

■ **FIGURE 4.12** *High-Frequency Words*

1. the	30. had	59. would	88. find	117. same	146. different	175. am
2. of	31. but	60. other	89. use	118. right	147. numbers	176. us
3. and	32. what	61. into	90. water	119. look	148. away	177. left
4. a	33. all	62. has	91. little	120. think	149. again	178. end
5. to	34. were	63. more	92. long	121. also	150. off	179. along
6. in	35. when	64. two	93. very	122. around	151. went	180. while
7. as	36. we	65. her	94. after	123. another	152. tell	181. sound
8. you	37. there	66. like	95. word	124. came	153. men	182. house
9. that	38. can	67. him	96. called	125. three	154. say	183. might
10. it	39. an	68. time	97. just	126. word	155. small	184. next
11. he	40. your	69. see	98. new	127. come	156. every	185. below
12. for	41. which	70. no	99. where	128. work	157. found	186. saw
13. was	42. their	71. could	100. most	129. must	158. still	187. something
14. on	43. said	72. make	101. most	130. part	159. big	188. thought
15. are	44. if	73. than	102. get	131. because	160. between	189. both
16. as	45. will	74. first	103. through	132. does	161. name	190. few
17. with	46. do	75. been	104. back	133. even	162. should	191. those
18. his	47. each	76. its	105. much	134. place	163. home	192. school
19. they	48. about	77. who	106. good	135. old	164. give	193. show
20. at	49. how	78. now	107. before	136. well	165. air	194. always
21. be	50. up	79. people	108. go	137. such	166. line	195. looked
22. this	51. our	80. my	109. man	138. here	167. mother	196. large
23. from	52. then	81. made	110. our	139. take	168. set	197. often
24. I	53. them	82. over	111. write	140. why	169. world	198. together
25. have	54. she	83. did	112. sat	141. things	170. own	199. ask
26. not	55. many	84. down	113. me	142. great	171. under	200. turn
27. or	56. some	85. way	114. day	143. help	172. last	
28. by	57. so	86. only	115. too	144. put	173. read	
29. one	58. these	87. may	116. any	145. years	174. never	

Source: T. G. Gunning, *Creating Literacy Instruction for All Children*, 3rd ed. (Boston: Allyn and Bacon, 2000). Copyright © 2000 by Allyn and Bacon. Reprinted by permission. Adapted from S. M. Zeno, S. H. Ivens, R. T. Millard, and R. Duvvuri, *The Educator's Word Frequency Guide* (Brewster, NY: Touchstone Applied Science Associates, 1995).

TEACHING WORD RECOGNITION, DECODING, AND WORD STUDY

Bradley, a third grader, is the lowest reader in his class and is not making progress in reading. When he reads orally first-grade level texts, the teacher assists him in pronouncing about 30 percent of the words. He reads slowly and cannot remember previously known words. He knows less than 30 sight words, and

he applies inconsistent strategies to decode words. Sometimes he attempts to sound out the word letter by letter, but he has difficulty with the letter–sound relationships beyond the first several letters, particularly the vowel sounds, as well as difficulty in accurately blending the sounds together. Hence, this strategy rarely results in him pronouncing the words correctly. Even though Bradley struggles in decoding the individual words, he can generally get the gist when reading these simple texts. He has good oral language skills and his life experiences result in him being familiar with much of the content of what he reads. His math skills are at a third-grade level, although he has not yet learned his math facts to the automatic level.

Lupita, another third grader, is also struggling to learn to read. Like Bradley she is reading at the first-grade level and has a sight vocabulary of about 40 words in Spanish and 25 in English. When she entered kindergarten she had limited oral language proficiency in both Spanish and English. She is in a bilingual program that initially taught reading in Spanish but began transitioning to English in second grade. This year much of the reading instruction is in English. Like Bradley, she has difficulty remembering words automatically, and her reading, even in very easy text, is slow and laborious. Her decoding strategies rely primarily on sounding out the words, but she does not know many of the letter–sound correspondences and has difficulty blending. Her most consistent strategy when she does not recognize a word is to look to the teacher for assistance. Lupita's oral language in both Spanish and English continues to be somewhat limited as measured on language assessments. Although she communicates with her friends, she is shy about responding in class and appears to have limited background experiences to assist her understanding what she is reading or learning. Lupita does well in basic math but has difficulty with word problems.

When beginning to work with students like Bradley and Lupita, who have limited sight words and word identification strategies, it is helpful not only to determine the students' current strategies but also to determine what approaches have been used previously, how consistently, for how long, and with what success. It is also helpful to use the intervention research to inform your decision-making.

Beginning reading approaches that emphasize explicit, direct teaching of phonological awareness and word identification strategies that rely on using phonics, onset-rime, and structural analysis result in greater gains in word recognition and comprehension than approaches in which phonological awareness and phonics are more implicitly taught (National Reading Panel, 2000; Swanson, 1999). Consequently, explicit code instruction approaches should a part of

a balanced reading approach for most students with special needs.

The rest of the chapter focuses on teaching approaches and techniques that build word recognition and word identification strategies. The first section presents several explicit code instruction approaches and the next section focuses on implicit code instruction approaches or approaches in which teaching phonic and structural analysis is not emphasized or less direct. The third section presents several techniques that provide students with repeated opportunities to practice identifying words until automatically recognized. It is important to remember that this is just one aspect of a reading program, although it is a very important one for students with reading problems. A reading program should also have multiple opportunities to teach listening and reading comprehension and to read for learning and enjoyment. It should also provide opportunities for students to write about what they are reading.

Explicit Code Instruction

Explicit code approaches teach phonological awareness, letter–sound correspondences, the alphabetic principle, and the use of phonic analysis, structural analysis, and syllabication to decode unknown words. They emphasize instructional features:

1. Introduce letter–sound correspondences systematically and teach students to blend the sounds to make words and segment sounds to spell words.
2. Scaffold instruction so that modeling, guidance, and positive and corrective feedback are integral features of instruction.
3. Provide multiple opportunities for practice and review in various contexts (e.g., games with words cards, constructing sentences, reading texts).

Typically the beginning reading materials associated with these approaches are controlled for the phonic and structural patterns they use, hence, they are referred to as *decodable text*. See Apply the Concept 4.2 for information about different text types and their purposes related to teaching students beginning reading.

APPLY THE CONCEPT 4.2

TEXT TYPES AND HOW THEY FACILITATE LEARNING TO READ

For students with learning and behavior problems who are learning to read as well as other students, it is important to match the type of text with the goals and purposes of reading instruction. When the text type matches the level and purpose for instruction, it can provide a scaffold that supports students as

they learn to read as well as provide them with opportunities to practice what they are learning (Brown, 1999/2000; Mesmer, 1999). Beginning text can be classified into five general categories, each of which serves a different but complimentary purpose for teaching students to read.

Type of Text and Characteristics	*Support for Beginning Reading*
Predictable/Pattern Language • Repeated language patterns with accompanying pictures that make it easy to predict what the rest of the text says • Control of language pattern, rhyme, rhythm, sentence structure with difficulty increasing gradually across levels of text • Example of text: I have a soccer ball (picture of soccer ball). I have a basketball ball (picture). I have a baseball (picture). I have a kick ball (picture). I like to play ball. Types: • Patterned text with picture/text match • Cumulative pattern with information added on each page (e.g., I ate an apple. I ate an apple and some grapes. I ate an apple, some grapes, and three bananas. I have a stomachache. • Familiar poems and songs	**Emphasizes student use of:** • Memory • Context and picture clues • Repeating language patterns • Repeating reading of text **Emphasizes teacher use of:** • Modeling the concept that print has meaning • Modeling how books work (e.g., concept of a sentence, word; directionality) • Developing oral reading fluency and expression
Decodable Text • Text that introduces sound/symbol relationships, onset-rimes, and sight words in a controlled sequence so that difficulty level increases across levels • Text that provides opportunities to apply the alphabetic principle and begin reading using the letter-sound correspondences and onset-rimes that have been taught • Control for words, sound/symbol relationships, onset-rimes, sentence structure • Example: Peg had a pet pup. The pup was sad. The pup wanted to get fed, but Peg was in bed. The pup ran to Peg's bed.	**Emphasizes student use of:** • Blending sounds and sounding out words to decode them • Using onset-rimes to make words and using analogy to decode words (e.g., "If I know "pit," then this word must be "lit") • Learning to recognize less predictable words by sight as whole words (e.g., was, come) **Emphasizes teacher use of:** • Modeling how to blend and segment sounds and providing independent practice in these skills

(continued)

APPLY THE CONCEPT 4.2 *Continued*

Types: • Emphasizes onset-rimes such as "The fat cat sat on the hat." Sometimes called linguistic readers. • Emphasizes systematic introduction of sound/symbol relationships usually starting with a few consonants and short vowels in CVC words. Sometimes called phonic readers.	• Developing students' letter-sound and simple spelling pattern knowledge • Sounding out words when unknown • Using onset-rime or word chunks to decode words • Developing independent, fluent reading of words, sentences, and connected text
Transitional Text • Integrates predictable and decodable text so that across levels predictability decreases and decodability increases • Example: So she said to Grandpa, "Can you rock Nick for a little while? Maybe you can get him to stop." "Sure," Grandpa said. "Now I can try." But Grandpa had no luck. So he said to me. "Can you play with Nick for a little while? Maybe you can get him to stop." "Sure," I said. "I will pick him up. It's my turn to try! (*Pick Up Nick* by Kate McGroven, pp. 10-14).	**Emphasizes student use of:** • Diminishing use of memory and context clues to identify words • Increasing use of blending sounds, sounding out words, and onset-rime to decode unknown words • Learning to recognize less predictable words by sight **Emphasizes teacher use of:** • Modeling how to blend and segment sounds • Modeling how to sound out and use onset-rime to decode unknown words • Developing independent, fluent reading of words, sentences, and connected text
Easy Reader Text • Series of books that gradually increase in difficulty across levels but are less controlled than predictable, decodable, or transitional texts • Less control of words with more difficult high-frequency words, more polysyllabic words, and more complex sentences • More complex plot and information and more text per page • Some use of short chapters • Example: "And it means that we can begin a whole new year together, Toad. Think of it," said Frog. "We will skip through the meadows and run through the woods and swim in the river . . . (*Frog and Toad Are Friends*, p. 8).	**Emphasizes student use of:** • Using simple syllabication, prefixes/suffixes, and chunking with polysyllabic words (e.g., unprepared) and using more complex spelling patterns (e.g., fright) • Using sight word knowledge and working on automaticity and fluency **Emphasizes teacher use of:** • Modeling more complex decoding strategies using more difficult words • Developing student's oral reading fluency and expression • Modeling comprehension strategies while reading aloud
Authentic Literature and Nonfiction • Text that is written with limited regard for word or sentence difficulty and provides more complex plots and information • Varies widely in style and genre	**Emphasizes student use of:** • Listening and reading comprehension strategies • Developing knowledge of different writing styles and genres

Examples:
- *Peter Rabbit* by Beatrix Potter
- *Owl Moon* by Jane Yolen
- *Bearman: Exploring the World of Black Bears* by Laurence Pringle

- Applying advanced decoding strategies in less controlled texts

Emphasizes teacher use of:
- Reading for enjoyment and model fluency when reading aloud
- Motivating students and creating interest in reading
- Discussing literature and teaching listening/ reading/ comprehension strategies

Predictable texts can be particularly beneficial for early or emergent readers because these texts provide opportunities for demonstration and student practice of how reading works. It gives beginning readers including older readers who are struggling to learn to read, a sense of successful reading by relying upon repetitive language patterns and their memory. However, it is decodable and transitional texts that provide these students with practice in using letter–sound relationships and word identification strategies to make them successful at decoding unknown words. The degree of decodability (i.e., control on the vocabulary and the systematic manner in which the letter–sounds and onset-rimes are introduced) is related to the degree of difficulty that the students with learning or reading problems are experiencing in developing decoding strategies, learning words so that they are recognized automatically, and reading fluently. In general, those students who are experiencing greater difficulties will require more decodable text and systematic instruction for a longer period of time. As students become more proficient, they move to easy readers. Thus, the use of highly decodable text is related to where students are in the process of learning to read (Beck and Juel, 1995). Throughout the "learning to read" process, it is important to include authentic literature and nonfiction for building listening and reading comprehension strategies, for learning about books, genre, and writing styles, and for the enjoyment of reading (Fountas and Pinnell, 1999; Watson, 1997).

Linguistic Approach: Onset-Rime and Word Families

The linguistic approach uses controlled text and word families (onset-rimes, phonograms, or spelling patterns) such as -at, -ight, and -ent to teach word recognition. This approach was introduced by the linguists Bloomfield and Barnhart (1961) and Fries (1963). It gained popularity in the late 1960s and early 1970s. Recent research has highlighted the effectiveness of teaching onset-rime (Ehri, 1998; Goswami, 1998), particularly for students who experience difficulties learning to read (see "Decoding Strategies for Identifying Words: Onset-Rime" on page 132).

— **PROCEDURES:** The linguistic approach is built on a salient feature of in the English language, that is, onset-rime. Figure 4.10 (page 132) presents a list of 37 common rimes with a more complete list found in Appendix 4.2. In teaching onset-rime, words are segmented and blended at the onset-rime level rather the phoneme level, and words are taught in related groups often referred to as word families (at: *cat*, *fat*, *bat*, *sat*, *rat*; *ight*: *right*, *might*, *fight*). Sight or less phonetically regular words are kept to a minimum. Figure 4.13 provides an example of a beginning text from a typical linguistic reader. These readers give the students extensive practice with the word families and systematically introduce onset-rime patterns. Figure 4.14 presents a selected list of linguistic reading programs and linguistic readers.

When students cannot identify a word-family word, one strategy is to use a synthetic method of decoding by having them segment it at the onset-rime level (e.g., for the word *flat* cover the /fl/ and have

■ **FIGURE 4.13** *Sample Linguistic Reading Story*

Nat and the Rat

Nat is a cat.

She is a fat cat.

She likes to sit on her mat.

Dad likes to pat Nat.

One day Nat sat on Dad's lap for a pat.

Nat saw a rat.

She jumped off Dad's lap and ran after the rat.

That made Nat tired.

So Nat sat on her mat.

---

the student read the /at/, then cover the /at/ and have them give the sound /fl/, and then expose the whole word and have them blend the two segments together to make the word *flat*). Another strategy is to use an analogy method where the students think of another word, or the key word, they know with the same rime pattern (e.g., *cat*) and then substitute the initial sound(s) to make the word *flat*. Activities such as word sorts in which students sort words by word families, constructing word walls using onset-rime patterns, making word family houses (see Figure 4.15), and playing games like Word Family Concentration

and Can You Write a Word that Rimes With are all ways of reinforcing onset-rime patterns.

— **COMMENTS:** Teaching students about onset-rime and word families provides them with another context for understanding the alphabetic principle and how English sounds map to print. It also reinforces the phonological awareness skill of rhyming. The use of a linguistic approach and linguistic readers provides struggling readers with multiple opportunities to learn and practice onset-rime patterns. Because of the highly controlled vocabulary, students are frequently able to experience success in comparison to learning to read whole words (Goswami, 1998; Levy and Lysynchuk, 1997; O'Shaughnessy and Swanson, 2000). It is unclear from research, however, whether decoding at the phoneme level (e.g., /c-a-t/) versus the onset-rime level (e.g., /c-at/) is more advantageous and for which students. Several cautions should be mentioned when using this approach. First, like other explicit code instruction, the texts oftentimes provide limited opportunities for the development of comprehension. Therefore, the use of children's narrative and expository literature should be incorporated into the reading program to develop listening comprehension. To demonstrate this point, reread the text given in Figure 4.13 and then try to generate five comprehension questions. Second, some words introduced in a family may represent unfamiliar or abstract concepts.

■ **FIGURE 4.14** *Selected Linguistic Reading Programs and Readers*

Foundations, 1999, Bothell, WA: The Wright Group.

Get Ready, Get Set, Read, 1991, Hauppauge, NY: Barron's Educational Series.

Let's Read: A Linguistic Reading Program, Bloomfield, L., Barnhart, R. K., and Barnhart, R. K., 1965, 1994–1997, Cambridge, MA: Educators Publishing Service.

Merrill Reading Program, Bertin, P., et al., 1999, Columbus, OH: SRA/McGraw-Hill.

New Way: Heads and Tails, 2000, Austin, TX: Steck-Vaughn.

Preventing Academic Failure, Bertin, P., and Perlman, E., 1999, Columbus, OH: SRA/McGraw-Hill.

Ready Readers, 1999, Parsippany, NJ: Modern Curriculum Press.

Sullivan's Programmed Reading (3rd ed.), Buchanan, C, 1988, St. Louis, MO: Phoenix Learning Resources.

Sundance Phonic Readers, 1998–1999, Littleton, MA: Sundance.

The Basic Reading Series, Rasmussen, D., and Goldberg, L., 2000, Columbus, OH: SRA/McGraw-Hill.

■ **FIGURE 4.15** *Word Family House*

For example, when learning the -og family, a student may be asked to read about "the fog in the bog."

Reading Mastery and Corrective Reading

Reading Mastery: Rainbow Edition (Englemann, Bruner, Hanner, Osborn, Osborn, and Zoref, 1995) and *Corrective Reading* (Engelmann et al., 1999) are highly structured, systematic reading programs that use a direct instruction model for teaching (Carnine, Silbert, and Kameenui, 1997) and a synthetic method for teaching phonics and structural analysis. These programs directly teach individual sound–symbol relationships, blending of sounds, and how to build these sounds into words. The programs include components in decoding and comprehension, with comprehension focusing on the systematic development of logical reasoning skills and the use of questioning to promote comprehension. Whereas *Reading Mastery* is designed for elementary-level students, *Corrective Reading* is designed for students in grades

4 through 12 who have not mastered decoding and comprehension skills. Both programs are best taught in small- to medium-sized groups.

— **PROCEDURES:** *Reading Mastery* and *Corrective Reading* are built on principles of direct instruction (Carnine et al., 1997) that for reading include:

— Design instruction to maximize the amount of student engaged time (e.g., students work in small groups with teacher; students give unison responses after adequate wait time so all students have time to think).

— Teach students to rely on strategies rather than require them to memorize information (e.g., teach several letter sounds such as /m/, /t/, /s/, /f/, /ă/, and /ĭ/ and the sounding-out strategy to decode words).

— Teach procedures to generalize knowledge (e.g., have students apply the sounding-out strategy to new sounds to build additional words).

— Use a teaching format that includes an introduction stage, followed by guided practice, independent practice, and review.

— Teach to mastery (specific criterion level).

— Teach one skill or strategy at a time.

— Systematically teach skills and strategies in a cumulative manner.

• Prerequisite knowledge or skills (e.g., sounds of letters are taught before words).

• Instances that are consistent with the strategy are introduced before exceptions (e.g., teach consistent CVCe words such as *gave* and *made* before exceptions such as *have*).

• High utility knowledge is introduced before less useful knowledge (e.g., teach frequent irregular words such as *of* and *was* before less frequent ones such as *heir* and *neon*).

• Easy skills are taught before more difficult ones.

• Introduce information and strategies that are likely to be confused separately (e.g., letters *b* and *d* and words *were* and *where*).

• Provide for systematic review and practice.

— Monitor student performance and provide corrective feedback.

■ **FIGURE 4.16**

— Use a reinforcement system that promotes student engagement and learning.

In both programs students are taught a consistent method of responding to sounds and sounding out words. Using the guide in Figure 4.16, teachers touch the first ball of the arrow and cue

"Say it with me or sound it out. Get ready."

They touch quickly under each sound, saying each sound, /rrreeed/. They repeat until students are consistent and then cue

"Say it fast. What sound or what word?"

Repeat until students consistently respond with the sound or word.

In both programs the teacher is given specific procedures to follow including scripted lessons. These scripted lessons specify what the teacher is to say and include hand signals. Part of an early lesson from *Corrective Reading: Word Attack Basics—Decoding A* is presented in Figure 4.17. Each lesson contains multiple exercises that focus on word attack skills such as sound identification, pronunciations, say the sounds, word reading, sentence reading, story reading, and spelling from dictation. Lessons are designed to last from 30 to 50 minutes with time provided for direct teaching, group reading, individual reading practice, and monitoring of progress with feedback. Both programs have placement tests. Whereas *Corrective Reading* uses standard print, the initial levels of *Reading Mastery* employ modified print that includes marking the long vowel sounds and reducing the size of silent letters (see Figure 4.18). Both programs provide for reading of decodable text with *Corrective Reading* having an emphasis on reading expository texts.

Corrective Reading teaches skills in word identification including word attack, decoding strategies, and skill application and skills in comprehension including thinking basics, comprehension skills, and

concept applications. The program provides daily feedback and has a built-in reinforcement system.

— **COMMENTS:** Research has demonstrated that these programs are effective for improving the reading skills of students with reading difficulties and students from disadvantaged backgrounds (Becker, 1977; Gersten, Carnine, and Woodward, 1987; Gregory, Hackney, and Gregory, 1982; Grossen, 1999; Kameenui, et al., 1998; Polloway, Epstein, Polloway, Patton, and Ball, 1986; Thorne, 1978; Vitale, Medland, Romance, and Weaver, 1993.) Much of the teaching of phonic analysis skills is conducted in an explicit manner, which has been demonstrated to be advantageous for students with learning and behavior problems (Swanson, 1999). Several cautions, however, should be noted. First, these programs rely heavily on oral presentation by the teacher and oral responses and reading by the students. Second, the programs are highly scripted, making modifications difficult. Third, the nonstandard print used with Levels I and II of *Reading Mastery* may limit some students' access to other decodable books. Although other books with the nonstandard print are available, the number is limited.

Phonic Remedial Reading Lessons

The *Phonic Remedial Reading Lessons* (Kirk, Kirk, and Minskoff, 1985) were originally developed in the 1930s to teach phonic analysis skills to students who had mild mental retardation. The lessons follow principles of systematic direct instruction in that they utilize such principles as minimal change, one response to one symbol, progress from easy to hard, frequent review and overlearning, corrective feedback, verbal mediation, and multisensory learning. The lessons are designed as an intensive phonics program to be used individually or in groups of no more than two to three students. They are not recommended as a general technique for teaching beginning reading, but rather as a technique for students who have not yet learned an efficient method of identifying unknown words (Kirk, Kirk, and Minskoff, 1985).

— **PROCEDURES:** The program begins by developing the readiness level for the lessons. These readiness skills include auditory discrimination and auditory sound blending. Figure 4.4 presented this

■ **FIGURE 4.17** *Portion of an Early Lesson from* Corrective Reading

EXERCISE 2
PRONUNCIATIONS
Note: Do not write the words on the board. This is
an oral exercise.

Task A

1. Listen. He was mad. (Pause.) **Mad.** Say it. (Signal.)
   Mad.
2. Next word. Listen. They wrestled on a mat. (Pause.)
   Mat. Say it. (Signal.) *Mat.*
3. Next word: **ram.** Say it. (Signal.) *Ram.*
4. (Repeat step 3 for **sat, reem, seem.**)
5. (Repeat all the words until firm.)

Task B Sit, rim, fin

1. I'll say words that have the sound iii. What sound?
   (Signal.) *iii.* Yes, iii.
2. (Repeat step 1 until firm.)
3. Listen: **sit, rim, fin.** Your turn: **sit.** Say it. (Signal.)
   Sit. Yes, sit.
4. Next word: **rim.** Say it. (Signal.) *Rim.* Yes, rim.
5. Next word: **fin.** Say it. (Signal.) *Fin.* Yes, fin.
6. (Repeat steps 3–5 until firm.)
7. What's the middle sound in the word rrriiimmm?
   (Signal.) *iii.* Yes, iii.
8. (Repeat step 7 until firm.)

EXERCISE 3
SAY THE SOUNDS
Note: Do not write the words on the board. This is
an oral exercise.

1. First you're going to say a word slowly without
   stopping between the sounds. Then you're going to
   say the word fast.
2. Listen: ssseee. (Hold up a finger for each sound.)
3. Say the sounds in (pause) ssseee. Get ready. (Hold
   up a finger for each sound.) *ssseee.* Repeat until the
   students say the sounds without stopping.)
4. Say it fast. (Signal.) *See.*
5. What word? (Signal.) *See.* Yes, see.
6. (Repeat steps 2–5 for sad, mad, mat, me, seed, in,
   if, sat, ran, rat.)

EXERCISE 4
SOUND INTRODUCTION

1. (Point to i.) One sound this letter makes is iii. What
   sound? (Touch.) *iii.*
2. (Point to d.) This letter makes the sound d. What
   sound? (Touch.) *d.*

3. Say each sound when I touch it.
4. (Point to 1.) What sound? (Touch under) **i.** iii.
5. (Repeat step 4 for d, e, d, r, t, s, ǎ, m.)
   To correct:
   a. (Say the sound loudly as soon as you hear an
      error.)
   b. (Point to the sound.) This sound is _____. What
      sound? (Touch.)
   c. (Repeat the series of letters until all the students
      can correctly identify all the sounds in order.)
6. (Point to the circled letters.) The sound for one of
   these letters is the same as the letter name. That's
   the name you say when you say the alphabet.
7. (Point to i.) Listen: iii. Is that a letter name? (Signal.)
   No. Right, it isn't.
8. (Point to a.) Listen: ăăă. Is that a letter name?
   (Signal.) *No.* Right, it isn't.
9. (Point to e.) Listen: eee. Is that a letter name? (Signal.)
   Yes. Yes, it is. Remember, the sound you're
   learning for eee is the same as the letter name.

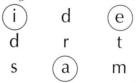

Individual test

I'll call on different students to say all the sounds. If
everybody I call on can say all the sounds without
making a mistake, we'll go on to the next exercise.
(Call on two or three students. Touch under each
sound. Each student says all the sounds.)

EXERCISE 6
WORD READING

Task A Sat

1. Say each sound when I touch it.
   (Point to a.) What sound?
   (Touch under s.) *sss.*
   (Point to a.) What sound?
   (Touch under a.) *ăăă.*
   (Point to t.) What sound?
   (Touch under t.) *t.*
2. Touch the ball of the arrow for sat.)
   Now I'm going to sound out the word. I won't stop
   between the sounds.
   (Touch under s, a, t as you say:) **sssăăăt.**
   (Point to t.) What sound?

(continued)

FIGURE 4.17 *Continued*

3. (Touch the ball of the arrow.) Do it with me. Sound it out. Get ready.
   (Touch under s, a, t.) **sssaaat.** (Repeat until the students say the sounds without pausing
4. Again. Sound it out. Get ready. (Touch under s, a, t.) **sssaaat.** (Repeat until firm.)
5. All by yourselves. Sound it out. Get ready. (Touch under s, a, t.) **sssaaat.** (Repeat until firm.)

6. Touch the ball of the arrow.) Say it fast. (Slash right, along the arrow. *Sat.)* Yes, you read the word sat.

s a t

Source: S. Engelmann, L. Carnine, and G. Johnson, *Corrective Reading: Word-Attack Basics, Teacher Presentation Book 1—Decoding A* (Columbus, OH: SRA/McGraw-Hill, 1999), pp. 26–29. Reprinted by permission of The McGraw-Hill Companies.

■ **FIGURE 4.18** *Sample from a Story from* Reading Mastery: Rainbow Edition.

the fat man and his dog had

a car. the car did not run.

Source: S. Engleman and E. C. Bruner, *Reading Mastery I: Rainbow Edition—Storybook I* (Columbus, OH: SRA/McGraw Hill, 1995), pp. 53–54. Reprinted by permission of The McGraw-Hill Companies.

simple procedure for teaching sound blending. Developing readiness also includes learning the sound-symbol associations for the short *a* sound and eleven consonant sounds (i.e., /c/, /d/, /f/, /g/, /h/, /l/, /m/, /p/, /s/, /t/, /w/).

Once these skills have been learned, the first lesson is introduced (see Figure 4.19). For each lesson, students sound out each word in each line, one letter at a time, and then give the complete word. Each lesson is organized into four parts and is based on the principle of minimal change. In the first part, only the initial consonant changes in each sequence; in the second part, only the final consonant changes; in the third part, both the initial and final consonants change; and in the fourth part, the space between letters in a word is normal.

In addition to these drill lessons, high-frequency sight words are introduced and highly controlled stories are interspersed throughout the program. Frequent review lessons are also provided.

— **COMMENTS:** This program provides for a systematic and intensive approach to teaching phonic analysis skills to beginning readers. However, the approach places little emphasis on comprehension and reading for meaning and incorporates limited practice in connected text. The authors suggest using other books to provide students with the opportunity to try both their word-identification and comprehension skills in other reading materials.

Multisensory Structured Language Instruction

Multisensory structured language programs combine the systematic explicit teaching of phonemic aware-

■ **FIGURE 4.19**   *First Lesson from Phonic Remedial Reading Lessons*

a

at	s a t	m a t	h a t	f a t
a m	h a m	S a m	P a m	t a m
s a d	m a d	h a d	l a d	d a d
w a g	s a g	t a g	l a g	h a g

s a t	s a p	S a m	s a d
m a p	m a m	m a d	m a t
h a g	h a m	h a t	h a d
c a t	c a p	c a d	c a m

s a t	a m	s a d	p a t	m a d
h a d	m a t	t a g	f a t	h a m
l a g	h a m	w a g	h a t	s a p
s a d	t a p	c a p	d a d	a t

map	hag	cat	sat	ham	tap
sap	map	hat	sad	tag	am
Pam	mat	had	tap	hat	dad
fat	mad	at	wag	cap	sag

Source: S. A. Kirk, W. D. Kirk, and E. H. Minskoff, *Phonic Remedial Reading Lessons* (Novato, CA; Academic Therapy Publications, 1985), p. 22. Reprinted by permission.

ness, the alphabetic principle, phonics and structural analysis, syllabication, and decoding with activities that incorporate the visual, auditory, tactile (touch) and kinesthetic (movement) (VAKT) modalities. Multisensory structured language instruction was developed in the 1930s by Samuel Orton, a neuropathologist, and Anne Gillingham, a school psychologist. They developed reading remediation methods that built associations between the modalities such as "having the child trace [the letter] over a pattern drawn by the teacher, at the same time giving its sound or phonetic equivalent" (Orton, 1937, p. 159) or teaching spelling through analysis and writing of the sequence of sounds in words. The content of multisensory structure language programs includes teaching: (1) phonology and phonological awareness, (2) sound–symbol associations that must be mastered in two directions: visual to auditory and auditory to visual, (3) syllable instruction, (4) morphology (5) syntax, and (6) semantics. These programs use the following instructional features or principles (McIntyre and Pickering, 1995):

— *Simultaneous, multisensory (VAKT) presentation:* visual, auditory, and kinesthetic–tactile modalities are used simultaneously to enhance memory and learning.

- *Systematic and cumulative progression* that follows the logical order of the language, moves from easy to difficult, and provides systematic review to strengthen memory.
- *Direct instruction* that entails the explicit teaching of all concepts, skills, and strategies.
- *Systematic practice of decoding and spelling skills* at the word, sentence, and text levels in controlled, decodable text.
- *Diagnostic teaching* that requires the teacher to be adept at individualizing instruction based on careful and continual assessment of the student's learning.
- *Instruction that incorporates* **synthetic methods** (teaching the parts and how they work together to make a whole) and **analytic methods** (teaching the whole and how it can be broken down into its component parts).

These programs are designed for students with dyslexia or those who are experiencing substantial difficulty in learning to read. Examples of multisensory structure language programs are presented in Figure 4.20. Described in more detail is the Gillingham-Stillman method (Gillingham and Stillman, 1973). It is designed for third- through sixth-grade students of average or above average ability and normal sensory acuity who are having difficulty learning to read. With some adaptations it can be modified to work with both older and younger students.

— **PROCEDURES:** This method is designed to teach students how to identify words by teaching phonic generalizations and how to apply these generalizations in reading and spelling. It is to be used as the exclusive method for teaching reading, spelling, and penmanship for a minimum of a two-year period. Initially students who use this method should read only materials that are designed to conform with the method. Other written information such as content area textbooks should be read to the students.

The method is introduced by discussing the importance of reading and writing, how some children have difficulty learning to read and spell using whole-word methods, and how this method has helped other students. Thereafter, a sequence of lessons is completed, beginning with learning the names of the letters and the letter sounds, learning words through blending sounds, and reading sentences and stories.

Teaching Letters and Sounds: The teaching of letter names and letter sounds employs associations between visual, auditory, and kinesthetic inputs. Each new sound-symbol relationship or phonogram is taught by having the students make three associations.

■ **FIGURE 4.20** *Examples of Multisensory Structure Language Programs*

Alphabetic Phonics and *Foundations for Literacy: Structures and Techniques for Multisensory Teaching of Basic Written English Language Skills* Cox, A. R., 1992, Cambridge, MA: Educators Publishing Service.

Language: A Curriculum for At-Risk and ESL Students, Greene, J. R., 1995, Longmont, CO: Sopris West.

Lindamood Phoneme Sequencing Program for Reading, Spelling, and Speech: The LiPS Program, Lindamood, P., and Lindamood, P., 1998, 3rd ed., Austin, TX: PRO-ED.

Multi-Sensory Approach to Language Arts for Specific Language Disability Children, Volumes: 1–3, rev.

ed., Slingerland, B. H., and Aho, M. 1994–1996, Cambridge, MA: Educators Publishing Service.

Project Read, Enfield, M. L., and Greene, V., 1997, Bloomington, MN: Language Circle Enterprise.

Recipe for Reading: A Structured Approach to Linguistics, Traub, N., Bloom, F., et al., 2000, Cambridge, MA: Educators Publishing Service.

The Herman Method for Reversing Reading Failure, Herman, R. D., 1993, Sherman Oaks, CA: The Herman Method Institute.

The Writing Road to Reading, 4th ed., Spalding, R. B., and Spalding, W. T., 1990, New York: Quill.

Wilson Reading System, Wilson, B. A., 1996, Millbury, MA: Wilson Language Training Corporation.

1. *Association I (Reading).* The students are taught to associate the written letter with the letter name and then with the letter sound. The teacher shows the students the letter. The students repeat the name. The letter sound is learned using the same procedure.
2. *Association II (Oral Spelling).* The students are taught to associate the oral sound with the name of the letter. To do this the teacher says the sound and asks the students to give its corresponding letter.
3. *Association III (Written Spelling).* The students learn to write the letter through the teacher modeling, tracing, copying, and writing the letter from memory. The students then associate the letter sound with the written letter by the teacher directing them to write the letter that has the _____ sound.

When teaching these associations:

1. Cursive writing is preferred and suggested over manuscript.
2. Letters are always introduced by a key word.
3. Vowels and consonants are differentiated by different colored drill cards (i.e., white for consonants, salmon for vowels).
4. The first letters introduced (i.e., ă, *b, f, h,* ĭ, *j, k, m, p,* and *t*) represent clear sounds and nonreversible letter forms.
5. Drill cards are used to introduce each letter and to provide practice in sound and letter identification.
6. The writing procedure is applied to learning all new letters. The procedure for writing is:
   a. The teacher makes the letter.
   b. The students trace the letter.
   c. The students copy it.
   d. The students write it from memory.

Teaching Words: After the first ten letters and sounds have been learned using the Associations, students begin blending them together into words. Words that can be made from the ten letters are written on yellow word cards and kept in student word boxes (jewel cases). Students are taught to read and spell words.

To teach blending and reading, the letter Drill Cards that form a word (e.g., *b—a—t*) are laid out on the table or put in a pocket chart. The students are asked to give the sounds of the letters in succession, repeating the series of sounds again and again with increasing speed and smoothness until they are saying the word. This procedure is used to learn new words. Drill and timed drill activities are used to give the students practice reading the words.

To teach spelling, the analysis of words into their component sound should begin a few days after blending is started. To teach this method of spelling the teacher pronounces a word the students can read, first quickly and then slowly. The teacher then asks the students, "What sound did you hear first?" and then asks, "What letter says /b/?" The students then find the *b* card. When all cards have been found, the students write the word. Gillingham and Stillman (1973) stress the importance of using this procedure for spelling. After the teacher pronounces /bat/:

		Child writes, naming each letter	
	Child names letters	Child while forming it	Child reads
Child repeats			
b-a-t	/*b-a-t*/		bat

This procedure is referred to as Simultaneous Oral Spelling, or SOS. Gillingham and Stillman comment that after a few days of practice in blending and SOS, it should be an almost invariable routine to have the students check their own errors. When a word is read wrong, the student should be asked to spell what he or she has just said, and match it against the original word. When a word is misspelled orally the teacher may write the offered spelling and say, "Read this (e.g., *bit*)." The student would respond, "Bit." The teacher would say, "Correct, but I dictated the word /bat/."

As the students continue to learn and practice new words, they also continue to learn new sound–symbol associations or phonograms. As new phonograms are introduced, more and more words are practiced and added to the word boxes. An example of a daily lesson might be:

Practice Association I with learned phonograms
Practice Association II with learned phonograms
Practice Association III with learned phonograms
Drill words for reading
Drill words for spelling and writing

Sentences and Stories: When the students can read and write three-lettered phonetic words, sentence and story reading is begun. This begins with reading simple, highly structured stories, called "Little Stories." These stories are first practiced silently until the students think they can read them perfectly. They can ask the teacher for assistance. The teacher pronounces nonphonetic words and cues the student to sound out phonetically regular words. Then the students read the sentence or story orally. The story is to be read perfectly with proper inflection. Later, the stories are dictated to the student. An example of a story is:

Sam hit Ann.
Then Ann hit Sam.
Sam ran and Ann ran.
Ann had a tan mitten.
This is Ann's tan mitten.
Ann lost it.
Sam got the mitten.
Sam sent the mitten to Ann.

Comments: For the most part, multisensory structured language programs have been designed and used as remedial programs for students who have not learned to read successfully. Much of the original research that supports their use was clinical case studies and summarized in a review by McIntyre and Pickering (1995). More recent studies of older students with reading disabilities, although limited, do indicate that these students do make substantial gains when the principles and content of multisensory structure language are employed (Green, 1996; Torgesen, Wagner, and Rashotte, 1997; Torgesen, Wagner, Rashotte, Alexan-

der, and Conway, 1997). Several considerations are worth keeping in mind when deciding to use structured language programs. First, it is best employed by teachers who have been trained in multisensory procedures. A list of institutions and organizations offering training can be obtained from the International Dyslexia Association (800-222-3123), Academic Language Therapy Association (972-907-3924), Academy of Orton-Gillingham Practitioners and Educators (914-373-8919), and International Multisensory Structured Language Education Council (972-774-1772). Second, in general these programs emphasize decoding skills and strategies and use text with such controlled vocabulary that it can be difficult to build comprehension skills. Hence, a number of the programs suggest simultaneously building listening comprehension until the students are able to read more conventional text. Finally, there is limited research to support that the addition of the tactile–kinesthetic component facilitates learning (Moats, 1999).

Word Study: Making Words, Word Building, and Word Walls

Both reading and special educators have stressed the importance of word study as a way of learning the relationships between speech sounds and print, of building word recognition and spelling skills, and of developing vocabulary (Bear, Invernizzi, Templeton, and Johnston, 2000; Cunningham, 2000; Gunning, 2001; Henry, 1997). For students with learning and behavior problems, opportunities to construct words using magnetic letters, letter tiles, or laminated letters provides them with experience in manipulating sounds to see how it affects the words. For example, the teacher might start with the sounds, /s/, /t/, /r/, /n/, and /ă/ and ask the students to do the following:

Teacher: What two sounds make the word *at?*
Now add a letter sound to the beginning to make the word *sat.*
Remove the /s/. What sound would you add to the beginning to make the word *rat?*

Now listen. We're going to make a three-letter word. Take off the /t/ sound at the end of the word. Now add the sound that will make the word *ran.*

■ **PROCEDURES:** There are many activities that can be developed around word sorts, building words, and words wall. A number of resource books are available, including the following:

■ *Building Words: A Resource Manual for Teaching Word Analysis and Spelling Strategies* (2001) by T. Gunning, Boston: Allyn and Bacon.
■ *Making Words* and *Making Big Words* (1994a; 1994b) by P. Cunningham and D. Hall, Parsippany, NY: Good Apple.
■ *Patterns for Success in Reading and Spelling: A Multisensory Approach to Teaching Phonics and Word Analysis* (1996) by M. Henry, Austin, TX: PRO-ED.
■ *Phonics They Use: Words for Reading and Writing* (3rd ed.) (2000), by P. Cunningham, New York: Longman.
■ *Word Journeys: Assessment-Guided Phonics, Spelling, and Vocabulary Instruction* (2000) by K. Ganske, New York: Guilford Press.
■ *Words Their Way: Word Study for Phonics, Vocabulary, and Spelling Instruction* (2000) by D. Bear, M. Invernizzi, S. Templeton, and F. Johnston, Upper Saddle River, NJ: Merrill.

Making Words (Cunningham and Hall, 1994a) is one activity that has been used and adapted for students with learning and behavior problems (Schumm and Vaughn, 1995). Using a specific set of letters (e.g., $\breve{a}$, *c, h, r, s, t*), students make approximately 15 words beginning with two-letter words (e.g., *at*) and progressing to three-, four-, and five-letter words (e.g., *tar, cart, star, cash*) until the final "mystery word" is made (e.g., *scratch*). To use *Making Words,* each student needs a set of letters and the teacher needs a large set of letters and a sentence strip chart to hold the cards and words that are constructed. Prior to the lesson, the letters the students will need during the lesson are put in plastic bags and given to each student. The three steps in the activity are

■ *Making Words*
After the students have identified their letters, the teacher writes the numeral on the board for the number of letters the students are to put in their words. Next, the teacher cues the students to make different two-letter words. For example, with the word *scratch* the teacher might ask the students to construct the word *at.* When working with a class of students, after each word is constructed the teacher selects one student who was correct to use the set of large letters and the chart to spell the word for the other students to check their work. Then, the teacher might ask the students to add /c/ to the word *at* to make *cat,* or to make the word *art* and then rearrange the letters to make the word *tar.* The teacher continues to guide students through the lesson by directing them to make words with their letters. The last word includes all the letters a student has been given for the lesson.

■ *Word Sorting*
The teacher puts up on the sentence strip chart all the words the students have constructed. The teacher then asks the students how some of the words are alike, and students sort the words by spelling patterns. For example, the teacher would take the word *car* and have the students find the other words that begin with *c—cars, cash, cart;* or take the word *art* and have the students find the other *art* words—*cart, chart.* Other students hypothesize why the words are alike, which assists the students in seeing the spelling patterns.

■ *Making Words Quickly*
Students write as many words as they can using the day's letters, writing the words in a Making Words Log. Students first write the letters from the lesson, and when the teacher says "Go," they write words for two minutes.

■ **COMMENTS:** Both special education and general education teachers have found this practice an effective and efficient way to organize for teaching word identification, and students report that they enjoy the activity and manipulating the letters (Cunningham, 1991;

Schumm and Vaughn, 1995). However, Schumm and Vaughn (1995) found it necessary to develop simpler lessons and to focus more on teaching word families with less able readers.

Implicit Code Instruction

In comparison to explicit code instruction approaches, implicit code instruction in general

- Places more emphasis on using context clues, including picture clues, when decoding unknown words
- Begins by teaching an initial set of sight words
- Uses known words to discover word patterns and phonic generalizations
- Teaches onset-rime and phonic and structural analysis within the context meaningful stories and books
- Puts less emphasis on systematically controlling the introduction of letter–sound relationships and spelling patterns
- Uses text in which the language patterns are at the sentence level (e.g., "I see a dog," "I see a cat," I see a bear.") rather than the word family or phoneme level (e.g., "The fat cat sat on a mat.")

This section presents two code implicit instruction approaches that have been used with students who experience difficulties in developing fluent word recognition and effective word identification strategies: Modified Language Experience and the Fernald (VAKT) Method.

Modified Language Experience Approach

This approach to teaching early reading facilitates the transfer from oral language to written language by capitalizing on the child's linguistic, cognitive, social, and cultural knowledge and abilities (Stauffer, 1970). Language experience approaches are congruent with principles based on Vygotsky's theory of cognitive development, and on learning frameworks such as whole language and process writing (Veatch, 1991). These approaches use the students' own language, repeated reading, visual configuration, and

context clues to identify words. Language experience approaches are often considered language arts approaches, since they integrate oral language, writing, and reading (Allen, 1976; Nelson and Linek, 1999). Several methods for teaching language experience approaches have been developed: Allen's Language Experience Approach in Communication (Allen, 1976; Allen and Allen, 1966–68; 1982); Ashton-Warner's Organic Reading (Ashton-Warner, 1958, 1963, 1972) and Stauffer's Language-Experience Approach (Stauffer, 1970). The modified language experience approach we describe is designed for students who have limited experience or success with reading and little or no sight vocabularies. The objectives are:

1. To teach the concept that text is talk written down
2. To teach the metalinguistic skills of sentence and word segmentation
3. To teach left-to-right progression
4. To teach use of semantic and syntactic clues
5. To teach recognition of words both within the context of the experience story and in isolation
6. To teach phonic and structural analysis by discovering patterns in known words

The approach is built on the idea that oral and written language are interdependent and that oral language can serve as the base for the development of written language.

- **PROCEDURES:** The procedures for this modified language experience approach are similar to those suggested by Stauffer (1970). However, more structure and practice have been incorporated into this modification to provide for the needs of students who experience difficulties in learning to read. It is designed to be used individually or with small groups of two to five students. At the heart of this approach is the language experience story, a story written by the students about events, persons, or things of their choice (see Figure 4.21).

First day: For the first day of instruction, guidelines for developing a language experience story are:

■ **FIGURE 4.21** *Dictated Language Experience Story*

Woody Woodpecker was

driving a jet to outer space and

saw some aliens. And he got on

his jet and went to Jupiter and

saw some people from outer space

and they were driving jets, too.

---

1. *Provide or select an experience.* Provide or have the students select an experience of interest to them. Sometimes a picture can help stimulate ideas, but be sure the students have experiences related to the picture. Remember—you are relying on the students' memory of the experience and their memory for the language used to describe the experience.
2. *Explain the procedure to the students.* Explain that the students are going to be dictating a story about the selected experience. This story will then become their reading text or book.
3. *Discuss the experience.* Discuss the experience with students so that they can begin to think about what they want to put in the dictated story. Students with learning and behavior problems sometimes have difficulty organizing their thoughts. The discussion can serve as time for the students to plan what they want to say. To facilitate the planning process you may want to write notes or construct a map or web.
4. *Write the dictated story.* Have the students tell the story while you write it. Students should watch as you write or type it. If you are work-

ing with several students you may want to write the story on large chart paper. Have each of the students contribute to the story. If you are working with an individual, sit next to the student so that he or she can see what you write. Encourage the students to use natural voices. The language experience story presented in Figure 4.21 was dictated by Sam, a third grader reading at the primer level.

5. *Read the story to the students.* Ask the students to listen to the story to see if they want to make any changes. Make changes accordingly.
6. *Have students read the story.* First have the students read the story together with you (choral reading) until they seem comfortable with the story. When you are choral reading point to the words so that the students focus on the text as they read. Next have the students read individually and pronounce words they cannot identify. In some cases a student may give you a lengthy story, yet his or her memory for text is limited. When this occurs, you may work on the story in parts, beginning with only the first several sentences or first paragraph.
7. *Encourage the students to read the story to others.* This is often a very intrinsically reinforcing activity.
8. *Type the story.* If not already typed, type the story and make one copy for each student. Also make a second copy for each student to keep and use for record keeping.

Second day: For the second day of instruction, guidelines for reading the story are:

1. *Practice reading the story.* Have the students practice reading the story using choral reading, individual reading, and reading to one another. When the students are reading individually and they come to a word they do not recognize, encourage them to look at the word and think of what word would make sense. Having the students read to the end of the sentence can also help them to think of a word that makes sense. If students cannot recall the word, pronounce it.
2. *Focus on individual words and sentences.* Have the students match, locate, and read individual

sentences and words in the story. Discuss what markers are used to denote sentences and words. Finally, have the students read the story to themselves and underline the words they think they know.

3. *Check on known words.* Have each student read the story orally. Record the words the student knows on your copy of the story.

4. *Type the words from the story on word cards.* Type the words each student knows from the story on word cards.

Third day: Guidelines for the third day are:

1. *Practice reading the story.* Repeat the type of activities described in step 1 of the second day.

2. *Focus on individual sentences and words.* Repeat the type of activities described in step 2 of the second day.

3. *Check on known words.* With the word cards in the *same order* as the words in the text, have each student read the word cards, recording the words the student knows.

4. *Practice reading the story.* Repeat the type of activities described in step 1 of the second day.

5. *Focus on sentences and words.* Repeat the type of activities described in step 2 of the second day.

6. *Check on known words.* With the cards in *random order,* have each student read the words, recording the words each student knows.

Fourth day: Guidelines for the fourth day are:

1. *Check on known words.* Repeat step 3 from the third day, using only the words the student knows from the previous day.

2. *Enter known words in word bank.* Each student should make word cards (3 × 5 inch index cards or scraps of poster board work well) for the words that he or she can identify in step 1. These words should be filed by the student in his or her word bank (index card box). Words the student cannot identify should not be included.

3. *Read, illustrate, and publish the story.* Have the students read the story and decide if they want to illustrate it and/or put it into a language experience book. Books can be developed for individual students or one book can be made for

the group. Students can then share these books with each other, with other interested persons, and place them in the library.

Once the students have completed at least one story and have developed 15 to 20 words in their word banks, they can begin to use the banks for a variety of activities, such as generating new sentences, locating words with similar parts (i.e., inflectional endings, beginning sounds, shapes), and categorizing words by use (e.g., action words, naming words, describing words).

As the number of sight words continues to increase, students can write their own stories, using the words from the word bank to assist them. More suggestions for developing activities based on the word bank are given in Figure 4.22.

— **COMMENTS:** The modified language experience approach provides a method for teaching children initial skills in reading, including the recognition of sight words. The approach utilizes the students' memory, oral language, and background experiences (Robertson, 1999), as well as visual configuration and context clues. Once the initial sight vocabulary has been built to between 30 and 100 words, students should be encouraged to read other books and stories. This approach also provides a way to monitor students' reading development, including word recognition and fluency (Stokes, 1989). Having students tape record their stories during initial reading and reading on the fourth day allows the teacher to monitor growth.

This approach lends itself to the use of computer technology (Duling, 1999), particularly with the use of word processing, desktop publishing, and multimedia software that incorporates voice and graphics such as Children's Writing and Publishing Center (Learning Company), *Kidwriter II* (Davidson and Associates) and *Kid Pix* (Broderbund) or language experience—based software programs such as *Writing to Read* (Martin and Friedburg, 1986). For example, Stratton, Grindler, and Postell (1992) integrated word processing and photography into a language experience with middle school students.

Activities are incorporated into the approach to encourage the development of the metalinguistic

■ **FIGURE 4.22** *Suggested Activities for Word Bank Cards*

1. Alphabetize words in word banks.
2. Match the word with the same word as it occurs in newspapers, magazines, etc.
3. Make a poster of the words known.
4. Complete sentences using word banks. Provide students with a stem or incomplete sentences and have students fill slot with as many different words as possible. Example:

   He ran to the _____. The _____ and _____ ran into the park.

5. Find or categorize words in word banks:

naming words	science words
action words	color words
descriptive words	animal words
words with more than one meaning	names of people
words with the same meaning	interesting words
opposites	funny words
people words	exciting words

6. Locate words beginning the same, ending the same, or meaning the same.
7. Locate words with various endings.
8. Match sentences in stories with words from word bank.
9. Use word bank cards for matching-card games, such as grab and bingo.
10. Organize words into a story. Students might need to borrow words for this use and may wish to illustrate or make a permanent record of it.
11. Delete words from a story. Have students use words from their word banks to complete the story.
12. Scramble the sentences in the story or words in a sentence.
13. Establish class word banks for different classroom centers, such as science words, number words, weather words, house words, family words.

Source: Adapted from R. J. Tierney, J. E. Readence, and E. K. Dishner, *Reading Strategies and Practices: Guide for Improving Instruction* (Boston: Allyn and Bacon, 1980), pp. 285–287.

skills of sentence and word segmentation. However, this approach does not present a systematic method for teaching phonic and structural analysis. For students who have difficulty with these skills, a more structured method of teaching phonic and structural analysis may be needed after they have developed an initial sight vocabulary. This approach may not provide some students with enough drill and practice to develop a sight vocabulary. In those cases, it will be necessary to supplement this approach with activities presented in the section on techniques for building sight words. For a research review of language experience approaches to teaching beginning reading, see Stahl and Miller (1989).

Fernald (VAKT) Method

The Fernald method (Fernald, 1943, 1988) uses a multisensory or visual-auditory-kinesthetic-tactile (VAKT) approach to teach students to read and write words. This method was used by Grace Fernald and her associates in the clinic school at the University of California at Los Angeles in the 1920s. It is designed for students who have severe difficulties learning and remembering words when reading, who have a limited sight vocabulary, and for whom other methods have not been successful. It is usually taught on an individual basis.

— PROCEDURES: The Fernald method consists of four stages through which students progress as they learn to identify unknown words more effectively. The first stage, which is the most laborious, requires a multisensory approach and utilizes a language experience format. By the final stage, the students are reading books and are able to identify unknown words from the context and their similarity to words or word parts already learned. At this stage, the students are no longer tracing or writing a word to learn it.

Stage One: Guidelines for Stage One are as follows:

1. *Solicit the student's commitment to learn.* Tell the student that you are going to be showing him or her a technique for learning to read unknown words that has been successful with many students who have not learned in other ways. Inform the student that this method will take concentration and effort on his or her part, but it should be successful.

2. *Select a word to learn.* Have the student select a word (regardless of length) that he or she cannot read but would like to learn to read. Discuss the meaning of the word and listen for the number of syllables.

3. *Write the word.* Sitting beside the student, have him or her watch and listen while you:

   a. Say the word.

   b. Using a broad-tipped marker on a piece of un-lined paper approximately 4" × 11", write the word in blackboard-size script, or in print if cursive writing is not used by the student. Say the word as you write it.

   c. Say the word again as you smoothly move your finger underneath the word.

   See Figure 4.23 for a model.

4. *Model tracing the word.* Model how the student is to trace the word so that he or she might learn it. Do not explain the process but simply say to the student, "Watch what I do and listen to what I say."

   a. Say the word.

   b. Trace the word using one or two fingers. The fingers should touch the paper in order to receive the tactile stimulation. As you trace

the word, say the word. When discussing this process, Fernald (1943) stresses that the student must say each part of the word as he or she traces it. This is necessary to establish the connection between the sound of the word and its form, so that the student will eventually recognize the word from the visual stimulus alone. It is important that this vocalization of the word be natural; that is, it should be a repetition of the word as it actually sounds—not a stilted, distorted sounding-out of letters or syllables in such a way that the word is lost in the process. The sound for each letter is never given separately nor overemphasized. In a longer word, like *important,* the student says *im* while tracing the first syllable, *por* while tracing the second syllable, and *tant* as he or she traces the last syllable.

   c. Say the word again while moving the tracing finger(s) underneath the word in a sweeping motion.

   Model this process several times and then have the student practice the process. If the student does not complete the process correctly, stop the student when he or she makes an error and cue, "Not quite. Watch me do it again." Continue this procedure until the student is completing the three-stage process correctly.

5. *Trace until learned.* Have the student continue tracing the word until the student thinks he or she can write the word from memory.

6. *Write from memory.* When the student feels he or she is ready, remove the model and have the student write the word from memory, saying the word as he or she writes. Fernald (1943) stresses that the student should always write the word without looking at the copy. She comments:

   When the child copies the word, looking back and forth from the word he is writing to the copy, he breaks the word up into small and meaningless units. The flow of the hand in writing the word is interrupted and the eye movements are back and forth from the word to the copy instead of those which the eye would make in adjusting to the word as it is being written. This

■ **FIGURE 4.23** *Sample Word Using Fernald Technique*

11 inches

4 inches

license

writing of the word without the copy is important at all stages of learning to write and spell. The copying of words is a most serious block to learning to write them correctly and to recognize them after they have been written (pp. 37–39).

It is also important that the student write the word as a unit. If the student makes an error in writing the word or hesitates unduly between letters, stop the student immediately, cross out the word, and have him or her again practice tracing the large model. The word is never erased and rewritten. Fernald states, "The reason for this procedure is that the various movements of erasing, correcting single letters or syllables, and so forth, break the word up into a meaningless total which does not represent a word" (p. 39). It also can interfere with the student's motor memory for the word. The student should write the word from memory correctly at least three consecutive times.

7. *File the word.* After the word has been written three times correctly, the student should place it in his or her word bank.

8. *Type the word.* Within an interval of twenty-four hours, each word learned using this process should be typed and read by the student. This helps establish the link between the written and typed word.

The number of words learned per session using this VAKT process depends on the number of tracings a student needs to learn a new word. This number varies greatly among students. We have worked with students who need less than five tracings to learn a new word, whereas other students required over fifty tracings when first beginning this approach.

Fernald (1943) reports, "As soon as a child has discovered that he can learn to write words, we let him start 'story writing'" (p. 33). As the student writes a story and comes to a word he or she cannot spell, the tracing process is repeated. These stories should be typed within 24 hours so that the student may read the newly learned words in typed form within the context of the story.

Fernald suggests no arbitrary limit be set for the length of the tracing period (Stage One). The student stops tracing when he or she is able to learn without it. This is usually a gradual process, with the student sometimes feeling the need to trace a word and sometimes thinking the word does not need to be traced.

Stage Two: When the student no longer needs to trace words to learn them, he or she moves to Stage Two. In this stage, the teacher writes the requested word in cursive (or manuscript) for the student. The student then simply looks at the word, saying it while looking at it, and then writes it without looking at the copy, saying each part of the word as he or she writes it from memory. As with Stage One, words to be learned are obtained from words the student requests while writing stories. The word bank continues to function as a resource for the student, but a smaller word box can be used since the teacher is writing the words in ordinary script size.

Stage Three: The student progresses to the third stage when he or she is able to learn directly from the printed word without having it written. In this stage the student looks at the unknown printed word, and the teacher pronounces the word. The student then says the word while looking at it and then writes it from memory. Fernald reports that during this stage, students still read poorly but are able to recognize quite difficult words almost without exception after once writing them.

During this stage the student is encouraged to read as much as and whatever he or she wants. Unknown words are pronounced, and when the passage is finished, the unknown words are learned by using the technique described in the preceding paragraph.

Stage Four: The student is able to recognize new words from their similarity to words or parts of words he or she has already learned. At first, a student may need to pronounce the word and write it on a scrap of paper to assist in remembering it, but later this becomes unnecessary. The student continues to read books of interest to him or her. When reading scientific or other difficult material, the student is encouraged to scan the paragraph and lightly underline each word he or she does not know. These words are then discussed for recognition and meaning prior to reading.

▬ **COMMENTS:** Empirical evidence lends support to this approach for teaching word identification to students with severe reading disabilities (Berres and Eyer, 1970; Coterell, 1972; Fernald, 1943; Kress and Johnson, 1970; Thorpe and Borden, 1985). Although this approach tends to be successful with such readers, the first several stages are very time-consuming for both the teacher and the student. Consequently, it should be used only if other approaches have not been successful.

Techniques for Building Sight Words

Students who read fluently recognize words automatically individually or when they are reading text (see sections on "What Is a Sight Word?," page 130, and "Automatic Word Recognition," page 134). Students with reading disabilities struggle with automatic word recognition. This is important not only for words that are decodable (e.g., *and, then, it*), but especially for high-frequency, less phonetically regular words (e.g., *the, you, was, have*). See Figure 4.12 for a list of high-frequency words. This section presents several techniques that teachers can use to assist students in remembering words. In addition, a number of games and computer programs can be used to provide students with practice in recognizing words presented individually and in text. These techniques can be incorporated into a reading program for the purpose of building automatic word recognition and can be used with either explicit or implicit code instruction.

Sight Word Association Procedure

The sight word association procedure (SWAP) (Bradley, 1975) uses corrective feedback and drill and practice to assist students in associating spoken words with written form. The procedure is appropriate to use with students who are beginning to learn to identify words across various contexts or texts, or with students who require more practice of new words than the amount provided in the current reading program. It is designed to be used individually or with small groups.

▬ **PROCEDURES:** Begin by selecting words from the text that the students consistently miscall or do not identify at an automatic level. Write each word on a word card. The procedure for teaching these words (usually three to seven words at a time) is:

1. Discuss the words with the students to assure that they understand the meanings of the words as the words are being used in the text.
2. Present the words to the students one word at a time. Each word is exposed for five seconds, with the teacher saying the word twice.
3. Shuffle the cards and ask the students to identify the word on each card. Provide corrective feedback by verifying the correctly identified words, giving the correct word for any word miscalled, and saying the word if the students do not respond in five seconds.
4. Present all the words again, using the same format given in step 2.
5. Have the students identify each word, using the same format given in step 3. Repeat this step at least two more times or until the students can automatically recognize all the words.

If students continue to have difficulty recognizing a word after the seventh exposure to the word, switch from a recall task to a recognition task. To do this, place several word cards on the table and have the learners point to each word as you say it. If the students still continue to have difficulty learning the words, use a different technique to teach the words, such as picture association techniques, sentence/word association techniques, or a cloze procedure. A record sheet for keeping track of individual student responses is presented in Figure 4.24.

After teaching the words on the initial day, the words should be reviewed for several days to determine if the words are being retained and to reteach if necessary.

▬ **COMMENTS:** This procedure provides a technique for systematically practicing unknown words. It utilizes principles of corrective feedback and mass and distributed practice to teach words. However,

■ **FIGURE 4.24** *Sight Word Association Procedure (SWAP) Record Sheet*

							✓ Correct		
							0 Incorrect		
Words	Initial Teaching					Retention			Comments
	1	2	3	4	5	1	2	3	

there are several important cautions regarding sight word association. First, it needs to be used in conjunction with an approach to reading that stresses reading text and utilizing other decoding strategies. Second, students should understand the meanings of the words being taught. Third, in addition to the isolated word practice provided by this technique, students should be given ample opportunity to read these words in context.

Picture Association Technique

Using a key picture to aid in identifying the word can be beneficial (Mastropieri and Scruggs, 1998). It allows the readers to associate the word with a visual image. It is on this premise that picture association techniques use key pictures to help students associate a spoken word with its written form.

— **PROCEDURES:** Select words that the students are having difficulty identifying when reading. At first, choose words that are easily imaged such as nouns, verbs, and adjectives. Write each word on a card (usually three to seven words). On a separate card, draw a simple picture or find a picture and

attach it to the card. In some cases, the students may want to draw their own pictures. Use the following procedure to teach the picture-word association:

1. Place each picture in front of the student, labeling each one as you present it. Have the students practice repeating the names of the pictures.
2. Place next to each picture the word it represents, again saying the name of the word. Have the students practice saying the names of the words.

3. Have the students match the words to the pictures and say the name of the word while matching it. Repeat this process until the students easily match the pictures and words.
4. Place the words in front of the students and have them identify the words as you say them. If they cannot identify the correct word, have them think of the picture to aid in their recognition. If they

still cannot point to the word, show them the picture that goes with the word.

5. Have the students recall the words by showing the word cards one at a time. Again, if the student cannot recall a word, have them think of the picture. If they still cannot think of the word, tell them to look at the picture that goes with the word.

6. Continue this procedure until the students can identify all the words at an automatic level. The same record sheet as the one used for SWAP (Figure 4.23) can be used for this procedure.

7. Have the students review the words on subsequent days and, most importantly, give the students plenty of opportunities to read the words in text. When a student is reading and cannot identify a word, encourage him or her to think of the picture.

— COMMENTS: This picture association technique assists students in forming visual images that facilitate their identification of words. As with the sight word association procedure, this procedure should be used only as a supplemental technique and the students should be given ample opportunities to read the words in text.

Picture associations have been used in beginning reading programs such as the *Peabody Rebus Reading Program* (Woodcock, Clark, and Davies, 1969) and word processing programs such as *Kid Writer Deluxe* (Davidson). Students learn to read these symbols and then transfer their skills to traditional print by making picture/word associations.

Sentence/Word Association Technique

The sentence/word association technique encourages students to associate an unknown word with a familiar spoken word, phrase, or sentence to aid in remembering the word when reading.

— PROCEDURES: Select from three to seven words that the students are consistently having difficulty recognizing. Discuss the words with the students and ask them to find the words in the text and read them in a sentence. Tell the students to decide on a key word, phrase, or sentence that will help them remember the word. For example, for the word *was* a sentence might be "Today he is, yesterday he _____." For the word *there* the sentence might be "Are you _____?" Put the words to be taught on word cards and put the associated word, phrase, or sentence on separate cards. Teach the associations between the key word, phrase, or sentence and the unknown word, using the same procedures described for the picture association technique. After teaching, when a student is reading and comes to one of the new words and cannot remember it, have the student think of the associated clue. If the student cannot think of the associated clue orally, tell him or her.

INSTRUCTIONAL ACTIVITIES

This section provides instructional activities that are related to phonological awareness, the alphabetic principle, and word identification. Some of the activities teach new skills; others are best suited for practice and reinforcement of already acquired skills. For each activity, the objective, materials, and teaching procedures are described.

■ Grocery Store

Objective: To increase the students' awareness of print in the environment and to provide practice in matching words.

Grades: Primary

Materials: (1) An area that is set up as a grocery store. (2) Commonly used packaged and canned goods with labels left on (e.g., Jello, toothpaste, corn flakes, chicken noodle soup). Remove the contents of packaged goods and reclose the box. (3) Cards with names of items written on them. (4) Baskets and/or bags children can use when shopping.

Teaching Procedures: This center can be used in a variety of ways. Word cards can be placed by each food item. When the student is shopping and selects a food item, he or she also picks up the card, reads it, and matches it to the label on the box. When the child goes through checkout, he or she can read each card and hand the cashier the item that goes with it. Or the teacher and child can decide which items the child wants to buy. The teacher gives those word cards to the child, and he or she shops for those items by matching the cards to the items on the shelves.

Children can serve as stock persons by reshelving the items the other children have purchased. When a stock person reshelves an item, he or she can find the card that matches the item and then place the card next to the item.

■ My Sound Book

Objective: To provide the students practice in finding pictures that start with a specific consonant or vowel sound.

Grades: Primary

Materials: (1) Three-ring binder or folder into which "Sound Pages" can be inserted. (2) Magazines, old books, or workbooks that can be cut up. (3) Stickers, scissors, and glue.

Teaching Procedures: Explain to the students that each of them will be making a book where they can collect and keep pictures and stickers that start with various sounds. Select one sound that the students are learning and have the students write the letter representing the sound on the top of the page. Then have them look through magazines, old books, and workbooks to find pictures starting with the sound. Once they have selected the pictures, have them say the names to you so that you both can determine if the pictures represent the designated sound. Then have the students glue the pictures on the sound pages, leaving room to add other pictures they find while looking for pictures representing other sounds. Have the student put the sound page in the notebook and share his or her pictures with other students. Continue until the book is complete. As students collect stickers, you may want to encourage them to put them in the sound book.

■ Vowel Match

Objective: To provide the students practice in decoding words that have various vowels sounds.

Grades: Primary and intermediate

Materials: (1) One file folder that is divided into two playing areas that consist of ten boxes for each player. In each box, paste a picture that illustrates a vowel sound. (2) Thirty to 40 playing cards with pictures illustrating vowel sounds.

Teaching Procedures: Explain the game to the students. Shuffle and place cards face down near the players. Each student draws a card and checks to see if the vowel sound illustrated on the card matches one of the pictures on his or her side of the game folder. If it does, the player places the card over the picture on the game folder. If the picture does not match, the card is discarded. The player to cover all the boxes first wins the game.

Adaptations: This game is easily adapted to teaching rhyming words and other sounds such as consonant digraphs or blends.

■ Sight Word Bingo

Objective: To provide the students practice in recognizing words.

Grades: Primary and intermediate

Materials: (1) Poster board cut into 10×8 inch pieces to use for Bingo cards. (2) List of new words students have encountered in their reading. Such lists can be found in the back of basal readers or in books of lists such as *The New Reading Teacher's Book of Lists* (Fry, Fountoukidis, and Polk, 1985). To make the Bingo cards randomly select words from the list and write them on the card as illustrated. (3) Colored markers.

Word Bingo			
happen	should	night	enough
below	never	complete	thought
grow	where	while	building
every	through	include	were
country	even	important	between

Teaching Procedures: One student (or the teacher) is designated as the caller. Each of the remaining students gets a Bingo card. The caller randomly selects a word from the list and says the word. The students place a colored marker on the square in which the word is written. The first person to cover all the squares in a horizontal, vertical, or diagonal row calls, "Bingo." The caller and the student then verify the words. If verified, that student wins.

Adaptations: Bingo is a generic game that can be adapted to provide practice for a variety of skills. For example:

> *Consonant Bingo:* Put pictures of objects that start with initial consonants, blends, or digraphs on the Bingo cards. The caller says the letter(s) and the students mark the picture(s) that has the same consonant, blend, or digraph. This can also be adapted for final consonants.
>
> *Prefix Bingo:* Write prefixes on the Bingo cards. The caller says a word with a prefix or gives

the definition of a prefix, and the students mark the prefix on their cards.

> *Math Fact Bingo:* Write the answers to math facts on the Bingo cards. The caller says a math fact and the students mark the answer.

■ Compound Concentration

Objective: To give the students practice in identifying compound words and to illustrate how words may be combined to form compound words.

Grades: Intermediate and secondary

Materials: Thirty-six index cards (3 × 5 inch) on which the two parts of 18 compound words have been written. Make sure that each part can only be joined with one other part.

Teaching Procedure: Explain the game. Have the students shuffle the cards and place the cards face down in six rows with six cards each. Each player takes a turn at turning over two cards. The student then decides whether the two words make a compound word. If the words do not make a compound word, then the cards are again turned face down and the next player takes a turn. If the words make a compound word, then the player gets those two cards and turns over two more cards. The student continues playing until two cards are turned over that do not make a compound word. The game is over when all the cards are matched. The winner is the player with the most cards.

Adaptations: Concentration can be adapted for many skills. Students can match synonyms, antonyms, prefixes, suffixes, initial or final consonants, categories, and math facts.

SUMMARY

Reading is one of the most important areas of education, and special education teachers who work with students with learning and behavior problems spend more time teaching reading than any other area. Reading is a skilled and strategic process in which learning to decode and read words accurately and rapidly is essential. It entails understanding the text and is dependent upon active engagement and interpretation by the reader. Therefore, the goal of reading instruction is to provide students with the skills, strategies, and knowledge to read fluently and understand the text for purposes of enjoyment and learning. Reading instruction can be organized into components or areas that include phonological awareness, letter–sound correspondence, and the alphabetic principle; word identification, decoding, and word study; fluency; vocabulary; and comprehension. It is the integration of these areas along with the integration of oral language, reading, and writing that makes successful instruction in reading.

Many students with learning or reading disabilities experience significant difficulties in developing phonemic awareness, letter–sound correspondence, and the understanding of how speech maps to print (i.e., alphabetic principle). For these students, systematically teaching these knowledge and skills will be crucial to their success in learning to read. The skills of blending, segmenting, and manipulating phonemes are particularly important. Taking into consideration the sequence in which phonological awareness skills and letter–sound correspondences are introduced can facilitate acquisition. For example, teaching a core set of frequently used consonants and short vowel sounds that represent clear sounds and nonreversible letters provides students with the opportunities to develop the skills to decode unknown words by sounding them out. Teaching words so that they are automatically recognized provides students with the necessary word recognition to develop fluent reading and to have the opportunity to allocate their attention to the comprehension of the text (i.e., teaching to automaticity).

In developing strategies for decoding words, students can rely on phonic analysis, using onset-rimes or spelling patterns, structural analysis (e.g., affixes and inflectional endings), syllabication, syntax, and semantics. Ideas for teaching these various decoding strategies are presented. In fact, teaching word recognition can be divided into two major types: explicit code instruction and implicit code instruction. Explicit code instruction systematically teaches letter–sound relationships, structural analysis, and syllabication skills and includes such programs or approaches as multisensory structured language instruction, phonic approaches, and linguistic approaches that emphasis teaching onset-rimes. Implicit code instruction that is used with students with learning or reading disabilities allows the students to induce or discover the relationship of speech to print and relies on the use of the student's own language and memory to learn to recognize words. Modified language experience and the Fernald (VAKT) method are two examples.

Although some words lend themselves to using decoding strategies such as phonic analysis, structural analysis, and syllabication, other words may be more effectively learned as whole units because they are less predictable phonetically. For these words a number of strategies for teaching sight words are presented including the sight word association, picture association, and cloze.

Teaching phonological awareness, letter–sound correspondences, the alphabetic principles, word recognition, decoding, and word study are the focus of this first chapter on teaching reading. As special education teachers, it is important to know a variety of teaching strategies, methods, and programs for teaching these skills so that we might meet the differing needs of these students.

WEBSITES AS RESOURCES TO ASSIST IN TEACHING READING

http://www.NationalReadingPanel.org

This Website is from the National Reading Panel and provides a current review of the research on teaching reading.

http://www.interdys.org

This Website is from the International Dyslexia Association and provides resources for teaching individuals with reading disabilities.

http://www.reading.org

This Website is from the International Reading Association and provides a wide variety of resources for teaching reading.

http://www.ncld.org

This Website is from the National Center for Learning Disabilities and provides resources related to reading and other learning disabilities.

http://www.ciera.org

This Website is from the Center for Improvement of Early Reading Achievement provides resources in teaching early reading.

http://www.texasreading.org

This Website is from the Texas Center for Reading and Language Arts at the University of Texas at Austin and provides a variety of resources and links for teaching reading.

http://cars.uth.tmc.edu

This Website is from the Center for Academic and Reading Skills at the University of Texas–Houston Health Science Center and the University of Houston provides resources on the assessment and teaching of reading.

http://www.ed.arizona.edu/rimes2000

This Website is from the University of Arizona and provides a resources for teaching early reading and spelling.

http://www.ldonline.org/ld_indepth/reading/ldrp_chard_guidelines.html

This Website provides information on phonics and word recognition instruction in early reading programs.

http://readbygrade3.com

This Website provides information on how to teach students how to learn to read with an emphasis on phonological awareness and word recognition.

http://www.interdys.org/article8.stm#content

This Website presents an article about phonological difficulties.

http://www.cec.sped.org/ericec/readlist.htm

This Website contains several links related to phonological awareness and word identification.

http://ericec.org/digests/e540.htm

This Website contains information on phonological awareness.

http://www.ldresources.com/readwrite/readingtolearn.html

This Website provides an overview of learning to read, including phonological awareness, word identification, etc.

http://www.ldonline.org/ld_indepth/reading/teaching_children_to_read.html
This Website contains information on alphabetical principle, phonemic awareness, and phonics.

http://www.ldonline.org/ld_indepth/reading/torgeson_catchthem.html
This Website contains information on identification and assessment of reading difficulties with a focus on phonemic awareness.

http://www.ldonline.org/ld_indepth/teaching_techniques/cld_hownow.html
This Website introduces phoneme awareness activities for collaborative classrooms.

http://www.successforall.net
This Website provides information about the Success for All program, including effective practice research.

http://pbskids.org/lions
The Website for the PBS show *Between the Lions,* which contains information and activities for learning to read with emphasis on phonological awareness and phonics.

THINK AND APPLY

— What are the characteristics of the reading process, and how are oral language and written expression related to reading?

— What are the components of reading instruction?

— Observe in a kindergarten classroom for evidence of each of the phonological awareness skills in the continuum of development.

— Review several early reading programs or basal readers and describe how they introduce letter–sound relationships.

— Compare and contrast code explicit and code implicit instruction. Describe what type of learner might profit from each.

— Develop several games for building sight words.

APPENDIX 4.1

Scope and Sequence for Teaching Phonics

Level	Categories	Correspondence	Model Word	Correspondence	Model Word
Preparatory	Letter names, phonemic awareness, rhyming, segmentation, perception of initial consonants				
1	High-frequency initial consonants	s = /s/ f = /f/ m = /m/ t = /t/ d = /d/	sea fish men toy dog	r = /r/ l = /l/ g = /g/ n = /n/ h = /h/	rug lamp game nine hit
	Long vowels: word-ending single-letter vowels and digraphs	e = /ē/ o = /ō/	he, me no, so	ee = /ē/	bee, see
	Lower-frequency initial consonants and x	c = /k/ b = /b/ v = /v/ j = /j/ p = /p/ w = /w/ k = /k/	can boy vase jacket pot wagon kite	c = /s/ g = /j/ y = /y/ z = /z/ x = /ks/ x = /gs/	city gym yo-yo zebra box example
	High-frequency initial consonant digraphs	ch = /ch/ sh = /sh/ th = /th/	church ship this	th = /th/ wh = /wh/	thumb wheel
	Short vowels	a = /a/ i = /i/ e = /e/	hat fish net	u = /u/ o = /o/	pup pot
2	Initial consonant clusters	st = /st/ pl = /pl/ pr = /pr/ gr = gr/ tr = /tr/ cl = /kl/ br = /br/ dr = /dr/	stop play print green tree clean bring drive	fr = /fr/ fl = /fl/ str = /str/ cr = /kr/ sm = /sm/ sp = /sp/ bl = /bl/	free flood street cry small speak blur
	Final consonant clusters	ld = /ld/ lf = /lf/ sk = /sk/ st = /st/	cold shelf mask best	mp = /mp/ nd = /nd/ nt = /nt/ nk = /dk/	lamp hand ant think
	Less frequent digraphs and other consonant elements	ck = /k/ dge = /j/	lock bridge		

Long vowels: final *e* marker	*a-e* = /ā/	save	*e-e* = /ē/	these
	i-e = /ī/	five	*u-e* = /ū/	use
	o-e = /ō/	hope		
Digraphs and trigraphs	*ee* = /ē/	green	*ow* = /ō/	show
	ai/ay = /ā/	aim, play	*igh* = /ī/	light
	oa = /ō/	boat	*ea* = /ē/	bread
	ea = /ē/	bean		
Other vowels	*ou/ow* = /ow/	out, owl	*oo* = / o͝o /	book
	oi/oy = /oi/	oil, toy	*oo* = /ō͞o/	tool
	au/aw = /aw/	author, paw		
r vowels	*ar* = /ar/	car	*are* = /air/	care
	er = /ər/	her	*air* = /air/	hair
	ir = /ər/	sir	*ear* = /i(ə)r/	fear
	ur = /ər/	burn	*eer* = /i(ə)r/	steer
	or = /or/	for		

3   Consonants

	ti = /sh/	action
	ssi = /sh/	mission
	t, ti = /ch/	future, question

Consonant digraphs	*ch* = /k/	choir	*kn* = /n/	knee
	ch = /sh/	chef	*wr* = /r/	wrap
	gh = /g/	ghost	*ph* = /f/	photo
Vowels	*y* = /ē/	city	*o* = /aw/	off
	y = /ī/	why	*al* = /aw/	ball
	y = /i/	gym	*ew* = /ū/	few
	a = /o/	father		
	e = /i/	remain		

APPENDIX 4.2 ▬▬▬▬▬▬▬▬▬▬▬▬▬▬▬▬▬▬▬▬▬▬▬▬▬

Common Rime/Spelling Patterns

	Vowel Sound	*Rimes*
Short Vowels	/a/	-ab, -ack, -ad, -ag, -am, -amp, -an, -and, -ang, -ank, -ant, -ap, -ash, -ask, -ast, -at, -atch
	/e/	-ead, -eck, -ed, -ell, -elt, -en, -end, -ent, -ess, -est, -et
	/i/	-ick, -id, -ig, ill, -im, -in, -ing, -ink, -ip, -ish, -iss, -it
	/o/	-ob, -ock, -od, -og, -op, -ot
	/u/	-ub, -uck, -ud, -udge, -uff, -ug, -um, -ump, -un, -unch, -ung, -unk, -us, -ust, -ut
Long Vowels	/ā/	-ace, -ade, -age, -ake, -ale, -ame, -ane, -ape, -ate, -aid, -ail, -ain, -aste, -ate, -ave, -ay
	/ē/	-e, -ea, -each, -ead, -eak, -eal, -eam, -ean, -ee, -eep, -eet
	/ī/	-ice, -ide, -ie, -ife, -ike, -ile, -ime, -ind, -ine, -ipe, -ite, -ive, -y
	/ō/	-o, -oe, -oke, -old, -ole, -oll, -one, -ope, -ow, -own
	/u/	-ute
Other Vowels	/aw/	-alk, -all, -aught, -aw, -awl, -awn, -ong, -ought
	/oi/	-oil, -oy
	/o͝o/	-ood, -ook, -ould
	/o͞o/	-ew, -oo, -ool, -oom, -oon, -oot, -ue, -oup
	/ow/	-ouch, -ound, -our, -ouse, -out, -ow, -owl, -own
r Vowels	/air/	-air, -are, -ear
	/ar/	-ar, -ard, -ark, -art
	/ər/	-ir, -ird, -irt, -urt
	/e(ə)r	-ear, -eer
	/i(ə)r/	-ire
	/or/	-oar, -ore, -ort, -orn

Note: Rimes containing few examples have been omitted. Because of dialect variation, some rimes (-*og,* for instance) may have more than one pronunciation. Depending upon onset, some rimes will vary in pronunciation: *mash* vs. *wash,* for example.

Source: T. G. Gunning, *Creating Literacy Instruction for All Children* 3rd ed. (Boston: Allyn and Bacon, 2000), p. 92. Copyright © 2000 by Allyn and Bacon. Reprinted by permission.

5

Reading: Fluency and Comprehension

OUTLINE

KEY TOPICS FOR MASTERY

- *Reasons why students with learning problems may have difficulty with fluency*
- *Strategies for reading aloud and previewing books, repeated reading, choral repeated reading, and peer-supported reading*
- *Making books acceptable and accessible to struggling readers*
- *Integrating fluency building into a reading program*
- *Reasons that students have difficulty comprehending what they read*
- *A framework for reading comprehension, including textually explicit, textually implicit, and scriptually implicit question-answer relationships*
- *Guidelines for promoting reading comprehension including activities for before, during, and after reading*
- *Strategies for previewing, predicting, and activating background knowledge including brainstorming, PreReading Plan, text preview, and K-W-L*
- *Strategies for promoting questioning including reciprocal questioning, question–answer relationship strategy, and self-questioning strategies*
- *Strategies for teaching text structure and summarization strategies including story mapping or retelling, paraphrasing, and summarization*
- *Teaching multicomponent cognitive strategy instruction, including reciprocal teaching, collaborative strategic reading, and POSSE*
- *Guidelines for adapting approaches to teach reading in inclusive classrooms including directed reading activity, directed reading–thinking activity, and literature-based reading and whole language*

 BRIGHT IDEA

> *Turn to pages 226–227 and read Think and Apply.*

Reading provides a window for learning in school and in later life. Research indicates that one key to becoming a good reader is to engage in reading for purposes of learning and enjoyment. Yet students with reading difficulties oftentimes do not have as many opportunities to engage in reading during school and do not choose reading as a leisure-time activity. As teachers our goal is to assist students in becoming fluent readers and provide them with a wide choice of literature and other materials to read and discuss so that reading becomes a source of learning, enjoyment, and satisfaction. To reach this goal it is important to plan instruction that focuses not only on

word recognition and decoding as discussed in the last chapter but also on strategies for building fluency and promoting active reading comprehension as presented in this chapter.

TEACHING FLUENCY

Although Jeff can recognize most of the words in his second-grade reader (i.e., word recognition is 90–95 percent or instructional level), he continues to sound out the words. Consequently, his reading, whether oral or silent, is very slow. He expends so much effort on identifying the words that he frequently misses the main points of the story.

Diane, a fourth grader, had great difficulty learning to read. After several years of failure, she finally learned to identify words by using multisensory structured language instruction. However, Diane's rate of reading is slow and she is experiencing some difficulties in comprehension. When asked to define reading, she places emphasis on "reading the word correctly" rather than on understanding what she reads. Though Jeff and Diane have developed a system for identifying words, they are having difficulties reading fluently (quickly and easily). Research indicates that students with significant reading disabilities have difficulty developing fluency and continue to be slow readers into adolescence and adulthood (Shaywitz and Shaywitz, 1996, Stanovitch, 1986; Torgesen, Wagner, and Rashotte, 1994). For these students, their ability to listen to text and understand the information usually exceeds their ability to gain understanding when reading text (Mosberg and Johns, 1994). Fluency instruction may be one means of improving their ability to recognize words automatically and to allocate more effort toward constructing meaning from what they are reading.

Fluency is the ability to read a text quickly, accurately, and with expression. Fluency instruction is designed to increase automatic word recognition or the "smoothness" of the reading, rate or "pace" of reading, and prosody or "expression, appropriate phrasing, and attention to punctuation" (Richards, 2000; Zutell and Rasinski, 1991). According to the theory of automaticity (LaBerge and Samuels, 1974; Samuels, 1997), fluent readers automatically process information at the visual and phonological levels, and are therefore able to focus most of their attention on the meaning of the text, integrating this information with their background knowledge. The "multitask functioning" of the fluent reader is made possible by the reduced cognitive demands needed for word recognition and other reading processes (i.e., processing in an almost effortless, unconscious fashion), thus freeing cognitive resources for comprehension (National Reading Panel, 2000). Since poor readers take much longer and require more exposures to automatically

recognize and rapidly recall words than do normally reading students (Ehri and Wilce, 1983), it is important that fluency instruction provide multiple opportunities for practice.

Fluency instruction and practice at reading is thus an important part of any reading program, particularly for students with learning and behavior problems. It provides students with repeated practice at reading materials at the students' independent or instructional reading levels. Therefore, let's look at several strategies for helping students develop fluency in their reading and for monitoring their progress as well as and ideas for making difficult text more accessible and easy books more acceptable.

Measuring Fluency and Monitoring Student Progress

Fluency is most frequently measured by the words correct per minute (WCPM) and through observations of phrasing, smoothness, and pace.

To measure progress in fluency, select two to three passages that are unfamiliar to the student and that are at the student's instructional or independent word recognition levels (i.e., word recognition from 90 to 100 percent). Have two copies of the texts: one for recording errors and one for the student to read. You can use a stopwatch for timing, and it is often helpful to audiotape the student's reading on a monthly basis so that he or she can hear as well as see their progress. Tell the student: "When I say 'begin,' start reading aloud at the top of the page. Do your best reading. If you come to a word that you don't know, I'll tell it to you." If a student does not read a word within three seconds, pronounce the word. Have the student read for one to three minutes. Follow along as the student reads and mark your copy by putting a slash (/) through words read incorrectly. This includes mispronunciations, substitutions, omissions, words pronounced after hesitations of more than three seconds, and reversals. Do not count insertions, self-corrections, or repetitions. Also note if the student is having difficulty with phrasing, ignoring punctuation, reading slow, word-by-word, or laboriously, and/or has frequent extended pauses, false starts, sound-outs, and repetitions. Note the last word read by the student within the allotted time and the number of minutes that he or she read. If the student is in the middle of a sentence when the time has finished, have him or her finish the sentence. Use this procedure with two to three passages.

To calculate fluency, use the following formula:

$$\frac{\text{Total Words Read } - \text{ Errors}}{\text{Number of Minutes of Reading}} = \frac{\text{Words Correct}}{\text{per Minute}}$$

For example, if a student reads 160 words during a two-minute sample and makes 6 errors, then the WCPM would be 160 minus 6 equals 154 divided by 2 equals 77. Average the scores across the two to three passages collected to get a mean rate.

Guidelines for fluency rates for grades 2 through 5 are presented in Table 5.1. They are based on the performance of 9,000 students in grades 2 to 5 between 1981 and 1990 in five midwestern and western states (Hasbrouck and Tindal, 1992). Rates are given for students reading at the 25th, 50th, and 75th percentiles during the fall, winter, and spring of each year. For example, if Maria, a fourth grader, was reading fourth-grade level materials at 90 wcpm during the winter, then she would be reading similar to other students at the 25th percentile.

Fluency information can be plotted in graphs such as the one shown in Figure 5.1. Having students record their own progress serves as a motivation for reading, provides immediate feedback, and allows the students to set goals and see concrete evidence of their progress. Generally for students with fluency problems, the goal is set by adding one to two more words correct per minute per week with fluency increasing more quickly in the earlier grades (Fuchs, Fuchs, Hamlett, Walz, and Germann, 1993). Audiotape recordings of the student reading allow students not only to graph their progress but also to hear their progress over time. Generally, these reading samples are collected once every one to two months and can be kept across the year.

Jeff's fluency instruction and progress as reported in Figure 5.1 was measured weekly using beginning second grade instructional level reading materials. He was making consistent progress and increased substantially from the third to fourth weeks (three words), when he began to rely less on sounding out words and to attempt to read the words automatically. This also resulted in better phrasing and reading with more expression.

■ **TABLE 5.1** *Reading Fluency Guidelines for Grades 2 through 5 (Medians)*

Grade	Student Percentile	Fall WCPM*	Winter WCPM	Spring WCPM
2	75	82	106	124
	50	53	78	94
	25	23	46	65
3	75	107	123	142
	50	79	93	114
	25	65	70	87
4	75	125	133	143
	50	99	112	118
	25	72	89	92
5	75	126	143	151
	50	105	118	128
	25	77	93	100

*Words correct per minute

Source: Adapted from J. E. Hasbrouck, and G. Tindal, "Curriculum-Based Oral Reading Fluency Norms for Students in Grades 2 through 5," *Teaching Exceptional Children, 24*(3) (1992): 41–44.

■ **FIGURE 5.1** *Fluency Monitoring*

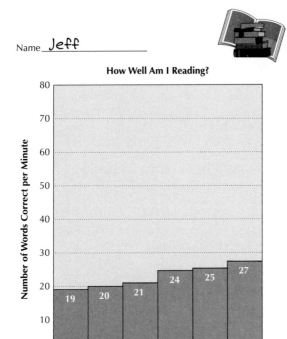

Name _Jeff_

How Well Am I Reading?

Reading Aloud and Previewing Books

Students develop the concept of fluent reading through listening and watching others read aloud, through previewing the book, and through practice reading materials that are at their instructional to independent word recognition levels (word recognition from 90 to 100 percent). In the last decade, a growing emphasis has been placed on the importance of reading aloud to children and previewing a book as a means for developing not only an enjoyment of literature and books but also as an avenue for modeling and building fluent reading (Reutzel and Hollingsworth, 1993; Rose, 1984; Shany and Biemiller, 1995; Trelease, 1995).

Reading aloud and previewing a book (e.g., listening to the teacher read the text and discuss the book and difficult vocabulary with the students) promotes the development of reading fluency in a number of ways. First, it allows the teacher to model fluent reading. When reading aloud to a group of students just learning to read, the use of big books can be helpful because it allows the teacher to make more visible the literacy act and creates interest in the story. If the teacher or parent or volunteer is reading aloud to one child, then sitting next to the child or having the child sit on the teacher's lap (depending on the age of the child) makes it easy for the child to interact with the print and the teacher. When reading aloud, read with expression and point to the words as you read or sweep your fingers underneath them.

Second, reading aloud and previewing a book provides background knowledge for the students so that they can read the book by themselves, with a partner, or while listening to an audiotape. It gives the teacher the opportunity to preview difficult words and unfamiliar concepts. Once children have listened to a book, they are more likely to select it as a book they want to read. In a study of kindergartners, Martinez and Teale (1988) found that children chose very familiar books (i.e., those read repeatedly by the teacher) to read during free time three times more frequently than unfamiliar books (unread). Rose (1984) compared the effects of teacher-directed previewing and not previewing texts with six students with learning disabilities and found that previewing substantially increased oral reading rates. Others studies have investigated the effects of taped previewing (Rose and Beattie, 1986) and peer previewing (Salend and Nowak, 1988). These procedures also increased fluency of the text, but not to the degree that teacher-directed previewing. Apply the Concept 5.1 presents guidelines for teacher-directed previewing. Since students have already listened to and previewed the book, they will have a wealth of knowledge about the book to assist them in reading.

Third, reading aloud allows the student to listen to and discuss books that may be too difficult for them to read. Many students with learning and behavior problems have listening comprehension that is several years more advanced than their reading

APPLY THE CONCEPT 5.1

GUIDELINES FOR IMPLEMENTING PREVIEWING FOR PROMOTING FLUENCY

1. *Decide on an appropriate book or text* (i.e., one that is of interest to the students and at their independent to instructional reading levels). For longer books, preview only a section of the book at a time.) Have student copies of the book or text.
2. *Introduce the book or text* using the title and looking through the text or section. With the students make predictions about their content. Introduce words that might be difficult for the students to automatically recognize or for which the meaning may be unfamiliar. Students may write these words in a personal dictionary or on word cards.
3. *Have students follow along as you read the book or text orally* at a relatively slow con-

versational rate (approximately 130 words per minute).
4. After you have read a section, *have students partner and take turns reading* the same section. Have the stronger partner read first and as one student reads have the other student provide support by pronouncing words the students does not know.
5. *Have the students review the difficult words* using techniques for building sight words discussed in Chapter Four.
6. On a regular basis *monitor the students' reading fluency* by using the procedures discussed in the section on monitoring student progress.

---

comprehension. Reading a book aloud affords the students the opportunity to talk about literature that is at a more advanced level.

Fourth, reading aloud can be orchestrated so that older, less adept readers can read books to young children and serve as cross-age tutors. This provides the opportunity for the older students to read aloud and to serve as the role model of a "good reader," an opportunity not often available in the regular or resource classroom.

Jim Trelease, author of *The New Read-Aloud Handbook* (1995), suggests that reading aloud:

— Provides a positive reading role model
— Furnishes new information
— Demonstrates the pleasures of reading
— Develops vocabulary
— Provides examples of good sentences and good story grammar
— Enables students to be exposed to a book they might not otherwise be exposed to
— Provides opportunity for discussions concerning the content of the book

Repeated Reading

Have you noticed how young children thoroughly enjoy having the same story read to them many, many times? As you sit with them and read a familiar book, they automatically begin to read along with you. At first, they join in on some of the words and phrases. Eventually, they are reading with you for most of the book. With repeated reading of a story, the children are becoming so familiar with the text that their memory becomes a great aid to them. Repeated reading is based on the notion that as students repeatedly read text, they become fluent and confident in their reading (Samuels, 1979, 1997). And because they are exposed to the same story several times, they have the opportunity to practice identifying unknown words while relying on their memory of the language flow to assist them.

— **PROCEDURES:** Repeated reading consists of rereading short, meaningful passages several times until a satisfactory level of fluency is reached. The procedure is then repeated with a new passage. The general format for this reading procedure is to have the student repeatedly read passages that range from 50 to 200 words in length, until they reach a more fluent reading rate (see Table 5.1) and with an adequate word recognition level (e.g., 90 to 100 percent word recognition). When a student reads under the direct supervision of a teacher, the words a student does not recognize are pronounced by the teacher. To foster comprehension, discussion of the book follows reading.

A number of researchers have investigated the use of tape-recorded books for this procedure (Carbo, 1978, 1997; Chomsky, 1976; Conte and Humphreys, 1989; Dowhower, 1987; Hasbrouck, Ihnot, and Rogers, 1999; Rasinski, 1990). Using taped books, the students listen to the stories and read and/or follow along with the written text. They listen to and read the same story until they can "read the book by themselves." The teacher then listens to students individually read the story and discusses the story with the students. Guidelines for tape-recording books, keeping records of students' reading, and using computers are presented in Apply the Concept 5.2.

— **COMMENTS:** Students reading below grade level who have used repeated reading have consistently demonstrated gains in both fluency and reading comprehension (for recent reviews see Dowhower, 1994; Mastropieri, Leinart, and Scruggs, 1999; Meyer and Felton, 1999; National Reading Panel, 2000; Strecker, Roser, and Martinez, 1998). From these reviews of research, several instructional guidelines for using repeated reading can be generated (Meyers and Felton, 1999):

— Consistently using repeated reading with poor readers increases reading speed, accuracy, expression, and comprehension.
— Text materials should be at the students' independent to instructional level (90 to 100 percent word recognition).
— Passages should be read three to five times.
— Multiple reading of phrases may also improve fluency.
— Specific strategies should take into account individual students' characteristics. For *more impaired readers:*

- Provide more adult guidance during reading.
- Use more decodable texts as reading materials.
- Practice on words and phrases from the text before reading the text.
- Practice reading shorter passages.
- Model expressive reading.

— Short, frequent sessions of fluency practice (generally 10 to 15 minutes) should be used.
— Transfer of fluency is increased when the overlap of words across passages is substantial (Rashotte and Torgesen, 1985).
— Having a way for students to set goals and record their progress should be provided.

Using tape-recorded stories, Carbo (1987) found that rereading small segments of text may be helpful. When Shany and Biemiller (1995) compared (a) teacher assistance during repeated reading with (b) students listening to taped readings on a speed-controlled recorder, they found that reading rates and reading comprehension increased in both cases. Students who used a tape recorder, however, read twice the amount and had higher listening comprehension scores. Dowhower (1987) compared the effects of independent repeated reading versus reading-along with tape-recorded books with second-grade, below average readers (reading rate less than 50 words per minute). While students in both methods improved in the reading fluency, students using the tapes improved more in their ability to reading meaningful phrases. Dowhower also noted that students reading between 25 and 45 words per minute were less frustrated in the read-along condition, while students reading more than 45 words per minute appeared more able to practice reading independently.

Choral Repeated Reading

Choral repeated reading is a technique that combines ideas and procedures from repeated reading and choral reading. It was developed by one of the authors (Bos, 1982), because of her concern that fluency-building strategies for less-adept readers tend to ignore the teaching of either word identification skills or comprehension (e.g., neurological impress). We have used the approach with students who have

APPLY THE CONCEPT 5.2

USING TAPED AND COMPUTER-BASED BOOKS FOR REPEATED READING

Selecting Books and Passages

Select books and passages that are of interest to the students and for which the students' word recognition is from 85 to 95 percent. For more impaired readers select more decodable texts (see Chapter Four). Pattern language books (see Chapter Four) can be another good source of books because they provide students with frequent repetition of language patterns and words. For older readers, high-interest, low-vocabulary stories provide another source.

Tape Recording the Books

Use a good quality recording tape and recorder. Audiotape a book speaking at a conversational rate and with expression. Use appropriate phrasing. Provide the students with cues to assist them in keeping their place in the text while listening to the recording.

- Allow ten seconds of blank tape before recording.
- Remind students of any strategies you want them to use (e.g., "Remember to use your finger or a marker as a guide.").
- Use a signal to cue turning the page.
- For a new page announce each page number.
- Direct students to put their finger on the first word on the page.

Record about ten minutes of reading on each side of tape so that it will be easy for students to find their place. Label each side of the tape by the title of the book and page numbers covered. You can instruct parent volunteers to record books. Kirk (1986) suggests forming student committees to select, practice, and record the books. You can also purchase prerecorded taped books but be aware that they may not provide the same level of cueing.

Store the books with their tapes in clear plastic bags. Inside the bag, place the book and tape. If you have multiple copies of the book with a tape, they can be stored together.

Keeping Student Records

Have each student make a reading folder. Staple forms inside the folder on which the student can record the name of the book, the author, the date, how he or she read the book, and with whom he or she discussed the book. In this way, both the teacher and the student have a record of the student's reading.

Computer-Based Reading Practice

Computer software provides another avenue for children to repeatedly read books using the computer. For example, *Living Book Series* (Discus Books) and *Wiggleworks* (Scholastic) both provide opportunities for students to listen to books being read, to read along with the computer, and, in the case of *Wiggleworks,* to record their own reading of the book. Reading software provides flexibility; the text can be read in sentences or phrases, or the students can highlight individual words and have them pronounced. Many of these programs easily switch languages (most commonly between English and Spanish), and have built-in record keeping systems so teachers know the number of times students read the books and the type of assistance they use.

Research suggests that computer reading programs help students with learning disabilities to build word recognition and reading comprehension (Leong, 1995; Lundberg, 1995; Torgesen and Barker, 1995).

Name of Book	Author	Dates	Read with				Discussed with	
			Self	Tape	Student	Teacher	Student	Teacher

Using Taped Books at Home to Support English-Language Learners

Taped books can also be integrated into a home reading component. In the *Dog Gone Good Reading Project,* first grade teachers provided additional opportunities for linguistically diverse students to repeatedly read books by audiotaping books and having students listen to them and read along at home (Koskinen, Blum, Bisson, Phillips, Creamer, and Baker, 1999). In preparing the tapes, the books were read twice, first at a slow but expressive "read-along" rate and second at a faster rate, more typical of fluent oral reading. Cues for turning pages and using a finger to point were inserted. Simple tape recorders were also provided. Students were taught how to use the taped books and notes went home with the audiotaped books reminding the children and their parents to read the books two or three times every day. While this technique promoted literacy for all students, it was particularly helpful for students who were learning to read in English but had limited access to English role models and books in English.

Using Voicemail to Support Summer Reading

Elementary-aged students with learning and behavior problems usually do not choose reading as a recreational activity during the summer. Ann Willman, a reading specialist, used her school voicemail to promote summer reading (Willman, 1999). She sent home books with the students along with directions on how to use the school voicemail. The students practiced reading a book until they were comfortable. Then she asked the students, with the assistance of their parents, to call her voicemail and read the book to her for three minutes or to summarize the book. She called backed to compliment the students. Ann also invited parents to leave a message about how the process was going. Parents noted that they liked the summer school connection that made their "sometimes reluctant reader more amenable to reading during vacation" (p. 788).

significant reading difficulties in word identification and reading rate.

■ **PROCEDURES:** Choral repeated reading is designed for students who are able to comprehend material read to them but, due to difficulties in word identification and reading rate, are unable to read material commensurate with their listening comprehension level. Students should have a sight vocabulary of at least 25 words. We suggest the following procedure:

1. Explain the technique to the student.
2. With the student, select a book of interest that is at a challenging reading level (85 to 90 percent word recognition) and that has frequent repetition of words and decodable text.
3. Establish a purpose for reading by introducing the book and making predictions. Read the book with the student, using the following three-step process:
   a. *Teacher reads:* Start at the beginning of the book and read a piece of text to the student, ranging from several sentences to a paragraph. (The length of each section should be short enough that the student can rely on his or her short-term memory as an aid for reading.) Read at a normal rate and move your finger smoothly along underneath the words as the student watches, making sure that your reading matches your movement from word to word.
   b. *Teacher and student read:* Read the same section together aloud with the student. Continue to point to the words. The two of you may read the section once or several times, rereading until the student feels comfortable reading the section independently.
   c. *Student reads:* Have the student read the section independently. Pronounce any unknown words and note words the student consistently has difficulty recognizing.
4. After reading each section, discuss how it related to your predictions and what you have learned. New predictions and purposes for reading can be set.

5. Repeat the three-step process throughout the book. The length of each section usually increases as the book is read, and the number of times you and the student read together usually decreases. For some students the first step is discontinued.

6. Write on word cards the words the student consistently has difficulty identifying automatically. Use a variety of activities to give him or her more experience with these words. For example, discuss the word meanings or locate the words in the text and reread the sentences. Use the supplemental sight word techniques discussed in Chapter Four.

7. Have the student keep records of his or her progress (see Figure 5.1). Check progress at least every third day when initially using the procedure.

In this method, reading sessions usually last 10 to 15 minutes, with most of the time focusing on oral reading. As the student becomes more confident in reading ability, use repeated readings with tape-recorded books or stories as independent reading activities. Spelling words can be selected from words in the books and words can be organized to teach phonic and structural analysis skills (see Chapter Four).

— COMMENTS: We have used this procedure with a number of students who have severe word identification and/or fluency problems. Because choral repeated reading allows the teacher and student to attend to word identification skills and comprehension as well as fluency. Using the three-step process also allows the student to read more difficult books. We have found this particularly rewarding for older nonreaders in that it quickly gives them success in reading books. Others have noted that choral reading is valuable not only for increasing fluency but also for helping students learn English as a second language (McCauley and McCauley, 1992; Van Wagenen, Williams, and McLaughlin, 1994).

Peer-Supported Reading

One concern for students with learning and behavior problems is that they read substantially less than high-achieving readers and spend less time engaged in academic behaviors (Allington, 1983; Greenwood, Delquadri and Hall, 1989). How can the amount of time devoted to text reading be increased? One strategy is to use peers to support each other when reading for the purpose of building fluency as well as supporting word recognition and comprehension. Techniques such as *assisted reading* (Hoskinsson and Krohm, 1974), *classwide peer tutoring* or *partner reading* (e.g., Delquardi, Greenwood, Whorton, Carta, and Hall, 1986; Fuchs, Fuchs, and Burish, 2000; Fuchs, Fuchs, Mathes, and Simmons, 1997; Simmons, Fuchs, Fuchs, Hodge, and Mathes, 1994; Vaughn, Hughes, Schumm, and Klingner, 1998; Vaughn, Schumm, and Forgan, 1995) and *dyad reading* (Eldredge and Quinn, 1988) all provide opportunities for students to work in pairs and provide support for each other while reading. For the most part, these techniques have been used in general education classrooms to provide more opportunities for students to actively engage in reading.

— PROCEDURES: Important considerations in planning for peer-supported reading is the pairing of students and the selection of reading materials. To pair students, it is advantageous to pair a stronger reader with a weaker reader. One example of pairing students is to rank order the class based on reading fluency and reading level. Then split the class in half and pair the top-ranked high performing student with the top-ranked lower performing student, the second-ranked high performing student with the second-ranked low performing student, and so on. Check to see that there are no partners who socially will not work well together and adjust accordingly. Keep pairing for three to four weeks. Reading materials should be at the lower performing student's independent to instructional reading levels. If peer-support reading is used three to four times per week, have enough materials selected so that students can work on two new passages per week. As in other fluency techniques, such as repeated reading and repeated choral reading, the reading materials will vary based on the students' needs. At first, it may be advantageous to use short passages or books as students learn the procedures, but high interest/low vocabulary chapter books can also be a good source of reading materials (see Figure 5.2 for a selected list of publishers and Websites).

■ **FIGURE 5.2** *Selected List of High Interest/Controlled Vocabulary Publishers and Websites*

Academic Communication Associates 888-758-9558
Narrative: classics

BMI 800-222-8100
Narrative: classics, adventures, mysteries
Expository: biographies

Capstone Press 888-574-6711
Narrative: classics, adventures, mysteries
Expository: biographies, family, communities, native peoples, states, wildlife, galaxies, countries, ethnic holidays, space, extreme sports, military, history

Carson-Dellosa 800-321-0943
Narrative: adventures, mysteries
Expository: biographies

Curriculum Associates 800-225-0248
Narrative: action, tales
Expository: nature, animals, sports

Educational Design 800-221-9372
Narrative: action
Expository: biographies, multicultural, world events

Educators Publishing Service 800-435-7728
Narrative: sports
Expository: biographies, multicultural, world events, history

Globe Fearon 800-872-8893
Narrative: classics, action, science fiction, suspense, adventures, mysteries
Expository: biographies, multicultural, world events, family, communities, native peoples, states, wildlife, galaxies, countries, ethnic holidays, space, extreme sports, military, history

High Noon Books 800-422-7249
Narrative: classics, adventures, mysteries, athletes
Expository: natural disasters, biographies

Incentives for Learning 888-238-2379
Narrative: personal challenges, thrillers, adventures, mysteries, athletes, classics
Expository: holidays, biographies

Michigan Products Incorporated 800-444-1773
Expository: health and fitness, finance, history, sports and leisure, jobs, general science

National Reading Styles Institute 800-331-3117
Expository: sports figures

New Readers Press 800-448-8878
Expository: heroes, bibliographies, friendships

News for You 800-448-8878
Narrative: national and international articles and essays
Expository: national and international news

PCI Educational Publishing 800-594-4263
Narrative: adventures, mysteries, classics, short stories
Expository: heros, escapes, disasters, body science, U.S. history, drivers education, job search

Perfection Learning 800-831-4190
Narrative: mysteries, action, adventure
Expository: science, technology, sports, myths

Phoenix Learning Resources 800-221-1274
Narrative: classics, art, poetry
Expository: life science, earth science, physical science

Remedia 800-826-4740
Expository: the solar system, biographies, insects, animals, inventors

Rigby 800-822-8661
Expository: journeys, survival, adventure, animals

Saddleback Educational 949-860-2500
Narratives: classics
Expository: history, biographies, sports, disasters

Scholastic 800-724-6527
Narrative: adventures, sports, mysteries
Expository: sports, science, technology, art, entertainment
Book Clubs: Firefly, SeeSaw, Lucky, Arrow, and Tab Book Clubs and Scholastic Software Clubs

Steck-Vaughn 800-531-5015
Narrative: classics, mysteries, true tales
Expository: geography, challenges, adventures, rescues, national disasters, foreign nations, entertainers, health

Sundance 800-343-8204
Narrative: classics, adventure, science fiction, thrillers, mysteries, sports
Expository: ships, animal attacks, biographies

Wright Group 800-523-2371
Narrative: mysteries, adventure
Expository: science, technology, sports, myths

Publishing Companies/Magazines
National Geographic 800-638-4077
National Wildlife Federation 800-611-1599
Smithsonian Institute 800-827-0227

(continued)

Websites

American Library Association
   www.ala.org/yalsa/booklists/2000quickpicks
   Quick Picks for Reluctant Young Adult Readers
   2000—list selected yearly

International Reading Association
   www.reading.org/ choices
   Children's, Teachers', and Young Adults' Choices
   Booklists—lists selected yearly

Source: Adapted from Texas Center for Reading and Language Arts, *Enhancing reading for secondary students — Part II* (Austin: Texas Center for Reading and Language Arts, University of Texas–Austin, 2000).

Teach students how to be both tutors/listeners and tutees/readers and provide role-play practice and feedback. For the tutors, give guidelines for how they should correct errors during oral reading (e.g., point out the word, pronounce the word, and have the tutee say the word) and the questions they should ask when the students has finished reading (e.g., What is the story about? What is happening in the story now? What do you think will happen next?). Also assist the students in giving positive feedback.

When the students work in partners, first the stronger reader reads aloud to serve as a model, and then the other reader reads. Because the lower performing students read what has just been read by the higher performing students, it is more likely that they will read fluently and comfortably (Fuchs et al., 1997). How much material is read before the student switch roles depends on the material and the readers, but it usually ranges from a sentence to a page or for a specified amount of time (e.g., five minutes). Partners can take turns reading a book or passage several times, thus adding a repeated reading component (Koskinen and Blum, 1984; Mathes and Fuchs, 1994; Simmons et al., 1994). Copies of guidelines for the tutor and reader can be posted and each pair can rate themselves on their effort (see Figure 5.3).

— COMMENTS: Research consistently indicates that peer-supported reading has positive outcomes on the reading fluency and comprehension of students with learning and behavior problems (see Mastropieri et al., 1999 for a review) even in first grade classrooms (Mathes, Grek, Howard, Babyak, and Allen, 1999). Such features as adding a repeated reading component (Simmons et al., 1994) did not differentially affect student progress. They suggest that the strength of the intervention may be related to the additional instructional time and student reading involvement afforded by peer-supported reading.

Reading Performance

While Ms. Thompson, the special education teacher, and Ms. Martinez, the fifth grade teacher, were pleased with the way in which the students with learning and behavior problems were participating with the other students in partner reading, they wanted the students to have the opportunity to practice reading for purposes other than to build fluency. Consequently, they used readers theater and buddy reading as techniques in which students practice reading a selection until fluent and then perform the reading, sometimes referred to as *reading performances* (Worthy and Broaddus, in press).

— PROCEDURES: In *readers theater,* students perform a play or a book adapted to script form by reading it aloud to an audience. Since the focus is on reading fluently, students are not expected to memorize the text, and props are minimal. Students with different reading skills can use the same text, since the different parts often vary widely in reading level. Once parts have been chosen, students practice reading their parts with a teacher, tutor, and/or other students in the performance. Finally, the group practices rehearsing the entire performance. Performances may be given to a variety of audiences including other groups of students in the class, other classes, and parents. Even simple texts can be adapted to a script form as demonstrated in Figure 5.4.

Buddy reading consists of the students practicing and reading texts to younger students. This provides opportunities for students with learning and behavior problems to practice reading texts that are not at

■ FIGURE 5.3 *Guidelines for Peer-Supported Reading*

Partner Reading Procedures

- First reader reads.
- Second reader reads.
- Students discuss reading with one student asking questions and other student answering.
- Repeat until story is complete.

Tutoring Rules

- Talk only to your partner.
- Talk only about partner reading.
- Be cooperative.

Kinds of Errors

- Saying the word wrong.
- Leaving out a word.
- Adding a word.
- Waiting longer than 4 seconds.

Feedback about Words

- Stop. You missed this word (point to it). Can you figure it out?
- That word is _____. What word? (Reader says word). Good! Read the sentence again.

their grade level but at their independent reading level without the stigma of reading "easy" books. When using buddy reading, it is important to choose books that the students can read easily and that are appropriate for and interesting to younger children.

— COMMENTS: While techniques such as readers theater and buddy reading do not provide the level of explicit instruction and support that are used with techniques such as repeated choral reading and peer-supported reading, they do provide students with learning and behavior problems the opportunities to practice and transfer their reading fluency to tasks other than practicing fluency. Furthermore, they lend themselves to implementation in general education classrooms.

Making Easy Books Acceptable and Difficult Books Accessible

One key to becoming a fluent reader is to read. Yet students with learning and behavior problems who have difficulty reading are generally not provided as many opportunities to read books in school and do not select reading books as a leisure time activity (Anderson, Wilson, and Fielding, 1988; Spear-Swerling and

■ FIGURE 5.4 *Example of Adapting a Simple Text to Script Format for Readers Theater*

Original Text	Scripted Text	
One day Mrs. Duck went to the pond. It was hot and she wanted a cool drink. Mr. Fox was sitting by the side of the pond. He told Mrs. Duck that she could not get a drink because he was in a bad mood and did not want anyone near his pond. Mrs. Bird heard Mr. Fox say this and she called down sweetly from her branch . . .	**Mrs. Duck:**	I have been working so hard and now I am so thirsty. I need to go to the pond for a nice, cool drink.
	Mr. Fox:	Hello, Mrs. Duck. I am in a very bad mood. No one can drink from my pond today.
	Mrs. Bird:	This is not your pond. It belongs to everyone.

Source: Adapted from Texas Center for Reading and Language Arts, *Professional development guide: Reading fluency: Principles of instruction and progress monitoring* (Austin: Texas Center for Reading and Language Arts, University of Texas–Austin, 2000).

Sternberg, 1996). Stanovitch (1986) has referred to this as the "Matthew effect" in that students who read well read more and improve their reading abilities, while those who read poorly read less, increasingly falling further behind in developing proficiency. Two reasons why these students may choose not to read are because they perceive easy books as unacceptable and embarrassing, and when they try to read books that they perceive as interesting, they are too difficult. Fielding and Roller (1992) discuss several strategies that teachers can use to make easy books more acceptable or legitimate, including:

- *Model your own use and enjoyment of easy books.* In adult life, most pleasure reading is easy reading.
- *Alter the purposes for easy reading.* Have students read easy books for the purpose of reading to younger students or children in preschool.
- *Have students make tape recordings of their reading.* Students will often choose easier books and reread them several times so that they "sound good" on the tape recording.
- *Broaden the definition of acceptable reading.* Poems, songs, raps, jump-rope chants, and cheers often are easier because of the predictable language and repetition such as Joanna Cole's (1989) collection of popular jump-rope chants in *Anna Banana* and Joanna Cole and Stephanie Calmenson's (1990) collection of children's street rhymes in *Miss Mary Mack.*
- *Make simple nonfiction books available.* Books that contain new information about a topic of student interest are often not perceived by the student as easy or boring.

Fielding and Roller (1992) and Worthy (1996) discuss several strategies for making difficult books more accessible to older readers with disabilities. These strategies include:

- Using tape recorded books and CD-ROM books for the computer (see Apply the Concept 5.2).
- Reading aloud to the students.
- Using partner reading, in which less able and more able readers are paired.

- Preceding difficult books with easier books about the same topic or genre (e.g., comets, solar system, scary books, fairy tales, mystery books), thereby familiarizing the child with the vocabulary and text structure in books that are easier.
- Using series books to increase students' comfort level. Reading books in a series provides benefits that are similar to those of repeated reading of the same text because of the consistent use of characters, language, and content. Examples are Bridwell's *Clifford the Big Red Dog,* Rylant's *Henry and Mudge,* Park's *Junie B. Jones,* Scieska's *Time Warp Trio,* and Applegate's science fictions, *Animorphs.*

Integrating Fluency Building into a Reading Program

Fluency building should be just one part of a reading program for a student with reading difficulties, and generally includes only 5 to 15 minutes of a lesson. Figure 5.5 describes several programs that have been developed specifically to build fluency. When teaching fluency, strategies for improving word identification skills and comprehension should also be instructional goals. As presented in previewing and repeated choral reading, word recognition and word extension activities can be developed naturally from the text. For example, the same activities recommended for the word cards generated from language experience stories (see Chapter 4) can be used with word cards generated from these fluency techniques. Although improving fluency can provide students with more attention to allocate toward comprehension, not all students will automatically acquire the skills associated with effective comprehension. For some students, methods of teaching comprehension may be required.

TEACHING COMPREHENSION

Comprehension is the ultimate goal and the essence of reading. It is understanding the text and constructing meaning by integrating the information provided by the author with the reader's background knowl-

■ **FIGURE 5.5**   *Selected List of Fluency Building Programs*

Peer-Assisted Learning Strategies-Reading (PALS)
(Classwide Peer Tutoring)

PALS Reading has been developed for students in kindergarten through high school. It is designed primarily for general education classrooms and as supplements to a teacher's more comprehensive reading program. PALS programs target key reading skills including fluency and, because students work with students on these skills, PALS provides students with intensive practice. Evaluative studies indicate that on average PALS accelerates the reading achievement of students with LD, low-achieving students, and average- and high-achieving students. PALS Math uses a similar format but focuses on math.

Contact: Douglas Fuchs/Lynn Fuchs
           Box 328
           Peabody/Vanderbilt University
           Nashville, TN 37220
           615-343-4782
           e-mail: doug.fuchs@vanderbilt.edu

Read Naturally

Students read along while listening to a tape of leveled, recorded high-interest passages and practice until they can read them at a predetermined rate. Students graph wcpm before and after practicing. Comprehension questions provided.

Contact: Read Naturally
           2329 Kressin Avenue
           Saint Paul, MN 55120
           800-788-4085

Website: www.readnaturally.com
e-mail: info@readnaturallly.com

Great Leaps

Great Leaps addresses fluency at three levels: Phonics—students identify sounds and decode simple word patterns; Sight Phrases—students read phrases with sight words; Reading Fluency—students read stories. Students graph progress.

Contact: Diarmuid, Inc.
           Box 35780
           Gainesville, FL 32635
           877-GRL-EAPS
           Website: www.greatleaps.com
           e-mail: KUC49@aol.com

Taped Books: National Reading Style Institute

The Carbo reading method has children listen to and repeatedly read along with audiotapes of books that have been recorded at a slow pace but with proper phrasing and intonation until they can read fluently. Books can be recorded by the teacher or can be purchased from the National Reading Style Institute.

Contact: National Reading Styles Institute, Inc.
           Box 737
           Syosset, NY 11791
           800-331-3117
           Website: www.nrsi.com
           e-mail: nrsi@mindspring.com

---

edge. It involves complex cognitive skills and strategies by which the reader interacts with the text to construct meaning. There are many reasons why students may have difficulty comprehending what they read.

As a fourth grader reading at second-grade level, Amanda would probably better comprehend what she reads if she did not have to allocate so much attention to word identification. On the other hand, Scott is a word caller. He thinks reading is "reading the words correctly." Even though he is able to read fluently, he does not attend to the meaning of the passage. He frequently has difficulty recalling both the gist

and details of a story. Carrie is diagnosed as having language disabilities, with difficulties in syntax and semantics. These low oral-language skills affect her comprehension of what she reads.

Sam can remember what he reads but does not relate it to what he already knows about the topic (schema). Therefore, he has particular difficulty answering questions that require him to use his background knowledge. Ron, on the other hand, relies too heavily on his background knowledge. This is adversely affecting his reading comprehension.

Kim fails to monitor her comprehension as she reads. She often reports that everything makes sense.

Yet when her teacher asks questions it becomes obvious that Kim has achieved limited comprehension.

All these students are struggling with reading comprehension although their problems are very different. For students such as Amanda, word identification difficulties get in the way of comprehension. Focusing on building word identification skills is probably appropriate for her. However, comprehension skills should not be ignored. This may mean building listening comprehension at her current grade level as well as working on reading comprehension at her current reading level. For Amanda, it is making sure that reading is perceived as understanding and interacting with the text to construct meaning, and not just reading the words correctly. Although word identification skill development will be important, it needs to be coupled with teaching comprehension.

For Scott, the major portion of reading instruction should focus on comprehension. The teacher needs to assist Scott in changing his definition of the reading process. Helping Scott set comprehension-oriented purposes for reading and teaching him how to ask questions as he reads should assist him in changing his definition of reading.

Carrie's difficulties relate to a language problem that affects her reading comprehension as well as her receptive language. For students such as Carrie, instruction in reading comprehension often parallels instruction in receptive language. Both reading and listening comprehension can be improved simultaneously. For example, when Carrie either listens to or reads a story she needs to learn to ask and answer such questions as, "Who is the story about?" "Where did it happen?" "What was the problem in the story?" "What happened to solve the problem?" "How did the story end?"

Some students fail to relate what they are reading to what they already know about the topic. This is the case with Sam. Other students have limited background knowledge to bring to the reading process. Research in schema theory has shown that the knowledge one brings to the reading task affects comprehension, particularly inferential comprehension (Anderson, Reynolds, Schallert, and Goetz, 1977; Carr and Thompson, 1996; Hansen and Pearson, 1983; McKeown, Beck, Sinatra, and Loxterman, 1992; Williams, 1998). Teaching strategies that encourage students to activate their knowledge, or activities that provide opportunities for students to enrich their backgrounds prior to reading, can facilitate comprehension.

Although some students do not rely enough on background knowledge, other students may rely too much on background knowledge, as is the case with Ron. Often these are the same students who tend to overrely on context clues when identifying unknown words. When these students begin reading informational and technical texts that require accurate recall of information, comprehension problems become more evident. Comprehension strategies that encourage self-questioning can encourage such students to pay closer attention to the information presented in the text.

Kim, like many other students with learning disabilities, has difficulty with the metacognitive skill of comprehension monitoring (Bos and Filip, 1984; Ellis, 1996; Palincsar and Brown, 1987; Pressley, 1998; Wong, 1987, 1996). Strategies that teach students to ask questions about their comprehension and that require them to paraphrase and summarize what they read should help them develop metacognitive skills.

Increasing emphasis is being placed on reading comprehension and teaching comprehension strategies for improving reading comprehension (e.g., Gattney and Anderson, 2000; National Reading Panel, 2000; Pearson and Camperell, 1994; Pressley, 2000). First, we will look at a framework for reading comprehension to better understand the scope of comprehension. Then we will focus on instructional strategies for improving reading comprehension. Finally, we will discuss approaches used for teaching reading and reading comprehension.

A Framework for Reading Comprehension

One way of guiding reading comprehension instruction is to determine the different reasoning and information processing skills that are required by readers in order to construct meaning from what they read. Read the passage in Apply the Concept 5.3.

APPLY THE CONCEPT 5.3

THINKING ABOUT READING COMPREHENSION

The Drive To Big Lake

Pat and her father were driving to Big Lake in the Blue Mountains. They were going to Big Lake to go fishing. As they drove Pat watched her father talk on the C.B. radio and watched the sun come up over the mountains.

When Pat and her father were near Big Lake it became very foggy. Pat's father drove slowly but did not see a sharp bend in the road. The car ran off the road and into a ditch. Pat was OK, but she knew that she needed to get help for her father.

She climbed out of the car and went to the road. She thought maybe a car would come by, but none did.

She walked down the road. She was looking for a house. As she walked, she yelled for help.

Then she remembered the C.B. radio that was in the car. She ran back to the car. She had never used the C.B., but she tried to call for help on it. A fisherman at Big Lake was listening to his C.B. Pat told him where she and her father were. Fifteen minutes later help came.

By this time Pat's father had opened his eyes and was OK. The police helped Pat and her father get the car out of the ditch and back on the road. Everyone was proud of Pat.

Source: C. S. Bos, *Inferential Operations in the Reading Comprehension of Educable Mentally Retarded and Average Students.* Doctoral dissertation. (Tucson: University of Arizona, 1979), p. 164.

Now answer each of the following questions and think about the processes that were needed for you to arrive at an answer.

1. What did Pat do first to get help?
2. Where did you find the information to answer the question?

The answer, of course, is in the text. If information is found in the text, then we say that the information is *textually explicit* or *literal* (i.e., taken directly from the text) or we are *reading the lines* (Dale, 1966).

3. What time of day was it in the story?
4. Where did you find that information?

You may have automatically answered question 3 as "early in the morning" or "in the morning" without looking back at the text. If you did this, now go back and read to see if that information is in the text. It is not. Instead, you will find in the first paragraph that "Pat watched the sun come up over the mountains." You may have automatically integrated that informa-

tion with your background knowledge to conclude, "It was in the morning." When information is not in the text but requires you to integrate your background knowledge with text information to generate the answer, then we say the information is *implicit* or *inferential* (e.g., not stated directly in the text). Can we be more specific about this kind of implicit information? Pearson and Johnson (1978) refer to this kind of relationship between the question and the answer as *scriptually implicit*. It requires you to use your schema or *script* about "morning" to generate the answer. Dale (1966) has referred to this as *reading beyond the lines.*

5. Was Pat successful in using the CB radio?
6. Where did you find that information?

It was in the text, but not nearly so clearly as in the case of the first question. In this case you had to read several sentences and piece the information together. The information was *implicit* in that it was not directly stated in the text, but it did not require you to use your background knowledge in the same way that question 4 did. Pearson and Johnson (1978) refer to this kind of implicit information as *textually implicit*. The relationship between the question and the answer required you to get the information from the text, but the relationship is not clearly (*explicitly*) stated. You had to use your knowledge about language and how ideas related to answer the question. Dale (1966) has referred to this relationship as *reading between the lines.*

Therefore, when teaching reading comprehension, we can divide comprehension into types of reasoning according to how readers have to activate their background knowledge to construct the meaning. These three arbitrary categories are:

— *Textually explicit:* Information is derived directly from the text with minimal input from the readers' background knowledge.
— *Textually implicit:* Information is derived from the text but readers are required to use their background knowledge to put together the ideas presented in the text.

— *Scriptually implicit:* Information is not stated in the text. Readers have to activate and use their background knowledge to obtain the information.

We can also categorize comprehension by the type of information or relationship it represents. For example, the first question, "What did Pat do first to get help?" requires the reader to focus on the sequence of the events in the story. Therefore, it requires a sequencing or temporal relationship. The question "Why was everyone proud of Pat?" requires a causal relationship. Barrett (1976) has identified a number of types of information or relationships that can be represented in text (e.g., main ideas, details, sequence, cause and effect) as part of his taxonomy of reading. We can combine types of information with processes required (i.e., textually explicit, textually implicit, and scriptually implicit) to form a matrix for reading comprehension (Figure 5.6).

■ **FIGURE 5.6**   *Matrix for Reading Comprehension*

	Type of Reasoning Based on Background Knowledge		
Type of Information or Relationship	*Textually Explicit*	*Textually Implicit*	*Scriptally Implicit*
Main idea/summary	X	X	X
Detail	X	X	X
Sequence	X	X	X
Comparative relationship	X	X	X
Cause/effect relationship	X	X	X
Conditional relationship	X	X	X
Vocabulary definition	X	X	X
Vocabulary application	X	X	X
Figurative language definition	X	X	X
Figurative language application	X	X	X
Conclusion	X	X	X
Application		X	X
Analysis		X	X
Synthesis		X	X
Evaluation			X

This matrix can be used in planning comprehension instruction, such as planning activities that will encourage students to engage in all the different facets of comprehension (cells in the matrix). For example, to work on sequencing of ideas, students could retell a story by having each student in the group tell one episode from the story; copy a story onto sentence strips and discuss how to arrange the sentences in a logical order; read an explanation of how to do something and write a list of the steps in order; ask each other sequence questions about a description of how to make something; and write a description of how to make something and then have the other students in the group read the description and make the object. Whereas all of these activities focus on sequencing, both explicit and implicit comprehension are required to complete the various activities.

A matrix rather than a taxonomy is used to depict the various aspects of comprehension because comprehension should not be thought of as a set of hierarchical skills. The comprehension process entails ongoing transactions between the text, the reader, and the author (Goodman, 1996; Rosenblatt, 1978) and the active use of comprehension strategies such as predicting, activating background knowledge, asking questions, clarifying, and checking for understanding (National Reading Panel, 2000; Pressley, 1998).

But comprehension goes further than this. We also read to reflect on and judge the quality of the information. Thus, we engage in *critical reading* including such skills as:

— Recognizing the author's purpose
— Distinguishing between facts and opinions
— Identifying words that signal opinions
— Verifying factual statements
— Detecting assumptions
— Judging sources
— Identifying persuasive language
— Detecting propaganda
— Drawing logical conclusions

Critical reading involves both affective and cognitive skills. To read critically, students must be able to suspend judgment, consider other viewpoints, and draw logical conclusions (Gunning, 2000).

We also engage in *aesthetic reading,* in which the reader's attention is centered on the literacy style of a piece and the feelings that are engendered by reading the piece (Rosenblatt, 1978). Reading aesthetically results in a deeper level of involvement with the reader identifying with the characters and picturing the story in his or her mind (Cox and Many, 1992).

Both critical and aesthetic reading involve thinking about the text in relation to the readers' beliefs. For example, when Mrs. Gomez, the intermediate-level inclusion teacher, was working on critical and aesthetic reading in a third grade classroom, she had the students read the passage about Pat and her father (Apply the Concept 5.3). After reading she asked the students, "Have you ever had an experience that made you feel like Pat?" Figure 5.7 lists sample areas of critical and aesthetic reading and sample comments teachers might use to encourage critical and aesthetic reading.

Guidelines for Teaching Reading Comprehension

If comprehension is the essence of reading, how do we go about teaching students with learning and behavior problems to be effective comprehenders? Twenty years ago observational research indicated that teachers spent little time teaching children how to comprehend (Duffy, Lanier, and Roehler, 1980; Durkin, 1978–1979). For example, in Durkin's observational studies of reading instruction in fourth grade classrooms, only 20 minutes of comprehension instruction was observed in more than 4,000 minutes of reading instruction. Much of what teachers did to "teach" comprehension was ask questions, have students respond, and provide feedback. Furthermore, they provided a steady diet of literal or textually explicit comprehension questions, a ratio of 4:1 literal to inferential, with lower reading groups getting asked even more literal questions than higher-level groups (Guszak, 1972).

Since then, instructional research and practice has focused on how to teach reading comprehension. One of the keys to teaching reading comprehension, particularly for students with learning and behavior problems, is to teach these students to use

■ **FIGURE 5.7** *Critical and Aesthetic Reading*

Critical Reading

Critical reading: The reader reflects upon and makes judgments about the content or information in the piece.

Sample Areas of Reflection or Judgment

Sample Comments

Reality or Fantasy	I don't think the author expected us to think this could really happen.
Fact or Opinion	You really get the idea they are pushing their point of view.
Adequacy and Validity	Some of this information just isn't right.
Worth	This piece really helped me write my report.
	I think this article could hurt his political campaign.

Aesthetic Reading

Aesthetic reading: The reader reflects upon and makes judgments about the literary style of a piece.

Sample Areas of Reflection or Judgment

Sample Comments

Plot	I like the way the author always kept me interested in what was happening.
Characters	I didn't know enough about the witch to really understand why she did it.
Imagery	I could just picture myself being there.
Language	When the author said, "That was one frightened man," I felt a chill in my body.

---

comprehension and comprehension monitoring strategies (for reviews see Mastropieri and Scruggs, 1997; Swanson, 1999b). This includes such strategies as:

— *Activating background knowledge:* Thinking about what you already know about the topic and how your knowledge relates to what you are reading.

— *Predicting:* Making predictions about what is going to happen or what will be learned from reading the text.

— *Generating questions:* Asking relevant questions that promote understanding such as who, what, when, where, why, and how questions.

— *Clarifying:* Clarifying unclear concepts or vocabulary.

— *Summarizing:* Determining the main ideas and important concepts related to the main idea.

— *Using text structure:* Using knowledge of different text structures (e.g., narrative, expositive) as a framework for comprehension.

— *Comprehension monitoring:* Checking for understanding and using "fix-up" strategies (e.g., rereading, clarifying a concept) to facilitate comprehension.

In other words, we need to teach these students cognitive strategies that will provide them with the tools for understanding and constructing meaning from what they are reading.

Not only has intervention research provided us information on the importance of teaching comprehension and comprehension monitoring strategies, it has also provided us with evidence of how to teach these strategies. As is the case with higher-level academic learning, this is particularly challenging because comprehension involves thinking processes that are not nearly so visible as in other skills such as spelling and math calculations. Therefore, our instruction in reading comprehension should incorporate many of the aspects of cognitive behavior principles and scaffold instruction (see Chapter Two) including explicit instruction in:

— Providing rationales and evidence for the effectiveness of its use
— Describing and modeling the strategy using "thinking aloud"
— Providing supported practice and feedback
— Providing independent practice
— Teaching for generalization (i.e., when and where strategies apply) and maintenance

This instruction can be accomplished through more direct explanations and mental modeling associated with cognitive strategy instruction and exemplified in the Strategies Intervention Model (Deshler and Schumaker, 1986) in Chapter Two, or through more interactive dialogues that are based on a sociocultural theory of cognitive development. This instruction engages students and teachers in instructional conversations and demonstrations about how the strategies work as is exemplified in the Early Literacy Project (Englert, Rozendal, and Mariage, 1994) described in Chapter Two and the Benchmark School Reading Program (Gaskins, Anderson, Pressley, Cunicelli, and Satlow, 1993; Pressley et al., 1992). Using scaffolded instruction, the teacher's instruction is guided as much out of the analysis of the learner's understanding as it is from the analysis of the text (Dole, Brown, and Tranthen, 1996; Pearson and Fielding, 1991; Pressley, Brown, El-Dinary, and Afflerbach, 1995).

Based on notions from information processing and schema theories, our instruction should also assist students in activating their prior knowledge about the topic before they read so that they can apply this knowledge during reading and after they read.

Our instruction should also demonstrate to students the importance of predicting and questioning as they read. In this way, comprehension is the association of new information with prior knowledge or experience (Perez and Torres-Guzman, 1992; Pressley, 2000).

Comprehension instruction should encourage students to engage actively in discussions not only related to the content of the text but also instructional conversations about the reading process. These discussions can be prompted by:

1. *Before reading,* activate the students' background knowledge for the selected passage and/ or provide experiences to enrich their backgrounds. Assist students in thinking about how this text may be related to other texts in terms of content, storyline, and text structure. Help them set purposes for reading by predicting and asking questions about what they are going to read.
2. *During reading,* encourage students to self-question and monitor their comprehension as they read.
3. *After reading,* use follow-up activities such as:
   a. Discussions that focus on the content of the reading as well as evaluation of the content and the writing style
   b. Discussions that encourage students to generate more questions and ideas for further reading and investigation
   c. Retellings that assist students in summarizing and organizing what they have read

The idea behind explicit instruction of comprehension is that comprehension can be improved by teaching students to use specific cognitive strategies or to reason strategically when they encounter barriers to comprehension when reading. The goal is to achieve competent and self-regulated reading (National Reading Panel, 2000). Tech Talk describes how text enhancements and speech feedback provided by the computer can support self-regulated reading.

Whether reading narrative or expository texts, comprehension strategy instruction should focus on (a) previewing, predicting, and activating background knowledge; (b) questioning to promote understanding, clarifying, and monitoring comprehension, and

TECH TALK 5.1

USING COMPUTER-BASED TEXT ENHANCEMENTS AND SPEECH FEEDBACK TO SUPPORT READING COMPREHENSION

Today, more textbooks and literature books are becoming available on CD-ROM. This provides students the opportunity to read with support. Through speech feedback students have the opportunity to listen as the text is read to them or to request the computer to read specific words, phrases, or sentences that are difficult. It also provides for text enhancements such as:

- Definitions for vocabulary
- Paraphrases of the text that have lower readability levels
- Supplemental background information
- Statements of the main ideas
- Pronunciation of individual words
- Word, phrases, or sentences read in another language

Researchers have investigated the use of text enhancements with students who have reading/learning problems. One would suspect that the results would be positive. For example, Reinking and colleagues (Rienking and Schreiner, 1988) found that students who had the option to use these enhancements or were required to do so had better reading comprehension than students who read on-line or read off-line. Using the enhancements was more important the more difficult the text. However, this has not necessarily been the case. In a later study with students who had more computer experience Reinking (1988) and several other researchers (Feldmann and Fish, 1991; Swanson and Trahan, 1992) found no clearcut advantage for using the text enhancements. What is important to consider in using these types of enhancements is the characteristics of the reader in relation to the text being read. For example, if students have limited background knowledge about a topic, then the supplemental information or simple definitions of key vocabulary may be helpful.

Speech feedback and the simultaneous visual and auditory presentation of the text have also been investigated and again the research suggests that it is important to consider the students' knowledge and skills (Okolo et al., 2000). For example, Elkind and colleagues (Elkind, 1998a; Elkind, Black, and Murray, 1996) found that simultaneous auditory and visual presentation of text through speech feedback was most advantageous for students who had poor reading rate, comprehension, or endurance when reading but had good oral language capabilities and strengths in integrating auditory and visual information. This was not the case for students who had difficulty integrating auditory and visual information, who read faster than the rate spoken by the computer, or who had relatively good comprehension reading off-line (Elkind, 1998b).

(c) summarizing information. The next three sections highlight specific teaching strategies associated with these three goals.

Previewing, Predicting, and Activating Prior Knowledge

Previewing, predicting, and activating/building background knowledge are all instructional techniques that help get students ready to read. Taking time to prepare students before they read can pay big dividends in terms of their understanding and finding reading an enjoyable experience (Graves, Juel, and Graves, 1998). Graves and his colleagues suggest that prereading activities should:

- Motivate and set purposes for reading
- Activate and build background knowledge
- Build text-specific knowledge
- Relate reading to students' lives
- Preteach vocabulary and concepts
- Provide opportunities for prequestioning, predicting, and direction setting

What instructional techniques can the teacher use that will help students with learning and behavior problems

APPLY THE CONCEPT 5.4

*STRATEGIES FOR PROMOTING READING COMPREHENSION
FOR STUDENTS WHO ARE CULTURALLY DIVERSE
AND/OR ENGLISH-LANGUAGE LEARNERS*

For students from culturally and linguistically diverse backgrounds and for English-language learners, a number of strategies can be used to promote reading comprehension.

Making Input More Comprehensible
- Begin teaching new concepts by working from the students' prior knowledge and incorporating the funds of knowledge from the students' communities.
- Use demonstrations and gesture to augment oral and written communication.
- Discuss connections between the concepts being read and the students' home cultures.
- Encourage students to share the new vocabulary in the first language and incorporate the first language into instruction.
- If students share a common first language, pair more proficient English-language learners with less proficient peers, and encourage students to discuss what they are reading.
- Provide opportunities for students to learn to read and to read in their first language.

- Highlight key words and phrases in text and incorporate them into semantic maps.
- Teach text structures and use visual representations of text structures.
- When asking questions or discussing new ideas or vocabulary, slow the pace.
- Repeat key ideas and write them.
- Use "think-alouds" to make comprehension strategies more explicit.

Incorporating Multicultural Literature into the Reading Program
- Select literature that reflects various cultures.
- Study authors from various cultures.
- Read literature that incorporates various dialects.
- Select genres that are typical of different cultures.
- Use book lists, directories, Websites, and textbooks on multicultural education as resources for multicultural literature.
- In the classroom and school libraries, have literature written in the students' first languages available to the students.

activate relevant background knowledge (schema), motivate them to read, assist students in making predictions about what they are going to be reading, preview the reading, and assist them in becoming familiar with difficult vocabulary? Four such techniques are discussed: brainstorming, the PreReading Plan (Langer, 1981), Text Preview (Graves, Prenn, and Cooke, 1985; Grave, Juel, and Graves, 2001), and K-W-L (Ogle, 1986).

Activating prior knowledge is particularly important for students with learning and behavior problems. It is also important for second language learners or students from culturally diverse backgrounds, for they bring unique real-world knowledge to learning situations (Bos and Reyes, 1996; Echevarria and Graves, 1998; Jiménez and Gersten, 1999). As with all learners, their prior knowledge is crucial to the

successful construction of meaning. Apply the Concept 5.4 presents ideas for facilitating and teaching comprehension with these students. While the strategies in this section may be used as specific activities, they should also be integrated into reading lessons and discussions about the literature and literacy.

Brainstorming
Brainstorming is a teaching strategy that activates the students' relevant prior knowledge, aids the teacher in determining the extent of the students' prior knowledge, and stimulates interest in the topic.

— PROCEDURES: Brainstorming works best with groups of students reading the same or related selections. Prior to beginning the activity, determine the major topic or concept presented in the selection(s).

Next, decide what to use as a stimulus to represent that topic. It might be a single word or phrase, a picture, a poem, or a short excerpt from the reading passage. Prior to reading, conduct the brainstorming session.

1. Present the stimulus to the students.
2. Ask the students to list as many words or phrases as they can associate with the stimulus. Encourage them to think about everything they know about the topic or concept. Allow several minutes for the students to think and get ready to report their ideas. (If appropriate, have students write their ideas.)
3. Record their associations on the board. Ask for other associations and add them to the list. Do not make judgments concerning the appropriateness of the associations.
4. With the students, categorize the associations. Clarify the ideas and discuss what titles to use for the categories.

You may also want to organize the ideas into a map. Strategies for organizing story maps are discussed later in this chapter, and strategies for developing content maps are discussed in Chapter Seven.

Although the brainstorming activity usually ends before reading begins, we recommend that you encourage students to continue to add to their list of associations as they read and after they read. Review the list and add new associations.

■ **COMMENTS:** Brainstorming is a quick and simple way of activating background knowledge. It usually takes five to ten minutes to complete. However, for some student and topic combinations, simple associations without further discussion may not provide enough input to activate and build the students' prior knowledge. The next procedure provides additional activities for further activating relevant schema.

PreReading Plan

The PreReading Plan (PReP) is a three-phase instructional/assessment strategy that builds on the instructional activity of brainstorming. Designed by Langer (1981), it assists students in accessing knowl-

edge related to the major concepts presented in a reading selection.

■ **PROCEDURES:** Prior to beginning the activity, provide a phrase or picture to stimulate group discussion about a key concept in the text. For example, if a science selection was about the types and characteristics of mammals, *mammals* might serve as the stimulus word. After introducing the topic, conduct the following three-phase process:

1. *Initial association with the concept.* Cue the students by saying, "Say anything that comes to mind when . . . (e.g., you hear the word *mammals*)." Have the students free associate, writing a list of their associations. Record the associations on the board, noting the student's name by each association.
2. *Reflections on initial associations.* Now ask the students, "What made you think . . . (the responses given by each of the students during Phase 1)?" This phase requires the students to bring to the conscious level their prior knowledge and how it relates to the key concept. It also allows the students to listen to each other's responses. Langer states, "Through this procedure they [students] gain the insight which permits them to evaluate the utility of these ideas in the reading experience" (1981, p. 154).
3. *Reformation of knowledge.* After each student has had an opportunity to think and tell about what triggered his or her ideas, ask the students, "Based on our discussion, have you any new ideas about . . . (e.g., mammals)?" This phase gives the students the opportunity to discuss how they have elaborated or changed their ideas based on the previous discussion. Because the students have the opportunity to listen to other students, new links between prior knowledge and the key concept are also formed.

Based on the information gathered during this three-phase procedure, Langer presents a means of assessing prior knowledge into levels to determine if further concept building will need to be completed prior to reading (see Figure 5.8). In a study with Nich-

■ **FIGURE 5.8** *PreReading Plan: Levels of Prior Knowledge*

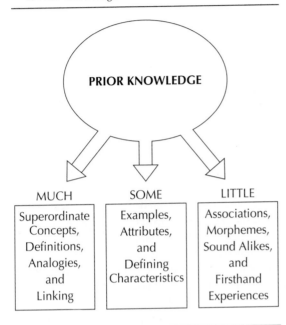

Source: J. A. Langer, "Facilitating Text Processing: The Elaboration of Prior Knowledge," in J. A. Langer and M. T. Smith-Burke, (Eds.). *Reader Meets Author/Bridging the Gap* (Newark, DE.: International Reading Association, 1982), p. 156. Reprinted by permission of Judith A. Langer and the International Reading Association.

olich (Langer and Nicholich, 1981), Langer found this assessment method a better predictor of reading comprehension for a particular passage than either IQ or standardized reading scores. The three levels and their instructional implications are:

1. *Much knowledge.* Students whose free associations reflect superordinate concepts, definitions, analogies, or a linking of the key concept to other relevant concepts demonstrate *much* integration of the key concept with concepts already in accessible memory. Comprehension for these students should be adequate.
2. *Some knowledge.* Students whose free associations are primarily examples, attributes, or defining characteristics have *some* knowledge concerning the concepts being taught. Com-

prehension should be adequate, but some instructional activities that assist the students in making the critical links between existing and new knowledge may be necessary.

3. *Little knowledge.* Students whose free associations reflect morphemes (prefixes, suffixes, root words), rhyming words, or unelaborated or unrelated firsthand experiences demonstrate *little* knowledge of the concept. These students need concept instruction before reading commences, with the reported firsthand experiences serving as a reference point for starting instruction.

— COMMENTS: The PreReading Plan provides a direct means of activating the students' background knowledge. The authors have frequently used both brainstorming and PReP, particularly with upper elementary and secondary students with learning and behavior problems. We find that taking the extra time to conduct the PreReading Plan is worthwhile since it requires the students to bring to the conscious level why they made their associations, and it gives them the opportunity to reflect on what they have learned through the discussion. Have students add to and adjust their lists during reading and after they read.

Text Preview

Text Preview is designed to increase students' prior knowledge, provide motivation for students to read, and provide a scaffold for text comprehension (Graves, et al., 1985; Graves, et al., 2001). Text Preview can be used with students at varying reading and grade levels and with narrative or expository texts.

— PROCEDURES: The two major steps in using Text Preview are preparing the preview and then using it with the students.

1. *Preparation and construction of Text Previews.* A Text Preview is a synopsis of a text that is written in an organized framework that enhances student comprehension of the text by bridging it to their real-world experiences. It has three sections: (a) one that piques student interest, (b) a brief discussion of the text's theme (e.g., for stories this could include the setting, character descriptions, and

essential story organization, and (c) questions or directions that guide student reading.

2. *Presentation of Text Previews.* The following steps are suggested for implementing the Text Preview and should take no longer than five to ten minutes (Graves et al., 1985):
   - Cue students about the new reading.
   - Discuss an interesting aspect of the story or content that will pique motivation.
   - Make connections to the students' lives and world knowledge.
   - Present the questions or directions that should guide student reading.
   - Have students read the text.

Discussing an interesting aspect of the story or content helps students delve into reading materials—knowing that there will be new knowledge, discoveries, and/or excitement. These motivation activities often involve hands-on experiences and intrigue that are then tied to the story being read. For example, "Feel these fabrics and tell me what it makes you think about and how it makes you feel. In the story, Robbie has a special blanket made out of these fabrics (satin and flannel). As you read the story think about what is special about this blanket and how it feels." Making connections to the students' lives and their world knowledge

also serves to activate background knowledge and create motivation. Using a Connections Chart such as the one in Figure 5.9 helps students think about connections they can make to their own lives and to world knowledge they have about a topic. For example, in reading about dolphins, students can list experiences they have had with dolphins as well as facts they know about dolphins before they read and then add to the list after they read.

— COMMENTS: While Text Previews take time to prepare, students report that previews enable them to understand the text to a fuller extent (Chen and Graves, 1995; Dole, Valencia, Greer, and Wardrop, 1991). Text Previews can be especially beneficial for students who have learning or behavior problems and with English-language learners.

When using Text Previews with expository text, the teacher may want to include important points, vocabulary, and more implicit and experience-based thinking (Readence, Bean, and Baldwin, 1995). Additionally, teachers can use Text Previews as potential writing assignments. Students can be assigned to develop Text Previews for other students' guided reading. Critical thinking about the ideas presented in a text selection will ensue as students create Text Previews for one another.

■ **FIGURE 5.9** *Connections Chart about Dolphins*

Connection to Dolphins

Connections to Our Experiences	Connections to World Knowledge
Reneé, Maria, Jon, Marcos petted the dolphins at Sea World	Skin is soft and smooth
Peter saw dolphins swim under boat when his family was sailing in Florida	Seem to communicate with one another
Everyone has seen dolphins on TV	Bottle nosed dolphin
	Have to come to surface to breathe

K-W-L

K-W-L is a strategy designed to activate students' background knowledge and to assist students in setting purposes for reading expository text (Bryant, 1998; Ogle, 1986, 1989). This strategy is based on research that highlights the importance of background knowledge in constructing meaning (e.g., Anderson, Reynolds, Schallert, and Goetz, 1977).

— **PROCEDURES:** The K-W-L strategy consists of three basic steps representative of the cognitive/metacognitive steps employed by the students as they utilize the strategy:

> accessing what I <u>K</u>now
> determining what I <u>W</u>ant to Learn
> recalling what I did <u>L</u>earn

To assist the students in using the strategy, Ogle developed a simple worksheet for the students to complete during the thinking-reading process (see Figure 5.10).

During the *Know* step the teacher and students engage in a discussion designed to assist students in thinking about what they already know about the topic of the text. For this step the teacher starts by using a *brainstorm* procedure (see section on Brainstorming). As in the PreReading Plan, students are encouraged to discuss where or how they learned the information so as to provide information concerning the source and substantiveness of their ideas. After brainstorming, the teachers and students discuss the general *categories of information* likely to be encountered when they read, and how their brainstormed ideas could help them determine the categories. "For example, the teacher might say 'I see three different pieces of information about how turtles look. Description of looks is certainly one category of information I would expect this article to include'" (Ogle, 1986, p. 566).

During the *Want to Learn* step, the teacher and students discuss what they want to learn from reading the article. While most of the W step utilizes group discussion, before students begin to read, they each write down the specific questions in which they are most interested.

During the *What I Learned* step, the students write what they learned from reading. They should also

---

■ **FIGURE 5.10** *K-W-L-Q Chart for Pond and Pond Life*

All about Ponds (K-W-L-Q)

What I Know	What I Want to Know	What I Learned	More Questions I Have
Contains water	How does the pond get its water?	Underground springs and rain	Why do ponds die?
Smaller than a lake	Why are ponds green and muddy?	Algae and other plants make it green	What happens to a pond in winter?
Fish	Does the temperature change?	Like the air but temperature is less affected the deeper you go	How does algae help or hurt a pond?
Ducks			
Frogs			
Muddy	What fish live in the pond?	Blue gill, trout, bass, catfish	
Algae	What insects live in the pond?	Dragon flies, mosquitoes, water fleas	
Insect on top	What plants live in the pond?	Algae, cattails, water lilies	
Birds eat insects			

Source: Adapted from P. R. Schmidt, "KWLQ: Inquiry and Literacy Learning in Science," *The Reading Teachers, 52* (1999): 789–792.

check the questions that they generated in the *Want to Learn* step to see if they were addressed in the article.

— **COMMENTS:** K-W-L represents a strategy for assisting students in actively engaging in the reading process and for assisting teachers in teaching reading using an interactive model of reading. Informal evaluation of the strategy indicates that students recalled more information in articles when they used K-W-L and that they enjoyed using the strategy and used it independently (Ogle, 1986). Carr and Ogle (1987) added mapping and summarizing activities to K-W-L to gain the advantage of these powerful comprehension tools. Ogle (1989) added a fourth column "what we still want to learn" and referred to this adaptation as KWL Plus. Bryant (1998) referred to it as K-W-W-L to assist students in generating questions and designing scientific experiments, and Schmidt (1999) referred to it as K-W-L-Q with the *Q* representing more questions. This addition encourages further research and reading.

Questioning Strategies

Asking questions is a major vehicle used by teachers to foster understanding and retention and check for comprehension. When questions are asked about information in text, that information is remembered better. Asking higher-level questions (see Figure 5.6) that require integration of background and text knowledge will promote deeper processing and therefore more learning (Sundbye, 1987), and simply asking "Why?" and "How?" can significantly increase retention of information (Menke and Pressley, 1994; Pressley, 1998).

However, simply asking questions does not ensure that students will develop questioning strategies. As already demonstrated, teacher and student questioning prior to reading helps to activate prior knowledge and to set purposes for reading. Self-questioning during reading (e.g., "Does this make sense?" "Am I understanding what I am reading?" "How does this relate to what I already know?" "What will happen next?") assist students in comprehension and monitoring comprehension (one of the metacognitive activities discussed in Chapter Two).

This section presents four techniques for teaching questioning strategies. These techniques require teachers to model comprehension questions and comprehension monitoring questions, teach students to recognize types of questions, and encourage students to self-question before, during, and after they read.

ReQuest or Reciprocal Questioning

The ReQuest procedure is a reciprocal questioning technique designed to assist students in formulating their own questions about what they read. The procedure was developed by Manzo (1969; Manzo and Manzo, 1993), who stressed the importance of students setting their own purposes for reading and asking their own questions as they read.

— **PROCEDURES:** This procedure relies heavily on modeling, which is a major premise of cognitive strategy instruction and sociocultural theory of learning (Chapter Two). To use this procedure, select materials at the students' instructional to independent reading levels. You and the students read a sentence or section of the passage and then take turns asking each other questions. Your role is to model "good" questioning and to provide feedback to students about their questions. In modeling, include higher level questions that require you to use scriptually and textually implicit information and that require critical and aesthetic reading. Also include monitoring questions (e.g. "Does this make sense?").

Manzo suggests that this procedure first be introduced on an individual basis and then used in small groups. The following explanation can be used to introduce ReQuest:

> The purpose of this lesson is to improve your understanding of what you read. We will each read silently the first sentence [section]. Then we will take turns asking questions about the sentence [section] and what it means. You will ask questions first, then I will ask questions. Try to ask the kinds of questions a teacher might ask in the way a teacher might ask them.
>
> You may ask me as many questions as you wish. When you are asking me questions, I will close my book (or pass the book to you if there is only one between us). When I ask questions, you close your book (Manzo, 1969, p. 124).

The rules are: (1) the answer "I don't know" is not allowed; (2) unclear questions are to be restated; and (3) uncertain answers are to be justified by reference to the text or other source material if necessary. In addition, you and the students may need to discuss unfamiliar vocabulary.

The procedure itself consists of the following steps:

1. *Silent reading.* You and the students read the sentence or section.
2. *Student questioning.* Close your book while the students ask questions. Model appropriate answers and reinforce appropriate questioning behavior. The students ask as many questions as possible.
3. *Teacher questioning.* The students close their books and you ask questions modeling a variety of question types (see Figure 5.6).
4. *Integration of the text.* After completing the procedure with the first sentence or section, repeat the process with subsequent sentences or sections. Integrate the new section with previous sections by asking questions that relate to new and old sections.
5. *Predictive questioning.* When the students have read enough to make a prediction about the rest of the passage, ask predictive questions (e.g., "What do you think will happen?" "Why do you think so?"). If the predictions and verification are reasonable, you and the students move to the next step.
6. *Reading.* You and the students read to the end of the passage to verify and discuss your predictions.

— **COMMENTS:** One important aspect of this strategy is the questions that the teacher models. Manzo and Manzo (1990, 1993) suggest that teachers employ a variety of questions including:

— *Predictable questions*—the typical *who, what, when, where, why,* and *how* questions
— *Mind-opening questions*—designed to help the students understand how written and oral language are used to communicate ideas

— *Introspective questions*—metacognitive questions oriented toward self-monitoring and self-evaluation
— *Ponderable questions*—questions that stimulate discussion and for which no right or wrong answer is apparent
— *Elaborative knowledge questions*—questions that require the students to integrate their background knowledge with the information given in the text.

The ReQuest procedure assists students in developing appropriate questions. We have used several variations of these procedures. For instance, we have introduced the ReQuest procedure as a game. The students and teacher take turns asking questions and keeping score of appropriate answers. We also recommend that the text be read in longer, more natural segments rather than individual sentences. Legenza (1974) has adapted this procedure by having kindergarten children ask questions about a picture rather than a text.

Question–Answer Relationships Strategy

The question–answer relationships (QARs) strategy (Raphael, 1982, 1984, 1986) is designed to assist students in labeling the type of questions being asked and to use this information to help guide them as they develop an answer. QARs was developed by Raphael and Pearson (1982) to facilitate correct responses to questions. The strategy is based on question–answer relationships developed by Pearson and Johnson (1978) (e.g., *textually explicit, textually implicit,* and *scriptually implicit*), discussed earlier in this chapter. It helps students realize they need to consider both the text and their prior knowledge when answering questions and to use strategic behavior to adjust the use of each of these sources.

— **PROCEDURES:** QARs was originally taught by Raphael (1984), using the three categories of information suggested in the Matrix for Reading Comprehension (Figure 5.6). The three categories were renamed for use with students.

1. *Right There.* Words used to create the question and words used for the answer are in the same sentence (textually explicit).

2. *Think and Search.* The answer is in the text, but words used to create the question and those used for an appropriate answer would not be in the same sentence (textually implicit).

3. *On My Own.* The answer is not found in the text but in one's head (scriptually implicit).

Based on input from teachers, Raphael (1986) modified these categories to include two major categories (*In the Book* and *In My Head*) and then further divided these categories, as shown on the cue card (Figure 5.11).

Raphael suggests the following procedure for introducing QARs. The first day, introduce the students to the concept of question–answer relationships (QARs), using the two major categories. Use several short passages (from two to five sentences) to demonstrate the relationships. Provide practice by asking students to identify the type of QAR, the answer to the question, and the strategy they used for finding the answer. The progression for teaching should be from highly supportive to independent:

1. Provide the text, questions, answers, QAR label for each question, and reason for why the label was appropriate.

2. Provide the text, questions, answers, and QAR label for each question. Have the students supply the reason for the label.

3. Provide the text, questions, and answers, and have the students supply the QAR labels and reasons for the labels.

4. Provide the text and questions, and have the students supply the answers, QAR labels, and the reasons for the labels.

When the students have a clear picture of the difference between *In My Head* and *In the Book,* teach the next level of differentiation for each one of the major categories. First, work on *In the Book,* then go to *In My Head.* The key distinction between the two subcategories under *In My Head* (i.e., *Author and You* and *On My Own*) is "whether or not the reader needs to read the text for the questions to make sense" (Raphael, 1986, p. 519). When the information must come from the reader, but in connection with the in-

formation presented by the author, then the QAR is *Author and You.* For example, in the story about Pat and her father (Apply the Concept 5.3), the question "How did the fisherman alert the police?" requires the reader to use his or her background knowledge but relate it to the information in the text. In comparison, the question "What would you have done if you were in Pat's shoes?" is an example of an *On My Own* QAR.

Once the students are effectively using the QAR strategy in short passages, gradually increase the length of the passages and the variety of reading materials. Review the strategy and model its use on the first question. Have the students then use the strategy to complete the rest of the questions.

■ **COMMENTS:** After teaching this strategy using the original three categories, Raphael (1984) found that groups of low-, average-, and high-achieving, fourth-grade students had higher performance on a comprehension test and gave evidence that the question-answer relationships strategy transferred to reading improvement in the content areas. This strategy helped lower-achieving students to answer all three types of questions, particularly their performance on textually explicit and implicit questions. Simmonds (1992) taught 24 special education teachers to implement either QARS or selected traditional methods of reading comprehension instruction including the skills of answering literal questions (recall of factual information and main ideas), locating supportive details, and drawing conclusions. Using a lesson sequence similar to the one just described, they found students who participated in the QARS instruction performed better than the other students on tests of comprehension over the social studies text they read. Labeling the types of questions and then using that information to assist in answering questions appears to be an effective strategy for students and one that encourages active involvement in the comprehension process.

Self-Questioning Strategies

Self-questioning strategies are a good example of how metacognition assists students in reading. These questions typically have the student focus on activating

■ **FIGURE 5.11**   *Cue Card for Question–Answer Relationships (QARS)*

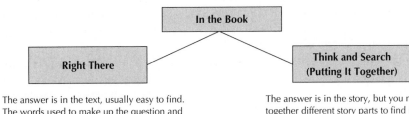

The answer is in the text, usually easy to find. The words used to make up the question and words used to answer the question are **Right There** in the same sentence.

The answer is in the story, but you need to put together different story parts to find it. Words for the question and words for the answer are not found in the same sentence. They come from different parts of the text.

The answer in *not* in the story. You need to think about what you already know, what the author tells you in the text, and how it fits together.

The answer is not in the story. You can even answer the question without reading the story. You need to use your own experience.

Source: Adapted from T. E. Raphael, "Teaching Question-Answer Relationships, Revisited," *The Reading Teacher, 39*(6) (1986), 516–523.

prior knowledge and setting purposes for reading, asking questions to assist the comprehension process, checking understanding during reading, and reviewing after reading to determine understanding. For example, Alvermann and her colleagues (Alvermann et al., 1989) suggest the following self-questions to foster comprehension:

Think Ahead
— What is this section about?
— What do I already know about the topic?
— What do I want to find out?
— What is my goal?
— How should I go about reading to meet my goal?

Think While Reading
— What have I read about so far?
— Do I understand it?
— If not, what should I do?
— What is the author saying, and what did I think about it?

Think Back
— Have I learned what I wanted to learn?
— How can I use what I read?

One strategy, developed by Wong and Jones (1982), focuses primarily on asking questions related to the main idea. When investigating the reading comprehension skills of upper elementary students with learning disabilities, Wong (1979) found that in text without inserted questions, the students had poorer recall of the thematically important ideas than average readers. She hypothesized that the students do not self-question when they read. To demonstrate this point, she inserted questions in the text for a second group of students with learning disabilities and average students, and she no longer found significant differences between the recall of the two types of readers. Whereas the inserted questions resulted in significantly better recall for the students with learning disabilities, no such effect was evident with average readers, indicating that the students with learning disabilities were not as effective at self-questioning.

Based on this research, Wong and Jones (1982) developed a self-questioning technique to determine if junior-high students with learning disabilities could be taught to self-question as they read.

— **PROCEDURES:** First, teach the students the concept of a main idea. During this stage, teach the students how to identify the main idea(s) in paragraphs. For Wong and her colleagues, this took up to three one-hour sessions.

During the next stage, teach the students the steps in self-questioning strategy:

1. *What are you studying this passage for?* (So you can answer some questions you will be given later.)
2. *Find the main idea(s) in the paragraph and underline it (them).*
3. *Think of a question about the main idea you have underlined. Remember what a good question should be like.* ("Good questions" are those that directly focus on important textual elements. Write the question in the margin.)
4. *Learn the answer to your question.* (Write the answer in the margin.)
5. *Always look back at the previous questions and answers to see how each successive question and answer provide you with more information.*

In teaching, model the strategy and then have the students study the steps in the strategy. Next, have the students practice using this strategy on individual paragraphs and provide them with immediate corrective feedback. Have the students use a cue card to assist them in remembering the steps in the strategy. When the students are successful, switch to multiple paragraph passages and gradually fade the use of the cue card. Give feedback at the end of each passage. At the end of each lesson, discuss the students' progress and the usefulness of the self-questioning strategy.

— **COMMENTS:** Results from the Wong and Jones (1982) study indicate the students with learning disabilities who learned the self-questioning strategy performed significantly higher on comprehension tests than students who were not taught the strategy.

Another self-questioning strategy was developed at the Kansas University Center for Research on Learning (Clark, Deschler, Shumaker, Alley, and Warner, 1984; Shumaker, Deshler, Nolan, and Alley, 1994). It was used to assist secondary-level students with learning disabilities in comprehending and remembering the important information presented in content area textbooks. Students read the title of a section and then ask questions regarding *who, what, when, where, why, which,* and/or *how.* They then read the section to answer their question(s).

We have used the WH Questions Plus HOW to facilitate the comprehension of elementary students with learning and behavior problems. When reading expository text, students mark in the text using symbols where they find the answers to the WH questions plus HOW and then record their answers on the textframe in Figure 5.12. (If students cannot mark in the text, Post-its with the different symbols can be placed in the text.) We have also used the WH Questions Plus HOW to assist students in journal writing. We have found that using this strategy helps students understand what they read and to write journal entries that are more elaborated and comprehensible.

For self-questioning strategies to be effective for students with reading difficulties, it is important that teachers provide modeling, direct coaching, prompting, and guidance so that they can become facile with questioning (Chan, 1991; Gersten, Williams, Fuchs, and Baker, in press; Mastropieri, Scruggs, Hamilton, Wolfe, Whedon, and Canevaro, 1996). Furthermore, teaching students to stop and question themselves before, during, and/or upon completion of reading is another key element of success (Mastropieri and Scruggs, 1997).

Text Structure and Summarization Strategies

Using text structures to facilitate reading comprehension can be helpful for students, particularly for students with learning and behavior problems (Mastroprieri and Scruggs, 1997; Swanson, 1999). Often teachers divide text into two major types: narrative and expository. *Narrative texts* tell a story and can be

■ **FIGURE 5.12** *Frame for Answering WH and HOW Questions*

Student Name: _____

Title: _____

Pages: _____

Date: _____

| Who? |
| What? |
| Where? |
| When? |
| Why? |
| How? |

organized into components such as setting, problem statement, goals, event sequences or episodes, and ending. This component analysis has been referred to as story grammar and is a set of rules designed to show how the parts of a story are interrelated (Mandler and Johnson, 1977; Stein and Glenn, 1979). Generally, stories are easier for students to comprehend than expository text because the structure is more consistent and has a linear orientation, therefore making it more predictable. Typical questions that focus on story grammar include:

Where does the story take place (setting)?

When does the story take place (setting)?

Who are the main people in the story (characters)?

What problems does the main character face (problem)?

What are the main character's goals (goal)?

What does the main character want to do to solve the problem (goal)?

What are the main things that happened in the story to solve the problem (plot)?

How did each thing work out (plot)?

Is the problem finally resolved? If so, how (outcome/ending)?

Expository texts are designed to explain phenomena or provide information. These are the informational texts students encounter not only in school content area subjects such as social studies, science, math, and vocational education, but also in newspapers, magazines, and on the Internet. Expository texts can be more difficult to comprehend because there is more variation in the text organization (e.g., describing an object, comparing and contrasting two ideas, explaining a cause–effect relationship), the content may be less familiar, and there may be a high proportion of technical terms. Teaching types of expository texts can help students with comprehension problems understand the more complex scientific style of thinking that is evident in expository text. Figure 5.13 presents six types of expository texts with signal words and cohesive ties that note the relationships and sample frameworks that depict the relationships. These text structures can also guide the type of questions that

promote comprehension. For example, here are some questions that might be asked to help students understand the process of rusting (cause/effect structure) and how it relates to their lives (Muth, 1987):

What causes rusting?

What are some of the effects of rusting?

What are the conditions needed to cause rusting?

What kinds of things rust in your home and why?

What can be done around your home to prevent rusting? Why would these things work?

While the type of text may vary within an expository passage or paragraph, thinking about the specific type can facilitate comprehension. This section first discusses strategies for using story grammar to facilitate comprehension and then strategies that focus on expository text. More techniques related to expository texts are presented in Chapter Seven when discussing content area learning.

Story-Mapping and Story-Retelling Strategies

Story-retelling strategies provide the students with a framework for retelling the key points of narrative texts. The strategies can be combined with story maps, which provide the students with a visual guide to understanding and retelling stories.

Figure 5.14 shows the visual framework for a simple story.

Teachers have taught students with reading problems how to use story maps and story strategies to aid in comprehending and retelling stories (Bos 1999; Cain, 1996; Gurney, Gersten, Dimino, and Carnina, 1990; Idol, 1987a, 1987b; Williams, Brown, Silverstein, and deCani, 1994; Williams, 1998). For example, Idol (1987a, 1987b) used a model-lead-test paradigm (Carnine, Silbert, and Kameenui, 1997) to teach story mapping to five intermediate-grade students with learning disabilities. Bos (1987) used a story-retelling strategy to assist intermediate students with learning and language disabilities in retelling stories.

While these first two strategies focus on the components of the story, Williams (1998) has developed

■ **FIGURE 5.13**   *Types of Expository Texts*

Text Type	Cohesive Ties and Signal Words	Sample Frameworks
Description/ Enumerative Describes the characteristics, attributes, examples, or a series of facts about a topic	for example for instance in addition besides to illustrate characteristics are can be described as moreover such as in other words	
Sequential/How To Tell how to do something or a series of events presented in order	first, second, third next then last, finally before, after soon in the past currently in the future	
Compare/Contrast Two or more topics are compared according to the their likenesses and differences	different from same as, alike however in contrast in comparison, compared to instead of on the other hand whereas although while similarly yet still	

(continued)

FIGURE 5.13 *Continued*

Text Type	Cohesive Ties and Signal Words	Sample Frameworks
Cause/Effect Explanation of the reason(s) for something or why something happened and the resulting effect(s)	cause because therefore thus as a result of if . . . then consequently for this reason	
Problem/Solution Statement of a problem and possible solutions, sometimes with resulting effects	problem is possible solutions are one, two, next, last, etc., solutions as a result	
Argument/Persuasion Statement of a position on an issue with justification	the point is first, second, next, last reasons major reason consequently therefore	

a instructional lesson to assist students with severe learning disabilities to identify the themes of stories and relate them to their lives.

— **PROCEDURES:** Idol (1987b) used the story map in Figure 5.14 to teach story mapping. She used the following procedure to teach story mapping:

1. During the *model* phase, model how to use the story map by reading the story aloud, stopping at points where information pertaining to one of the story components is presented. Ask the students to label the part and then demonstrate how to write the information onto the story map. Have the students copy the information onto their own maps. If the information is implicit in the story, model how to generate the inference.

2. During the *lead* phase, have students read the story independently and complete their maps, prompting when necessary. Encourage the students to review their maps after completing the story, adding details that may have been omitted.

■ **FIGURE 5.14** *Simple Story Map*

NAME _____ DATE _____

| The Setting |
| Characters: Time: Place: |

↓

| The Problem |

↓

| The Goal |

| Action |

←→

↓

| The Outcome |

Source: "Group Story Mapping: A Comprehension Strategy for Both Skilled and Unskilled Readers," L. Idol, *Journal of Learning Disabilities, 20* (1987): 199. Reprinted by permission.

3. During the *test* phase, ask students to read a story, generate their map, and then answer questions such as: Who were the characters? Where did the story take place? What was the main character trying to accomplish?

One of the authors (Bos, 1987) used principles based on cognitive strategy instruction to teach a story-retelling strategy. The procedures are:

1. Motivate the students to learn the strategy by demonstrating how it will help them remember what they have read.

2. Describe the components in a story and the steps used to identify and remember the different components:

STORE the Story
Setting: Who, What, When, Where
Trouble: What is the trouble that the main character(s) needs to solve?
Order of Action: What action(s) does the main character(s) take to solve the problem?
Resolution: What was the outcome (resolution) for each action? How does the main character(s) react and feel?
End: What happened in the end?

Explain how this answering these questions will help the students STORE, or remember, the important parts of the story.

3. Practice together reading stories, labeling the components, and retelling the stories. The students can retell their stories to the teacher, to each other, tape record their retellings, or answer questions about the stories.

4. Have the students independently read stories and retell them by using the STORE the Story strategy.

Williams (1999) has developed an instructional program to assist students with learning disabilities generate themes for the stories and relate them to the students' lives. The lesson was organized around a single story and had five parts as demonstrated for the story. "Kate Shelly and the Midnight Limited." This story is about how Kate experienced great danger to warn the stationmaster that a railroad bridge had collapsed, and thereby avert the wreck of the Midnight Limited.

— *Prereading discussion about lesson purpose and story topic.* This includes discussion of the importance of identifying and understanding the theme.

— *Story reading.* Students listen to and/or read the story, discussing the story grammar components and the story (e.g., What do you think will happen next? Do you think Kate was brave? Why?).

— *Discussion to generate theme.* Teacher and students discuss five questions designed to help generate the theme.
  • Who is the main character? (Kate Shelly)
  • What did he or she do? (She ran more than a mile in a terrible storm to warn the stationmaster about a collapsed railroad bridge; she persevered.)
  • What happened? (She reached the station in time to save the train and the passengers.)
  • Was this good or bad? (Good.)
  • Why was this good or bad? (It was good that Kate persevered because she saved lives.)

— *Writing the theme.* The teachers and students write the theme using the format, "Kate should have persevered. We should persevere."

— *Generalization to real-life experiences.* Discussion is focused around the questions:
  • To whom would this theme apply?
  • When would it apply? In what situations?

Williams compared this theme discussion framework to more traditional discussions about stories.

— **COMMENTS:** Results from the Idol (1987b) and Bos (1999) studies indicate that students were able to recall substantially more relevant information after learning each strategy. They were also able to answer more explicit and implicit comprehension questions about the stories. Students were also more likely to label the parts of the story in their retellings, thereby providing the listener with a framework for listening. Results from the Williams (1999) study indicate that students were able to generate and apply qualitatively better themes. These same strategies have also been adapted and used to help students plan and write stories.

One aspect that is particularly challenging for students to comprehend is different characters' perspectives and internal reactions as the story progresses (Emery, 1996; Shannon, Kameenui, and Baumann, 1988). Emery (1996) suggests using story guides in which the story events are outlined in one column and different characters' perspectives are listed in subsequent columns. This assists the students in seeing how different characters react to different events in the story. Using "why" questions about the characters during discussions (e.g., "Why did the characters act that way?" "Why did the characters feel that way?") also promotes comprehension.

Paraphrasing Strategy

Getting the main idea(s), paraphrasing, and/or summarizing when reading expository materials is an important skill, particularly in content area subjects such as science and social studies. The paraphrasing strategy, developed and validated at Kansas University Center for Research on Learning (Schumaker, Denton, and Deshler, 1984) instructs students in recalling the main ideas and specific facts of materials they read.

— **PROCEDURES:** To teach the strategy, you would use the Strategy Intervention Model presented in Chapter 2.

The steps in the strategy that the students learn are as follows:

1. *Read a paragraph.* Read the paragraph silently. As you read, be sure to think about what the words mean.

2. *Ask yourself, "What were the main ideas and details of this paragraph?"* After reading the paragraph, ask yourself, "What were the main ideas and details?" This question helps you to think about what you just read. To help you, you may need to look quickly back over the paragraph and find the main idea and the details that are related to the main idea.

3. *Put the main idea and details in your own words.* Now put the main idea and details into your own words. When you put the information into your own words, it helps you remember the informa-

tion. Try to give at least two details related to the main idea.

The acronym for the steps in the strategy is RAP. (Paraphrasing is like rapping or talking to yourself.) Students are also given rules for finding the main idea. They are:

1. Look for it in the first sentence of the paragraph.
2. Look for repetitions of the same word or words in the whole paragraph (Schumaker, Denton, and Deshler, 1984, p. 59).

The criteria used when generating a paraphrase are: (1) must contain a complete thought, and have a subject and verb; (2) must be accurate; (3) must make sense; (4) must contain useful information; (5) must be in your own words; and (6) only one general statement per paragraph is allowed (Schumaker, Denton, and Deshler, 1984). Specifics for teaching the strategy, including a scripted lesson, cue cards for learning and generalizing the strategy, record and worksheets, and suggested materials for practicing the strategy, are presented in the instructors' guide, *The Paraphrasing Strategy* (Learning Strategies Curriculum) (Schumaker, et al., 1984).

— **COMMENTS:** Students with learning disabilities who learned and used the paraphrasing strategy increased their ability to answer comprehension questions about materials written at their grade level from 48 percent to 84 percent (Schumaker, et al., 1984). This strategy provides an example of how metacognitive skills can be taught to students. Although the research was conducted with high school students, we have used the strategy with upper elementary students and found it successful.

When using this strategy, the students orally repeat the paraphrases into a tape recorder rather than writing them. This approach seems particularly advantageous for students with learning and behavior problems, since many of them also experience writing problems. However, once the students have mastered the skill, it may be helpful for students to write their paraphrases. These can then serve as an overview from which the students can integrate the information across the entire passage.

We have had students put their paraphrases for each paragraph or section on Post-it notes so that they can then arrange the notes to make a summary of the whole reading selection. You and the students may also want to vary the size of the unit that the students paraphrase. For example, in some books it may be more advantageous to paraphrase each section or subsection rather than each paragraph.

Summarization Strategies

Summarization also requires the student to generate the main idea and important details from a text. Based on analyses of informational or expository texts, Brown and Day (1983) generated five rules for writing summaries:

1. Delete irrelevant or trivial information.
2. Delete redundant information.
3. Select topic sentences.
4. Substitute a superordinate term or event for a list of terms or actions.
5. Invent topic sentences when none are provided by the author.

Gajria and Salvia (1992) used these same rules to teach sixth through ninth grade students with learning disabilities how to summarize expository passages. Gajria and Salvia (1992) employed many of the principles of cognitive strategy instruction (see Chapter Two). The teaching principles include explicit explanation of the rules, modeling of the strategy, guided practice in controlled materials, monitoring with corrective feedback, independent practice, and teaching each rule to criterion.

— **PROCEDURES:** To teach the summarization strategy, use sets of short paragraphs, each set highlighting a different rule. In this way the rules can be explained, modeled, and practiced individually. Then apply the rules to informational passages. Gajria and Salvia (1992) adapted passages from the *Timed Reading Series* (Spargo, Williston, and Browning, 1980). As the students learn the rules and their application, give them greater responsibility for practicing the rules and checking that each rule has been applied. Figure 5.15 presents a

■ **FIGURE 5.15**   *Student Checklist for Monitoring Summaries*

How Good Is That Summary?

Student: _____   Date: _____

Title: _____

Pages: _____

Summary:

_____

_____

_____

Rating: 3 = Clear, Concise Summary
          2 = Somewhat Clear, Concise Summary
          1 = Several Sentences That Do Not Accurately Summarize Information
          0 = Not Completed

____   Does the summary state the **main idea**?

____   Is the **main idea** stated first?

____   Does the summary give *only* **the most important information**?

____   Is the summary brief with **unimportant and redundant information** deleted?

____   Is the summary written well and clear?

checklist students can use to judge the qualities of their summaries and teachers can use to monitor student progress.

■ **COMMENTS:** When Gajria and Salvia (1992) taught the summarization strategy to 15 students with learning disabilities they found that at the end of instruction (ranging from 6.5 to 11 hours), students in the trained group performed significantly better than an untrained control group of students with learning disabilities on main idea/inference questions and factual questions, better than a group of average-achieving students on main idea/inference questions, and similar to the average group on factual questions. Students who participated in the strategy instruction also generalized these skills as demonstrated by increased performance on a reading test.

Malone and Mastropieri (1992) taught middle school students with learning disabilities how to summarize and self-question using two questions:

■ Who or what is the passage about?
■ What is happening (to them)?

Using principles of direct instruction and explicit teaching of the summarization and self-questioning, they found that these middle school students outperformed students receiving traditional comprehension instruction on recall of the passage content and that they could generalize the strategy to new texts.

Using Multicomponent Cognitive Strategy Instruction to Teach Comprehension

So far we have discussed techniques to facilitate the use of specific comprehension skills such as activating prior knowledge, predicting, asking and answering questions, getting the main idea, and summarizing the text. Students with learning and behavior problems often have difficulty with a number of these skills. For example, even when Shane, an eighth-grade student with decoding and reading comprehension problems, is reading text that is easy for him to decode (about fifth grade level), he still has difficulty understanding what he reads. His approach to reading comprehension is to "just begin reading and read to the end." He reads quickly and when finished can answer detailed questions about what he has read if the information is provided in the text. If he is not sure about an idea, Shane reports, "I usually just skip it." He has difficulty generating a summary and reports that he does not make predictions during reading and does not think about how what he is reading relates to what he already knows. For students like Shane, who have several comprehension skills that need attention, research would suggest that it is more efficient and effective to teach a multicomponent strategy that includes several robust strategies such as predicting, questioning, and summarizing than to teach individual strategies (National Reading Panel, 2000; Swanson, 1999b). This section discusses one such multicomponent approach to teaching comprehension, reciprocal teaching (Palincsar and Brown, 1984; 1986; Rosenshine and Meister, 1994 for a review), and two adaptations of reciprocal teaching, collaborative strategic reading (Klingner and Vaughn, 1996; Vaughn and Klingner, 1999), and POSSE (Englert and Mariage, 1991).

All three are built on notions associated with metacognition, schema theory, and a sociocultural theory of learning. From metacognition comes the strong emphasis on comprehension monitoring (e.g., checking to see if understanding is adequate given the purposes for reading). From schema theory, these approaches incorporate activities that encourage students to activate and use relevant background knowledge. From a sociocultural theory of learning comes scaffolded instruction in which the teacher and students take turns assuming the leader role.

These instructional techniques build on the notion that successful comprehension and learning is based on six activities:

1. Clarifying the purpose of reading (i.e., understanding the task demands, both explicit and implicit)
2. Activating relevant background knowledge
3. Allocating attention on the major content at the expense of trivia
4. Evaluating content for internal consistency and compatibility with prior knowledge and common sense
5. Monitoring ongoing activities to see if comprehension is occurring, by engaging in such activities as periodic review and self-questioning
6. Drawing and testing inferences including interpretations, predictions, and conclusions (Brown, Palincsar, and Armbruster, 1984)

While all three approaches build on these activities, reciprocal teaching was developed first and collaborative strategic reading and POSSE further elaborate on reciprocal teaching.

Reciprocal Teaching

In the initial research on reciprocal teaching Palincsar and Brown (Palincsar, 1982; Palincsar and Brown, 1984) chose four comprehension strategies to teach seventh-grade students who had average decoding skills but had significant difficulty with comprehension. The four strategies were

— Predicting
— Clarifying
— Questioning
— Summarizing

They used an interactive mode of teaching that emphasized modeling, feedback, and scaffolded instruction.

— **PROCEDURES:** The procedure used to teach the four strategies was *reciprocal teaching,* a technique in which the teacher and students took turns leading a dialogue that covered sections of the text. The procedure is similar to, but more extensive than, the reciprocal questioning used with the ReQuest procedure (Manzo, 1969, 1993), discussed in the section on questioning. Palincsar and Brown (1984) described the teaching procedure as follows:

> The basic procedure was that an adult teacher, working individually with a seventh-grade poor reader, assigned a segment of the passage to be read and either indicated that it was her turn to be the teacher or assigned the student to teach the segment. The adult teacher and the student then read the assigned segment. After reading the text, the teacher (student or adult) for that segment asked a question that a teacher or test might ask on the segment, summarized the content, discussed and clarified any difficulties, and finally made a prediction about future content. All of these activities were embedded in as natural a dialogue as possible, with the teacher and student giving feedback to each other. (Palincsar and Brown, 1984, pp. 124–125)

The teacher initially modeled the leader role and as the students assumed the role provided feedback by using:

> *Modeling.* "A question I would have asked would be . . ."
>
> *Prompting.* "What question do you think might be on a test?"
>
> *Instruction.* "Remember, a summary is a short version—it doesn't include details."
>
> *Modifying the activity.* "If you can't think of a question right now, go ahead and summarize and then see if you can think of one."
>
> *Praise.* "That was a clear question, because I knew what you wanted." "Excellent prediction—let's see if you're right."
>
> *Corrective feedback.* "That was interesting information. It was information I would call a detail. Can you find the most important information?"

Palincsar (1988) suggests that to introduce reciprocal teaching, it is logical to start with a discussion regarding why text may be difficult to understand, why it is important to have a strategic approach to reading and studying, and how reciprocal teaching will help students understand and monitor their understanding. The students are given an overall description emphasizing the use of interactive dialogues or discussions and of a rotating leader. To ensure a level of competency, each strategy is introduced individually and in a functional manner (e.g., summarize a television show or movie) and opportunities provided for the students to practice using the strategy. Palincsar (1988) provides a number of suggestions regarding each comprehension strategy:

Predicting
- Begin a new passage by having students predict based on the title.
- Encourage students to share information they already know about the topic.
- Refer to, and interweave the text with, their predictions and background knowledge as you read.
- Use headings to help students make predictions.
- Use other opportunities to predict, such as when the author asks questions or gives information about what will be covered next.
- Predictions should be used in an opportunistic and flexible manner.

Questioning
- Encourage students to ask "teacherlike" questions.
- Fill-in-the-blank questions should be discouraged.
- If the students cannot think of a question, have the students summarize first.
- Provide prompts if needed (e.g., identify the topic, provide a question word).

Summarizing
- Encourage students to identify the "main idea" and an example of supportive information.
- Encourage students to attempt their summaries without looking at the passage.
- Remind students of the rules for generating summaries:
  - Look for a topic sentence.
  - Make up a topic sentence if one is not available.

- Give a name to a list of items.
- Delete what is unimportant or redundant.

Clarifying
— Opportunities for clarifying generally occur when:
  - Referents (e.g., *you, he, it*) are unclear.
  - Difficult or unfamiliar vocabulary is presented.
  - Text is disorganized or information incomplete.
  - Unusual, idiomatic, or metaphorical expressions are used.
— Clarifying will not always be necessary.
— It may be helpful if students are asked to point out something that might be unclear to a younger student.

— **COMMENTS:** Palincsar and Brown studied the effectiveness of reciprocal teaching with poorly comprehending seventh-grade students who were taught individually or in groups of four to seven students (Brown, Palincsar, and Armbruster, 1984; Palincsar, 1986; Palincsar and Brown, 1984). They found the effects of this instruction to be substantial, reliable, durable over time, and generalizable to classroom settings. Even substantial improvements in standardized reading comprehension scores were reported. Lovett and her colleagues (1996) found reciprocal teaching to result in significant improvements in the comprehension skills of seventh- and eighth-grade students with reading disabilities compared to control students. Like Palincsar and Brown (1984) they also found reciprocal teaching to transfer to new texts. Lederer (2000) found reciprocal teaching improved the ability of fourth through sixth graders with learning disabilities to compose summaries of what they read but not in their ability to answer comprehension questions. When reciprocal teaching was used by three student teachers, the teachers reported that "once they got started, there were two specific trouble spots: teaching the clarification and question-generating strategies and bridging the transition from teacher to students control" (Speece, MacDonald, Kilsheimer, and Krist, 1997, p. 186). They reported that marking children's copies of the text with cue pictures, implementing a reward system to maintain focus, and selecting interesting and challenging literature were important for student success.

Collaborative Strategic Reading

By adding a cooperative learning component to reciprocal teaching and simplifying the cues for the different strategies, Vaughn, Klingner, and Schumm (1996; Klingner, Vaughn, and Schumm, 1998) developed collaborative strategic reading (CSR). This approach uses cooperative learning in diverse classrooms to help students read content area materials more efficiently and effectively (Klingner and Vaughn, 1998, 1999, 2000).

— **PROCEDURES:** As with reciprocal teaching, students learn four strategies: Preview (i.e., brainstorming and predicting), Click and Clunk (i.e., comprehension monitoring and clarifying), Get the Gist (i.e., summarization), and Wrap Up (i.e., self questioning and summarization). Preview is used before reading, and Wrap Up after reading the entire text.

Previewing: The goals of previewing are for students to: (a) learn as much about the passage as they can in 2 to 3 minutes, (b) activate their background knowledge about the topic, (c) make predictions about what they will read, and (d) pique their interest in the topic to foster active reading. Using the analogy of a movie preview is a good way to teach previewing. In previewing students are taught to "check-out" the headings, key words, pictures, tables, graphs, and other key information to identify what they know about the topic and to make predictions. Klingner and Vaughn (1998) report that Tiffany Royal, who teaches a fifth grade class with a number of students with learning and behavior problems, gives her students 1.5 minutes to write down everything they already know about the topic, 1 minute to share with the group, 1.5 minutes to write down predictions, and 1 minute to share. Figure 5.16 presents the four strategies for CSR with key questions the students can ask as they complete the process.

Click and Clunk: Students "click and clunk" while reading each section of the text. "Clicks" refer to the

■ **FIGURE 5.16** *Plan for Collaborative Strategic Reading (CSR)*

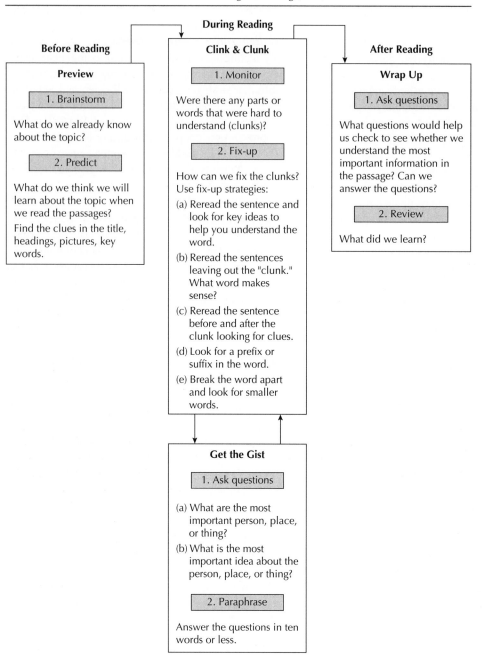

Source: Adapted from J. K. Klinger, and S. Vaughn, "Promoting Reading Comprehension, Content Learning, and English Acquisition through Collaborative Strategic Reading (CSR)," *The Reading Teacher, 52* (1999): 738–747.

portions of the text that make sense, and "Clunks" are the portions in which comprehension isn't clear, (e.g., students do not know the meaning of a word). Clicking and clunking is designed to assist students in monitoring their comprehension and to employ "fix-up strategies" to clarify their understanding. Tiffany has placed the fix-up strategies on clunk cards so that the cooperative groups can use them during reading.

— Reread the sentence and look for ideas that help you understand the word.
— Reread the sentence leaving out the clunk. What word makes sense?
— Reread the sentences before and after the sentence with the clunk.
— Look for prefixes or suffixes in the word.
— Break the word apart and look for smaller words you know.

Getting the Gist: Students learn to get the gist by reading each section and then asking themselves:

— "Who or what is it about?"
— "What is most important about the who or what?"

The goal is to teach the students to restate in their own words the most important point as a way of making sure they understood what they read (Klingner and Vaughn, 1998). Students are taught that a "good" gist:

— Answers the two questions, "Who or what is it about?" and "What is most important about the who or what?
— Is paraphrased in your own words.
— Contains ten words or less (Fuchs et al., 1997).

In teaching how to get the gist we have used the analogy of a sand sieve to demonstrate that the sand (i.e., details) go through and all that is left are the rocks (i.e., main details that answer the two questions). Using the gists from several students or groups to discuss and construct a "best" gist is another technique that can assist students in understanding how to

get the gist or main idea. Students repeat the second and third strategies (Clink and Clunk and Get the Gist) for each paragraph or section of the passage. Having students keep a CSR Learning Log such as the one presented in Figure 5.17 can provide students with information that will assist them in completing the last strategy, Wrap Up.

Wrap Up: In the Wrap Up step students formulate questions and answers about the key ideas from the entire passage and discuss what they have learned. The goal is to improve students' knowledge, understanding, and memory for what they read (Klingner and Vaughn, 1998). For students with learning and language disabilities, it may be necessary to explicitly teach them to ask questions using the WH + How questions. Like reciprocal teaching, students are to think about questions that a teacher might ask. To assist students in generating higher-level questions, it is important to model question stems such as "What do you think would happen if . . . ?" "How were _____ and _____ the same? Different?" "Why do you think . . . ?" Students can use the gists they have generated for the different sections to think about the most important information in the whole passage.

Cooperative Learning Groups: Once students have developed proficiency in applying the comprehension strategies through teacher-led activities, the students learn to use CSR in peer-led cooperative learning groups of about four or five students. Typical roles used during CSR include:

— *Leader.* Leads group by saying what to read and what strategy to use next.
— *Clunk expert.* Reminds students to use clunk strategies to figure out a difficult word or concept.
— *Announcer.* Calls on different members to read and share ideas.
— *Encourager.* Watches the group and give encouragement and feedback.
— *Reporter.* During whole class wrap-up, reports to class the important ideas learned and favorite questions.
— *Time-keeper.* Keeps time and lets the group know when it is time to move on.

■ **FIGURE 5.17**   *Example of CSR Learning Log*

CSR Learning Log

Name: _____

Title: _____   Date: _____

Pages: _____

Preview
What I already know about the topic: _____

_____

What I predict I will learn: _____

_____

Clicks and Clunks
List your clunks and what they mean.

Getting the Gist
Write/tell the gists for the sections you read.

Wrap Up
What was the most important thing the entire passage was about? _____

_____

Write questions you may have for your classmates. _____

_____

What I learned. _____

_____

Roles should change on a regular basis. After wrapping up in their cooperative groups, a whole-class wrap up is completed to give the teacher and groups the opportunity to report and to discuss the content.

— **COMMENTS:** Collaborative strategic reading has been used by a number of classroom teachers who have students with learning and behavior problems and English-language learners included in their classrooms (Klingner, et al., 1998; Klingner and Vaughn, 1996; 2000). For example, seventh and eighth grade English-language learners with learning disabilities were taught to apply CSR while working on social studies content (Klingner and Vaughn, 1996). Students' reading comprehension scores for the passages they read as well as on standardized tests improved significantly. It has also been a successful practice with upper elementary and middle school students with reading problems (Klingner et al., 1998; Bryant, Vaughn, Linan-Thompson, Ugel, Hamff, and Hougen, 2000). For these students more intensive instruction including instruction in word recognition is recommended. Overall, the results demonstrate the effectiveness of explicit instruction of cognitive strategy training and comprehension monitoring in improving a range of reading comprehension skills.

POSSE (Predict, Organize, Search/Summarize, Evaluate)

Englert and Mariage (1990; 1991) combined reciprocal teaching and the teaching of expository text structure to develop a strategy called POSSE (Predict, Organize, Search, Summarize, and Evaluate).

— **PROCEDURES:** In the POSSE process, two of the strategies were presented before reading, Predict and Organize, and were led by the teacher. The other three strategies were used during reading, Search, Summarize, and Evaluate, and students took turns leading the discussion. The Predict step included having the students brainstorm and preview the text, similar to the procedure in CSR. In the Organize step, students categorized and labeled their ideas from the Predict process and generated a semantic map (see Figure 5.18). This map was then reviewed to help students identify unknown information and set the purpose for learning. During the Summarize step, the group leader began the dialogue by giving the main idea for the section and then discussing it with the students. When they agreed, it was recorded on the map. The group leader then asked questions to help the group generate supporting details about the main idea that were also recorded on the map. This was completed for each section until a semantic map was generated for the article. The Evaluate step included three reading strategies to further guide the group's discussion: *compare, clarify,* and *predict.* First, the student compared the map they generated prior to reading with the map they generated during reading. Second, the students asked questions to clarify unfamiliar vocabulary and unclear information. Third, the students predicted what the next section would be about. Finally, after reading the entire selection, they reviewed the Prediction and the Search/Summarize maps to compare their prior knowledge with what they read and to see if their prior concepts were confirmed or disconfirmed by the text.

To facilitate the students' use of the strategy in their discussions about the text, they emphasized the following cues through the use of a cue card:

> Predict
>> I predict that . . .
>> I'm remembering . . .
> Organize
>> I think one category might be . . .
> Search/Summarize
>> I think the main idea is . . .
>> My question about the main idea is . . .
> Evaluate
>> I think we did (did not) predict this main idea (Compare)
>> Are there any clarifications?
>> I predict the next part will be about . . . (p. 128).

— **COMMENTS:** Englert and Mariage (1991) taught fourth through sixth graders with learning disabilities to use POSSE during a two-month period. They found that students who learned the strategy recalled significantly more information from the expository

■ **FIGURE 5.18** *POSSE Strategy Sheet for Article on Bermuda Triangle*

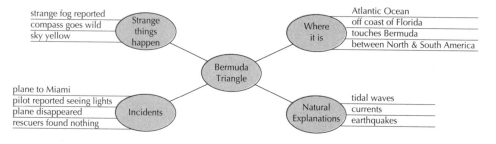

Search for the structure.

Summarize. Summarize the Main Idea in your own words. Ask a "Teacher" Question about the Main Idea.

Evaluate. Compare. Clarify. Predict.

Source: C. S. Englert and T. V. Mariage, "Making Students Partners in the Comprehension Process: Organizing the Reading 'POSSE'," *Learning Disabilities Quarterly, 14* (1991): 129. Reprinted by permission, Council for Learning Disabilities.

texts than students who read the texts using usual classroom reading and discussion. However, they also noted that the teacher had an effect on how well the students learned the POSSE strategy. In reviewing videos of the discussions during POSSE, they found that one of the keys to success was the teachers' ability to transfer of control for completing the steps in the strategy to the students and fade reliance on the POSSE strategy sheet as the students became successful at implementing the POSSE process.

Adapting Approaches to Teaching Reading in Inclusive Classrooms

In this chapter and the last chapter we have talked about a number of techniques and strategies that can be used to teach students with learning and behavior problems how to read. These have included strategies for building phonological awareness, knowledge of letter–sound correspondence and the alphabetic principle, techniques for teaching word recognition, decoding strategies, and word study, techniques for building reading fluency, and strategies for teaching reading comprehension. In this section we discuss three lesson frameworks or approaches to teaching reading that are often used in general education elementary classrooms and found in basal reading programs. They include aspects of all the areas of reading we have discussed (e.g., word recognition, fluency, comprehension). The first approach, the Directed Reading Activity (Betts, 1946) has been a standard framework used for organizing the reading lesson in basal readers. The Direct Reading–Thinking Activity (Stauffer, 1969, 1970) is an adaptation of this framework that encourages more active participation on the part of the reader. Literature-based reading (Cullinan, 1992; Holdaway, 1979) and whole language (Goodman, 1986; 1996) emphasizes the use of literature as the major medium for teaching reading; it integrates reading, writing, speaking, and listening and focuses on reading comprehension and implicit code instruction for teaching word recognition. Each of these three approaches is summarized and modifications for students with reading difficulties are discussed. For more comprehensive discussions of these approaches see textbooks on methods for teaching reading in elementary schools (e.g., Graves, Juel, and Graves, 1999; Gunning; 2000).

Directed Reading Activity

The Directed Reading Activity (DRA), developed by Betts (1946), is the general framework or lesson plan used in many basal readers (Gunning, 2000; Wilkinson and Anderson, 1995). The DRA is a systematic method for providing instruction in reading, including procedures for teaching word identification as well as comprehension.

— PROCEDURES: This general method for teaching reading is designed to be used with students reading at any level who are reading the same selection. The following outline presents the stages usually found in a DRA (Betts, 1946).

1. Readiness
   a. Developing conceptual background
   b. Creating interest
   c. Introducing new vocabulary
   d. Establishing purposes for reading
2. Directed silent reading
   a. Constructing meaning
   b. Monitoring comprehension
3. Discussion and comprehension check
   a. Revisiting purposes for reading
   b. Clarifying concepts and vocabulary
   c. Correcting difficulties in applying word identification and comprehension strategies
   d. Evaluating student performance
4. Rereading
   a. Clarifying information
   b. Obtaining additional information
   c. Enhancing appreciation and understanding
   d. Providing opportunities for purposeful oral reading
5. Follow-up activities
   a. Extending skill development
   b. Enriching and generalizing

— COMMENTS: Although the DRA is suggested as a framework for teaching in basal readers, modifications will be necessary for students who experience reading difficulties. For example, both at the earlier and later elementary grades many of these students will need more systematic, explicit instruction in phonics and decoding strategies than are usually provided. Incorporating fluency building through repeated and partner reading will also assist in providing the needed practice required of these students. The PreReading Plan and previewing could be added to the readiness stage of the DRA to activate and build prior knowledge, and explicit instruction of comprehension and comprehension monitoring strategies such as self-questioning and summarizing would also support students with reading difficulties. Finally, it is important that reading materials used with a DRA framework are at the students' instructional level.

One concern about the DRA is that it is teacher-dominated and, therefore, may not facilitate the development of independent reading skills. Encouraging the students to set their own purposes for reading, to self-question as they read, and to generate their own questions and follow-up activities is emphasized in the next framework, the Directed Reading–Thinking Activity.

Directed Reading–Thinking Activity (DR-TA)

The Directed Reading–Thinking Activity (DR-TA) was developed by Stauffer (1969, 1970, 1976) as a framework for teaching reading that stresses students' abilities to read reflectively and to use prediction and preview strategies to set their own purposes for reading (Gunning, 2000). The purpose of the DR-TA is to provide readers with the ability to:

— Determine purposes for reading
— Extract, comprehend, and assimilate information
— Use prediction while reading
— Suspend judgments
— Make decisions based on evidence gained from reading

It is based on the notion that reading is a thinking process that requires students to relate their own experiences to the author's ideas, and thereby construct meaning from the text.

In using this approach, the construction of meaning starts by setting purposes for reading and generating hypotheses about meaning. It continues as the students acquire more information and confirm or disconfirm hypotheses and establish new hypotheses. It ends when the hypotheses have been confirmed and the purposes for reading have been met.

Stauffer (1969) describes a number of distinguishing features about group DR-TA activities:

1. Students of approximately the same reading level are grouped together.
2. The group size ranges from two to ten students to promote interaction and participation.
3. All students in a group read the same material at the same time. This permits each student to compare and contrast predictions, justifications for answers, and evaluations with those of his or her peers.

4. Purposes for reading are declared by the *student;* students ask questions to become active readers and thinkers.
5. Answers to questions are validated. Proof is found and tested, with the group judging whether or not the offered proof is trustworthy.
6. Immediate feedback helps develop integrity and a regard for authenticity.
7. The teacher serves as a facilitator or moderator and asks provocative questions that require the students to interpret and make inferences from what they have read.

The DR-TA can be used with reading materials written at any level and having either narrative or expository structures. Stauffer (1969) suggests that primer and preprimer materials that have limited plots will not lend themselves to this procedure.

— **PROCEDURES:** Adapt the following procedures when using a DR-TA:

1. After each student receives a copy of the material, direct the students to identify a purpose for reading by studying the title, subtitles, pictures, and so on, to develop a hypothesis about what the passage is about. Questions you might ask to stimulate hypotheses are:
   a. What do you think a story with this title might be about?
   b. What do you think might happen in this story? Have students share these hypotheses, discussing how they arrived at them. Have students use information from their prior knowledge to substantiate their predictions.
2. Once each student has stated his or her hypothesis, encourage the students to adjust their rate of silent reading to their purpose for reading.
3. Teach or remind the students of the strategies they can use when they come to a word they cannot identify, such as sounding out the word parts and thinking what makes sense, and asking for assistance.
4. Select a logical segment of the passage and direct the students to read it to themselves to check

on their predictions. Be responsible for ensuring that students read for meaning by observing reading performance and helping those who request help with words.

5. When the students have finished reading, have them discuss their predictions. Target questions to ask are:
   a. Were you correct?
   b. What do you think now?

   Have students reread orally the sections of the text that confirm or contradict their hypotheses. Assist the students in determining if other source materials may be necessary to clarify meaning, and have the students discuss concepts and vocabulary that are critical to the comprehension process.
6. Repeat the procedure (hypothesis setting, silent reading to validate, oral reading to prove, and discussion) with subsequent segments of the text.
7. Once the passage is completed, use skill activities to teach "skill training" (Stauffer, 1969). This entails rereading the story, reexamining selected words, phrases, pictures, and/or diagrams for the purpose of concurrently developing the students' reading–thinking abilities with the other reading-related skills (Tierney and Readence, 2000). These might include word attack skills and concept clarification and development.

The processing entailed in a DR-TA is summarized as follows:

1. Pupil actions
   a. Predict (set purposes)
   b. Read (process ideas)
   c. Prove (test answers)
2. Teacher actions
   a. What do you think? (activate thought)
   b. Why do you think so? (agitate thought)
   c. Prove it! (require evidence) (Stauffer, 1969)

Stauffer (1969) suggests that once the students are comfortable with the DR-TA process they should be encouraged to use an individualized DR-TA. In other words, the students should use this systematic, predictive process as they read individually. Figure 5.19 presents a sample worksheet that students might use to guide them as they complete individual DR-TAs.

— **COMMENTS:** The DR-TA provides the teacher with a procedure for teaching students to become active thinkers as they read. This is particularly relevant for students with learning and behavior problems since it requires the students to assume responsibility for the reading–learning process. Dixon and Nessel (1992) present strategies for using the DR-TA with second language learners. In comparison to the DRA, where the teacher sets the purpose for reading and preteaches vocabulary, the DR-TA encourages the students to set their own purposes and decide which vocabulary warrants further development.

Widomski (1983) suggests incorporating DR-TA with semantic mapping, thereby enabling students to construct a visual representation on which to test their predictions in much the same way that the predictions are tested by the students in POSSE, presented in the preceding section.

Two cautions, however, seem relevant to the DR-TA. First, it requires a great deal of self-directiveness on the part of the students, particularly the individualized DR-TA. It will be important for instruction to be scaffolded so that there is a systematic movement from teacher modeling and control to student control. Second, it does not teach word identification or fluency building skills in a direct or systematic manner. Like DRA, providing direct instruction in these areas and having students work in instructional-level materials will be important modifications to make in inclusive classes.

Literature-Based Reading and Whole Language

Literature-based reading and the whole language philosophy of reading and learning are based on the assumption that students will learn to read by having multiple opportunities to engage in listening, talking about, reading, and writing about interesting and engaging literature. This orientation is reflected in basal

■ **FIGURE 5.19**   *Directed Reading-Thinking Activity Individual Prediction Sheet*

Name:

Passage/Book

Pages	*Prediction*	*Outcome*

Summary

reading programs that include literature anthologies and patterned language books (for early readers) and the wide use of children's literature as core reading materials for instruction. Whole language and, to a varying degree, literature-based reading are derived from a more student-centered, sociolinguistic model of teaching and learning and from a psycholinguitic model of reading as articulated by Goodman (1984, 1986, 1996). The philosophy is evident in the following statements:

> A "psycholinguistic approach" to reading would be the very antithesis of a set of instructional materials. . . . The child learning to read seems to need the opportunity to examine a large sample of language, to generate hypotheses about the regularity underlying it, and to test and modify these hypotheses on the basis of feedback that is appropriate to the unspoken rules that

he happens to be testing. (Smith and Goodman, 1971, pp. 179–180)

> In this method there are no prereading skills, no formalizing reading readiness. Instead, learning is expected to progress *from whole to part,* from general to specific, from familiar to unfamiliar, from vague to precise, from gross to fine, from highly contextualized to more abstract. Children are expected to read, first, familiar meaningful wholes—easily predictable materials that draw on concepts and experiences they already have. These may be signs, cereal boxes, or books.... By carefully building on what children already know, we assure their readiness. (Goodman and Goodman, 1982, p. 127)

Literature-based programs and whole language emphasize that language be kept as a whole, children use language in ways that relate to their lives and cultures, and strategies for reading be taught within the context of meaningful activities and texts (Baumann, Hooten, and White, 1999; Freppon and Dahl, 1998, Weaver, 1998).

— **PROCEDURES:** The focal points of whole language and literature-based reading programs center on: (1) involving students in lots of reading and writing; (2) creating an environment that accepts and encourages risk-taking; (3) maintaining a focus on meaning (Goodman, 1986; 1996; Weaver, 1990).

In a literature-based or whole-language classrooms, the curriculum is often organized around themes and units that integrate oral language, reading, and writing. With the focus on meaning, phonics and word recognition skills are generally not taught in isolation but within the context of connected text, when children are writing during writer's workshop, and based on the needs of the students (Dahl and Scharer, 2000; Dahl, Scharer, Lawson, and Grogan, 1999; Stahl, Pagnucco, and Suttles, 1996). Strategies for comprehension are taught within the context of books; teachers and students discuss not only the content but also the processes used in constructing meaning from text (Goodman, Watson, and Burke, 1996; Jewell and Pratt, 1999; Rosenblatt, 1978). *Literature circles, literature discussion groups, book clubs,* and *reader response journals* are techniques that have been used to structure discussions about books and to promote critical reading.

Literature circles are often used to structure discussions about books (Short and Harste, with Burke, 1995; Short, 1997). Literature circles facilitate literacy in that they provide opportunities for students to explore ideas about the content and craft of literacy and to think critically and deeply about what they read. In literature circles, the teacher initially introduces several books for which there are multiple copies and the group decides which book to read. Students read the book or, if too long, chapters or smaller segments of the book and then meet in literature circle to discuss the book. The first day the discussion starts with a broad focus (e.g., "What was the story about?"). In the discussion the teacher listens to what the students highlight as interesting or challenging and also leads the students to talk about the outstanding characteristics of the book (e.g., charac-

ter development, plot development, use of dialogue). As the discussions progress across several meetings, the teacher models and guides the students in making connections between the book they read and their personal experiences and other literature they have read or written (Bos, 1991; Martinez-Roldain and López-Robertson, 1999/2000; Raphael, 2000). Apply the Concept 5.5 presents a list of sample questions that fosters discussion and understanding of literature both from the reader's and writer's perspectives. The questions focus on character development, authenticity, mood, voice, writing style and genre, text structure, comparison across literature, and tying reader to author. At the end of each discussion, the group decides what they want to discuss the next time. They prepare for the next discussion by rereading sections of the book or related literature. Students also keep notes about the discussion and their reading in Literature Logs (Atwell, 1984).

In literature-based and whole-language classrooms, writing is reciprocally tied to reading so that the students have opportunities to work in the roles of both reader and author. Process writing (see Chapter Six) and conferencing about books and written pieces allows the teacher to facilitate the students' understanding of the processes associated with language learning.

Literature for reading and topics for writing are oftentimes self-selected, giving the students the opportunity to explore topics of interest to them. Students also learn about the authors and illustrators of the books they are reading. With this approach, the librarian, annotated bibliographies of children's literature, and teacher resource books are important tools for teaching.

— **COMMENTS:** Using literature-based reading programs and whole language emphasizes the purposeful reading, writing, discussion, and analyzing of literature for purposes of learning to read, critically analyzing, and appreciating literature and literacy. These approaches are student-oriented and the social nature of activities such as literature circles fits well with the sociocultural theory of learning and teaching (see Chapter Two). Research investigating the use of literature-based programs and whole

APPLY THE CONCEPT 5.5

DISCUSSION QUESTIONS TO FOSTER UNDERSTANDING OF READING AND WRITING

- Is the story like any other story you have heard, read, or watched? How are they alike? (comparisons across literature)
- What questions would you ask if the author were here? How might the author answer these? (tying reader to author)
- Who are the main characters of the story? What kind of people are they? How does the author let you know? (character development)
- Do the characters change during the story? How do they change? What changes them? Do the changes seem believable? (character development)
- How does the author make the story seem possible? (authenticity)
- Does the language used in the story seem real for the character? (authenticity)
- Did you notice any natural breaks in the book where it seemed like a good place to stop? (text structure)

- Think of a different ending or beginning to the story? How would the rest of the story have to change to have the different ending or beginning work? (text structure)
- Are there any signs or clues that the author gives you to help you with the break? If so, what are they? (writing style and genre)
- Does the story create a specific feeling or mood? What words does the author use to create the mood? (mood)
- Is there anything unique about this author's style? If so, what? (writing style)
- What does the author do to help you feel like you are part of the story? (writing style)
- Who is the teller or narrator of the story? How would the story change if the narrator were someone different? (voice)

Source: Adapted from G. D. Sloan, *The Child as Critic,* 2nd ed. (New York: Teachers College Press, 1984); and K. Vandergrift, *Child and Story* (New York: Neal-Schuman, 1980).

language indicates that there is some evidence using primarily case studies that such approaches facilitate the reading and attitudes toward reading of students with learning and behavior problems (e.g., Allen, Michalove, Shockley, and West, 1991; Mills, O'Keefe, and Stephens, 1992; Morrow, 1992; Stires, 1991). At the same time, there is substantial evidence to support that students with learning and behavior problems need more direct and intensive instruction than is usually associated with these approaches (National Reading Panel, 2000; Snow et al., 1998; Swanson, 1999b). What kinds of modifications might be helpful for students with reading problems? For Jessie, a second grade student who was struggling with learning to read, explicitly teaching sound/symbol relationships and word patterns (e.g., *-ight, -ate*) and how to segment and blend the sounds and patterns to decode the words assisted her. Providing her with

ample opportunities to read the words using word sorts and word games and simple decodable books allowed her to practice the relationships and patterns she was learning. Benjamin, a fourth grader with learning disabilities, was having particular difficulty finding the main idea and summarizing what he had read, both in reading and social studies. Ms. Lin, his resource special education teacher, supported him by teaching him how to use the paraphrasing strategy as part of his instruction in the resource room. Because several students with learning disabilities or difficulties similar to Benjamin's were in Mrs. Brown's fourth grade class, she and Mrs. Brown cotaught social studies so that they could teach the entire class how to use collaborative strategic reading (see Chapter Eleven for information on coteaching). In both cases, the adaptations that were provided used teaching strategies that emphasized explicit teaching of skills and strategies using modeling, cuing, guided and independent practice, corrective feedback, and progress monitoring as would be suggested by research (Pressley and Rankin, 1994; Mastroprieri and Scruggs, 1997; Swanson, 1999a).

INSTRUCTIONAL ACTIVITIES

This section provides instructional activities that are related to reading comprehension and fluency. Some of the activities teach new skills; others are best suited for practice and reinforcement of already acquired skills. For each activity, the objective, materials, and teaching procedures are described.

■ Critiquing Oral Reading

Objective: To provide students the opportunity to critique their oral reading.

Grades: Primary and intermediate

Materials: (1) A book or story the student is reading. (2) A tape recorder and a labeled blank tape for each student.

Teaching Procedures: Explain that the purpose of the activity is to give the students an opportunity to listen to how they read. Let the students know that they are to listen for things they do well and things they want to work on. Model the process by practicing, recording, listening, and critiquing a passage you read. Before the students read into the tape recorder, have them practice the segment. Each student should practice and then read and record a passage of about 100 to 500 words. After the students record, they should listen to their tapes and finish writing the following statements:

When I read orally, I do a really good job of

_____ .

One thing I could do better when I read out loud is _____ .

It is important to have students start with the things they do well.

Listen to and discuss each tape and then ask the students to critique each presentation. Have the students record their oral reading every three to six weeks so that they can compare and hear how they are improving.

Adaptations: Each student can record two passages—one that has been practiced and one that is unpracticed.

■ Story Jumble

Objective: To provide students practice in sequencing a story.

Grades: Primary and intermediate

Materials: Short stories written at the students' independent reading levels that have been cut into story parts (e.g., setting, episodes, endings), paragraphs, or sentences. Mount each segment of the story on an index card.

Teaching Procedures: Present the cards to the students and have them read each part and arrange them so that the story makes sense. Then have the students read the story again to check to see if it makes sense. If students disagree as to the order, have them explain why they prefer a certain order.

Adaptations: Students can work on this activity in groups of two or three students or individually.

■ Predict the Plot

Objective: To provide students practice in predicting the events and plots in stories.

Grades: Intermediate and secondary

Materials: Cartoon strips such as Peanuts, Broomhilda, or Beetle Bailey.

Teaching Procedures: Select a cartoon strip and expose one frame at a time for the students to read.

Then have them predict the plot by asking such questions as:

> What do you think is going to be pictured in the next frame? Why?
>
> Of the ideas we have generated, which one do you like best? Why?
>
> How do you think the cartoonist will end this story? Why?

Read the next frame, discussing the previous predictions and making predictions about the next frame. After the story is completed, have the students draw and write their own cartoons, using the characters presented in the strip or creating new characters. Then the students may share their cartoons with each other.

Adaptations: Mystery and adventure stories also lend themselves to this type of plot prediction. Segments of the story could be read and then predictions made. Students could also finish this activity by writing a mystery or adventure story.

■ Stake-Out

Objective: To give students the opportunity to arrange the paragraphs of articles in a logical order.

Grades: Intermediate and secondary

Materials: (1) At least two newspaper articles with at least four paragraphs written at the students' instructional to independent reading levels. Cut each article up by paragraphs, and mount each paragraph from the same story on the same color index card. (2) Write clues on another set of index cards that will help the students find the various paragraphs located in a given area (e.g., room, school).

Teaching Procedures: Place the paragraphs to the articles around the room or school. Divide the students into teams that consist of two or three members. Explain to the teams that their goal is to use the clues to find the various parts to their newspaper article, and then to arrange the article so that it makes sense.

Explain that the parts to their article will all be on the same color index cards. Use either the rule that the first team that completes the task wins, or that a certain time limit is available for the stake-out and the team must complete it by that time if they are to win.

Give each team the clues and have them begin. When time is complete, have each group read the article. The class then determines if the order is correct. Have the students justify the order they selected.

■ Judge the Ad

Objective: To provide students the opportunity to think critically about advertisements.

Grades: Intermediate and secondary

Materials: Ads cut from newspapers and magazines.

Teaching Procedures: Select examples of ads that provide a fair representation of a product and ones that present a biased or unfair representation. Discuss with the students what makes the ad fair, unfair, or biased. Then have the students each select an ad for a product they know about and would like to purchase. Ask them to study the ad to determine if it is "fair." Have each student present his or her ad to the other students and build a case for why the ad is fair or unfair. Encourage the students to provide evidence for their opinions.

■ WH-Game

Objective: To provide students practice in answering who, what, when, where, why, and how questions.

Grades: All grades

Materials: (1) Generic gameboard, spinner or die, and markers. (2) WH Cards, which are small cards with "WH-Game" written on one side and one of the following words written on the other side: Who, What, When, Where, Why, How. (3) Sets of Story and Article Cards, which are copies of short stories and articles mounted on cards. There should be one copy for each player. Select topics of interest for the age level of students.

Teaching Procedures: Explain the game to the students or have them read written directions. First, the players set up the game. Next, they select a set of Story or Article Cards. All players read the story or article and place their cards face down. Then, each player takes a turn by throwing the die or spinning and selecting a WH-Card. The player must make up a question using the WH word indicated on the card and answer it correctly in order to move his or her marker the indicated number of spaces. If another player questions the validity of a player's question or answer, the players may look at the story or article card. Otherwise, these cards should remain face down during play. After ten questions have been asked using one Story or Article card, another set is selected. The students read this card and then the game continues. The first player to arrive at the finish wins.

Adaptations: Students may also work in pairs, with one person on the team making up the question and the other person answering it.

SUMMARY

Many students with learning and behavior problems struggle with learning word identification skills. We, as special education teachers, spend a considerable amount of our instructional time focusing on these skills, assuming that fluency and comprehension will follow. What we have found is that these students also experience difficulties in reading fluently and comprehending what they read. Consequently, we need systematically to plan and implement fluency and comprehension instruction.

Strategies for fluency instruction first focus on providing students frequent opportunities to listen to literature being read aloud and on having students read familiar books. In addition, the techniques of repeated reading, repeated choral reading, and peer-supported reading, are stressed because they provide students with additional instructional support when developing fluent reading patterns.

Much of what teachers refer to as instruction in reading comprehension is, in fact, better described as the assessment of students' comprehension after they have read. So as to draw attention away from teacher questioning, this chapter presents a framework for reading comprehension that is not tied to level of reading comprehension questions. Instead, it is tied to the reasoning processes required (i.e., textually explicit, textually implicit, or scriptually implicit) and the types of information or relationships represented. We can use this matrix in planning instruction in that we can implement techniques and strategies that will assure many different facets of comprehension are tapped.

In discussing methods for teaching reading comprehension, emphasis is placed on the importance of planning activities before the students read that will help them preview the text and activate their background knowledge or schemas. Techniques such as brainstorming, the PreReading Plan, Text Preview, and K-W-L can facilitate this process. In the area of questions, emphasis is placed on helping students learn to predict and ask their own questions rather than just respond to the questions of the teacher.

Teaching students to paraphrase, summarize, monitor their comprehension, and use fix-up strategies when there are problems are also critical skills for effective reading. Rather than a steady diet of teacher questions, what is needed is explicit, cognitive strategy instruction in these comprehension strategies. Using multicomponent strategies such as reciprocal teaching, collaborative strategic reading, and POSSE can be both effective and efficient for students with reading problems.

Most students with learning and behavior problems receive instruction in reading in their general education classrooms using such frameworks as directed reading activities, directed reading–thinking activities, and literature-based reading and whole language. Adapting these frameworks to make instruction more explicit with greater opportunities for modeling, practice, and feedback is important.

WEBSITES AS RESOURCES FOR TEACHING READING (ALSO SEE CHAPTER 4 WEBSITES)

http://www.bowker.com/catalog/home/entry_child.html
This Website contains lists of reference books about different types of children's literature.

http://www.ala.org
This is the Website of the American Library Association, which provides recommendations for books for children including reluctant and struggling readers.

http://www.reading.org
This is the Website for the International Reading Association Website, which includes numerous resources including children's and teacher's choices for children's books.

http://www.ncte.org
This is the Website for the National Council of Teachers of English, which includes numerous resources on teaching literature and children's literature.

http://www.ldonline.org/ld_indepth/reading/teaching_children_to_read.html
This Website contains information on fluency and comprehension.

http://www.ldonline.org/ld_indepth/teaching_techniques/collab_reading.html
This Website introduces Collaborative Strategic Reading to improve reading comprehension and fluency.

http://www.dk.com
This Website features programs that build reading comprehension and vocabulary.

THINK AND APPLY

— Describe several reasons why a student might have difficulty with fluency or reading comprehension.

— Why is it important to read aloud to a student who is having difficulty learning to read?

— Describe the framework for reading comprehension presented in this chapter. After reading a piece of text, write several questions/answers of each of the following types: textually explicit, textually implicit, and scriptually implicit.

— Select an informational text that you plan or might plan to read with students. Describe how you would use brainstorming, PreReading Plan, Text Preview, or K-W-L to assist students in activating background knowledge.

— Describe how a "think-aloud" would be used with a paraphrasing or retelling strategy. Select a passage and a strategy (e.g., RAP, STORE) and do a think-aloud by describing what you are thinking as you carry out the steps in the strategy.
— Compare and contrast the Directed Reading Activity and the Directed Reading–Thinking Activity.
— What four comprehension and comprehension monitoring strategies are taught in reciprocal teaching and collaborative strategic reading and why?
— Describe how you would adapt the directed reading activity, the directed reading–thinking activity, and literature-based reading and whole language to support students with reading problems.

6

Written Expression

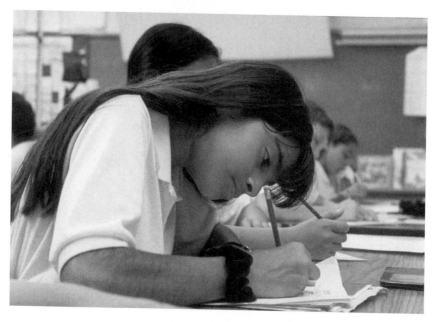

KEY TOPICS FOR MASTERY

- *The **writing process approach** to written language instruction—its elements, implementation, and benefits to students*
- *The many positive outcomes that occur when students with learning and behavior problems are given **choices** about writing topics, **encouragement** and support in their writing, and sufficient **time** for that writing*
- *The **writing conference**—its importance in helping a student improve a piece of writing*
- *The principles for establishing a **writing community** within the classroom*
- *Why **error analysis** must be the first step in developing an effective spelling program*
- *Principles and strategies for teaching spelling skills to students with learning disabilities, including empirically based instructional practices*
- *Special considerations to be made in deciding appropriate handwriting instruction for students with learning disabilities*

 BRIGHT IDEA

Turn to page 278 and read Think and Apply.

A high school teacher of students with learning disabilities reports, "The adolescents in my program do not want to write. They do not even want to answer questions in writing. Writing a theme for a class is torture."

Most young children love to scribble. They enjoy writing and drawing on paper, sidewalks, chalkboards, and, unfortunately, even on walls. On the first day of school when first graders are asked if they know how to write, most of them say yes. What happens to the interest and joy in writing from age 3 to age 13?

Many researchers in the field feel that students do not spend enough time on writing as a craft and are given too little choice about what they write. Writing has many negative associations for students because it is often used as a form of punishment and when their writing is returned to them it is filled with corrections.

The good news is that we have made more progress in written expression for students with disabilities than in any other academic area (Vaughn, Gersten, and Chard, 2000). This includes students with disabilities who are bilingual (Echevarria and Graves, 1998; Graves, Valles, and Rueda, 2000). When teachers implement effective intervention approaches that use both the conventions of teaching writing, (e.g., capitalization, punctuation, sentence structure) with strategies for improving written expression, (e.g., planning, composing the results) the results are quite positive (Gersten and Baker, 2001). This chapter is about what happens in writing when students are given choices in topics, and time and encouragement to write. The chapter presents background and instructional procedures for using the writing process approach to instruction. Getting started in writing, the writing process, and establishing a writing community are discussed. In addition, this chapter presents approaches to teaching spelling and handwriting to students who have learning difficulties, and provides a table showing the pros and cons of teaching cursive versus manuscript or both.

TEACHING THE WRITING PROCESS

Several years ago Marynell Schlegel, a resource room teacher who works with students who have learning and emotional disabilities, decided she disliked teaching writing almost as much as the students hated learning it. An interview with these students on the characteristics of good writing revealed that they perceived good writing as spelling words correctly, writing "correct" sentences, and having good handwriting—the very skills these students often have the most difficulty developing. None of the children included a purpose for writing in their description of good writing. Writing was not perceived by them as a means of conveying a message, which is considered by experts to be the most important element in writing (Murray, 1984, 1985).

During the summer Ms. Schlegel decided to read about writing and to change her writing instruction. She decided to implement the writing process approach to written expression (Graves, 1983; MacArthur, Graham, Schwartz, and Schafer, 1995).

The Writing Process for Students with Learning and Behavior Problems

After spending the summer preparing for the changes in her instructional approach to writing, Ms. Schlegel decided she was ready to begin. She arranged for students with writing problems to come to the resource room for four fifty-minute periods a week. During this time they were to write and participate in skills groups. Writing included initially selecting topics of their choice and, within each written piece, focusing first on the message and only later on the mechanics of writing. Skills such as organizing ideas and editing for capitalization, punctuation,

and spelling would be taught based on the students' individual needs and within the context of their written pieces rather than through the familiar drill and practice activities. Ms. Schlegel initiated the program with many reservations. She was concerned that this writer-centered format for teaching writing would require her to have a built-in scope and sequence for the development of written expression. She had taught reading and math for a number of years and had developed a scope and sequence of the skills required at each grade level, but written expression was much less developed in her mind and in the various teachers' guides she consulted. Ms. Schlegel knew that to implement the writing process approach to instruction she would need to consider setting, scheduling and preparing materials, teaching skills, and the teacher's role as a writer.

Setting

To ensure a successful writing program for her students who had already experienced failure in writing, Ms. Schlegel decided that one of the most important components would be the setting. According to Graves (1983), the setting should create a working atmosphere similar to a studio, which promotes independence and in which students can easily interact. Figure 6.1 depicts how Ms. Schlegel arranged her room to create such an atmosphere. Materials and supplies for writing, and the students' individual writing folders were stored in specific locations in the room. Students knew where materials could be found, so they did not have to rely on the teacher to get them started at the beginning of the writing period. The room was arranged so students could work together or individually. The room arrangement facilitated conferencing between small groups of students, teacher and student, and student and student.

Scheduling and Preparing Materials

Ms. Schlegel set up individual writing folders. In the daily writing folders, illustrated in Figure 6.2, students kept all their unfinished writing, a list of possible writing topics, a list of all writing pieces they had

APPLY THE CONCEPT 6.1

KNOWLEDGE OF WRITING STRATEGIES

Students identified as learning disabled differ from low-achieving and high-achieving students in their knowledge of strategies related to writing. They are less aware of steps in the writing process and ideas and procedures for organizing their written text. Students with learning disabilities are also more dependent on external cues such as how much to write, teacher feedback, and mechanical presentation of the paper. They demonstrate significant difficulties planning, writing, and revising text (Englert, Raphael, Fear, and Anderson, 1988).

■ **FIGURE 6.1**   *Setting the Stage*

1. Create a working atmosphere that is similar to a studio.
2. Create an atmosphere where students can interact easily.
3. Create an atmosphere which encourages independence.

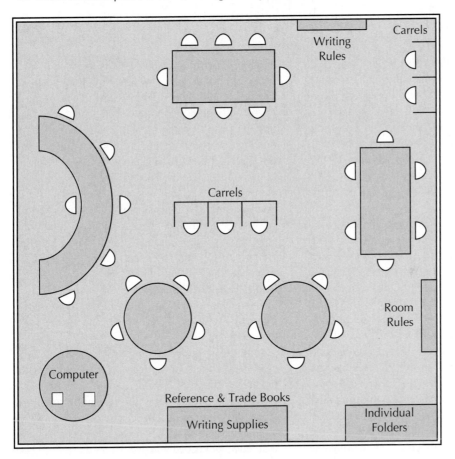

■ **FIGURE 6.2**   *Individual Writing Folder*

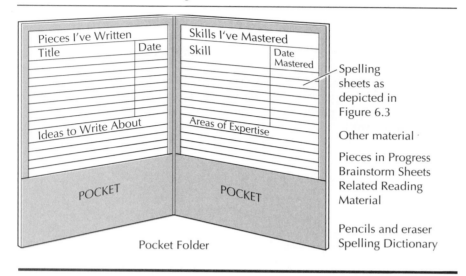

Pocket Folder

completed, a list of writing skills they had mastered, a list of skills and topics in which they had expertise, and dates when conferences with the teacher were held. A list of the words an individual student was learning to spell, along with a procedure for learning the words and measuring mastery, was also included in the folder (see Figure 6.3). In addition to this current writing folder, students had access to their permanent writing folder, which included all of the writing they had completed.

Ms. Zaragoza is an elementary teacher who used the writing process with all of her students. Ms. Zaragoza felt that the writing process approach was successful with all learners in her classroom because she organized short skill lessons, five to ten minutes each day, for small groups of youngsters, and individual skill lessons for students who had specific difficulties. When Ms. Zaragoza noticed that several students were having difficulty with a particular skill (e.g., quotation marks), or she felt that several students were ready to learn a more advanced writing procedure (e.g., the difference between first and third person when writing), she would organize a skill group. She taught approximately one skill group a day and advertised the skill group by writing the

name of it on the board as well as the time it would occur. She would write the names of the students who she felt would benefit from the skill group on the board but would also allow other students to "sign up" for the skill group. A skill group would last for one day or several depending upon the difficulty of the skill. Ms. Zaragoza also taught daily skill lessons to individual students. These skill lessons sometimes were responses to the "teachable moment"—for example, a student might ask how to develop an ending for a story—and other times the individual skill lessons were planned and scheduled. Ms. Zaragoza's viewpoint was that "practice in writing is essential to enhancing writing skills, but practice alone is insufficient. Skill groups are an essential way to keep students moving and learning as writers." See Figure 6.4 for a list of conventions and when they are demonstrated.

In setting up the writing program Ms. Schlegel also made a time commitment. Her previous written language instruction had focused on short periods of time several days a week—just enough time for the student to complete a skill activity or a piece of writing on an assigned topic. Her research convinced her that students needed adequate time on a daily basis

■ **FIGURE 6.3** *Sample Spelling Form for the Individual Spelling Folder*

Student: _____

Words I'm Learning to Spell

Date	Word	Written on Card	Practiced Using Strategy	Learned for Test	Learned in Writing	Date Mastered
3/12	1. mystery	✓	✓	✓		
	2. chasing	✓	✓	✓		
	3. haunted	✓	✓	✓		
	4. wouldn't	✓	✓			
	5. elsewhere	✓	✓	✓		
	6. whatever	✓	✓	✓		
	7. their	✓	✓	✓		
	8. there	✓	✓	✓		
	9.					
	10.					

if they were to develop as writers. So, coordinating with the regular classroom teachers, they scheduled 40 minutes per day, four days per week, for writing.

Teaching Writing Conventions

Students with learning disabilities display a wide range of abilities in writing (Berninger, Abbott, Witaker, Sylvester, and Nolen, 1995). They are also very different in terms of the writing skills they need to acquire and the ways in which they respond to instruction (Berninger et al., 1995). Variables such as motivation and attitude must be considered as well as writing conventions when designing effective writing skills programs for students with learning problems.

Therefore, the skills (e.g. spelling, capitalization and punctuation) that Ms. Schlegel taught during each writing period varied in response to the students' needs. Most of the time was devoted to individual writing and conferences with classmates and the teacher. Time for sharing ideas and drafts was often scheduled near the end of the period.

Ms. Schlegel conducted short (5 to 15 minutes) skill lessons with individuals or small groups of students. The topics and groupings for these lessons were based on the students' needs. Skill lessons were decided based on observations of student writing, requests for help, and data collected from conferences. Students were selected to participate in the skill lessons contingent on their abilities and needs. The same topic with different activities was usually covered for four lessons to help provide sufficient practice. To help promote generalization, Ms. Schlegel and

■ **FIGURE 6.4** *Instructional Timeline: Awareness to Mastery*

Instructional Concept	K	1	2	3	4	5	6	7	8
End Punctuation	*	*	*						
Commas in Dates	*	*	*						
Commas in Series	*	*	*	*					
Commas in Addresses	*	*	*	*					
Apostrophes in Contractions		*	*	*	*				
Periods in Abbreviations		*	*	*	*				
Commas in Compound Sentences			*	*	*				
Punctuation in Dialogue				*	*	*			
Apostrophes in Possessives				*	*	*			
Commas in Complex Sentences				*	*	*			
Quotation Marks and Underlining in Published Titles				*	*	*			
Commas in Series of Adjectives				*	*	*			
Commas to Set Off Appositives					*	*	*	*	
Commas after Introductory Words					*	*	*	*	
Commas after Introductory Phrases					*	*	*	*	
Commas in Compound-Complex Sentences						*	*	*	*
Commas to Set Off Parenthetical Expressions						*	*	*	
Dashes and Parentheses to Set Off Parenthetical Expressions						*	*	*	*
Colons in Sentences						*	*	*	*
Semicolons in Sentences						*	*	*	*
Capital Letters to Begin Sentences	*	*	*						
Capital Letters in Names	*	*	*						
Capitalizing	*	*	*						
Capital Letters in Days and Months	*	*	*	*					
Capital Letters in Place Names	*	*	*	*					
Capital Letters in Person's Title		*	*	*	*				
Capital Letters in Published Titles		*	*	*	*				
Capital Letters to Show Nationality, Ethnicity, and Language		*	*	*	*				
Capital Letters in Trade Names, Commercial Products, and Company Names		*	*	*	*				
Capital Letters in Names of Institutions, Associations and Events		*	*	*	*				

Source: From L. Fearn and N. Farnan, *Writing Effectively: Helping Children Master the Conventions of Writing* (Boston: Allyn and Bacon, 1998). Copyright © 1998 by Allyn and Bacon. Reprinted by permission.

students would use conferences to discuss how the skill was working in the writing process. She would maintain records on each skill area so she could carefully monitor students' progress.

Remember the following critical points about teaching conventions (Fearn and Farnan, 1998):

— Attention to conventions does *not* disrupt the flow of writing but is part of the discipline of writing.

— Focus on the conventions of writing does not inhibit growth in writing but facilitates it.

— Even very young children can learn simple conventions and perform then automatically (see Figure 6.5).

— Students with learning and behavior disorders need about 20 percent of their instructional time in writing addressing the use and application of these conventions.

■ **FIGURE 6.5**   *Questions to Consider in Monitoring Student Progress*

Assessing Progress

How does the student respond during the activity?

- Can the student complete the task?
- How comfortably and proficiently is the task completed?
- Can the student explain the process used to complete the task?
- Can the student apply the skills and knowledge to other contexts?
- Are there aspects of the task that are causing difficulties?

Adjusting Instruction

Will a different approach, materials, or setting improve student progress?

Different approaches

- Simplify tasks into small steps
- Do more modeling or demonstration
- Provide more review
- Give more guidance

Different materials

- Decrease difficulty of the material
- Use different types of writing genres
- Provide checklists or cue card

Different setting

- Use peers to assist
- Change time of day of instruction
- Change location of task

Sources: Adapted from I. C. Fountas and G. S. Pinnell, *Guided Reading: Good First Teaching for All Children* (New Hampshire: Heinemann, 1996); T. G. Gunning, *Assessing and Correcting Reading and Writing Difficulties* (Boston: Allyn and Bacon, 1998); and B. Rosenshine, "Advances in Research on Instruction." In J. W. Lloyd, E. J. Kameenui, and D. Chard (Eds.), *Issues in Educating Students with Disabilities* (Mahwah, NJ: Lawrence Erlbaum Associates, 1997), pp. 197–220.

Monitoring Student Progress

How do I monitor students' progress? When you monitor students' progress on critical elements regularly (at least every two weeks), students make improved progress (Gunning, 1998). Record students' progress so you, students, and parents can see progress, such as the number of words written for younger children and/or a checklist of story elements and their quality for older students.

As you teach, monitor students' progress by noting:

— Whether students can complete the written project.
— How proficient they are at each element of the writing process (e.g., planning, spelling, handwriting, composing).
— If they can apply the skills and knowledge to other context (e.g., at other times during the day).
— How they explain the process they are using.

For example, as students write, notice what strategies they use to compose text (e.g., outline, notes, keywords). Reflect upon the appropriateness of the

task and teaching presentation. Keep written records to document student progress, such as notes, checklists, and samples of students' work. Monitoring students' progress in writing involves evaluating written products and observing the writing process. You can observe students as they write and use conference times to assess and record their progress. By observing and examining writing processes and products, teachers can plan instruction to meet individual needs. Keep anecdotal records by creating a record sheet to quickly document students' progress on writing projects. Include a summary of what you observe, the date, and context. List skills and writing strategies that need to be taught. Collections of students' written work help you, parents, and students document growth and development as it occurs during the school year. Journals and writing folders also provide insight into writing growth. Periodically review and select representative pieces to show writing development.

Teachers as Writers

Writing with the students was also an important part of Ms. Schlegel's writing program. Ms. Gervasi, a teacher of emotionally disturbed adolescents, thinks that a teacher's writing is the most important ingredient to success with the students. Ms. Gervasi frequently writes with her students and shares her writing with them. Because she writes, she feels she can better understand their writing difficulties and can speak with them author to author.

Setting the tone for writing requires the teacher to write, to share his or her writing, to be genuinely interested in what the students say in their writing, to listen carefully, and to confer and provide feedback. According to Graves (1983), the tone for writing is set by what the teacher does.

Using the Writing Process in General Education Classrooms

Ms. Zaragoza conducts workshops for teachers on the use of writing process. During these workshops she is frequently asked whether youngsters who are at risk for learning problems or identified as learning disabled can successfully use this approach. She conducted three year-long case studies with students who were identified as gifted, low-achieving, and learning disabled in which she examined their progress in writing and writing related skills (e.g., capitalization, spelling, punctuation) (Zaragoza and Vaughn, 1992). For the first two months the student with learning disabilities was very hesitant about writing. He asked for constant teacher assistance and would not write unless a teacher worked closely with him. He wrote slowly and neatly even on first drafts. His first piece of writing was untitled and incomplete. He was insecure about working with other students and never volunteered to share his writing. His piece, entitled "Disneyworld," demonstrated an understanding that you can write down what you really think. He included his own dog in a Disneyworld theme ("Goofy is a dog I like to play with but Goofy is not better than my dog."). The other students loved this story, and asked him to read it over and over again. Subsequently, he volunteered frequently to share his writing in front of the class. He had a flair for good endings and became the class expert on developing endings. For example, in "The Spooky Halloween," he ended with this sentence, "Halloween is nothing to play with." "Freddy Is In My Room" ended with the sentence, "Give it up." The ending that was most appreciated by all was from "Part 4." This story was about a child who, because he did not get a Christmas present, wanted to die. He went to the graveyard and started to lie down, but then said, "Holy macaroni not this dead." These case studies revealed that students across achievement groups benefit from participating in writing process. These students demonstrated gains on standardized writing measures as well as increased confidence and skills in their daily writing. Their teacher was most satisfied with their increased active learning style in the classroom.

Elements of the Writing Process

The elements of the writing process include prewriting, composing, revising, editing, and publishing. Authors do not pass through these elements as stages in the order they are listed. In fact, many authors circle back through previous elements and jump ahead to later ones while they are writing their drafts. For example, Steven realized after he read his draft to his friend Jacob that he needed to have more information about what submarines look like on the inside. He returned to the prewriting stage and checked out several books on submarines so he could complete his story.

Some elements of the writing process are not used at all. For example, Sheryl decided she was going to write about her first date with Jerry, and she used little of what we describe as prewriting as she began her writing. Mark discussed an idea for writing with his teacher and then, after writing a draft and reading it to a friend, decided he was unhappy with the topic and left it. These elements are not stages that a writer passes through but merely processes that are often used in writing.

In prewriting, a writer collects information about a topic through observing, remembering, interviewing, and reading. In composing, the author attempts to get ideas on paper in the form of a draft. This process tells the author what he or she knows and does not know. During revising, points are explored further, ideas are elaborated, and further connections are made. When the author is satisfied with the content, he or she edits the piece, reviewing it line by line to determine that each word is necessary. Punctuation, spelling, and other mechanical processes are checked. The final element is publication. If the piece is a good one for the author, it is published. Obviously, not all pieces are published.

Stires (1983) and Zaragoza and Vaughn (1992), who have used the writing process approach with students with learning disabilities, concluded that students with disabilities differ from other students in the degree to which components of the writing process are difficult for them. Many students with learning disabilities experience significant problems in editing and writing final copies because they have difficulty with mechanical skills such as spelling, punctuation, and handwriting. These students often produce well-developed stories but they are hard to read because of the mechanical errors. Other students with learning disabilities have difficulty organizing their first drafts and need to rethink sequencing and order during their revisions.

Graham, Harris and their colleagues (e.g., De La Paz and Graham, 1997; Sexton, Harris, and Graham, 1998; Troia, Harris, and Graham, 1999) have successfully taught students with learning disabilities to use the following strategy with improvements in their composition:

1. Think: who will read this, and why am I writing it?
2. Plan what to say using TREE (note Topic sentence, note Reasons, Examine reasons, note Ending).
3. Write and say more.

Prewriting: Getting Started

The first hurdle in starting the writing process approach with your students is topic selection.

Selecting Topics. "The most important thing children can learn is what they know and how they know it" (Graves, 1985, p. 39). This is the essence of topic choice. Once students can identify what they know and talk about it, they have completed the first step in topic selection.

Give each student and yourself a piece of paper. Say to them, "You know lots of things about yourself, about your family, and about your friends. You have

hobbies and activities that you like to do. You have stories about things that have happened to you and/or to others you know. You have lots of things to share with others. I want you to make a list of things you would like to share with others through writing. Do not put them in any specific order—just write them as you think of them. You will not have to write on all of these topics. The purpose of this exercise is to think of as many topics as you can. I will give you about ten minutes. Begin." Model the process for the students by writing as many topics as you can think of during the assigned time. When time is up, tell the students to pick a partner and share their topics with him or her. They may add any new topics they think of at this time. When they finish sharing their topics with their partner, share your list with the entire group and comment on topics you are looking forward to writing about as well as the topics you feel you may never write about. Ask for volunteer students to read their topic lists to the entire group. Now ask the students to select the three topics they are most interested in writing about and to write them at the top of their lists and then place their topic lists in their writing folders. Explain that these lists can be consulted later for possible topics. Also, if the students think of new topics they want to write about, they may add them to their lists. Finally, ask the students to select a topic and begin writing. Throughout the day, consider what you are reading, discussing, and doing, and make opportunities for students to identify topics for writing.

Topic selection is often decided by the student. It may be supported by the teacher through story starters, picture cues, or other stimuli. Every student knows things and has stories to tell. We need to have confidence in them and give them an opportunity to discover what they know.

Problems in Topic Selection. There are two common problems in topic selection: difficulty in finding a topic and persistence in writing about the same topic.

Maintaining a supply of writing topics is difficult for some students and rarely a problem for others. When students tell you stories, ask them if the story generates a topic they want to write about. When students are reading or you are reading to them, ask if the reading has given them ideas for their own writing. If they were going to write the ending of this story, how would they do it? If they were going to continue this story, what would happen? If they were going to add characters to the story, what type of characters would they add? Would they change the setting?

You can also facilitate topic selection by presenting a range of writing styles including stories, factual descriptions, mysteries, and observations. Students often begin writing by telling personal experiences. Through your writing and the writing of other authors, the students can be introduced to a wide range of categories that can provide alternative topics. One teacher sent student reporters to other classrooms to interview students about what topics they thought would be interesting to write about.

Ms. Schlegel's resource room contained a list of suggestions for what the students should do when they are stuck about a topic for writing (see Figure 6.6). A good example of how a friend can help was observed in Ms. Schlegel's classroom.

Ruth Ann, a student in Ms. Schlegel's classroom, was stuck for a topic. "What can I write about?" she asked as Ms. Schlegel observed during writing period.

■ **FIGURE 6.6**   *Up in the Air for a Topic?*

- Check your folder and reread your idea list.
- Ask a friend to help you brainstorm ideas.
- Listen to others' ideas.
- Write about what you know: your experiences.
- Write a make-believe story.
- Write about a special interest or hobby.
- Write about how to do something.
- Think about how you got your last idea.

"Check on the poster, check in your folder, or ask a friend," Ms. Schlegel suggested.

Ruth Ann got up and went over to another table where Cary was working on the first draft of a piece about a talking dishwasher. "Can you help me?" Ruth Ann asked. "I don't know what to write about."

"Let me find my idea sheet so I can help you out," replied Cary. "And go get a piece of paper while I finish this." The rest of the interview between Cary and Ruth Ann is described in Apply the Concept 6.2.

In addition to difficulty in thinking of a topic, students often repeat the same topic. Many children with learning and behavior problems find security in repeating the same topic or theme in their writing. They like the control they have over the language, spelling, and content. Look carefully at their work and determine whether or not the stories are changing through vocabulary development, concept development, story development, or character development. It could be that the student is learning a great deal about writing even though the story content is changing very little. Continue to confer and ask questions about the student's writing. If you feel the student is not moving forward, then suggest a change in topic.

Another problem that may concern some teachers is when one student selects a topic and other students copy the idea. For example, Scott wrote a story about a talking dictionary that was stolen and how Scott endangered his life to recover the dictionary. The idea had special meaning for him since he generally misspelled about 50 percent of the words he used in his writing. Once the story was shared with his classmates, over half of the other children wrote about talking objects, including dishwashers, brooms, and shoes. These stories written by other students (repeating Scott's theme) served as a vehicle for several students to write better developed stories than they had written previously, and for one rather good storyteller, Cary, to expand the story format into a traditional murder mystery for her next story. Of course, when she shared her story, many students followed by copying the theme.

Brainstorming.   Many students with learning and behavior problems begin writing without much planning about what they are going to write. They find that

APPLY THE CONCEPT 6.2

A FRIEND HELPS WITH TOPIC SELECTION

Ruth Ann returned with a piece of blank paper, which she handed to Cary. Cary wrote Ruth Ann's name on the paper and underlined it. Then she conducted a rather sophisticated interview.

"Think of three ideas. Want to write about your first day of school?"

"I can't remember. That was five years ago," answered Ruth Ann.

"How about the first day in the learning lab?" continued Cary.

"I don't remember that either. It was over a year ago."

Looking at her idea sheet, Cary commented, "I'm writing about a talking dishwasher. Do you want to write about that?"

"Not really," replied Ruth Ann.

"Where do you go on vacations?" asked Cary.

"To Iowa, but I've already written about that."

"Well, have you ever been to a circus?" Cary pursued.

"No."

"How about a zoo?"

"The Los Angeles zoo," Ruth Ann answered.

"Do you want to write about that?" asked Cary.

"Yeah," remarked Ruth Ann, "that's a good idea."

Cary wrote the number 1 on the paper she had labeled with Ruth Ann's name, and wrote, "las angels zoo" beside it. She remarked, "I don't know how to spell Los Angeles."

"Don't worry," Ruth Ann commented. "I can find that out when I start writing about it."

"OK, let's think up another idea. Have you ever ridden a horse?" asked Cary as she continued the interview.

"No," replied Ruth Ann.

"Do you have any pets?" asked Cary.

"Yeah, I have a cat named Pierre."

"Do you want to write about him?" continued Cary.

"Yes, I could do that," replied Ruth Ann enthusiastically.

Cary wrote the number 2 on the paper and beside it wrote, "writing about your cat."

The interview continued, with Cary explaining that it is helpful to think up three ideas so that you have some choice when you decide what to write about. After more questioning, Ruth Ann decided it would be okay to write about a talking shoe, so Cary wrote down Ruth Ann's third idea. Then Cary helped Ruth Ann decide that she was first going to write about her cat. Cary wrote this idea at the bottom of the page and starred it to note that Ruth Ann had selected this topic. Cary ended the interview with the request, "Put this paper in your writing folder so that the next time you have to select a topic we'll already have two ideas thought up."

when they read their drafts aloud, others have difficulty understanding the story or following the sequence. Sometimes we need to teach students prewriting skills so the writing and rewriting stages are easier.

Students with learning disabilities are limited in text organization skills because they have difficulty categorizing ideas related to a specific topic, providing advanced organizers for the topic, and relating and extending ideas about the topic (Englert and Raphael, 1988).

In teaching the thinking that goes into a piece, teachers need to model their thinking as they move from topic selection to writing a first draft. Some teachers have found it helpful to teach this thinking process by writing their ideas in an organized structure (Bos, 1991; Thompkins and Friend, 1986) and by asking students to set goals, brainstorm ideas, and sequence their ideas while they are writing (Troia et al., 1999).

In Ms. Schlegel's classroom this was referred to as brainstorm sheets; however, they have also been called structured organizers (Pehrsson and Robinson, 1985), semantic maps (Pearson and Johnson, 1978), and story frames or maps (Fowler and Davis, 1985).

Although these visual organization devices have been used as aids to reading comprehension, they also serve to facilitate the writing process (Pehrsson and Robinson, 1985). Ms. Turk, a resource teacher who works with Ms. Schlegel, used a "think-aloud" technique to model how to use the brainstorm sheet presented in Apply the Concept 6.3. She drew a large brainstorm sheet on the board and then introduced the brainstorming technique to the students.

Ms. Turk began, "I want to write a story about a time when I was really scared. So I decided to write about the time when I was about ten years old and my dad and I went for a horseback ride. He got hurt and I wasn't sure we'd get back to the car. There is so much to remember about this story that I am going to jot down a few ideas so that when I begin to write my story, I can remember them all and put them in order. To help me organize my ideas, I'm going to use a brainstorm sheet."

At this point, Ms. Turk explained the brainstorm sheet and the parts of a story. Through class discussion, the students identified a story they had written recently and each part in their story.

Ms. Turk continued modeling, using the brainstorm sheet. "I am going to call my story the 'Horseback Ride' for now. I may want to change the name later since it's easier for me to think of a title after I write the story. Well, it happened when we were on a trip to Mount Graham. So I'm going to write 'Mt. Graham' by 'Where.' I'm not sure how to spell Mt. Graham, but it doesn't matter that I spell it correctly now. I can find out later. Also, since the brainstorm sheet is for me, I don't have to write sentences—just ideas that will help me remember when I'm writing my first draft of the story." Ms. Turk continued to think aloud as she completed the sheet.

Ms. Turk demonstrated that the students did not have to fill in the brainstorm sheet in a linear fashion. Sometimes it is easier to fill out the ending first. She also demonstrated how, after she listed all the ideas under the action section, she could go back and number them in the order that made the most sense.

In subsequent lessons Ms. Turk demonstrated how to write a story from the brainstorm sheet. She also worked individually with students to write brainstorm sheets and to use them in their writing.

APPLY THE CONCEPT 6.3

SAMPLE BRAINSTORM SHEET

Name: **Mrs. Turk**

Date: **2/7**

Working Title: **Horseback Ride**

Setting:

Where: **Mt. Graham**

start at trash dump

When: **When I was ten years old**

Who: **Dad and I, also mom and brother**

Dad and I were riding on trail. Trail got bad.

Action: **Dad's horse stumbled on rock. Dad fell off + hurt his arm. Finally he got on horse. I helped. Rode to top of mt. Mom met us. So did brother. Went to hospital.**

Ending: **Dad was OK.**

During the year several different brainstorm sheets were used in Ms. Turk's classroom. Figure 6.7 shows a brainstorm sheet that was developed for expository writing (writing that describes the facts or information about a subject area; often associated with social studies and science). However, the students also used this brainstorm sheet for stories. They wrote the title in the center circle, and information related to the setting, problem, action, and ending in the four other circles and their accompanying lines. Students also developed their own brainstorming sheets. For example, Cary combined topic selection and brainstorming together and developed the brainstorm sheet presented in Figure 6.8. Her rationale was, "You really need to pretty well think through a piece before you decide if you want to write about it."

Teaching students to think about what they are going to say before they write is generally a helpful technique. However, completing a visual representation prior to writing may not facilitate writing for all students (see Apply the Concept 6.4).

Composing

Many students with learning and behavior problems begin the writing process here. They think of a topic and, without much planning, begin to write. They write ideas as they think of them and each idea they

write serves as a stimulus for the next idea (Graham, Harris, and MacArthur, 1995). Thus, the goal is to guide students to be more reflective as they write (Graham, Harris, and MacArthur, 1995).

Some authors suggest using cue cards to assist students in writing better developed stories or essays (De La Paz, 1999). A cue card used by Montague and Leavell (1994) asks students to consider these elements when composing: Where and when; character (have them think and feel just like real people); problem and plan; and story ending. Englert and her colleagues (Englert et al., 1991) developed think sheets to assist students in planning and then organizing their ideas prior to writing. Figure 6.9 on page 244 presents the plan think sheet, and Figure 6.10 on page 245 presents the organizing think sheet for the text structure associated with explanations.

Once children begin composing, sharing their work with others plays an important role. Children need time to read and discuss their pieces with individual students, small groups of students, and the teacher. The author's chair (Graves and Hansen, 1983)

■ **FIGURE 6.7**   *Brainstorm Sheet*

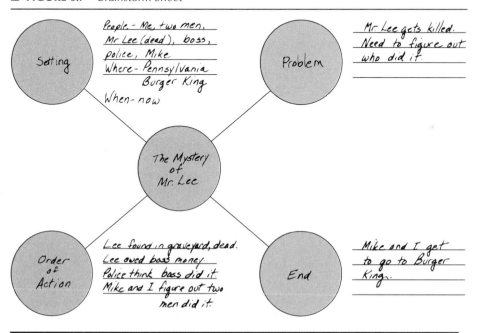

■ **FIGURE 6.8** *Cary's Brainstorm Sheet*

is a formal opportunity to share writing. Leila, a behaviorally disturbed fifth grader, signed up for "author's chair" early during the week. She thought her story about a dog who could fly was pretty good and she looked forward to reading it to the entire class. During "author's chair," she sat in a special chair in a circle, which included all students and the teacher. She enjoyed the attention from the group while she prepared to read. During her reading she could tell the story was going over well because the students were laughing and listening carefully. After the reading she asked them if they had any comments or questions. She called on several students who commented on sections of the story they liked and other students who asked questions. Mike wanted to know more about what the wings on the dog looked like. Rhonda wondered why the story ended the way it did. Leila answered the questions with the ownership of a professional author and made some decisions about parts she would change and how she would add more description about what the dog looked like. Sharing, as Leila did in the "author's chair," motivates her to keep writing and will help her with rewriting.

Teachers often need to set rules about students' behavior when a classmate is sharing their work in the "author's chair." These rules may include: raise your hand, ask a question or make a positive comment and give feedback when asked. Apply the Concept 6.5 discusses using the writing process approach in a heterogeneous classroom.

APPLY THE CONCEPT 6.4

THE BIG PICTURE

"The most difficult thing for me to teach my students," said Ms. Zaragoza, "is to think about the ideas in their writing, and to be willing to revise. My students thought good writing and good spelling were the same thing."

A common problem with poor writers is that the surface structure of their writing—the spelling, grammar, and punctuation—prevents them from expressing their ideas in writing. Many students with learning problems do not focus on thinking about their story. Their stories are often poorly organized and their ideas are disconnected and/or missing. These same students can *tell* you about the story, but have a hard time getting all of the ideas about the story in writing.

Following is the description of a procedure developed by Kucer (1986) to help poor writers focus on the "big picture" of writing:

1. Give students notecards and allow them to write possible topics on the cards (one topic per card). Students then share ideas about topics and make additions on their topic cards.
2. Students select a writing topic about which they would like to write.
3. Major ideas related to the writing topic are written on notecards. The major ideas may come from the student's knowledge and experience, or, if the writing is in a content area, the student may need to seek the assistance of class notes, books, and magazines. Major ideas are written as key concepts or thoughts rather than complete sentences.
4. Students share their major ideas about the topics with each other. They make any additions or comments about the ideas they feel will be helpful in writing about the topics.
5. Once major ideas are selected, they are organized in a meaningful sequence.
6. With their cards as a guide, students write their pieces.

Revising

Revising is a difficult task for all authors, and especially for students with learning problems. Getting the entire message down on paper the first time is difficult enough; making changes so the piece is its best and can be understood by others is a most formidable task. Many authors need to go back to prewriting and obtain more information, or they spend time conferring with others to find out what parts of the piece are going over well and what parts need additional work. It is also at this stage that some authors abandon the piece. They feel it can never be really good, and so they start again with a new idea.

Most students with learning and behavior problems have difficulty revising. They approach revision as a "housekeeping" task, making few or no substantive changes (MacArthur, Graham, and Schwartz, 1991). Many would like to move straight to publication, with little or no revision. Teachers often find it is best to allow students initially to move to publication without much revision, and then, through conferencing and reading the work of others, encourage students to see the benefits of revision. Ms. Gervasi, a middle school teacher, suggests modeling and patience. From her experience in using the writing-process approach with students, she finds they will eventually revise their pieces, but it usually takes time.

At first, their writing is more like a journal—a chance to write about how they feel and what is happening in their relationships. It is an intimate exchange between them and the teacher, and eventually between them and selected students, and finally between them and a larger audience. This progression does not happen quickly, nor in this order. For some students, it takes the entire school year. Ms. Gervasi helps students with revising by demonstrating how she rewrites pieces. She even brings in letters she is writing to ex-students and discusses the revision process she uses.

■ **FIGURE 6.9** *Plan Think Sheet*

PLAN

Name _____   Date _____

TOPIC: _____

WHO: Who am I writing for?

_____

_____

WHY: Why am I writing this?

_____

_____

WHAT: What do I know? (Brainstorm)

1. _____
2. _____
3. _____
4. _____
5. _____
6. _____
7. _____
8. _____

HOW: How can I group my ideas?

[_____]	[_____]
_____	_____
_____	_____
[_____]	[_____]
_____	_____
_____	_____

How will I organize my ideas?

___ Comparison/Contrast   ___ Problem/Solution
___ Explanation   ___ Other

Source: C. S. Englert, T. E. Raphael, and L. M. Anderson, Cognitive Strategy Instruction in Writing Project (East Lansing, MI: Institute for Research on Teaching, 1989). Reprinted by permission.

■ **FIGURE 6.10**   *Organization Think Sheet for Explanation of Text Structure*

Explanation Organization Form

What is
being
explained?

Materials/things you need?

Setting?

What are
the steps?

First,

Next,

Third,

Then,

Last.

Source: C. S. Englert, T. E. Raphael, and L. M. Anderson, Cognitive Strategy Instruction in Writing Project (East Lansing, MI: Institute for Research on Teaching, 1989). Reprinted by permission.

APPLY THE CONCEPT 6.5

CAN THE WRITING PROCESS APPROACH MEET THE NEEDS OF ALL STUDENTS IN A HETEROGENEOUS CLASSROOM?

A study that demonstrated the practicality and effectiveness of the writing process approach for meeting the diverse writing skill needs of students in a heterogeneous classroom was conducted by Zaragoza and Vaughn (1992). For six months they studied three second graders in a regular classroom setting as the writing process approach was implemented with their class.

One of the three youngsters in this study was a girl previously identified as low-achieving. The second youngster was a boy who had been diagnosed as having a learning disability in the areas of reading and written language and who had problems with distractibility and behavior as well. The third youngster was a gifted child from India; she had lived in the United States from the age of three and was highly verbal, cooperative, and self-motivated.

When the writing process approach was initiated, the writing skills of the low-achiever and those of the student with learning disabilities were so underdeveloped that it was difficult to read anything that either of them wrote. In addition, they had difficulty thinking about what they might write and were reluctant to put any words on paper. The gifted learner spelled imperfectly, but she enjoyed writing and had no difficulty expressing her thoughts in writing.

Progress was initially slow for both the low-achiever and the student with learning disabilities. However, as they witnessed their peers busily discussing and writing their ideas, and as their teacher worked with them to develop their own ideas for writing, they grew increasingly comfortable and confident in expressing those ideas in writing. Realizing that errors in spelling, punctuation, capitalization, and language were not the priority in the initial stages of their writing encouraged the children to take risks. Mistakes could wait to be corrected during the final stages of the writing process.

All three children made gains in written expression, spelling, punctuation, usage (grammar), proofing (identifying errors), and dictation (writing correctly from dictation). In addition, a writing-attitude scale administered at the conclusion of the study showed that all three students developed positive attitudes toward writing. Their positive attitudes were further demonstrated by the fact that all three children continued to write during the summer following the six-month period of study.

Source: Adapted from N. Zaragoza and S. Vaughn, "The Effects of Process Writing Instruction on Three Second-Grade Students with Different Achievement Needs," *Learning Disabilities Research and Practice, 7,* (1992): 184–193.

Ms. Gervasi writes a lot of poetry and shares her poetry with her students. Figure 6.11 shows a drawing and a poem written by an adolescent with behavior disorders in response to a poem written by his teacher.

Students with learning disabilities, particularly adolescents (Wong, Butler, Ficzere, and Kuperis, 1997) can learn procedures such as diagnose, compare, and operate to assist them during the revision process (De La Paz, Swanson, and Graham, 1998).

When teachers model, demonstrate, and provide feedback using the following procedure, students revisions and writing improve:

Compare and Diagnose
Read your writing and consider the following:
— Ignores the obvious point against my idea.
— Too few ideas.
— Part of the essay doesn't belong with the rest.
— Part of the essay is not in the right order.

Tactic Operations
— Rewrite
— Delete
— Add
— Move

■ **FIGURE 6.11** *Sample Poem Written by Student*

Shyness

My Shyness is like the color white
It is wanting to tell a girl how you feel
Shyness is girls who look up with a smile
Shyness is wishing I could disappear
From a crowd

Compare
— Reread the paper and highlight problems.

Diagnose and Operate
— This doesn't sound right.
— This isn't what I intended to say.
— This is an incomplete idea.
— This part is not clear.
— The problem is _____.

Editing

In addition to editing their own work, students serve as editors for the work of their peers. This can work several ways. One way is to have students edit their own work first and then to ask a friend to edit it. Another possibility is to establish a class editor. The responsibility of the class editor is to read the material and search for mechanical errors. The role of the class editor could rotate so that every student has an opportunity to serve in that capacity.

Whereas revision focuses mainly on content, editing focuses mainly on mechanics. After the student and teacher are happy with the content, it is time to make corrections for spelling, capitalizing, punctuation, and language. Students are expected to circle words they are unsure how to spell, put boxes in places where they are unsure of the punctuation, and underline the sentences where they feel the language may not be correct. Students are not expected to correct all errors but are expected to correct known errors. Figure 6.12 provides a poster that can be used in a classroom to remind students of the editing rules. Figure 6.13 depicts a form that can be included inside the students' folders to remind them of editing skills they know how to use. Figure 6.14 provides guidelines for how teachers and peers might respond to writing.

Although many spelling, punctuation, and language modifications are made during writing and revising, when students edit they focus solely on mechanical errors. Often they need to read the text for each type of error. First, they read the text, looking for spelling difficulties; next, they read the text, looking for punctuation and capitalization difficulties; and finally, they read the text, looking for language problems such as noun–verb agreement. Young students may not know what noun–verb agreement is, so they should simply look for sentences that do not "sound right" when they read them aloud.

■ **FIGURE 6.12** *Editing Rules*

Circle misspelled words.

Put a box around punctuation.

Underline writing that doesn't sound so good.

Add a ∧ to insert a word or phrase.

Add a ①∧ with a number to insert a sentence.

■ **FIGURE 6.13**   *Editing Skills I Know*

Spelling

1. done
2. was
3. from
4. come
5. girl
6. because
7. what
8. where
9. children
10. playground

Punctuation

1. Put a period at the end of a sentence.
2. Put a question mark at the end of an asking sentence.

Capitalization

1. Capitalize the first letter of a sentence.
2. Capitalize the first letter of a person's name.
3. Capitalize the name of a town.

The following suggestions are designed to assist students in removing the mechanical barriers from their writing (Isaacson and Gleason, 1997):

- Have students dictate their story to improve the flow of their writing.
- Provide students with a list of key words and difficult to spell word to assist with writing and editing.
- Teach students to use a "word" book.
- Promote peer collaboration in editing.
- Teach students to use technology to support editing and writing.

Tech Talk provides information about the Computers and Writing Instruction Project.

Publishing

Not all writing is published; often only one in five or six pieces is published. What does it mean to have a piece published? A piece is prepared in some way that it can be read and shared by others. Often this is in the form of books that have cardboard binding decorated with contact paper or scraps of wallpaper. Sometimes these books include a picture of the author, a description of the author, and a list of books published by the author.

Young children who are writing shorter pieces may be publishing every two weeks, whereas older students who spend more time composing and revising would publish less frequently. Why publish? Pub-

---

■ **FIGURE 6.14**   *Ways for Teachers and Peers to Respond to Writing*

Suggestions to Compliment Writing

- I like the way your paper began because . . .
- I like the part where . . .
- I like the way you explained . . .
- I like the order you used in your paper because . . .
- I like the details you used to describe . . .
- I like the way you used dialogue to make your story sound real.
- I like the words you used in your writing, such as . . .
- I like the facts you used like . . .
- I like the way the paper ended because . . .
- I like the mood of your writing because it made me feel . . .

Questions and Suggestions to Improve Writing

- I got confused in the part about . . .
- Could you add an example to the part about . . .
- Could you add more to this _____ part because . . .
- Do you think your order would make more sense if you . . .
- Do you think you could leave this part out because . . .
- Could you use a different word for _____ because . . .
- Is this _____ paragraph on one topic?
- Could you write a beginning sentence to "grab" your readers?

TECH TALK 6.1 ▬▬▬▬▬▬▬▬▬▬▬▬▬▬▬▬▬▬▬▬▬▬

COMPUTERS AND WRITING INSTRUCTION PROJECT

"Computers are powerful and flexible tools for writing that have the potential to help students write more effectively if they are used in ways that support the social and cognitive aspects of writing" (MacArthur, Schwartz, and Graham, 1991, p. 231).

The Computers and Writing Instruction Project (CWIP) curriculum is a process approach to writing that integrates word processing and strategy instruction. CWIP has been shown to be effective in improving students' writing performance and in developing writers who possess basic writing skills, including a range of strategies for planning, writing, and revising their work, and the ability to use writing to achieve a range of purposes (MacArthur et al., 1991). CWIP incorporates three key components that are associated with effective writing instruction:

1. Meaningful writing in a social context
2. Development of cognitive processes
3. Word processing to support the writing process

More information on this project is available from a technical report by MacArthur and Schwartz (1990).

---

lishing is a way of confirming a student's hard work and sharing the piece with others. Writing requires an audience, and periodically we need to share what we write. It is important for *all* students to publish—not just the best authors. Publishing is a way of involving others in school and home with the students' writings.

Aspects of the Writing Process

The Writing Conference

Conferring, which occurs throughout the writing process, is the heart of the writing procedure. The student comes to the writing conference prepared to read his or her piece, to describe problem areas, and to be asked questions. When students confer with the teacher, they know they will be listened to and responded to. The teacher's nonverbal and verbal interactions communicate to them that he or she wants to listen and help.

Students also know that they will be asked challenging questions about their work. Questions are not asked in a rapid-fire sequence with little time for the student to formulate answers. Instead, questions should be carefully selected and enough time should be allowed for the student to respond. Conferences need to focus on specific areas and should not cover all parts of the writing. During the conference with the author of "My best football game" (see Apply the Concept 6.6), the teacher realized there were many problems with the piece of writing. She was aware

of grammatical, spelling, and punctuation errors. She was also aware the story rambled, did not provide sufficient details, and lacked the voice of the author. However, she was ecstatic that this 14-year-old student with severe emotional problems had produced a piece of writing that he was excited about. Apply the Concept 6.7 presents the conference the teacher had with the student.

Some key points about conferring with students are:

1. Follow the lead of the student during the conference. Do not attempt to get the writer to write about a topic because it is of interest to you or to write the story the way you would write it.
2. Listen and accept what the student says. When you talk more than the writer during conferences you are being too directive.
3. Ask questions the student can answer.
4. Ask questions that teach. (Apply the Concept 6.8 on page 252 illustrates a conference in which the teacher asks questions that teach.)
5. Conferences should be frequent and brief. Although conferences can range from thirty seconds to ten minutes, most of them last only two to three minutes.

During conferences we listen to what students have written and we tell them what we hear. We

APPLY THE CONCEPT 6.6

SAMPLE STUDENT WRITING

"My best football game"

Football is my favorite game I like to play it even when I was little I played for a good team the bandits and one game we played against Macarther school and it started off with us 0 and them 7 and then the game was tied 7 to 7 and then it was time for me to sit on the bench and the score was 7-14 we was winning soon they told me to go back into the game it was getting close to the end and we wanted to win they said it was my turn to run a play and so I ran fast down the feild after the ball was Mike and I look back and see the ball coming right at me and I thought I was going to miss it but I kept looking at it and after I watched it I reached up and pulled the ball down and I kept on running and we won the game 7 to 21.

---

and other students make comments and suggestions based on what we have learned from writing. As Nancy Atwell (1985) suggests, we can only offer—writers may reject our advice.

Establishing a Writing Community

Writing requires trust. For students to write well within their classroom, an environment of mutual trust and respect is essential. The writer must also be able to depend on the predictability of the classroom structure. Establishing a writing community requires the following:

1. *Write every day for at least 30 minutes.* Students need time to think, write, discuss, rewrite, confer, revise, talk, read, and write some more. Good writing takes time.

2. *Encourage students to develop areas of expertise.* At first, students will write broadly about what they know. However, with encouragement, they can become class experts in a particular area, subject, or writing form. It will take them time and inducement before they discover their own writing "turf."

3. *Keep students' writing in folders.* Folders should include writing as documentation of what each student knows and has accomplished. This means students' work stays with them during the year. Work can be referred to for illustration of gains made, to indicate skills learned, and to demonstrate range of topic. Selected pieces from the year should be with the student for the next year.

4. *The teacher writes.* Teachers write outside of the classroom and with the students in the class-

APPLY THE CONCEPT 6.7

CONFERENCING WITH THE AUTHOR OF "MY BEST FOOTBALL GAME"

Teacher: "Mark, this football game was a special one for you. I bet you have a lot of feelings about this game. What are some of your feelings about this game?"

Mark: "I felt good."

Teacher: "Did you feel good like when you remember your homework or was it stronger than that?"

Mark: "It was stronger. I felt great. Like I was a hero or something."

Teacher: "Like a hero?"

Mark: "Yeah, like in the movies. I really saved the game. Well, I guess not really saved the game because we were already winning. But it was, like, 'cause I made the last touchdown it really said something."

Teacher: "What do you think it said?"

Mark: "It said, hey, watch out 'cause I'm good. Also, that we won and I scored the final points. It was great."

Teacher: "What could you do so the reader of your piece would know all of the things you just told me?"

Mark: "I guess I could include more about how I felt and all."

Teacher: "How could you do that? Where would it go?"

The teacher decided it was too early to focus on mechanical errors such as spelling and punctuation. Besides being discouraging to Mark, focusing too early on mechanical errors would sidetrack this writer from the story. After the author's story is complete, then working on mechanical errors could begin.

---

room. Using an overhead or easel, teachers may share with the students how they compose. Just as students share their writing with each other, the teacher shares his or her writing with the students.

5. *Share writing.* Conclude the writing time with an opportunity for students to read their writing to others and to exchange comments and questions.

6. *Read to the students.* Share and discuss books, poems, and other readings. There is a strong connection between reading and writing.

7. *Expand the writing community outside of the classroom.* Place published books by students in your class in the library for use by other students and allow students to share their writing with other classes. Encourage authors from other classrooms to visit and read their writings.

8. *Develop children's capacity to evaluate their own work.* Students need to develop their own goals and document their progress toward them. By conferring with the teacher, they will learn methods for evaluating their own work.

9. *Facilitate spelling during writing.* Teachers and students can provide instructional feedback to support students in spelling correctly during the writing process (See Figure 6.15 for suggestions).

10. *Considerations for culturally and linguistically diverse students.* Students from diverse cultures and whose first language is other than English often have specific needs in writing. With a few adjustments, teachers can create classroom communities that promote their success and learning. See Apply the Concept 6.9 for suggestions.

The writing process approach to instruction with children who have special needs requires time—time to set up the classroom, follow the progress of students, confer with students, and teach skills. More importantly, it requires time each day for the students to write. (See Apply the Concept 6.10 on page 255.) Suzanne, a teacher of emotionally disturbed adolescents who has used the writing process approach for the first time this year, comments, "Yes, it takes a great deal of time but it is worth it. The students want to write. They

APPLY THE CONCEPT 6.8

CONFERENCING: FOLLOWING THE LEAD OF THE STUDENT

During conferences, the teacher listens to what students say, follows the lead of the students, and asks questions that teach.

Teacher: "How's it going, Karin?"

Karin: "Not very good. I don't know what to write about."

Teacher: "You are having trouble with a topic?"

Karin: "I was going to write about how I want to go and live with my real mom again but I don't know what to say. All I do is write that I want to live with my real mom and then the story is over."

Teacher: "It's hard to think of what else might go in the story?"

Karin: "Well, yeah. I guess I could tell why, but I don't know why, I just want to."

Teacher: "Would it be any easier to get started if you told the story as though it were about someone else?"

Karin: "Like I could tell about a kid who wanted to go and live with her real mom. Then I could tell it like a story."

Teacher: "What are some of the things you might write if you told the story this way?"

---

have even started their own school newsletter. Best of all, they are seeing the connection between reading and writing. I feel it is worth the time."

Using Computers to Facilitate Writing

The use of word processors, spelling checks, and speech synthesizers to facilitate writing effectiveness for students with learning disabilities has been well documented (MacArthur, 1988; McNaughton, Hughes, and Ofiesh, 1997; Morocco, Dalton, and Tivnan, 1992; Morocco and Neuman, 1986). Of particular importance is the way these tools can be used to assist students whose writing or motor skills interfere with their ability to develop independent writing skills. The computer can also provide public visibility of the writing by displaying it on the monitor. This provides easy discussion between students and teachers and allows for immediate and facile editing (Zorfass, Corley, and Remz, 1994). When a computer-based speech recognition program was provided to college students with learning disabilities, the students performed significantly better on tasks of written expression than those without the speech recognition program, and as well as those who were provided an assistant (Higgins and Raskind, 1995).

Computers facilitate writing for students with learning problems because they:

— Make revising and editing easier
— Increase the amount and quality of revision completed
— Provide spell checking features
— Produce neat printed copies that enhance readability
— Allow for easy error correction (MacArthur, Graham, Schwartz, and Schafer, 1995)

TEACHING SPELLING

Most students with learning and behavior disorders need specific instruction in the mechanics of writing, such as spelling and handwriting. This is in part due to the fact that students with spelling difficulties do not have visual memory problems (Lennox and Siegel, 1996) but poor phonological processing skills (Lennox and Siegel, 1998). That is to say that the core phonological deficit, discussed in the reading chapter as causing reading problems, also causes spelling difficulties.

■ **FIGURE 6.15** *Providing Instructional Feedback to Facilitate Spelling Correctly*

Prompts to help students notice errors

- Check to see if that looks/sounds right.
- There is a tricky word on this line.
- You are nearly right.
- Try that again.
- Try it another way.
- You have almost got that. See if you can find what is wrong.

Prompts to help students find errors

- Find the part that is not right.
- Look carefully to see what's wrong.
- You noticed something was wrong.
- Where is the part that is not right?
- What made you stop?
- Can you find the problem spot?

Prompts to help students fix errors

- What do you hear first? Next? Last?
- What word starts with those letters?
- Do you think it looks/sounds like _____?
- What does an *e* do at the end of a word?
- What do you know that might help?
- What could you try?
- You said _____. Does that make sense?
- (Repeat what child said) Can you think of a better way to say _____?

Prompts to help students write errors

- You have only one letter to change.
- That sounds right, but does it look right?
- One more letter will make it right.
- It starts like that. Now check the last part.
- Did you write all the sounds you hear?
- Did you write a vowel for each syllable?
- What do you hear first? Next? Last?
- It starts (ends) like _____.
- There is a silent letter in that word.
- You wrote all the sounds you hear. Now look at what you wrote—think!

Prompts of encouragement

- I like the way you worked that out.
- The results are worth all your hard work.
- You have come a long way with this one.
- That was some quick thinking.
- that looks like an impressive piece of work.
- You are right on target.
- You are on the right track now.
- That is an interesting way of looking at it.
- Now you have figured it out.
- That is quite an improvement.
- That is quite an accomplishment.

- That is a powerful argument.
- That is coming along.
- You are really settling down to work.
- You have shown a lot of patience with this.
- You have been paying close attention.
- You have put in a full day today.
- I knew you could finish it.
- You make it look so easy.
- You have really tackled that assignment.
- This shows you have been thinking/working.
- It looks like you have put a lot of work into this.

Sources: Adapted from I. C. Fountas and G. S. Pinnell, *Guided Reading: Good First Teaching for All Children* (New Hampshire: Heinemann, 1996); I. C. Fountas and G. S. Pinnell, *Word Matters: Teaching Phonics and Spelling in the Reading/Writing Classroom* (New Hampshire: Heinemann, 1998); and E. B. Fry, J. E. Kress, and D. L. Fountoukidis, *The Reading Teacher's Book of Lists* (New York: The Center for Applied Research in Education, 1993).

Manuel hates spelling and finds it the most frustrating part of writing. He is an eighth-grade student who is adjusting to the transition from a self-contained classroom for emotionally disturbed students to a resource room in a junior high setting. He has been involved in the writing process approach for the past two years and has learned to use writing to express his feelings, convey information, and create stories. Manuel is proud of the way his writing has improved and he often shares his

APPLY THE CONCEPT 6.9

CONSIDERATIONS FOR CULTURALLY AND LINGUISTICALLY DIVERSE STUDENTS

Creating a learning community in the classroom that provides opportunities for all students to succeed is essential to promoting effective written expression. A few guidelines follow:

- Have high expectations for all students. Teachers demonstrate respect and provide opportunities when they treat each student as an able writer and provide the support necessary to assure their success.
- Allow students to write about topics they know and have experienced. Students with diverse backgrounds and experiences should be viewed as possessing a rich source of material for writing. Students benefit when they are encouraged to tap into their backgrounds and experiences and to share them with others.
- Allow students to teach all of us about their backgrounds and experiences through their writing. Students' writing can be viewed as an opportunity for them to better inform us about themselves, their families and communities and their interpretations of them. Students will want to write when they perceive that their writing has a purpose and is instructive to others.

- Encourage parent or family involvement in writing. Parents and/or family members often have a rich bank of stories and experiences that they are willing to share with the class if encouraged to do so. These experiences and stories can provide background for students' writing or can be used to prompt stories and ideas.
- Create a classroom setting that is culturally compatible. The social organization of the classroom can facilitate or impair the written expression of students from diverse cultures. Whole class instructional formats with high expectations for students to volunteer to answer questions may not be compatible with their cultural backgrounds. Read and ask questions about the cultures of the students in your classroom so you can establish a writing lab that is responsive to their learning styles.
- Use materials, stories, and books that are culturally relevant. Read stories about a range of cultures to students. Encourage students to exchange stories that are culturally familiar. Provide examples of cultures that are similar and different from the ones represented in your classroom.

stories with others. But he has difficulty with spelling. Manuel has learned to use inventive spelling (spelling words the way they sound or the way he thinks they are spelled) to aid in getting his ideas on paper, but he has difficulty editing because he is unable to detect or correct most of his spelling errors. Manuel, like many students with learning and behavior disorders, needs specialized instruction in spelling in order to be a successful writer.

Spelling is an important tool in our society. Many people measure one's intelligence or education by the ability to spell. Spelling is particularly difficult in the English language because there is not a one-to-one correspondence between the individual sounds of spoken words and the letters of the written words.

We learn to spell many words by remembering the unique combination or order of letters that produce the correct spelling of that word. Spelling facilitates the writing process by freeing the writer to concentrate on content. Although most students with learning disabilities have spelling difficulties (Johnson and Myklebust, 1967), spelling is often difficult even for those without a learning disability. Most beginning writers identify spelling as the key problem they need to solve in writing (Graves, 1983). Many good readers are poor spellers, and almost all poor readers are poor spellers (Carpenter and Miller 1982; Frith, 1980).

Students who have a very difficult time learning to read perform worse than average readers on

APPLY THE CONCEPT 6.10

TEN POINTERS FOR TEACHING WRITING TO STUDENTS WITH SPECIAL LEARNING NEEDS

1. *Allocate adequate time for writing.* Adequate time is a necessary but not sufficient criterion for improving the writing skills of special learners. Students who merely spend ten to fifteen minutes a day practicing the craft of writing are not spending adequate time to improve their skills. Students need a minimum of thirty minutes of time for writing every day.

2. *Provide a range of writing tasks.* Writing about what students know best—self-selected topic—is the first step in writing. After students' skills improve, the range of writing tasks should broaden to include problem solving, writing games, and a variety of writing tasks.

3. *Create a social climate that promotes and encourages writing.* Teachers set the tone through an accepting, encouraging manner. Conferences between students, students and teachers, and students and other persons in the school are conducted to provide constructive feedback on their writing and to provide an audience to share what is written.

4. *Integrate writing with other academic subjects.* Writing can be integrated with almost every subject that is taught. This includes using writing as a means of expression in content area subjects such as social studies and science as well as part of an instructional activity with reading and language arts.

5. *Focus on the processes central to writing.* These processes include prewriting activities, writing, and rewriting activities.

6. *During the writing phase focus on the "higher order" task of composing, and attend to the basic elements of spelling and punctuation after the writing is complete.* With some students, their mechanics of writing are so poor that they interfere with their ability to get ideas down on paper successfully. With these students, focus first on some of the basic elements so that the writing process can be facilitated.

7. *Teach explicit knowledge about characteristics of good writing.* The implicit knowledge about writing needs to be made explicit. For example, different genres and their characteristics need to be discussed and practiced.

8. *Teach skills that aid "higher level" composing.* These skills include conferencing with teachers and peers, and strategy instruction. Strategy instruction may provide guidelines for brainstorming, sentence composition, or evaluating the effectiveness of the written piece.

9. *Ask students to identify goals for improving their writing.* Students can set realistic goals regarding their progress in writing. These goals can focus on prewriting, writing, and/or rewriting. Both the students and the teacher can provide feedback as to how successful the students have been in realizing their goals.

10. *Do not use instructional practices that are not associated with improved writing for students.* Several examples of instructional practice not associated with improved writing are grammar instruction, diagramming sentences, and overemphasis on students' errors.

Source: Adapted from S. Graham and K. R. Harris, "Instructional Recommendations for Teaching Writing to Exceptional Students," *Exceptional Children, 54*(6) (1988): 506–512.

tasks of phonological awareness (see Phonology in Chapter 3) (e.g., Vellutino and Scanlon, 1987). Ehri (1989) suggests that they have phonological difficulties because they have not learned to read and spell.

This section will focus on teaching spelling to students who have learning difficulties. Techniques for analyzing students' spelling errors will be discussed first, followed by a discussion of principles to be applied in developing spelling programs, approaches to teaching spelling, and what the research has to say about teaching spelling.

Spelling Instruction

The first step in developing an appropriate spelling program is to determine the type and pattern of the students' spelling errors. After completing an error analysis, a spelling approach based on students' needs can be implemented.

Error Analysis

Error analysis should be done by using both dictated spelling tests and a student's written work. Random errors do not occur in the spelling of most students with learning disabilities. They are consistent in the types of misspellings to which they are prone (DeMaster, Crossland, and Hasselbring, 1986).

When Manuel and his teacher, Mr. Larkin, attempted to develop Manuel's spelling program, they began by selecting samples of Manuel's written work, which included writing he created and work written from dictation. Mr. Larkin examined these pieces to determine if there was a pattern to Manuel's spelling errors. He asked himself the following questions about Manuel's spelling:

1. Is he applying mistaken rules?
2. Is he applying rules that assist him in remembering spellings?
3. Is he making careless errors on words he can spell?
4. Is he spelling words correctly in isolation but not in context?
5. Are there frequently used words that he is consistently misspelling?

After examining Manuel's work and answering these questions, Mr. Larkin discovered:

1. Manuel did not apply the "ing" rule appropriately. For example, *run* became *runing*.
2. Manuel did not use the spelling rule "*i* before *e* except after *c*." For example, he spelled *believe* as *beleive* and *piece* as *peice*.

3. He was inconsistent in spelling words. He would spell them correctly in one piece of written work but not in another.
4. He spelled several words correctly on spelling tests but not in context.
5. He misspelled many frequently used words, such as *there, was, because, somewhere, very,* and *would.*

After answering the questions, Mr. Larkin examined Manuel's work to look for the following error patterns.

1. Additions of unneeded letters (e.g., *boxxes*)
2. Omissions of letters (e.g., *som*)
3. Reflections of mispronunciations (e.g., *ruf* for *roof*)
4. Reflections of dialect (e.g., *sodar* for *soda*)
5. Reversals of whole words (e.g., *eno* for *one*)
6. Reversals of consonant order (e.g., *cobm* for *comb*)
7. Reversals of consonant or vowel directionality (e.g., *Thrusday* for *Thursday*)
8. Phonetic spellings of nonphonetic word parts (e.g., *site* for *sight*)
9. Neographisms, which are spellings that don't resemble the word (e.g., *sumfin* for *something*)
10. Combinations of error patterns

In addition to examining Manuel's work, Mr. Larkin interviewed and observed Manuel to determine what strategies he used when he was unable to spell a word and whether he used any corrective or proofreading strategies after he wrote. Mr. Larkin observed Manuel's writing and then asked him the following questions:

1. *When you finish writing a piece, what do you do?* (Mr. Larkin was attempting to determine if Manuel rereads for spelling errors.)
2. *If you are writing and do not know how to spell a word, what do you do?* (Mr. Larkin was attempting to determine what, if any, strategies Manuel used. Did he use invented spelling to facilitate the writing process and underline the word so he could check the spelling later? Did

he stop and try to visualize the word or look for how it was spelled in another location? Did he continue writing and go back later to check the spelling?)

Mr. Larkin discovered that Manuel used few strategies to check or recall spelling when he was writing. In addition to teaching and rehearsing spelling rules, Manuel needed to learn and apply strategies for improving his spelling. After error analysis, intervention included discussing with Manuel the types of errors he was making, teaching him proofreading skills, teaching him techniques for remembering the correct spelling of words, and teaching him one of the spelling approaches (discussed in a later section of this chapter, Spelling Approaches). Before looking at specialized approaches to teaching spelling to students with learning and behavior disorders, we will first examine traditional approaches to spelling instruction.

Traditional Spelling Instruction

Spelling is taught in most classrooms through an integrated whole language approach or the use of spelling basal programs. Typical spelling basals included a prescribed list of weekly words to be mastered by all students. The usual procedure is that a pretest occurs on Monday, followed on Tuesday by a description of the spelling theme (e.g., long *e* words, homophones, *au* words, etc.). Wednesday and Thursday are usually assignments from the text that students work on independently. These assignments usually include dictionary activities, sentence or paragraph writing using the spelling words, writing the words a designated number of times, using the words in sentences, stories, or crossword puzzles, and so on. Friday is usually designated for the post-test in spelling. Although variations on this format occur, such as the teacher who attempts to individualize the spelling program, most classrooms follow a procedure similar to this.

How effective is this procedure for teaching spelling to students with learning disabilities? What other procedures might need to be considered to develop effective spelling strategies for students with learning problems? Spelling practices used in most classrooms are based more on tradition than they are on research (Gettinger, 1984; Gordon, Vaughn, and Schumn, 1993; Graham, 1999). For students with learning difficulties, the introduction of all the words at once, often words that are not in the students' reading vocabularies, and the lack of systematic practice and specific feedback make spelling difficult if not impossible for most. Before discussing specific strategies for teaching spelling to students with learning disabilities, the following section will discuss the role of phonics rules in teaching spelling.

Phonics Rules for Spelling

How much emphasis should be given to teaching phonics rules to improve spelling? There is probably no area of the language arts curriculum that has been more carefully reviewed, researched, and debated than spelling. At the heart of many of the debates is the efficacy of using a phonics approach to teaching spelling. Some researchers suggest that a phonics approach increases spelling ability (Baker, 1977; Gold, 1976; Thompson, 1977), whereas others argue that students learn the rules without direct instruction in phonics (Schwartz and Doehring, 1977), and still others insist that intensive phonics instruction is not necessary (Grottenthaler, 1970; Personkee and Yee, 1971; Warren, 1970). Recent evidence suggests that students who are taught spelling alongside a code-based (phonics) reading instruction improve in both spelling and word reading (O'Connor and Jenkins, 1995; Snow, Griffin, and Burns, 1998). At least for young children, a code-based approach to reading and spelling is likely to be both necessary and helpful.

Since there is a lack of consistency with phonics rules, primary emphasis should be given to basic spelling vocabulary with supplemented instruction in basic phonics rules (Graham and Miller, 1979). According to Graham and Miller (1979), the phonetic skills that should be taught include base words, prefixes, suffixes, consonants, consonant blends, digraphs, and vowel sound–symbol associations.

The important relationship between rhyming and spelling is illustrated in Apply the Concept 6.11.

APPLY THE CONCEPT 6.11

RELATIONSHIP BETWEEN RHYMING AND SPELLING

Rhyming and alliteration are positively and significantly related to progress in spelling (Bradley and Bryant, 1985). A possible explanation is that rhyming teaches students to identify phonological segments and it demonstrates how words can be grouped together according to common sounds. Students' participation at an early age, prior to school, in rhyming games and activities may be an important prerequisite to spelling success.

Principles for Teaching Spelling to Students with Learning Difficulties

Several principles should be included in any spelling approach used with students who have learning problems.

Teach in Small Units. Teach three words a day rather than four or five a day (or fifteen at the beginning of the week). In a study (Bryant, Drabin, and Gettinger, 1981) in which the number of spelling words allocated each day to students with learning disabilities was controlled, higher performance and less distractibility and less variance in overall performance were obtained from the group with learning disabilities assigned three words a day, when compared with groups assigned four and five words a day.

Teach Spelling Patterns. If the spelling lists each week are based on spelling patterns (Bloodgood, 1991; Carrekar, 1999), students have a better chance of learning and remembering them. A sample of several word lists based on patterned spelling follow:

List 1	List 2	List 3
cat	am	aim
bat	slam	claim
rat	clam	chain
fat	tram	rain
sat	tam	train
can	Pam	gain
fan	same	regain
ran	fame	brain
man	tame	pain

tan	blame	afraid
	flame	braid
	frame	

Zutell (1993) and Graham, Harris, and Loynachan (1996) recommend the use of contrast words to assist in identifying and teaching spelling patterns. Thus, the spelling patterns that are taught in the sample word lists 1–3 would be supplemented with several words that do not fit the pattern. Students would then be encouraged to identify the pattern and sort the words that do not fit.

Provide Sufficient Practice and Feedback. Give students opportunities to practice the words each day with feedback. Many teachers provide this by having students work with spelling partners who ask them their words and provide immediate feedback. The following methods can be used for self-correction and practice. Fold a paper into five columns. Write the correctly spelled words in the first column. The student studies one word, folds the column back, and writes the word in the second column. The student then checks his or her spelling with the correctly spelled word in column one. Folding the column back, the student writes the word in the third column. The student continues writing the word until it is spelled correctly three times. The student then moves to the next word. He or she continues until the word is spelled correctly three times in a row. This procedure should not be confused with spelling assignments that require the student to write the assigned spelling words a designated number of times. These procedures are often ineffective because the student

APPLY THE CONCEPT 6.12

PEER TUTORING AND SPELLING

Use of peer tutors to teach spelling can be helpful in improving spelling for the tutors and the tutees. When a peer tutoring system was used with a mainstreamed student with learning disabilities and a good speller from the classroom, the spelling performance of the student with learning disabilities improved and both students rated the peer tutoring system favorably (Mandoli, Mandoli, and McLaughlin, 1982). To increase effectiveness, peer tutors should be trained to implement the spelling approach most suitable for the target student.

does not attend to the details of the spelling word as a whole, the student often writes the word in segments, and he or she usually copies rather than writes from memory. The student also fails to check words after each writing, sometimes resulting in words being practiced incorrectly. Adding peer tutoring can help alleviate these problems (see Apply the Concept 6.12).

Select Appropriate Words.   The most important strategy for teaching spelling is that the students already should be able to read the word and know its meaning. Spelling should not focus on teaching the students to read and know the meaning of the word. Selection of spelling words should be based on the students' reading and meaning vocabularies. Ideally, high frequency words should be used (Graham and Voth, 1990).

Teach Spelling Through Direct Instruction.   Incidental learning in spelling is primarily reserved for good spellers. Spelling words can be selected from the students' reading or written words or can be part of a programmed text, such as lists provided in basal readers. Direct instruction includes mastery of specific words each day, individualized instruction, and continual review.

Use Instructional Language.   The language of instruction, or the dialogue between the teacher and the student, is critical to success in spelling, particularly for youngsters with learning and behavior problems. Gerber and Hall (1989) indicate that teachers' language provides a structure that calls attention to critical relationships within and between words and also isolates critical letter sequences. For example, "You wrote "nife"; however, the word *knife* starts with a silent letter. It is very unusual and you just have to remember that it is there. Think about the letter *k* as looking like an open jacknife and remember that the word *knife* starts with a *k*."

Maintain Previously Learned Words.   Maintenance of spelling words requires previously learned words to be assigned as review words, interspersed with the learning of new spelling words. Previously learned words need to be frequently reviewed to be maintained. Gettinger, Bryant, and Fayne (1982) conducted a study with students with learning disabilities to determine the efficacy of a spelling procedure designed to practice the principles of teaching smaller units, sufficient and distributed practice, and maintenance of words learned. Experimental group students with learning disabilities were able to reach an 80 percent criterion on more of the spelling words and were able to spell 75 percent of the transfer words when compared with a control group of students with learning disabilities involved in a spelling program that did not emphasize these principles.

Teach for Transfer of Learning.   After spelling words have been mastered, provide opportunities for students to see and use spelling words in context.

Motivate Students to Spell Correctly.   Using games and activities, selecting meaningful words, and providing examples of the use and need for correct spelling are strategies that help motivate students and give them a positive attitude about spelling (Graham and Miller, 1979).

Include Dictionary Training.   As part of the spelling program, dictionary training should be developed, which includes alphabetizing, identifying target words, and locating the correct definition when several are provided. Some students can develop a personal spelling dictionary to assist with their writing (Scheuremann, Jacobs, McCall, and Knies, 1994).

Spelling Approaches.   There are many approaches to teaching spelling. No one approach has been proven to be superior to others with all students with learning disabilities. Some students learn effectively with a multisensory approach, such as the Fernald method, and others learn best with a combination of several approaches. The following are several approaches to teaching spelling, all of which make use of the principles discussed in the previous section. Apply the Concept 6.12 describes the effects of peer tutoring as a procedure for teaching spelling.

Test-Study-Test Method.   This method of learning spelling words is superior to the study-test method (Fitzsimmons and Loomer, 1978; Yee, 1969). In using the test-study-test method, students are first tested on a list of words and then instructed to study the missed words. Strategies are taught for recalling the correct spelling of these words. These strategies often include verbal mediation—saying the word while writing it or spelling it aloud to a partner. After instruction and study, students are then retested over the words. Using this process, students then correct their own spelling test, which is an important factor in learning to spell.

Several word study techniques that can be applied when using the test-study-test method are presented in Figure 6.16.

Visualization Approach.   This approach to spelling teaches students to visualize the correct spelling as a means to recall. The visualization approach uses the following procedures:

1. The teacher writes a word that the child can read but cannot spell on the board or on a piece of paper.
2. The student reads the word aloud.
3. The student reads the letters in the word.
4. The student writes the word on paper.
5. The teacher asks the student to look at the word and "take a picture of it" as if his or her eyes were a camera.
6. The teacher asks the student to close his or her eyes and spell the word aloud, visualizing the letters while spelling it.
7. The teacher asks the student to write the word and check the model for accuracy.

The Five-Step Word-Study Strategy.   This strategy requires the student to learn and rehearse the following five steps and practice them with the teacher and then alone. The steps are: (1) say the word; (2) write and say the word; (3) check the word; (4) trace and say the word; (5) write the word from memory and check; and (6) repeat the five steps. When the student learns this technique the teacher models the procedure, then the student practices the procedure with assistance from the teacher, and finally the student demonstrates proficiency in the application of the procedure without teacher assistance. This procedure has been effectively used with elementary students with learning disabilities (Graham and Freeman, 1986).

Johnson and Myklebust Technique.   Johnson and Myklebust (1967) suggest working from recognition to partial recall to total recall when teaching new spelling words. Recognition can be taught by showing the students a word and then writing the word with several unrelated words, asking the students to circle the word they previously saw. The task can gradually be made more difficult by writing distracting words that more closely resemble the target word. In teaching partial recall, the correct word can be written with missing spaces for completing the spelling under it. For example,

with

w __ th

wit __

__ ith

wi ___ ___

w __ __ __

__ __ __ __

Total recall requires the students to write the word after it is pronounced by another or write the word in a sentence. This approach gives repeated practice and focuses the students on the relevant details of the word. Johnson and Myklebust (1967) also suggest that when initial spelling tests are given, the teacher may need to say the word very slowly, emphasizing each syllable. As students learn to spell the words correctly, the test is given in a normal voice and rate.

Cloze Spelling Approach.   This is referred to as the cloze spelling approach because the student needs systematically to supply missing letters in much the same way the students supply words in the cloze reading procedure. The cloze spelling approach uses a four-step process for teaching students to spell words.

1. *Look-study.* The student is shown the word on a card. He or she looks at the word and studies the letters and their order.
2. *Write missing vowels.* The student is shown the same word on a card with blanks where the vowels usually appear. The student writes the entire word, supplying the missing vowel(s).
3. *Write missing consonants.* The student is shown the word with blanks where the consonants

---

■ **FIGURE 6.16**   *Effective Word Study Procedures*

Kinesthetic Method (Graham and Freeman, 1986)

1. Say the word.
2. Write and say the word.
3. Check the word and correct if needed.
4. Trace and say the word.
5. Write the word from memory, check it, and correct if needed.
6. Repeat steps one through five.

Copy-Cover-Compare (Murphy et al., 1990)

1. Examine the spelling of the word closely.
2. Copy the word.
3. Cover the word and write from memory.
4. Check the word and correct if needed.
5. If spelled correctly, go to next word.
6. If spelled incorrectly, repeat steps one through four.

Connections Approach (Berninger et al., 1998)

1. Teacher says word, points to each letter, and names it.
2. Child names word and letters.
3. Child shown a copy of the word with the onset and rime printed in different colors.

4. Teacher says the sound and simultaneously points to the onset and rime in order.
5. Child looks at, points to, and says the sound of the onset and rime in order.

Simultaneous Oral Spelling (Bradley, 1981)

1. Teacher reads the word.
2. Child reads the word.
3. Child writes the word saying the name of each letter.
4. Child says word again.
5. Teacher examines correctness of written response; child corrects if needed.
6. Repeat steps one through five two times.

Visual Imagery (Berninger et al., 1995)

1. Look at word and say its name.
2. Close your eyes and imagine the word in your mind's eye.
3. Name letters with your inside voice.
4. Open eyes and write word.
5. Check spelling and repeat steps one through four if the word is not spelled correctly.

Source: S. Graham, "Handwriting and Spelling Instruction for Students with Learning Disabilities: A Review," *Learning Disability Quarterly, 22*(2) (1999): 78–98. Reprinted with permission.

usually appear. The student writes the entire word, supplying the missing consonant(s).

4. *Write the word.* The student writes the word without the model.

Fernald Method.   Fernald (1943) felt that most spelling approaches were useful for the extremely visual student but not for those students who need auditory and kinesthetic input for learning. Because poor spellers are characterized as having poor visual imagery, many may need to be taught through multisensory approaches such as the Fernald method.

According to Fernald (1943), specific school techniques that tend to produce poor spellers include:

1. Formal spelling periods in which children move through a series of practice lessons, writing, and taking dictation with little time to think about how the word is spelled before writing it.
2. Focus on misspellings and spelling errors, because it builds a negative attitude toward spelling.

A brief description of the Fernald approach to teaching spelling includes the following procedures:

1. The teacher writes the word to be learned on the chalkboard or paper. The word can be selected from the spelling book or by the child.
2. The teacher pronounces the word clearly. The student repeats the pronunciation of the word while looking at the word. This is repeated several times.
3. The teacher allows time for the student to study the word for later recall. If the student is a kinesthetic learner, the teacher writes the word in crayon and has the student trace the letters of the word with his or her finger. Fernald found that tracing is necessary in learning to spell only when the spelling difficulty is coupled with a reading disability.
4. Remove the word and have the student write it from memory.
5. The student turns the paper over and writes the word a second time.
6. The teacher creates opportunities for the student to use the word in his or her written expression.
7. The teacher gives written, not oral, spelling drills.

In contrast with Fernald's approach, which recommends not focusing on the student's errors and suggests blocking out errors immediately, other researchers have found some support for a spelling strategy that emphasizes imitation of students' errors plus modeling (Kauffman, Hallahan, Haas, Brame, and Boren, 1978; Nulman and Gerber, 1984). Using the imitation plus modeling strategy, the teacher erases the misspelled word and imitates the child's error by writing it on the board. The teacher then writes it correctly with the student and asks the student to compare what he or she wrote with the correct spelling of the word.

Gillingham and Stillman Approach.   According to Gillingham and Stillman (1973), "spelling is the translation of sounds into letter names (oral spelling) or into letter forms (written spelling)" (p. 52). Spelling is taught by using the following procedures:

1. The teacher says the word very slowly and distinctly and the student repeats the word after the teacher. This is referred to as *echo speech.*
2. The student is asked what sound is heard first. This process continues with all of the letters in the words. This is referred to as *oral spelling.*
3. The student is asked to locate the letter card with the first letter of the word on it and then write the letter. The student continues with this process until the cards for each letter are found, placed in order, and written. This is referred to as *written spelling.*
4. The student reads the word.

When writing the word, the student orally spells the word letter by letter. This establishes visual–auditory–kinesthetic association.

Correctional procedures in the Gillingham and Stillman approach include:

1. The student checks his or her own written word and finds errors.
2. If a word is read incorrectly, the student should spell what he or she said and match it with the original word.
3. If a word is misspelled orally, the teacher writes what the student spelled and asks him or her to

read it, or the teacher may repeat the pronunciation of the original word.

Constant Time Delay Procedure.　The time delay procedure is a method designed to reduce errors in instruction. Stevens and Schuster (1987) applied the procedure this way:

1. The verbal cue, "Spell _____ (target word)," is immediately followed with a printed model of the target word to be copied by the student.
2. After several trials in which there is no time delay between asking a child to spell a word and providing a model of the word, a five-second delay is introduced. This allows the child to write the word, or part of the word, if he or she knows it, but does not require him or her to wait very long if he or she is unable to correctly write the word.
3. The amount of time between the request to spell the word and the presentation of the model can be increased after several more trials.

The time delay procedure has been effective with students with learning disabilities and has several advantages as a spelling instructional method. It is a simple procedure that is easy to implement. It is fun for the student because it provides for nearly errorless instruction.

Self-Questioning Strategy for Teaching Spelling. Wong (1986) has developed the following self-questioning strategy for teaching spelling.

1. Do I know this word?
2. How many syllables do I hear in this word?
3. Write the word the way I think it is spelled.
4. Do I have the right number of syllables?
5. Underline any part of the word that I am not sure how to spell.
6. Check to see if it is correct. If it is not correct, underline the part of the word that is not correct and write it again.
7. When I have finished, tell myself I have been a good worker.

Morphographic Spelling.　Developed by Dixon (1976, 1991), Morphographic Spelling provides a highly structured and sequenced approach to teaching remedial spelling to fourth graders through adulthood. This teacher-directed approach assumes that students have some spelling skills and begins with teaching small units of meaningful writing (morphographs). Students are taught to spell morphographs in isolation, then to combine them to make words.

From the Research:
Instructional Practices in Spelling

Most students with learning disabilities have problems with spelling. Yet students with learning disabilities have been the focus of relatively few research studies on spelling acquisition. Gordon, Vaughn, and Schumm (1993), in a search for empirically based instructional practices for improving the spelling skills of students with learning disabilities, reviewed fifteen studies on spelling acquisition, dated from 1978 to the present, in which students with learning disabilities were the focus of the research.

Findings from the studies can be grouped into six areas of instructional practice: (1) error imitation and modeling; (2) unit size; (3) modality; (4) computer-assisted instruction (CAI); (5) peer tutoring; and (6) study techniques.

1. *Error imitation and modeling.* Students with learning disabilities need to compare each of their incorrectly spelled words with the correct spellings. The teacher imitates the student's incorrect spelling and, beside it, writes the word correctly. The teacher then calls attention to features in the word that will help the student remember the correct spelling.
2. *Unit size.* Students with learning disabilities tend to become overloaded and to experience interference when required to study several words at once. Students with learning disabilities can learn to spell if the unit size of their assigned list is reduced to only three words per day and if effective instruction is offered for those three words.
3. *Modality.* It has long been thought that students with learning disabilities learn to spell most easily when their modality preferences are considered. An investigation of the usefulness of a spelling study by: (1) writing the words;

(2) arranging and tracing letter shapes or tiles; and (3) typing the words at a computer, revealed that students with learning disabilities learned equally well when studying words by any of these procedures. Of significance, however, was the fact that most of the students preferred to practice their spelling words at a computer. Because students' preferences are likely to affect their motivation to practice, teachers are wise to consider students' personal preferences.

4. *Computer-assisted instruction (CAI).* Computer-assisted instruction (CAI) has been shown to be effective in improving the spelling skills of students with learning disabilities. CAI software programs for spelling improvement often incorporate procedures that emphasize awareness of word structure and spelling strategies, and make use of time-delay, voice simulation, and sound effects. Such capabilities make the computer an instructional tool with much potential to aid and motivate students with learning disabilities in learning to spell.

5. *Peer tutoring.* While a teacher's individual help is preferable, the realities of the classroom frequently make individualized instruction difficult to offer. Structured peer tutoring can be a viable alternative. In a study conducted by Harper and colleagues (1991), peer tutoring was extended to a classwide setting and incorporated a team game format into daily peer tutoring sessions. The students with learning disabilities tutored by their peers for the game achieved 100 percent mastery of their weekly spelling words.

6. *Study techniques.* Study techniques help students with learning disabilities organize their spelling study by providing a format for that study. As they approach the study of a new word, they know exactly how to go about their study; this is in contrast to the haphazard, unproductive study used by students who follow no such strategy.

Most of the research investigating the effectiveness of spelling interventions for students with learning and behavior problems has involved the use of teaching single words from lists rather than spelling in context (Fulk and Stormont-Spurgin, 1995). Nevertheless, spelling instruction for students with learning problems is best conducted explicitly and directly rather than through indirect methods that are often part of whole-language approaches (Graham and Harris, 1994).

TEACHING HANDWRITING

Often described as the most poorly taught subject in elementary curriculum, handwriting is usually thought of as the least important. Unfortunately, handwriting difficulties provide barriers to efficient work production and influence grades received from teachers (Briggs, 1970; Markham, 1976). Many students dislike the entire writing process because they find the actual motor skill involved in handwriting so laborious.

Despite the use of word processors, typewriters, and other devices that can facilitate the writing process, handwriting is still an important skill. Taking notes in class, filling out forms, and success on the job often require legible, fluent writing.

Handwriting Problems

Students with dysgraphia have severe problems learning to write. Hamstra-Bletz and Blote (1993, p. 60) define dysgraphia as follows:

> Dysgraphia is a written-language disorder that concerns the mechanical writing skill. It manifests itself in poor writing performance in children of at least average intelligence who do not have a distinct neurological disability and/or an overt perceptual-motor handicap. . . . Furthermore, dysgraphia is regarded as a disability that can or cannot occur in the presence of other disabilities, like dyslexia or dyscalculia.

Students with dysgraphia may exhibit any or all of the following characteristics:

1. Poor letter formation
2. Letters that are too large, too small, or inconsistent in size
3. Incorrect use of capital and lower case letters

4. Letters that are crowded and cramped
5. Inconsistent spacing between letters
6. Incorrect alignment (letters do not rest on a base line)
7. Incorrect or inconsistent slant of cursive letters
8. Lack of fluency in writing
9. Slow writing even when asked to write as quickly as possible (Weintraub and Graham, 1998)

Fortunately, with direct instruction and specific practice many of these problems can be alleviated. It is important to alleviate handwriting problems for several reasons: (a) they are associated with reduced interest in writing and thus influence written expression; and (b) students with handwriting difficulties spell worse than those without handwriting problems even when spelling interventions are provided (Berninger et al., 1998).

Manuscript and Cursive Writing

Traditionally, most students learn manuscript writing first and then, in about second or third grade, make the transition to cursive writing. Although this procedure seems to be effective for most students, many students with learning disabilities have difficulty with the transition from one writing form to another. Many learning-disability specialists advocate the use of instruction in only one form of handwriting, either manuscript or cursive. Some argue that manuscript is easier to learn, is more like book print, is more legible, requires less difficulty in making movement (Johnson and Myklebust, 1967), and should be the only writing form taught. Others feel cursive is faster, is continuous and connected, is more difficult to reverse letters, teaches the student to perceive whole words, and is easier to write. They feel cursive should be taught first as the only writing form. (See Table 6.1 for a summary of arguments for manuscript versus cursive.) Some critics maintain time could be better spent in teaching students to keyboard.

The greater bulk of evidence appears to be in the direction of teaching students with learning disabilities to use manuscript effectively and neatly, with the exception of learning to write their name in cursive. For most students with learning disabilities and with handwriting difficulties, manuscript should be taught in the early years and maintained throughout the educational program. Some students with learning disabilities can and want to make the transition to cursive, and benefit from its instruction. On some occasions, students who have struggled with manuscript writing feel learning cursive is "grown up" and thus respond well to the introduction of a new writing form.

Reversals

When five-year-old Abe signed his name on notes to his grandmother, he often reversed the direction of the *b* in his name. When writing other letters he would often write them backwards or upside down.

■ **TABLE 6.1** *Manuscript versus Cursive*

Manuscript	*Cursive*
1. It more closely resembles print and facilitates learning to read. 2. It is easier for young children to learn. 3. Manuscript is more legible than cursive. 4. Many students write manuscript at the same rate as cursive and this rate can be significantly influenced through direct instruction. 5. It is better for students with learning disabilities to learn one writing process well than to attempt to learn two.	1. Many students want to learn to write cursive. 2. Many students write cursive faster. 3. Many adults object to students using manuscript beyond the primary grades.

His mother was very concerned because she worried that it might be an indication that Abe was dyslexic or having reading problems. Many parents are concerned when their children make reversals and often their alarmed response frightens their children. Most children, age five and younger, make reversals when writing letters and numbers. Reversals made by students before the age of six or seven are not an indication that the student has learning disabilities or is dyslexic and are rarely cause for concern.

Teachers should recognize that:

1. Reversals are common before the age of six or seven. Teachers should provide correctional procedures for school-age students who are reversing letters and numbers but should not become overly concerned.
2. A few students after the age of seven continue to reverse numbers and letters and may need direct intervention techniques.

For students who persist in reversing letters and numbers, the following direct instructional techniques may be helpful.

1. The teacher traces the letter and talks aloud about the characteristics of the letter, asking the students to model the teacher's procedure. For example, while tracing the letter *d* the teacher says, "First I make a stick starting at the top of the page and going down, and then I put a ball in front of the stick." The student is asked to follow the same procedure and to talk aloud while tracing the letter. Next, the student is asked to do the same procedure, this time drawing the letter. Finally, the student is asked to draw the letter and say the process to himself or herself.

    Tracing letters is a frequently used method of improving legibility; however, there is little research that suggests tracing is an effective method of teaching letter formation. Hirsch and Niedermeyer (1973) found that copying is a more effective technique for teaching letter formation than tracing.
2. The teacher and the student can develop a mnemonic picture device that helps the student recall the direction of the letter. For example, with a student who is reversing the direction of the letter *p*, the teacher might say, "What letter does the word *pie* begin with? That's right, *pie* begins with the letter *p*. Now watch me draw *p*." Drawing the straight line, the teacher says, "This is my straight line before I eat pie, then after I eat pie my stomach swells in front of me. Whenever you make *p* you can think of pie and how your stomach gets big after you eat it, and that will help you make a *p* the right way." This procedure can be repeated several times, with the student drawing the letter and talking through the mnemonic device. Different mnemonic devices can be developed to correspond with the specific letter or number reversal(s) of the child.

The next section focuses on teaching handwriting, including discussions on posture, pencil grip, position of the paper, and legibility and fluency in writing. Specific instructional techniques such as the Hanover approach and Hagin's Write Right-or-Left are also discussed.

Components of Handwriting

Teaching handwriting requires the teacher to assess, model, and teach letter formation, spacing, and fluency as well as posture, pencil grip, and position of the paper. A brief description follows of these important components to an effective handwriting program.

Legibility
Legibility is the most important goal of handwriting instruction, and incorrect letter formation the most frequent interference.

The following six letters account for many of the errors (48 percent) that students make when forming letters: *q, j, z, u, n,* and *k* (Graham, Berninger, and Weintraub, 1998). Spacing between letters, words, and margins, connecting lines, and closing and crossing of letters (e.g., *t, x*) also influence legibility (Kirk and Chalfant, 1984).

The following remedial procedures for teaching letter formation are suggested by Graham and Miller (1980):

1. Modeling
2. Noting critical attributes (comparing and contrasting letters)
3. Physical prompts and cues (physically moving the student's hand or using cues such as arrows or colored dots)
4. Reinforcement (providing specific reinforcement for letters or parts of letters formed correctly, and corrective feedback for letters that need work)
5. Self-verbalization (saying aloud the letter formation and then verbalizing it to self while writing)
6. Writing from memory
7. Repetition

A summary of approaches to teaching letter formation is presented in Figure 6.17.

Fluency

Nine-year-old Marta's handwriting has improved considerably during the past year. She and her teacher have identified letters that were not formed correctly and Marta has learned to write these letters so they are legible. Now that her handwriting is easier to read, the teacher realizes Marta has another handwriting problem. In the regular classroom Marta has difficulty taking notes and writing down assignments that are given orally, because she is a very slow writer. She needs to learn writing fluency, which is the ability to write quickly and with ease without undue attention to letter formation. Marta's teacher decides to teach fluency by gradually increasing expectations about the speed at which letter formation occurs. Marta selects two paragraphs and is told to write them as quickly as she can while still maintaining good letter formation. The teacher times her in this procedure. They decide to keep a graph of her progress by indicating the time it takes her each day to write the two paragraphs legibly. Marta finds the graphing of her progress very reinforcing (see Figure 6.18 on page 270 and Apply the Concept 6.13). Since Marta's fluency problems were not just for copying but also for writing from dictation, her teacher implemented the same program, this time requiring Marta to time herself on oral dictations. Marta's time for completion of the passage decreased considerably over a three-week period.

Posture, Pencil Grip, and Position of the Paper

Many students have handwriting problems because they do not correctly perform three important components of the handwriting process.

Posture. The hips should touch the back of the chair and the feet should rest on the floor. The torso leans forward slightly, in a straight line, with both forearms resting on the desk and elbows slightly extended.

Pencil Grip. The pencil should be held lightly between the thumb and first two fingers, about one inch above the point. The first finger rests on top of the pencil. The back of the pencil points in the direction of the shoulder and rests near the large knuckle of the middle finger.

Position of the Paper. When writing manuscript, the paper should be in front of the student. For a righthander, the left hand holds the paper in place, moving it when necessary. In writing cursive, the paper is slanted counterclockwise for a righthander and clockwise for a lefthander.

Instructional Principles

The following instructional principles are suggested for any effective handwriting program:

1. Use direct instruction.
2. Provide individualized instruction.
3. Use a variety of techniques and methods, matching the students' individual needs.
4. Teach handwriting frequently, several times a week.
5. Give short handwriting lessons in the context of the students' writing assignment.
6. Handwriting skills should be overlearned in isolation, then applied in context and periodically checked.
7. Students should evaluate their own handwriting and, when appropriate, the handwriting of others.
8. The teacher's handwriting should be a model for the students to follow.
9. Teach handwriting not just as a visual or a motor task, but as both (Hagin, 1983).

■ **FIGURE 6.17** *Letter Formation Strategies*

Fauke Approach (Fauke et al., 1973)

1. The teacher writes the letter, and the student and teacher discuss the formational act.
2. The student names the letter.
3. The student traces the letter with a finger, pencil, and magic marker.
4. The student's finger traces a letter form made of yarn.
5. The student copies the letter.
6. The student writes the letter from memory.
7. The teacher rewards the student for correctly writing the letter.

Progressive Approximation Approach (Hofmeister, 1973)

1. The student copies the letter using a pencil.
2. The teacher examines the letter and, if necessary, corrects by overmarking with a highlighter.
3. The student erases incorrect portions of the letter and traces over the teacher's highlighter marking.
4. The student repeats steps 1–3 until the letter is written correctly.

Furner Approach (Furner, 1969a, 1969b, 1970)

1. The student and teacher establish a purpose for the lesson.
2. The teacher provides the student with many guided exposures to the letter.
3. The student describes the process while writing the letter and tries to write or visualize the letter as another child describes it.

4. The teacher uses multisensory stimulation to teach the letter form.
5. The student compares his or her written response to a model.

VAKT Approach

1. The teacher writes the letter with crayon while the student observes the process.
2. The teacher and student both say the name of the letter.
3. The student traces the letter with the index finger, simultaneously saying the name of the letter. This is done successfully five times.
4. The student copies and names the letter successfully three times.
5. Without a visual aid, the student writes and names the letter correctly three times.

Niedermeyer Approach (Niedermeyer, 1973)

1. The student traces a dotted representation of the letter 12 times.
2. The student copies the letter 12 times.
3. The student writes the letter as the teacher pronounces it.

Handwriting with Write and See (Skinner & Krakower, 1968)

The student traces a letter within a tolerance model on specially prepared paper. If the student forms the letter correctly, the pen writes gray; if it is incorrect, the pen writes yellow.

Source: From S. Graham and L. Miller, "Handwriting Research and Practice: A Unified Approach," *Focus on Exceptional Children, 13*(2) (1980):11. Reprinted by permission of Love Publishing Company.

Self-instructional strategies can be taught to students to improve their handwriting (Graham, 1983; Kosiewicz, Hallahan, Lloyd, and Graves, 1982). The self-instructional procedure that was used in the Graham (1983) study was based on a cognitive-behavioral model. The six-step procedure follows:

Step 1: The teacher models the writing of the target letter and describes the formation of the letter. The student then describes the formation of the letter. This step is repeated three times.

Step 2: The teacher writes the letter while describing the process. This continues until the student can recite the process for writing the letter.

Step 3: The student traces the letter, and the teacher and the student recite the process of the letter formation together.

Step 4: The teacher writes the letter, traces it, and then verbally discusses the process, including corrections (e.g., "My letter is too slanted.") then provides self-reinforcement (e.g., "Now,

APPLY THE CONCEPT 6.13

OBTAINING A FLUENCY SAMPLE

The following procedures can be used to obtain a fluency sample:

1. Have the student become familiar with the test sentence.
2. The teacher tells the student to write the test sentence a designated number of times at his or her usual rate (two- to three-minute sample).

3. After relaxing, have the student write the sentence as well and as neatly as he or she can.
4. After relaxing, have the student write the sentence as quickly and as many times as he or she can in three minutes.
5. After relaxing, the student and the teacher repeat this process with the same sentence.

that looks a lot better."). The procedure continues with and without errors, until the student can model the process.

Step 5: The teacher writes the letter and the student copies it while defining the process and providing self-correction. The student needs to complete this process successfully three times before moving to step 6.

Step 6: The student writes the letter from memory.

Following are several methods devised for teaching students who have handwriting difficulties.

Write Right-or-Left

Hagin (1983) suggests a process for teaching cursive that is based on manuscript and the vertical stroke learned in manuscript. In Hagin's Write Right-or-Left approach, the student learns cursive writing in the following manner:

1. The student learns motifs which form the foundation for later letter formation. These motifs are taught and practiced on the chalkboard. See Figure 6.19 for an illustration of the motifs and the letters that correspond with them.
2. After the motifs are learned at the chalkboard, the student learns and practices the letters associated with each of the motifs at the chalkboard.
3. At the desk, the student traces the letters while verbal cues as to letter direction and formation are given by the teacher.

4. In this step the student writes the letters without a model.
5. Through matching, the student compares the model with the product produced in step 4. Both the teacher and the student give feedback and determine whether additional practice is needed before the next step.
6. The student writes a permanent record of the letters that have been mastered.

The Hanover Method

Hanover's method (1983) of teaching cursive writing is founded on a single principle—the grouping of letters based on similar strokes into letter families. The letter families include:

e, l, h, f, b, k	This is the *e* family and is taught first.
b, o, v, w	This family has a handle to which the next letter is attached.
n, s, y	This family is grouped together to emphasize the correct formation of hump-shaped letters.
c, a, d, o, q, g	This is the *c* family.
n, m, v, y, x	This is the hump family.
f, q	This family has tails in the back.
g, p, y, z	This family has tails in the front.

■ **FIGURE 6.18**   *Marta's Fluency*

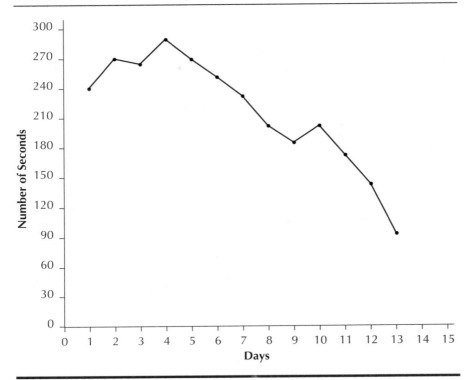

Some letters are included in more than one group. According to this approach, cursive letters are learned faster and easier when they are taught in their grouped families because of the similar strokes within the groups.

Teaching Handwriting at the High School Level

Handwriting often becomes important in the junior high and high school period because of the emphasis on taking notes and submitting written assignments. Many students have found that although the content of their assignment is correct they have lost points or were given a lower grade because their handwriting was difficult to read. Teaching handwriting to older students is difficult because the immediate needs of most older students are content-related and it is often difficult for the teacher to justify instructional time for handwriting, and because most materials for handwriting instruction are developed for younger students and are insulting to high school students. The teacher needs to carefully evaluate the handwriting problems of the students to determine if handwriting instruction could be helpful in a relatively short period of time, or if the students should learn compensatory methods such as typing or word processing. The two most important criteria for evaluating handwriting at the high school level are legibility and fluency.

In selecting curriculum for older students, specific attention should be given to the students' letter formation and fluency within context. Corrective feedback, short trace and copy exercises, and content exercises that require little thinking and allow the stu-

■ **FIGURE 6.19**   *Write Right-or-Left: Learning Motifs*

Ferry boats

Teaches smooth movements across the page.

Waves

Foundation for the letters *a, c, d, g,* and *q*

Pearls

Foundation for the letters *e, i, h, j, m, n, u, y,* and *z*

Wheels

Foundation for the letters *o, v, b, w,* and *x*

Arrows

Foundation for the letters *k, l, t, r,* and *f*

Source: Adapted from R. H. Hagin, "Write Right or Left: A Practical Approach to Handwriting," *Journal of Learning Disabilities, 16*(5) (1983): 266–271.

dents to concentrate on letter formation and fluency should be emphasized when teaching handwriting to older students (Ruedy, 1983).

INSTRUCTIONAL ACTIVITIES

This section provides instructional activities that are related to written expression, including spelling and handwriting. Some of the activities teach new skills; others are best suited for practice and reinforcement of already acquired skills. For each activ-

ity, the objective, materials, and teaching procedures are described.

■ Proofreading with "SCOPE"

Objective: To teach students a mnemonic strategy ("SCOPE") to help with proofreading their writing.

Grades: Intermediate and advanced.

Materials: A student-generated writing piece that needs to be edited.

Teaching Procedures: Discuss with the students how they often get into difficulty because they are not sufficiently skilled at proofreading their papers before they submit them and therefore get low grades because their papers have many errors. Teach the students a mnemonic strategy, "SCOPE," that will assist them in proofreading their work before they submit it.

> *S*pelling: Is the spelling correct?
> *C*apitalization: Are the first words of sentences, proper names, and proper nouns capitalized?
> *O*rder of Words: Is the syntax correct?
> *P*unctuation: Are there appropriate marks for punctuation where necessary?
> *E*xpress Complete Thought: Does the sentence contain a noun and a verb or is it only a phrase?

Next, demonstrate using SCOPE with a sample piece of writing on an overhead projector. Give the students ample practice and opportunity to apply SCOPE to their own work.

■ Writing an Autobiography

Objective: To provide students practice in developing written expression and to learn more about self and family.

Grades: Adapted for all levels

Materials: Writing materials

Teaching Procedures: During the academic year, read autobiographies to the students and discuss their contents. Ask the students what information they feel they would need to write an autobiography and how they might be able to obtain that information (e.g., students may need to interview parents and grandparents). Have the students write an autobiography, conferencing frequently with other students and teachers.

Autobiographies, with pictures, are then displayed in the classroom and school library.

The Life of JUAN GONZALES
by Juan Gonzales

My mother says she remembers
very well the day I was born.
She was at my grandmothers
She said all of a sudden she
had   great pain and went
oh my God !! My mother knew
I was going

■ Interview a Classmate

Objective: To give students practice in developing and using questions as a means for obtaining more information for the piece they are writing.

Grades: Adapted for all levels

Materials: (1) Writing materials and a writing topic; (2) a list of possible questions; and (3) a tape recorder (optional).

Teaching Procedures: Using the format of a radio or television interview, demonstrate and role-play "mock" interviews with sport, movie, music, and po-

litical celebrities. Give the students opportunities to play both roles.

Discuss what types of questions allow the interviewee to give elaborate responses (e.g., open questions), and what types of questions do not allow the interviewee to give a very expanded answer (e.g., closed questions). Practice asking open questions.

Use a piece that you are writing as an example, and discuss who you might interview to obtain more information. For example, "In writing a piece about what it might be like to go to the St. Louis World's Fair in 1904, I might interview my grandfather, who was there, to obtain more information."

Ask the students to select an appropriate person to interview for their writing piece and to write possible questions. In pairs, the students refine their questions for the actual interview. The students then conduct the interviews and later discuss how information from the interview assisted them in writing their piece.

■ Johnny Can Write!

By Sandra Stroud

Objective: To help a beginning writer increase his writing fluency, and to provide a model for correct sentence construction.

Grades: K–8

Materials: Pencil and paper

> My best Friend name is
>
> michell IS my best Friend because He lat me paly with has games and ride has bike we play Football and boket ball to.

> # My Best Friend
>
> Michael Pearson is my best friend. Michael is in the eighth grade at this school and he lives near me. I have known Michael for two years. Sometimes I go over to Michael's house and he lets me play with his games and ride his bicycle. We like to play football and basketball, and sometimes we go fishing. I'm glad that I have a good friend like Michael.

Teaching Procedure:

Step One: A list of story titles is shown and, if necessary, read to the students. They are each encouraged to select a topic about which they would enjoy writing. The students then write their titles at the top of their papers and write about their topic as well as they can. They are cheerfully told the spelling of any words for which they ask. An example is shown in the first box at the top of this page.

Step Two: As the students finish their paragraphs, they take turns reading them to their teacher or other helper. They are then asked to tell their teacher more about their topic. With input from the student, the teacher rewrites the paragraph. The student then orally reads the revised paragraph with the help of the teacher. An example is shown in the second box at the top of this page.

Step Three: The student copies the paragraph from the teacher's paper and then orally reads the revised

paragraph with the help of the teacher. An example is shown in the box at the top of the next page.

■ Expressing an Opinion

By Sandra Stroud

Objective: To evoke students' thoughts and opinions on topics of vital interest to them, so that they will write those thoughts and opinions with enthusiasm.

Grades: Middle and high school, with a fourth-grade reading level as a minimum.

Materials: Pencil, paper, computers for word processing.

Teaching Procedure: The teacher is alert for newspaper and magazine articles that are sure to be of interest to students in the class, and makes photocopies of an article for every student. After building

> ## My Best Friend
>
> Michael pearson is my best Friend. Michael is in the eighth grade at this school and he lives near me. I have known michael For two years. Sometimes I go over to michael's house and he lets me play with his games and ride his bicycle. we like to play Football and base+ball, and somdimes we go Fishing. I'm glad that I have a good Friend like Michael.

the students' interest in the topic of the article, the teacher requests that the students follow along, reading silently as the teacher reads aloud. The teacher takes care to read the article smoothly, with lots of expression, and at an appropriate pace for these students.

When the reading is finished, a class discussion ensues. Once the discussion has reached some intensity, the students are asked to turn to pencil and paper to write their thoughts and opinions on this topic. They are told not to worry about spelling or other errors.

The following day, the students are taken to a computer lab to type their articles at the computers. (While keyboarding skills are not required, students should first have some knowledge of the word-processing program and operation of the computers.) The teacher

will find that, as they type, most of the students will correct and greatly expand upon their compositions.

The preceding activity is beneficial to students for the following reasons:

1. *Encourages students to write.* Students who are reluctant to write are far more willing and interested in writing when asked to react to a topic of great interest to them. When assured that spelling and other kinds of mechanical errors (which can be corrected later on) will not be held against them, they express themselves using the rich and varied language of their thoughts.

2. *Builds vocabulary and word recognition.* As students listen and read silently while the teacher is

reading orally, new words enter their reading vo-cabulary. They simultaneously see a word, hear it pronounced, and learn its meaning from its use in the context.

3. *Encourages student participation.* When the topic for reading and discussion is one that is very close to students' hearts, they are eager to read silently with their teacher. Even the most reticent student will usually wish to participate in the class discussion that follows.

■ What would you do if . . . ?

By Alison Gould Boardman

Objective: To give students experience developing ideas for narrative writing and following simple story structure.

Grades: 4–8

Materials: pencil, blank paper, writing paper

Teaching Procedures: Have students fold a blank piece of paper in half. Ask students what they would do if they were invisible for 24 hours. Share ideas and probe students to add details (e.g., "You would go to the moon. Great, how would you get there? Would you take anyone with you?).

Tell the students that now that they have some ideas, they are going to make a rough drawing of four possible things they would do if they were invisible for 24 hours. Students should use pencil or one color to draw pictures of their ideas, one in each box. Pictures can be a rough drawings or sketches. The purpose of the drawings is to help students re-member and become interested in what they want to write about without the pressure of having to write it down.

Now that students are excited about their "adven-ture," they are ready to start writing. Begin with the introduction. Students write about how they become invisible. For the body of the story, students choose three of their four ideas to expand on. They use their pictures and build from there. The ending of the story details what happens when they become visible again and concludes their invisible day.

Adaptations: This assignment can be repeated with topics (from the teacher or students) such as "What would you do if you could fly, run 50 miles an hour, drive a car, etc." Depending on students' skill levels, length and content requirements can be adjusted.

■ Peer Revision

By Alison Gould Boardman

Objective: To give students the opportunity to work together in pairs to elaborate on their writing as one part of the revision process.

Grades: All levels

Materials: (1) A student-generated rough draft; (2) peer editing check-list; and (3) sticky notes

Teaching Procedures: Explain to students that all writers get help from their friends and colleagues to improve their writing. One way to do this is to get ideas for elaborating or expanding on what you have already written. Each student needs a rough draft that is ready to be revised (neat enough to be read by another student and checked by the teacher). Stu-dents work in pairs to complete the following revision steps, which are outlined on a peer revision checklist. It is helpful to model peer revision or to do a whole group revision before pairs work independently.

1. Read your rough draft out loud to your partner. While you are reading you may catch a few mis-takes. It is okay to correct them.
2. The partner reads the same rough draft out loud while both students check to make sure that each sentence is complete. Each sentence begins with a capital letter, ends with a period, and is a com-plete idea. The purpose of this editing step is to make sure the draft makes sense. This is not the final mechanical edit.
3. The partner reads through the rough draft again, this time focusing on the content. He makes three sticky note comments and puts them on the rough draft. One comment is positive. "I really liked the part when . . ." The other two

comments are helpful. "Tell me more about . . ." and "I don't understand the part when . . ."

4. Repeat the process for the second partner.
5. Each student works individually to elaborate on his draft by addressing the peer sticky note comments.

■ Step-By-Step Cartoon Writing

By Alison Gould Boardman

Objective: To give beginning or reluctant writers experience sequencing steps, using transition words, and writing a paragraph.

Grades: Elementary

Materials: (1) Index cards without lines; (2) colored pencils; (3) tape; and (4) writing materials.

Teaching Procedure: Discuss as a group the types of things students do to get ready for school in the morning. Tell students they will be drawing a comic strip about what they do when they get up in the morning. Students draw one event on each index card (e.g., waking up, getting dressed, eating breakfast). Students are encouraged to add detail to their pictures to help them remember exactly what happens. Now students put their ideas in order and tape them together like a comic strip. Before students begin writing, they use their comic strip as a guide to tell the story out loud. Encourage students to use transition words such as *first, next, later,* and *finally*. Teachers can post a list of transition words for students to use while telling and writing their paragraphs. Students then write one descriptive sentence about each frame of their comic strip to form a paragraph. Attach the final copy to the comic strip and display in the classroom.

Adaptations: Students can use this procedure to write any sequenced or "how-to" paragraph such as how to bake a cake, make a peanut butter and jelly sandwich, play checkers, or make the bed.

SUMMARY

Students start school feeling confident they know how to write. It is not uncommon to see young children writing notes to grandparents and other significant persons, making up letters and words as they go along, assured they are able to communicate in print. Most of these same students later find expressing themselves in writing one of the most difficult tasks required of them in school. The chapter described a process approach to writing instruction and discussed how to teach spelling and handwriting skills as aids to written expression. The assumption underlying the writing process approach presented in this chapter is that all children know something, and writing gives them the opportunity to share what they know. This approach has potential with students who have learning and behavior problems, as it focuses on writing from their own experiences and feelings, allowing them a systematic process for interacting with peers and teachers and providing consistent opportunities to write and receive feedback.

This chapter presented procedures for starting the writing process approach, including a description of materials needed, skills taught through the process approach, and the teacher as writer, modeling through writing and sharing with students. The elements of the writing process approach, which include prewriting, composing, revising, editing, and publishing were defined, and examples were presented of how they are taught and integrated into the writing process approach with students who have learning and behavior problems. Guidelines for conducting effective writing conferences, the key to successful writing, were described, and examples of students conferring with each other as well as with the teacher were provided.

In addition to describing the writing process as an approach to written expression this chapter discussed how to teach spelling and handwriting skills to students with learning and behavior problems. Most of those students need direct instruction in spelling and handwriting, and this chapter provided specific instructional techniques that have been successful. Since effective spelling instruction begins with understanding the types of spelling errors the student makes, how to conduct an error analysis in spelling was presented. Principles for teaching spelling to students with learning difficulties were discussed and spelling approaches were presented.

The handwriting section of the chapter discussed the advantages and disadvantages of teaching manuscript and/or cursive, as well as information all teachers should know about reversals. Approaches to teaching handwriting were also presented.

WEBSITES AS RESOURCES TO ASSIST IN TEACHING WRITING TO STUDENTS WITH LEARNING AND BEHAVIOR PROBLEMS

http://www.ldonline.org/ld_indepth/writing/isaacson_obstacles.html
This Website introduces eight methods that teachers can use to help students deal with the spelling or writing obstacle: collaboration, precueing, word books, asking the teacher, invented spelling, peer collaboration, self-checking, and computer-assisted writing.

http://www.ldonline.org/ld_indepth/writing/ERIC_E590.html
This Website contains information on effective strategies for writing and other useful links related to writing instruction.

http://www.ldonline.org/ld_indepth/teaching_techniques/strategies.html#anchor1001355
This Website provides several useful links on written language and spelling.

http://www.ldresources.com/readwrite/index.html
This Website provides several useful links on the writing process.

http://www.interdys.org/parents_.stm#spelling
This Website provides an overview of spelling difficulties and strategies.

http://www.edbydesign.com/parentres.html
This Website contains practical resources for spelling and writing.

http://www.quasar.ualberta.ca/ddc/incl/lamod.html
This Website provides a sample lesson plan for writing in inclusive setting.

http://www.Idonline.org/ld_indepth/technology/raskind1.html
This Website introduces technology to facilitate the learning of written expression.

http://www.Idonline/ld_indepth/technology/eric529.html
This Website introduces technology to assist writing process.

http://www.specialed.about.com/education/specialed/gi/dynamic/offsite.htm?site=http:www.schwablearning.org/main.asp%3Fpage=2.4.5
This Website provides an overview of using technology to facilitate the learning of written language.

http://www.ldonline.org/ld_indepth/technology/tech_writing.html
This Website provides information on using technology to enhance the writing processes of students with learning disabilities.

K AND APPLY

- Think about the elements of the writing process approach to instruction. How can you integrate them in your instruction?
- What is a writing conference and how can it be used with students with learning and behavior problems?
- What are several critical aspects to establishing a writing program for students with learning and behavior problems?
- In what ways can the computer facilitate writing for students with learning problems?
- How do you conduct and apply error analysis to the spelling errors of students with learning problems?
- What are the key principles for teaching spelling to students with learning problems?
- Can you describe several methods of teaching spelling to students with learning and behavior problems?
- Can you describe several methods of teaching handwriting to students with learning and behavior problems?
- What instructional principles are suggested for an effective spelling program?
- What key findings should you consider when increasing the spelling performance of students with learning disabilities?
- "Rhyming and alliteration are positively and significantly related to progress in spelling" (Bradley and Bryant, 1985). What is a possible explanation of this phenomenon?
- What instructional principles are suggested for an effective handwriting program?

7 Content Area Learning and Study Skills

KEY TOPICS FOR MASTERY

- *The role that concepts and related vocabulary play in content learning*
- *Strategies for determining which concepts and vocabulary to teach*
- *How to evaluate the considerateness of texts including readability*
- *How to adapt textbooks using study guides, highlighting, and alternative reading materials*
- *How to develop listener-friendly lectures*
- *How to make and adapt class assignments, homework, and tests*
- *How to use before, during, and after learning activities such as advance organizers, semantic feature analysis, semantic mapping, discussion webs, and concept diagrams to teach content*
- *How to teach personal development skills such as scheduling, self-regulation, notebook organization, and classroom participation*
- *How to teach students to take notes from lectures and learning from text using learning strategies such as Multipass*
- *Strategies for remembering content information such as key word mnemonics and strategies for taking tests*

 BRIGHT IDEA

Turn to pages 330–331 and read Think and Apply.

When Ms. Cho moved from her elementary resource room job to a high school resource position, her experience and education in teaching learning strategies and writing process serves her well for part of the school day. However, in addition to the two English periods she teaches daily, she is also expected to teach sections of American history and American government to students with learning and behavior problems. Although she minored in political science and history in college, she feels as if her content knowledge is rusty in these areas and her techniques for teaching content information are limited. She has also been asked to teach a section of general science, but she has chosen to team-teach the class with a science teacher, because of her limited content knowledge and desire to integrate the students in special education into general education classes.

When Desmond entered Bailey Middle School, he had been receiving help in a special education resource room since second grade. During that time, Mrs. Jackson, the resource room teacher, had been working with Desmond on word identification and basic comprehension skills as well as spelling and writing compositions. In elementary school, Desmond went to the resource room for forty-five minutes every afternoon. He consistently missed either social studies or science in the general education classroom while he was receiving special assistance in the resource room.

Desmond made many changes when he transitioned to middle school. While he attends resource English and reading, he also has social studies, science, and home economics classes in general education classes. All of these classes require him to listen to lectures in class and take notes, read chapters with technical vocabulary and answer the questions at the end of each section, take timed tests, write reports, and keep track of assignments and turn them in on time. By the end of the first nine weeks, Desmond is receiving failing slips in all three classes. He is frustrated by his classes and is becoming disruptive.

Doreen worked hard in high school and, despite her reading and writing disabilities, graduated with a high enough grade point average to enter college. However, as a freshman in a large university, she is finding herself overwhelmed by the demands of her classes. She is barely passing freshman English and classical literature and is even struggling in her math and science courses—areas that were her strengths in high school. Doreen can't seem to get organized. She has difficulty estimating how long it will take her to complete an assignment, and she is unable to keep up with the reading assignments in literature class. Doreen is a bright student with good potential to succeed as an architect or engineer, but she may never get through the basic liberal arts courses required for her degree.

Both Desmond and Doreen need strategies to assist them in being more effective learners. They need study skills in managing their time, organizing their notebooks, taking notes, studying for tests, taking tests, reading textbooks, learning new vocabulary, and writing reports and essays. Desmond and Doreen have mastered many of the basics of reading and writing, but they are having difficulty applying them in content area classes.

Ms. Cho, Desmond, and Doreen are experiencing difficulties functioning in the secondary and postsecondary school environments. In these environments the task demands for teachers and students change dramatically. The special education teacher often coteaches, teaches content subjects, or needs to provide content area teachers with learning and teaching strategies to support students so that they can have access to the general education curriculum. The students are asked to apply learning strategies and study skills as well as skills in listening, reading, writing, and math, in order to learn content area subjects such as biology, American history, art history, welding, computer programming, and home

economics (Bryant, Ugel, Thompson, and Hamff, 1999; Putnam, Deshler, and Schumaker, 1993; Tralli, Colombo, Deshler, and Schumaker, 1996; Vaughn, Bos, and Schumm, 1998).

Link (1980) surveyed 133 secondary and upper elementary teachers and administrators and asked them to rank 24 academic skills on a 1–7 Likert scale. Putnam (1992, Putnam, Deshler, and Schumaker, 1993) interviewed 120 at the seventh- and tenth-grade levels about the use of tests. The top ten skills identified by Link are:

1. Follow oral and written directions.
2. Make logical deductions.
3. Read at grade level.
4. Recall information for tests.
5. Locate answers to questions.
6. Turn in assignments on time.
7. Ask relevant questions.
8. Clearly express ideas in writing.
9. Locate information in textbooks.
10. Participate in discussions.

These skills reflect study skills rather than basic skills in reading and writing. The importance of study skills is clear when one considers that Putnam found almost 50 percent of grades are determined by tests. Students with learning and behavior problems often need instruction in study and test taking skills.

This chapter focuses on strategies for teaching content area subjects, making adaptations, and teaching learning strategies and study skills. The chapter is divided into three sections. First, we will look at teaching strategies to assist students with learning and behavior problems learn content area information. These strategies are useful to special education teachers whether they are directly teaching the content or collaborating with content area teachers (Bos and Duffy, 1991; Bulgren and Scanlon, 1997; Deshler, Ellis, and Lenz, 1996; Larkin and Ellis, 1998; Schloss, Smith, and Schloss, 2001; Tindal and Nolet, 1996). Next, we will discuss what general education teachers and their students think about teachers making adaptations. In the same light, we will also present some general strategies for making adaptations for textbooks, lectures, assignments, and tests.

Finally, we will examine methods of teaching students to be more effective and efficient learners. Many of the reading comprehension and writing strategies highlighted in Chapters Five and Six are effective in promoting content area learning and effective studying and learning. In addition, the Strategies Intervention Model in the section on cognitive behavior modification presented in Chapter Two can be used to teach many of the study skills and learning strategies suggested in this chapter.

Although the focus of this chapter is on teaching and learning strategies for secondary and postsecondary level students, many of the techniques presented are appropriate for upper elementary students. Both students and teachers alike have commented that using such techniques in upper elementary grades would greatly facilitate low-achieving students in secondary settings.

TEACHING CONTENT AREA INFORMATION AND VOCABULARY

If you are going to teach content, whether it be in courses of home economics, history, auto mechanics, biology, or government, then one of your major tasks is to teach the important concepts, vocabulary, and their relationships (Bos and Anders, 1990c; Readence, Bean, and Baldwin 1998; Vacca and Vacca, 1999). The goal is to enhance the content and teach related vocabulary so that the "critical features of the content are selected, organized, manipulated, and complemented in a manner that promotes effective and efficient information processing" (Lenz, et al., 1990, p. 132). Both the content enhancement (Lenz and Bulgren, 1995) and the teaching steps described in the interactive model for teaching concepts (Anders and Bos, 1984), as presented in the following pages, highlight the importance of using teaching routines. These researchers also recommend using instructional devices such as semantic or content maps and word maps or concept diagrams to organize and guide the learning of content information.

Concepts are general ideas that are associated with smaller but related ideas (Anders and Bos, 1984;

Vacca and Vacca, 1999). The following concept might be used in a science course:

> Bacteria are a class of microscopic plants that help people, other animals, and plants; however, bacteria also do things that hurt people, other animals, and plants.

Several related ideas that elaborate on the concept of bacteria are:

> Bacteria are small; you use a microscope to see them; bacteria multiply; bacteria live in soil, water, organic matter, plants, or animals; bacteria can make you ill; bacteria can spoil food.

The vocabulary associated with the general concept and its related concepts is the *conceptual vocabulary*. These are the words that are necessary for understanding the general idea and are associated with it. Examples of the conceptual vocabulary for a unit on bacteria in a science text are: *bacteria, microscope, colony, multiply, reproduce,* and *decay.* These words and their meanings facilitate understanding of the general concept.

Process for Teaching Concepts and Vocabulary

A six-step process or teaching routine (Bos and Anders, 1984; Lenz and Bulgren, 1995) can be used to teach concepts and their labels. The first step in teaching content area information is planning and deciding what concepts and related conceptual vocabulary to teach. Admittedly, some concepts and vocabulary are more important than others. Deciding what concepts and labels to teach is a crucial part of content area teaching. The six-step process is presented in Figure 7.1 and discussed in more detail in the following sections.

Step One: Selecting Concepts and Related Vocabulary

The first step in getting ready to teach content information is selecting the major concepts and related vocabulary to be taught, and generating a frame-

---

■ FIGURE 7.1   *Process for Teaching Concepts*

A six-step process can be used to teach concepts and their labels:

1. Decide what concepts and related conceptual vocabulary to teach.
2. Evaluate the instructional materials to be used for "friendliness or considerateness."
3. Assess the students on their background knowledge for the concepts and related vocabulary.
4. Use prelearning or prereading activities to facilitate and support learning.
5. Conduct the learning or reading activity.
6. Provide postlearning activities that further reinforce and extend the concepts and information learned.

---

work for facilitating understanding of the ideas to be learned. Selecting the major concepts and related vocabulary to be taught in a unit, a chapter, a section of a book, or a lecture is best completed prior to having the students interact with the material (Bos and Anders, 1990b; Readence et al., 1998). As the teacher, you need to determine the conceptual framework for the unit so that the information might be presented in an organized fashion based on this framework.

The process a teacher uses for determining the major concepts depends on his or her expertise and knowledge in the content area, knowledge of the structure of the textbook information, and knowledge about the students' background for the content and their study/reading skills (Bulgren and Lenz, 1996; Reyes and Bos, 1998). A teacher who has specialized in a given content area can probably generate concepts from expert knowledge and experiences, and use the assigned textbook along with key resource books and Websites as the primary resources for verifying the appropriateness of those concepts. A teacher with limited background knowledge could use a variety of resources, such as the assigned textbooks, trade books, state or local curriculum guides, Websites and other computer-based resources, and other teachers or experts in the field. Some texts—especially those written for students with reading problems—tend to include too much detail and fail

to explain the overall concept or to relate the concepts (Armbruster and Anderson, 1988; Scanlon and Anders, 1988).

After articulating the major concepts to be learned, you next generate and organize the related vocabulary. To do this, study the assigned text and instructional materials and compile a list of relevant related words and phrases. As you read, you may realize that some important vocabulary is missing from the text; if so, add it to the list.

To organize the list of vocabulary, group words that are related together. Then create a semantic or content map to visually represent the relationships among these terms (Scanlon, Duran, Reyes, and Gallego, 1992). Figure 7.2 depicts a map developed with the conceptual vocabulary a teacher generated from a chapter in a biology text. The map highlights the critical vocabulary and the organization and relationships of the concepts (Anders and Bos, 1984; Lenz and Bulgren, 1995). The map helps to solve an all too common problem that confronts content area teachers: deciding what concepts and related vocabulary to teach in a content lesson.

Step Two: Evaluating Instructional Materials

Before teaching the concepts and related vocabulary, teachers need to evaluate the instructional materials they intend to use in teaching the unit. Whether you are teaching the content yourself or collaborating with a content teacher, this evaluation is critical to support students with learning and behavior problems and to know how to make adaptations so that students have access to the content. While the breadth of instructional materials has increased with the use of the Internet and other media, textbooks still continue to be the predominant medium of instruction (Ciborowski, 1992; O'Brien, Stewart, and Moje, 1995; Vacca and Vacca, 1999). In terms of the general education curriculum, textbooks structure from 65 to 90 percent of secondary classroom instruction (Woodward and Elliott, 1990). How concepts are presented in a text, whether it is the class textbook, a resource book, or on the Internet, will affect how easily they are comprehended and learned

■ **FIGURE 7.2**   *Content Map of a Biology Chapter on Mollusks*

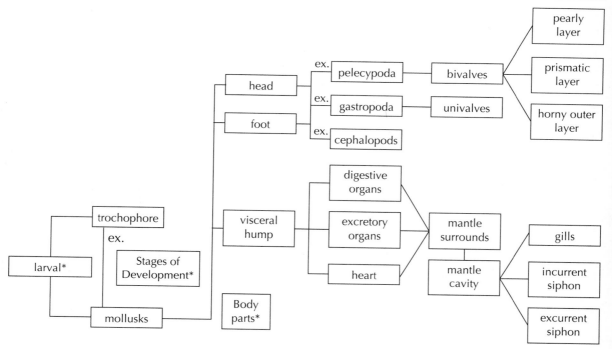

*Note: There seem to be two concepts being developed (apologies to the biologists among us):
1. When classifying animals biologists look for relationships between animals during the various stages of development from birth to adulthood.
2. Biologists describe the body parts of animals and the functions of each part.

Source: P. L. Anders and C. S. Bos, "In the Beginning: Vocabulary Instruction in Content Classes," *Topics in Learning and Learning Disabilities* 3(4) (1984): 56. Reprinted with permission of PRO-ED.

by the students (Bryant et al., 1999; McKeown, Beck, Sinatra, and Loxterman, 1992).

The manner in which the text is organized (e.g., use of headings and subheadings, highlighted words, marginal notes) will also affect comprehensibility of the text.

Readability

Traditionally, emphasis in evaluating content area texts was placed on the readability of the text as determined by readability formulas (e.g., Dale and Chall, 1948; Fry, 1977). Most readability formulas, including the Fry readability formula presented in

Figure 7.3, are based on two factors: sentence complexity as measured by sentence length and word difficulty as indexed by word length or frequency.

Readability formulas should be used cautiously and as only one aspect of evaluating a text for several reasons (Alvermann and Phelps, 1998; Anders and Guzzetti, 1996). First, the typical standard error of measurement for readability formulas is plus or minus approximately 1.5 grade levels (Singer and Donlan, 1989). Consequently, a text whose readability formula is predicted as 7.5 can range by chance from 6.0 to 9.0. Second, readability formulas do not take into account many characteristics of *text* that

■ **FIGURE 7.3**   *Fry Readability Graph for Estimating Readability—Extended*

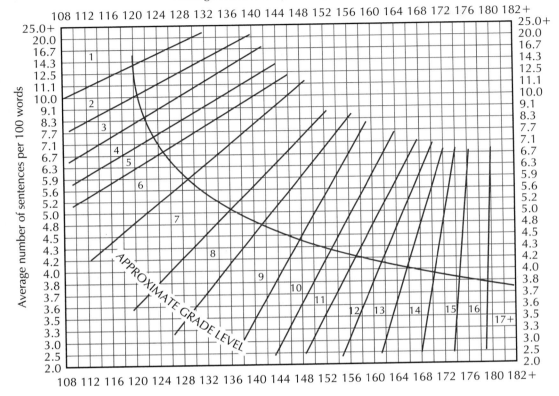

1. Randomly select three text samples of exactly 100 words, beginning with the beginning of a sentence. Count proper nouns, numerals, and initializations as words.
2. Count the number of sentences in each 100-word sample, estimating the length of the last sentence to the nearest one-tenth.
3. Count the total number of syllables in each 100-word sample. Count one syllable for each numeral or initial or symbol; for example, 1990 is one word and four syllables, LD is one word and two syllables, and "&" is one word and one syllable.
4. Average the number of sentences and number of syllables across the three samples.
5. Enter the average sentence length and average number of syllables on the graph. Put a dot where the two lines intersect. The area in which the dot is plotted will give you an approximate estimated readability.
6. If there is a great deal of variability in the syllable or sentence count across the three samples, more samples can be added.

Source: Edward Fry, "Fry's Readability Graph: Clarifications, Validity, and Extension to Level 17," *Journal of Reading, 21* (1977): 242–252.

are important in comprehension and learning. For example, to reduce the reading level or difficulty as measured by readability formulas, textbooks and, particularly, adapted textbooks that are designed for students with learning and behavior problems are written using short sentences. Oftentimes this means that important relational words such as *and, or, because,* and *if . . . then* have been eliminated to shorten the length of the sentences, and consequently reduce the readability level as predicted by the formula. However, it is these relational words that signal the reader to the relationships among the concepts (Davison, 1984). Consequently, although the readability according to the formula may be reduced, the text is actually more difficult to understand. Third, students' prior knowledge of the content and the concepts and technical vocabulary associated with the content can dramatically affect how easy the text is to comprehend. Fourth, readability formulas neglect to consider other characteristics of the *reader* that affect comprehension such as interest, purpose, and perserverance.

Considerate or User-Friendly Text

What characteristics should be considered when evaluating how considerate or user-friendly a text is? Armbruster and Anderson (1988) conducted a program of research to develop salient criteria for determining the considerate text. Their criteria fall into three broad categories: structure, coherence, and audience appropriateness.

1. *Structure* refers to the manner in which the text is organized and how the text signals its structure. Use of titles, headings, subheadings, introductions, and summary statements, informative and relevant pictures, charts, and graphs, highlighted key concepts, marginal notes, and signaling words (e.g., *first, second, then, therefore*) can facilitate comprehension. In evaluating the text, it is important not only to check if such structural features are used, but if they match the content. For example, sometimes headings will not relate well to the text contained under the headings. In this case, the structural features may serve more as a source of confusion than as an aide. Also,

check to see if the highlighted words in the text represent the important concepts or simply the words that are difficult to decode.

Also, consider if the format and the Table of Contents assist the reader in drawing relationships between the various chapters by using such devices as sections and subsections? Do introductions to each section or chapter encourage the reader to draw connections between previous ideas and concepts already discussed and the new ideas to be presented? Some key features to consider in assessing the structure are:

- Introduction is clearly identified.
- Introduction provides purpose, relevance, and overview.
- Titles, headings, and subheadings reflect main ideas of content.
- Key vocabulary are highlighted and reflect important concepts.
- Definitions of key terms are provided.
- Margin notes provide summaries or expand on information.
- Illustrations and pictures enhance important information.
- Summary is clearly identified.
- Summary reviews goals and most important concepts.
- Review questions require students to think about the key concepts and ideas.
- Questions have good balance among main concepts, fact/detail, and critical thinking (application, analysis, reactions).

2. *Coherence* refers to how well the ideas in a text "stick together" (Armbruster and Anderson, 1988). With coherent text the relationships among concepts are clear. For example, when Herman, Anderson, Pearson, and Nagy (1987) rewrote text about the circulatory system and made explicit the connections between motive and action, form and function, and cause and effect, student learning improved. Coherence is also facilitated by using different kinds of *cohesive ties*—linguistic forms that help convey meaning across phrase, clause, and sentence boundaries (Anders and Guzzetti, 1996). Examples of cohesive ties are *conjunctions* and *con-*

nectives, *pronoun referents* (using a pronoun to refer to a previously mentioned noun), and *substitutions* (using a word to replace a previously used noun or verb phrase).

3. *Audience appropriateness* refers to how well the textbook is suited to the readers' content knowledge, reading and study skills. The text needs to provide enough explanation, attributes, examples, and analogies to provide readers with adequate information to relate to their background knowledge. Superficial mentioning of new topics for which the reader has limited background knowledge does little to build understanding. On the other hand, too many or too technical supporting details can obscure the important concepts.

Another area to consider with relation to the audience is the explicitness of main ideas. As was discussed in the chapter on reading (Chapter Five), many students with learning and behavior problems have difficulty identifying and comprehending the main ideas of a text. Therefore, text in which the main ideas are explicit and regularly placed at the beginning of paragraphs and sections should facilitate learning. However, in examining social studies textbooks designed for the second, fourth, sixth, and eighth grades, Baumann and Serra (1984) found that only 27 percent of the short passages contained explicitly stated main ideas, only 44 percent of the paragraphs contained them, and only 27 percent of the paragraphs began with them.

Part of the process of preparing to teach content knowledge is evaluating instructional materials for readability and friendliness. By considering the structure, cohesion, and audience appropriateness when evaluating text or other types of instructional materials (e.g., films, lectures, demonstrations), the teacher develops a good idea of how considerate or user-friendly the materials are. Based on this evaluation, the teacher may decide to modify, augment, or adapt the instructional materials (see the section on adapting textbooks in this chapter).

The ultimate judge of the readability and friendliness of a textbook is the reader. The FLIP Chart strategy helps students learn to evaluate text on their own (Schumm and Mangrum, 1991). FLIP stands for Friendliness, Language, Interest, Prior knowledge. By filling out charts like the one shown in Figure 7.4, students learn what is comfortable for them individually as readers. After students have completed the FLIP chart you can learn (through class discussions and individual conferences) what is difficult for them in terms of text friendliness, language, interest, and prior knowledge. Students with reading and learning problems especially need to learn how to talk about the textbook and any problems they have with it. Classroom discussions based on the FLIP chart strategy also help students think as a group about effective strategies for coping with text they find difficult.

Step Three: Assessing Students' Prior Knowledge

Before content area teachers assign a specific chapter or text to read or present a lecture on a topic, they need to assess the students' background knowledge for the concepts and related vocabulary to be covered. Prior knowledge plays a critical role in determining how effectively students will comprehend and retain the information and vocabulary to be presented. One technique for assessing prior knowledge is using the PreReading Plan, with which you are familiar (see Chapter Five). This plan not only assesses students' knowledge, but also serves to activate their knowledge, thus facilitating comprehension.

A second procedure that can be used to assess and activate students' background knowledge is semantic mapping (Johnson, Pittelman, and Heimlich, 1986; Pearson and Johnson, 1978; Scanlon, et al., 1992). Like PReP, this technique uses brainstorming ideas about the topic to generate a list of words and phrases related to the key concept. The teacher and students take the ideas given by the students and relate them to the key concept, developing a network that notes the various relations (e.g., categories, subcategories, definition, class, examples, properties, or characteristics). A semantic map for the concept of "desert" was developed with a group of fifth-grade students with

■ **FIGURE 7.4**   *The FLIP Chart*

Title of assignment _____

Number of pages _____

General directions: Rate each of the four FLIP categories on a 1–5 scale (5 = high). Then determine your purpose for reading and appropriate reading rate, and budget your reading/study time.

Friendliness: How friendly is my reading assignment?

Directions: Examine your assignment to see if it includes the friendly elements listed below.

Friendly text features

Table of contents	Index	Glossary
Chapter introductions	Headings	Subheadings
Margin notes	Study questions	Chapter summary
Key terms highlighted	Graphs	Charts
Pictures	Signal words	Lists of key facts

1 ——————— 2 ——————— 3 ——————— 4 ——————— 5

No friendly text features   Some friendly text features   Many friendly text features

Friendliness rating _____

Language: How difficult is the language in my reading assignment?

Directions: Skim the chapter quickly to determine the number of new terms. Read 3 random paragraphs to get a feel for the vocabulary level and number of long, complicated sentences.

1 ——————— 2 ——————— 3 ——————— 4 ——————— 5

Many new words;   Some new words: No new words;
complicated sentences   somewhat complicated sentences   clear sentences

Language rating _____

Interest: How interesting is my reading assignment?

Directions: Read the title, introduction, headings/subheadings, and summary. Examine the pictures and graphics included.

1 ——————— 2 ——————— 3 ——————— 4 ——————— 5

Boring   Somewhat interesting   Very interesting

Interest rating _____

Prior knowledge: Who do I already know about the material covered in my reading assignment.

Directions: Think about the title, introduction, headings/subheadings, and summary.

1 ——————— 2 ——————— 3 ——————— 4 ——————— 5

Mostly new information   Some new information   Mostly familiar information

Prior knowledge rating _____

Overall, this reading assignment appears to be at:
- ❏ a comfortable reading level for me
- ❏ a somewhat comfortable reading level for me
- ❏ an uncomfortable reading level for me

Source: J. S. Schumm and C. T. Magnum, "FLIP: A Framework for Textbook Thinking," *Journal of Reading, 35* (1991): 120–124. Copyright by the International Reading Association.

learning disabilities preparing to study deserts, using the ideas they gave. The map, shown in Figure 7.5, indicates that the students can give examples and characteristics of a desert. However, the students did not produce a superordinate class (landform) or a definition ("What is it?"). Additionally, the property and example relations that were generated lacked technical vocabulary despite further probing on the part of the teacher. The semantic map in Figure 7.5 serves not only as a visual representation for the students' current understanding of the concept of deserts, but the map also functions as an initial blueprint for teaching (Bos and Anders, 1992; Reyes and Bos, 1998).

Using activities such as semantic mapping and PReP not only provides the teacher with valuable information concerning the students' knowledge, it also activates their knowledge. This is particularly important for second language and culturally diverse learners with learning and behavior problems who may have limited knowledge of more formalized content. In our work we have found that promoting discussions during these activities and encouraging students to relate firsthand experiences helps both the students and teacher to make connections (Reyes and Bos, 1996). For second language learners, having the student clarify concepts in their first language can also facilitate activation of background knowledge and understanding of key concepts (Bos and Reyes, 1996;

Echevarria and Graves, 1998; Reyes, Duran, and Bos, 1989).

Based on assessment information from such procedures as PReP or semantic mapping, decisions can be made as to the need and type of further prelearning activities to provide.

Step Four: Using Prelearning Activities

Limited background knowledge signals the teacher that students need more instruction to learn the information that will be presented in the text or lecture. Teachers can present any number of prelearning activities—advance organizers, semantic feature analysis, semantic mapping, concept diagrams—that students can use before reading an assigned text or listening to a lecture. All these activities enhance the content and have been referred to as content enhancement devices (Bulgren, Schumaker, and Deshler, 1988; Walther-Thomas and Brownell, 2000). Teachers can also use other learning experiences such as field trips, experiments, computer simulations, Internet investigations, and films.

Advance Organizers

Advance organizers are activities that orient students to the material before reading or class presentation (Ausubel, 1963; Slavin, 2000). It is based on schema theory and the notion that students profit from having a framework provided for the material to be learned to help them assimilate the new information into their current schemas or cognitive structure. Reviews of studies that have explored the effectiveness of advance organizers on learning have drawn the following conclusions (Corkill, 1992; Mayer, 1979):

1. Groups given advance organizers consistently perform better than control groups with none. This advantage diminishes when material is familiar, when learners have an extensive background of knowledge about the area, when learners have high IQs, and when tests fail to measure the breadth of transfer ability.
2. Advance organizers particularly aid students of lower ability and/or limited background knowledge.

■ **FIGURE 7.5** *Concept Map of Fifth Grade Students' Knowledge of Deserts*

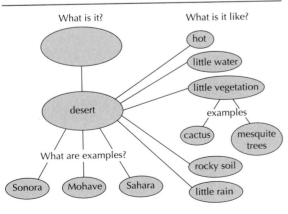

3. Advance organizers are more effective when presented prior to a learning task rather than after the task.

Using this information, Lenz (1983; Lenz, Alley, and Schumaker, 1987) demonstrated that both the quality and quantity of learning for adolescents with learning disabilities could be significantly improved by using advance organizers. He found that regular content area teachers are able to implement advance organizers.

▬ **PROCEDURES:** Lenz identified ten steps in using an advance organizer (see Figure 7.6). The resource teacher trained the students in the resource classroom to use advance organizers by giving the students a worksheet with each of the ten steps as headings. The students then practiced listening to advance organizers given by the resource teacher and completing the worksheets. Next, the students used the advance organizer worksheet in mainstreamed content area classes, with the resource teacher and students meeting afterward to discuss the success of the worksheets. They discussed how the advance organizer information can be used to organize notes and how the worksheet can be modified to assist the students to cue in on the most common organizing principles used by particular teachers.

In giving an advance organizer, the teacher provides an organizational framework for the information to be learned (see Figure 7.6, step 3). This framework might be an outline, a diagram in which the parts are labeled, or a picture semantic map, as discussed earlier. Townsend and Clarihew (1989) found that a pictorial component in a verbal advance organizer was necessary to improve the comprehension of eight-year-old students with limited background knowledge. The use of visual representations or pictures is particularly salient for students with learning and behavior problems (Schwartz, Ellsworth, Graham, and Knight, 1998).

▬ **COMMENTS:** Lenz and his colleagues found that regular content area teachers are able to implement advance organizers with minimal teacher training (45 minutes). The teachers who utilized the

advance organizers expressed satisfaction with the students' response to the instruction as well as the improvement in the overall quality of their own instruction. However, Lenz did find that teacher use of an advance organizer alone was not enough to facilitate student learning. "Learning disabled students had to be made aware that advance organizers were being presented and then had to be trained in the types of information presented in the advance organizer and ways in which that information could be made useful" (Lenz, 1983, p. 12).

Concept Diagrams and Comparison Tables

The concept diagram as part of *The Concept Mastery Routine* (Bulgren, Schumaker, and Deshler, 1988, 1996), is a content enhancement tool that can be used to assist students in understanding important key concepts in the reading or lecture and works well as a prelearning activity. Using the research on concept development, the concept diagram is a visual tool that supports students as they delineate a concept by:

▬ Exploring their prior knowledge of the concept
▬ Understanding the relationship of the concept to the overall concept class to which it belongs
▬ Classifying characteristics of the concept
▬ Generating examples and nonexamples
▬ Constructing a content-related definition of the concept

▬ **PROCEDURES:** When using a concept diagram, (See Figure 7.7) the first step is to prepare the diagram. First, the teacher identifies major and related concepts of which the students need a deeper or more technical understanding. In a science chapter on fossils, Mr. Thomas felt that it was important that the students develop a more technical understanding of the concept of fossils, so this became the concept to diagram. Second, Mr. Thomas used the instructional materials and his knowledge to list important characteristics of fossils. He also thought about whether or not each characteristic is "always present," "sometimes present," or "never present." Third, he located examples and nonexamples of the concepts in the instructional materials. He found in reviewing the

■ **FIGURE 7.6** *Steps in Using an Advance Organizer*

Step 1: Inform students of advance organizers
    a. Announce advance organizer
    b. State benefits of advance organizer
    c. Suggest that students take notes on the advance organizer

Step 2: Clarify action to be taken
    a. State teachers' actions
    b. State students' actions

Step 3: Identify topics of tasks
    a. Identify major topics or activities
    b. Identify subtopics or component activities

Step 4: Provide background information
    a. Relate topic to the course or previous lesson
    b. Relate topic to new information

Step 5: State the concepts to be learned
    a. State specific concepts/ideas from the lesson
    b. State general concepts/ideas broader than the lesson's content

Step 6: Clarify the concepts to be learned
    a. Clarify by examples or analogies
    b. Clarify by nonexamples
    c. Caution students of possible misunderstandings

Step 7: Motivate student to learn
    a. Point out relevance to students
    b. Be specific, short-term, personalized, and believable

Step 8: Introduce vocabulary
    a. Identify the new terms and define
    b. Repeat difficult terms and define

Step 9: Provide an organizational framework
    a. Present an outline, list, or narrative of the lesson's content

Step 10: State the general outcome desired
    a. State objectives of instruction/learning
    b. Relate outcomes to test performance

Source: Adapted from B. K. Lenz, "Promoting Active Learning Through Effective Instruction," *Pointer,* *27*(2) (1983): 12.

chapter that nonexamples were not provided, so he decided to show the students fossils and nonfossils to help them to start thinking about examples and nonexamples. Finally, Mr. Thomas constructed a definition. Lenz and Bulgren (1995) specify a concept definition as the "naming of the superordinate concept which includes the concept under consideration, a listing of the characteristics which must always be present in the concept, and a specification of the relationships among those characteristics" (p. 33).

After preparing the concept diagram, the next step is using it with the students to develop their understanding of the concept. After giving an advance organizer to explain its purpose, how the diagram works, and the expectations, the teacher can use what Bulgren and her colleagues refer to as the linking steps to teach the concept:

— <u>C</u>onvey the concept name and why it is the focus of study.

— <u>O</u>ffer the overall or overarching concept.
— <u>N</u>ote the key words by having the students brainstorm words related to the concept.
— <u>C</u>lassify the characteristics by using the key words and other ideas to generate characteristics that are always, sometimes, and never present.
— <u>E</u>xplore and list examples and nonexamples.
— <u>P</u>ractice with the examples by having students discuss how the examples relate to the characteristics.
— <u>T</u>ie down a definition by generating a content-related definition that includes the concept, the overall concepts and the characteristics that are always present.

The acronym CONCEPT can be used to help remember the teaching routine. The routine should employ interactive discussion that encourages the students to fine-tune and deepen their understanding of the concept being studied (Bulgren et al., 1988).

■ **FIGURE 7.7** *Concept Diagram*

CONCEPT DIAGRAM

Concept

| fossils |

Overall
Concept

| past geologic age |

Classifying Characteristics

Always Present	Sometimes Present	Never Present
remains or prints	frozen in ice	still alive
plants or animals	trapped in tar	still decaying
thousands of years old	crushed by water	
preserved in the earth	in volcanic ash	

Example:

(tigers in La Brea tar pits)

(Siberian mammoth)

(petrified forest in Arizona)

(fish skeleton in limestone layers)

Nonexample:

(your pet cat)

(elephant in Africa today)

(tree limbs and leaves in your yard)

(fish in supermarket)

Definition:

| Fossils are remains or prints of plants or animals who lived thousands of years ago which have been preserved in the earth. |

— **COMMENTS:** When Bulgren and her colleagues (Bulgren et al., 1988) worked with content area high school teachers in whose classes students with learning disabilities were mainstreamed, they found that when the teachers used the concept diagrams and the concept teaching routine, the learning performance of both the students with learning disabilities and the other students in the class improved.

Bulgren and her colleagues have extended the idea of concept diagrams to allow students to visually represent the comparison of two concepts (Bulgren, Lenz, Deshler, and Schumaker, 1995). Figure 7.8 presents a sample comparison table and includes the steps used in generating the table (see the steps in the upper right hand corner, which use the acronym COMPARING). An important part of this table and

■ **FIGURE 7.8**   *Comparison Table for the Concepts of Decimals and Fractions*

COMPARISON TABLE

2. Overall Concept NUMERALS		**C** Communicate targeted concepts

C Communicate targeted concepts
O Obtain the Overall Concept
M Make lists of known characteristics
P Pin down Like Characteristics
A Assemble Like Categories
R Record Unlike Characteristics
I Identify Unlike Categories
N Nail down a summary
G Go beyond the basics

2. Overall Concept
NUMERALS

1. Concept
FRACTION

1. Concept
DECIMAL

3. Characteristics

Represents parts of a whole

Written with one number on top of a line and another below the line (e.g., 4/10)

The number of parts contained in the whole is any number except zero

3. Characteristics

Represents parts of a whole

Written with one or more numbers and a decimal point (e.g., .4)

The number of parts contained in the whole is 10 or any multiple of 10

9. Extensions

Create two word problems, one involving fractions and the other involving decimals

4. Like Characteristics

Represents parts of a whole

5. Like Categories

Use

3. Unlike Characteristics

Written with one number on top of a line and another below the line (e.g., 4/10)

The number of parts contained in the whole is any number except zero

3. Unlike Characteristics

Written with one or more numbers and a decimal point (e.g., .4)

The number of parts contained in the whole is 10 or any multiple of 10

9. Unlike Categories

Written form

Number of parts in the whole

4. Summary

Two types of numerals are fractions and decimals. They are similar in their use (they are both used to represent parts of a whole). They are different in their written form and the number of parts contained in the whole.

Source: J. A. Bulgren, B. Lenz, D. D. Deshler, and J. B. Schumaker, *The Concept Comparison Routine* (Lawrence, KS: Edge Enterprises, Inc., 1995), p. 55. Reprinted with permission.

the steps in generating it is outlining the similar and dissimilar characteristics.

Bulgren and her colleagues note that both the concept diagram and the comparison table as shown in Figures 7.7 and 7.8 are "instructional tools developed and researched at the University of Kansas Center for Research on Learning. They represent a number of organizing and teaching devices designed for teachers to use as they teach content information to classes containing diverse student populations. They are data-based teaching instruments that have been found effective when used in instructional routines that combine cues about the instruction, specialized delivery of the content, involvement of the students in the cognitive processes, and a review of the learning process and content materials (Bulgren, Lenz, Deshler, and Schumaker, 1995). They have not been shown to be effective tools if they are simply distributed to students" (J. Bulgren, personal communication, November 20, 2000).

Semantic Feature Analysis/ Relationship Charts

Like an advance organizer, semantic feature analysis (SFA) is a prelearning activity that serves to organize the major concepts and related vocabulary to be taught in a unit, chapter, or lecture. Whereas the concept diagram can be used to clarify a concept that is difficult for the students, this activity aids students in seeing the relationships between the major concepts, the related vocabulary, and their current knowledge of the topic.

The theoretical foundation for the SFA teaching strategy is schema theory (Rumelhart, 1980), concept attainment theory (Klausmeier and Sipple, 1980), and a Vygotskian perspective of cognitive development (Vygotsky, 1978) (see Chapter Two). These theories suggest that knowledge is hierarchically organized, that relating the new concepts to students' prior knowledge will help students learn these new concepts, that teaching attributes of a concept as well as teaching examples and nonexamples are important to concept learning, and that principles of scaffold instruction and interactive dialogues will promote learning.

— PROCEDURES: The first step in preparing for the SFA activity is to develop a relationship chart. This chart is based on the notion that ideas or concepts are related to one another in terms of a hierarchy of abstractness. The most inclusive or abstract ideas are called *superordinate concepts;* the most concrete or narrow ideas are identified as *subordinate concepts.* Ideas or concepts that fall in between the superordinate and subordinate concepts are referred to as *coordinate concepts* (Frayer, Frederick, and Klausmeier, 1969). These ideas are then organized into a relationship chart, and the students and teacher discuss the relationship between the various levels of concepts and their own background knowledge. This SFA activity was originally developed for use in teaching a specific concept, such as is used with concept diagrams (Johnson and Pearson, 1984). In their interactive teaching research, Bos and her colleagues have adapted this strategy to text (Anders and Bos, 1986; Bos and Anders, 1992; Reyes and Bos, 1998).

When Ms. Cho used this technique in her American government class, she first read the assigned American government chapter on contracts. As she read, she listed the important concepts or vocabulary and then arranged them according to superordinate, coordinate, and subordinate concepts. She used words as well as relevant phrases.

Contracts	Counter Offer
Promise	Holding Good
Contracting Parties	Conditions
Buyer	Acceptance
Seller	Consideration
Written Contracts	Statute of Frauds
Verbal Contracts	Legal Obligation
Contractual Offer	Legal Action

Next, she organized the vocabulary into a relationship chart (see Figure 7.9). The superordinate concept "Contracts" is used as the name for the chart. The five coordinate concepts (main ideas in the text) serve as the column headings and are listed as the important or major ideas. The related vocabulary or subordinate concepts are listed down the side of

■ **FIGURE 7.9** *Relationship Chart: Contracts*

CONTRACTS

Name _____

Period _____

Important Ideas

Important Vocabulary	Contract	Promise	Written Contracts	Verbal Contracts	Conditions			
Legal Action								
Consideration								
Legal Obligation								
Holding Good								
Contractual Offer								
Counteroffer								
Acceptance								
Statute of Frauds								
Contracting Parties								

+ = positive relationship
– = negative relationship
0 = no relationship
? = unknown relationship

the chart. Notice that Ms. Cho left blank spaces for adding important ideas and important vocabulary. Students are encouraged to add relevant information from their background knowledge.

The relationship chart became Ms. Cho's instructional tool. She made a copy for each student and a transparency so that they could complete it as a group. To do this, she introduced the topic (superordinate concept) of the assignment. The students then discussed what they already knew about contract. Next, she introduced each coordinate concept (important idea) by assisting the students in generating meanings. During this introduction and throughout the activity, she encouraged students to add their personal experiences or understandings of the terms. For example, when Ms. Cho presented the major idea of "contract," Joe inquired if a contract had to be written to be legal. This led to Anne's conveying a first-hand experience of her dad making a verbal contract and having the contract honored in court even though it was not written. The discussion ended with one of the purposes for reading being the clarification of what was needed for a verbal contract to be considered legal.

Following the discussion of the coordinate concepts, Ms. Cho introduced each subordinate concept. Again, Ms. Cho and her students predicted what the meanings would be in relation to the topic of "contracts." For the more technical vocabulary (e.g., *contractual offer, Statute of Frauds*), sometimes Ms. Cho provided the meaning or the students decided to read to clarify the concept. After introducing each concept, she and the students discussed the relationship between each coordinate concept or phrase and each subordinate term or phrase. They used the following symbols to signify each of the relationships: a plus sign (+) represented a positive relationship, a minus sign (−) represented a negative relationship, a zero (0) signified no relationship, and a question mark (?) represented that no consensus could be reached without further information.

Ms. Cho found that student involvement during the discussion was important to the success of the SFA strategy. One key to a successful discussion was to encourage students to ask each other "why" they reached a certain relationship rating. This seemed to encourage students to use their prior knowledge regarding the topic, and in turn, seemed to encourage other students to activate what they already knew about the vocabulary.

After completing the relationship chart, Ms. Cho guided the students in setting purposes for reading. These purposes, for the most part, focused on the chart, reading to confirm their predictions and to determine the relationships between the terms for which no agreement could be reached. After completing the reading, Ms. Cho and the students reviewed the relationship chart, using discussion. They changed any of the relationships if necessary and reached consensus on those previously unknown.

Sometimes when Ms. Cho and her students used a relationship chart, they found that some information was still unclear after reading the text. Then, they checked other sources such as experts in the field, technical and trade books, the Internet, and other media. Ms. Cho also taught the students how to use the relationship chart to study for chapter tests by asking each other questions based on the meanings of the concepts and vocabulary and on their relationships (e.g., What is a contractual offer? What are the conditions necessary to have a contract?). She also taught how the chart could be used to write a report about the concepts.

— **COMMENTS:** One of the authors and her colleagues have conducted a series of intervention studies using the SFA teaching strategy with secondary students who have learning disabilities. Whether comparing it to the more traditional activity of looking the words up in the dictionary (Bos, Anders, Filip, and Jaffe, 1985; Bos, Anders, Jaffe, and Filip, 1989) or the direct instruction of word meanings (Anders, Bos, Jaffe, and Filip, 1986; Bos, Allen, and Scanlon, 1989; Bos and Anders, 1990a, 1992), they found that when teachers and researchers used this strategy, students consistently learned more vocabulary and had better comprehension of the chapters they read. One of the most important questions asked during discussion is "Why?" (e.g., "Why is *evidence* positively related to *evidence in court?*"). Students need to justify their reasoning. By answering "Why?" questions, students think through concepts, reaching a deeper understanding and more effectively relating new information to old.

Mapping and Graphic Organizers

Semantic mapping (Pearson and Johnson, 1978) and graphic organizers (Barron, 1969) are ways of visually representing the concepts and important vocabulary to be taught (see Figure 7.5). These content enhancement devices can be used as prelearning activities that assist students in activating their prior knowledge and in seeing the relationships between new concepts and related vocabulary.

— **PROCEDURES:** In using maps and organizers the teacher can begin by putting the major concept for the lecture or text on the board and then having the students generate a list of related vocabulary from their background knowledge, as was described in the section on brainstorming (see Chapter 5). However, when presenting more technical vocabulary, the teacher could begin by writing on the board the list of important vocabulary he or she generated in reviewing the text chapter or developing the lecture. After the words have been listed, discuss the meanings of the words, using a procedure similar to the one just presented in the section on semantic feature analysis. Next, arrange and rearrange the vocabulary with the students until you have a map that shows the relationships that exist among the ideas.

For example, when presenting the following words for a chapter on "Fossils," the students and teacher first grouped the animals together.

trilobites	small horses
crinoids	winged insects
ferns	geography of the present
dinosaurs	land masses
lakes	brachiopods
bodies of water	saber-tooth tigers
animals	guide fossils
geography of the past	rivers
trees	plants
oceans	continents

Next, they grouped the plants together. In the case of guide fossils and several other types of fossils with which the students were not familiar (e.g., crinoids, trilobites), they decided to wait until they had read before placing the concepts on the map. Finally, they grouped together the geography terms.

After the map is completed, instruct the students to refer to the map while reading and/or listening to the lecture. Like the relationship chart the semantic map can provide a framework for setting purposes for reading. The students read to confirm and clarify their understanding in relation to the map and make changes in it during discussions held as they read or after completing a chapter. The map can also serve as a blueprint for studying and for writing reports.

— COMMENTS: A number of researchers have investigated the use of mapping and graphic organizers with students who are low achievers or have learning disabilities. In some cases the students generated the maps as described above (Bos, Allen, and Scanlon, 1989; Bos and Anders, 1990a; Boyle, 1996; Scanlon, Deshler, and Schumaker, 1996), while in other studies the framework for the map or organizer was already generated and the students filled in the information (Horton, Lovitt, and Bergerud, 1990; Idol, 1987a,b; Lovitt and Horton, 1994). In other studies, the map or visual spatial display (see Figure 7.10) is presented to the students in completed form, and systematic Direct Instruction (Carnine, 1989) is used to assist the students in learning the information contained in the display (Bergerud, Lovitt, and Horton, 1988; Darch and Carnine, 1986). Consistently the research has been encouraging in this area: the use of semantic maps or visual representations of information increases the learning performance of students with learning and behavior problems.

Steps Five and Six: Reinforcing Concept Learning During and After Learning

In a typical "learning from reading" or "learning from lecturing" assignment, the teacher has three opportunities to enhance the learning of concepts and the related vocabulary: *before* the reading or listening, *during* the actual reading or lecture, and *after* the assignment has been read or heard. The previous section discussed prelearning activities that can be used to enhance content and facilitate concept learning.

Whether using an advance organizer, semantic feature analysis, semantic map, concept diagram, or comparison table, these frameworks can be used to guide students as they read the text or listen to the lecture and as they react to their learning. For example, the list of major ideas obtained from the advance organizer can serve as the framework in which students can take notes when listening to a lecture. After the lecture, students can meet in small groups and share

■ **FIGURE 7.10** *Visual Spatial Display*

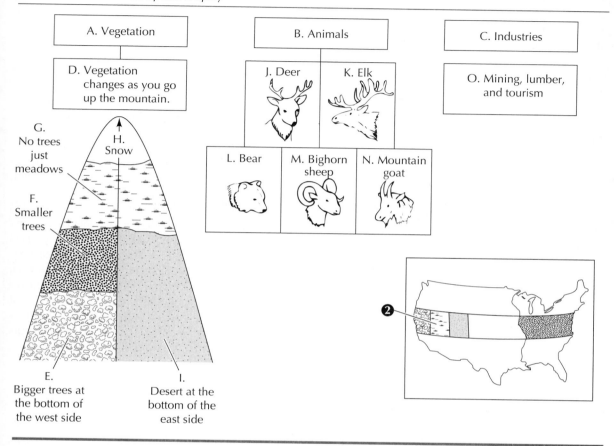

Source: From "Teaching Content Area Material to Learning Disabled Students" by C. Darch and D. Carmine, *Exceptional Children, 53,* 1986, p. 243. Copyright 1986 by The Council for Exceptional Children. Reprinted with permission.

their notes to create one overview that can serve as a study guide for the test. Students can be instructed on how to develop questions based on a concept diagram or semantic map. These questions can serve as self-questions to be asked when reading and when studying for a test.

Students generally require considerable practice in using these content enhancement devices. Additionally, devices used for one content area may not be transferred to other areas automatically (Scan-

lon, Deshler, and Schumaker, 1996; Swanson, 1999). Thus, numerous applications of each strategy may need to be taught explicitly (Bryant et al., 1999; Bulgren and Lenz, 1996; Hudson, Liqnugarls-Kraft, and Miller, 1993; Pressley, 1998). Second language learners who have learning disabilities are sometimes referred to as doubly challenged when learning content information. Apply the Concept 7.1 presents ideas for promoting content learning for these students.

APPLY THE CONCEPT 7.1

TEACHING CONTENT TO ENGLISH-LANGUAGE LEARNERS

English-language readers who may also have learning disabilities, have specific difficulties with vocabulary, syntax, and background knowledge when learning to read English. The *Cognitive Academic Language Learning Approach* (CALLA) (Chamot and O'Malley, 1994) is an interactive content-based approach to content learning that makes use of interactive teaching and metacognitive strategies that increase general reading skills in English-language learners (Chamot, 1998; Chamot and O'Malley, 1994). Some of these strategies include: elaboration and active use of prior knowledge, planning or setting a purpose for learning, monitoring for comprehension with questions, and self-evaluation.

Metacognition is more prevalent in the latter two strategies listed above. In monitoring comprehension with questions, teachers can teach students to make inferences or self-question for clarification, by explicitly modeling either or both techniques. Self-evaluation allows students to reflect on what they have learned, read, or discussed. Self ratings and learning logs can be used with all grade levels (Echevarria and Graves, 1998). The benefits of having students think about their learning can be transferred to their becoming more successful both in the content and in the use of English.

MAKING ADAPTATIONS

What Do Teachers and Students Think About Making Adaptations?

Special and general education teachers understand the need to make adaptations for those students in their classrooms who have special learning needs, and they express the desire to make those modifications. In actuality, however, research indicates most content area teachers seldom implement many adaptations for a number of reasons (Moody, Vaughn, and Schumm, 1997; Schumm and Vaughn, 1992; Schumm, Vaughn, and Saumell, 1992; Vaughn, Schumm, Jallad, Slusher, and Saumell, 1996). First, adapting textbooks takes time, and teachers' time for planning and preparing for instruction is already limited. Second, textbook adaptations often slow down instruction, and teachers cannot cover as much material as they would like. Third, some teachers think that making adaptations for the few students who need them is not fair to the higher achieving students who are ready to work at a faster pace. When asked to make specific modifications for a student with learn-

ing disabilities in her high school French class, a teacher commented, "I have a number of students in my class who would benefit from the modifications you are asking me to make for John. I'm not sure it would be fair to the other students for me to do these things for John and not offer the other students the same opportunities."

We have investigated how students feel when teachers make adaptations for individual students within the regular classroom, and the kinds of adaptations students view as acceptable and unacceptable. Some of the findings of these studies surprised us and should put to rest some of the concerns teachers have about taking the time to make adaptations (Elbaum, Schumm, and Vaughn, 1997; Klingner and Vaughn 1999; Klingner, Vaughn, Schumm, Cohen, and Forgan, 1998; Vaughn, Schumm, and Kouzekanani, 1993; Vaughn, Schumm, Niarhos, and Daugherty, 1993).

Both elementary and secondary students overwhelmingly preferred teachers who made adaptations for students who needed more help. They liked teachers who used flexible grouping for learning, who met with and assisted students with individual needs, and who varied instruction to meet those needs. They liked mixed-ability grouping and working in pairs with mixed ability. They also preferred teachers who gave all students the same homework assignments. Elementary students didn't mind if some students were given different tests as long as the tests were the same length and took the same amount of time. Secondary students preferred teachers who gave all students the same tests and textbooks.

An especially interesting finding was that students who are high achieving not only were aware that certain students in their classrooms needed extra help, but they also preferred a teacher who made adaptations to help all the students learn. No high-achieving student in these studies expressed concern that instructional time would be taken away from him or her if the teacher took the time to give extra help to those who needed it. The following comment by one high-achieving high school student illustrates the altruism that was typical: "Even though I am smart enough to deal with any method of teaching, I realize not everyone else is. I like to see a diversified method of teaching in which the individual needs of students are met. Often students who do not perform as well are overlooked as ignorant and stupid, unable to learn. But these students are the ones that must be concentrated on so that they can develop better." (Vaughn, Schumm, Niarhos, and Daugherty, 1993). These nonreaders were the ones for whom same ability grouping was perceived as advantageous (Elbaum et al., 1997).

In contrast to the high-achieving students, low-achieving students were more likely to prefer a teacher who made no adaptations for students with special needs. Two possible reasons that low-achieving students felt negatively about teacher adaptations were that, (1) they were concerned about "fitting in" socially and did not wish to have their deficiencies revealed to their peers and, (2) many low-achieving students are passive learners (Torgesen, 1982; Torgesen and Licht, 1983). If they have a teacher who makes adaptations, they may be forced to take a more active role in their own learning—something that many low-achieving students are reluctant to do.

Adapting Textbooks

Despite these concerns, however, research indicates that students at all achievement levels feel that they need textbook adaptations and are not getting the adaptations they need (Schumm et al., 1992). Apply the Concept 7.2 lists textbook adaptations you might consider, three of which are discussed here in greater depth.

Study Guides

Study guides are tools teachers can use to lead students through a reading assignment. A typical study guide is a series of questions or activities that students complete while they read a selection. As Wood, Lapp, and Flood (1992, p. 1) put it, "Study guides are designed to accompany reading, not follow it." Study guides help direct students to the key points to be learned. They also provide structure for students to reflect about what they are reading and to engage in higher-order thinking. In short, study guides can help "tutor" a student through a chapter.

Commercially prepared study guides can be purchased or obtained through the Internet as supplements to some textbooks. The advantage of commercially prepared study guides is that they are already done. Real time savers! The disadvantage is that the publisher does not know your style of teaching, your emphasis, or your school district's requirements. Moreover, the publisher does not know your students. Many teachers elect to construct their own study guides.

Many types of study guides exist. Some are designed to help students activate prior knowledge, others to help students understand literal or inferential information in the textbook, others to foster peer interaction and discussion, and still others to help students recognize meaning patterns in text (e.g., cause and effect, compare and contrast). Following are some general suggestions for developing study guides (Wood et al., 1992):

- *Decide whether a guide is needed.* Is textbook information particularly dense? Are there few considerate features? Will student with special

APPLY THE CONCEPT 7.2

GUIDELINES FOR ADAPTING CONTENT AREA TEXTBOOKS

Substitute the textbook for students who have severe word-recognition problems:

- Audiotape textbook content.
- Read textbook aloud to students.
- Pair students to master textbook content.
- Use direct experiences, films, videotapes, recorders, and computer programs as substitutes for textbook reading.
- Work with students individually or in small groups to master textbook material.

Simplify the textbook for students whose reading level is far below that of the textbook used in class:

- Construct abridged versions of the textbook content or use the publisher's abridged version.
- Provide students with chapter outlines or summaries.
- Use a multilevel, multimaterial approach.

Highlight key concepts for students who have difficulty comprehending textbook material:

- Preview reading assignments with students to orient them to the topic and provide guidelines for budgeting reading and study time.
- Provide students with a purpose for reading.
- Provide an overview of an assignment before reading.
- Structure opportunities for students to activate prior knowledge before starting a reading assignment.

- Introduce key vocabulary before assigning reading.
- Develop a study guide to direct learning.
- Summarize or reduce textbook information to guide classroom discussions and independent reading.
- Color-code or highlight textbooks.
- Reduce length of assignments.
- Slow down the pace of reading assignments.
- Provide assistance in answering text-based questions.
- Demonstrate or model effective reading strategies.
- Place students in cooperative learning groups to master textbook content.
- Teach comprehension-monitoring techniques to improve ongoing understanding of text material.
- Teach students to use graphic aids to understand textbook information.

Increase idea retention for students who have difficulty with long-term memory.

- Structure postreading activities to increase retention of content.
- Teach reading strategies to improve retention.
- Teach students to record key concepts and terms for study purposes.
- Teach memory strategies to improve retention of text material.

Source: Adapted from J. S. Schumm and K. Strickler, "Guidelines for Adapting Content Area Textbooks: Keeping Teachers and Students Content," *Intervention in School and Clinic, 27*(2) (1991): 79–84.

needs need support and guidance to get through the chapter and to grasp the most important ideas?

— *Analyze the chapter.* Can some parts be omitted? Are some parts easier to understand than others?

What skills will your students need to read and understand this material?

— *Decide how you want to structure your study guide.* Create one that includes the suggested components.

All study guides should also include the following components (Hudson, Ormsbee, and Myles, 1994; Readence et al., 1998):

— Specific information about the reading assignment (page numbers, title)
— Learning objectives of the assignment
— Purpose statement for the assignment
— Introduction of key terms or vocabulary
— Activities for students to complete
— Questions for students to answer as they read

Text Highlighting

Students with comprehension problems have difficulty sifting out important information. Underlining or highlighting key points in the textbooks can help students attend to the most salient information (Echevarria and Graves, 1998). In reading the textbook, highlight the information you think is most important. Then student or adult volunteers can use your book as a guide to highlight the same information in books for students with reading and learning disabilities. Keep in mind that you will also want to teach students this and other textbook study skills (see the section on teaching study skills).

Using Alternative Reading Materials

For students with very low reading skills who are able to learn by listening:

— *Audio-tape textbook chapters.* Adult and student volunteers can read the chapters on audio tape. Students can then listen to the tapes at home or in their resource classes. Tech Talk 7.1 provides ideas for taping content area textbooks.
— *Read text aloud to students.* Encourage students to follow along, reading silently. Pause frequently to assess student learning from the reading.
— *Pair a good reader with a poor reader.* The good reader reads the textbook material aloud and, together, the two students learn the content.

Sometimes you will find it necessary to use alternative materials that present similar content. Films, videotapes, and trade books provide good sources.

Computer software programs in which the text can be read by the computer, such as encyclopedias on CD-ROM, are other resources.

Developing Listener-Friendly Lectures

People today discuss software programs in terms of their "user friendliness." Is the program easy to understand? Does the program use familiar language or at least define unfamiliar terms? Does the program give you cue words or icons to signal the important ideas and processes? If you don't understand something, does the program allow you to ask questions? Does the program have more than one way to explain a difficult concept or process? If the program has these features, then one might consider it "user friendly."

Now take a minute to go back and reread the previous paragraph but substitute the word *lecture* for the word *program* (hence the term *listener-friendly lecture*). Just as using "considerate" or "user friendly" text assists students in learning the critical information, a well-organized lecture makes the students' work easier in that it assists them in seeing relationships among concepts and in distinguishing important from supplementary information. It also helps them relate new information to old. Well-designed lectures seem particularly beneficial for students with learning/language disabilities, English-language learners, and listeners with relatively limited language skills and /or little prior knowledge of the content.

As you plan your teaching, the following guidelines can make your lectures *"listener-friendly"*:

— Use advance organizers.
— Use cue words or phrases to let students know what information is important (e.g., "It is important that you know . . . ," "They key information to remember is . . . ," "In summary . . . ").
— Repeat important information.
— Write important information on board, transparency, and handout.
— Stress key points by varying the tone and quality of your voice.

TECH TALK 7.1

AUDIOTAPING AND SCANNING CONTENT AREA INFORMATION

Students who have limited reading skills should still have access to content area information. Since much of this is provided through text, it may be necessary to record or scan content-area reading materials, including textbooks. Recordings for the Blind and Dyslexic (800-803-7201, http://www.rfbd.org) is a nonprofit organization that records trade books and textbooks for individuals who are blind, have low vision, dyslexia, or learning disabilities. This organization provides on-loan recorded books at all academic levels.

If you are recording your own textbooks or content-area information, some suggestions for audiotaping are:

- Instead of recording an entire chapter verbally, read the key sections and paraphrase the less important sections.
- Code the text so that readers or listeners will know whether the person on the tape is reading or paraphrasing.
- Provide a short advanced organizer on the tape to help students get ready to read and listen.
- Insert questions that readers or listeners can stop and think about.

- Remind readers or listeners to stop periodically and think about what they have read.
- Use a natural tone of voice and a comfortable rate.
- Have students experiment with taped texts to see whether they comprehend better with or without the text.

Computer programs that scan text into computer-readable files using a scanner are available. These programs, such as the Kurzweil 3000 (http://www.lhs.com, 888-537-6688) allow the student to listen or read along as the text is being read, take notes, and highlight right on the computer screen. Also built into reading system are tools such as a dictionary, thesaurus, and phonetic spell checker. Students can look up unfamiliar words, have them spelled, broken into syllables, or defined. Once a book is scanned into the computer, it can be read and used by multiple students. Like many other CD-ROM books, dictionaries and pronunciations in Spanish and other languages are available.

Source: Lernout & Hauspie Speech Products N.V. Copyright © Kurzweil Educational.

- Number ideas or points (e.g., first, second, next, then, finally).
- Write technical words or words that are difficult to spell.
- Use a study guide that lists the major concepts, with space for students to add other information.
- Use pictures, concept diagrams, and content maps to show relationships among ideas.
- Provide examples and nonexamples of the concepts you are discussing.
- Ask questions and encourage discussion that requires students to relate the new information to ideas they already know (from their own background or your previous lectures).
- Stop frequently and have students work with partners and discuss what they have learned.
- Allow time at the end of a lecture for students to look over their notes, summarize, and ask questions.

Table 7.1 provides cues that can assist students in "seeing" the key information. By using these guidelines you will naturally incorporate cues that indicate what information is important.

Using the Pause Procedure

One technique that has demonstrated its effectiveness for students with learning and behavior problems in enhancing the understanding and recall of information presented through lectures is the pause procedure (e.g., Ruhl, Hughes, and Gajar, 1990; Ruhl, Hughes, and Schloss, 1987). The procedure consists of pausing during natural breaks in the lectures and having students work in partners for about two minutes to discuss what they are learning and review their notes. At the end of the two minutes, ask students whether they have any questions or concepts that need further discussion or clarification. Then resume lecturing.

Using this procedure, college students with and without learning disabilities performed better than listening to the lectures without the pauses for discussion on both multiple-choice tests and on free recalls of the information presented (Ruhl et al., 1990).

Adapting Class Assignments and Homework

One area in which students with learning and behavior problems oftentimes struggle is with the completion of assignments and homework. In a survey of students with and without learning disabilities in grades 6 through 8, the students with learning disabilities had greater difficulty completing homework assignments because of problems with attention, motivation, and study skills (Gajria and Salend, 1995). At the same time, homework has become a significant part of schooling. In the 1996 National Assessment of Educational Progress in math and science, more than half of all 8th and 12th graders and nearly half of the 4th graders reported having at least one hour of homework every night (Bursuck, Harniss, Epstein, Polloway, Jayanthi, and Wissinger, 1999) and accounting for more than 20 percent of the time students spend on academic tasks (Cooper and Nye, 1994). In a recent survey of middle school students, students indicated that they preferred adaptations in which assignments are finished at school, extra credit is allowed, assignments are graded according to effort, and assignments are begun and checked for understanding in class (Nelson, Epstein, Bursuck, Jayanthi, and Sawyer, 1998). At the same time these students were least approving of adaptations in which shorter or different assignments were given to students with learning problems or that for these students assignments are graded easier. After conducting a comprehensive review of the literature, Cooper and Nye (1994) concluded that homework assignments for students with disabilities should be brief, focused on reinforcement rather than new material, monitored carefully, and supported through parental involvement.

The most important aspect of making assignments is to give complete information. You need to let students know why the assignment is important, when it is due, what support they will have for completing the task, and steps necessary for getting the job done. Having complete information helps to motivate students as does giving the students real-life assignments (i.e., assignments that connect homework to events or activities in the home) plus rein-

■ **TABLE 7.1**   *Cues to Listen and Watch for in Lectures*

Type of Cue	Examples
Organizational Cues	Today, we will be discussing . . .
	The topic I want to cover today . . .
	There are (number) points I want you to be sure to learn . . .
	The important relationship is . . .
	The main point of this discussion is . . .
	Any statement that signals a number of position (e.g., first, last, next, then).
	To review/summarize/recap . . .
Emphasis Cues	
Verbal	You need to know/understand/remember . . .
	This is important/key/basic/critical . . .
	Let me repeat this . . .
	Let me check, now do you understand . . .
	Any statement is repeated.
	Words or terms are emphasized.
	Teacher speaks more slowly, loudly, or with more emphasis.
	Teacher stresses certain words.
	Teacher spells words.
	Teacher asks rhetorical question.
Nonverbal	Information written on overhead/board.
	Information handed out in study guide.
	Teacher emphasizes point using gestures.

Source: Adapted from S. K. Suritsky and C. A. Hughes, "Notetaking Strategy Instruction," in D. D. Deshler, E. S. Ellis, and B. K. Lenz, *Teaching Adolescents with Learning Disabilities,* 2nd ed. (Denver: Love, 1996), p. 275.

forcement, using homework planners, and graphing homework completion (Bryan and Sullivan-Burstein, 1998). The tips in Figure 7.11 can help you provide students with a complete set of directions.

Class assignments and homework can be adapted for special learners so that they can experience success without undue attention being brought to their learning difficulties. The key to success is to make assignments appropriate in content, length, time required to complete, and skill level needed to accomplish the task. It is also important to explain the assignments, model several problems if appropriate, and check for understanding (Sawyer, Nelson, Jayanthi, Bursuck, and Epstein, 1996). Students should know how and where to get help when they get stuck.

Constructing and Adapting Tests

The best way to discover what students have learned is to construct student-friendly tests, adapt test administration and scoring as necessary, consider alternatives to testing (such as assessment portfolios), and teach test-taking skills.

Student-friendly tests are considerate to the test taker in content and format. The content has been covered in class or assigned readings, and students have been told explicitly that they are responsible for learning it. The format is clear and easy to understand.

To construct student-friendly tests, you must first decide what skills and concepts to include.

In test format, directions should be clear and unambiguous, and items should be legible and properly

■ **FIGURE 7.11**   *Tips for Giving Assignments*

1. Explain the purpose of the assignment. Stress what you expect students to learn and why learning the skill or concept is important. Connect the skill or concept to real-life applications.
2. Explain in detail the procedures for completing the assignment. Ask one or two students to summarize the procedures, to check for understanding.
3. Get students started by modeling one or two problems or by providing an example.
4. Describe the equipment and materials needed to complete the assignment.

5. Anticipate trouble spots and ask students how they might tackle difficult parts in the assignment.
6. Explain when the assignment is due.
7. Explain how the assignment will be graded and how it will impact students' grades.
8. Describe appropriate ways to get help or support in completing the assignment.
9. For an in-class assignment, explain your expectations for student behavior while they complete the assignment, and what students who finish early should do.
10. Address student questions.

spaced. Students should have sufficient room to place their answers, and specific guidelines if answers are to be written on a separate sheet (Salend, 1995, 2001). Attention to format is important for all students, but particularly for those who have difficulty reading and taking tests and who are very anxious about test taking.

Even with student-friendly tests, students with learning and behavior problems may have difficulty reading tests, working within time constraints, or resisting distractions during a test. Poor or laborious writing may cause them to tire easily and inhibit performance on a test. Figure 7.12 suggests accommodations for test administration and scoring. As you decide which, if any, adaptations to use, consider the material to be covered by the test, the test's task requirements (e.g, reading, taking dictation), and the particular needs of special learners.

In addition to or instead of tests, consider using portfolios as an assessment tool. Apply the Concept 7.3 presents ideas for developing and using portfolios.

■ **FIGURE 7.12**   *Testing Accommodations*

- Teach students test-taking skills.
- Give frequent quizzes rather than only exams.
- Give take-home tests.
- Test on less content than rest of the class.
- Change type of questions (e.g., essay to multiple choice).
- Give extended time to finish tests.
- Read test questions to students.
- Use tests with enlarged print.
- Highlight key words in questions.
- Provide extra space on tests for answering.
- Simplify wording of test questions.
- Allow students to answer fewer questions.
- Give extra help preparing for tests.

- Give practice questions as a study guide.
- Give open-book and note tests.
- Give tests to small groups.
- Allow use of learning aids during tests (e.g., calculators).
- Give individual help with directions during tests.
- Allow oral instead of written answers (e.g., tape recorders).
- Allow answers in outline format.
- Allow word processors.
- Grade for content, not for spelling and writing mechanics.
- Give feedback to individual students during test.

Source: Adapted from M. Jayanthi, M. H. Epstein, E. A. Polloway, and W. D. Bursuck, "Testing Adaptions: A National Survey of the Testing Practices of General Education Teachers," *Journal of Special Education, 30* (1981): 99–115.

APPLY THE CONCEPT 7.3

USING PORTFOLIOS TO MONITOR STUDENT PROGRESS

Assessment portfolios are collections of work samples that document a student's progress in a content area. You can use portfolios to provide tangible evidence of student performance over a period of time. Portfolios can include writing samples of all stages of the writing process in all genres. Suggestions for developing assessment portfolios include:

- Develop a portfolio plan consistent with your purposes for the assignment.
- Clarify what work will go into portfolios.
- Start with only a couple of different kinds of entries and expand gradually.
- Compare notes with other teachers as you experiment with portfolios.
- Have as a long-term goal the inclusion of a variety of assessments that address content, process, and attitude goals across the curriculum.
- Make portfolios accessible in the classroom. Students and teachers should be able to add to the collection quickly and easily.
- Develop summary sheets or graphs that help to describe a body of information (e.g., "I can do" lists, lists of books read, or pieces of writing completed). Let students record these data when possible.
- Work with the student to choose a few representative samples that demonstrate the student's progress.
- Review portfolios with students periodically (at least four times during the school year). The review should be a time to celebrate progress and to set future goals.

- Encourage students to review portfolios with a classmate before reviewing with the teacher. Students should help make decisions about what to keep.
- In preparation for a parent conference, have students develop a table of contents for the portfolio (Radencich, Beers, and Schumm, 1993 pp. 119–120).

Examples of items you can include in a portfolio are as follows:

- Student assignments and work samples
- Student interviews
- Self-assessments
- Audiotapes
- Videotapes
- Diagnostic tests
- Achievement tests
- Teacher-made tests
- Pages from writing journals
- Awards
- Personal reading and writing records
- Interest and attitude inventories
- Photographs
- Copies of passages read fluently
- Contributions from parents
- Report cards
- List of accomplishments
- Observation checklists

STUDY SKILLS AND LEARNING STRATEGIES

In addition to learning content-area information making user-friendly lectures, and making adaptations, students with learning and behavior problems also need to develop study skills, learning strategies, and habits. Particularly as students move into sec-

ondary and postsecondary settings, the task demands require more emphasis on such skills as time management, self-monitoring and feedback, listening and notetaking, studying from textbooks, and test-taking skills (Brinckerhoff, Shaw, and McGuire, 1992). Surveys and observational studies conducted in secondary settings show: (1) a heavy reliance on written products as a means of evaluating performance,

(2) the need to listen to lectures containing few advance organizers and limited opportunities for interactions, and (3) a limited amount of individual help and teacher feedback (Putnam, 1992; Schumaker, Wildgen, and Sherman, 1982; Schumm, Vaugh, Haager, McDowell, Rothlien, Saumell, 1995).

Study skills can be defined as those competencies associated with acquiring, recording, organizing, synthesizing, remembering, and using information and ideas (Devine, 1987; Pauk, 2001). Study skills are the key to independent learning, and they help students gain and use information effectively. Students with effective study skills can be characterized as executive learners (Schumm and Post 1997) in that they:

— Are knowledgeable about personal learning strengths and challenges
— Have clear understanding about tasks to be accomplished
— Have a repertoire of learning strategies that can be applied in independent learning situations
— Have developed a set of help-seeking behaviors to activate when additional assistance is needed

Study skills can be divided into three areas:

1. *Personal development skills:* personal discipline, management and organizational skills, self-monitoring and reinforcement, and positive attitudes toward studying
2. *Process skills:* technical methods of studying such as notetaking, outlining, learning information from a text, and library reference skills
3. *Expression skills:* retrieval skills, test-taking skills, and using oral and/or written expression to demonstrate understanding

As would be expected, these are the skills and strategies that students with learning and behavior problems have difficulty developing. One reason for this may be that most study skills are not directly and systematically taught in the same manner in which reading and math skills are taught (Devine, 1987; Larkin and Ellis, 1998).

Personal Development Skills

Personal development skills include personal discipline, goal setting, management and organizational skills, self-monitoring and reinforcement, and positive attitudes toward studying. Many of the personal development skills related to school focus on time management, scheduling, organization, self-monitoring, and reinforcement.

Time Management and Scheduling

Jon's mom is concerned because Jon, her son with learning disabilities, falls asleep while trying to finish book reports the night before they are due. Even if she gets him up early in the morning, there is little chance Jon will have time to finish. Even though Jon knows about the assignments for three weeks, he waits until they're due to start reading, despite her queries about homework. Granted, it takes Jon longer than the other students, but his teacher, gives him the assignment early. He has the skills to get a B or C if he would just start earlier.

Many parents and teachers can identify with this scenario. Jon has the skills to complete the assignment successfully, but he lacks the personal management skills, particularly time management. Teaching a unit on time management at the beginning of the year and then reinforcing students during the year for the effective use of time can be well worth the effort. Here are the steps to follow.

Building a Rationale. The first step in getting students to schedule and manage their time is to build a rationale for its importance to success in school and later life. Discuss the following ideas with your students to build a rationale for effective time management:

— Parents will "get off your back" when they see you are getting your work done on time.
— If you write down what you have to do, you don't have to try to remember everything.
— If you set a time to begin, it is easier to get started and not procrastinate.
— When you set a time frame to complete an assignment it helps you work for a goal and concentrate.

— When you have a schedule, you're less likely to let a short break become a long break.

— Being in control of time makes you feel like you have more control of your life.

— When you get assignments and jobs done on time, then you can really enjoy your free time.

— Scheduling your time helps you get jobs done and have more time for fun and your friends.

Determining How the Time Is Spent.　Before students can decide how to schedule their time they need to determine how they are currently spending it. Using a schedule, have students keep track of their activities for one or two weeks. Also have them list the school assignments they have for the time period and if they have "too little," "enough," or "too much" time to complete them.

Estimating Time.　As part of the time management process, have students determine how long it takes them to complete regularly scheduled tasks such as meals, commuting, reading assignments in their various textbooks, writing a paragraph on a topic, completing a ten-problem math assignment, and so on. Although there will probably be considerable variability in the time taken to complete a task, most students with learning and behavior problems underestimate the time it takes. Having students get an idea of the time required can be helpful when planning a schedule.

Scheduling.　If students feel that they do not have enough time to get their tasks completed or if they do not have regular times for studying, encourage them to set up a schedule. Some suggestions that students might want to use when setting up their schedules are:

1. Plan regular study times.
2. Plan at least one-hour blocks of time in which to study.
3. Plan which assignments you are going to work on during the study time.
4. Take the first five minutes of each study activity to review what you have done already and what you have learned, and to plan what you are going

to accomplish today. This helps promote long-term learning and a sense of accomplishment.

5. When studying longer than one hour, plan breaks and stick to the time allowed for the breaks.
6. Use daytime or early evening for study if possible. Most people are less efficient at night.
7. Work on your most difficult subjects when you are most alert.
8. Distribute your studying for a test rather than cram.
9. Balance your time between studying and other activities. Allow time for recreational activities.
10. Reward yourself by marking through your schedule each time you meet a scheduled commitment and by crossing off items you complete on your "to do" list.

Not only should regular times for studying be listed on the schedule, but due dates for assignments and dates for other events should be noted so that the schedule also serves as a calendar. Students should also be encouraged to set aside some time they can use as they please, if they accomplish their tasks on schedule during the day or week. This type of self-determined reinforcer may serve as an extra motivation for some students.

Monitoring and Using a "To-Do" list:　Setting up a schedule will do little good unless students follow and monitor their schedules. Using a weekly schedule have students fill in those activities they feel are important to monitor. Figure 7.13 presents a schedule for Jon and a To-Do list. His study time, time spent working out, time spent on his after-school job, and TV time were the most important tasks for him to monitor, so he scheduled them in each week. He also noted when the next book report was due and used his To-Do list to schedule reading each day, crossing off tasks as they are accomplished.

　　Jon developed a contract with himself. If he studied at least 80 percent of the time he had scheduled during the week, then he could work out at the gym or "goof off" two extra hours on Saturday. In this way Jon is not only monitoring his schedule but setting goals and providing rewards for meeting his goals.

■ **FIGURE 7.13** *Jon's Weekly Schedule and To-Do List*

NAME: __Jon__

WEEK OF: __Oct 14__

	MON.	TUES.	WEDS.	THURS.	FRI.	SAT.	SUN.	
6:00 a.m.	get up and eat ———————————————————→							6:00 a.m.
7:00	ride ——————————————————→					sleep	sleep	7:00
8:00	bus							8:00
9:00	History	*same every day*				house &		9:00
10:00	English					yard	go to	10:00
11:00	PE					chores	church	11:00
12:00	Welding						eat	12:00
1:00 p.m.	Lunch					eat	read for fun	1:00 p.m.
2:00	Algebra					go		2:00
3:00	General science					to gym	goof off and	3:00
4:00	ride bus						eat	4:00
5:00	recreational activity			study	eat have fun	eat and have fun		5:00
6:00	eat ———————————————→							6:00
7:00	study	study	study	study			study	7:00
8:00								8:00
9:00	↓	↓	↓	↓			↓	9:00
10:00	sleep ———————————————→						sleep	10:00
11:00	↓				sleep ————→		↓	11:00

TO-DO LIST						
history paper due math assign finish book	math assign	math assign book report due	math assign welding project due	science test math test	chores mow grass pull weeds fix cooler	start English paper

TECH TALK 7.2

TECHNOLOGY FOR STUDENTS SELF-MANAGEMENT

Personal data assistants (PDAs) such as palm computers, schedulers, and address books are available and quickly becoming more affordable. In addition, software programs for laptop and standard computers provide a way of keeping track of schedules, assignments, addresses, phone numbers, e-mail addresses, Websites, and other important information. If streamlined in design and accessible, these high-tech tools can be ideal for students with planning and self-management needs. Personal management software and PDAs might include the following features: note taker, planner, calendar, spreadsheet, databases, programmable clock, timer or stopwatch, e-mail/Internet programs, and fax capabilities. Companies that specialize in PDAs and software include: Palm, Inc., http://www.palm.com, 800-881-7256; Handspring, Inc., http://www.handspring.com, 888-565-9393, and Compaq, http://www.compaq.com, 800-888-0220.

Many low-tech applications are available as well that have been developed specifically for student use, such as the familiar assignment notebooks and notebook organizers that students carry. Directly teaching students how to use these devices increases their ability to apply personal development skills and become independent learners. Adaptations of notebook organizers for students with special needs include, for example, a time management program called "Plan Your Day," which uses a system of picture prompts, laminated cards, pocket folders, and stickers. Information about self-management products from a variety of manufacturers for students with special needs, including print, video, and software products may be obtained from PCI Educational Publishers, (http://www.pcicatalog.com, 800-594-4263; or Franklin Covey, http://www.franklincovey.com, 800-360-8118.

Although Jon realizes that schedules need to be flexible, he has found that planning, even when plans change, helps him get more work accomplished in a timely manner. Tech Talk 7.2 describes some high- and low-tech approaches to scheduling.

Self-Monitoring and Reinforcement

For students with learning and behavior problems there is much evidence to support the notion that they have difficulty goal setting and self-monitoring, whether it be in the areas of attention and memory, reading comprehension, or personal and management skills (Bos and Filip, 1984; Larkin and Ellis, 1998; Schunk, 1996; Wilson and David, 1994).

Van Reusen and Bos (1992) developed a strategy that students can use to assist them in setting goals and keeping track of their progress. The strategy uses the acronym MARKER (it gives students a *mark* to work toward and is a *marker* of their progress), and includes the following steps:

Make a list of goals, set the order, set the date.
Arrange a plan for each goal and predict your success.
Run your plan for each goal and adjust if necessary.
Keep records of your progress.
Evaluate your progress toward each goal.
Reward yourself when you reach a goal, and set a new goal.

For each goal, students use a Goal Planning Sheet (see Figure 7.14) to answer the following questions:

— Can I describe my goal?
— What is the reason or purpose for the goal?
— Where am I going to work on and complete this goal?
— How much time do I have to complete the goal?
— What materials do I need to complete the goal?

■ **FIGURE 7.14**   *Goal Planning and Monitoring Sheet*

Name: _____   Class: _____   Date: _____

1. Goal: _____

2. Reason(s) for working on goal: _____

3. Goal will be worked on at: _____

4. Date to reach goal (due date): _____

5. Materials needed: _____

_____

_____

_____

_____

6. Steps used to reach the goal: _____

_____

_____

_____

_____

7. Progress toward the goal: Record in each box the date and progress rating.

  3—Goal reached   2—Good progress made   1—Some progress made   0—No progress made

Date / Rating					

8. Reward for reaching goal: _____

Source: Adapted from A. K. Van Reusen and C. S. Bos, *Use of the Goal-Regulation Strategy to Improve the Goal Attainment of Students with Learning Disabilities* (Final Report) (Tucson: University of Arizona, 1992).

— Can I divide the goal into steps or parts? If so, in what order should I complete each step or part?
— How am I going to keep records of my progress?
— How will I reward myself for reaching my goal?

The teacher can use the steps in the Strategies Intervention Model (see Chapter Two) to teach the students the strategy. After learning the strategy, students usually work on one to three goals at a time, keeping progress data on each goal.

When Van Reusen and Bos (1992) used this strategy with middle and high school students with learning disabilities and behavior disorders, they found that students accomplished more goals and gained a more informed perspective of their educational and personal goals.

Hughes and his colleagues (Hughes, Ruhl, Deshler, and Schumaker, 1995) have developed an assignment completion strategy for the Strategies Intervention Model that is similar. The steps in this learning strategy include:

Psych up. Prepare your assignment monitoring form and your mind.

Record and ask. Record the assignment, think about it, and ask questions.

Organize. Break the assignment into parts, estimate and schedule the number of study sessions, and organize your materials.

Jump to it. Survey the assignment, set goals and a reward.

Engage in the work. Follow the instructions, note questions, and get help if you need it.

Check the work. Check for requirements and quality, store the assignment and reward yourself.

Turn it in. Take it to class, turn it in, record the date, and praise yourself.

Set your course. Record your grade, evaluate your assignment, and think about future assignments.

Classroom Participation

Students who participate actively in class tend to be more successful academically than their quieter, less attentive peers (Ellis, 1991; Larkin and Ellis, 1998). Students with learning and behavior problems may benefit from specific strategies to enhance their classroom participation. The SLANT strategy is part of the Strategies Intervention Model (see Chapter Two) and was designed for the purpose of increasing active participation in class. The acronym SLANT stands for

> Sit up
> Lean forward
> Activate your thinking
> Name key information
> Track the talker

Examples of Activate your thinking include asking yourself questions ("What is this about?" "What do I need to remember?"); answering your questions ("This is about _____." "I need to remember _____."); and asking the teacher a question when you do not understand. Examples of Name key information include answering the teach-er's questions, sharing your ideas, and additions to other's comments (Ellis, 1991). This general set of activities can be used in any learning situation to improve students' active participation as can the SHARE behaviors (See Apply the Concept 1.1 p. 14)

An important part of assignment completion and class participation in inclusive classrooms is recruiting positive teacher attention. Students with learning and behavior problems often get the attention of the teacher for their negative behaviors rather than the positive behaviors in class. To assist students with gaining positive teacher attention in general education classes, the special education teacher taught four middle school students with learning disabilities to recruit positive teacher attention in their general education classrooms (Alber, Heward, and Hippler, 1999). Through instruction, role-playing, and reinforcement students were taught to raise their hands and wait quietly or at an appropriate time ask such questions as "How am I doing?" or "I don't understand," or "Would you please look at my work?" Observations in the general education classrooms demonstrated that students increased their amount of positive teacher recruiting and teachers increased their rate of student praise. Teaching students strategies for self-monitoring, self-reinforcement, and classroom participation is an important part of the special education curriculum in that like study skills, these skills support student success in the general education classroom and curriculum.

Process Skills

Process skills include the technical methods of studying such as notetaking, outlining, learning information from text, and research and library skills.

Listening and Taking Notes

In school, students spend more time listening than reading, speaking, or writing. On the average, teachers in secondary settings spend at least half of their class time presenting information through lectures (Putnam, Deshler, and Schumaker, 1993). Furthermore, teachers rely on information presented in class discussion and lectures as the basis for a significant number of items on tests (Putnam et al., 1993). Notetaking is one of the most efficient ways to record this information. It has several important functions:

— Notetaking increases students' attention.
— Notetaking, as opposed to just listening, requires a deeper level of cognitive processing in that the student must make sense of the information and write the ideas.
— Because the information has been processed more deeply, notetaking helps the student learn and remember the information more easily.

These three statements are supported by research which demonstrates that notetaking gives students an advantage over simply listening (Anderson and Armbruster, 1986; Kiewra, 1985). Even if students do not go back and review their notes, just the act of taking them results in greater recall of information on tests.

Students with learning and behavior problems often have difficulties with listening and notetaking. For some students with severe writing disabilities, it will be important that they have a notetaker. Lightweight laptop computers or devices designed specifically for taking notes, such as the AlphaSmart (www.AlphaSmart.com, 888-274-0680) are also very beneficial if students are instructed on how to use them. Students with learning disabilities may have difficulty with:

— Paying attention
— Writing fast and legibly
— Deciding what information to write
— Spelling
— Making sense of notes after the lecture

They also have limited use of abbreviations and limited use of a comprehensive notetaking system (Suritsky and Hughes, 1996). Given the importance of taking notes and the difficulty some students encounter with this skill, as a teacher you will want to teach students how to take notes, and consider using "listener-friendly lecturers" to make notetaking easier.

Teaching Students to Take Notes. Numerous formats for notetaking have been suggested (Bragstad and Stumpf, 1982; Langan, 1982; Pauk, 2001; Roberts, 1999). One aspect that these systems have in common is the focus on making notetaking and reviewing an interactive learning process (Schumm and Post, 1997). To facilitate this interactive process, two- or three-column notetaking systems have been developed. Figure 7.15 gives an example of each. Students take class notes in the far right-hand column in both systems, using only the front side of the paper. Modified outlining is the format that is most often suggested for taking these notes. In the two-column system, students note the key concepts in the left-hand column, sometimes referred to as *triggers* since they are meant to "trigger" the ideas noted in the other column (Devine, 1987). Later, in reviewing, students should be able to cover the right column and use their personal triggers to help them remember the ideas covered in the class notes. In three-column systems, the additional column generally serves as a space to write textbook notes so that they can be integrated with class notes. This is most helpful when the teacher's lectures make frequent, direct ties to the textbook.

The following list gives several hints for helping students develop efficient notetaking skills.

— Take notes using either a two- or three-column system.
— Take notes on only one side of the paper.
— Date and label the topic of the notes.
— Generally use a modified outline format, indenting subordinate ideas and numbering ideas when possible.
— Skip lines to note changes in ideas.
— Write ideas or key phrases, not complete sentences.
— Use pictures and diagrams to relate ideas.
— Use consistent abbreviations (e.g., w/ = with, & = and).
— Underline or asterisk information the lecturer stresses as important.

■ **FIGURE 7.15** *Formats for Notetaking*

SAMPLE TWO-COLUMN SYSTEM

Topic: _____

Date: _____

Triggers or Key Concepts	Class Notes

SAMPLE THREE-COLUMN SYSTEM

Topic: _____

Date: _____

Triggers or Key Concepts	Class Notes	Text Notes

— Write down information that the lecturer writes on the board or transparency.

— If you miss an idea you want to include, draw a blank _____ so that you can go back and fill it in.

— If you cannot automatically remember how to spell a word, spell it the way it sounds or the way you think it looks.

— If possible, review the previous sessions' notes right before the lecture.

— If the lecture is about an assigned reading topic, read the information before listening to the lecture.

— As soon as possible after the lecture, go over your notes, filling in the key concept column and listing any questions you still have.

— After going over your notes, try to summarize the major points presented during the lecture.

— Listen actively! In other words, think about what you already know about the topic being presented and how it relates.

— Review your notes before a test!

Direct Instruction in Notetaking. For many students with learning and behavior problems, just telling them how to take notes is insufficient. Teachers may want to develop and conduct a unit on listening and notetaking. The following is a list of teaching ideas for developing such a unit:

1. *Have students evaluate the effectiveness of their current notetaking skills and determine if they will profit from instruction.* Generally, this can be assessed in two ways. First, have the students bring to class current examples of notes and have them evaluate them for completeness, format, ease of use for review, and legibility. Second, present a simulated 10- to 15-minute lecture or a videotape of a lecture and ask the students to take notes. Give a test covering the information on the following day. Have the students again evaluate their notes and their test results.

2. *Use videotaped lectures when teaching students to listen effectively and to take notes.* The use of videotaped lectures is particularly helpful because it allows the students to replay the tape so that they can watch or listen for main ideas. For example, you may be teaching students to watch and listen for cues the lecturer gives to note the important information. After listening to a short segment of videotape, have the students list the cues and then discuss why they are important. Then replay the segment so that students can verify their list of cues and add other cues.

3. *Control the difficulty of the lectures.* When first introducing new listening or notetaking skills such as listening for cues or using a two-column system, begin with short, well-organized lectures with ample use of advance organizers and visual aids, covering fairly simple, relatively familiar materials. As students reach proficiency, gradually increase the length of the lectures, reduce the use of organizers and visual aids, and increase the difficulty and novelty levels of the materials.

4. *Have students learn how to review their notes for tests.* Although students may learn to take more effective notes, they may fail to use them to study for tests. Teach students how to review their notes and ask themselves questions, using the "triggers" column to develop questions over the "notes" column.

5. *Have students monitor the use and effectiveness of notetaking in other classes.* To increase the probability that students will generalize the notetaking skills to other classes, have them discuss in which classes the skills would be helpful and then have them monitor and discuss their effectiveness in those classes.

6. *Have students determine the effects that notetaking has on learning.* Students need to know there is a payoff for their increased effort. Have students rate how well they feel they have taken notes over a unit or lecture and have them monitor their performance on tests over the material. This will aid them in determining if better notetaking leads to better learning.

Learning from Text

Probably the best-known technique for learning information from text is SQ3R, developed by Robinson (1946). This acronym stands for the five steps in this study skill: Survey, Question, Read, Recite, Review. The purpose of this technique is to provide students with a systematic approach to studying text. The following is a brief description of each one of the five steps in the process.

Survey: Read through the headings quickly to learn what is to be studied.

Question: Change each heading into a question (to have in mind what is to be learned from the reading).

Read: Read to answer the question.

Recite: At the end of each heading, either write brief notes about the highlights of the reading or engage in self-recitation.

Review: After completing the above steps on the entire selection, review the main points of the notes by self-recitation and check to see if the information is correct. (Adapted from F. P. Robinson, Effective Study [New York: Harper and Brothers], 1946.)

Although SQ3R seems well based in information processing theory, research has yet to support its effectiveness (Adams, Carnine, and Gersten, 1982; McCormick and Cooper, 1991). One of the major difficulties associated with the SQ3R method is the complexity of the process, particularly for students who are experiencing reading problems. In content area classes, these students are often attempting to read and learn information from textbooks written above their instructional reading levels.

Multipass. Schumaker, Deshler, Alley, Warner, and Denton (1982) have developed a strategy based on SQ3R. It incorporates the learning acquisition and generalization stages from the Strategy Intervention Model (see Chapter 2) and it is designed for students who experience problems learning information from textbooks. This strategy is referred to as *Multipass* because the students make three passes through the text while carrying out the process. Each pass through the text (i.e., Survey, Size-up, and Sort-out) entails the use of a different substrategy. Because each substrategy represents a fairly complex set of behaviors, each of the substrategies is taught as a unit, with the students reaching proficiency in the first substrategy before they learn the next substrategy. Prerequisite skills include the ability to paraphrase and a reading level of fourth grade or above. Research conducted with eight high school students with learning disabilities indicated that the students were able to master the strategy in instructional level materials and were able to use the strategy in grade-level materials without further training or practice. The students' grade on content tests improved—from barely passing to grades of C or better.

Survey. During the Survey Pass, students become familiar with the main ideas and organization of the chapter (Deshler, Schumaker, and McKnight, 1997). In completing the Survey Pass, students are directed to do the following:

1. *Title.* Read the chapter title and think about how it fits with what you have already studied. Predict what the chapter is going to be about.
2. *Introduction.* Read the introduction and make a statement about the main idea of the chapter. If there is no introduction, read the first paragraph, which is generally the introduction.
3. *Summary.* Turn to the last page of the chapter, read the summary, and make a summary state-

ment. If there is no summary, check the last paragraph to see if it is a summary. If it is not a summary, make a mental note so that you can summarize later.
4. *Organization.* Look through the chapter to see how the chapter is organized. Use the major headings to make a written outline. Paraphrase each heading.
5. *Pictures, maps, charts.* Look at the illustrations. Think about why they might have been included.
6. *Table of Contents.* Find out how this chapter fits in with the other information in the book by perusing the table of contents. Decide what relationships this chapter has with the others, especially the chapters immediately preceding and following. For example, in a history book, chapters are often related because of chronological sequence. Chapters might also have a causal relationship (e.g., Chapter 6 talks about the causes of the Depression; Chapter 7 talks about its effects). Other types of frequently occurring relationships include: general/specific, compare/contrast, and related concepts.

After completing this process, close the book and think about what the chapter is going to be about and what you already know about the topic.

Using the Strategies Intervention Model, the teacher first describes and then models this survey process. The students should practice with guidance and feedback in materials at their reading instructional level until they are effective and efficient at surveying a chapter.

Size-up. During the Size-up Pass, students gain more specific information from the chapter without reading the chapter from beginning to end. Whereas the Survey Pass provides a general framework for the chapter, the Size-up Pass allows the students to look for the information that fits into that general framework using *textual cues*. In learning the Size-up Pass, students do the following:

1. *Illustrations.* Again, look over the pictures, maps, and charts and read the captions. Think about why they are included.

2. *Questions.* Read the questions, including those found at the beginning or interspersed in the chapter. If you can already answer a study question, put a check by it.
3. *Words.* Read over the vocabulary words, including any vocabulary list and words highlighted in the chapter.
4. *Headings. Read* the heading. *Ask* yourself a question that you think will be answered in the section. *Scan* for the answer. When you find the answer, *paraphrase* it orally or state something you have learned from the information under the heading. *Note* on your outline what information you have learned from the section.

Like the Survey Pass, the teacher will need to describe the Size-up process and the students should practice in instructional level material until they are proficient.

Sort-out. During this third and final pass, the students test themselves on the material in the chapter. This pass assists them in determining what they have learned and on what information they should still concentrate. In the final pass, the students read and answer each question at the end of the chapter, using the following process.

1. *Read.* Read the study question at the end of the chapter or each question provided by the teacher.
2. *Answer.* Answer the question if you can.
3. *Mark.* If you can answer a question, put a check by it; if you cannot, put a box in front of it. If you do not know the answer, scan the headings on your outline to determine in which section it most likely will be answered. When you find the likely section, look for the answer. If you find the answer, paraphrase it and check the box. If you do not find the answer, scan the headings a second time for another likely place to find the answer. Again, look for the answer and paraphrase it if you find it. If you do not find the answer after trying twice, circle the box so you know you need to come back to it later and possibly get help.

Like the other two steps, the students should practice with materials at their instructional level until they are effective and efficient at answering questions over the material presented in the chapter.

— **COMMENTS:** From the description of Multipass, it should be clear that when students use this strategy they do not have to read the text in its entirety. Instead, they study the text to determine the main ideas, its overall framework and related details, and to answer the study questions. In this way students can use this strategy in textbooks that are written above their instructional level. However, several cautionary notes are in order. First, remember to have the students reach proficiency on each substrategy before they begin learning the next substrategy. Second, when the difference between the students' instructional reading level and reading level of the textbook is greater than one to two years, students may have difficulty moving from instructional-level materials to grade-level materials. Teachers will generally need to provide graduated instructional materials. (For example, Hector's instructional reading level is fifth grade and he is a ninth grader. Hector will probably need to practice using the strategy in seventh-grade material as an intermediary step.) Third, do not expect students with learning and behavior problems to transfer this study strategy automatically to various content area textbooks. You will need to instruct for generalization.

Expression Skills

Expression skills include memory, retrieval, and test-taking skills, as well as other oral and/or written expression skills used to demonstrate understanding and application of knowledge.

Remembering Information

Have you ever arrived at the grocery store without your grocery list? What are the strategies that you use to help you remember what was on the list? Maybe you counted the items on the list and now you just need to see how many of the items you can jot down. Or maybe you read the list over several times almost rehearsing it; so it was easier to recall. Or you might use association by thinking of the meals that you were planning for the next few days and seeing if you can associate the needed items with the meals. Or you might visualize your kitchen and quickly think about the refrigerator and each cabinet and the items needed from each. Finally, you might categorize the items based on the sections in the grocery store (i.e., produce, cereal, bread, frozen foods). Clearly, there are many strategies for remembering information.

In many ways, remembering information for a test is not unlike remembering the items on a grocery list. Often we are asked to remember a list of things (e.g., the major exports of England, the different kinds of flour and their uses, the names of the cranial nerves). During tests we may be asked to take this information and apply it to specific situations (e.g., to support why England's economy is struggling), but we still need to remember the basic information.

Students with disabilities often have difficulty memorizing information whether it be for tests, presentations, or written work (Ashbaker and Swanson, 1996). Sometimes the students may not understand the information to be learned, but in other cases the poor performance may be due to difficulties with retrieval of the information (Swanson and Cooney, 1991), failure to use deliberate memory strategies (Ceci, 1985), and/or poor motivation for school tasks (Licht, 1983). Research suggests that these students also have difficulty with metamemory (i.e., awareness of memory strategies and the ability to use and monitor these strategies) in that they have trouble with one or more of the following:

— Knowing, selecting, and using appropriate strategies
— Estimating their own memory capacity for specific tasks
— Predicting accuracy on a memory task
— Allotting appropriate time to study
— Deciding when they have studied enough (Hughes, 1996)

Consequently, it's important to teach students memory strategies and "tricks" for remembering. Because teachers are regularly asking students to remember information (e.g., for tests, class discussions), it is relatively easy to incorporate teaching memory strategies into the content curriculum.

Furthermore, incorporating the general teaching principles presented in Apply the Concept 7.4 makes the information more memorable and encourages learning and remembering the information.

Many content area learning strategies such as semantic mapping, advance organizers, and semantic feature analysis can be thought of as teaching procedures that facilitate memory. In addition to these kinds of activities, a number of formal strategies have been deliberately designed to improve memory. These are often referred to as *mnemonics*.

Mnemonics are strategies for improving memory. The word *mnemonics* literally means "aids memory." Mnemonics aids memory and retrieval by forming associations that do not exist naturally in the content (Eggen and Kauchak, 1992). To use mnemonics, the information needs to be distilled so that the students are learning conceptual lists or frameworks. This information is then operated on using mnemonics. Mnemonic strategies can be grouped into three types: organization and association, visualization or mental imagery, and rehearsal.

Organization and Association. Organizing and associating information refers to arranging the information or associating it with other information in such a way that it is easier to remember. Study the list of terms below in order to remember them:

Democracy	Mammals
Socket Wrench	Judiciary
Biology	Anatomy
Photosynthesis	Drill Press
Lathe	Blow Torch
Freedom of Speech	Constitution

Chances are that you categorized the words according to three superordinate categories, possibly labeled *tools, science concepts,* and *social studies concepts.* Now, instead of learning twelve unrelated words you are learning three sets of four related words. Research would show that the second task is considerably easier. Research and practice have

APPLY THE CONCEPT 7.4

GENERAL TEACHING PRINCIPLES FOR INCREASING STUDENT'S MEMORY OF INFORMATION

- Orient student attention before presenting information, emphasize important vocabulary and concepts when they occur.
- Activate prior knowledge and help students make connections between old and new knowledge.
- Use visual aids such as graphic organizers to highlight the important information and make it more memorable.
- Control the amount of information presented; group related ideas.

- Control the rate at which the information is presented.
- Provide time to review, rehearse, and elaborate on the information.
- Teach the students how to use and apply memory strategies and devices.
- Provide time and guidance in developing associations and mnemonics such as acronyms and acrostics.
- Provide opportunities for distributed review of information, and encourage overlearning.

also demonstrated that students experiencing learning problems do not tend to make these associations spontaneously (Howe, O'Sullivan, Brainerd, and Kingman, 1989). Therefore, one mnemonic to teach students when trying to remember lists of information is to associate or categorize related ideas.

Another type of association is the use of acrostics and acronyms. *Acrostics* are sentences created by words that begin with the first letters of a series of words.

Do you remember learning the names of the spaces on the musical staff as the word *FACE* and the names of the lines as *"Every Good Boy Does Fine"*? *Acronyms* are words created by joining the first letters of a series of words. Examples are *radar* (radio detecting and ranging), *scuba* (self-contained underwater breathing apparatus), and *laser* (light amplification by stimulated emission of radiation). If needed, extra letters can be inserted, or the letters can be rearranged. This technique has been used extensively in the development of learning strategies for students with learning and behavior problems (Deshler, et al., 1996). By teaching students to construct acronyms and acrostics, sharing them in class, and then cuing students to use them when they study and take tests, you help them to learn and retrieve information.

The FIRST-letter mnemonic strategy (Nagel, Schumaker, and Deshler, 1986) is one strategy you

can teach to help students construct lists of information to memorize and develop an acronym or acrostic for learning and remembering the information. The strategy includes an overall strategy (LISTS) and a substrategy for making the mnemonic device (FIRST). The steps in the overall strategy include the following:

Look for clues. In the class notes and textbooks, look for lists of information that are important to learn. Name or give a heading to each list.

Investigate the items. Decide which items should be included in the list.

Select a mnemonic device, using FIRST. Use the FIRST substrategy, explained shortly, to construct a mnemonic.

Transfer the information to a card. Write the mnemonic and the list on one side of a card and the name of the list on the other side of the card.

Self-test. Study by looking at the heading using the mnemonic to recall the list.

To complete the Select step, students use the FIRST strategy to design an acronym or acrostic:

Form a word. Using uppercase letters, write the first letter of each word in the list; see whether an acronym—a recognizable word or nonsense word—can be made.

Insert a letter(s). Insert letter(s) to see whether a word can be made. (Be sure to use lowercase letters so that you know they do not represent an item on the list—BACk, for example.

Rearrange the letters. Rearrange the letters to see whether a word can be made.

Shape a sentence. Using the first letter of each word in the list, try to construct a sentence (an acrostic).

Try combinations. Try combinations of these above steps to generate the mnemonic.

This strategy is taught using the Strategies Intervention Model presented in Chapter Two. It can be used with most content, but is particularly effective with science and social studies in which lists of information are to be learned. The strategy provides a systematic method for students to review text and class notes, construct lists, and develop acronyms and acrostics that help them remember and retrieve information.

Visualization and Key Word Method.   Another strategy that is helpful in remembering information is visualization. *Visualization* is seeing in your mind or making a visual image of what you are to remember. Sometimes the visual image is simply the information that needs to be remembered. For example, it is not unusual to notice students closing their eyes when they are trying to remember how to spell a word. They may be using visualization to recall "what the word looks like."

If the information is complex, however, it may be helpful for the students to change the image that they are to remember into a picture that will trigger or cue the information to be remembered. One strategy used to do this is the *key word method* (e.g., Mastroprieri and Scruggs, 1998; Mastroprieri, Sweda, and Scruggs, 2000). Using this visualization strategy, students construct a picture that represents an interactive relationship between a concept and its definition. Figure 7.16 shows a key word picture generated for the concept of *allegro* and its definition (i.e., to move quickly). This picture is used to link the vocabulary

■ **FIGURE 7.16**   *Key Word Picture Generated for the Concept "Allegro"*

Source: C. A. Hughes, "Memory and Test-Taking Strategies," in D. D. Deshler, E. S. Ellis, and B. K. Lenz, *Teaching Adolescents with Learning Disabilities,* 2nd ed. (Denver: Love, 1996), p. 223. Reprinted with permission.

word with the definition using a key word(s) that sounds like the vocabulary word. In Figure 7.16 *leg* and *row* are the keywords and are used to construct a picture that triggers the definition of *allegro*.

The following steps are suggested for creating the key word picture (King-Sears, Mercer, and Sindelar, 1992) and uses the acronym IT FITS.

I̲dentify the word or term.

T̲ell the definition or answer information.

F̲ind a key word that sounds like the new word or word you need to remember.

I̲magine an interaction, that is, something that the key word and the answer information can do together. If you draw a sketch of the interaction, you may review it later for improved memory.

T̲hink about the key word and the interaction.

S̲tudy your vocabulary and the information using your keyword to help you remember. Review by asking for each item? "What was my key word for (word)? What was happening in my picture (or image)? What is the information I am supposed to remember?

Mastropieri and Scruggs (1989) suggest three rules that help a teacher decide the type of reconstructive elaboration that might work best:

Rule A: If the stimulus-response information is already concrete and meaningful to the learners, simply provide an interactive elaboration between the stimulus and response. Use of picture or mental images is particularly helpful.

Rule B: If the information is familiar but abstract, reconstruct that stimulus into something more concrete and more meaningful for the learners, and then provide an interactive illustration or image for the learners with the reconstructed stimulus and the response. This may be accomplished by concretizing abstract concepts like "justice" or "liberty" with symbolic representations, such as scales, or Uncle Sam as a symbolic representation of United States policy.

Rule C: If the information is unfamiliar, such as with unfamiliar names, places, and vocabulary words, reconstruct the item into something more concrete and familiar for the learner by means of the keyword method, and then depict that more concrete and familiar response in an interactive elaborative picture or image. (p. 76)

The key word method has been shown to be most effective in increasing the recall of information by students with learning disabilities when the key word relationships were presented to the students rather than having individual students generate them (Fulk, Mastropieri, and Scruggs, 1992; Mastropieri and Scruggs, 1989; Scruggs and Mastropieri, 1989). Students should have ample opportunities to create the key word associations as a class or in cooperative groups before having students work individually.

Verbal Rehearsal.   Repeating the information aloud or to yourself can help facilitate memory. Verbal rehearsal is the major cognitive strategy used to enhance short-term memory (Hughes, 1996). Rehearsal, however, is most effective if there is limited interference between the time of the rehearsal and the time of recall, if the number of items to be remembered is limited, and if the information is clustered or chunked.

General Memory Strategies.   Often several mnemonics are used simultaneously. For example, after you categorized the words in a list you could use acronyms within each category to help you remember the specific words, and then use rehearsal to practice, review, and test your memory. Teaching students with learning and behavior problems which strategies to use for which types of information and how to combine strategies will generally be necessary. In addition to teaching students how to use the various memory strategies, it is also important to teach students to use periodic review to minimize forgetting.

Studying and Taking Tests

Studying and taking tests are important study skills in secondary schools. Tests are the primary means that teachers use to determine if students have learned new concepts and can apply them. For example, Putnam (1992) surveyed 120 English, science, social studies, or mathematics teachers grades 7 to 12 to determine how frequently they used tests. In a nine-week grading period, students were expected to take an average of 11 tests in each content area. On the average teachers used scores on tests to determine approximately half of a grade for a course. While a great deal of effort is placed on tests to measure learning, only 25 percent of the teachers surveyed indicated that they taught strategies for taking tests. Yet research on students with disabilities and students at risk indicates that they have limited study and test taking strategies to employ (Hughes and Schumaker, 1991; Scruggs and Mastropieri, 1988). For example, the only strategy college students with learning disabilities regularly reported using when taking objective tests was skipping over difficult/unknown items. For essay questions, only half the students reported rereading the question or proofreading their response.

Studying for Tests.   Studying for a test means that students are reviewing information on a regular basis so they are not left cramming the day before the test. To help promote positive study habits Teri Martinez, a middle school resource social studies teacher, taught the following guidelines for studying:

1. *Manage your study time.* Keep up with assignments and do daily and weekly reviews. Teri planned five minutes each day at the end of her social studies class for students to review the material. On Monday, she took an extra five minutes and had the students review the previous week's work. She used individual, small group and whole-class discussion to review.

2. *Create study aids.* Create a semantic map or other graphic organizer to help students remember key information. Teri often used an on-going map during review sessions so that the students added to the map each day. Teri also taught the students how to create and use flashcards for key concepts and vocabulary. She taught the students the following procedures.
   - When learning vocabulary, put the word on one side and the definition and an example on the other side.
   - When learning other information, put the question on one side and the answer on the other side.
   - When learning a formula, put the formula on one side and examples of how it is used on the other side.
   - Review the flashcards in random order or after sorting the cards into categories or making a semantic map.
   - Keep index cards in notebooks and on desks during class.
   - Make a card when learning about a key concept or idea.

3. *Learn about the test.* The more information students learn about the format, type, and time allotted for the test, the more effectively they can prepare for it. Rather than telling the students about the test, Teri would start the discussion with, "Let's talk about the test, what do you want to ask me?" She used the following checklist to guide the students' questioning:
   - Format of test; types of questions
   - How much test is worth
   - Date of test
   - Time allotted for test
   - Whether or not books or notes allowed
   - Information covered
   - Teacher recommendations for *how to study*
   - Teacher recommendations for *what to study*

4. *Predict questions.* Teri also demonstrated how the students can predict the questions that will be asked. Have the students use what they know about the teacher's testing style, their class notes, their maps and other study aids to predict questions. Two days before a test, Teri had the students work in cooperative groups and write what they thought would be the most important questions on the test and then answer them.

5. *Think positive.* An important part of doing well on a test is having a positive attitude and believing that you are going to do well. Teri finds that she enjoys working with the students on having positive attitudes. Each day during their review, she asks the students about the following:
   - What they learned today
   - How it relates to what they already know
   - What will they be working on tomorrow
   - How well they have learned the information

   She also has them rate how well they think they will do on the test and think about what they could do to improve their ratings. Just before a test, Teri also takes several minutes to review test-taking strategies and have the students visualize themselves being successful as they take the test.

Test-Taking Strategies.   There are a number of test-taking hints that help students be more successful on tests. The following are consistently noted as important for success:

— Bring the necessary materials.
— Be on time and sit where you will not be disturbed.
— Survey the test.
— Read the directions carefully and check that you understand them. If not, ask for assistance.
— Schedule your time.
— Be sure you understand the scoring system (i.e., Is guessing penalized?).

- If you have memorized specific outlines, formulas, mnemonics, etc., write that information before you forget it.
- When answering questions, place a mark in the margin for those questions about which you are unsure and/or want to review.
- Place the question in the context of what has been discussed in class and what you have read.
- Avoid changing answers arbitrarily.
- Review your answers and proofread written responses.

Taking Objective Tests.   For students with learning and behavior problems, it may be beneficial to teach specific test-taking strategies. The test-taking strategy can be used for taking objective tests (Hughes, Schumaker, Deshler, and Mercer, 1988) and uses the Strategies Intervention Model described in Chapter Two. Research indicated that students with learning disabilities increased their performance 20 to 40 percentage points by learning and applying this strategy. The steps in the strategy are:

Prepare to succeed
    Put your name and PIRATES on the test
    Allot time and order the sections
    Say affirmations
    Start within 2 minutes
Inspect the instructions
    Read instructions carefully
    Underline what to do and where to respond
    Notice special requirements
Read, remember, reduce
    Read the whole question
    Remember what you studied
    Reduce your choices
Answer or abandon
    Answer the question
    Abandon the question for the moment
Turn back
Estimate your answer
    Avoid absolutes
    Choose the longest or most detailed choice
    Eliminate similar choices

Survey
    Survey to ensure all questions are answered
    Switch an answer only if you're sure

Like many learning strategies, this strategy uses an acronym to help students remember the steps in the strategy (PIRATES). When using this strategy a student repeats, for each section of the test, the second, third, and fourth steps (i.e., inspect the instructions; read, remember, reduce; answer or abandon).

In addition to this strategy, there are a number of hints for taking objective tests. Apply the Concept 7.5 presents information that is helpful when answering objective questions (e.g., true-false, multiple-choice, matching, and completion).

Taking Essay Tests.   Essays tests are not used as frequently as objective tests (Putnam, 1992), but when essay questions are incorporated into a test, they make up a sizable portion of the test grade (Hughes, 1996). This type of test can be particularly difficult for students with disabilities. Not only do they have to recall the information, they have to write clearly in terms of thought, legibility, spelling, and grammar. Students with difficulties in written expression may be able to orally express the answer to the question, but their writing skills make it difficult for them to communicate that knowledge. You may want to record the student's answers on audiotape. For some students it may be advantageous to teach a strategy for answering essay questions so that the students organize the information and communicate it effectively. One strategy developed to assist students in organizing better responses to essay questions is called ANSWER (Hughes, Schumaker, and Deshler, in preparation). The steps include:

Analyze the situation
    Read the question carefully
    Underline key words
    Gauge the time you need
Notice requirements
    Scan for and mark the parts of the question
    Ask and say what is required
    Tell yourself you will write a quality answer

APPLY THE CONCEPT 7.5

TIPS FOR ANSWERING OBJECTIVE QUESTIONS

True-False Questions
- Remember, *everything* in a true statement must be true. One false detail makes it false.
- Look for qualifying words that tend to make statements false, such as: *all, always, everyone, everybody, never, no, none, no one, only.*
- Look for qualifying words that tend to make statements true, such as: *generally, most, often, probably, some, sometimes, usually.*
- Simplify questions that contain double negatives by crossing out both negatives and then determining whether the statement is true or false.
- Don't change an answer unless you have a good reason to. Usually your first impression is correct.

Matching Questions
- Read directions carefully. Determine whether each column contains an equal number of items and whether items can be used more than once.
- Read both columns before you start matching, to get a sense of the items.
- Focus on each item in one column and look for its match in the other column.
- If you can use items only once, cross out each item as you use it.

Multiple-Choice Questions
- Determine whether you are penalized for guessing.
- Answer the questions you know, putting a check in the margin next to items you want to return to later.

- Read all possible options, even when you are pretty sure of the right answer.
- See whether multiple options are available (e.g., c. A and B; d. All of the above).
- Minimize the risk of guessing by reading the stem with each option to see which option is most logical.
- Use a process of elimination, crossing out options you know are wrong.
- When you do not know the answer and you are not penalized for guessing, use the following signals to help you select the right option:
  - The longest option is often correct.
  - The most complete answer is often correct.
  - The first time the option "all of the above" or "none of the above" is used, it is usually correct.
  - The option in the middle, particularly if it is the longest, is often correct.
  - Answers with qualifiers such as *generally, probably, sometimes,* and *usually* are frequently correct.

Completion Questions
- Determine whether more than one word can be put in one blank.
- If blanks are of different lengths, use length as a clue for the length of the answer.
- Read the question to yourself so that you can hear what is being asked.
- If more than one answer comes to mind, write them down; then reread the question with each answer to see which one fits best.
- Make sure that the answer you provide fits grammatically and logically.

Source: Selected ideas adapted from J. Langan, *Reading and Study Skills,* 2nd ed. (New York: McGraw-Hill, 1982).

Set up an outline
   Set up main ideas
   Assess whether they match the question
   Make changes if necessary
Work in details

Remember what you learned
Add details to the main ideas using abbreviations
Indicate order
Decide if you are ready to write

Engineer your answer
    Write an introductory paragraph
    Refer to your outline
    Include topic sentences
    Tell about details for each topic sentence
    Employ examples
Review your answer
    Look to see if you answered all parts of the question
    Inspect to see if you included all main ideas and details
    Touch up your answer

In her social studies class, Teri taught the ANSWER strategy since essay questions were one format she used in her tests. She also gave to the students the list of direction words for essay questions (see Figure 7.17). She demonstrated how taking one concept such as *democracy* and using different direction words will change the response. In her daily reviews Teri frequently discussed one of the cue words in relation to the content covered that day. She provided examples of how to write an answer to a question using that cue word.

INSTRUCTIONAL ACTIVITIES

This section provides instructional activities that are related to content area learning and study skills. Some of the activities teach new skills; others are best suited for practice and reinforcement of already acquired skills. For each activity, the objective, materials, and teaching procedures are described.

■ **FIGURE 7.17**   *Direction Words for Answering Essay Questions*

Cue	Meaning	Cue	Meaning
Analyze	Break into parts and examine each part.	Interpret	Explain and share your own judgment.
Apply	Discuss how the principles would apply to a situation.	Justify	Provide reasons for your statements or conclusion.
Compare	Discuss differences and similarities.	List	Provide a numbered list of items or points.
Contract	Discuss differences and similarities, stressing the differences.	Outline	Organize your answer into main points and supporting details. If appropriate, use outline format.
Critique	Analyze and evaluate, using criteria.		
Define	Provide a clear, concise statement that explains the concept.	Prove	Provide factual evidence to support your logic or position.
Describe	Give a detailed account, listing characteristic, qualities, and components as appropriate.	Relate	Show the connection among ideas.
		Review	Provide a critical summary in which you summarize and present your comments.
Diagram	Provide a drawing.	State	Explain precisely.
Discuss	Provide an in-depth explanation. Be analytical.	Summarize	Provide a synopsis that does not include your comments.
Explain	Give a logical development that discusses reasons or causes.	Trace	Describe the development or progress of the idea.
Illustrate	Use examples or, when appropriate, provide a diagram or picture.		

Add your own direction words and definitions!

■ Jeopardy

Objective: To provide students practice in using reference and trade books to obtain information and to generate questions.

Grades: Secondary

Materials: (1) Reference and trade books; (2) Jeopardy board with four categories and five answers per category; (3) index cards to fit in the Jeopardy board.

JEOPARDY

Pop Music	Presidents	Football	Southwest
20	20	20	20
40	40	40	40
60	60	60	60
80	80	80	80
100	100	100	100

Teaching Procedures: Divide the students into three teams of two to four students. Explain to them that each team is going to make a Jeopardy game for the other students to play.

To make the game, each team needs to select four categories. Then have the students use reference books, trade books, and other sources to generate five questions and answers for each category that other students could possibly answer. Have them write the questions and answers on separate index cards and order the questions and answers from easy to difficult.

Each team then takes a turn directing its Jeopardy game. First, the team inserts their category names and answer cards into the Jeopardy board. Then they direct the game as the two other teams compete against each other. To direct the game, one student should serve as master of ceremonies, another as timekeeper, and the rest of the students as judges.

To play, each team takes a turn selecting a category and a level underneath the category. The answer is then exposed and the team members have 15 seconds to give the question. If the question is correct, they get the number of points indicated and are allowed to make another selection. If the answer is incorrect, the other team has 15 seconds to give an answer.

■ Study Groups

Objective: To provide students the opportunity to work in groups when studying a textbook for a test.

Grades: Secondary

Materials: (1) Content area textbook chapter or sections over which the students are going to be tested; (2) index cards

Teaching Procedures: Have students who are studying for tests covering the same material work in groups of two to three students. (Note: When students first do this activity the teacher will generally need to demonstrate and guide the students through the process.)

Have the students read the assigned materials together, stopping at the end of each paragraph or section to discuss the main ideas and the important vocabulary. Each main idea and important vocabulary for each section should be written on an index card. After the students finish reading the assignment using this technique, they should take all the main idea cards and arrange them in logical groupings or in a logical order. The students then take each important vocabulary card and write a simple definition that makes sense according to the text. Then they arrange the important vocabulary next to the related main idea. Next, each student copies onto paper the arrangement that was organized for the main ideas and vocabulary (with definitions). Finally, the students should study the paper and then take turns quizzing each other on the information.

■ Get Their Opinions

Objective: To provide students the opportunity to collect, interpret, and present information about controversial topics and to increase awareness of current topics in social studies.

Grades: Intermediate and secondary

Materials: Tape recorder and blank tapes if respondents are interviewed.

Teaching Procedures: Discuss the meanings of surveys and polls and how they are conducted. Have the students study examples of surveys to determine the topics asked and the kinds of questions asked. Tell the students to select a topic about which they want to obtain other people's opinions. Then have them develop three to five questions that one could ask someone to determine their opinion. Have them write the survey and decide who they should survey.

Discuss how to conduct a survey and how not to bias a person who is answering the survey. Next, have the students conduct the survey, recording the responses in writing or on a tape recorder. Then the students need to tabulate the results of the survey, indicating what percent of persons answered the questions in the same manner. Finally, the students report the results of the survey to the rest of the class.

Adaptations: Results can also be written as an article for a school or community newspaper.

■ Smell and Taste

Objective: To provide students the opportunity to learn the relationship between the two senses of smell and taste.

Grades: Elementary

Materials: (1) Fruit, bread, crackers, and other foods that are easy to prepare in a classroom. Cut food into bite-size pieces; (2) Smell and Taste Worksheet; (3) blindfolds

Smell and Taste Worksheet		
Food	Taste	Smell and Taste
apple	apple	apple
pear	apple	pear
watermelon cantaloupe honey dew	cantaloupe honey dew cantaloupe	watermelon cantaloupe honey dew
Findings:		

Teaching Procedures: Explain the instructions and pair off the students. Give each pair of students similar foods to try and a worksheet on which to record their results. Have one student in each pair hold his or her nose and close the eyes (or use a blindfold). The other student then gives the blindfolded student one type of food at a time and asks, "Is it a(n) (pear) or a(n) (apple)?" The student then records the results on the worksheet. The student who is blindfolded then releases the hold on his or her nose and the procedure is repeated. Then the students switch places and the experiment is run again.

The students then return to the general group and discuss their findings, stating the relationship between taste and smell. The findings can be written in each student's Science Idea Notebook which contains a log of the various experiments conducted and their results.

■ Learn Those Words!

Objective: To teach students a simple strategy for memorizing vocabulary words—either English words or those of a foreign language.

Grades: Fifth through high school

Materials: Index cards used whole, or cut in half or in thirds, a pen, and papercutter or scissors

Teaching Procedures: When there are words that must be memorized, the student writes a word on one side of an index card and its definition or translation on the reverse side.

The student studies the words and then tests himself. He forms two piles of cards as he works, a pile for those words he knows and another for those he doesn't know. He continues to study the words he doesn't know until there are no more cards in the unknown pile.

Students should always keep a set of words with them. While they are waiting in line, or waiting for class to begin, they can test themselves on their words. They make new sets of words, and continuously review the old sets. When it comes time for a big test, they're ready!

■ Homework Treasure Hunt

Objective: To provide students with a definite purpose for their homework reading assignments.

Grades: Fourth through college

Materials: Textbooks or supplementary content area materials.

Teaching Procedures: Instead of asking your students to read pages 28–43 for homework tonight, which causes them to focus just on covering those pages as quickly as possible without really learning the material, ask them to begin reading on page 28 and to continue reading until they have answered the five questions you've written on the chalkboard or photocopied for them. They'll have to read to page 43 to answer all the questions, but they'll be reading actively and for a purpose. Tomorrow, during your presentation, you'll have students who are prepared to participate in, and learn from, your presentation!

SUMMARY

For secondary and postsecondary settings as well as the upper elementary grades, the success with which students with learning and behavior problems are included in general education classrooms and participate in the general education curriculum is dependent on the teaching effectiveness of the content area teacher and the study skills of the student. This chapter focused on those topics as well as adaptations, capitalizing on the relationship between the teacher and the learner.

Utilizing teaching strategies that assist students to organize and relate information has been shown to increase their ability to learn from text and from lectures. Therefore, it behooves us to be listener-friendly lecturers and to use such instructional techniques as advance organizers, semantic feature analysis, concept diagrams, and content mapping.

At the same time, we can work with students to teach them effective methods of studying. This includes time management and organization skills, strategies for learning from lectures and texts, and strategies for remembering and retrieving information, and strategies for taking tests.

If we can provide students with sound content area instruction while at the same time teaching them study skills, then we have facilitated their success in secondary school settings and in later life.

WEBSITES AS RESOURCES FOR TEACHING CONTENT AREA LEARNING AND STUDY SKILLS

http://www.ldonline.org/ld_indepth/teaching_techniques/strategies.html#anchor1001355
This Website provides several useful links on content area learning.

http://www.reading.org
This is the International Reading Association Website, which includes resources for content area learning.

http://www.ldonline.org/ld_indepth/parenting/sedita_studyskills.html
This Website introduces a variety of study skill strategies.

http://www.ncld.org/tips/tips21.html
This Website provides a few brief tips for good study skills.

http://www.ku-crl.org/htmlfiles/core.html
This Website is from the University of Kansas's Center for Research on Learning and provides resources for teaching learning strategies and study skills.

http://www.rfbd.org
This Website is from the Recordings for the Blind and Dyslexic and provides information on getting books on tape.

http://www.ldanatl.org
This Website is for the Learning Disabilities Association of America and provides resources related to learning disabilities including study skills.

http://www.mtsu.edu/~studskl
This Website is authored by the study skills coordinator at a university and provides resources for developing effective study skills.

http://www.nsta.org
This Website is from the National Science Teachers Association and provides resources for teaching science.

http://www.lhs.berkeley.edu:80
This Website is from the Lawrence Hall of Science, SAVI/SELPH materials.

http://www.gsfc.nasa.gov/education/education_home.html
This Website provides NASA links to student activities

http://www.sunburst.com
This Website provides Voyage of the Mimi materials.

http://www.socialstudies.org
This Website is from the National Council for the Social Studies and provides resources for teaching social studies.

http://www.teleport.com/~vincer/social.html
This Website provides teaching resources for teaching social studies.

THINK AND APPLY

— Why is it difficult for students with learning problems to succeed in content area classes in secondary schools?
— What is a content analysis? Select a chapter from a content area text and complete a content analysis.

- What is "considerate" text? Using the ideas in the section on "Evaluating the Considerateness of Instructional Materials," select a text and evaluate it for considerateness and appropriateness for your students.
- Explain the difference between a concept diagram, a map, and a relationship chart. Select a chapter and develop each of these instructional aids for the chapter. Compare the differences and similarities.
- What should teachers keep in mind when they are adapting a textbook? Select a chapter from a text and adapt it for students with learning and behavior problems.
- What should you include in a unit on self-management? Plan the unit for a group of students with learning and behavior problems.
- What are the characteristics of listener-friendly lectures? Plan a lecture that is listener-friendly.
- Conduct a content analysis and then develop key word mnemonics to teach the "hard to learn" technical vocabulary.

8

Mathematics

OUTLINE

KEY TOPICS FOR MASTERY

— *Factors that influence mathematics ability in all people*
— *Characteristics of students with learning disabilities that frequently interfere with the mastery of mathematics*
— *Teaching perspectives to consider when planning mathematics instruction for students with learning disabilities and for those with emotional and/or behavior problems*
— *Teaching an understanding of the prenumber skills, numeration, and place value*
— *Teaching the basic facts—addition, subtraction, multiplication, and division*
— *Calculators—why they are a "must" for students with learning disabilities*
— *Fractions and measurements—why overlearning at the concrete stage is critical to students' mastery of these skills*
— *How to help students with learning disabilities overcome problems with traditional written story problems*
— *Cognitive and operant approaches to increasing math performance*
— *The importance of teaching students with learning and behavior problems the mathematics necessary to operate in the "real world"*
— *Curriculums and materials that focus on the needs of students with learning disabilities*

 BRIGHT IDEA

Turn to page 380 and read Think and Apply.

Esteban, a third-grade student identified as having behavior disorders, spends most of his day in the regular third-grade classroom. He is in the top math group and is proud of this achievement. His special education teacher is pleased that he is fulfilling his behavior contract and has not had any serious disturbances since he has been included in the regular classroom.

Claudia, a seventh-grade student who spends part of her day in a classroom for students with learning disabilities, is not nearly so successful in math. In fact, when asked what her favorite academic time is during the day, she quickly answers, "I love to write. In fact, I think I will be an author. I have already written several books for the classroom and one was even selected for

the library." When asked what she thinks of math, she looks away and says, "No way—Don't even mention it. I can't do math. We don't get along."

Claudia has had difficulty with mathematics since she was in the primary grades. Her first-grade teacher just thought she was not very interested in math, and asked her parents to obtain special tutoring help during the summer. Her parents found that the special help did little good, and when Claudia continued to have serious difficulty with math in second grade, the teacher referred her for assessment for possible learning disabilities. The assessment results suggested she had difficulty with spatial relations and using memory to recall rote math facts. She has received special help in math for the past four years, and though she seems to have made progress, her math skills are still her weakest academic area.

Some students with learning and behavior problems have difficulty with language arts (reading, writing, and spelling), some have difficulty with mathematics, and some have difficulty with both. However, despite the number of students who have math problems, the skill that has received by far the most attention from researchers, writers, and even clinicians is reading. Reading is often viewed as an essential skill for survival in our society, whereas math is often considered less important. With an increased need for students to understand problem solving for success in the workplace, the inferior status of mathematics instruction may need to change.

This chapter's purpose is to increase your understanding of how to teach mathematics to students who have difficulty learning. The chapter begins by discussing factors and characteristics that interfere with math performance and then presents teaching perspectives that provide general guidelines for teaching math. The chapter follows with teaching suggestions for prenumber skills, followed by numbers and place value, computation, fractions, and measurement. The chapter ends by discussing strategies for teaching problem solving and approaches to increasing math performance.

FACTORS INFLUENCING MATH ABILITY

Kosc (1981) identifies the following four variables as significant influences on mathematics ability:

1. *Psychological factors* such as intelligence/cognitive ability, distractibility, and cognitive learning strategies
2. *Education factors* such as the quality and amount of instructional intervention across the range of areas of mathematics (e.g., computation, measurement, time, and problem solving
3. *Personality factors* such as persistence, self-concept, and attitudes toward mathematics
4. *Neuropsychological patterns* such as perception and neurological trauma

Considering these four factors, it is not surprising that many students with learning and behavior problems have difficulty in math. Whereas most students with learning difficulties have average or above-average intelligence, they have been identified as inactive learners and as less likely to use cognitive strategies. Because much of their educational intervention has focused on computation, they often have limited exposure to other elements of math, including measurement, time, and practical problem solving. They are unable to apply the computation skills to everyday math problems. Many of these students have lowered self-concepts and lack persistence, which are characteristics that may interfere with learning math skills. The fourth factor identified, unique neuropsychological patterns, certainly characterizes many students with learning and behavior problems.

The following difficulties may interfere with the mathematics performance of a student with learning disabilities (Ginsburg, 1997; Homan, 1970):

1. *Perceptual skills.* Because students with learning disabilities often have difficulty with spatial relationships, distances, size relationships, and sequencing, these difficulties will interfere with such math skills as measurement, estimation, problem solving, and geometry. Students with weak perceptual skills will need practice in estimating size and distance and then in verifying estimates with direct measurement.
2. *Perseveration.* Some students may have difficulty mentally shifting from one task or operation to the next. This may interfere with a student's performance on problems that require multiple operations or on applied mathematics problems that often require several steps. The teacher can provide cues to illustrate the number of steps involved in each operation. After the skills for two operations have been mastered (e.g., addition and subtraction), the teacher can provide worksheets that include both types of problems.
3. *Language.* The student may have difficulty understanding such mathematical concepts as *first, last, next, greater than, less than,* and so on.

When teaching arithmetic, the teacher's instructions should be precise. Presenting unnecessary concepts and rules is interfering and confusing to the students and distracts them from concentrating on the concept being presented. The teacher should demonstrate as well as provide instruction. Concrete objects should be used to illustrate abstract concepts. Give plenty of examples and allow students to provide examples to demonstrate understanding of concepts.

4. *Reasoning.* Reasoning is often difficult because it requires a great deal of abstract thinking. Teachers should use concrete materials and real-life application whenever possible. After students understand the mathematical concept at an automatic level, introduce tasks that ask students to think through the process, explain the rationale, and apply reason. Some students acquire "bugs" (Ginsburg, 1997) in their thinking, in which they have faulty ideas about how practices in mathematics work. These bugs need to be "reprogrammed" so children can understand the operation correctly.

5. *Memory.* Many students with learning and behavior problems have difficulty remembering information that was presented to them. Teachers can assist students with memory problems by reducing the amount of new information the students are required to learn, increasing the number of exposures to the new materials, and giving the students opportunities to verbalize and demonstrate the new material.

6. *Symbolism difficulty.* Many children with learning disabilities have a difficult time understanding what mathematics symbols refer to or even gaining the vaguest idea of what they mean. These children may know the rote behavior for what they are supposed to do but cannot tell you the meaning or use of the symbols such as equals, subtract, and multiply.

Johnson and Myklebust (1967) referred to students with dyscalculia—poor skills in numerical calculating—as demonstrating such social difficulties as disorientation, deficiencies in self-help skills, and poor organization. Rourke's (1993) research supports the finding that social deficits are associated with individuals who have good reading and poor math skills.

In a study by Badian and Ghublikian (1983), students with significantly lower math than reading skills (low math) were compared with two other groups, students with significantly higher math than reading skills and students who had similar math and reading skills. The results indicated that the low math group demonstrated lower scores overall on the following abilities:

- Paying sustained attention
- Working in a careful and organized manner
- Accepting responsibility

These findings partially explain why students with learning and behavior problems have difficulty with mathematics. Students with learning disabilities often have difficulty applying learning strategies and are frequently characterized as having perceptual and neurological complications. Students with emotional disturbances may have greater difficulties with mathematics than other areas because it requires persistence and concentration. Students with mild mental retardation have more difficulty with mathematics than students with learning disabilities (Parmar, Cawley, and Miller, 1994). Furthermore, adolescents with learning disabilities perform in many areas of mathematics, such as multiplication, in ways that are similar to much younger non–learning disabled students (Barrouillet, Fayol, and Lathuliere, 1997).

TEACHING PERSPECTIVES

When developing math programs for students with special needs, several teaching perspectives need to be considered for all ages and programs. These teaching perspectives include:

1. *Comprehensive programming.* Mr. Noppe was not happy with his math program. He taught a varying exceptionalities classroom (a special

education classroom that serves all mildly handicapped students) at an elementary school, and 90 percent of his math program consisted of teaching math computation. In discussing his math program with a coteacher, he said, "I know I need to include more than just computation, but I'm not sure what else I should be teaching. I guess I should ask the students to apply some of their math computation. Next year, I want to concentrate on my math program and make it more comprehensive."

Students need to be taught and involved in a full range of mathematics skills, including basic facts, operations, word problems, mathematical reasoning, time, measurement, fractions, and math application. Teachers should not focus their entire mathematics program on math facts and the four basic operations: addition, subtraction, multiplication, and division. The National Council of Teachers of Mathematics (NCTM) has issued new standards for a comprehensive mathematics program. These standards are listed in Apply the Concept 8.1.

Remember that a relevant feature of a comprehensive math program is to teach concepts and vocabulary—to make sure students understand the language of mathematics. Students with disabilities are less likely to know the relevant concepts related to mathematics learning. Thus when they are participating in problem-solving in real-life contexts, they may not understand key words such as *perimeter* or *diameter*, and for younger students, words like *minus, half,* or *percentage.*

2. *Individualization.* Esteban and Claudia, the two students described in the beginning of this chapter, have very different needs in math. Students with learning difficulties are different from each other in their math abilities and disabilities. Individualized programs that respond to the needs of each student are necessary. Individualization in math programming refers not just to the task but also to the way the task is learned (Carnine, 1991). Some students learn math facts through rote drill, whereas other students learn math facts by associating them with known facts. We often

assume that an individualized program means the student works alone. Individualization, however, means the program is designed to meet the individual needs of the student; thus it is often beneficial for the students to work in small groups to learn new skills and rehearse and practice problems. In addition, small groups that focus on solving the same problem can include students of different abilities, particularly when the teacher creates a cooperative environment for solving the problems and allowing the students to learn from each other.

3. *Correction and feedback.* Receiving immediate feedback about performance is particularly important in math. If students are performing an operation incorrectly, they should be told which parts are correct and which parts are incorrect. Showing students patterns in their errors is an important source of feedback. Students also need to learn to check their own work and monitor their own errors. Remember, feedback includes noticing improvements as well as monitoring needed changes.

Students in Ms. Wong's math class were given a worksheet to practice their new skill of using dollar signs and decimal points in their subtraction problems. Ms. Wong told the students to do only the first problem. After they completed the first problem they were to check it and make any necessary changes. If they felt problem one was correct they should write a small *c* next to the answer. If they felt it was incorrect they should mark a small *i* next to the answer. They were also to indicate with a checkmark (✓) where they felt they had made a mistake. Ms. Wong moved quickly from student to student, checking their first problem. Students who had the first problem correct were given encouragement and directions for the rest of the problems. "Good for you. You got the first problem correct and you had the confidence, after checking it, to call it correct. I see you remembered to use both a decimal point and a dollar sign. After you finish the first row, including checking your problems, meet with another student to see how your answers compare. Do you

APPLY THE CONCEPT 8.1

NCTM STANDARDS 2000

Instructional programs from prekindergarten through grade 12 in the following areas should enable all students to use the following concepts:

1. Number and operations
- Understand numbers, ways of representing numbers, relationships among numbers, and number systems
- Understand meanings of operations and how they relate to one another
- Compute fluently and make reasonable estimates

2. Algebra
- Understand patterns, relations, and functions
- Represent and analyze mathematical solutions and structures using algebraic symbols
- Use mathematical models to represent and understand quantitative relationships
- Analyze change in various contexts

3. Geometry
- Analyze characteristics and properties of two- and three-dimensional geometric shapes, and develop mathematical arguments about geometric relationships
- Specify locations and describe spatial relationships using coordinate geometry and other representational systems
- Apply transformations and use symmetry to analyze mathematical situations
- Use visualization, spatial reasoning, and geometric modeling to solve problems

4. Measurement
- Understand measurable attributes of objects and the units, systems, and processes of measurement
- Apply appropriate techniques, tools, and formulas to determine measurements

5. Data analysis and probability
- Formulate questions that can be addressed with data and collect, organize, and display relevant data to answer them

- Select and use appropriate statistical methods to analyze data
- Develop and evaluate inferences and predictions that are based on data
- Understand and apply basic concepts of probability

6. Problem solving
- Build new mathematical knowledge through problem solving
- Solve problems that arise in mathematics and in other contexts
- Apply and adapt a variety of appropriate strategies to solve problems
- Monitor and reflect on the process of mathematical problem solving

7. Reasoning and proof
- Recognize reasoning and proof as fundamental aspects of mathematics
- Make and investigate mathematical conjectures
- Develop and evaluate mathematical arguments and proofs
- Select and use various types of reasoning and methods of proof

8. Communication
- Organize and consolidate their mathematical thinking through communication
- Communicate their mathematical thinking coherently and clearly to peers, teachers, and others
- Analyze and evaluate the mathematical thinking and strategies of others
- Use the language of mathematics to express mathematical ideas precisely

9. Connections
- Recognize and use connections among mathematical ideas
- Understand how mathematical ideas interconnect and build on one another to produce a coherent whole
- Recognize and apply mathematics in contexts outside of mathematics

(continued)

APPLY THE CONCEPT 8.1 *Continued*

10. Representation
- Create and use representations to organize, record, and communicate mathematical ideas
- Select, apply, and translate among mathematical representations to solve problems
- Use representations to model and interpret physical, social, and mathematical phenomena

Source: National Council of Teachers of Mathematics, *Principles and Standards for School Mathematics* (2000). Available online at http://www.nctm.org/standards/.

know what to do if there is a discrepancy in your answers? That's right. You'll need to check each other's problem to locate the error." When Ms. Wong locates a student who incorrectly solved the problem, she says, "Talk aloud how you did this. Start from the beginning and as you think of what you're doing, say it aloud so I can follow." Ms. Wong finds that students often notice their own errors, or she will identify some faulty thinking on the part of the students that keeps them from correctly solving the problem.

4. *Alternative approaches to instruction.* If a student is not succeeding with one approach or program, make a change. Despite years of research, no single method of mathematics instruction has been proven to be significantly better than others. This includes using a range of formats such as textbooks, workbooks, math stations, manipulatives, and so on.

5. *Applied mathematics.* Concrete materials and real-life applications of math problems make math real and increase the likelihood that students will transfer skills to applied settings such as home and work. Students continue to make progress in math throughout their school years. Emphasis needs to be on problem solving rather than rote drill and practice activities (Cawley and Miller, 1989).

The term *situated cognition* refers to the principle that students will learn complex ideas and concepts in the contexts in which they occur in day-to-day life. Students need many opportunities to practice what you want them to learn in the ways they will eventually use it. This is

a critical way to promote the generalization of mathematical skills. For example, when teaching measurement, give students opportunities to measure rooms for carpet, determine the mileage to specific locations, and so on.

After Ms. Wong's students were successfully able to use dollar signs and decimals in subtraction, she gave each of them a mock checkbook, which included checks and a ledger for keeping their balance. In each of their checkbooks was written the amount $100.00. During math class for the rest of the month she gave students "money" for the checkbook when their assignments were completed and their behavior was appropriate. She asked them to write her checks when they wanted supplies (pencils, erasers, chalk) or privileges (going to the bathroom, free time, meeting briefly with a friend). Students were asked to maintain their balance in their checkbooks. Students were penalized $5.00 for each mistake the "bank" located in the checkbook ledgers at the end of the week.

6. *Generalization.* Generalization or transfer of learning needs to be taught. As most experienced teachers know, students can often perform skills in the special education room and are unable to perform them in the regular classroom. In order to facilitate the transfer of learning between settings, teachers must provide opportunities to practice skills by using a wide range of materials such as textbooks, workbooks, manipulatives, and word problems. Teachers also need to systematically reduce the amount of help they provide students in solving problems. When students are first learning a math concept or operation, teachers provide a lot of assistance to students in performing it correctly. As students become more skillful, less assistance is needed.

After Ms. Wong's students were able to apply subtraction with dollars and decimals to their checkbooks, she asked students to perform similar problems for homework. Ms. Wong realized that before she could say the students had mastered the skill, they needed to perform the skill outside of her classroom and without her assistance.

7. *Allow students to participate in setting their own goals for mathematics.* Participation in goal selection is likely to increase the individual's commitment to the goal. Students who selected their own math goals improved their performance on math tasks over time more than did those students whose math goals were assigned to them by a teacher (Fuchs, Bahr, and Rieth, 1989). Even very young children can participate in selecting their overall math goals and keep progress charts on how well they are performing.

8. *Discovery versus didactic instruction.* Many teachers wonder whether and how they should use more discovery-oriented approaches to teaching mathematics. Based on the literature available at this time (Dixon, Carnine, et al., 1998), very little evidence favors discovery learning for mathematics unless it is in the application of already known principles. Students are more likely to be successful if you use a guided discovery mode ore didactic mode.

The National Research Council (NRC) has conducted an examination of U.S. mathematics education from kindergarten through graduate study (National Research Council, 1989). This joint activity was conducted by the Mathematical Sciences Education Board, Board on Mathematical Sciences, Committee on the Mathematical Sciences in the Year 2000, and National Research Council. The extensive report resulting from the work of these committees not only outlines problems in mathematics education

but charts a course for remedying them. The suggestions that relate to students with learning and behavior problems follow:

— Do not alter curricular goals to differentiate students; change the type and speed of instruction.
— Make mathematics education student-centered, not an authoritarian model that is teacher-focused.
— Encourage students to explore, verbalize ideas, and understand that mathematics is part of their life.
— Provide daily opportunities for students to apply mathematics and to work problems that are related to their daily lives. Instill in them the importance and need for mathematics.
— Teach mathematics so that students understand when an exact answer is necessary and when an estimate is sufficient.
— Teach problem solving, computer application, and use of calculators to all students.
— Teach students to understand probability, data analysis, and statistics as they relate to daily decision making, model building, operations research, and applications of computers.
— Shift from primarily performing paper-and-pencil activities to use of calculators, computers, and other applied materials.

The National Research Council (1989) reports that mathematics is "the invisible culture of our age" and emphasizes that mathematics is embedded in our lives in many ways:

Practical. Mathematical knowledge can be put to immediate use. This includes figuring unit prices, comparing interest rates on loans, appreciating the effects of inflation, calculating the effects of a salary increase, and calculating risks.

Civic. Mathematical concepts relate to public policy. This includes understanding taxation, inferences drawn from statistics on crime, health issues, and other related public issues, and reading charts and graphs depicting change in spending.

APPLY THE CONCEPT 8.2

INSTRUCTIONAL PRACTICES FOR MATHEMATICS

Based on several recent syntheses on mathematics instruction for students with learning and behavior problems (Cawley, Parmar, Yan, and Miller, 1998; Dixon, et al., 1998; Montague, 1997; Rivera, Smith, Goodwin, and Bryant, 1998; Xin and Jitendra, 1999) the following instructional practices are recommended:

1. *Instructional routines* that focus on cognitive behavioral techniques benefit students with learning and behavior problems and engage them in the learning process.
2. *Instructional design features* are effective ways to teach students to differentiate problem types, use a wide range of examples, separate confusing elements, and provide opportunities for students to reach performance levels before introducing more new principles.
3. *Teach students the principles of mathematics to mastery* and then move to more advanced principles. Many students with special needs

are provided the same instructional math curriculum (e.g., subtraction with regrouping) from second through ninth grade.

4. *Establish realistic goals* for progress in mathematics with students by providing information to students about their present performance and what they need to learn.
5. *Monitor progress* on a weekly basis through graphing or visual display so students can chart and see how they are performing. Make adjustments in teaching, materials, grouping, or other features of instruction if students are not making adequate progress.
6. *Provide evidence* that hard work and effort yield good outcomes and progress. Students can also learn to reinforce themselves for setting and meeting goals in mathematics.
7. *Computer-assisted instruction* can provide an effective way to learn arithmetic computation and mathematical problem solving.

Professional. Mathematics is a tool for success on the job. This includes all knowledge of basic and theoretical mathematics that is necessary for success in the workplace.

Recreational. Mathematics can be a source of recreation and relaxation. This includes participating in games of strategy, puzzles, lotteries, and other related activities.

Cultural. Mathematics is the appreciation of mathematics for its beauty and power to solve problems. Like language, art, and music, mathematics is an important part of our human culture.

As a teacher, you may want to be sure your curriculum includes all five dimensions of mathematics: practical, civic, professional, recreational, and cultural. See Apply the Concept 8.2 for suggested instructional practices.

It is particularly important for teachers to design mathematics programs that enhance learning for all students, especially students with diverse cultural or

linguistic backgrounds. See Apply the Concept 8.3 for suggestions.

CURRICULUM-BASED MEASUREMENT

How can teachers best make decisions about whether students are learning mathematics effectively? Also, how can teachers monitor the progress of their students so that they can document the rate and progress they are making in mathematics? Bryant and Rivera (1997, p. 63) stated "one would be hard-pressed to find a more effective technique than curriculum-based measurement (CBM) for directing, monitoring, and redirecting remedial efforts." There is considerable and growing evidence that when teachers use CBM to monitor their students' progress and to adjust their instruction accordingly, students make gains at much more rapid rates than when CBM is not used.

APPLY THE CONCEPT 8.3

CONSIDERATIONS FOR CULTURALLY AND LINGUISTICALLY DIVERSE STUDENTS: ENHANCING SKILLS IN MATHEMATICS

An essential part of implementing a successful mathematics program is to provide instructional practices and assignments that facilitate learning in mathematics for all students, particularly those from diverse cultures and language backgrounds. Here are some suggestions to consider:

1. Continually consider ways to infuse the various cultures of students in your classroom and the cultures of students not represented in your mathematics curriculum. Students will appreciate, feel accepted, and learn a great deal about other cultures when cultural diversity is infused in their daily learning routines.

2. Develop story problems that reflect events from diverse cultures. Encourage students to design story problems that are reflective of the happenings of other cultures.

3. Read books about youngsters from other cultures. Use the stories and data from these books to design story problems.

4. In designing mathematical problems, use the data from newspapers or magazines that provide information about individuals or events representing other cultures.

5. Design mathematical studies that address real problems of individuals or groups who are not from the mainstream culture. Assign these studies to individuals, students in pairs, or small groups.

6. Assure that goals are challenging for all students and provide adequate support for their participation and effort. These challenges should provide opportunities for success, with infrequent failure.

7. Model an enthusiastic and positive attitude about appreciating and learning more about the cultures and languages of other groups.

8. Link students' accomplishments to their hard work and effort. Remind students that they performed the task well because they worked hard, persisted, reread, rethought, revisualized, modeled, and so forth (Mercer and Mercer, 1993).

9. Use manipulatives to concretely explore the meaning of mathematical symbols and problems. Manipulatives enhance learning, and provide an easy means of crossing potential language barriers.

10. Use culturally relevant materials as a "springboard" for mathematics learning (D'Ambrosio, Johnson, and Hobbs, 1995). The ways in which mathematics are practiced in various cultures, mathematical games that are played, and the use of mathematics cross-culturally can be imbedded into mathematics instruction.

11. Use the languages of the students throughout the instruction. Ask students to provide the word that means the same as "_____" and then use both words when referring to the term. Encourage all of the students in the room to use and apply multiple terms that represent the languages of the students in the class. Communicate to students that you value their home language.

12. Use technology to enhance learning and understanding of mathematical principles (Woodard, 1995). Computers provide a language that should be available to all students. Encourage expertise on the computer and provide multiple opportunities to practice math skills on the computer.

Professional Resources

1. N. S. Bley and C. A. Thornton (1995). *Teaching Mathematics to Students with Learning Disabilities* (3rd ed.). Austin, TX: PRO-ED. Each chapter provides information on a different mathematical topic (e.g., money and time, number and place value), and provides a description of the errors commonly made by students with learning disabilities. The book provides procedures for appropriate instruction across all areas of the mathematics curriculum.

2. J. F. Cawley, A. M. Fitzmaurice-Hayes, and R. A. Shaw (1988). *Mathematics for the Mildly Handicapped*. Boston: Allyn and Bacon.

(continued)

APPLY THE CONCEPT 8.3 *Continued*

This book provides a long-term, systematic approach to providing a comprehensive curriculum in mathematics for students with mild learning disabilities. Assessment, instruction, and component analysis are an integral part of the book's focus.

3. G. Cuevas and M. Driscoll (Eds.). (1993). *Reaching all Students with Mathematics.* Reston, VA: National Council of Teachers of Mathematics.

The book discusses the current trends in mathematics instruction, with special emphasis on assisting teachers to capitalize on the increasing diversity in their classrooms. The book presents procedures for improving the performance of special student populations and programs aimed at their success.

What is CBM for math? Simply stated, it is a way of documenting the extent to which the student is learning the critical elements in the curriculum that you have targeted. To illustrate, let's consider the case of Ricky, a fifth-grade boy with learning and attention problems, who has been struggling with math. His goals for the next ten weeks are to know all subtraction facts up to 100 automatically and quickly, to be able to do addition with regrouping word problems, and to be able to use basic measurement terms such as *inches, feet,* and *yards* appropriately. Here is how he and his teacher use CBM:

— The teacher pretested Ricky on all 100 subtraction facts in random order, timing him while he completed the worksheet. She then showed Ricky how to graph his performance in two ways: first, by graphing how long it took him to complete the worksheet, and second, by graphing the number of problems correct. Together they agreed that he would take a version of this test once every week to determine whether he could decrease the amount of time he needed to complete the test and increase the number of problems he got correct. Together, they established a schedule of work assignments and practice sessions. (See Figure 8.1 as an illustration of the graph that Ricky kept).

— His teacher followed a similar procedure with measurement and problem-solving to determine what he knew and what he needed to know, and

then he established a simple graph that Ricky could complete to monitor his progress.

— Ricky and his teacher frequently discussed Ricky's progress and modified assignments and instruction to facilitate his learning.

As a teacher, you may want to consider using a computerized application of CBM procedures, which are available for mathematics as well as spelling and reading (Fuchs, Hamlett, and Fuchs, 1990).

PRENUMBER SKILLS

Many students come to school with few experiences that allow them to develop important prenumber skills, such as one-to-one correspondence, classification, and seriation. The following section focuses on these important prenumber skills.

One-to-One Correspondence

Matching one object with another is a core skill in any mathematics curriculum. It eventually leads the student to a better understanding of numeration and representation. Early man used one-to-one correspondence when he kept track of how many bags of grain he borrowed from a neighbor by placing a rock in a bucket to represent each one. One-to-one correspondence is used today when we set the table, one

■ FIGURE 8.1   *Ricky's Progress Monitoring Chart*

Ricky's teacher developed three versions of a subtraction fact sheet that had 30 problems representing the 100 subtraction facts he was learning. Once a week he was timed on one version of the test and the number of problems correct were counted. Ricky kept the following two charts to demonstrate his progress.

Number of Problems Correct

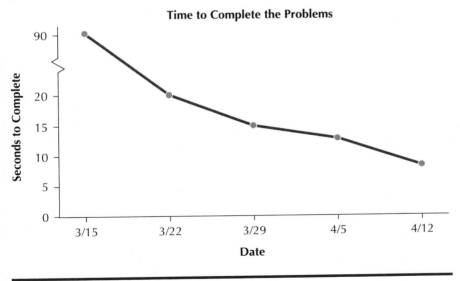

Time to Complete the Problems

place setting for each person; go to the theater, one ticket and seat for each person; and distribute paper in the classroom, one piece for each student. Activities for teaching one-to-one correspondence include:

1. Use every opportunity to teach students the relationship between number words (e.g., *one, two, three, four*) and objects. For example, "Here are two scissors, one for you and one for Margo." "There are five students in our group and we need one chair for each student."

2. Use familiar objects such as small cars or blocks and give a designated number (e.g., three) to each student. Pointing to the objects, ask the student to place one block next to each of the objects. "You have one block here and you placed one block next to it. You have a second block here and you placed a block next to it. And you have a third block here and you placed a block next to it."

3. Give the student a set of cards with numbers the student recognizes. Ask the student to put the correct number of blocks on top of each number card. Reverse the task by giving objects to the student and asking him or her to put the correct number card next to the objects.

Classification

Classification is the ability to group or sort objects based on one or more common property. For example, classification can occur by size, color, shape, texture, or design. Classification is an important prenumber skill because it focuses the student on common properties of objects and requires the student to reduce large numbers of objects to smaller groups. Most students are naturally interested in sorting, ordering, and classifying. A sample of activities for teaching classification includes:

1. Ask students to sort articles into groups. Ask them which rule they used for sorting their articles.

2. Give students an empty egg carton and a box of small articles. Ask the students to sort the articles according to one property (e.g., color). Now ask

them to think of another way they can sort them (e.g., size, texture).

3. Using an assortment of articles, ask students to classify several of the articles into one group. Other students then try to guess the property(ies) that qualifies the articles for the group.

4. Students can use pictures for sorting tasks. Animals, foods, plants, toys, and people can all be sorted by different properties.

5. Board games and bingo games can be played by sorting or classifying shapes, colors, or pictures.

Seriation

Seriation is similar to classification in that it depends on the recognition of common attributes of objects. With seriation, ordering depends on the degree to which the object possesses the attribute. For example, seriation can occur by length, height, color, or weight. A sample of activities for teaching seriation might include:

1. Give students some objects of varied length and ask them to put them in order from shortest to longest.

2. Ask students to stack their books from biggest to smallest.

3. Using a peg with varied sizes of rings, put the rings on the peg from largest to smallest.

4. Fill jars of the same size with varied amounts of sand or water and ask students to put them in order.

NUMERATION AND PLACE VALUE

Teachers and parents often assume that children understand numerals because they can count or name them. Understanding numerals is a very important and basic concept; many children who have trouble with computation and word problems are missing numeral concepts. For example, Michael's beginning experiences with math were positive. He had learned to read and write numerals and even to perform basic addition and subtraction facts. However, when Michael was asked to perform problems that involved addition with regrouping, he demonstrated he had very little knowledge of numerals and their meaning (as shown here), and thus quickly fell behind his peers in math.

48	37	68
+26	+55	+17
614	812	715

Understanding numeration and place value is necessary for:

1. *Progress in computation.* Like Michael, many students fail to make adequate progress in math because they lack understanding of numerals and place value.
2. *Estimation* (e.g., "number sense"). Many students with learning difficulties in math do not have a sense of how much $1.00 is, what it means to have 35 eggs, or "about" how much 24 and 35 equals. They cannot check their answers by looking at problems and determining which answers could not be correct because the answer doesn't make "sense."
3. *Reducing conceptual errors.* Students who understand the meaning of the numerals 43 and 25 would be less likely to make the following error:

$$
\begin{array}{r}
43 \\
-25 \\
\hline
22
\end{array}
$$

4. *Understanding place value.* Students who know the meaning of the numeral 28 are going to have far less difficulty understanding the value of the "2 place" and the "8 place." Students need to understand the 2 in 28 represents two tens and the 8 represents eight ones.
5. *Understanding regrouping.* Regrouping errors, such as those below, are less likely to occur if a student understands numeration.

39	56	41
+27	−18	−24
516	42	23

6. *Application of math computation to everyday problems.* Students who do not understand the real meaning of numerals have difficulty applying computation to everyday problems.
7. *Understanding zero.* Students need to understand that 0 (zero) has more meaning than just "nothing." For example, in the number 40, students need to understand the meaning of the 0 as a place holder.

Readiness for Numeration: Seventeen Concepts

Engelhardt, Ashlock, and Wiebe (1984) identified seventeen numeration readiness concepts that can be assessed through paper-and-pencil assessment and interview. A list of the behaviors that correspond to each concept, along with examples of how each concept can be assessed, follows.

Concept 1
Cardinality—The face value of each of the ten digits (0 through 9) tells how many.

1. Identify sets with like numerousness (1 through 9). Circle the groups with the same number of *x*s.

2. Identify, write, and name the numeral that corresponds to the numerousness of a set (1 through 9). Circle the numeral showing how many mice there are.
   How many mice are there?

3 2 6 4 9

3. Construct sets with a given numerousness (1 through 9). "Draw five dots."
4. Recognize sets of one to five without counting. Place from one to five objects behind a book. Say to the students, "As soon as I move this book I want you to tell me how many objects there are." Without counting, the students should tell you how many objects are in the group.
5. Represent and name the numerousness of the empty set (zero). "The box has 2 hats in it. Make 0 hats in the circle."

Concept 2
Grouping Pattern—When representing quantity, objects are grouped into sets of a specified size (base) and sets of sets.

1. Form sets of ten from a random set of objects or marks. Circle the *x*s to make as many groups of ten as possible.

   xxxxxxxxxxxxxx   xxxxx   xxxxxxx

   xxxxxxxxxxxxxx   xxxxx   xxxxxxx

2. Construct appropriate groups to show how many. Give students about 125 popsicle sticks and rubberbands. Say, "Bundle these sticks so it will be easy to tell how many there are."

Concept 3
Place Value—The position of a digit in a multidigit numeral determines its value (places are assigned values).

1. Given two multidigit numerals with the same digits but in different orders, identify the position of the digits as distinguishing the two numerals. How are 145 and 154 alike? Different?

2. Explain that the value of a digit in a multidigit number is dependent on its position. Using the number 5, place it in each column and ask, "How does the number change?" "How much is it worth?"

100s	10s	1s

Concept 4
Place Value (base 10)—A power of ten is assigned to each position or place (the place values).

1. Identify, name, and show the values for each place in a multidigit numeral. Show the number 1,829 and say, "What is the name of the 8s place?"
2. Select the place having a given value. Show the number 6,243 and say, "Circle or point to the number in the thousands place."

Concept 5
One Digit per Place—Only one digit is written in a position or place.

1. Identify and name which numerals (digits) can be assigned to a place. Say to the students, "Tell me the numbers that can be written in the tens place."
2. State that no more than one digit should be written in a place or position. Then ask, "What's wrong with these problems?"

85	27	13
+39	+35	+48
1114	512	511

3. Rewrite or restate a nonstandard multidigit numeral (or its representation) as a numeral with only one digit in each place or position. Say to the students, "Write the number for this:"

10s	1s
5	4

Concept 6

Places-Linear/Ordered—The places (and their values) in a multidigit (whole number) numeral are linearly arranged and ordered from right to left.

1. Identify the smaller-to-larger ordering of place values in a multidigit numeral. Show the number 6,666 to the students and say, "Underline the 6 that is worth the most and put an *x* through the 6 that is worth the least."
2. Describe how the place values are ordered. Show the number 8,888 to the students and ask, "How can you tell which 8 is worth more?"
3. State or demonstrate that the places in a multidigit numeral are linearly arranged. Say to the students, "Rewrite this problem correctly."

$$
\begin{array}{cccc}
7 & & 1 & \\
& 2 & & 4 \\
6 & 3 & & 8 \\
+ & & 0 & \\
\hline
\end{array}
$$

Concept 7

Decimal Point—The decimal point in a decimal fraction indicates the location of the units (ones) and tenths places.

1. Given a decimal fraction, identify the digit in the units (ones) place. Show the number 29.04 to the students and say, "Circle the number in the ones place."
2. Given juxtaposed digits and a digit's value, identify and place the decimal point to show the appropriate multidigit numeral. Show the number 284 to the students and say, "Place the decimal in the correct place to show 4 tenths, 2 tens, and 8 ones."
3. State the meaning (function) of the decimal point.

Concept 8

Place Relation/Regrouping—Each place in a multidigit numeral has a value ten times greater than the place to its right and one-tenth the value of the place to its left (place relationships and regrouping).

1. Describe the relationships between the values of two adjacent places in a multidigit number.

Show the number 222 to the students and say, "How does the first 2 in the number compare with the second 2?"

2. Express the value of a multidigit numeral in several ways. Give the following problem to the students: 1 hundred, 8 tens, and 6 ones can also be expressed as ___ tens and ___ ones.

Concept 9

Implied Zeros—All numerals have an infinite number of juxtaposed places, each occupied by an expressed or implied digit. In places to the left of nonzero digits in numerals for whole numbers, zeros are understood; in places to the right of nonzero digits and the decimal point in decimal fractions, zeros are understood.

1. Name the digit in any given place for any multidigit numeral. Tell the students to rewrite each numeral and show a digit in each place.

	100s	100s	10s	1s
683				
27				
79				

2. Rewrite a given numeral with as few digits as needed. Tell the students to cross out the zeros that are not needed.

0301	004
1010	105

3. State a rule for writing zeros in a multidigit numeral. Ask the students, "When do we need to write zeros in a number?"

Concept 10

Face Times Place—The value of any digit in a multidigit numeral is determined by the product of its face and place values (implied multiplication).

1. Show, name, and identify the value of a specified digit within a multidigit numeral. Show the number 1,468 to the students and ask, "How much is the 6 worth: 0, 6, 10, 60, or 16?"

2. Name and identify the operation used to determine the value of a digit in a multidigit numeral. Ask the students, "In 1,468 we find 6 is worth 60 when we: add, subtract, multiply, or divide?"

3. State a rule for finding the value of a specified digit in a multidigit numeral. Ask the students, "How do you know 6 is worth 60 in the number 1,468?"

Concept 11

Implied Addition—The value of a multidigit numeral is determined by the sum of the values of each digit (implied addition).

1. Express any multidigit numeral as the sum of the values of each digit.

   294 = ___ ones + ___ tens + ___ hundreds

2. Express the sum of digit values as a multidigit numeral. Ask the students to write the numeral for:

   4 ones + 3 tens + 6 hundreds = _____

3. Identify the operation used to determine the value of a multidigit numeral. Ask the students, "To know the value of 287, do we add, subtract, multiply, or divide the value of each numeral?"

Concept 12

Order—Multidigit numerals are ordered:

1. Order multidigit numerals. Say to the students, "Put these numbers in the correct order from smallest to largest: 1689, 1001, 421, 1421."

2. Describe a procedure for determining which of two unequal multidigit numerals is larger. Show the numbers 984 and 849 to the students and ask, "How do you know which is larger?"

Concept 13

Verbal Names (0 through 9)—In English, the verbal names for the numbers zero through nine are unique.

1. Identify the oral/written names of the ten digits. Ask the students to write the name next to each digit:

0 ____   4 ____   7 ____
1 ____   5 ____   8 ____
2 ____   6 ____   9 ____
3 ____

2. State the name for the ten digits.

Concept 14

Verbal Names with Places—In English, the verbal names for multidigit numbers (except ten through twelve) are closely associated with the written numerals (i.e., combining face and place names).

1. Give a multidigit numeral, identify the verbal name for one of the digits that includes both a face and place name. Show the number 2,847 and ask the students, "How is the 8 read?"

   a. eight   c. eighty
   b. eight hundred   d. eighteen

2. Identify the digit in a multidigit numeral that is stated first when giving the verbal name. Say to the students, "Write the number that is said first when reading the number."

   44 _____   6,186 _____
   284 _____   37 _____

3. Select two-digit numerals whose naming pattern is different from most. Ask the students to circle the numbers that when read aloud are different from the others: 17, 43, 126, 11, 281.

Concept 15

Periods and Names—Beginning with the ones place, clusters of three (whole numbers) adjacent places are called periods and are named by the place value of the right-most member of the number triad (e.g., ones, thousands, millions, etc.)

1. Given a multidigit numeral, insert commas to form "periods." Ask the students to put commas in the correct places: 28146 682 7810 192642

2. Name the periods of a given multidigit numeral. Ask the students, "Which number represents the periods?"

   284,000,163 _____

   ones, tens, hundreds, thousands, millions

Concept 16

Naming in Ones Period—Numerals in the ones period are named by stating, from left to right, each digit's name (except zero) followed by its place name (ones being omitted). (Special rules exist for naming tens.)

1. Name three-digit numerals (tens digit not 1). Tell the students to write the name for 683.
2. Name three-digit numerals (tens digit of 1). Tell the students to write the name for 718.

Concept 17

When naming a multidigit numeral, the digits in each period are read as if they were in the ones period, followed by the period name (ones period name being omitted).

1. Name multidigit numerals up to six digits. Tell the students to write the name for 284,163.
2. Name multidigit numerals over six digits. Ask the students to read the following numbers:
   1,846,283   27,219,143
   103,600,101   3,078,420*

Teaching Place Value

Place value is directly related to the students' understanding of numeration. Students need to be able to:

1. *Group by ones and tens.* Using manipulatives, pictures, and then the numerals, students need practice and instruction in grouping by ones and tens. Students can sort manipulatives such as buttons or sticks in groups of tens. Students can also use a table grid to record their answers.

Tens	Ones	Numerals
2	3	23
6	2	62
4	7	47

Source: From *Helping Children Understand and Use Numerals* (pp. 89–149) by J. M. Engelhardt, R. B. Ashlock, and J. H. G. Wiebe, 1984, Boston: Allyn and Bacon. Copyright 1984 by Allyn and Bacon. Adapted by permission.

Use "tens blocks" and "single blocks" to represent numerals. For example, 24 can be represented as:

Flannel boards can also be used to group tens and ones.

2. *Naming tens.* Teach students to identify numerals by the number of tens. For example, six tens is 60, four tens is 40, eight tens is 80, and so on. Give students opportunities to count by tens and then name the number. For example, "Count by tens three times." "Ten, twenty, thirty." "Counting by tens seven times." "Ten, twenty, thirty, forty, fifty, sixty, seventy." Also give students opportunities to draw picture diagrams that represent the place values of tens and ones and to identify the number from diagrams.

3. *Place value beyond two digits.* Once students can accurately group and identify numbers at the two-digit level, introduce them to three- and four-digit numbers. It is a good idea to be certain students have overlearned the concept of two-digit place value before introducing numerals and place value greater than two digits. Many of the principles students have learned with two-digit place value will generalize to three digits and beyond. Give students plenty of opportunity to group, orally name, and sequence three- and four-digit place values.

4. *Place value with older students.* Since place value is a skill that is taught in the math developmental sequence during the primary grades, students who have not adequately learned the skill will likely

have problems with computation and word problems, and yet may have little opportunity to learn place value. Many of the games and activities designed to teach place value focus on young children and are less appropriate for older students. The following sources of numbers may be useful for teaching place value to older students:

a. An odometer
b. Numbers from students' science or social studies texts
c. Numbers from the population of the school (e.g., number of freshmen, sophomores, juniors, seniors, etc.)
d. Population data from the town, county, state, or country
e. The financial data page from the newspaper

COMPUTATION: ADDITION, SUBSTRACTION, MULTIPLICATION, DIVISION

Most of students' time in math is spent on computation. Memorizing facts and practicing addition, subtraction, multiplication, and division problems are the major parts of many math programs. Students spend lots of time completing math sheets, workbook pages, and problems copied from a book that require the continued practice and application of math computation principles. It is probably for this reason that many students find math boring and not applicable.

Teachers can help make computation exercises and fact learning less boring by using computer-assisted instruction (see Tech Talk), which is equally effective for teaching basic arithmetic facts as the conventional drill and practice (Okolo, 1992).

Computing math problems is much easier for students if they understand numeration and place value and if they are given frequent practical application of the math problems.

When students are having difficulty performing math computation, it may be because they:

1. Do not have an understanding of numeration and/or place value
2. Do not understand the operation they are performing

3. Do not know basic math facts and their application to more complicated computation

Students with attention deficit disorder often demonstrate difficulty in computation because they fail to automatize computational skills at an appropriate age (Ackerman, Anhalt, and Dykman, 1986). By *automatize* we mean learning computational facts so they are automatic. Students with attention deficit disorder require time for computation.

Understanding the Operation

Ask the students to demonstrate their understanding of the operation by drawing picture diagrams and illustrating with manipulatives. For example, Sylvia was able to write the correct answer to the multiplication fact $3 \times 2 = 6$. However, when asked to draw a picture to represent the problem, she drew three flowers and two flowers. She seemed totally undisturbed that the number of flowers she drew was different from the answer she wrote. When asked why she drew the number of flowers she did, Sylvia said, "I drew three flowers for the 3 and two flowers for the 2." When the teacher questioned her further, she discovered that Sylvia had no understanding of multiplication. By rote, she had memorized the answers to some of the elementary multiplication facts. The teacher used manipulatives such as chips and buttons to illustrate multiplication.

The following activities can be helpful in teaching students to understand the operation.

1. The following drawing illustrates how chips in rows can be used to illustrate multiplication. For example, ask, "How many 4s make 20? Fours are placed on the board ____ times."

$$4 \times \underline{} = 20$$

TECH TALK 8.1

USING COMPUTER-ASSISTED INSTRUCTION

Although computer-assisted instruction (CAI) alone is not as effective as teacher-directed instruction in teaching mathematics skills to children with disabilities (Wilson, Majsterek, and Simmons, 1996), CAI when used in an augmentative capacity can produce achievement gains that are greater than teacher-directed instruction alone (Watkins and Webb, 1981). In addition, transferability from CAI practice to paper-and-pencil tasks has been supported (Chiang, 1986).

Majsterek and Wilson (1989) stated that effective CAI applications would incorporate the following elements:

- Prompting, checking for understanding, individualized pacing, and reinforcement of correct performance
- Use of a database of academic information gained through use of an extensive questioning routine to elicit what the learner knows
- Transcendence of traditional teaching methods through use of animation, voice synthesis, interaction, and response monitoring

- Adaptability or modification by the teacher
- Data collection procedures so that student progress can be easily monitored by teachers
- The ability to elicit and sustain the student's attention

Source: Stickybear's Word Problems by Optimum Resource, Inc.

2. Have students "talk aloud" what is involved in solving a problem. Do not let them merely *read* the problem; ask them to *explain* what it means. For example, "63–27 means that someone had 63 pieces of gum and gave 27 pieces to a friend."

3. Have students explain the process to another student by using block manipulatives. For example, "24 + 31 is the same as adding 4 one-block pieces to 1 one-block piece and 2 ten-block pieces to 3 ten-block pieces."

4. Have students close their eyes and use noises to illustrate operations. For example, to illustrate multiplication, the teacher can tap in groups of six. "How many times did I tap a group of 6?"

       tap-tap-tap-tap-tap-tap
       tap-tap-tap-tap-tap-tap
       tap-tap-tap-tap-tap-tap

"Yes, I tapped a group of 6 three times. Now I am going to tap a group of 6 three times again and I want you to tell me how many taps there are altogether." "Yes, when you tap a group of 6 three times there are 18 total taps." This same process can be used for addition and subtraction (Bley and Thornton, 1981).

Knowing Basic Math Facts

Two of the reasons students may have difficulty with computation have been discussed: (1) they do not understand numeration and/or place value, and (2) they do not understand the computation process. A third reason students may have difficulty with computation is they do not know the basic math facts. A common instructional misconception is that if students learn basic arithmetic facts they will no longer have difficulties with other arithmetic operations and problems. Arithmetic facts do not help the student in analyzing or understanding the application of arithmetic operations; however, they do aid in the acquisition and speed of performing arithmetic operations. Students who do not know the basic math facts are going to be considerably slower and less accurate in math computation. It is difficult for them to understand the math process because so much of their attention is focused on computing one small segment of the problem.

Using thinking strategies assists in the acquisition and retention of basic math facts (Thornton and Toohey, 1985). Without direct instruction, students with learning disabilities often do not discover and use these strategies and relationships for learning and retaining math facts (Thornton, 1978).

Some of the thinking strategies used by students who are successful at solving basic math facts (Thornton and Toohey, 1985; Thornton, Tucker, Dossey, and Bazik, 1983) can be taught to students who are having difficulties.

1. *Using doubles.* Students can learn to use doubles to solve basic math facts. If the student knows $6 + 6 = 12$, then the student can easily compute $6 + 7$. Apply the Concept 8.4 illustrates picture devices to associate with learning doubles.

2. *Counting-on.* Students do not need to resort to counting from one to solve math facts. They can learn to count on from the largest numeral in an addition fact. For example:

$$7 + 2 = \underline{\hspace{1cm}}$$

The student counts on two more from 7: "seven, eight, nine." Students can use this same principle when subtracting, only they count backwards. For example:

$$7 - 2 = \underline{\hspace{1cm}}$$

The student counts backwards two from 7: "seven, six, five." Students can be taught counting-on before operations, and then they will only need to learn to apply the principle.

3. *Using the commutative idea.* The commutative property means that adding or multiplying any two numbers always yields the same answer re-

gardless of their order. Students can be taught that with addition and multiplication, if they know it one way they know it the other. For example:

$$3 + 5 = 8$$
$$5 + 3 = 8$$
$$2 \times 9 = 18$$
$$9 \times 2 = 18$$

4. *Thinking one more or less than a known fact.* Yvette knew several basic math facts but had trouble with the more difficult ones. When her teacher taught her how to use the math facts she knew to solve the more difficult ones, her math performance improved. For example, Yvette knew $5 + 5 = 10$, but when she was presented with $5 + 6$, she began counting on her fingers. Her teacher taught her to think of $5 + 6$ as one more than $5 + 5$, and $5 + 4$ as one less than $5 + 5$. Pictures such as the following can help to illustrate the principle:

$$5 + 5 = 10 \quad \cdots \quad + \quad \cdots \quad =$$

$$5 + 6 = \quad \cdots \quad + \quad \cdots \quad =$$

$$5 + 4 = \quad \cdots \quad + \quad \cdots \quad =$$

5. *Using tens.* Students can learn that 10 + any single-digit number merely changes the 0 in the 10 to the number they are adding to it.

6. *Using nines.* There are two strategies students can apply to addition facts that involve nines. First, they can think of the 9 as a 10 and then subtract 1 from the answer. As illustrated here, the student is taught to "think" of the 9 as a 10.

$$\begin{array}{c} 9 \\ +6 \end{array} \qquad \text{think} \qquad \begin{array}{c} 10 \\ +6 \\ \hline 16 - 1 = \underline{15} \end{array}$$

APPLY THE CONCEPT 8.4

7. *Counting by twos, threes, and fours.* Being able to count by multiples helps in addition, multiplication, and division. Multiplication facts can be taught by interpreting 3×4 as counting by threes four times. Division facts, such as $8 \div 2$ can be interpreted as, "How many times do you count by twos before you reach 8?"

8. *Relationship between addition and subtraction; multiplication and division.* After students learn addition facts, they can be shown the relationship between the addition fact and subtraction. For example, if a student knows $7 + 6 = 13$, students can learn the relationships between the known addition fact and the subtraction fact, $13 - 7 = \underline{\quad}$. Whenever possible, reinforce this principle as students are working, "You know $8 + 4 = 12$, so $12 - 4 = $ must be $\underline{\quad}$." Give students known addition facts and ask them to form subtraction problems. These sample relationships can be used to teach multiplication and division facts (see Figure 8.2).

Luit and Naglieri (1999) have been successful in teaching students multiplication and division by ensuring that they learn the following skills: (a) multiplication is repeated addition; (b) reversibility means that 4×7 is the same as 7×4; (c) the need to memorize the basic multiplication facts below 100; (d) division is repeated subtraction; (e) the need to memorize the basic division facts below 100; and (f) ways to apply multiplication and division in real-life problems.

If you think these strategies for assisting students in learning math facts seem logical and automatic, you are right. They are for most students. However, students with learning difficulties in math do not use these strategies automatically and it prevents them from acquiring the needed math facts for accurate and speedy computation.

■ **FIGURE 8.2** *Relationships between Addition and Subtraction; Multiplication and Division*

Known Addition Facts	Made-up Subtraction Facts
5 + 5 = 10	$10 - 5 = 5$
3 + 2 = 5	_____
8 + 8 = 16	_____
6 + 4 = 10	_____

Known Multiplication Facts	Made-up Division Facts
7 × 4 = 28	$28 \div 4 = 7$
8 × 8 = 64	_____
5 × 9 = 45	_____
5 × 10 = 50	_____

When these strategies are directly taught, students' math performance improves. When Ms. Zaragoza taught math strategies to students who were having difficulty in math she used the math strategies summarized in Apply the Concept 8.5, and she used other students who were performing the math skill accurately to help her. She interviewed students who knew how to perform the skill and asked them to "talk aloud" while they solved the problems so she could learn what strategies they used. She then taught these strategies to students who were having problems.

Peer-Assisted Instructional Practices

Perhaps one of the most effective procedures for teaching math facts to students with learning and behavior problems is the use of cross-age tutors. Cross-age tutors refers to the use of older students, often students without learning or behavior problems, to serve as tutors for younger students with learning difficulties. Cross-age tutors are particularly effective in teaching math facts because the skills they need to be effective can be acquired quickly, in as little as two 45-minute periods. In a study that successfully used cross-age tutors to teach addition facts to students with learning disabilities (Beirne-Smith, 1991), tutors were trained to do the following:

- Use contingent reinforcement
- Use task and error correction procedures
- Use procedures for "counting on"
- Use procedures for rote memorization of facts
- Repeat skills and instruction till mastery

Cooperative learning groups, usually small groups of students (three to five per group), can be used to have students work together to solve problems. Maheady, Harper, and Sacca (1988) conducted a cooperative learning math instruction program for ninth and tenth grade students with mild disabilities. Students who participated in the cooperative teams performed better in mathematics and received higher grades than those who did not.

Constant Time Delay Procedure

Constant time delay is a procedure for teaching math facts that provides for systematic assistance from the teacher through near errorless control of the prompt to ensure the successful performance of the student (Gast, Ault, Wolery, Doyle, and Belanger, 1988; Mattingly and Bott, 1990; Schuster, Stevens, and Doak, 1990; Stevens and Schuster, 1988; Wolery, Cybriwsky, Gast, and Boyle-Gast, 1991). Students are presented with a math fact. The student is allowed a specific amount of time to provide the correct answer. If the student does not respond within the time allotted, a controlling prompt, typically the teacher modeling the correct response, is provided. The student then repeats the teacher's model. Correct responses before and after the prompt are reinforced; however, only correct responses provided before the prompt are counted toward criterion.

Math Computation Errors

How could students make the errors in Figure 8.3? It appears as though all the students did was guess. Yet each of the students who computed the problems can tell you what they did to get the answer. Most errors that students make are rule governed. Although the rule they are applying may not always be obvious, they are using some rule to tell them how to compute a problem. In Figure 8.3 problem (A), Erika said, "I took 1 away from 7 to get 6, and 0 away from 5 to get 5." In problem (B), Jeff added across, adding the 3 and 1 to get 4, and 2 and 3 to get 5. In problem (C), Yolanda said, "I knew this wasn't right but it was the best I knew how to do. I multiplied 3 × 4 to get 12, and then 6 × 4 to get 24." In problem (D), Shawn knew that 7 plus 7 plus 7 was 21, but he was operating under the faulty rule that you always carry the smaller number, so he wrote the 2 in the ones column and carried the 1. Paulette, in problem (E), said, "I added 4 plus 1 because it was easier than adding 4 plus 3." When given several similar problems, she had no concerns about placing the number in the ones or tens column depending upon where it was easier for her to add. All of these students applied faulty rules as they performed math computations. Once the teacher discovered the faulty rules they were applying, she was able to teach them the underlying concept and the correct rule for completing computations.

APPLY THE CONCEPT 8.5

STRATEGIES FOR TEACHING ADDITION FACTS

Addition Facts Groups by Strategy for Recall

	Fact Group	Examples	Most Popular Strategy for Working Out Unknown Answers
	Count Ons	(+1, +2, +3, facts)	"Feel" the count
No fingers needed!	Zero facts	(6 + 0, 0 + 4)	Show it
	Doubles	(4 + 4, 7 + 7)	Use pictures (e.g., 7 + 7 is the 2-week fact; 7 + 7 = 14)
	10 sums	(especially 6 + 4)	Use 10-frame
	9s	(4 + 9, 9 + 6)	Use pattern
	Near Doubles	(4 + 5, 7 + 8)	Relate to doubles (via pictures)
	four last facts	(7 + 5, 8 + 4, 8 + 5, 8 + 6)	Make 10, add extra

Note: Turn-arounds (commutatives of facts within each group) would be learned before moving to a different group of facts.

Verbal Prompts Used in the Addition Program

Fact Group	Sample Facts		Sentence Patterns (Verbal Prompts)
Count Ons	8 +2	3 +7	Start BIG and count on.
Zeroes	6 +0	0 +3	Plus zero stays the same.
Doubles	5 +5	7 +7	Think of the picture.
Near Doubles	5 +6	7 +8	Think doubles to help.
9s	4 +9	9 +6	What's the pattern?
Near 10s	7 +5	6 +8	Use 10 to help.

Source: C. A. Thornton and M. A. Toohey, "Basic Math Facts: Guidelines for Teaching and Learning," *Learning Disabilities Focus* 1(1) (1985): 50, 51. Reprinted with permission of the Division for Learning Disabilities.

■ **FIGURE 8.3**   *Math Computation Errors*

(A)	15		(B)	31		(C)	63
	− 7			+ 23			× 23
	65			45			2412

(D)	37		(E)	13
	27			+ 4
	17			53
	72			

Teachers can learn a great deal about students' thinking in mathematics through an oral diagnostic interview (Lankford, 1974). Such an interview will provide information about what each student is doing and why he or she is doing it that way. For the diagnostic interview to yield accurate, helpful information, the teacher must ask the student questions about math computation in a nonthreatening way. For example, "I am interested in learning what you say to yourself while you do this problem. Say aloud what you are thinking." It is often most effective to use a problem different from the one the student has performed incorrectly. The assumption behind this interview is that there is an underlying reason behind the mistakes, and understanding why a student is making errors provides valuable diagnostic information which leads directly to instruction. Roberts (1968) identified four common "failure strategies" in computation. These are summarized in Apply the Concept 8.6.

Students with learning problems are slower, but not necessarily less accurate, when it comes to doing and learning math facts (Garnett, 1992). When you teach mathematics in your classroom, consider that students with learning problems may need additional practice to learn math facts and longer time to perform mathematics computations because they often lack the "automatization" to perform math computation effectively and efficiently (Garnett and Fleischner, 1983).

Language of Math Computation

"What do you mean by 'find the difference'? Am I supposed to add or subtract? Why don't you just say it in plain English?" Many students with learning and behavior problems have difficulty with the language of computation. Yet understanding the vocabulary is important for success in the regular classroom, application to math story problems, and communication with others. Understanding the terminology of the four basic operations as well as the symbols associated with the processes is important. Students also need to understand the vocabulary that is associated with the answer derived from each of these processes. Table 8.1 illustrates the relationship between the process, symbol, answer, and problem.

After teaching the information on the chart, you can use the following activities:

1. Cover one column (e.g., the symbols) and ask the student to write the answer.
2. Place each of the symbols, answers, and problems on a separate index card and ask the student to sort them by process.
3. Play concentration with two columns. Two columns of index cards (e.g., the symbol cards and answer cards) are laid answer down and each student takes turns searching for matching pairs by selecting two cards. When the student picks up a corresponding pair, he or she keeps the pair and takes another turn.

Use of Calculators

Many students with learning and behavior problems let computation interfere with their ability to learn problem solving. They spend so much time learning to compute the problem accurately that they miss the more important aspects of mathematics such as concept development and practical application.

In 1974, the National Council of Teachers of Mathematics issued a statement that urged teachers to use calculators in mathematics instruction (NCTM, 1974). Teachers did not adequately respond to this plea, with fewer than 20 percent of elementary teachers using calculators as part of their instructional program (Suydam, 1982). Many teachers did not use calculators because they felt the use of calculators threatened the acquisition of basic skills. Mr. Coffland, a third-grade teacher, put it this way: "If I let my students use calculators to solve problems, they will not have adequate practice in basic skills. They will become too dependent on using the calculator." Research suggests that Mr.

APPLY THE CONCEPT 8.6

ERRORS IN COMPUTATION

1. *Wrong operation.* The pupil attempts to solve the problem by using the wrong process. In this example the student subtracted instead of adding.

$$\begin{array}{r} 24 \\ + 11 \\ \hline 1\,3 \end{array}$$

2. *Computational error.* The student uses the correct operation but makes an error recalling a basic number fact.

$$\begin{array}{r} 24 \\ + 35 \\ \hline 5\,8 \end{array}$$

3. *Defective algorithm.* The pupil attempts to use the correct operation but uses a wrong procedure for solving the problem. The error is not due to computation.

$$\begin{array}{r} 24 \\ - 17 \\ \hline 1\,3 \end{array}$$

4. *Random response.* The student has little or no idea how to solve the problem, and writes numbers randomly.

$$\begin{array}{r} 304 \\ - 196 \\ \hline 3\,9\,6 \end{array}$$

Source: Adapted from G. H. Roberts, "The Failure Strategies of Third Grade Arithmetic Pupils," *The Arithmetic Teacher,* 15 (1968): 442–446.

■ **TABLE 8.1** *Relationship of Process, Symbol, Answer, and Problem*

Process	Symbol	Answer	Problem
Addition	+	Sum	$6 + 4 =$
Subtraction	−	Difference	$5 - 3 =$
Multiplication	×	Product	$8 \times 5 =$
Division	÷	Quotient	$12 \div 6 =$

Coffland has little to fear. The results of a summary of 79 studies (Hembree, 1986) on the use of calculators suggest:

1. The use of calculators does not interfere with basic mathematics skill acquisition. In fact, calculator use can increase skill acquisition.
2. Only in fourth grade does sustained calculator use interfere with skill development.
3. The use of calculators in testing situations results in much higher achievement scores, particularly when students are low in problem-solving ability.
4. Using calculators improves students' attitudes towards mathematics.
5. Calculators can be introduced at the same time that the paper and pencil practice exercises are introduced.
6. Calculators can be used by students to solve complex problems that they construct. This also provides support for improved self-concept with math skills.

In summary, as long as students are involved in basic skills instruction, the use of calculators is a positive aid to mathematics instruction. There are several ways calculators can be used with students who are having difficulty with mathematics instruction.

1. *Develop a positive attitude.* Using a calculator removes the drudgery associated with solving computations and makes problem solving fun.
2. *Increase self-concept.* Being able to compute extremely complex problems on the calculator gives students confidence in their mathematics abilities.
3. *Improve practice in problem solving.* Students are willing to tackle difficult problem-solving tasks when they have the assistance of the

calculator in solving the problem. Students still have to decide what numbers are used, what operation is used, and whether additional operations are necessary. Using the calculator can free students from the burden of computation and allow more focus on thinking about the problem.

4. *Develop their own problems.* Using the calculator lets students develop their own problems. They can then exchange their problems with each other, and use their calculators to solve them.

FRACTIONS

Fractions is one of the most difficult concepts to teach. Because of the availability of calculators, teachers place less emphasis on being able to compute fractions and greater emphasis on understanding the meaning and use of fractions.

The *concept* of a fraction can be introduced before the actual fractions are even discussed. For example, Figure 8.4 shows the relationship between common fractional terminology and its represented unit.

Children as young as ages three, four, and five are introduced to the concept of fractions as they help cook. "We use 1 cup of milk and 1/2 cup of flour." "You'll need to share the cookie with your brother. You each may have one-half of a cookie." Teachers often use cooking activities to enhance students' understanding of fractions.

Many manipulative aids can be used to teach fractions: colored rods, cardboard strips and squares, blocks, fractional circle wheels, cooking utensils such as measuring cups, and any unit dividers such as egg cartons and muffin pans.

Teaching fractions, as in teaching most concepts, proceeds from concrete to abstract. Apply the Concept 8.7 demonstrates the teaching sequence.

However, the use of intuitive procedures for the acquisition of knowledge in fractions is unlikely to be successful with low achievers (Kelly, Gersten, and Carnine, 1990). Success in understanding fractions is likely to occur when the following variables are presented (Kelly et al., 1990):

■ **FIGURE 8.4**   *Unit Representation of Fractions*

1. *Systematic practice in discriminating among different problem types.* Students with learning and behavior problems often confuse algorithms when computing fractions. For example, they learn to compute denominators and then use this procedure when adding, subtracting, multiplying and dividing.

2. *Separation of confusing elements and terminology.* Much of the language of learning fractions is unfamiliar and confusing to youngsters. If the language is well explained and the concepts illustrated, students are more likely to be successful in learning fractions.

3. *Use a wide range of examples to illustrate each concept.* Students have a difficult time generalizing beyond the number of examples provided by the teacher; thus, a wide range and large number of examples facilitates understanding.

MEASUREMENT

Measurement includes weight, distance, quantity, length, money, and time. Measurement can be taught almost entirely with applied problems. For example,

APPLY THE CONCEPT 8.7

SEQUENCE FOR TEACHING FRACTIONAL CONCEPTS

The student

1. Manipulates concrete models (e.g., manipulating fractional blocks and pegs)
2. Matches fractional models (e.g., matching halves, thirds, fourths)
3. Points to fractional model when name is stated by another (e.g., the teacher says "half" and the student selects a model of "half" from several distractors)
4. Names fractional units when selected by another (e.g., the teacher points to a fractional unit such as a "fourth" and the student names it)

5. Draws diagrams or uses manipulatives to represent fractional units (e.g., the teacher says or writes fractional units such as "whole," "half," and "third," and the student uses manipulatives or drawings to represent these units)
6. Writes fraction names when given fractional drawings (e.g., next to ▮▮▯ the student writes "half")
7. Uses fractions to solve problems (e.g., place $1\frac{1}{2}$ cups of sugar in a bowl)

---

students learn time by using the clock in the classroom or by manipulating a toy clock; they learn money by making purchases with real or toy money; and they learn measures like cup, pint, and teaspoon through following recipes. With each measurement unit taught (e.g., weight, distance, money), the students need to learn the vocabulary and concepts for that unit. Only after students understand the terminology and concepts and have had experience applying the concepts in real measurement problems should they be exposed to measurement instruction through the use of less applied procedures such as textbooks and worksheets. Lerner (1985) refers to this as the "concrete-to-abstract progression" (p. 364). Lerner states that the teacher should plan three instructional states: (1) concrete or applied; (2) representational (e.g., toy money); and (3) abstract (e.g., workbook page with money problems). It is particularly important when teaching measurement to have overlearning occur at the concrete or applied stage. This section will focus on two forms of measurement: time and money.

Time

Even before coming to school, most children can tell time by the hour or know when the clock says it is time to go to bed or time for dinner. The following teaching sequence assists students in understanding time.

1. Teach students to sequence events. Younger students can sequence the normal routine of the school day. For instance, "First we have a group story, then reading, then we go to recess." Additional practice in sequencing events can occur with story cards, events that occur at home, field trips, and so on.
2. Ask students to identify which events take longer. Name two events (e.g., math time and lining up for recess) and ask the student to identify which event takes longer. Name several events and ask students to put them in order from the event that takes the longest to the one that is quickest to complete.

one twenty-five

A scope and sequence of skills for teaching time is presented in Figure 8.5.

Money

Students with learning disabilities often have difficulty applying money concepts because they have not mastered many of the earlier concepts such as the value of coins, how coins compare (e.g., a quarter is more than two times as much as a dime), and how the value of the coins relates to what can be purchased. One parent reported that her child was frequently taken advantage of because he would trade coins of high value for coins of less value. Students with learning difficulties often do not know the price of common goods. Although they may not need to know the exact price of a loaf of bread or a television set, they should have an estimate of what these items cost.

When initially teaching students to identify money, start with real coins. After they learn to recognize real coins, switch to play money, and then to representations of money on workbook pages. The following sequence is useful when teaching money identification:

1. Teach students to match the same coins. Give students several different coins and ask them to place all of the same coins in the same group.
2. Ask students to point to the coin when you name it. Depending on the students' skill level you may want to start with two coins (e.g., a penny and

a nickel) and then progress to three and four. At this point the students do not need to be able to tell the name of the coin but merely to locate it when it is named.
3. Students name the coin. At this level the students tell the name of the coin.

After students are able to identify accurately the name of the coins, the value of the coins is discussed. Coins and dollars are discussed, both in terms of their purchase power and how they relate to each other. Activities and problems that require students to use money and make change assure students that they can apply what they have learned about money. For example, students can learn to balance and keep a checkbook and to give change when role-playing a clerk in a store.

A scope and sequence for teaching money is presented in Figure 8.6.

PROBLEM SOLVING

"I can read the arithmetic all right; I just can't read the writing" (Barney, 1973, p. 57). Many students with learning problems have trouble with traditional

■ **FIGURE 8.5**   *Time—Scope and Sequence of Skills*

- Tells time to the hour
- Tells time to the half hour
- Knows the days of the week
- Knows the names of the months
- Tells time to the quarter hour
- Knows the number of days in a week
- Knows the number of months in a year
- Can use a calendar to answer questions about the date, the day, and the month
- Writes time to the hour
- Writes time to the half hour
- Writes time using five-minute increments
- Can solve simple story problems using time

■ **FIGURE 8.6**   *Money—Scope and Sequence of Skills*

- Correctly identifies penny, nickel, and dime
- Knows how many cents are in a penny, nickel, and dime
- When shown combinations of pennies, nickels, and dimes, can add to the correct amount
- Can describe items that can be purchased with combinations of pennies, nickels, and dimes
- Can solve simple word math problems involving pennies, nickels, and dimes
- Correctly identifies quarter, dollar, 5 dollars, 10 dollars, and 20 dollars
- Knows the value of combination of quarters and dollars
- Can solve verbal math problems with quarters and dollars

story problems in mathematics because their difficulty in reading makes understanding the math problem almost impossible. In addition, students with learning problems often have difficulty with logical reasoning, which is the basis of many story problems. It is also common that their mathematics education has focused primarily on the operation and not on understanding the why of doing it, or even a thorough understanding of the numbers involved in the operation. So, because of their difficulties with reading and logical reasoning, and perhaps because of insufficient instruction in mathematics, students with learning problems often find problem solving the most difficult part of mathematics.

Despite its difficulties, teaching problem solving may be the most important skill we teach students who have learning and behavior problems. Whereas most other students are able to apply the operations they learn to real-life problems with little direct instruction, students with learning problems will be less able to apply these skills without instruction, rehearsal, and practice. Students with learning disabilities lack metacognitive knowledge about strategies for math problem solving. Poor math performance is not solely a function of math computation difficulties (Montague and Bos, 1990). Students who are taught strategies for problem solving are more likely to be successful than students who are taught the sequence for solving problems (Wilson and Sindelar, 1991).

Students need to know when and how to add, subtract, multiply, and divide. Knowing *when* involves understanding the operation and applying it in the appropriate situation. Knowing *how* is the accurate performance of the operation. Most students are better at *how* than at *when;* problem solving gives students practice at these skills.

Factors Affecting Successful Verbal Problem Solving

The factors that affect successful verbal problem solving or story problems (Carnine, 1997; Goodstein, 1981; Jitendra, Hoff, and Beck, 1999) need to be considered by teachers when writing and selecting story problems and instructing students.

1. *Teach big ideas.* When students understand the big idea or principle, all of the subordinate concepts around that big idea make more sense and are easier to learn and remember (Carnine, 1997). An example of a big idea is "volume." You can teach students the principle of volume and then provide examples of real-life problems that students can solve applying the big-idea principles they learn about volume.

2. *Sameness analysis.* The quality of sameness in mathematical problem solving was developed by Carnine and colleagues through a series of research investigations (Engelmann, Carnine, and Steely, 1991). The idea is to connect math concepts so that students see the ways in which aspects of mathematical problem solving are the same. They identify "types" of word problems and then explicitly teach students the ways in which these word problems are alike.

3. *Cue words.* The presence or absence of cue words can significantly affect students' abilities to solve verbal word problems. The cue word *altogether* is illustrated in the following example: "Mary has 4 erasers. Joe has 7 erasers. How many erasers do they have *altogether*?" The cue word *left* is illustrated in the following example: "Jackie has 9 pieces of candy. She gave 3 pieces to Tom. How many does she have *left*?" Students need to be taught to look for cue words that will guide them in solving problems.

4. *Reasoning.* Ask students to think about the idea behind the story problem. Does it appear the person in the problem will get more or less? Why? What operation will help solve this? What numbers in the story do we have to use? Are there numbers we do not have and need to compute? Ask students to explain the way in which they set up and calculated the problem so that they can justify what they've done and why they've done it that way.

5. *Syntactic complexity.* The sentence structure within the story problem needs to be kept simple. Learner performance can be significantly impaired when the sentence contains a complex interrogative sentence structure (Larsen, Parker, and Trenholme, 1978). The sentence length

and vocabulary may also affect verbal problem solving.

6. *Extraneous information.* Extraneous information in word problems causes difficulties because the majority of students attempt to use all of the information in solving the problem. For example: "Mary's mother baked 10 cookies. Mary's sister baked 8 cookies. Mary's brother baked 3 cupcakes. How many *cookies* were baked?" The information regarding Mary's brother baking three cupcakes is extraneous, yet many students will use the information in attempting to solve the problem. Extraneous information introduced into story problems is associated with decreases in accuracy and computation speed with students. Blankenship and Lovitt (1976) explain students' difficulties with extraneous information by suggesting that the difficulties are based not on reading the entire story problem but merely on knowing which numbers are needed to solve the problem. Students will construct the problem using the numbers available in the story problem, disregarding the question and the content available in the story problem. After students are successfully able to complete story problems without extraneous information, teach them to complete story problems with extraneous information.

7. *Content load.* The content load refers to the number of ideas contained within a story problem. The story problem should not be overloaded with concepts (West, 1978) and, if it is, the students need to be taught to discriminate between relevant and irrelevant concepts.

8. *Suitable content.* The story problems should contain content that is interesting and appealing to the students and relevant to the types of real problems the students have or will encounter.

9. *Monitor progress.* Use weekly tests of word-problem solving to monitor study progress on each type of word problem students have mastered and/or are learning. Reteach when necessary.

10. *Provide guided practice.* Use diagrams to demonstrate how to solve the problem and guide students through the development and use of these diagrams. As students demonstrate more and more proficiency with independent use of diagrams and strategies for effective problem solving, reduce the amount of support provided.

Methods of Teaching Story Problem Solving

There are three important considerations in preparing students for success in solving story problems: (a) provide anchored instruction that relates to a real-life problem the students might encounter (Goldman, Hasselbring, et al., 1997), (b) provide story problems in an appropriate sequence, and (c) make students aware of the types of errors that are commonly made. Students also need to learn specific strategies that will assist them in using a successful process for mastering story problems in class and applying those principles to the mathematics of everyday life.

A step-by-step strategy for teaching sixth-grade students to solve story problems is illustrated in Apply the Concept 8.8 (Smith and Alley, 1981). Students need first to learn the strategies, practice them with support from a teacher, and then practice them independently until they can apply the principles with success. After continued success, students make adaptations in or condense the steps they use. The section on cognitive behavior modification in Chapter Two discusses how to teach students learning strategies.

Fleishner, Nazum, and Marzola (1987, p. 216) devised the following instructional program to teach arithmetic problem solving to students with learning disabilities:

READ	What is the question?
REREAD	What is the necessary information?
THINK	Putting together = addition
	Taking apart = subtraction
	Do I need all the information?
	Is it a two-step problem?
SOLVE	Write the equation

APPLY THE CONCEPT 8.8

STEPS FOR TEACHING STUDENTS TO SOLVE STORY PROBLEMS

Story Problem: Mark had $1.47 to spend. He spent $0.34 on gum. How much money does he have left?

I. Read the Problem
   A. Find unknown words
   B. Find "cue words" (e.g., *left*)

II. Reread the Problem
   A. Identify what is given
      1. Is renaming needed?
      2. Are there unit changes?

B. Decide what is asked for
   1. What process is needed?
   2. What unit or category is asked for? (e.g., seconds, pounds, money)

III. Use Objects to Show the Problem
   A. Decide what operation to use

IV. Write the Problem

V. Work the Problem

CHECK   Recalculate
          Label
          Compare

Another strategy for solving word problems was used by Hutchinson (1993). She taught adolescent students with learning problems to solve algebra word problems by asking themselves questions and using graphs to monitor their progress. The self-questions she used included:

— Have I read and understood the sentence?
— Do I have the whole picture, a representation, for this problem?
— Have I written the representation on the worksheet?

Montague and Bos (1986a, 1986b) demonstrated the efficacy of the learning-strategy approach, described in Apply the Concept 8.9, with high-school adolescents with learning disabilities.

In summary, when teaching story problems to students with learning and behavior problems, keep the following guidelines in mind:

1. Be certain the students can perform the arithmetic computation before introducing the computation in story problems.

2. Develop a range of story problems that contain the type of problem you want the student to learn to solve.

3. Instruct with one type of problem until mastery is attained.

4. Teach the students to read through the word problem and visualize the situation. Ask them to read the story aloud and tell what it is about.

5. Ask the students to reread the story—this time to get the facts.

6. Identify the key question. In the beginning stages of problem solving, the students should write the key question so it can be referred to when the computation is complete.

7. Identify extraneous information.

8. Reread the story problem and attempt to state the situation in a mathematical sentence. The teacher plays an important role in this step by asking the students questions and guiding them in formulating the arithmetic problem.

9. Tell the students to write the arithmetic problem and compute the answer. (Some problems can be computed by the students in their heads without completing this step.)

10. Tell the students to reread the key question and be sure they have completed the problem correctly.

11. Ask the students if their answer is likely, based on their estimate.

APPLY THE CONCEPT 8.9

TEACHING ADOLESCENTS TO SOLVE STORY PROBLEMS

The eight steps in the verbal math problem-solving strategy are described below:

1. *Read the problem aloud.* Ask the teacher to pronounce or define any word you do not know. (The teacher will pronounce and provide meanings for any words if the student asks.)

   Example: In a high school there are 2,878 male and 1,943 female students enrolled. By how many students must the enrollment increase to make the enrollment 5,000?

2. *Paraphrase the problem aloud.* State important information giving close attention to the numbers in the problem. Repeat the question part aloud. A self-questioning technique such as What is asked? or What am I looking for? is used to provide focus on the outcome.

   Example: Altogether there are a certain number of kids in high school. There are 2,878 boys and 1,943 girls. The question is by how many students must the enrollment increase to make the total enrollment 5,000. What is asked? How many more students are needed to total 5,000 in the school?

3. *Visualize.* Graphically display the information. Draw a representation of the problem.

4. *State the problem.* Complete the following statements aloud. I have . . . I want to find . . . Underline the important information in the problem.

   Example: I have the number of boys and the number of girls who go to the school now. I want to find how many more kids are needed to total 5,000.

5. *Hypothesize.* Complete the following statements aloud. If I . . . then . . . how many steps will I use to find the answer? Write the operation signs.

   Example: If I add 2,878 boys and 1,943 girls, I'll get the number of kids now. Then I must subtract that number from 5,000 to find out how many more must enroll. First add, then subtract. + − This is a two-step problem.

6. *Estimate.* Write the estimate. My answer should be around . . . or about . . . (The skills of rounding and estimating answers should be reinforced at this step.) Underline the estimate.

   Example: 2,800 and 2,000 are 4,800. 4,800 from 5,000 is 200. My answer should be around 200.

7. *Calculate.* Show the calculation and label the answer. Circle the answer. Use a self-questioning technique such as, Is this answer in the correct form? (Change from cent sign to dollar sign and decimal point should be reinforced when solving money problems.) Correct labels for the problems should be reinforced.

   Example: 2,878   5,000
             + 1,943   − 4,821
             ─────   ─────────
              4,821   179 students

8. *Self-check.* Refer to the problem and check every step to determine accuracy of operation(s) selected and correctness of response and solution. Check computation for accuracy. (Checking skills will be reinforced at this step.) Use the self-questioning technique by asking if the answer makes sense.

Source: M. Montague and C. S. Bos, "The Effect of Cognitive Strategy Training on Verbal Math Problems Solving Performance of Learning Disabled Adolescents," *Journal of Learning Disabilities, 19* (1986): 26–33. Copyright 1986 by PRO-ED, Inc. Reprinted by permission.

Teaching math story problems does not have to be limited to the content area of math. Cawley (1984) discusses how story problems can be integrated with instruction in reading so that reading level does not interfere with understanding the math story problem. At the same time, story problems can enhance and support what the student is doing in reading. For example, a story about a mother duck and her babies was part of a student's reading lesson. During mathematics, the teacher makes minor changes in the story and uses it for instruction in story problems in mathematics (see Figure 8.7).

This same procedure can be used with junior high and high school students' content area textbooks. Math story problems can be taken from social studies and science tests; Cawley and Miller (1986) refer to these as knowledge-based problems. Usually these problems require specific knowledge in the content area. Cawley (1984) identifies the integration of math into other content areas as an important means of promoting generalization of math concepts.

Pictures can be used to facilitate processing information in solving mathematic word problems. For example, using Figure 8.8, the teacher could say, "The small monkeys have four bananas and the large monkeys have six bananas. How many bananas would they have if they put them all together?"

Instructional manipulatives can also be used to assist students with learning problems in solving mathematical word problems. Cuisenaire rods can be

■ **FIGURE 8.7** *Example of Teacher-Altered Story for Use in Story Problem Instruction*

The mother duck went to the pond with her *eight* babies. They looked for their new friend. *Two* more baby ducks joined them. How many baby ducks were there?

■ **FIGURE 8.8** *Pictures Help Solve Math Story Problems*

used to represent the numerical values in the problem and assist students in better understanding and solving mathematical word problems (Marsh and Cooke, 1996).

APPROACHES TO INCREASING MATH PERFORMANCE

There are three types of interventions for mathematics instruction for individuals with learning disabilities (for review, see Mastropieri, Scruggs, and Shiah, 1991; Parmar and Cawleg, 1997). One type of intervention is cognitive, one is behavioral and the third is alternative instructional delivery systems, which includes cooperative learning, computer-assisted instruction, and interactive video disks. Mastropieri, Scruggs, and Shiah (1991) reflect that a broad array of interventions are effective, including: strategy instruction, worksheets, computers, peer-assisted instruction, and direct measurement.

Cognitive Approaches

Cognitive behavior modification (CBM) can be used with instructional procedures in mathematics. Cognitive behavior modification often takes the form of self-instruction, which relies on using internalized language to facilitate the problem-solving process.

Based largely on the work of Meichenbaum and his associates (Meichenbaum, 1977, 1985; Meichenbaum and Goodman, 1971), CBM is receiving attention as an alternative strategy for teaching arithmetic to students with learning difficulties. Lovitt and Curtiss (1968) found that when students verbalize the answer before writing it, as opposed to just writing the answer, they make fewer computational errors. It could be that the process of verbalization focuses the students on the answer and gives them a second opportunity to check whether the answer makes sense and is correct. When verbalizations are added to the arithmetic process, either by naming the sign before proceeding (Parsons, 1972) or verbalizing the steps in the arithmetic process while solving the problem (Grimm, Bijou, and Parsons, 1973), there is a significant improvement in performance. Leon and Pepe (1983) taught a five-step self-instructional sequence to special education teachers. Students participating in arithmetic instruction from these teachers who were trained in the sequence improved greatly in both arithmetic computation and in generalizing skills acquired.

The following sequence for using self-instruction in mathematics is a modification of the approach used by Leon and Pepe (1983).

1. *Modeling.* The teacher demonstrates how to compute the problem by using overt self-instruction. This overt self-instruction, or talking aloud of the process, assists students who have learning problems in knowing what they should say to themselves and what questions they should ask to keep them focused on the process.
2. *Coparticipation.* Both teacher and students compute the problem together by using overt self-instruction. This step helps the students put the procedure in their own words and yet supplies the support of the teacher while they are still learning the process.
3. *Student demonstration.* The students compute the problem alone by using overt self-instruction and the teacher monitors the students' performance. The students are more independent in this step; however, the teacher is still available to give correction and feedback.

4. *Fading overt self-instruction.* The students continue to demonstrate the computation of the problem with internal self-instruction. Often students have a check sheet of symbols or key words to cue them to the key points.
5. *Feedback.* The students complete the problem independently by using covert self-instruction and providing self-reinforcement for a job well done.

Behavioral Approaches

Behavioral techniques can be used to increase students' math performance. As you know, stimulus cues precede responses and often control or provide information to control responses. In arithmetic instruction, the teacher needs to identify the relevant cues and determine whether the students are aware of these cues and are using them appropriately. In Figure 8.9 three different problems are presented; there are many different cues a student must understand and attend to before accurately performing these problems. For example, in problem 1 of Figure 8.9 the student must know what "+" means, what the numbers represent, and what procedure to follow to perform the problem. In problem 2 the student must know what the picture represents, the difference between the short and long hands of the clock, and what each of the numbers represents. Problem 3 requires the student's understanding of the cue *long*, and what type of tool is needed to address the problem. Math provides many stimulus cues and the teacher needs to be certain that the students recognize and understand the cues and attend to them.

■ **FIGURE 8.9** *Math Problems Enlisting Various Cues*

(1)   37
       24
    + 89

(2) [clock face showing approximately 3:30]

What time is it? _____

(3) How long is this line? _____

Teachers can also provide cues to assist students in learning new skills. For example, the following illustrates cues a teacher provided when students were first learning long division.

÷ (divide) $6\overline{)478}$ $8\overline{)521}$
× (multiply)
− (subtract)
↓ (bring down)

Providing corrective feedback reinforces students' performances. Corrective feedback involves telling the students what they are doing well, including procedures, accuracy of responses, and work style. It also involves identifying in what area a student needs further assistance. Corrective feedback should be given frequently. Do not wait until students have completed tasks; give feedback while they are working on the task. Be precise with feedback; rather than saying, "You are doing a good job," say, "You remembered to carry. All of the answers in the first row are correct. Good job."

Task analysis is a process of specifying the behaviors needed for a particular task that can help shape student responses. The student is taught behaviors from the simple to the more complex until he or she can perform the target behavior. For example, the teacher's goal may be for a student to complete two-place addition with carrying by solving a verbal math problem. The student's present level of performance is knowledge of math facts when adding numbers between 0 and 9. Through task analysis, the teacher identifies the many behaviors that need to be shaped through instruction and practice before the student is performing the target behavior.

For example, the teacher identified the skills needed between knowing math facts between 0 and 9 and being able to solve a verbal math problem with two-place addition.

1. Number concepts
   0–9
2. Number concepts
   10–100
3. Place value
4. Simple word   Answers require
   problems (oral) 0–9   addition facts
5. Simple word   Answers require
   problems (written)   addition facts
   0–9
6. Two-place addition
   problems
7. Word problems   Answers require
   (oral) addition   two-place addition
   computation
8. Word problems   Answers require
   (written) addition   two-place addition
   computation

The teacher decided that it would take approximately three months to reach the goal. She knew that her mathematics program would focus on other skills during that period (e.g., time, measurements, and graphs).

FOCUS ON REAL-WORLD MATHEMATICS

Many students with learning and behavior problems manage to graduate with only a minimal understanding of mathematics skills. Many, relieved to escape formal education in mathematics, have the unfortunate misconception that they are finished with mathematics. Unfortunately, they are sadly mistaken and they soon find that functioning as an adult requires applying mathematic concepts. Managing money, checkbooks, interest on loans, and credit cards is only the beginning. Adults must file taxes, complete employment forms for deductions, and use basic math skills in their jobs. Figure 8.10 lists the mathematics skills all students need to acquire because they are essential for survival in the real world. To function completely in society, all students should be able to demonstrate applied knowledge and understanding of these skills.

Functional Math

Mathematics instruction for students with learning disabilities needs to focus on teaching functional skills necessary for independent living (Patton et al., 1997). Many of the skills most important for students with learning disabilities are not contained in

■ **FIGURE 8.10** *Mathematical Concepts for the Everyday World*

More and more science and technology are permeating our society and with this, the need for more mathematics to understand the scientific and technological concepts is increasing. The new level of mathematical competencies, skills, and attitudes toward mathematics required of modern citizenry is much higher than what was expected 25 years ago. The following represent the skills and competencies considered necessary for adults to participate effectively in contemporary society:

1. Numbers and Numerals
   - Express a rational number using a decimal notation.
   - List the first ten multiples of 2 through 12.
   - Use the whole numbers (four basic operations) in problem solving.
   - Recognize the digit, its place value, and the number represented through billions.
   - Describe a given positive rational number using decimal, percent, or fractional notation.
   - Convert to Roman numerals from decimal numerals and conversely (e.g., data translation).
   - Represent very large and very small numbers using scientific notation.

2. Operations and Properties
   - Write equivalent fractions for given fractions such as 1/2, 2/3, 3/4, and 7/8.
   - Use the standard algorithms for the operations of arithmetic of positive rational numbers.
   - Solve addition, subtraction, multiplication, and division problems involving fractions.
   - Solve problems involving percent.
   - Perform arithmetic operations with measures.
   - Estimate results.
   - Judge the reasonableness of answers to computational problems.

3. Mathematical Sentences
   - Construct a mathematical sentence from a given verbal problem.
   - Solve simple equations.

4. Geometry and Measurement
   - Recognize horizontal lines, vertical lines, parallel lines, perpendicular lines, and intersecting lines.
   - Recognize different shapes.
   - Compute areas, surfaces, volumes, densities.
   - Understand similarities and congruence.
   - Use measurement devices.

5. Relations and Functions
   - Interpret information from a graphical representation.
   - Understand and apply ratio and proportion.
   - Construct scales.

6. Probability and Statistics
   - Determine mean, average, mode, median.
   - Understand simple probability.

7. Mathematical Reasoning
   - Produce counter examples to test invalidity of a statement.
   - Detect and describe flaws and fallacies in advertising and propaganda where statistical data and inferences are employed.
   - Gather and present data to support an inference or argument.

8. General Skills
   - Maintain personal bank records.
   - Plan a budget and keep personal records.
   - Apply simple interest formula to calculate interest.
   - Estimate the real cost of an item.
   - Compute taxes and investment returns.
   - Appraise insurance and retirement benefits.

Source: M. C. Sharma, "Mathematics in the Real World" in J. F. Cawley (Ed.) *Developmental Teaching of Mathematics for Learning Disabled* (Austin, TX: PRO-ED, 1984), pp. 224–225. Reprinted with permission of PRO-ED, Inc.

mathematics curricula because they do not need to be taught through direct instruction to nonlearning-disabled students. Halpern (1981) suggests students with learning disabilities learn (1) the realistic prices of products, (2) how to estimate, and (3) how to tell time and estimate time intervals. According to Halpern (1981), most arithmetic done in the real world is done orally, and yet arithmetic done in classrooms is done with pencil and paper. More attention to oral practice in the classroom is needed.

Math curricula for students with disabilities requires the teacher to consider the functional math skills students need. Figure 8.11 presents an outline of content for teaching functional math.

Schwartz and Budd (1981) recommend an eight-step sequence useful for initiating teaching strategies for a functional math curriculum. This approach appears to be particularly useful with junior high and high school students.

1. *Become motivated.* Students need to feel there is a valid reason for learning to solve mathematics problems. This may include identifying how math is used at home and on the job. Students

---

■ **FIGURE 8.11** *Content for Teaching Functional Math*

Consumer Skills
Making change
Determining cost of sale items utilizing percentages
    (e.g., "25% off")
Determining tax amounts
Doing cost comparisons
Buying on "time"
Balancing a checkbook
Determining total cost of purchases

Homemaking Skills
Measuring ingredients
Budgeting for household expenses
Calculating length of cooking and baking time when
    there are options (e.g., for a cake using two 9"
    round pans vs. two 8" round pans)
Measuring material for clothing construction
Doing cost comparisons

Health Care
Weighing oneself and others
Calculating caloric intake
Determining when to take medication

Auto Care
Calculating cost of auto parts
Measuring spark plug gaps
Determining if tire pressure is correct
Figuring gas mileage

Home Care
Determining amount of supplies (paint, rug shampoo)
    to buy

Determining time needed to do projects
Measuring rods and drapes
Finding cost of supplies
Finding cost of repairs

Vocational Needs
Calculating payroll deductions
Determining money owed
Knowing when to be at work
Doing actual math for various jobs

Leisure Activities
Comparing travel expenses
Magazine and newspaper costs
Membership fees
Entertainment: movies, video rentals, sporting and ar-
    tistic events

Home Managment
Determining where to live
Moving expenses
Move in expenses
Utilities
Insurance
Furniture
Additional expense

Transportation
Public or automobile
Insurance
Maintenance

Source: Adapted from J. R. Patton, M. E. Cronin, D. S. Bassett, and A. E. Koppel, "A Life Skills Approach to Mathematics Instruction: Preparing Students with Learning Disabilities for the Real-Life Demands of Adulthood," *Journal of Learning Disabilities, 30*(2) (1997): 178–187; and S. E. Schwartz and D. Budd, "Mathematics for Handicapped Learners: A Functional Approach for Adolescents," *Focus on Exceptional Children 13*(7) (1981): 7–8. Reproduced by permission of Love Publishing Company.

can interview their parents to determine all of the ways they use functional math. Ask former students or speakers to discuss the need for math as they join the work world.

2. *Choose the operation.* When students are able to identify the question being asked, it is much easier for them to identify the appropriate operation for resolving the question. Students must understand how the operation is performed before they use the operation in functional mathematics.

3. *Understand the problem.* Students need to understand the type of question being asked in verbal problem solving. They need to understand such terminology as *fewer, greater, more, all together, in addition to,* and so on, in order to be successful at functional math. Present realistic problem situations and discuss the questions being asked. Ask students to focus on key words and discuss their meaning. Assist students in identifying unnecessary information.

4. *Estimate the answer.* This step encourages students to check to determine if their selected operation is reasonable. For example, give the following problem:"How much money will John have left after he lends half of his total savings of $8.40 to his sister?" The student selects multiplication as the operation for solving the problem. The student estimates the answer and has a second opportunity to check whether the correct operation was chosen. Questions such as the following should be asked of the student: "After multiplying, will John have more money or less?" "When we lend money to people do we usually have more money or less?" "Is multiplying the correct operation?"

5. *Do the operation.* The students should be able to perform the operation, but a review of skills may be necessary.

6. *Check the answer.* The student checks to be sure the numbers were copied correctly and the problem was performed correctly. Students are encouraged to answer the question, "Is this a reasonable answer to the problem?"

7. *Understand the answer.* After determining the answer, the student should be able to interpret

it. The teacher may ask additional questions that allow the student to demonstrate more fully understanding of the answer and the problem.

8. *Apply the skill.* The application of the first seven steps is discussed relative to problems generated by the students and the teacher.

CURRICULUM AND MATERIALS

Traditional math curricula have provided problems for students with learning disabilities. These problems have been summarized by Blankenship (1984):

1. The reading vocabulary is difficult and the reading level is too high.
2. The sequencing of material presented is poor, multiple concepts are introduced, and focus skips from one concept to another.
3. There are insufficient problems covering each concept.
4. There are insufficient opportunities and problems focusing on application.
5. There is too much variance in the formatting of the pages.
6. Students often do not have the prerequisite skills that the text assumes they possess.

Teachers who attempt to use traditional curricula with students who have learning difficulties will need to control for these factors in their teaching.

Recently a number of curricula have been developed that focus on teaching math skills to students with learning difficulties.

Project Math

Project Math (Cawley, Fitzmaurice, Sedlak, and Althaus, 1976) is a well-recognized math curriculum designed specifically for students with mild disabilities. The program includes work on sets, patterns, numbers, operations, fractions, geometry, measurement, and lab activities. It is both a developmental and remedial program and it has eliminated many of the problems associated with traditional arithmetic programs. Project Math reduces the reading level, provides a direct link between assessment and instruction, teaches to mastery, and provides procedures for individualizing instruction. It appears to be a very useful program for teaching mathematics to students with learning difficulties.

DISTAR Arithmetic

The DISTAR arithmetic program (Englemann and Carnine, 1972, 1975, 1976) stresses direct instruction through a highly sequenced format that provides immediate feedback to the student. The DISTAR Arithmetic Kits come complete with a detailed teacher's guide, workbooks, teaching book, and take-homes. The teacher's guide tells the teacher exactly what to say and do—even such directions as, "Say 'Good'." The materials are designed to be fast-paced with lots of oral drill. The DISTAR Arithmetic programs have been effectively used in teaching skills to economically disadvantaged children (Abt Associates, 1976; Becker and Englemann, 1976; Stallings and Kaskowitz, 1974).

Additional Sources of Curriculum and Materials

There are many other sources of curriculum suitable for teaching mathematics to students who have learning problems.

1. The *Computational Arithmetic Program,* developed by Smith and Lovitt (1982), provides 314 worksheets to teach basic math skills from grades one through six.
2. The *Corrective Mathematics Program,* by Englemann and Carnine (1982), provides remedial basic math for students in grades three through twelve.
3. *Structural Arithmetic* by Stern (1965) involves students in kindergarten through third grade making, discovering, and learning math concepts and facts.
4. *Cuisenaire Rods,* by M. Georges Cuisenaire, to give conceptual knowledge of the basic structure of mathematics.

5. *Milliken Wordmath,* developed by Coffland and Baldwin (1985), uses computer programs to teach problem solving within the mathematics curriculum to children in fourth grade and up who are unable to apply their computational knowledge to the solving of everyday problems.
6. *Key Math Teach and Practice* by Connolly (1985) was developed to provide diagnosis of math difficulties and remedial practice. Materials include a teacher's guide, student progress charts, and sequence charts. Activities and worksheets are also provided.
7. *Applied Mathematics Program,* developed by Chambers and Kepner (1985), is a description of an integrated mathematics program for non–college-bound students in the last three years of high school.
8. *This Is Your Life* by Lindsay (1979), exposes high school students to true and familiar situations from the adult world to help them realize which skills they need.
9. *Economics and the Real Life Connection,* developed Murphy and Walsh (1989), teaches the impact of economics and consumerism on day-to-day life.
10. *Integrating Math Skills into Vocational Education Curricula,* developed by Pickard (1990), reinforces academic concepts and suggests hands-on activities in a vocational setting.
11. *Noncareer Mathematics* by Sonnabend (1985) teaches students mathematics topics that adults need (e.g, consumer math, media math, applied math in leisure and theme, and mathematical content and processes).
12. *Civics Mathematics,* developed by Vatter (1994), teaches students math in the context of important social issues of concern to teenagers.

INSTRUCTIONAL ACTIVITIES

This section provides instructional activities related to mathematics. Some of the activities teach new skills; others are best suited for practice and reinforcement of already acquired skills. For each activity, the objective, materials, and teaching procedures are described.

■ Two-Digit Numbers: Focus on Reversals

Objective: To help students understand and use two-digit numbers successfully. (For use with students who write 23 for 32; 41 for 14; and so on.)

Grades: Primary

Materials: Objects that can be grouped by tens (e.g., pencils, paper, chips, sticks).

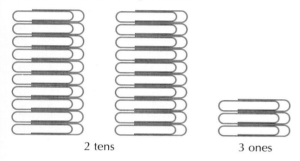

2 tens   3 ones

Teaching Procedures: Four steps are recommended: First, tell the children to group objects such as popsicle sticks or chips in tens, and then to tell the number of tens and number of ones left over. Next, the children count orally by tens and use objects to show the count (e.g., 2 tens is twenty; 6 tens is 60; and so on). When multiples of ten are established, extra ones are included (e.g., 2 tens and 3 is 23). Because of naming irregularities, teens are dealt with last.

Children then group objects by tens and write to describe the grouping. The tens-ones labels, used in early stages, are gradually eliminated. On separate sheets of paper, the students write the number that corresponds with the grouping. The children use objects (tens and ones) to help compare and sequence numbers.

■ "Two Up"

Objective: To practice multiplication facts by rehearsing counting by twos, threes, fours, etc.

Grades: Primary through intermediate

Prerequisite Behaviors: Counting by twos, threes, etc.

Materials: A set of forty-eight cards made by printing the multiples of two from 1 to 12, using a different color of pen for each set (e.g., 2, 4, . . . , 12 in red, blue, green, and brown).

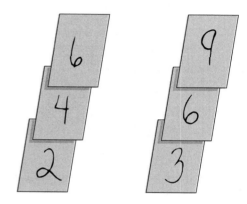

Teaching Procedures: Directions for playing the game are: The cards are shuffled and dealt, giving an equal number of cards to each player. The player who has the red 2 starts the game by placing the red 2 in the middle of the table. The next player must place a red 4 on top of the red 2 *or* pass. Next a red 6 is needed, and so on. Each of the players play in a similar manner. A player can only play one card each turn.

The object of the game is to play the cards from 2 on up. The first player to play all of his or her cards is the winner.

Adaptations: This game can be played with decks of threes, fours, sixes, and so on, called "Three Up," "Four Up," etc. A different deck of cards must be made for each multiple.

■ Bingo Clock Reading

Objective: To give the students practice in associating the time on a clock face, to its written form on a game board, to its spoken form.

Grades: Primary

three o'clock	seven o'clock	fifteen minutes after four	twenty minutes after twelve
fifteen minutes after six	twenty minutes after twelve	twenty minutes to eleven	twenty minutes after eleven
five minutes after five	fifteen minutes after ten	twenty-five minutes after one	twenty-five minutes to eleven
nine thirty	five minutes to seven	twenty-five minutes after twelve	ten o'clock

Materials: (1) Cards that show times on a standard clock. (2) Large game boards with sixteen squares and with times written at the bottom of each square. (3) Sixteen "clock" chips (made by placing gummed labels on gameboard chips and drawing a clock on the face of the label). (4) Markers.

Teaching Procedures: A caller holds up a clock face. The players must decide if the time shown by that clock is on their gameboard. If it is, the player places a marker in the square that contains the written form. The winner is the first person who completes a row in any direction and reads the time in each winning square.

■ **Coin Concentration**

Objective: To practice reading money amounts in four different notations and to reinforce coin recognition.

Grades: Primary, intermediate to high school (see adaptation for older students)

Prerequisite Behaviors: Coin value, value placement, coin recognition of dollars and cents

Materials: (1) Money picture card; (2) money-word card; (3) money-decimal card; (4) money-cents card.

Teaching Procedures: The game of coin concentration can be played at several levels of difficulty, with varying skill emphasis depending on specific classroom needs. At the simplest level, use only one kind of money card (make two copies of the card and cut apart on solid lines so students play with a total of twenty cards). Decide on the number and type of cards to be used, and place them face down on the table.

The first player turns over two cards, one at a time, trying to match values. If the cards match, the player keeps them. If not, he or she simply turns them back over on the table in their same location. Then the next player tries to make a match by turning over two more cards, and so on, until all the cards are matched with their pair.

The winner is the one with the most matched cards. For variety, ask the students to add the total value of their cards and the player with the highest value wins. To add variety and increase difficulty, put different type cards down and players can match 4¢ to $.04 or to *four cents*.

Adaptations: This activity can be used with older students by increasing the difficulty of the coin values represented and by adding a fifth card. On the fifth card is the name of an object that costs the corresponding amount. For example, if the money value is $329.00 the fifth card may have "Video Cassette Recorder" written on it.

■ **Shopping Spree**

Objective: To give students practice using money and understanding the concept of addition and subtraction with money.

Grades: Elementary-age students who are having difficulty with the money concepts. (See adaptations for use with older students.)

Materials: (1) Coins and dollar bills (when teaching the more advanced concepts); (2) pictures of items.

Teaching Procedures: Cut out magazine pictures of things children would like to buy and put a price on the pictures. Start with easy amounts, such as 5¢, 10¢, 25¢, and then in further lessons, increase the complexity of the amounts, to such things as 63¢, 51¢, etc. For higher grades, use of dollar bills can be implemented. Have the students divide into two groups and have half the groups be storeclerks, and have the other half be shoppers. The shoppers buy picture items from the clerk. The shoppers are responsible for giving the correct amount of money. The clerks are responsible for giving the correct change. Then the children trade places.

At a later date, specific amounts of money can be distributed and the children are to select several items without going over their designated amount. Also with a specific amount of money, show two or three different items and ask which item they can afford.

Adaptations: For older students, "pretend" checkbooks can be made and distributed. Each student is given a specified amount in his or her checkbook and must make appropriate deductions as he or she makes purchases.

■ **"99"**

Objective: To generalize and practice adding numbers in one's head or on paper.

Grades: Intermediate to high school

Materials: (1) Playing cards; (2) paper and pencils.

Teaching Procedures: Explain that the objective of this game is to add cards up to a score of 99. Establish the following rules:

> Jacks and Queens = 10
> Kings = 99
> Nines = "free turn" pass; to be used anytime
> Fours = pass
> Aces = 1
> Other cards = face value

Each player is dealt three cards. The rest of the cards go face down on a draw pile. The players take turns discarding one card from their hand face up on a discard pile and drawing one card from the draw pile to put back in their hand. As a player discards his or her card, he or she must add the number from the card to any previous score acquired up to that point in the game and give the new score out loud. Note the exception: If a player plays a nine, he or she receives a free-turn pass. If a player plays a four, he or she has to pass a turn with no score. The first player to score higher than 99 loses the game.

■ **Shopping**

Objective: To provide practice in addition, subtraction, and comparing prices (problem solving).

$3.00   .25¢ $25.00

Shopping List
1 lb hamburger
1 pkg buns
1/2 gallon milk
1 box cereal
1 dozen eggs
onions
vegetables
bread

MILK $1.09 $.98

$1.03 $1.27

Grades: Junior high

Materials: (1) Newspaper from which to cut out various supermarket sale ads that include price per item. Mount individual items on cardboard and cover them with clear plastic or just bring the ads; (2) made-up shopping lists to hand out to the class; (3) pencil and paper.

Teaching Procedures: Divide the class into small groups. Tell the students that their shopping list contains the items that they will need this week. Assign each group a designated amount for groceries (e.g., $30.00). The object is to buy everything on the list and spend the least. Place on each desk the supermarket sale ads each with the name of its store. After students buy their item they record the price and the store where they bought it. (It's easier if one student in each group buys the meats, one buys the dairy products, and so on.) When the students have bought all the items on the list, tell them to total their bills and be ready to present the results.

■ **Cake for Four—No, Make that Six!**

By Sandra Stroud

Objective: Developing students' *concept of fraction* by having them partition an object into equal parts.

Grades: Second through fourth grade (possibly higher)

Materials: For each student: (1) A 6-inch paper circle; (2) 5 strips construction paper—¼-inch wide by eight inches long, in a contrasting color to the paper circle; (3) 8 Teddy Grahams (or other small cookies), placed in a small sandwich bag.

Teaching Procedure: Students move desks together so that each has a partner with whom to compare his or her work. Materials are distributed. The teacher introduces the lesson by telling the students that they are going to take part in a *Let's Pretend* activity that will help them learn that when they eat a piece of cake that has been divided into equal parts they are actually eating a *fraction* of that cake.

The students are asked to imagine that they have just helped their mother (or other grown-up) bake a cake for their supper. It is their favorite kind of cake and, because there are four people in their pretend family, they are planning to divide it into four equal pieces. They are asked to think of the paper circle on their desk as the top of the cake, and to show the teacher—and their partners—how they would use the strips of paper to divide the cake into four equal parts. When each child has successfully demonstrated this first partitioning task, they are asked what fraction of the whole cake each piece is, and how that fraction is written.

Next, they are asked to imagine that their grandmother and grandfather have arrived unexpectedly and that the grandparents have accepted the family's invitation to stay for supper. The family certainly wants to share the cake with their grandparents, so into how many pieces will they now divide their cake? The teacher makes sure that each student shows six equal portions and that they understand that each piece of cake is now 1/6 of the whole—just enough for the six people at the dinner table. However, before that cake is served, Uncle Bob and Aunt Doris arrive! Now the cake will be divided into how many equal pieces? Finally, the time comes to decorate the cake with the Teddy Grahams and to cut and serve the cake. (As a reward for all their good thinking, the students now get to eat the decorations—1/8 at a time!)

Students enjoy the story associated with this activity, and they enjoy comparing their partitioned cakes with those of their peers. (This is a good example of cooperative learning.) They especially enjoy eating their cookies at the end of this activity.

■ The Values of Coins

By Ae-Hwa Kim

Objective: To help students learn the relative values of coins. For example, students will determine a quarter is worth 25 times as much as one cent.

Grade: Primary

Materials: Models with real coins for each step

Teaching Procedures: For the initial instruction, the teacher shows all models and coins and addresses the objective of the lesson. During the lesson, the teacher models and verbally explains each step, provides students with guided and independent practice, and gives them feedback.
  Steps to the objective:

1. Show students proportionate models to represent the values of coins.

1	1	1	1	1	1	1	1	1	1
1	1	1	1	1	1	1	1	1	1
1	1	1	1	1	1	1	1	1	1
1	1	1	1	1	1	1	1	1	1
1	1	1	1	1	1	1	1	1	1
1	1	1	1	1	1	1	1	1	1
1	1	1	1	1	1	1	1	1	1
1	1	1	1	1	1	1	1	1	1
1	1	1	1	1	1	1	1	1	1
1	1	1	1	1	1	1	1	1	1

2. Teach the values of coins and their relative values with models, which visually represent the values

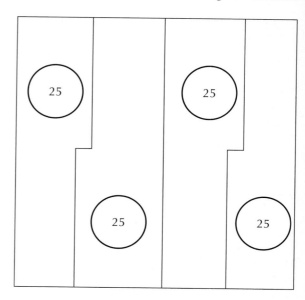

of coins and their relative worth. For example, one nickel is worth five pennies, and so takes up the space of five pennies.

3. Teach the value of a set of coins with models, which visually represent the value of a set of coins.
4. Teach the students to compare the values of sets of coins with models.

5. Teach the students to use models to create a set of coins with a given value. Allow students to use different combinations of coins to make the given value.
6. Teach the students to create a set of coins with a given value by using the fewest coins with models.

Source: Based on an activity by R. L. Drum and W. G. Petty, "Teaching the Value of Coins," *Teaching Children Mathematics,* 5(5) (1999): 264–268.

■ Learning Addition!

By Ae-Hwa Kim

Objective: To help students understand how to do addition with three-digit numbers and provide practice in addition through activities.

Grade: Primary

Materials: (1) Pictures of three animals; (2) three lengths of bricks (e.g., short, medium, long); (3) scratch paper.

Teaching Procedures:

1. Seat three volunteer "animals" (e.g., lion, donkey, and dog) on chairs side by side in front of a chalkboard. Hang a sign with a picture of each animal around the neck of the student who acts as that animal. The sign on the right (dog) also has the word *ones* or *1s,* signifying the units place of the number. The middle sign (donkey) shows the word *tens* or *10s,* signifying the tens place of the number. The sign on the left (lion) has the word *hundreds* or *100s,* signifying the hundreds place of the number. Throughout the activity, the place-value words are visible.
2. Give each animal a supply of bricks. Long bricks signify hundreds; medium bricks signify tens; and short bricks signify units. Give two long bricks to the hundreds lion, five medium bricks to the tens donkey, and eight short bricks to the ones dog. (First number = 258.)
3. Ask each animal to tell what he or she has been given, as the teacher writes the combined number on the chalkboard.

4. Teach students the rules to this activity.
   - All business exchanges begin with the ones dog, then the tens donkey, and finally the big boss hundreds lion. The animals receive their shipments in turn and take inventory of their bricks as they are received.
   - The inventory process ensures that the ones dog never has ten ones bricks (short), and the tens donkey never has ten tens bricks (medium); nor the hundreds lion, ten hundreds bricks (long; i.e., each animal's total is nine or less). If any animal has more than ten bricks, he or she must trade ten bricks for one brick of the next greater value.
5. The brick suppliers will arrive to deliver more bricks to each animal. For example, the supplier may bring four hundreds bricks, seven tens bricks, and three ones bricks. (Second number = 473.)
6. When the ones dog inventories 11 bricks, a teacher reminds him or her of the rules and establishes that he or she must deliver a stack of 10 short bricks back to the supplier in exchange for one medium brick, which must then be given to the tens donkey. The single short brick that remains is recorded on the chalkboard. When the 7 newly delivered medium bricks are added to the original 5 medium bricks and the medium brick passed from the ones dog, the tens donkey then has 13 medium bricks. Thus, he or she delivers one set of 10 bricks to the supplier in exchange for one long brick, which is then given to the hundreds lion. The tens donkey then reports an inventory of 3 medium bricks remaining. Our hundreds lion then reports a total inventory of 7 long bricks, or hundreds. (Final answer: 258 + 473 = 731)

Source: Based on an activity by M. M. Bartek, "Hands-on Addition and Subtraction with the Three Pigs," *Teaching Children Mathematics,* 4(2) (1997): 68–71.

■ Addition and America!

By Ae-Hwa Kim

Objective: To motivate students to solve addition problems as well as to increase their accuracy of solving problems.

Grade: Second through fourth grade (possibly higher)

Materials: (1) The map of the United States; (2) "tickets" made of cards on which math addition facts are printed.

Teaching Procedures:
1. Show students the map of the United States to get their attention.
2. **Show the map and explain the rules of game:**
   a. The students start from their home state to another state across the nation.
   b. Students have to have their ticket in order to travel from state to state.
   c. Students must solve the addition problem printed on the ticket and also read the name of the state. (The name of the state will be printed on the map, so students just need to read the word.)
   d. Only when students get the right answer are they allowed to move to the next state. If students miss the problem, they have to stay in their current state until their next trial time.
3. Let the students play a game. During the game, the teacher assists them and also records the speed and accuracy of their answers.

Note: This game can be extended to subtraction, multiplication, and division.

Source: Based on an activity by D. E. Miller, "Math Across America," *Teaching Exceptional Children, 24*(2) (1997): 47–49.

Grade: Primary

Materials: (1) Popsicle sticks; (2) rubber bands to group the ice cream sticks; (3) a sign; (4) number cards; (5) three boxes to hold 1s, 10s, and 100s of popsicle sticks.

Teaching Procedures:
Practice:
1. Count the number of popsicle sticks.
2. Model putting a rubber band around a group of 10 sticks; then ask students to put a rubber band around each new group of 10 sticks.
3. Model putting 1s in the 1s box, 10s in the 10s box, and so on. Ask students to put 1s in the 1s box, 10s in the 10s box, and so on.

Activity:
4. Show the students a sign that says "Thank you for the ___ popsicle sticks" (e.g., 157).
5. Model putting that number of popsicle sticks in the boxes; then ask students to put the number of popsicle sticks in the boxes.
6. Change the numbers on the sign over and over and allow students to practice grouping popsicle sticks according to the sign.

Source: Based on an activity by C. Paddock, "Ice Cream Stick Math," *Teaching Exceptional Children, 24*(2) (1997): 50–51

■ **The Value of Numbers**

By Ae-Hwa Kim

Lesson Objective: To help students understand the value of numbers (1s value, 10s value and 100's value).

SUMMARY

Developing appropriate mathematics instruction for students with learning and behavior problems involves comprehensive programming with an emphasis on its application to daily living skills. Special attention is given to factors that might influence the math learning abilities of special students. Psychological factors, educational factors, neuropsychological factors, perceptual skills, language skills, and reasoning need to be considered when developing a student's instructional program.

When developing comprehensive programming it is necessary to consider all facets of math instruction including: numeration, place value, facts, computation, time, money, fractions, and verbal problem solving. Success in teaching math is directly related to the student's ability to apply the concepts to math problems that occur in daily living.

Traditional math curricula have provided problems for students with learning and behavior problems. Often the reading level is difficult, the material is not sequenced, and there are not enough problems covering each concept so mastery can be assured before the next concept is introduced. These students need math problems to be directly linked to their real-world application.

Teaching math to students with learning and behavior problems is a challenge—potentially, a very rewarding challenge. Students with learning difficulties have evidenced greater gains through appropriate instruction in math than in most other content areas. Although students have access to computers and calculators which can assist them in solving math problems they understand, they must know what problems they want to solve, the operation needed, and the procedures for computing the answers before they can fully use these instruments to assist in solving problems. Because of the increased need to use mathematics at the workplace, students need to understand mathematics now more than ever before.

WEBISTES AS RESOURCES TO ASSIST IN TEACHING MATHEMATICS TO STUDENTS WITH LEARNING AND BEHAVIOR PROBLEMS

http://ericir.syr.edu/Virtual/Lessons/Mathematics/index/html
This Website contains math lesson plans and ideas (e.g., algebra, measurement, etc.)

http://www.ofcn.org/cyber.serv/academy/ace/math/elem.html
This Website contains math lesson plans and ideas (e.g., problem solving, geometry, multiplication, etc.)

http://www.ed.gov/pubs/parents/Math/index.html
This Website provides parents with instructional materials to increase math skills.

http://www.ldonline.org/ld_indepth/math_skills/math-1.html
This Website contains an overview of math difficulties of students with LD.

http://www.ldonline.org/ld_indepth/math_skills/adapt_cld.html
This Website contains information on instructional adaptation of mathematics for students with learning disabilities in regular classes.

http://www.ldonline.org/ld_indepth/math_skills/math_jld.html
This Website contains information on math instruction for secondary students with LD.

http://www.ldonline.org/ld_indepth/math_skills/mathld_mercer.html
This Website provides information on educational aspects of math difficulties (e.g., learner characteristics, effective strategies, etc.)

http://www.ldonline.org/ld_indepth/math_skills/coopmath.html
This Website contains information on cooperative learning in math instruction.

http://www.ldonline.org/ld_indepth/teaching_techniques/strategies.html#anchor1001355
This Website provides several useful links on math.

http://users.black-hole.com/users/rsch/indexnew.html
This Website provides worksheets for addition, subtraction, multiplication, division, and word problems.

http://www.edbydesign.com/parentres.html
This Website contains practical resources for mathematics.

http://www.awesomelibrary.org/Classroom/Mathematics/Mathematics.html
This Website contains a variety of resources on mathematics for students in K–12 (e.g., lesson plans, materials, projects, worksheets, etc.)

http://specialed.about.com/education/specialed/gi/dynamic/offsite.htm?site=http://www.schwablearning.org/main.asp%3Fpage=2.4.5
This Website introduces technology to help mathematics.

THINK AND APPLY

— What factors and learning difficulties might interfere with mathematics learning for students with learning and behavior problems?

— What are five important teaching perspectives that should be considered when designing a math intervention program for students with learning and behavior disorders?

— What are the mathematical skills that need to be taught so that students will have an adequate knowledge of numeration and place value?

— What are the strategies that can be taught to students who are having difficulty with basic math facts?

— How would you convince a fellow teacher that the use of calculators can be helpful when learning mathematics?

— What factors affect successful problem solving and what problem-solving strategy might be effective to assist students in becoming better math problem solvers?

— Why is it so important that learning disability teachers make use of concrete materials and stress the real-life application of math problems?

— Why are traditional math curricula and materials often inadequate for meeting the needs of students with learning disabilities?

9

Socialization and Classroom Management

OUTLINE

SOCIAL COMPETENCE AND SOCIAL DIFFICULTIES
Definitions of Social Competence
Perceptions of Students with Social Difficulties
Characteristics of Students with Social Disabilities
Social Difficulties Prevalent During Adolescence

INTERVENTION STRATEGIES
Interpersonal Problem Solving
Behavior Therapy
Mutual Interest Discovery
Principles for Teaching Social Skills
Classroom Management
Classroom Management and Student Behavior

Positive Behavioral Support

INSTRUCTIONAL ACTIVITIES

SUMMARY

WEBSITES AS RESOURCES TO ASSIST IN SOCIALIZATION AND CLASSROOM MANAGEMENT

THINK AND APPLY

KEY TOPICS FOR MASTERY

- *Social characteristics of students who have learning and behavior problems*
- *Externalizing behaviors and internalizing behaviors: two dimensions of the social interaction style of students with behavior disorders*
- *How the inactive learning style of students with learning disabilities translates to an inactive style of communication*
- *Low self-concept: an unfortunate trait of many students with learning and behavior problems*
- *Internal locus of control, external locus of control, and learned helplessness: how these concepts relate to student behavior*
- *Appropriate responses to adolescent suicide threats and attempts*
- *Nonverbal learning disability: why a student with this type of learning disability is particularly at-risk for suicide*
- *Symptoms of substance abuse in students*
- *Intervention programs that assist students with learning disabilities and behavior disorders in developing more positive and rewarding social skills and overall life satisfaction*

 BRIGHT IDEA

Turn to page 430 and read Think and Apply.

As Donna Douglas listened to her son, Jeff, playing with a classmate in his room, she closed her eyes and flinched as she heard him say, "That's not how you do it. I know how to do it, give it to me." She hoped the classmate would understand Jeff and not find her son's difficulty interacting with others so disagreeable that he would not return. Donna knew her son was not mean or cruel, but he had a difficult time communicating interpersonally with others. He had trouble making and maintaining friends. He didn't seem to know how to listen and respond to others, and often he expressed himself harshly and inconsiderately.

Mark's special education teacher's first comment to the school counselor was, "I feel let down. Mark and I had an agreement that I would give him free time at the end of the day if he brought a signed note from his regular classroom teachers that indicated his behavior was appropriate in class. After three days of signed notes and free time, I checked with his regular classroom teachers only to find out that Mark had his friends forge the teachers' initials. The teachers had not seen the note. Though this experience is discouraging, I comfort myself with the thought that two years ago Mark was incapable of spending even thirty minutes in a regular classroom without creating havoc. He has improved and he even has a friend in the regular classroom. It is comforting to know that despite periodic setbacks his social skills have gradually improved."

Jeff and Mark both have social skills difficulties. Many students with learning and behavior problems have difficulties in school, at home, and work because of their interaction with others. This chapter will help you understand the social characteristics of students who have learning and behavior problems. How these students are perceived by others and how they respond to others will be discussed. In addition, interventions you might use to improve the social behaviors of your students will be presented, along with programs and activities that may assist in teaching interpersonal social skills. The first issue to be discussed is social competence.

SOCIAL COMPETENCE AND SOCIAL DIFFICULTIES

Social difficulties often characterize students with behavior problems, but what about students with learning disabilities? Since many students with learning disabilities demonstrate difficulties with social skills, a definition of learning disabilities has been proposed that includes social skills deficits. The Interagency Committee on Learning Disabilities offers the following changes to the definition by the National Joint Committee for Learning Disabilities (NJCLD). Changes made to the NJCLD definition are italicized.

> *Learning disabilities* is a generic term that refers to a heterogeneous group of disorders manifested by significant difficulties in the acquisition and use of listening, speaking, reading, writing, reasoning, or mathematical abilities, *or of social skills*. These disorders are intrinsic to the individual and presumed to be due to central nervous *system* dysfunction. Even though a learning disability may occur concomitantly with other handicapping conditions (e.g., sensory impairment, mental retardation, social and emotional disturbance), *with socio*environmental influences (e.g., cultural differences, insufficient or inappropriate instruction, psychogenic factors), *and especially with attention deficit disorder, all of which may cause a learning problem, a learning disability* is not the direct result of those conditions or influences. (Kavanagh and Truss, 1988, 550–551)

This definition of learning disabilities has not been adopted by the U.S. Department of Education and is presently not used by school districts to identify youngsters. It does indicate, however, that many professionals perceive that the social disabilities of youngsters with learning disabilities should be considered as a manifestation of their disabling condition.

Understanding the social difficulties of students with learning and behavior problems begins with an understanding of social competence and the characteristics associated with it. This section discusses the social characteristics of students with learning disabilities along with a description of the social problems associated with adolescents.

Definitions of Social Competence

We have all met people who seem to know what to say and what to do no matter who they are with or what situation they are in. Sometimes we watch with envy as they move from person to person, group to group, sometimes listening, sometimes talking, but always seemingly at ease. We often refer to these people as *socially competent.*

According to Foster and Ritchey (1979), *social competence* is defined as ". . . those responses, which within a given situation, prove effective, or in other words, maximize the probability of producing, maintaining, or enhancing positive effects for the interactor" (p. 626) and, it should be added, without harm to others. Social skills are not a specific skill to be acquired, but rather a set of skills that allow one to adapt and respond to the expectations of society. Social competence is a process that begins at birth and continues throughout the life span. The process of social competence begins within the confines of our immediate family and expands to include extended family, friends, neighbors, and social institutions.

Vaughn and Hogan (1990) have described a model of social competence that is analogous to intelligence in that it describes social competence as a higher-order, global construct that is made up of many components. Their model of social competence includes the following four components:

1. *Positive relations with others.* This includes the ability to make and maintain positive relations with a range of people including classmates, teachers, parents, and at later ages, intimate relations. With students the focus is usually on peer, parent, and teacher relations.

2. *Accurate/age-appropriate social cognition.* This component includes how the child thinks about self and others, as well as the extent to which the child understands and interprets social situations. This component includes self-perceptions, social problem solving, attributions, locus of control, empathy, and social judgment.

3. *Absence of maladaptive behaviors.* This component focuses on the absence of behavior problems that interfere with social functioning such as disruptive behaviors, anxiety, attention problems, and lack of self-control.

4. *Effective social behaviors.* This includes the range of social behaviors that are often included in social skills intervention programs. These social behaviors include initiating contact with others, responding cooperatively to requests, and giving and receiving feedback.

The most discriminating characteristic of students with behavior problems is their lack of social competence. These students are referred for special education because of severe difficulty in adapting to society and interacting successfully with others. Whereas the common characteristic of students with learning disabilities is problems in learning, many students with learning disabilities are perceived by their peers and others as having social difficulties. Thus most students with behavior problems and many students with learning disabilities have difficulties with social skills.

Figure 9.1 provides suggestions for teachers in dealing effectively with minority students with behavior problems.

■ **FIGURE 9.1**   *Minority Students and Behavior Problems*

The behavior of minority students is often misunderstood by teachers and responded to inappropriately (Irvine, 1991; Morgan, 1980; Partington, 1998). Discipline problems and ultimately discouragement on the part of the minority student can result from frequent misunderstanding between teachers and students. Grossman (1995) has identified several considerations for teachers in dealing effectively with the behavior of minority students.

• The home and community often accept and encourage behaviors that may be incompatible with the behaviors in the school setting. Thus, students may receive conflicting messages between home and school about their behavior and may be forced to chose between loyalty to home and community or school. When teachers learn as much as they can about the behaviors that the home and community accept, the teacher may distinguish for the student what behaviors are acceptable in what settings. For example, aggressive and highly emotionally charged behavior may be expected of African American males at home and in their community, but unacceptable in the class setting. Many Hispanic students are viewed by teachers as dependent, passive, and reticent to participate and respond to the teacher. Yet, these behaviors are expected and nurtured in their home and community.

• The same behaviors that reflect problems with some students may not with students from other cultural groups. For example, African American students with internalizing problems may go unnoticed because it is expressed differently. Hispanic students may need help from the teacher, but may not ask for it, therefore, it may be necessary to check frequently with these students to determine if they need assistance, knowing they are unlikely to request assistance when needed. Fitting into the group for some African Americans may mean displaying aggressive and acting-out behavior.

• Some behaviors exhibited by students from different cultural groups may be wrongly attributed and interpreted by teachers. For example, some students who are English language learners may fail to respond, make limited eye contact with the teacher, or appear defiant because of their lack of confidence in using English. Also, some students from other cultures (e.g., Asian groups) are accustomed to clearly defined rules and regulations and may have difficulty interpreting rules that are more implicit.

Perceptions of Students with Social Difficulties

The social interaction of students with behavior disorders is often described as having two dimensions: externalizing and internalizing (Achenback, 1991; Achenback and Edelbrock, 1978). Externalizing behaviors are those behaviors that are extremely disturbing or intolerable to *others* (e.g., aggression, hyperactivity, delinquency). Conversely, internalizing behaviors are behaviors that are more likely to adversely affect the student displaying them rather than other people (e.g., depression, immaturity, obsessive-compulsive behavior, shyness).

Students with behavior disorders who exhibit externalizing behaviors appear to be experts at identifying and performing behaviors that are most disturbing to others. Donald, in the following example, is a student who exhibits externalizing behaviors.

When Mr. Kline discovered Donald was to be placed in his fourth-grade class next year, his stomach did a flip flop. "Any student but Donald," thought Mr. Kline, "he's the terror of the school." Every teacher who had Donald in class had come to the teachers' lounge at the end of the day exhausted and discouraged. The real catastrophe was the effect he seemed to have on the rest of the class. Students who were only mild behavior problems seemed to blossom with Donald's encouragement. Donald's hot temper and foul language left him continually fighting with other students. This year he had socked his teacher in the chest when she tried to prevent him from running out of the classroom. While escaping, he shouted, "I'll sue you if you touch me." As he was thinking of next year's plight, Mr. Kline saw Donald running full speed down the hall, knocking over students along the way, screeching as though he were putting on brakes as he turned into his classroom. Mr. Kline knew it was going to be a difficult year.

Students like Donald are frequently avoided by more socially competent students in class and are disliked and feared by other members. They are either loners who move from one group to the next after alienating its members or they develop friendships with other students whose behavior is also disturbing to others. These students are extremely difficult classroom management problems.

Students with behavior disorders who exhibit internalizing behaviors are often less disturbing to others but frequently concern others because of their bizarre behavior. Elisa, in the following example, is a student who exhibits internalizing behaviors.

Elisa, a fifth grader, was brought to the school office by her mother. Elisa's parents had just moved to the area and her mother brought Elisa to register for school but refused to speak with the school secretary. She demanded to register Elisa with the school principal. In meeting with the school principal, Elisa's mother told him Elisa would sometimes act "funny." She told the principal Elisa only acted that way to get attention and she should be told to "stop" as soon as she tried it. The principal noted that Elisa had not said one word. In fact, she had sat in a chair next to her mother looking down and rocking gently. Elisa's mother said she had been receiving special education services during part of the day and was in a regular classroom most of the day. In the regular classroom, Elisa was a loner. She spoke to no one. When another student approached her, she reared back and scratched into the air with her long nails, imitating a cat. If other children said something to her, she would "hiss" at them. She would sit in the room, usually completing her assignments and, whenever possible, practicing scrolling cursive letters with her multicolored pen. She spent most of the day rocking. She even rocked while she worked.

Problems like Elisa's are usually thought of as being internal and related to their own pathology. Other classmates, recognizing that these children are very different, may make attempts to be compatible, but they are usually rebuked. Students with internalizing behaviors are easy victims for students whose behaviors are more externalizing.

It is important to note that not all youngsters with behavior problems demonstrate either externalizing or internalizing problems. Many youngsters with behavior disorders display *both* externalizing and internalizing problems. Is this difficult to understand? Well, imagine a child who is often shy and withdrawn who, when frustrated or forced to interact with others, acts out and is aggressive.

Externalizing and internalizing behaviors are more frequently characteristics of students with behavior problems rather than students with learning disabilities. Students with learning disabilities typically display less severe emotional and behavior difficulties. However, many students with learning disabilities have difficulties making and maintaining positive interpersonal relationships with others.

When compared with their non-learning-disabled peers, students with learning disabilities are:

1. Inconsistent and less effective in displaying appropriate conversational skills (Hartas and Donahue, 1997).
2. Identified as being more poorly accepted by their peers (Bryan, 1974; Bryan 1976; Vaughn, Elbaum, and Schumm, 1996; Vaughn, McIntosh, and Spencer-Rowe, 1991; Wiener, Harris, and Shirer, 1990)
3. At greater risk for social alienation from teachers and classmates (Seidel and Vaughn, 1991)
4. Less frequently selected to play (Hutton and Palo, 1976)
5. Perceived as having lower social status (Stone and LaGreca, 1990)
6. Less accepted by peers even prior to being identified as learning-disabled (Vaughn, Hogan, Kouzekanani, and Shapiro, 1990)
7. More willing to conform to peer pressure to engage in antisocial activities (Bryan, Pearl, and Fallon, 1989; Farmer, Pearl, and VanAcker, 1996)
8. Less likely than other students to interact with teachers and classmates (McIntosh, Vaughn, Schumm, Haager, and Lee, 1993)

Unfortunately, the lowered social status of students with learning disabilities reflects not only the perceptions of peers but of teachers as well. Teachers perceive students with learning disabilities as less socially competent and less desirable to have in the classroom (Garrett and Crump, 1980; Juvonen and Bear, 1992; Keogh, Tchir, and Windeguth-Behn, 1974; Vaughn, Schumm, Jallad, Slusher, and Saumell, 1996). This negative perception of students with learning disabilities may be related to their academic problems. For example, in a study conducted by Juvonen and Bear (1992), teachers perceived socially adjusted students with learning disabilities as less socially competent than similarly adjusted non-learning-disabled. In this study, teachers perceived students negatively even though there were no significant differences between students with and without learning disabilities in the proportions of students accepted and rejected by peers.

One possible interpretation of the lowered social status of students with learning disabilities is that it is a reflection of how the teacher feels about them. The teacher's negative perception of a student with learning disabilities is conveyed to other students in the classroom, thus lowering the child's social status and how the child is perceived and responded to by peers. Some research suggests this may not completely explain the lowered social status of students with learning disabilities, since strangers, after viewing a few minutes of students' social interaction on videotapes, perceive students with learning disabilities more negatively than their non-learning-disabled peers (Bryan, Bryan, and Sonnefeld, 1982; Bryan and Perlmutter, 1979; Bryan and Sherman, 1980). Additionally, students who are later identified as learning disabled, as early as two months into their kindergarten year are already more often rejected and less frequently chosen as best friends than other students in the kindergarten class (Vaughn, Hogan, Kouzekanani, and Shapiro, 1990). Whereas teachers view students with learning disabilities more negatively than their non-learning-disabled peers, they are more favorably disposed toward having students with learning disabilities in their classroom than they are students identified as emotionally disabled or mentally retarded (Abroms and Kodera, 1979; Moore and Fine, 1978). Teachers regard students with emotional disabilities as the most disruptive and the most difficult students to work effectively within the regular classroom.

In general education classrooms where youngsters with learning disabilities are accepted by their teachers, they are also accepted by their peers (Vaughn, McIntosh, Schumm, Haager, and Callwood, 1993). In these classrooms students with learning disabilities were as well accepted and had as many mutual friends as other students.

The educational setting in which students are placed can affect the number of reciprocal friendships made and maintained by students. Reciprocal friends are when two students independently nominate each other as friends. For example, both Martha and Kathy write down each other's names on a list of friends. Low-achieving students, average-achieving students, and those with learning disabilities demonstrated an increased number of reciprocal friendships in inclusive settings. In these settings, the special and general education teachers co-planned, and the special education teacher provided a range of services in the classroom, such as working individually or with small groups of students with learning disabilities and leading lessons and demonstrating adaptations. However, students in classrooms where the special education teacher co-taught with the general education teacher for the entire day did not make similar gains (Vaughn, Elbaum, Schumm, and Hughes, 1998). This study suggests that a classroom climate of high acceptance and expectations can enhance mutual regard and acceptance of students with learning disabilities, and low-achieving students.

When discussing the social skills of students with learning disabilities and how they are perceived by others, it is important to realize we are talking about students with learning disabilities as a group. Not all students with learning disabilities have social difficulties. Whereas students with behavior disorders are characterized by deficits in social skills, many students with learning disabilities are socially competent, making and maintaining friends and struggling to please their teachers and parents. Many adults with learning disabilities who are participating in postsecondary education programs identify their social skills as their strengths.

An additional point to consider is that the findings on the social and behavioral functioning of youngsters with learning disabilities mostly reflect how they compare with their nondisabled peers. Recent studies that compare students with learning disabilities to their low-achieving classmates find few differences in their social or behavioral functioning (Vaughn, Haager, Hogan, and Kouzekanani, 1992; Vaughn, Zaragoza, Hogan, and Walker, 1993).

Characteristics of Students with Social Disabilities

We expect students with behavior disorders to have difficulty in successfully interacting with others. Students with behavior disorders are identified and placed in special programs because their social problems are so interfering that they are unable to function adequately with only the services provided by the regular classroom. Why is it that almost 75 percent (Kavale and Forness, 1996) of students with learning disabilities have difficulty developing and maintaining relationships with others? It may be because some students with learning disabilities display profiles of verbal difficulties that influence their academic and social performance. This is often referred to as a *verbal learning disability* (Rourke and Fuerst, 1992; Shapiro, Lipton, and Krivit, 1992). Figure 9.2 provides suggestions for creating a learning community that celebrates student differences.

Social Interaction

The type and quality of interactions that students with disabilities engage in are different from those of their non-learning-disabled peers. Students with learning disabilities are more likely to approach the teacher and ask questions (Dorval, McKinney, and Feagans, 1982; McKinney, McClure, and Feagans, 1982). Teachers interact almost four times as often with students with learning disabilities as with their peers; however, 63 percent of teachers' initiations towards students with learning disabilities involve managing their behavior (Dorval, McKinney, and Feagans, 1982). The interactions students with learning disabilities have with their teachers are often not appropriate to the situation. They impulsively attempt to display their knowledge, request more time to complete assignments, and request time to speak individually with the teacher to ask questions. Teachers report that questions from students with learning disabilities are inappropriate, as they often ask questions when the answer to the question was just stated.

■ **FIGURE 9.2** *Create a Learning Community That Celebrates Diversity*

- Students are children or adolescents first. Look beyond the ways students differ and respect their common needs and goals to be accepted, recognized, and valued members of the community. The classroom community is a primary source of students' perceptions of acceptance. Teachers' attitudes need to celebrate the diversity of students and at the same time recognize that students are more alike than different.

- Focus on abilities. Establish an environment where teachers and students seek and use knowledge about the abilities and expertise of all class members. Myrna Rathkin, a sixth-grade teacher, framed a picture of each student in a decorated star and hung them from the classroom ceiling. Attached to each star were lists of self- and teacher-identified strengths or abilities. All students were encouraged to recognize the knowledge and skills of their fellow students and to discover new ways their fellow students were special. When they did so, they would add them to the list of attributes under the individual's star.

- Celebrate diversity. Teachers can view students' differences as something to be tolerated, mildly ac-

cepted, or celebrated. Celebrating diversity means conveying to students the values added by having students as part of their learning community who have different learning styles, behavior profiles, physical abilities, languages, and cultural backgrounds. Sharon Andreaci, a sixth-grade teacher, was thrilled that many students she taught spoke Spanish and represented the cultural backgrounds of several Hispanic groups (e.g., Cuban, Nicaraguan, Columbian, Mexican). She often asked children about their backgrounds and encouraged them to share their knowledge and practices with others. She looked for ways to learn from others by asking such questions as, "Juan, how would you say that in Spanish? Anna, do you agree with Juan? Is there another way to say it in Spanish?"

- Demonstrate high regard for all students. Demonstrating high regard for all students means treating each one of them as special and extraordinary in their own way. It means not having "favorites" even if you think you disguise it. Listen carefully to each student and find something meaningful in what each student says.

Source: Adapted from S. Vaughn, C. S. Bos, and J. S. Schumm, *Teaching Mainstreamed, Diverse, and At-Risk Students in the General Education Classroom* (Boston: Allyn and Bacon, 1997).

Although classroom teachers spend more time with students with learning disabilities, the nature of the involvement during that time is not viewed positively by the teachers (Siperstein and Goding, 1985). One teacher describes it this way: "When Carlos raises his hand, I dread it. He usually asks me what he is supposed to do. I find myself trying to reexplain a thirty-minute lesson in five minutes. I'm sure he can tell I'm frustrated."

In one of the few studies conducted to examine general education teachers' behavior toward middle and high school students with learning disabilities (McIntosh, Vaughn, Schumm, Haager, and Lee, 1993), the findings indicated that middle- and high-school teachers do not treat students with learning disabilities differently from other students in the classroom. There is, of course, a positive and negative side to this finding. From a positive perspective teach-

ers treated all students fairly and impartially, and although praise was infrequently given, it was given at the same rate both to students with learning disabilities and students without learning disabilities. From a negative perspective, youngsters with learning disabilities interacted infrequently with the teacher, other students, and classroom activities, and teachers made few, if any adaptations, to increase the involvement or assure the learning of students with learning disabilities.

However, students with learning disabilities can be taught specific behaviors to increase positive teacher attention (Alber, Heward, and Hipple, 1999). Students with learning disabilities were taught to show their work to the teacher and ask questions such as, "How am I doing?" The results indicate that students received more positive teacher attention and instructional feedback. Furthermore, these students also completed their workbook assignments with increased accuracy. This study suggests that although students with learning disabilities often play a passive role in the classroom, they can be taught specific behaviors to actively solicit positive teacher attention. This is a simple but valuable tool special education teachers can use to assure that their students are displaying behaviors in general education classrooms to increase their likelihood for teacher acceptance and feedback.

Communication Difficulties

Expressing our ideas and feelings and understanding the ideas and feelings of others is an integral part of socialization. Adults and children with good social skills are able to communicate effectively with others, whereas students with learning and behavior problems frequently have trouble in this area. Torgeson (1982) describes the learning style of students with learning disabilities as inactive. An inactive learner is one who is passively involved in the learning process, does not attempt to integrate new information with previously learned information, and does not self-question or rehearse. It appears students with learning disabilities also demonstrate an inactive style during the communication process. While communicating with others, students with learning disabilities are less likely to make adaptations in their communication to accommodate the listener. When most of us speak with a young child, we make modifications in how we speak to them, such as using simpler words and asking questions to be sure they understand us. Many students with learning disabilities fail to make these modifications (Bryan and Pflaum, 1978; Soenksen, Flagg, and Schmits, 1981). When discussing the reading difficulties of students with learning disabilities, we talked about their difficulty in responding to ambiguous information in print. In much the same way, students with learning disabilities do not request more information when given ambiguous information through oral communication (Donahue, Pearl, and Bryan, 1980). They also have difficulty interpreting the emotions expressed by their social partner and identifying deceptive statements (Jarvis and Justin, 1992; Pearl, Bryan, Fallon, and Herzog, 1991). For example, students were presented with stories that

had sincere, deceptive, sarcastic, and neutral versions. Each story was followed by questions to determine the students' understanding of facts in the story, assessment of the speaker's belief, intent, and evidence used to determine the speaker's belief and intent. Students with learning disabilities were more likely to believe that the speaker was sincere but wrong, whereas non-learning-disabled peers were more likely to believe that the speaker was insincere (Pearl et al., 1991).

The student with learning disabilities is often a difficult communication partner who makes few adaptations to his or her audience, does not question inappropriate verbal statements, and does not "code switch," that is, pick up on what was said by the other. For example, boys with learning disabilities and normal-achieving boys were involved in a task in which they were asked to give essential information about a game of checkers (Knight-Arest, 1984). The adult they were supposed to give the information to claimed not to know how to play the game. As found in other studies, the communication skills of students with learning disabilities were less effective than those of normal-achieving students. Students with learning disabilities:

1. Talked more
2. Provided less information
3. Were more likely to use gestures and demonstrations
4. Were less able to respond to the needs of the listener

If the listener appeared confused, they were more likely to repeat the message without reformulating it. It is interesting to note that familiarity with one's partner positively affects the performance on communication tasks of students with learning disabilities, but has no impact for children without learning disabilities (Mathinos, 1987). Perhaps knowledge of one's partners serves as a motivator for students with learning disabilities to use the communication skills they have.

The communication style of students with learning disabilities appears to be egocentric. That is, they do not appear to be interested in the responses of their partner, and they demonstrate less shared responsibility for maintaining a social conversation (LaGreca, 1982; Mathinos, 1987). In a study of the friendship-making and conversation skills of boys with and without learning disabilities, LaGreca (1982) reports that the boys with and without learning disabilities did not differ in how to handle social situations (positive and negative), nor did they differ in their knowledge of how to make friends. Naive observers identified the boys with learning disabilities as less adept in social situations, as more egocentric and lacking in reciprocity in their conversations. The impression is that many students with learning disabilities display communication styles that suggest they are just waiting for the speaker to stop rather than being interested in what the speaker is saying.

Individuals with learning disabilities are less able to display interpersonal decentering (Horowitz, 1981) and less able to take on an alternative viewpoint (Dickstein and Warren, 1980; Wong and Wong, 1980). We know from the communication skills of populations with learning disabilities that they are less likely to make adjustments in their communication with others. It could be that their difficulty taking on the role of the "other" influences both their social relationships with others and their ability to communicate successfully with others.

Since students with learning disabilities are frequently rejected by peers, it could be that this communication pattern is sufficiently frustrating to others that they find the student with learning disabilities an undesirable social partner.

Stone and LaGreca (1984) compared students with and without learning disabilities on their ability to comprehend nonverbal communication. Their findings indicated that when attention is controlled for with students with learning disabilities by reinforcing their attendance to the social cues given, they perform as well as their non-learning-disabled peers. These authors suggest that the attention problems of students with learning disabilities often appear as poor social skills.

Problem Solving

Students with learning disabilities often demonstrate difficulties involving their ability to perceive, inter-

pret, and process social information (Rudolph and Luckner, 1991), which in turn leads to inappropriate social responses and poor social problem-solving skills. For example, when students were presented vignettes depicting an age-appropriate dilemma, students with learning disabilities performed below average in defining a problem and generating effective solutions (Shondrick, Serafica, Clark, and Miller, 1992). Tur-Kaspa and Bryan (1994) compared the social information processing and social problem-solving skills of elementary and middle school students with learning disabilities with low-achieving and average-achieving students. Results indicated that students with learning disabilities demonstrated an increased tendency to select incompetent self-generated solutions to social situations. Similarly, adolescents with learning disabilities were found to experience difficulties generating solutions to interpersonal problems (Hartas and Donahue, 1997). Hence, asking students to generate solutions to problems and discussing the consequences of each of the solutions may help students in developing their own ideas about solutions to problems. Additionally, it may help students choose more appropriate solutions for specific situations after taking into account the consequences of those solutions. All students will benefit from activities designed to help them generate solutions to specific problems and connecting the effectiveness of the solutions to their consequences.

Aggression

Many children with severe behavior disorders are characterized by aggressive behavior. *Aggressive behaviors* include assaultiveness, fighting, temper tantrums, quarrelsomeness, ignoring the rights of others, negative tone of voice, threatening, and demands for immediate compliance. Apply the Concept 9.1 describes five types of aggressive behavior. Aggression does not go away without treatment and is related to such negative outcomes as alcoholism, unpopularity, aggressive responses from others, academic failure, and adult antisocial behaviors. Specific skills for teaching students to deal more effectively with their aggressive responses is an important component of social skills programs for students with behavior disorders.

APPLY THE CONCEPT 9.1

AGGRESSION AND PEER ACCEPTANCE

In a study conducted by Lancelotta and Vaughn (1989) five types of aggressive behavior and their relation to peer social acceptance were examined. The five types of aggression were:

Provoked Physical Aggression—A youngster who attacks or fights back following provocation from another. An example is a student who hits someone back after being hit by that person.

Outburst Aggression—A youngster who responds in an uncontrollable, outburst manner without apparent provocation. Outburst aggression may or may not be directed at another person. An example is a student who gets angry and throws a fit.

Unprovoked Physical Aggression—A youngster who attacks or acts aggressively toward another person without provocation. An example is a student who starts a fight for no reason.

Verbal Aggression—A youngster who says verbally aggressive things to another person in order to attack or intimidate them. An example is a student who threatens to beat up another.

Indirect Aggression—A person who attacks or attempts to hurt another indirectly so that it is not likely to be obvious who did it. An example is a student who tells the teacher that another student does bad things.

The study demonstrated that girls are less tolerant of all types of aggression than are boys. Also, there was a negative relationship between peer acceptance and subtypes of aggression, with the exception of provoked aggression for boys. This means that boys who fight back when they are attacked first by other boys are not any more likely to be poorly accepted. This, however, is not true for girls who fight back when they are attacked. All of the other subtypes of aggression are related to poor peer acceptance.

Appearance

Appearance may be a more important factor influencing the social status of students with learning difficulties than was previously thought. In a study evaluating the social status, academic ability, athletic ability, and appearance of students with learning disabilities (Siperstein, Bopp, and Bak, 1978), researchers found that whereas academic and athletic ability were significantly related to peer popularity, the correlation between physical appearance and peer popularity was twice as great as the other two.

Two children from a study (Vaughn, Lancelotta, and Minnis, 1988) illustrate this point. Chris was a fourth-grade student with learning disabilities who worked as a model for children's clothing in a large department store. Her position gave her access to the latest children's fashions and she was well recognized by both girls and boys in her class as attractive. She ranked first when sociometric data asking peers to rate the extent to which they liked others in the classroom were analyzed. Her best friend, Carmen, who was also identified as learning-disabled, ranked second from the bottom by her classmates on the same sociometric test. In looking at the tests of social skills administered to these students, there was little difference between the scores of Chris and Carmen.

In another study, 35 percent of junior high students with learning disabilities exhibit some problem in grooming, neatness of clothing, posture, and general attractiveness, as compared with 6 percent of the junior high students without learning disabilities. (Schumaker, Wildgen, and Sherman, 1982). Bickett and Milich (1987) found boys with learning disabilities were rated as less attractive than boys without learning disabilities. Since appearance is highly related to popularity, it could be helpful to give feedback and pointers to students who display problems with appearance. Many students with behavior disorders display atypical appearance as a means of demonstrating identification with a group or gang. These students may wear their hair or clothing in nonconforming ways in order to let others know their allegiance. This style may be highly accepted by a particular group and highly rejected by others. These nonconforming appearances often become stylish, as did styles of the punk-rock movement in the late seventies and early eighties.

Attention Problems/Hyperactivity

Attention deficits and hyperactivity are characteristics often observed in students with learning and behavior disorders. In fact, according to one study, 25 to 68 percent of students with Attention Deficit Disorder are also identified as learning disabled (McKinney, Montague, and Hocutt, 1993). Students with attention deficits frequently display a pattern of inattention, while students with hyperactivity often exhibit patterns of impulsivity; these patterns are evident in a variety of contexts including home and school.

In the classroom, inattention is manifested in a failure to pay attention to details, careless mistakes, messy work, and difficulty in persisting with a task until completion (American Psychiatric Association, 1994). Hyperactivity may be exhibited through fidgetiness, inability to engage in quiet activities, blurting out answers, and excessive talking (American Psychiatric Association, 1994).

Students with attention deficits and/or hyperactivity may be treated with medication. Several stimulant medications (e.g., Dexedrine, Ritalin) are available to help students to focus by adjusting those parts of the brain that regulate attention, impulse control, and mood (Hallowell and Ratey, 1995). As with any medication, unwanted side effects may occur. Some of the side effects of stimulant medications include facial tics, loss of appetite, and difficulty sleeping (Swanson et al., 1993). Some children respond with unpleasant physical symptoms, and are affected by the drugs in some settings but not others. Most children who receive medication for hyperactivity are under the care of a physician whom they see infrequently. Thus the monitoring of the effectiveness of the drug is often the responsibility of parents and teachers. Perhaps the most effective technique for monitoring the effects of the drug is through behavior management. The teacher identifies and defines specific behaviors that are indicative of hyperactivity and then charts the occurrence of these behaviors. Whereas medication may be necessary for some children, attempts to treat the student's learning disability through changing his or her hyperactivity have not been very successful (Routh, 1979).

A learning characteristic frequently associated with hyperactivity is *selective attention,* which is the ability to attend to relevant information and ignore irrelevant information (Hallahan, Tarver, Kauffman, and Graybeal, 1978; Pinel, 1993). This characteristic occurs in children with learning disabilities about two years later than in normal children (Tarver, Hallahan, Kauffman, and Ball, 1976; Tarver, Hallahan, Cohen, and Kauffman, 1977). The delayed development of selective attention with populations with learning disabilities may be related to the conceptual tempo of students with learning disabilities, which is more impulsive than reflective. A more reflective conceptual tempo is associated with success in academic subjects such as reading and math, whereas a more impulsive tempo is associated with learning difficulties. One characteristic of impulsive responders is that they do not stop and think before responding. Students with learning disabilities demonstrate symptoms very similar to those of students with some behavior disorders and are at risk for demonstrating a number of other difficulties (Goldstein, 1995; Merrell and Stein, 1992). Recent interest has focused on the overlap between learning disabilities and attention deficit disorder. Students with learning disabilities displayed significantly more attention problems, but not conduct problems or anxiety, than average achievers (LaGreca and Stone, 1990). In a study conducted by Lambert and Sandoval (1980), 40 percent of the elementary children with attention problems also met stringent criteria for the presence of a learning disability. Since students with attention problems are at high risk for also demonstrating difficulties with their peers, it is important to evaluate the presence (or absence) of attention problems with children with learning disabilities prior to initiating social interventions.

Self-Concept

What we think of ourselves and how we view ourselves is highly related to our comparison group. Thus, it is not surprising that students with learning and behavior difficulties often have poor self-concepts. When, however, students perceive their disability in more positive terms, they also tend to report more positive global self-concepts (e.g., Rothman and Cosden, 1995). These students are aware of how their learning performance compares with others. There is some evidence that students with learning difficulties make higher gains in self-esteem and perception of their abilities when they are placed in special education classes (Battle and Blowers, 1982; Beltempo and Achille, 1990; Vaughn, Elbaum, and Schumm, 1996), whereas other research suggests the special education placement has not significantly affected either self-concept or peer acceptance (Whinnery, 1995). Students with learning disabilities who also experience reading difficulties view themselves more negatively than do students with learning disabilities and normal reading scores (Black, 1974) and older students with learning disabilities view themselves more negatively than do younger students with learning disabilities. In an attempt to interpret the sometimes conflicting results of studies, Morrison (1985) demonstrated that two factors significantly influence self-perception with students with learning disabilities: type of classroom placement (e.g., self-contained, regular classroom) and what aspect of self-perception is being evaluated (e.g., academic, social, behavioral, or anxiety-laden). When achievement is controlled, for example, there are no differences in self-perception measures between students with learning disabilities in resource rooms and self-contained settings (Yauman, 1980).

The self-concept of youngsters with learning disabilities was evaluated prior to and following identification as learning disabled. When compared with classmates without learning disabilities, the self-concept of students with learning disabilities was not significantly lower either before or after identification (Vaughn, Haager, Hogan, and Kouzekanani, 1992). This suggests that placement in a special education resource room had no negative effects on their self-concept.

The self-perceptions of students with learning disabilities have been surprisingly accurate. In general they rate themselves as low on academic ability (Chapman and Boersman, 1980) and like other children on overall feelings of self-worth (Bear, Clever, and Proctor, 1991; Bryan, 1986). They identify reading and spelling as the academic areas in which they are lower than other children and yet perceive themselves as being relatively intelligent (Kloomok and Cosden, 1994; Renik, 1987). A longitudinal study of students with learning disabilities suggests that they may differ from low-achieving students in that they do not become more negative about themselves as they grow older (Kistner and Osborne, 1987).

However, students who excel in extracurricular activities such as sports or music demonstrate levels of self-concept similar to those of average-achieving students (Kloomok and Cosden, 1994). Teachers and parents need to be aware of the effects of learning and behavior difficulties on self-concept and provide opportunities for students to demonstrate and recognize their abilities. Teachers and parents can provide opportunities for students to demonstrate what they do well and provide encouragement in the areas of difficulty. One parent described it this way: "The best thing that happened to my son is swimming. We knew from the time Kevin was an infant that he was different from our other two children. We were not surprised when he had difficulties in school and was later identified as learning-disabled. His visual motor problems made it difficult for him to play ball sports so we encouraged his interest in swimming. He joined a swim team when he was six and all his friends know he has won many swimming awards. No matter how discouraged he feels about school, he has one area in which he is successful."

Teachers may want to discuss with students the nature of their learning and behavior difficulty and how it affects their performance in specific situations. Assisting students in identifying and predicting how they might respond in situations allows them to prepare for the situation and develop strategies for more successfully dealing with it.

Locus of Control and Learned Helplessness

Persons with an *internal locus of control* view events as controlled largely by their own efforts, whereas persons with an *external locus of control* interpret the outcome of events as due largely to luck, chance, fate, or other events outside of their own influence. Attributing success to external factors and failures to lack of personal ability fosters an external locus of control (Perry, 1999). Locus of control proceeds along a continuum, with learning- and behavior-disordered children frequently having a high external locus of control, unable to view the cause of events as related to their own behavior. For this reason, they are not motivated to change events that are undesirable to them because they feel there is little they can do to improve the situation.

Mrs. Mulkowsky, a junior high learning disabilities teacher, said, "My students act as though there is nothing they can do to improve their grades in their regular classes. They feel they are unable to succeed in most of these classes, and they give up. They come to my class, sit down, and expect me to tutor them in their regular classes. They act as though it is *my* responsibility. These students are actually the ones who are still working; others have given up entirely and expect little from themselves and little from me."

When students with learning disabilities were compared with two other groups of students without learning disabilities, students with learning disabilities were more likely to interpret positive results as luck than were either of the other two groups (Sobol, Earn, Bennett, and Humphries, 1983). This suggests that when students with learning disabilities perform well, they are less likely to attribute it to their own effort and therefore may be less likely to maintain the effort that produced the positive outcome. In contrast, students with learning disabilities do attribute their failures to being within their own control and not to external factors outside of their control (Dudley-Marling, Snider, and Tarver, 1982). When students with learning disabilities are compared with behavior-disordered students and students who are both learning-disabled and behavior-disordered on three dimensions of locus of control: intellectual, social, and physical (Morgan, 1986), students with learning

disabilities had higher internal locus of control on all three dimensions than did the other two groups. The students with learning disabilities and behavior disorders had the most external scores on all three dimensions of locus of control.

It could be that students with learning disabilities have difficulties in social situations because they fail to realize that successful interaction with others can be influenced by their behavior. To assist students in developing an internal locus of control, teachers need to show students the relationships between what they do and its effect on others and reciprocally on themselves. Giving students ownership of their tasks and behavior and teaching them to set their own goals are first steps toward increasing their internal locus of control (Cohen, 1986). Also, teachers may want to interview children to learn more about their locus of orientation (Lewis and Lawrence-Patterson, 1989). Borkowski and colleagues (Borkowski, Weyhing, and Carr, 1988; Borkowski, Weyhing, and Turner, 1986) have used attributional training paired with specific strategy training (e.g., in the area of reading) to influence students' use and generalization of strategies. Attributional training helps the student see the role of effort in academic success or strategy use. Reasons for not doing well that do not relate to controllable factors are discouraged. Students are encouraged to see the relationship between strategy use and success, "I tried hard, used the strategy, and did well" (Borkowski, Weyhing, and Carr, 1988, p. 49).

The concept of *learned helplessness* was introduced by Seligman (1975) to explain the response animals and humans have when exposed to a number of trials in which they are unable to influence the outcome. When subjects learn there is no relationship between what they do and their ability to impact the environment or reach their goal, they give up and respond passively. Although learned helplessness, or the perceived inability to influence a situation, may be situation-specific, it often generalizes to other learning situations. For example, when a student with learning disabilities and severe reading problems approaches a reading task, the student is frequently unable to reach his or her goal—being able to read the passage successfully. Whereas the student may initially be very persistent in attempting to read, the student who meets with continued failure learns his or her attempts are useless and there is nothing he or she can do to impact the situation, thus the individual responds as though he or she is "helpless."

Many students with learning problems act is if they have learned helplessness (Thomas, 1979). Learned helplessness leads to lowered self-concept, lethargy, reduction in persistence, and reduced levels of performance. There is a remarkable resemblance between the descriptions of learned helplessness and the observations of special education teachers about students with learning disabilities and behavior disorders. "Learning-disabled children have been portrayed as no longer able to believe that they can learn" (Thomas, 1979, p. 209).

The concepts *learned helplessness* and *locus of control* are highly related. Students who have a feeling of learned helplessness toward a particular academic task perceive there is nothing they can do to impact their ability to perform the task successfully. It is also likely they view results from their "work" on that task as "external" and not related to what they do. Thus there is a high correlation between learned helplessness and external locus of control. Apply the Concept 9.2 describes what teachers might be able to do to affect learned helplessness and locus of control.

Social Difficulties Prevalent During Adolescence

In addition to the characteristics of students with learning and behavior disorders discussed earlier, several difficulties are prevalent during adolescence that may affect students with special needs. These are social alienation, suicide, anorexia nervosa, and drug and alcohol abuse.

Social Alienation

Social alienation is the extent to which youngsters feel they are part of or have an affinity for the school or the people in the school. Social alienation has been interpreted to refer to alienation from teachers or peers (Seidel and Vaughn, 1991). The notion of alienation has been linked with school dropouts in that youngsters who are socially alienated from their teachers or peers are more at risk for leaving school than are those who are not (Finn, 1989). Not surprising, social alienation begins early in the youngsters' school career but is most obvious during adolescence. According to Seidel and Vaughn (1991) students with learning disabilities who dropped out of school differed from those who did not on such items as: "I thought of my teachers as friends," "The thing I hated most about school was my teachers," and "Most of my teachers liked me." Students with learning disabilities who dropped out also felt that their classmates "would not have missed them if they moved away," and they did not look forward to seeing their friends at school. Interestingly, these students did not differ on their academic achievement scores but did differ on the extent to which they felt they were socially accepted and liked by their teachers and classmates.

Social alienation is often associated with loneliness. Different school environments trigger feelings of loneliness in students depending on the individual student's temperament. For example, Asher, Gabriel, and Hopmeyer (1993) found that aggressive students reported the highest levels of loneliness in classroom settings, whereas students described as withdrawn reported increased levels of loneliness in less structured contexts, such as the playground or lunch room (Asher et al., 1993). Thus, as a teacher it is important to realize that students who are more withdrawn will need additional support in less structured settings to be comfortable. It may be useful to rehearse with them what they can do or to assist them in establishing routines with which they are comfortable in these settings. Pavri and Monda-Amaya (2000) interviewed fourth and fifth grade students with learning disabilities to determine their experience with school-related loneliness and which coping strategies students used, and to determine intervention strategies perceived as useful by students. Students indicated self-initiated and peer-initiated strategies to be most helpful followed closely by teacher-initiated strategies.

What can teachers do so students feel less socially alienated?

- Try for a small class size that encourages all students to participate.
- Set the tone in the class that all students are valuable and have something important to contribute.

APPLY THE CONCEPT 9.2

*HOW TEACHERS MIGHT AFFECT LEARNED HELPLESSNESS
AND LOCUS OF CONTROL*

In order to reduce the impact of learned helplessness and external locus of control on students' behavior, teachers may want to:

1. Offer process-directed praise or criticism (Dweck and Kamins, 1999) such as, "This paper is clearly written," or, "You really concentrated and finished this biology assignment." Focus on the activity the students are engaged in such as reading, writing, art, and avoid person-directed praise or comments such as, "You are good in biology." This will help reduce the amount of external reinforcement needed and instead reinforce student performance.

2. Reduce the amount of external reinforcement and focus on reinforcing student performance. Rather than saying, "Good work" or "Excellent job," focus on the behaviors, such as, "You really concentrated and finished this biology assignment. You needed to ask for help but you got it done. How do you feel about it?"

3. Link students' behaviors to outcomes. "You spent ten minutes working hard on this worksheet and you finished it."

4. Provide encouragement. Because they experience continued failure, many students are discouraged from attempting tasks they are capable of performing.

5. Discuss academic tasks and social activities in which the student experiences success.

6. Discuss your own failures or difficulties and express what you do to cope with these. Be sure to provide examples of when you persist and examples of when you give up.

7. Encourage students to take responsibility for their successes. "You received a B on your biology test. How do you think you got such a good grade?" Encourage students to describe what they did (e.g., how they studied). Discourage students from saying, "I was lucky," or, "It was an easy test."

8. Encourage students to take responsibility for their failures. For example, in response to the question, "Why do you think you are staying after school?" encourage students to take responsibility for what got them there. "Yes, I am sure Billy's behavior was hard to ignore. I am aware that you did some things to get you here. What did you do?"

9. Structure learning and social activities to reduce failure.

10. Teach students how to learn information and how to demonstrate their control of their learning task.

11. Teach students to use procedures and techniques to monitor their own gains in academic areas.

— Take a moment between classes to ask about students and demonstrate you care.

— Allow students to participate in decision making regarding class rules and management.

— Identify youngsters who demonstrate uninvolvement and/or detachment and refer them to the counselor.

— Encourage students to participate in school-related extracurricular activities.

— Ask students who are lonely if there is a person in the class they like and seat them nearby.

— Try grouping students into small groups or pairing students during activities.

— Provide students with activities to engage in with peers (e.g., hide and go seek) during less structured times such as recess and lunch. Encourage students to play together.

Suicide

Two Leominster, Massachusetts, teenagers died in a shotgun suicide pact next to an empty bottle of champagne, after writing farewell notes that included "I love to die I'd be happier I know it! So please let me go. No hard feelings" (*The Boston Herald*, November 10, 1984, p. 1). Although the autopsy showed high levels of alcohol in the girls' bloodstreams, there were no indications that either girl was involved with drugs or was pregnant. It appeared as though both girls willingly participated in the suicide act. In another note left by one of the girls, she wrote, "I know it was for the best. I can't handle this sucky world any longer" (*The Boston Herald,* November 10, 1984, p. 7). The cause of the suicide pact is unknown.

After being forbidden to see each other, a 14-year-old-boy and a 13-year-old-girl ran away. Shortly thereafter, the two leaped into a river and drowned (*Miami Herald,* November 9, 1995, p. 10).

Suicide of a child or adolescent is a shocking event. Suicides between birth and the age of 15 are termed *childhood suicides.* Between 15 and 19 they are referred to as *adolescent suicides.* Many deaths of adolescents are viewed as accidents and not reported as suicide; therefore, the statistics on adolescent suicide are meaningless (Toolan, 1981). However, suicide is one of the top three causes of death for persons under 24 years of age. There is agreement, however, that the rate of adolescent suicide is on the rise (Cimbolic and Jobes, 1990; Henry, Stephenson, Hanson, and Hargett, 1993; Popenhagen and Qualley, 1998), and that female attempts at suicide greatly outnumber male (Hawton, 1982); however, male attempts are more frequently successful.

The suicide attempts of adolescents can frequently be explained by one or more of the following factors:

1. Relief from stress or from stressful situations
2. A demonstration to others of how desperate they are
3. An attempt to hurt or get back at others
4. An attempt to get others to change (Wicks-Nelson and Israel, 1984)

Suicide attempts most frequently occur following interpersonal problems with boyfriends or girlfriends, parents, or teachers (Wannen and Fombonne, 1998). Often these relationships have had prolonged difficulties. Disturbed peer relationships are a large contributing factor to suicide attempts. Adolescents feel unique, as if there are no solutions to their problems. In addition, adolescents often feel responsible for their problems and are unlikely to seek assistance,

thus, leaving them isolated (Culp, Clyman, and Culp, 1995). "Life is a chronic problem. There appears no way out. Solutions previously tried have failed. To end the chronic problem, death appears to be the only way left" (Teicher, 1973, p. 137 in Sheras, 1983).

"Suicidal patients are often very difficult because they so frequently deny the seriousness of their attempts" (Toolan, 1981, p. 320). They often make comments such as, "It was all a mistake. I am much better now." Even though they may attempt to discount the attempt, it should be treated with extreme seriousness.

Early detection of students at risk for suicide can help in providing services and reducing the risk. Students contemplating suicide may provide subtle verbal clues such as, "don't bother grading my test, because by tomorrow it really won't matter what I got on it" (Guetzloe, 1989; Hicks, 1990; Kalafat, 1990; Popenhagen and Qualley, 1998). Hopelessness may be the best indicator of risk for suicide (Beck, Brown, and Steer, 1989). Other variables that are related to suicide include depression, flat affect, an emotion-laden event, and isolation. Sheras (1983) discusses the following general considerations when dealing with adolescent suicide attempts:

1. All suicide attempts must be taken seriously. Do not interpret the behavior as merely a plea for "attention." Do not try to decide whether the attempt is real or not.
2. Develop or reestablish communication with the person. Suicide is a form of communication from a person who feels he or she has no other way to communicate.
3. Reestablish emotional or interpersonal support. Suicide is an expression of alienation and the person needs to be reconnected with significant others.
4. Involve the adolescent in individual and/or family therapy. Often the adolescent feels unable to establish communication with a significant person (e.g., a parent) and needs assistance from another to do so.
5. Work with the youngster to identify the problem or problems and provide realistic practical solutions to the problems.

6. Devise a "no-kill contract" that requires a student to promise in writing to not inflict harm upon him- or herself. Students who have agreed to such a contract tend to find it more difficult to follow through with plans of suicide (Pfeffer, 1986).

Rourke and colleagues (Rourke, Young, and Leenaars, 1989) identify a specific subtype of learning disabilities as being at risk for depression and suicide. This subtype is referred to as *nonverbal learning disability* and includes such characteristics as: bilateral tactile-perceptual deficits, bilateral psychomotor coordination problems, severe difficulties in visual-spatial-organizational abilities, difficulty with nonverbal problem solving, good rote verbal capacities, and difficulty adapting to novel and complex situations. Fletcher (1989) urges that students with nonverbal learning disabilities be identified early and treated. Since verbal skills are highly valued, particularly in school settings, it is likely that many students with nonverbal learning disabilities go unnoticed.

Eating Disorders

Eating disorders may take a variety of forms, and different definitions exist (Button, 1993; Tylka and Subich, 1999). Central to each definition, however, is the presence of abnormal patterns of behavior and thought related to eating (American Psychiatric Association, 1994). Levine (1987) indicates that these patterns include:

1. A person's health and vigor reduced or threatened by his or her eating habits
2. Obligations to self and others affected by isolation and secretiveness related to eating problems
3. Emotional instability and self-absorption associated with food and weight control
4. Persistence of dysfunctional eating habits despite warnings that they are affecting the person's health and functioning

Interestingly, eating disorders are not fundamentally about eating, but are multidetermined and multidimensional reflections of the person's disturbance (Ashby, Kottman, and Shoen, 1998). Eating disorders

are much less prevalent among males, with more than 90 percent of cases of bulimia or anorexia nervosa occurring in females (American Psychiatric Association, 1994).

The highest incidence is in females between the ages of 15 and 24, and it occurs most frequently in higher socioeconomic levels (Jones, Fox, Haroutun-Babigian, and Hutton, 1980). Characteristics associated with anorexia include:

1. Loss of menstrual cycle
2. Sensitivity to cold
3. Sleep disturbance
4. Depression

Characteristics associated with bulimia include:

1. Loss of dental enamel
2. Low self-esteem
3. Anxiety
4. Depression

Because our society places a premium on thinness, exercise, and dieting, the symptoms of eating disorders are often overlooked or not recognized soon enough. The target person insists on remaining thin and does not perceive that she or he has a problem.

Why someone would deliberately starve herself or himself is puzzling. In attempting to unravel the mystery of eating disorders, researchers have examined several factors that may contribute to the disease, including biological factors, such as malfunctioning of the hypothalamus; and psychodynamic factors, such as an enmeshed family which makes it difficult for the adolescent to express individual identity; thus, the adolescent's refusal to eat becomes a form of rebellion. There is little doubt that a combination of these biological and psychological factors contributes to anorexia and bulimia.

Drug and Alcohol Abuse

Parents probably fear nothing more than the possibility their child will abuse drugs. With the increase in drug availability and use in the early to mid-1960s, parents became aware of the numbers of adolescents using drugs. There is a great deal of media attention focusing on the consequences of drug use. Stories of youngsters from stereotypically "normal" families becoming addicted to drugs and committing crimes to maintain their habits are featured in magazines and newspapers across the country.

Parental concerns about the availability and use of drugs among adolescents seem to have strong support. According to a summary by Wicks-Nelson and Israel (1984) of reports from the Department of Justice (1980) and the FBI (1980), 90 percent of a sample of high-school seniors reported that marijuana was very easy or fairly easy to get. Some 59 percent said the same thing about amphetamines and 49.8 about barbiturates. Availability of drugs is not the only concern. According to the 1990 National Household Survey on Drug Abuse, 48 percent of adolescents (aged 12 to 17 years) had used alcohol at least once; 40 percent had used cigarettes; 15 percent had used marijuana and hashish, and 8 percent had used inhalants.

The pattern of drug and alcohol consumption is the most important issue. Typically the pattern is conceptualized along five points: nonusers, experimenters, recreational users, problem users, and addicts (Krug, 1983).

Since daily marijuana use is second only to cigarette use, teachers need to be familiar with some of the outcomes of marijuana use so they can identify and counsel users. Users may have these adverse psychological effects:

1. Occasional anxiety and suspiciousness
2. Impairment of immediate memory recall
3. Long-term memory disorders
4. Loss of goal-related drive
5. Inability to think and speak clearly
6. Lung damage
7. Increased risk for certain types of cancer
8. Flashbacks
9. Possible suppression of the immune system

It is quite difficult to use characteristics from checklists to identify drug users. Many drug users are aware of the behavioral and physiological consequences of drug use and use disguises such as eyedrops and sun glasses to hide the "red eyes." They have also learned to control their behavior to avoid calling undue attention to themselves. Teachers most often rely on identifying drug abusers through the abusers' self-disclosures or disclosures by concerned others.

Understanding the difference between drug and alcohol use and abuse is difficult. As Zinberg (1984) explains, what would be drug abuse for one person is manageable use for another. Zinberg interviewed many drug users who were functioning well in society and used drugs on a daily basis. This pattern is unusual, however; the majority of daily users have a difficult time functioning in society.

Elementary, junior high, and high school programs are preparing materials and disseminating information about drug and alcohol use. Teachers, particularly at the junior high and high school levels, should be aware of drug and alcohol terminology, characteristics of users, and consequences (Maxwell and Liu, 1998). Familiarity with local referral agencies providing guidance and assistance to students involved with drugs and alcohol is important for all teachers.

Now that we understand social competence and how students with behavior and learning difficulties feel about themselves, are perceived by others, and interact socially with others, let us focus on intervention theory and specific programs and activities for teaching social skills.

INTERVENTION STRATEGIES

Understanding and using different interventions when attempting to affect the social skills of students with learning disabilities and behavior disorders is extremely important. The variety of social difficulties exhibited by students with learning and behavior disorders is great; using a particular intervention may be effective with one student, yet considerably less effective with another student or another problem. By understanding many approaches, we increase the likelihood of success with all students. The real challenge to teachers is knowing when to use which approach with which child under which condition.

Whereas there is a range of intervention strategies to assist in teaching appropriate social skills to students with learning disabilities and behavior disorders, effective social skills training programs share the same goals (McIntosh, Vaughn, and Zaragoza, 1991). The purpose of social skills training is to teach the students a complex response set that allows them to adapt to the numerous problems that occur in social situations. Common goals of social skills training programs include the ability to do the following:

1. Solve problems and make decisions quickly
2. Adapt to situations that are new or unexpected
3. Use coping strategies for responding to emotional upsets
4. Communicate effectively with others
5. Make and maintain friends

Interpersonal Problem Solving

We spend an extraordinary amount of time preventing and solving interpersonal problems. Whether we are concerned about what to say to our neighbor whose dog barks long and loud in the middle of the night, how to handle the irate customer at work, or our relationships with our parents and siblings, interpersonal problems are an ongoing part of life. Some people seem to acquire the skills necessary for interpersonal problem solving easily and with little or no direct instructions; others, particularly students with learning and behavior disorders, need more direct instruction in how to prevent and resolve difficulties with others.

The goal of interpersonal problem-solving training is to teach students how to employ a wide range of strategies that allow them to develop and maintain positive relationships with others, cope effectively with others, solve their own problems, and resolve conflict with others. The problem-solving approach attempts to provide the student with a process for solving conflicts.

Interpersonal problem solving has been used successfully with a wide range of populations, including adult psychiatric patients (Platt and Spivack, 1972), preschoolers (Ridley and Vaughn, 1982), kindergartners (Shure and Spivack, 1978), students identified as mentally retarded (Vaughn, Ridley, and Cox, 1983), students with learning disabilities (Vaughn, Levine, and Ridley, 1986), and aggressive children (Vaughn, Ridley, and Bullock, 1984). Spivack, Platt and Shure (1976), along with their colleagues at the Hahnemann Medical College, have conducted a comprehensive examination of the relationship between interpersonal problem solving and adjustment. Their research has led them to explore the effects of interpersonal problem-solving training programs with emotionally disturbed adolescents, disadvantaged preschoolers, and impulsive kindergartners (Spivack, Platt, and Shure, 1976; Shure and Spivack, 1978, 1979, 1980). Based on their work, adaptations and extensions of techniques for teaching interpersonal problem solving to special populations have evolved.

Components of Interpersonal Problem-Solving Programs

Four skills appear to be particularly important for successful problem resolution (Spivack, Platt, and Shure, 1976). First, the student must be able to identify and define the problem. Second, the student must be able to generate a variety of alternative solutions to any given problem. Third, the student must be able to identify and evaluate the possible consequences of each alternative. Finally, the student must be able to implement the solution. This may require rehearsal and modeling. Whereas these four components are characteristic of most interpersonal problem-solving programs, many programs include additional components and procedures.

For example, a social problem-solving intervention was conducted with 50 students with serious emotional disturbances (Amish, Gesten, Smith, Clark, and Stark, 1988). The intervention consisted of 15 structured lessons which occurred for 40 minutes once each week. The following problem-solving steps were taught:

1. Say what the problem is and how you feel.
2. Decide on a goal.
3. Stop and think before you decide what to do.
4. Think of many possible solutions to the problem.

5. Think about what will happen next after each possible solution.
6. When you find a good solution, try it.

The results of the intervention indicated that students with serious emotional disturbances who participated in the intervention improved their social problem-solving skills and were able to generate more alternatives to interviewing and role-playing measures.

Following are descriptions of several interpersonal problem-solving (IPS) programs that have been developed, implemented, and evaluated with students who have learning and behavior disorders.

FAST and SLAM

FAST is a strategy taught as part of an IPS program to second-, third-, and fourth-grade students with learning disabilities identified as having social skills problems (Vaughn and Lancelotta, 1990; Vaughn, Lancelotta, and Minnis, 1988; Vaughn, McIntosh, and Spencer-Rowe, 1991). The purpose of FAST is to teach students to consider problems carefully before responding to them and to consider alternatives and their consequences. Figure 9.3 presents the FAST strategy. In step one, Freeze and Think, students are taught to identify the problem. In step two, Alterna-

■ **FIGURE 9.3** *FAST: An Interpersonal Problem-Solving Strategy*

FAST

FREEZE AND THINK!
What is the problem?

ALTERNATIVES?
What are my possible solutions?

SOLUTION EVALUATION
Choose the best solution:
    safe?
    fair?

TRY IT!
Slowly and carefully
Does it work?

---

tives, students are taught to consider possible ways of solving the problem. In step three, Solution Evaluation, students are asked to prepare a solution or course of action for solving the problem that is both safe and fair. The idea is to get students to consider solutions that will be effective in the long run. The fourth step, Try It, asks students to rehearse and implement the solution. If they are unsuccessful at implementing the solution, students are taught to go back to alternatives. Students with learning disabilities practiced this strategy by using real problems generated by themselves and their peers.

▬ PROCEDURES:

1. In each classroom ask peers to rate all same-sex classmates on the extent to which they would like to be friends with them. Students who receive few friendship votes and many "no friendship" votes are identified as rejected. Students who receive many friendship votes and few "no friendship" votes are identified as popular. See Coie, Dodge, and Coppotelli (1982) for exact procedures in assessing popular and rejected students.

2. Rejected students with learning disabilities are paired with same-sex popular classmates and the pair becomes the social skills trainers for the class and school. The school principal announces to the school and to parents through a newsletter who the social skills trainers are for the school.

3. Children selected as social skills trainers are involved in learning social skills strategies and are removed from the classroom two to three times a week for approximately 30 minutes each session.

4. Social skills training includes learning the FAST strategy as well as other social skills such as accepting negative feedback, receiving positive feedback, and making friendship overtures.

5. At the same time period that social skills trainers are learning social skills strategies, their classmates are recording problems they have at home and at school and placing their lists in the classroom from the problem-solving box are used by trainers as they learn the strategies outside of class, as well as for in-class discussion which occurs later and is led by the social skills trainers.

APPLY THE CONCEPT 9.3

ACTIVITY SHEET FOR FAST

This activity sheet can be used to give children written practice in using the FAST strategy.

You are in the cafeteria. Another student keeps bugging you. He hits you, pokes you, tries to steal your food, and will not stop bullying you. You start to get angry. What would you do? Use FAST to help you solve the problem.

1. *Freeze and think.* What is the problem?

   _____

   _____

2. *Alternatives.* What are your possible solutions?

   _____

   _____

3. *Solution evaluation.* Choose the best one. Remember: safe and fair; works in the long run.

   _____

   _____

4. *Try it.* Do you think this will work?

   _____

   _____

A friend of yours is upset. She is teased a lot, especially by a boy named Kenny. She told you that she wants to run away from school. What could you tell your friend to help her solve the problem? Use FAST to help you.

1. _____

   _____

   _____

   _____

2. _____

   _____

   _____

   _____

3. _____

   _____

   _____

   _____

4. _____

   _____

---

6. After the social skills trainers have learned a strategy, such as FAST, they teach it to the entire class with backup and support from the researcher and classroom teacher.

7. During subsequent weeks, social skills trainers leave the room for only one session per week and practice the FAST strategy as well as other strategies with classmates at least one time per week. These reviews include large group explanations and small-group problem-solving exercises.

8. Social skills trainers are recognized by their teacher and administrator for their special skills.

Other students are asked to consult the social skills trainer when they have difficulties.

— **COMMENTS:** The above approach to teaching social skills and increasing peer acceptance has been successfully applied in two studies with youngsters with learning disabilities (Vaughn, Lancelotta, and Minnis, 1988; Vaughn, McIntosh, and Spencer-Rowe, 1991) but has not been evaluated for behavior-disordered students or adolescents.

Apply the Concept 9.3 shows an activity sheet used as part of a homework assignment for students participating in the training.

Based on principles similar to those of the FAST strategy, SLAM is a technique that can be used to assist students in accepting and assimilating negative feedback and comments from other people (McIntosh, Vaughn, and Bennerson, 1995). The SLAM is practiced in small groups, and presented to the class. The four components of the SLAM strategy are:

1. *STOP*—Stop whatever you are doing.
2. *LOOK*—Look the person in the eye.
3. *ASK*—Ask the person a question to clarify what he or she means.
4. *MAKE*—Make an appropriate response to the person.

Figure 9.4 presents the lyrics to the SLAM Strategy Song.

LLW: Living, Learning, and Working

Living, learning, and working (LLW) is a program designed to enhance listening, attending, empathy, social problem solving, and contributing skills among fourth and fifth graders (Brigman and Molina, 1999). This program can be implemented throughout the school with the cooperation of other teachers or the school counselor. The fourth and fifth graders work

---

■ **FIGURE 9.4**   *Lyrics to the SLAM Strategy Song*

Accepting negative feedback, feedback, feedback.
Accepting negative feedback, feedback, feedback.
Stop what you're doing. Look them in the eye.
Fix your face. We'll tell you why.
Accepting negative feedback, feedback, feedback.
Accepting negative feedback, feedback, feedback.
Listen with your ears to what they say.
This is no time for you to play.
Accepting negative feedback, feedback, feedback.
Accepting negative feedback, feedback, feedback.
Ask a question if you don't understand.
Don't stand there in wonderland.
Accepting negative feedback, feedback, feedback.
Accepting negative feedback, feedback, feedback.
Make a response to their concerns.
Accepting negative feedback is the way to learn.

---

with a younger reading partner and the pair read books that deal with specific issues such as difficulty making friends. This program is designed to be implemented in a group setting. The goals of the program are achieved in three phases: working together, learning together, and living together. Figure 9.5 presents the specific goals for each session. Bibliotherapy is a counseling strategy similar to LLW that can be used in the classroom to enhance the self-concept of students. Bibliotherapy also requires the use of age-appropriate books that focus on specific problems that the students are experiencing such as difficulty making friends. Students discuss how they are like or unlike the characters in the book, emotions of the character, make predictions about events, and share similar life experiences with the class (Sridhar and Vaughn, 2000). Tables 9.1 and 9.2 present a list of books along with their summaries to help teachers choose books.

TLC: Teaching, Learning, and Caring

Teaching, Learning, and Caring (TLC) (Vaughn, 1987; Vaughn, Cohen, Fournier, Gervasi, Levasseur, and Newton, 1984) is an interpersonal problem-solving skills training program based on the work of Vaughn and Ridley (e.g., Vaughn, Ridley, and Bullock, 1984).

The TLC program was developed to teach specific social problem-solving strategies to students with severe emotional disorders and learning disabilities. The program was developed and initiated within a self-contained classroom for severely learning- and behavior-disordered students.

The TLC curriculum includes six major components: goal identification, cue sensitivity, empathy, alternative thinking, consequential thinking, and skills implementation. In addition to these core components, a communication mode was identified as a process for listening, responding, and addressing the needs of others, which would facilitate the acquisition of all program components. Figure 9.6 on page 411 provides a list of the core components of the program.

Social Decision-Making Skills (Elias and Clabby, 1989) is a curriculum based on cognitive interpersonal problem solving and designed for both regular

■ **FIGURE 9.5** *Living, Learning, and Working*

Session 1

Developing group norms and learning about each other.

Session 2

Learning specific encouragement skills and behaviors.

Session 3

Learning cooperation skills for working in a group. Students learn that they will be helping younger students by learning specific strategies for reading, discussing, and role playing. The younger students are introduced and paired with the older students midway through the session.

Session 4–8

Each session follows a six-step format. Different books can be used for each session.

1. Read a developmentally appropriate story that involves diversity such as cognitive, physical, or social.
2. Process the story using story structure and the five Ws (*Who* were the main characters? *When* did the story take place? *What* were the main events? *What* were the main problems encountered in the story? *Where* did the story take place? *Why* did the characters have the problem?) and two Hs (*How* did the characters feel at the beginning, middle, and end of the story? *How* was the problem solved?).
3. Discuss similarities and differences between story characters and group members.
4. Brainstorm other ways to solve the problem introduced in the story.
5. Role play various problem-solving solutions
6. Provide feedback on role playing.

Session 9

Involve the whole group of older and younger students and discuss ground rules for reading, discussing the story, and role playing.

Session 10

Have each pair of older and younger students read a story. Ask the older child to use a structured guide to discuss the story and role play the solution to the problem identified in the story.

Session 11

Conduct a closure activity with the whole group.

Session 12

Bring both the older and younger groups of students together at the beginning of the session to discuss what the experience was like for them. Involve only the older students at the end of the session and debrief them.

and special education elementary-age students. The curriculum provides for readiness areas and steps for social decision making and problem solving. The teacher's guide is very complete and includes sample worksheets, tips for teaching the skills, and directions for how to structure role plays.

Behavior Therapy

Behavior Therapy, or Applied Behavior Analysis (ABA), is based primarily on operant learning principles. The application of these principles to change maladaptive behaviors is referred to as behavioral therapy.

The major components of ABA include:

1. *Target behaviors are defined operationally.* For example, a teacher described the behaviorally disturbed child in her classroom as "emotional." Although most of us know what *emotional* means, it is likely that each of us imagines a somewhat different behavioral repertoire when we think of a student as behaving in an emotional way. In the same way, if we were asked to chart the emotional behavior of a student, it is unlikely that any two observers would get the same results. For this reason, the teacher is asked to describe the behaviors she observes when the student is acting emotional. "*When I ask her to turn in her work she puts her head down on her desk, sighs, and then crumples her paper.*"

■ **TABLE 9.1**   *Books for Young Children*

Topic	*Book Citation and Cost*	*Summary*
Self-acceptance; retention	Aseltine, L. (1988). *First Grade Can Wait*. Virginia Wright-Frierson. Niles, IL: Whitman.	Luke is a first grader who is behind his classmates in many skills. Although he enjoys kindergarten, the prospect of first grade frightens him. His parents and teacher decide Luke should be retained. The book focuses on reassuring Luke that he is growing and developing well and will be ready to go to first grade next year.
Breaking a habit	Hughes, S. (1983). *Alfie Gives A Hand*. New York: Lothrop.	Alfie clings to his security blanket all during Bernard's birthday party. When the overexcited Bernard makes a little girl cry, Alfie comforts her. While comforting the little girl Alfie finds his blanket is in the way and puts it down. The book focuses on painlessly breaking a habit.
Breaking a habit	Cooney, N. E. (1987). *Donald Says Thumbs Down*. New York: Putnam.	Donald still sucks his thumb when he is tired or unhappy and his friends at school make fun of his thumb sucking. His mother helps him break the habit by diverting him. Eventually he learns to divert himself. The book focuses on Donald's process of breaking a habit.
Accepting difference in people	Spier, P. (1980). *People*. New York: Doubleday.	Celebrating the variety of human beings, the book encourages acceptance and appreciation of all kinds of people with all kinds of eyes, noses, hair colors, languages, and so on.
Self-acceptance; tolerance of others.	Cohen, M. (1985). *Liar, Liar, Pants on Fire*. New York: Greenwillow.	Alex, a new boy in first grade, brags about his pony and rocket car. The other children consider him a liar and reject him. Their teacher gently explains that Alex really wants to be noticed and needs friends. So Alex is given another chance at making friends. The book focuses on being yourself and tolerating others.
Handling criticism; dealing with emotional hurt.	Doleski, T. (1983). *The Hurt*. New York: Paulist.	Justin finds dealing with criticism particularly painful. Each criticism is shown as a hurt that grows larger and larger until it begins to crowd him out of his bedroom. His father suggests the hurt will go away if he stops thinking about it, and it never becomes big again. The book focuses on effectively dealing with criticism.
Making and keeping friends; expressing emotions.	Rogers, F. (1972). *Making Friends*. New York: Macmillan.	The process of making and keeping friends is discussed, which include angry quarrels as well as happy playtimes. The book focuses on the emotional growth involved in maintaining friendships.

(continued)

TABLE 9.1   *Continued*

Topic	Book Citation and Cost	Summary
Reassuring late bloomers.	Kraus, R. (1987). *Leo the Late Bloomer.* New York: Harper.	Leo the tiger cub is behind other animals in reading, writing, drawing, and eating neatly. Although his father is worried, his mother assures him that Leo will bloom with time, and he does. The book focuses on assuring late bloomers that children develop at different rates.
Self-acceptance; making friends.	Wells, R. (1981). *Timothy Goes To School.* New York: Dial.	Timothy starts school with feelings of inadequacy that is made worse by Claude, who is condescending, critical, and annoyingly good at everything. Luckily, Violet, another animal child, is having similar problems and the two left-out animal children become happy friends. The book focuses on making friends and accepting different kinds of people.
Self-acceptance.	Waber, B. (1972). *Ira Sleeps Over.* Boston: Houghton.	Ira is invited to spend the night with Reggie. Ira wonders if taking his teddy bear would be babyish and decides to leave his behind. The boys do several things together, including reading a ghost story. The scary story helps them discover that they both have teddies that comfort them. They are greatly relieved that they can be themselves. The book deals with accepting yourself and growing up at your own pace.
Acceptance and usefulness of wearing glasses.	Brown, M. (1979). *Arthur's Eyes.* Boston: Little.	Arthur is embarrassed about wearing glasses and often tries to lose them. One day a teacher he admires shows Arthur the usefulness of his glasses. Arthur's arithmetic and basketball improve, and his classmates also begin to want glasses. The book emphasizes the value of wearing glasses.
Acceptance of physical appearance.	Brown, M. (1981). *Arthur's Nose.* New York: Avon.	Arthur is unhappy with his long nose and consults a "rhinologist" about changing it. He tries out several other noses such as an elephant's and a toucan's. Finally, he decides to keep his own, much to the relief of his friends. The book effectively deals with accepting physical acceptance.
Acceptance and assurance that rate of development can vary for individual children.	Brown, M. (1986). *Arthur's Tooth.* Boston: Atlantic Monthly.	Arthur is the only one in his class who hasn't lost a baby tooth. His friends make fun of him, and the problem is solved when the main teaser accidentally swats him in the mouth, and the tooth pops out. The issue of different rates of development is effectively dealt with.

TABLE 9.1 *Continued*

Topic	Book Citation and Cost	Summary
We are all special; treating classmates kindly.	Yashima, T. (1955). *Crow Boy.* New York: Viking.	Chibi has attended the village school for six years but has been too fearful to learn or make friends. Finally the beauty of his drawings and pictographs and the depth of his knowledge of nature, particularly crows, is recognized by a kind teacher. The book emphasizes individual uniqueness.
We are all special.	Leaf, M. (1977). *The Story of Ferdinand.* New York: Puffin.	A bull calf in enjoys sitting quietly smelling the flowers instead of goring the matador in the bull-ring. He will not lose his temper even when tormented by *banderilleros* and *picadors*. The book focuses on the value of individuality.
Accepting people of various origins; accepting various handicaps; all children enjoy similar things.	Brown, T. (1984). *Someone Special Just Like You.* New York: Holt.	Children of different origins with different handicaps all enjoy similar activities that normal children enjoy. The idea that children are more alike than different regardless of origin and disability is emphasized.
Inclusion of a blind child; accepting and understanding visual impairment.	Cohen, M. (1983). *See You Tomorrow Charles.* New York: Greenwillow.	The inclusion of a blind first grader into a general education first grade classroom is described. The class accepts the boy with friendliness, protectiveness, and interest.
Children with certain disabilities sometimes go to special schools; children with disabilities also have loving, caring families.	Fassler, J. (1975). *Howie Helps Himself.* Chicago: Whitman.	A boy must go to a special school because his legs are weak. However, he learns the same things that all children learn such as reading and counting. Although he learns many things, his greatest achievement is to wheel his wheelchair across the classroom to his father, who demonstrates love and caring.
People with disabilities may use different things but they are more similar than different from us.	Hamm, D. (1987). *Grandmom Drives A Motor Bed.* Virginia Wright-Frierson. Niles, IL: Whitman.	A cheerful grandmother with paralyzed legs has to spend almost all her time in a motorized hospital bed. But she enjoys telephoning, visits from friends, watching television, and, most of all, seeing her grandson. The idea that she is like most grandmothers regardless of her paralyzed legs is emphasized.
Children with learning disabilities also enjoy doing the same things that other children do; children with learning disabilities have home lives similar to those of other children.	Lasker, J. (1974). *He's My Brother.* Chicago: Albert Whitman.	Although Jamie has a learning disability, he enjoys activities that most children his age enjoy. His brother describes Jamie's problems, abilities, and likes at home and school.

(continued)

TABLE 9.1   *Continued*

Topic	*Book Citation and Cost*	*Summary*
Recognizing and appreciating individual differences.	Bradman, T. *Michael*. New York: Macmillan.	Michael is not like the other students in class. He is usually late and frequently in trouble. However, Michael has special abilities that have not yet been recognized. His special abilities are indicated through the illustrations.
Having a sibling with mental retardation; managing conflicting emotions caused by individual differences.	Wright, B. R. (1981). *My Sister Is Different*. Milwaukee: Raintree.	Carlo finds it difficult to accept his older sister Terry, who is mentally retarded. He finally realizes how special Terry is when he almost loses her.
Accepting spectacles; the value of wearing glasses.	Raskin, E. (1968). *Spectacles*. Atheneum.	Iris, a little girl, sees strange things such as a fire-breathing dragon and a fat kangaroo because she cannot see clearly. She is taken to an eye doctor who decides she needs glasses. Iris initially does not want to wear glasses, but later realizes that they really help her see better.
Teasing can hurt.	Hines, A. G. (1989). *They Really Like Me!* New York: Greenwillow.	Two mischievous older sisters tease their little brother who is left in their care. The little boy teaches them a lesson by hiding under the staircase after they pretend to abandon him in the woods. He finally reappears and they promise to stop teasing him.
Adjusting to a new baby.	Brown, M. (1987). *Arthur's Baby*. Boston: Little.	Arthur is apprehensive about the new baby since his friends tell him it will be noisy, smelly, and need him to baby-sit, but he discovers with great satisfaction that he can cope with the new baby better than his bossy sister.
The positive and negative aspects of having a baby sister.	Edelman, E. (1984). *I Love My Baby Sister (Most of the Time)*. New York: Lothrop.	The difficult things about having a baby sister, such as hair pulling, crying, and demanding mother's attention are balanced by her cute antics and the happy expectation that when she gets bigger, she will be a friend and a playmate.
Teasing among siblings.	Chorao, K. (1987). *George Told Kate*. New York: Dutton.	In an elephant family, a big brother teases and frightens his little sister about going to school. The book focuses on effectively deal with teasing.

■ **TABLE 9.2** *Books for Second through Fourth Grade*

Topic	Book Citation and Cost	Summary
What it is like to live to live with siblings with diabetes, asthma, and spina bifida.	Rosenburg, M. B. (1988). *Finding a Way: Living with Exceptional Brothers and Sisters.* New york: Lothrop.	Children talk about how it is to live with siblings who have diabetes, asthma, and spina bifida. They talk about ways in which they help and about the mixed feelings they have about the siblings with medical conditions.
Children with disabilities also enjoy activities that other children enjoy.	Rosenburg, M. B. (1983). *My Friend Leslie.* New York: Lothrop.	A bubbly, happy kindergartner with multiple handicaps is mainstreamed in a public school. She enjoys activities such as music, painting, exercise, and friendships, which most children enjoy. The book focuses on the normalcy of children with handicaps.
Sibling rivalry.	Viorst, J. (1969). *I'll Fix Anthony.* New York: Macmillan.	The book is about a little boy fantasizing about all the ways in which he will become better than his older brother when he reaches the powerful age of six. His fantasies include becoming stronger, taller, and healthier.
Experiences of having a new infant from the perspectives of children from different ethnicities.	Cole, J. (1985). *The New Baby at Your House.* New York: Morrow.	Describes the experiences of young children of various ethnicities with new infants in their families.
The experience of having a new baby in the house from the perspectives of a young boy and girl.	Stein, S. B. (1974). *That New Baby.* New York: Walker.	The experiences of a young boy and girl dealing with the entry of a new baby into their family is described with all the usual upsets, but eventually things become better. The text for children is accompanied by explanatory passages interpreting their feelings to adults.
The value of a sibling.	Zolotow, C. (1987). *If It Weren't for You.*	A little boy dreams about how much better life would be without his younger brother to share things such as cake, the bedroom, and Christmas presents. While dreaming, he suddenly realizes that he would then be alone with all the grown-ups and begins to see the value of having a little brother.
We are all unique and universal.	Shan, E. L. (1972). *What Makes Me Feel This Way?* New York: Macmillan.	Feelings common to all children such as anger, fear, and shyness are treated as natural, and suggestions are made about understanding and expressing them acceptably.
Overcoming disabilities.	White, E. B. (1970). *The Trumpet of the Swan.* New York: Harper.	Louis, a trumpeter swan, is born mute. However, he overcomes his handicap by learning to read, write, and play the trumpet. The book deals with the idea of overcoming disabilities.

(continued)

TABLE 9.2   *Continued*

Topic	Book Citation and Cost	Summary
Normality of children with handicaps.	Wolf, B. (1988). *Don't Feel Sorry for Paul*. Philadelphia: Lippincott.	Paul is a young boy born with unfinished hands and feet and wears prostheses to substitute for his missing body parts. However, he rides in horse shows, wrestles with his sisters, and leads an active life. The normality of Paul's life is emphasized without ignoring his problems.

Source: D. Sridhar and S. Vaughn, "Enhancing Reading Comprehension, Self-Concept, and Behavior through Bibliotherapy for Students with Learning and Behavior Disorders," *Teaching Exceptional Children* (in press). Reprinted by permission.

Identifying the specific behaviors the student exhibits assists the teacher in clarifying what is disturbing to her, and it also assists in the second step, measurement.

2. *Target behaviors are measured.* To determine the student's present level of functioning and to determine if the selected intervention is effective, target behaviors must be measured before and during intervention. Some behaviors are easy to identify and measure. For example, the number of times John completes his arithmetic assignment is relatively easy to tabulate. However, behaviors such as "out of seat" and "off task" require more elaborate measurement procedures.

The three types of measurement procedures most frequently used are event, duration, and interval time sampling. *Event sampling* measures the number of times a behavior occurs in a designated amount of time. Sample behaviors include the number of times the bus driver reports misconduct regarding a student, the number of times a student is late for class, or the number of times a student does not turn in a homework assignment. *Duration sampling* measures the length of time a behavior occurs. Sample behaviors include the amount of time a student is "out of seat," how long a student cries, or the amount of time a student is "off task." You can see that it is possible to use event and duration samplings for the same behavior. You may want to measure the behavior both ways or select the measurement

procedure that will give you the most information about the behavior. *Interval sampling* designates whether or not a behavior occurs during a specific interval of time. For example, a teacher may record whether a student is reported for fighting during recess periods. Interval sampling is used when it is difficult to tell when a behavior begins or ends and also when a behavior occurs very frequently.

In addition to the measurement of the target behavior, it is helpful to identify the antecedents and consequences of the target behavior. A listing of what occurs before the behavior and what occurs immediately after gives important information that assists in developing an intervention procedure. If every time the student cries, the teacher talks to the student for a few minutes, it could be the teacher's attention is maintaining the behavior. The listing of antecedents may provide information about the environment, events, or people who trigger the target behavior. An analysis of antecedents and consequences facilitates the establishment of a successful intervention procedure.

3. *Goals and treatment intervention are established.* Based on observation and measurement data and an analysis of antecedents and consequences, goals for changing behavior and intervention strategies are established. The purpose of establishing goals is to determine the desired frequency or duration of the behavior. Goal setting

■ **FIGURE 9.6**   *Teaching, Learning, and Caring Skills*

Communication Mode

1. Repeat the content of another's message.
2. Identify the main idea of the content of another's message.
3. Identify the stated feelings in another's message.
4. Identify the underlying feelings in another's message.
5. Identify the main idea of the content of one's message.
6. Identify the underlying feeling in one's message.
7. Use self-disclosure appropriately.
8. Use open and closed questions appropriately.
9. Listen to the problems of another without discounting.
10. Listen to the problems of another and hypothetical situations which influence behavior.

Goal Identification

1. Define own goal(s) when in a problem situation.
2. Define the goal(s) of another when in a problem situation.
3. Identify immediate and long-term goals.
4. Share identified goals with the student group and accept feedback.
5. List the steps to reaching identified goals.
6. Chart progress towards reaching goals.
7. Identify and describe the needs and goals of others.

Empathy

1. Identify words which convey emotions, e.g., jealous, hurt, angry, hostile, shy, afraid, furious.
2. Match past situations and the feelings associated with the situation.
3. Discuss the relationship between identifying emotional states as the first step in responding appropriately to them.
4. Identify how you would feel in hypothetical situations.
5. Identify the feelings of others in pictures, films, and hypothetical situations.

Cue Sensitivity

1. Identify environmental cues in pictures and respond by asking questions and summarizing content and feelings.
2. Identify environmental cues in real situations which influence behavior.
3. Identify the personal cues people use and what they mean in role plays and films.
4. Identify the personal cues used by others in real situations.
5. Identify own cues when interacting with others and what they mean.
6. Identify several cues you want to include in your repertoire.
7. Identify cues of others, your typical response to them, and possible alternative responses.

Alternative Thinking

1. Identify likely alternatives to solving hypothetical problems.
2. Identify likely alternatives to solving real problems.
3. Identify nonaggressive alternatives to solving hypothetical problems.
4. Identify nonaggressive alternatives to solving real problems.

Consequential Thinking

1. Predict the likely consequences to a series of events not involving them.
2. Predict the likely consequences to hypothetical stories and role play situations.
3. Predict the likely consequences to interpersonal interactions of others.
4. Identify short-run and long-run solutions to solving hypothetical problems.
5. Identify problems in the long run when implementing short run solutions to hypothetical situations.
6. Identify the consequences of selected behaviors in interpersonal situations involving others.
7. Identify the consequences of selected behaviors in interpersonal situations involving self.
8. Implement a "stop and think" approach to solving interpersonal difficulties.

Skills Implementation

1. Identify the best procedure for implementing the selected alternative.
2. Identify a person who implements the alternative well and describe what he or she does.

(continued)

■ FIGURE 9.6 *Continued*

3. Describe the step-by-step process for implementing the selected alternative.
4. Role play, practice, and rehearse the selected alternative.
5. Use feedback from self and others to make changes in the procedure.
6. Implement selected alternative.
7. Evaluate the outcome and the procedure.

Integration

1. Observe models (counselors, teachers, and peers) integrate the problem solving process in solving hypothetical problems.

2. Observe models (counselors, teachers, and peers) integrate the problem-solving process in solving real problems.
3. Integrate the problem-solving process in solving group problems.
4. Integrate the problem-solving process in solving hypothetical problems.
5. Integrate the problem-solving process in solving real problems.

Source: S. Vaughn, "TLC—Teaching, Learning, and Caring: Teaching Interpersonal Problem-Solving Skills to Behaviorally Disordered Adolescents," *The Pointer, 31*(2) (1987): 25–30. Reprinted with permission of the Helen Dwight Reid Educational Foundation. Published by Heldref Publications, 1319 18th Street, N.W., Washington, DC 20036-1802. Copyright 1987.

is most effective when the person exhibiting the target behavior is involved in establishing the goals. For example, Dukas is aware he gets into too many fights and wants to reduce his fighting behavior. After the target behavior is identified and measured, the teacher and student examine the data and identify that the only time he gets into fights is during the lunch-time recess. They set up a contract in which the teacher agrees to give Dukas ten minutes of free time at the end of each day in which he does not get into a fight. The student agrees with the contract. The teacher continues to measure the student's behavior to determine if the suggested treatment plan is effective.

There are many treatment strategies in behavior therapy that can be used by the teacher to effect change. For example, the teacher may use reinforcers to shape new behaviors, reinforce incompatible behaviors, or maintain or increase desired behavior. The teacher may use extinction, punishment, or time-out to eliminate undesired behaviors. Guidelines for using time-out are presented in Figure 9.7. The teacher may use contracts or token economies to change behavior. These strategies are discussed

in Chapter Two, in the section on operant learning theory. With these intervention strategies, consequences are controlled by another (e.g., the teacher). Self-management is a procedure in which the consequences are controlled by the target person. These procedures are particularly effective with older children, adolescents, and adults because the control and responsibility for change is placed in their hands. With assistance from a teacher, counselor, or other influential adult, the adolescent implements a self-management program by following three processes.

1. Identify the behavior he or she wants to change (e.g., being late for school).
2. Identify the antecedents and consequences associated with the behavior (e.g., Doreen says, "When the alarm rings I continue to lie in bed. I also wait until the last minute to run to the bus stop and I frequently miss the bus").
3. Develop a plan that alters the antecedents and provides consequences that will maintain the desired behavior. Doreen decides to get up as soon as the alarm rings and to leave for the bus stop without waiting until the last minute. Doreen arranges with her parents to have the car on Friday

■ FIGURE 9.7　*Time-Out: Guidelines for Effective Implementation*

- Use time-out as a last resort.
- Discuss time-out procedures with school administrators and parents before implementation.
- Put time-out procedures in writing and file with school rules.
- Provide students with information in advance about what behaviors will result in time-out.
- Place students in time-out only for brief time periods (15 to 20 minutes).
- Specify the amount of time the student will be in time-out prior to placement.
- Tell the student to go to time-out. If the student does not comply, the teacher should unemotionally place the student in time-out.
- Use time-out *immediately* following the inappropriate behavior.
- Establish contingencies in advance for the student who fails to comply with time-out rules.
- Always monitor the time-out area.
- When the time specified for time-out is over, the student should join his or her classmates.
- Provide reinforcement for appropriate behavior after time-out.

nights if she has arrived at school on time every day that week. An obvious disadvantage of a self-control model of behavior change is that it relies on the motivation of the student for success. Students who are not interested in changing behaviors and who are not willing to analyze antecedents and consequences and develop potentially successful intervention strategies will be unsuccessful with self-determined behavior change plans.

ASSET: A Social Skills Program for Adolescents

The purpose of ASSET is to teach adolescents the social skills they need to interact successfully with peers and adults (Hazel, Schumaker, Sherman, and Sheldon-Wildgen, 1981). The eight social skills considered fundamental to successful relationships are:

1. *Giving positive feedback.* This skill teaches students how to thank someone and how to give a compliment.
2. *Giving negative feedback.* This skill teaches students to give correction and feedback in a way that is not threatening.
3. *Accepting negative feedback.* This skill teaches students the all-important ability to receive negative feedback without walking away, showing hostility, or other inappropriate emotional reactions.
4. *Resisting peer pressure.* This teaches students to refuse their friends who are trying to seduce them into some form of delinquent behavior.
5. *Problem solving.* This teaches students a process for solving their own interpersonal difficulties.
6. *Negotiation.* This teaches students to use their problem-solving skills with another person to come to a mutually acceptable resolution.
7. *Following instructions.* This teaches students to listen and respond to instructions.
8. *Conversation.* This teaches students to initiate and maintain a conversation.

The Leader's Guide (Hazel, Schumaker, Sherman, and Sheldon-Wildgen, 1981) that comes with the ASSET program provides instructions for running the groups and teaching the skills. Eight teaching sessions are provided on videotapes that demonstrate the skills. Program materials include skill sheets, home notes, and criterion checklists.

━ PROCEDURES: Each lesson is taught to a small group of adolescents. There are nine basic steps to each lesson: (1) review homework and previously learned social skills; (2) explain the new skill for the day's lesson; (3) explain why the skill is important and should be learned and practiced; (4) give a realistic and specific example to illustrate the use of the skill; (5) examine each of the skill steps that are necessary to carry out the new social skill; (6) model the skill and provide opportunities for students and others to demonstrate correct and incorrect use of the skills; (7) use verbal rehearsal to familiarize the students with the sequence of steps in each social skill and provide a procedure for students to be automatic with their knowledge of the skill steps; (8) use behavioral rehearsal to allow each student to practice and demonstrate the skill steps until they reach criterion; (9) assign homework that provides opportunities for the students to practice the skills in other settings. These nine steps are followed for each of the eight specific social skills listed above.

■ **COMMENTS:** The ASSET program has been evaluated with eight students with learning disabilities (Hazel, Schumaker, Sherman, and Sheldon, 1982). It demonstrated that the students with learning disabilities involved in the intervention increased in the use of social skills in role-play settings. The curriculum guide provides specific teaching procedures and is particularly relevant to teachers working with adolescents.

Mutual Interest Discovery

Rather than specifically teaching social skills, *Mutual Interest Discovery* is an approach to increasing peer acceptance which has been used with students with learning disabilities (Fox, 1989). The rationale is that people are attracted to persons with whom they share similar attitudes. The more we know about someone the more likely it is that we will like them. Structured activities are provided for students with and without learning disabilities to get to know each other with greater acceptance being the outcome.

■ **PROCEDURES:** The overall goal of mutual interest discovery is to participate in structured activities with a partner (one partner with learning disabilities and the other without) to identify things you have in common and to get to know your partner better.

1. All students in the class are paired; students with learning disabilities are paired with non-learning-disabled classmates.
2. Students interact on preassigned topics for approximately 40 minutes once each week for several weeks. Preassigned topics include interviewing each other on such things as sports, entertainment preferences, hobbies, and other topics appropriate for the specific age group with which you are working.
3. After the structured activity each member of the pair writes three things he or she has in common or three things he or she learned about the other person.
4. Partners complete a brief art activity related to what they learned about their partner and place it in a mutual art book to which they contribute each week.
5. At the bottom of the art exercise each partner writes two sentences about something new he or she learned about his or her partner. If there is time, art activities and sentences are shared with members of the class.

■ **COMMENTS:** Partners who participated in the mutual interest discovery intervention demonstrated higher ratings of their partners over time than did a control group of students. This intervention is not designed to teach specific social skills but to increase the acceptance and likability of students with learning disabilities in the regular classroom. It is likely that this intervention, paired with social skills training, has promise for success with students with learning disabilities.

Structured Learning

Structured learning is a psychoeducational and behavioral approach to teaching prosocial skills to students both with and without disabilities (Goldstein, Sprafkin, Gerhsaw, and Klein, 1980). The procedure has four components and can be implemented by teachers, social workers, psychologists, or school counselors.

The first component is *modeling* and involves a verbal and behavioral description of the target skill as well as the steps that comprise the target skill. At this point the teacher might role play the steps in the skill and other models may also role play, exhibiting the target skill itself. During the second step, students are encouraged to enact role plays based on actual life experiences. These role plays are facilitated by coaching and cues from the teacher. Next, the teacher and other observers provide feedback. Specific attention is paid to elements of each role play that were effective and appropriate. Skills that were not role-played effectively are modeled by the teacher. In the final step, students are provided with opportunities to practice the steps and skills in the real world (e.g., outside the classroom).

The structured learning program for elementary students offers 60 prosocial skills and their constituent steps, arranged into five groups: classroom survival skills, friendship-making skills, skills for dealing with feelings, skill alternatives to aggression, and skills for dealing with stress. The structured learning program for adolescents also has 60 prosocial skills. It differs from the program for elementary students by including skills related to planning and decision making.

Social Life Program

The social life program developed by Griffith (1991) for use with developmentally handicapped adults was modified and used successfully with 9- to 12-year-old students with learning disabilities (Wiener and Harris, 1997). The program is delivered through a board game similar in format to Monopoly and can be played by three to five students. Students take turns throwing the dice. After throwing the dice, the student moves to a colored square and must solve the social problem read by the teacher from a color-coded chart. Depending on the solution, the child receives or returns Monopoly money. The cards are designed specifically to encourage role playing, modeling of appropriate social behavior and problem solving, and performance feedback.

Principles for Teaching Social Skills

There are several points teachers need to consider, no matter what social skills program they utilize. These include:

1. *Develop cooperative learning.* Classrooms can be structured so there is a win-lose atmosphere in which children compete with each other for grades and teacher attention, or classrooms can be structured so children work on their own with little interaction between classmates, or classrooms can be structured for cooperative learning so children work alone, with pairs, and with groups, helping each other master the assigned material. Cooperative learning techniques in the classroom result in increases in self-esteem, social skills, and learning (Johnson and Johnson, 1986). Teachers can structure learning activities so they involve cooperative learning and teach students techniques for working with pairs or in a group. The following four elements need to be present for cooperative learning to occur in small groups (Johnson and Johnson, 1986):

    a. Students must perceive they cannot succeed at the required task unless all members of the group succeed. This may require appropriate division of labor and giving a single grade for the entire group's performance.

    b. Assure individual accountability so each member of the group is assessed and realizes his or her performance is critical for group success.

    c. Teach students the necessary collaborative skills so they are able to function effectively in a group. This may include managing conflicts, active listening, leadership skill, and problem solving.

    d. Allow time for group process. This may include discussing how well the group is performing, developing a plan of action, and identifying what needs to happen.

2. *Involve peers in the training program for low-social-status students.* An important function of social skills training is to alter the way peers perceive students identified as low in social status. Including popular peers in the social skills training program increases the likelihood that they will have opportunities to observe the changes in target students and to cue and reinforce appropriate behavior in the classroom. For example, a study conducted by Vaughn, McIntosh, and Spencer-Rowe (1988), found that popular students involved in the social skills training with low-social-status students were more likely to increase the social-status ratings of the low-social-status students than were popular students not involved in the training.

Even when a social skills program is effective in producing the desired change in target students, it does not always alter the way these students are perceived by their peers (Bierman and Furman, 1984). Involving students with high social status with those with lower social status will improve the way the low-social-status students are perceived by others.

3. *Use principles of effective instruction.* Many teachers claim they do not know how to teach social skills. Considering the social skills difficulties of special education students, methods of teaching social skills to students may need to become part of our teacher training programs (Vaughn, 1985).

Teaching social skills requires implementing principles of effective instruction. These have been used and explained throughout this text and include: obtain student commitment, identify target behavior, pretest, teach, model, rehearse, role play, provide feedback, practice in controlled settings, practice in other settings, posttest and follow-up. A list of social skills that learning- and behavior-disordered students frequently need to be taught follows:

a. *Body language.* This includes how the student walks, where he or she stands during a conversation, what his or her body "says," gestures, eye contact, and appropriate facial reactions.

b. *Greetings.* This may include expanding the student's repertoire of greetings, selecting appropriate greetings for different people, and interpreting and responding to the greetings of others.

c. *Initiating and maintaining a conversation.* This includes a wide range of behaviors such as knowing when to approach someone; knowing how to ask inviting, open questions; knowing how to respond to comments made by others; and maintaining a conversation with a range of persons, including those who are too talkative and those who volunteer little conversation.

d. *Giving positive feedback.* Knowing how and when to give sincere, genuine, positive feedback and comments.

e. *Accepting positive feedback.* Knowing how to accept positive feedback from others.

f. *Giving negative feedback.* Knowing how and when to give specific negative feedback.

g. *Accepting negative feedback.* Knowing how to accept negative feedback from others.

h. *Identifying feelings in self and others.* Being able to recognize feelings both in self and others is how the student is able to predict how he or she will feel in a given situation and prepare appropriately for it. Responding appropriately to one's own and others' feelings.

i. *Problem solving and conflict resolution.* Knowing and using problem-solving skills to prevent and solve difficulties.

4. *Teach needed skills.* According to Perlmutter (1986), many social skills training programs fail because youngsters are trained to do things they already know how to do. For example, in a social skills training group with students with learning disabilities, the trainer was teaching the students to initiate conversations with others. Through role playing, the trainer soon learned that the students already knew how to initiate conversations but they did not know how to sustain them. In addition to being taught appropriate skills, students need to learn when and with whom to use the skills. One student put it this way: "I would never try problem solving like this with my father, but I know it would work with my mom."

5. *Teach for transfer of learning.* Many programs for teaching social skills effectively increase students' performance in social areas during the skills training or within a particular context, but the skills do not generalize to other settings (Berler, Gross, and Drabman, 1982). In order for social skills to generalize to other settings, the program must require the rehearsal and implementation of target skills across settings. Social skills training programs need to assure learned skills are systematically demonstrated in the classroom, on the playground, and at home.

6. *Empower students.* Many students with learning difficulties feel discouraged and unable to influence their learning. They turn the responsibility for learning over to the teacher and become "passive" learners. How can we empower students?

a. *Choice.* Students need to feel they are actively involved in their learning.

b. *Consequences.* Students will learn from the natural and logical consequences of their choices.

c. *Document progress.* In addition to teacher documentation of progress made, students need to learn procedures for monitoring and assessing their progress.

d. *Control.* Students need to feel as though they can exercise control over what happens to them. Some students feel as though their learning is in someone else's hands and therefore is someone else's responsibility.

7. *Identify strengths.* When developing social skills interventions for students with special needs, be sure to consider their strengths as well as their needs. Since appearance and athletic ability relate to social acceptance, these areas need to be considered when determining the type of social intervention needed. For example, if a youngster's physical appearance is a strength, the teacher can compliment him or her on hair appearance, what they are wearing, or how "neat" and "sharp" they look. Also, knowing something about the students' areas of strength might be helpful in identifying social contexts that may be promising for promoting positive peer interactions (Vaughn and LaGreca, 1992). For example, it is possible that a student with learning disabilities who is a particularly good swimmer and a member of a swim team would find friendship-making on the swim team an easier task than friendship-making in the academic setting. Students with learning disabilities may benefit from acquiring strengths in appearance and athletic activities so they can have areas of strength from which to build their social skills. While athletic skills are associated with peer success, particularly for boys, many children with learning disabilities do not have the motor ability or eye-hand coordination to succeed in the athletic area. Other areas such as hobbies or special interests can be presented in the classroom so that the student with learning disabilities has an opportunity to be perceived as one who is knowledgeable.

When developing social skills interventions, it may be important to consider the nature of children's friendships or social support outside of the school setting (Vaughn and LaGreca, 1992). It is possible that students with learning and behavior disorders who are not well accepted by their classmates have friends in the neighborhood or within their families (e.g., cousins). Perhaps the most important point to remember is that because a child is not well accepted by peers at school does not necessarily mean that the child does not have effective social relationships outside of the school setting.

8. *Reciprocal friendships.* Reciprocal friendship is the mutual identification as "best friend" by two students. Thus, a student who identifies a youngster as his or her best friend is also identified by that same youngster as a best friend. It has been hypothesized that reciprocal friendships could play an important role in reducing the negative effects of low peer acceptance (Vaughn, McIntosh, Schumm, Haager, and Callwood, 1993). From this perspective, it may be less important to increase the overall acceptance of a student in the classroom and more effective to concentrate on the development of a mutual best friend. Since it is quite unlikely that all youngsters in the classroom are going to like all of the other youngsters equally, the notion of developing a reciprocal friendship is a more realistic goal for most youngsters with learning and behavior problems.

Classroom Management

When someone mentions classroom management, most teachers think of discipline and classroom management rules. Duke and Meckel (1980) refer to classroom management as the procedures needed to establish and maintain an environment in which instruction and learning can occur. Classroom rules, routines, and order play an important part in classroom management (Doyle, 1986). Students need to have expectations for the behaviors and routines of the classroom.

Early in the year it is important to establish processes and procedures that sustain order (Doyle,

1979; Emmer, Evertson, and Anderson, 1980). One way to inform students of the classroom rules is to discuss the rules with them. As new children enter the class during the year, assigning a "veteran" student as a guide or mentor can help the new student understand the rule system of the classroom.

The purpose of some classroom rules is to regulate student behaviors that are likely to disrupt learning and teacher activities or cause damage or injury to property or others. In addition to explicit conduct rules, most classrooms also have a set of implicit rules under which they function (Erickson and Shultz, 1981). Sharing the explicit conduct rules and demonstrating the rewards of working within the rule system is particularly important for students with behavior problems. Making rewards contingent on full class participation can also assist a teacher, because students will encourage each other to work within the rule system.

Ms. Schiller works with junior high students with emotional disorders in a self-contained setting. Establishing conduct rules early in the year and setting up a reward system for "good behavior" is an important part of her program. Ms. Schiller comments:

> As far as I know, all of the students in this class are here primarily because they cannot cope with the rule systems in regular classrooms. This is due to a variety of reasons, and as a part of our social skills program we discuss some of the reasons and how to cope with them. But the majority of the day is focused on academic learning. To accomplish effective learning, we have a set of written and unwritten rules that the students and I are willing to operate under. We establish these rules at the beginning of the year during class meetings. In these meetings we talk about how the school operates and the rules it operates under, and then we decide what rules we want the classroom to function under. Usually it takes several days to establish these rules. The rules we generally decide on are:
>
> During discussions, one person talks at a time.
> When a person is talking, it is the responsibility of the rest of us to listen.
> Work quietly so you won't bother others.
> No hitting, shoving, kicking, etc.
> No screaming.
> Do not take other people's possessions without asking.
> Treat classmates and teachers with respect and consideration.
> When outside the classroom, follow the rules of the school or those established by the supervisor.
>
> Each day when we have a class meeting, we discuss the rules, our success with using these rules, and how the rules have operated. Sometimes we add new rules based on our discussions. I involve the students in this evaluation and decision making. Eventually we begin to decide when the rules can be made more flexible. In this way I hope that I am helping the students assume more responsibility for their own behavior, while at the same time maintaining a learning environment that is conducive to academic as well as social growth.
>
> I think there are three main reasons this rule system works in my classroom. First, the students feel like they own the system and have a responsibility to make it work. We have opportunities to discuss the system and to make changes. Second, we also establish a token system [see Chapter Two] for appropriate behavior and learning. Third, I communicate regularly with the parents, letting them know how their child is performing.

The classroom rules a teacher establishes are dependent on the social context of the school and the classroom, and the teaching–learning process as described in Chapter One. Some guidelines to use in developing and implementing classroom rules and management systems follow.

- Have the students help in selecting rules for the classroom.
- Select the fewest number of rules possible.
- Check with the principal or appropriate administrative personnel to determine if the rules are within the guidelines of the school.
- Select rules that are enforceable.
- Select rules that are reasonable.
- Determine consistent consequences for rule infractions.
- Have students evaluate their behavior in relation to the rules.
- Modify rules only when necessary.

TECH TALK 9.1

CLASSROOM MANAGEMENT PROFESSIONAL DEVELOPMENT

As the student population in the United States has become more diverse, teachers need to know more about an effective classroom management (Burns and Allen, 1998). Especially for students with disabilities, an effective classroom management system is vital for their success in mainstream classrooms (Burns and Allen, 1998). Successful classroom management is viewed as a process of establishing an effective learning environment rather than maintaining teachers' role as authority figures or disciplinarians (Brophy, 1998).

The series of professional development videos produced by SunBurst is an excellent tool for preparing teachers to successfully implement classroom management aiming at establishing an effective learning environment. *Good Discipline, Good Kids* addresses ways to develop and practice a nonpunitive approach to discipline (e.g, self-discipline, respect, cooperation, etc.), which can be particularly useful for children with behavior problems. *Building Student Success* teaches the use of strategies such as self-reflection and peer conferencing. *Respectful Schools and Classrooms* focuses on creating an atmosphere of respect in the classroom. More information about this series is available online (http://sunburstdirect.com/cgi-bin/SunburstDirect.storefront/).

— Have frequent group meetings in which students provide self-feedback as well as feedback to others about their behavior.

— Allow students to provide solutions to nagging class or school issues through problem solving.

Tech Talk presents information on a video series on implementing effective classroom management.

Classroom Management and Student Behavior

Lisa Rosario is a first-year, middle school resource room teacher in a suburban school district. She is not happy with the behavior of the students who come to the resource room. She was telling an experienced special education teacher in the same middle school, "I feel like I know what to teach and how to teach, but I just can't seem to get the students to behave so that they can learn. What can I do to make the students change?" The experienced teacher responded by suggesting that Lisa Rosario first look at her own behavior in order to change the behavior of the students in her classroom. Figure 9.8 provides a checklist for teachers to evaluate the effectiveness of their interventions.

■ **FIGURE 9.8** *Implementation Checklist*

If your intervention is not working, consider the following:

• Have you adequately identified and defined the target behavior?

• Have you selected the right kind of reinforcer? (What you decided on may not be reinforcing to the student.)

• Are you providing reinforcement soon enough?

• Are you providing too much reinforcement?

• Are you giving too little reinforcement?

• Are you being consistent in your implementation of the intervention program?

• Have you made the intervention program more complicated than it needs to be?

• Are others involved following through (e.g., principal, parent, "buddy")?

• Is the social reinforcement by peers outweighing your contracted reinforcement?

• Did you fail to give reinforcers promised or earned?

Source: From B. Larrivee, *Strategies for Effective Classroom Management: Creating a Collaborative Climate* (Boston: Allyn and Bacon, 1992). Reprinted with permission.

Lisa is not alone. Classroom management is identified by teachers as a cause of stress and is frequently cited as the reason they leave the teaching profession (Elam and Gallup, 1989; Fettler and Tokar, 1982). Following are some guidelines for Lisa to consider to assist in facilitating more appropriate behavior on the part of her students.

1. *Look for the positive behavior and let students know you recognize it.* Most teachers indicate that they provide a lot of positive reinforcement to their students. However, observations in special and general education teachers' classes indicate relatively low levels of positive reinforcement (McIntosh, Vaughn, Schumm, Haager, and Lee, 1993). Teachers need to provide a lot more positive feedback than they think is necessary.

   One of the fundamental rules about positive feedback is that it needs to be both specific and immediate. "Carla's homework is completed exactly the way I asked for it to be done. She has numbered the problems, left space between answers so that they are easy to read, and written the appropriate heading at the top of the paper." A second fundamental rule about positive feedback is that students need to be clear about what behaviors are desirable and undesirable.

   A clear list of class rules and consequences is an important step in making classroom management rules clear. Rules and procedures form the structure for classroom management (Brophy, 1988). Procedures that are part of the classroom routines need to be taught to students. Rules provide the structure for the behaviors that are acceptable and unacceptable. Teacher's criteria for what constitutes a behavior problem is the basis for the rules (Emmer, Evertson, Sanford, Clements, and Worsham, 1989). Think back to Lisa Rosario who indicated she had difficulty with classroom management. What became clear after further discussion was that she had difficulty establishing and enforcing classroom procedures. Once the experienced teacher observed in her classroom and assisted her in establishing routines, Lisa experienced significantly fewer difficulties with classroom management.

Positive reinforcement is more effective at the elementary level than in middle school, and least effective with high school students (Forness, 1973; Stallings, 1975). This does not suggest that positive reinforcement should be avoided with older students, but merely that it should be handled in a different way. Elementary students find public recognition in front of the entire class more rewarding than do older students, who prefer to receive individual feedback.

2. *Reinforcers can be used to encourage positive behavior.* As explained in Chapter One, both positive and negative reinforcement increases behavior. Most people think negative reinforcement means something harmful or "negative." As described in Chapter One, positive reinforcement is the presentation of a stimulus (verbal response, physical response such as touching, or a tangible response such as a reward) following the target behavior, intended to maintain or increase a target behavior. A list of reinforcers that teachers may want to consider for use in their classrooms is provided in Figure 9.9.

3. *Token economy.* A token economy is a structured plan for delivering reinforcers (tokens) following the display of target students behaviors and/or the absence of undesirable student behaviors. Token economies can be adapted for use in a variety of settings, and have been used extensively in special education (Kazdin, 1989). For example, teachers can post in the classroom a list of desirable behaviors (e.g., raising a hand and waiting to be called on by the teacher before talking) as well as undesirable behaviors (e.g., hitting classmates). Posted along with the behaviors are the corresponding number of tokens (e.g., points, chips, tickets) that students may earn for exhibiting target behaviors and eliminating noxious behaviors. Teachers can award tokens as target behaviors occur and/or may deliver tokens after a specific period of time has elapsed (e.g., Johnny receives one token at the start of each hour providing he has not hit a peer during the previous 60 minutes). Teachers can award tokens to individuals as in the previous example, or

■ **FIGURE 9.9** *Reinforcers Teachers Can Use to Increase Appropriate Behavior*

Student Provides Self-Reinforcers

- Student gives points to self for behaving well.
- Student says positive things to himself or herself, "I'm working hard and doing well."
- Student monitors his or her own behavior.

Adult Approval

- Verbal recognition from the teacher that the student is behaving appropriately, "John you are following directions on this assignment."
- Physical recognition from the teacher that the student is behaving appropriately. Teacher moves around the classroom and touches students on the shoulder who are behaving appropriately.
- Teacher informs parents or other professionals of the appropriate behavior of the student. This can be accomplished with "good news notes" or verbally.

Peer Recognition

- Teacher informs other students of the appropriate behavior of a student. "The award for Student of the Day goes to the outstanding improvement in behavior demonstrated by (student's name)."
- A box is established in the class where peers can write the names of students who have demonstrated appropriate behavior. These names can be read at the end of the week.
- A designated period of time is allocated at the end of the class period (high school) or day (elementary school) to ask students to recognize their fellow classmates who have demonstrated outstanding behavior.

Privileges

- Students are awarded free time after displaying appropriate behavior.
- Students are allowed to serve in key classroom roles after demonstrating outstanding behavior.
- Students are awarded passes that they can trade in for a night without homework.

Activities

- Students can perform an activity they like (e.g., drawing) after they complete the desired activity (e.g., the activity during that class period).
- Students can perform their tasks on the computer.
- Students can perform their tasks with a partner they select.

Tokens

- Tokens are items (e.g., chips, play money, points) that can be exchanged for something of value.
- Use tokens to reward groups or teams who are behaving appropriately.
- Allow groups of individuals to accumulate tokens that they can "spend" on privileges such as no homework, or free time.

Tangibles

- Tangibles refer to rewards that are desirable objects to students, but usually not objects they can consume (e.g., toys, pencils, erasers, paper, crayons).
- Tokens can be exchanged for tangible reinforcers.
- Tangible reinforcers can be used to reward the class for meeting a class goal.
- Tangible reinforcers may be needed to maintain the behavior of a student with severe behavior problems.

Consumables

- Consumables refer to rewards that are desirable objects to students that they consume (e.g., raisins, pieces of cereal, candy).
- Tokens can be exchanged for consumable reinforcers.
- Consumable reinforcers can be used to reward the class for meeting a class goal.
- Consumable reinforcers may be needed to maintain the behavior of a student with severe behavior problems.

Source: Adapted from S. Vaughn, C. S. Bos, and J. S. Schumm, *Teaching Mainstreamed, Diverse, and At-Risk Students in the General Education Classroom* (Boston: Allyn and Bacon, 1997).

award the entire class. Either way, the underlying principle is that students will be motivated to earn tokens that are collected and exchanged for previously determined privileges (e.g., a class pizza party, or first choice of equipment at recess).

4. *Changing inappropriate behavior.* Behaviors that are interfering are the ones that teachers can most easily identify. It is much easier for teachers to list the behaviors they would like to see reduced than to identify behaviors they would like to have increased. Morgan and Reinhart (1991) identify the following guiding principles to assist in changing inappropriate behavior of students.

- Do not use threats. Consider carefully the consequences you intend to use. Do not threaten students with a consequence you are actually unwilling to use or that will force you to back down.
- Follow through consistently on the rules you make, with the consequences you have predetermined.
- Do not establish so many rules that you spend too much time applying consequences. You will find yourself continually at war with the students.
- Do not establish consequences that are punishing to you. If you are stressed or inconvenienced by the consequence you may eventually begin to resent the student, which would interfere with your relationship.
- Listen and talk to the student but avoid disagreements or arguments. If you are tempted to argue, set another time to continue the discussion.
- Use logic, principles, and effective guidelines to make decisions. Avoid using your power to make students do something without connecting it to a logical principle.
- Do not focus on minor or personal peeves. Focus on the problems that are the most interfering.
- Treat each student as an individual with his or her own problems and abilities. Avoid comparing students' behaviors or abilities, as this does not assist students in self-understanding or in

better understanding the problems and abilities of others.

- Remember that students' problems belong to them and are not your problems. Although their problems may interfere with your work, they are not your problems. Students with behavior or emotional problems are often successful at transferring their problems to others. Students need to learn to resolve their own conflicts.
- Students often say or do things that are upsetting to teachers. Recognize your feelings and do not let them control your behavior. Do not respond to the upsetting behavior of a student by "striking back," humiliating, embarrassing, or berating the student.
- Solicit the assistance of parents and students in putting the problem in writing to assure that all of you agree on what needs to be changed.
- Get student and parent input on the behavior problem and suggestions for what might reduce it.
- Set up a plan that identifies the problem, consequence, and/or rewards for changes in behavior. See Figure 9.10 and Figure 9.11 for a sample behavioral contract and a self-management plan.

Positive Behavioral Support

In recent years, the principles of behavior management have been applied in various community settings (school, family) with supports to reduce problem behaviors and develop appropriate behaviors that lead to enhanced social relations and lifestyle. This modification of behavior management principles is called *positive behavioral support* (PBS).

The focus of PBS is to develop individualized interventions that stress prevention of problem behaviors through effective educational programming to improve the individual's quality of life (Janney and Snell, 2000). Behavior is one way of communication and is often a product of a combination of the environment and the individual. Hence, PBS involves careful observation of circumstances and the purpose of the problem behavior. A significant number of

■ **FIGURE 9.10** *Sample Behavior Contract*

DATE: _____

Mr. Reynolds will give one point to Joleen when she exhibits any of the following in his classroom:

1. Raises her hand appropriately and waits for the teacher to call on her before responding to a question or seeking information.
2. She sits appropriately (in chair with all four legs on the ground).
3. When annoyed by other students, she ignores them or informs the teacher instead of yelling at and/or hitting others.

After Joleen has earned 10 points, she may select one of the following:

1. She may obtain a 20-minute coupon to be used at any time to work on the computer.
2. She may serve as the teacher's assistant for a day.
3. She may obtain a 15-minute coupon for free time.

4. She may have lunch with the teacher and brought by the teacher.

Joleen may continue to select awards for every 10 points earned. New awards may be decided upon by the teacher and Joleen, and added to the list. I, Joleen Moore, agree to the conditions stated above, and understand that I will not be allowed any of the rewards until I have earned 10 points following the above stated guidelines.

_____
(student's signature)

I, Mr. Reynolds, agree to the conditions stated above. I will give Joleen one of the aforementioned rewards only after she has earned 10 points.

_____
(teacher's signature)

---

negative behaviors can be dealt with by modifying the environment (e.g., altering seating arrangements). PBS also emphasizes teaching appropriate behaviors to replace the inappropriate behavior in a normalized setting (Janney and Snell, 2000).

Rick is a fourth-grade student who has a learning disability, poor social skills, and difficulty interacting with peers. He was seen hitting other students and is known to get into fights for no apparent reasons. A careful observation of Rick's interactions with peers and his behaviors suggested that hitting was Rick's way of saying, "Get off my back." Rick was taught to say, "Get off my back" and walk away instead of hitting. All the teachers in the school reminded Rick to "use his words instead of his hands" to communicate. He was taught other specific skills necessary for successful social interactions such as joining a group and initiating and maintaining a conversation. Teachers tried to pair Rick with other students during classroom activities to provide him with opportunities to practice his new skills.

In this case, Rick's behavior and the environment in which target behaviors occurred were observed. Once the causes, circumstances, and purposes of the

behaviors were identified, the classroom teacher met with other teachers to discuss and enlist their help in providing Rick with the support he would need. The teachers also developed a list of specific social skills to teach Rick. Over time, Rick's problem behaviors decreased, his social skills improved, and he made friends with a few students.

John is a first-grade student with behavior problems. He gets in trouble for taking materials from his neighbors without requesting their permission. John's teacher moved his desk closer to the end of the row so he would have only three neighbors. She also taught John to think and take out all the materials he needed to do a particular assignment such as completing the worksheet requires the worksheet, pencil, and eraser. She even placed a small box labeled "materials needed" on his table so John could place all the materials he needed for a particular work in his box and not have to borrow from his neighbors. The teacher also taught John appropriate ways of asking others to lend him their materials.

In this case, John's target behaviors and the environment in which they occurred were observed, and then the causes, circumstances, and purposes of the

■ **FIGURE 9.11** *Self-Management Plan*

Name: Kiernen Smathers

Target Behavior: Submit completed homework to the teacher on time or meet with teacher prior to when the assignment is due to agree on an alternative date and time.

Where Behavior Occurs: Mathematics and Science

Goals:

1. Kiernen will use an assignment book and write down the assignments, guidelines, and due dates. The teacher will initial these to assure he understands them and has written them correctly.
2. Kiernen will interpret what he needs to do for each assignment and ask questions as needed.
3. Kiernen will discuss any assignments with the teacher ahead of time if he anticipates not having them ready on time.

Time Line: Meet each Friday to review progress and assignments. Revise plan as needed.

Reinforcer: Kiernen will receive 15 minutes of extra time to work on the computer each day his assignments are completed.

Evaluation: Kiernen will write a brief description of the program's success.

---

behavior were determined. The teacher then decided to alter the physical environment (move John's desk) to reduce the circumstances in which John could intrude on his neighbors. She also taught him alternative behaviors (organizing his materials) to replace his old inappropriate behaviors (taking materials from neighbors).

INSTRUCTIONAL ACTIVITIES

This section provides instructional activities related to developing socialization skills. Some of the activities teach new skills; others are best suited for practice and reinforcement of already acquired skills. For each activity, the objective, materials, and teaching procedures are described.

■ **Please Help**

Objective: To teach students a process for asking for help when needed and yet continuing to work until assistance is given. To have a record-keeping system that allows the teacher to monitor how many times each day he or she assists each student.

Grades: Primary and intermediate

Materials: A 6 × 8 inch card that states "Please Help _____ (student's name)" and then a place to list the date and comments.

Teaching Procedures: Construct the "Please Help" card for each student, including a place to mark the date and comments. Give all the students a card and inform them that they are to place the card on their desks when they need help. They are to continue working until you or someone else is able to provide assistance.

When you or your assistant is able to provide help, mark the date and time on the card and any appropriate comments such as, "We needed to review the rules for long division," or "She could not remember the difference between long and short vowels," or "He solved the problem himself before I arrived."

PLEASE HELP JENNIFER		
DATE	TIME	COMMENTS

■ Problem Box

Objective: To give students an opportunity to identify problems they are having with others and to feel their problems will be heard and attended to.

Grades: All grades

Materials: Shoe box decorated and identified as "Problem Box."

Teaching Procedures: Show the students the box that is decorated and identified as the "Problem Box." Place the box in a prominent location in the classroom. Tell the students that when they have problems with other students, teachers, or even at home they can write the problems down and put them in the box. At the end of every day, you and the students will spend a designated amount of time (e.g., 15 minutes) reading problems and trying to solve them as a class. Be sure to tell students they do not need to identify themselves or their notes.

During the designated time, open the problem box and read a selected note. Solicit assistance from the class in solving the note. Direct students' attention to identifying the problem, suggesting solutions, evaluating the consequences of the solutions, and identifying a solution and describing how it might be implemented.

■ A Date by Telephone

Objective: To give students structured skills for obtaining a date by telephone.

Grades: Secondary

Materials: Two nonworking telephones.

Teaching Procedures: Discuss with the students why preplanning a telephone call with a prospective date might be advantageous. Tell them that you are going to teach them some points to remember when calling to ask for a date. After you describe each of the following points, role play them so the students can observe their appropriate use:

1. Telephone at an *appropriate time.*
2. Use an *icebreaker,* such as recalling a mutually shared experience or a recent event in school.
3. *State what you would like to do and ask him or her to do it.* Ask the person what kinds of things he or she likes to do on the weekend. After there is an initial lull in the conversation, state you would like to take her or him to the movies, state when, and to see what. Then ask the person if he or she would like to go with you.
4. If yes, *make appropriate arrangements* for day, time, and transportation. If no, ask if you can call again.

Be sure that each student has an opportunity to role play.

■ Making and Keeping Friends

Objective: To have students identify the characteristics of students who are successful at making and keeping friends and, after identifying these characteristics, to evaluate themselves in how well they perform.

Grades: Intermediate and secondary

Materials: Writing materials

**How Good Are You at Making
and Keeping Friends**

Next to each item, circle the face that best
describes how well you do.

1. I tell friends the truth.

2. I call friends on the phone.

3. I share my favorite toys and games
with friends.

Teaching Procedures: Ask the students to think
of children they know who are good at making and
keeping friends. Brainstorm what these children do
that makes them successful at making and keeping
friends. On an overhead projector or chalkboard,
write the student-generated responses to the characteristics of children good at making and keeping
friends. Then select the most agreed on characteristics and write them on a sheet of paper with smiley
faces, neutral faces, and frowny faces so students
can circle the face that is most like them in response to that characteristic. Finally, ask students to
identify one characteristic they would like to target
to increase their skills at making and maintaining
friends.

■ **Identifying Feelings**

Objective: To identify the feelings of others and
self, and to respond better to those feelings.

Grades: Primary and intermediate

Materials: Cards with pictures of persons in situations where their feelings can be observed or
deduced.

Teaching Procedures: Select pictures that elicit
feeling words such as *happy, angry, jealous, hurt,*

sad, mad, and so on. Show the pictures to the students
and ask them to identify the feelings of the people in
the pictures. Discuss what information in the picture
cued them to the emotional states of the people. Then
ask the students to draw a picture of a time when they
felt as the person in the picture feels. Conclude by
asking students to discuss their pictures.

■ **I'm New Here (and Scared)**

By Sandra Stroud

Objective: To help students who are new to your
community and school make a positive adjustment.

For many students, moving to a new school can be an especially traumatic experience.

Grades: K–12

Materials: The *good will* of a group of socially competent student volunteers, and their adult leader—a teacher, guidance counselor, or school administrator.

Teaching Procedures: The adult in charge organizes a school service club whose purpose it is to take new students under its wing and help them feel welcome at their school. Students in this organization can be given sensitivity training to help them understand how new students feel when they move to a new area of the country and enter a new school. The group can discuss and decide upon the many strategies they can use to help new students feel "at home." One of their functions could be to speak to whole classes about how it feels to be a new student at a school, and to suggest how each student at this school can help new students when they arrive.

For a new student, nothing is quite as traumatic when they enter a new school as having no friend or group with whom to sit when they go to the cafeteria for lunch. Therefore, one of a new student's greatest needs is for someone to invite him or her to have lunch with them. This should be the number-one priority of the members of the welcoming club. New students may eventually become members of this club, joining in the effort of welcoming and helping the new students who follow them.

Note: This instructional activity was written by a mother who would have been so grateful if her son's middle school had had such a program when he entered the eighth grade there. As it was, things were pretty rough for him until his band teacher realized that he was skipping lunch. She paved the way for him to begin eating lunch with a group of boys who became his best friends!

■ I'm in My Own Little House

By Sandra Stroud

Objective: To help young children acquire a sense of personal "space" as well as an understanding of

"other people's space." Many young children have not acquired an inner sense of space—of their own space and of space that belongs to others. As a result, the more active of these youngsters—usually little boys—tend to intrude on other children's space and, in the process, annoy the other children. As a result, they may not be well liked by their classmates. The problem is made worse by the fact that many primary children sit at long tables where the space of one student often overlaps the space of others.

Grades: Primary

Materials: Individual student desks, and colored masking tape.

Teaching Procedure: The teacher arranges the room so that each student desk sits in an area that is three-feet-square. The desks are barely close enough to each other to make it possible for students to pass materials from one student to another without leaving their seats. On the floor around each desk, the teacher outlines the three-square-foot block with colored masking tape.

The teacher explains the taped areas, or blocks, by telling a story about a child who wanted a little house that was all his own where no one would bother him or his belongings. This was "his" house. Just as his house was his, he knew that the other children needed their houses and that he shouldn't bother them or their houses either. (Teacher makes up the story according to his or her imagination or to fit the situation in his or her classroom.)

■ Introducing People

By Dheepa Sridhar

Objective: To teach students to introduce friends to one another appropriately.

Grades: Intermediate and secondary

Materials: None required

Teaching Procedures: Discuss the importance of introducing people. Allow students to share experiences such as when they were with a friend who was either good at or had difficulty introducing them to his or her other friends. Tell students that you are going to teach them some points to remember when they introduce people to each other. After describing each of the following points, ask students to role play to demonstrate their use:

1. Provide additional information about the person being introduced such as "This is Mark, he's new to our class" or "This is Mark, he's good at baseball."
2. Provide additional information about people in the group who share common interests with the new person such as "Steve plays basketball."
3. Talk about those common interests.

■ Invitation to Play

By Dheepa Sridhar

Objective: To teach students to invite a classmate to play with them.

Grades: Primary

Materials: Toys

Teaching Procedures: Tell students that they should do the following when requesting a classmate to join them in play.

1. Decide what you want to play (e.g., jump rope, building with Legos).
2. Check to see if you have the materials (rope or Legos).
3. Check to see what the person you want to play with is doing.
4. Wait for a lull in the activity that the person is engaging in.
5. Ask him or her if they would like to play (rope or Legos).
6. If they refuse, ask them what else they would like to play.
7. Have students role play and provide feedback.

■ In Your Shoes

By Dheepa Sridhar

Objective: To facilitate students in taking a different perspective.

Grades: Intermediate and high school

Materials: Cardboard cut-outs of two pairs of shoes. Let the pairs be of different colors. Masking tape, index cards with social problems written on them. For example, "Jake was supposed to go to a baseball game with Pete over the weekend. He has been looking forward to this event all week. On Friday Pete says he would rather go to a movie instead of the game."

Teaching Procedures: Discuss the importance of taking the other person's perspective. Tell them this activity will help them see a different perspective.

1. Tape a line on the floor with the Scotch tape. Write the name of a character (e.g., Jake and Pete) on each pair of shoes. Place each pair of shoes on either side of the line.
2. Have two students volunteer to be Jake or Pete.
3. Ask one student to stand on Jake's shoe and the other student to stand on Pete's shoes.
4. Let them talk about the problem.
5. Ask the students to exchange places and discuss the problem.
6. Help the students reach a solution that is acceptable to both parties.

Note: This activity can also be used with students experiencing problems with each other instead of hypothetical situations. Although only two students can participate at a time, the rest of the class can help by generating solutions and discussing the consequences of those solutions.

SUMMARY

This chapter described the social behaviors of students with learning and behavior disorders. Students identified as behavior-disordered display behaviors that are inappropriate and/or harmful to self or others. Many behavior-disordered students have appropriate social skills but do not use them or do not know when and with whom to use them. Other students do not have the skills and need to be taught them.

Students with learning disabilities are frequently identified as having social difficulties. As a group, they are more frequently rejected by their peers and teachers. They have been characterized as having social interaction difficulties, communication difficulties, low role-taking skills, and low self-concepts.

Five interventions to increase appropriate social behavior and decrease inappropriate social behavior were presented: intervention by prescription, interpersonal problem solving, behavior therapy, positive behavioral support, and ASSET. Intervention by prescription is a model that focuses on the student's impulse management. Appropriate intervention procedures are applied according to the student's need for external control or ability to utilize internal control. Behavioral approaches are utilized when the student has low impulse control and needs external controls; more cognitively oriented interventions are used as the student demonstrates more internal impulse control. Interpersonal problem solving teaches students strategies for communicating effectively with others and solving and preventing interpersonal conflicts with others. Behavioral therapy is based on the principles of applied behavior analysis for increasing and decreasing behaviors.

Positive behavioral support is based on the principles of behavior therapy, but it focuses on improving the quality of life of students along with increasing positive behaviors. The goal of positive behavioral support is to provide individualized educational programs to prevent problem behaviors and enhance social relations of students.

A number of intervention approaches have been effectively implemented to increase appropriate social behaviors. Five of these approaches were discussed in this chapter and provide effective techniques for developing appropriate social behaviors.

WEBSITES AS RESOURCES TO ASSIST IN SOCIALIZATION AND CLASSROOM MANAGEMENT

http://www.usoe.k12.ut/us/sars/Upi/behavior_management.htm
This Website provides several links related to behavior management (e.g., positive behavior support, supporting students with challenging behavior).

http://www.ldonline.org/ld_indepth/social_skills/lavoie_teach.html
This Website contains information on teachers' role in developing social skills and other links related to social skills.

http://www.ldonline.org/ld_indepth/teaching_techniques/class_manage.html
This Website provides information on adjustments in classroom management.

http://www.ldonline.org/ld_indepth/teaching_techniques/nasp_adhdclsrm.html
This Website provides information on general behavior intervention and environment arrangement.

http://www.ldonline.org/ld_indepth/teaching_techniques/strategies.html#anchor1001355
   This Website provides several useful links on social skills training.

http://www.ldonline.org/ld_indepth/social_skills/behavior_management.html
   This Website provides an overview of behavior management.

http://specialed.about.com/education/specialed/gi/dynamic/offsite.htm?site=http://
www.geocities.com/Athens/Styx/7315/subjects/behavior.html
   This Website provides various classroom management links.

THINK AND APPLY

- What is social competence?
- What are the characteristics of students with social disabilities?
- What are two types of social interventions used with students with learning and behavior problems? What are the procedures for implementing these social interventions?
- What are several principles for teaching social skills to students with learning and behavior problems?
- Why can the communication style of students with learning disabilities be termed egocentric?
- How are student appearance and popularity related?
- Why do students whose behavior is aggressive require professional help?

10

Transition Planning and Life Skills/ Transition Education

by James R. Patton, Ed.D.

O U T L I N E

KEY TOPICS FOR MASTERY

- Various transitions that exist across a person's life span
- Key elements that contribute to successful transitions
- Introduction to the federal and professional definitions of transition
- Major themes that should guide transition practice
- Nature and implications of transition education
- Various approaches to teaching real-life content
- Key aspects of the transition planning process, including assessing transition needs and developing transition goals
- Major components of the individual transition plan
- Importance of active student involvement in the transition planning process
- The need to begin discussion of transition/real-life topics as early as possible

 BRIGHT IDEA

Turn to page 453 and read Think and Apply.

Kevin is a typical student with learning disabilities, and his case illustrates one of the many possible scenarios that exist in schools today.

Kevin is a 15-year-old who has a learning disability, and was identified as being eligible for special education services when he was in elementary school. He currently attends high school and participates in general education classes for most of the day.

Kevin is a bright student who works very hard to maintain his grades. He excels in his art classes, as he is a very talented artist. He does struggle in certain areas: written expression, organizational skills, and a variety of study skills, including note taking, test taking, and time management.

Kevin would like to become a commercial artist and is interested in attending a local community college when high school is over. The prospect of this happening is good if certain issues are considered and appropriate plans are developed.

Kevin's situation underscores the reality that all students have strengths along with areas that need some attention. As you read this chapter, think about

Kevin, and we'll discuss Kevin's transition needs and education further.

FUNDAMENTAL ISSUES RELATED TO TRANSITION

The notion of *transition* implies a period in time when change occurs. Specifically, transition relates to the movement from one situation to another. Many different transitions are part of the daily lives of all individuals, as explained in the next section. Transition, in Kevin's case, refers to "an outcome-oriented process" (Will, 1984) that considers various features of his future adult life. The actual act of transition planning is a set of activities that assists in preparing a person for the transition that is to take place.

As important as transition planning might seem, specific transition planning activities are mandated for only two of the many possible transitions through which children and youth with learning disabilities pass. The first mandated transition involves very young children (usually age 2 to 3) who are receiving services under the Individuals with Disabilities Education Act (IDEA) and who are exiting early-intervention programs. An Individual Family Service Plan (IFSP) has been developed for each of these toddlers. One component of this plan serves to smooth the movement of these young children from the early intervention program to an early childhood special education or another preschool program.

The second mandated transition affects students like Kevin who are preparing to exit the school system. Currently, transition planning must be initiated by age 14 for all youth who receive special and related services under IDEA. We'll discuss transition planning later in this chapter.

Types of Transitions

Important transitions occur throughout everyone's life. Some are normal and predictable (vertical), whereas others are specific to the individual and occur at unpredictable points in time (horizontal). Figure 10.1 presents the vertical transitions that individuals with disabilities will predictably experience along with select horizontal transitions that they may encounter during their lives. The life span–related (i.e., vertical) transitions are associated with predictable life events, such as beginning school, leaving elementary school, and growing older. Coordinated planning for these transitions can minimize the anxiety that may arise and make such transitions smoother. But in reality, little comprehensive planning occurs in the lives of most individuals.

Horizontal transitions refer to movement from one person-specific situation or setting to another. One of the most important and frequently discussed horizontal transitions is the movement from separate settings to more inclusive ones. This is an example of a transition that is not age specific, as opportunities for such movement are available throughout the life span for people with disabilities.

Key Elements of Successful Transitions

A few key provisions allow students to navigate the many transitions faced throughout their lives. All transitions can be accomplished more smoothly if the following elements are in place:

— Comprehensive planning (needs assessment and individual planning)
— Implementation of a plan of action
— Coordination, communication, and collaboration

Although other factors such as motivation or personal goals of the student making the transition are important to consider, these basic elements are the *sine qua non* for successful transition.

Comprehensive planning includes two related components. First, the special education teacher or transition specialist completes a thorough *needs assessment*. This includes talking with the student who is getting ready to transition and his or her parents, as well as exploring the possible programs or settings (e.g., technical school, community college, university, work) into which the student will be transitioning. In other words, the more the professional knows about the setting into which the student is transitioning (i.e., what is required to be successful, what kinds of accommodations are available if needed) and the student's existing competencies (strengths and needs), the better the chances are for an effective transition. In Kevin's case, the results of an initial needs assessment indicate certain areas where attention must be directed. Kevin's personal transition needs must be considered in relation to the demands of the community college he will attend if admitted.

The second component, *individual planning,* entails developing a plan of action based on the needs assessment. Although this plan may be formalized in a written document, for most of the transitions listed in Figure 10.1, ideas are discussed but a written document is not generated. Regardless of format, the key issue is that a plan of action is developed in which the student's current values, future preferences, and personal interests are balanced with the realistic demands of the new settings. A list of transition goals that need to be developed for Kevin is provided later in the chapter.

The second element is *implementing the plan of action*. Of course, needs assessments and individualized plans are useless if the plan of action is not

■ **FIGURE 10.1**   *Vertical and Horizontal Transition*

Source: Adapted from G. Blalock and J. R. Patton, "Transition and Students with Learning Disabilities: Creating Sound Futures," *Journal of Learning Disabilities, 29*(1) (1996): 8. Copyright 1996 by PRO-ED, Inc. Adapted with permission.

implemented effectively. Far too often, good plans are not put into effect. Whether the transition involves the transitioning a young child with severe language or learning disabilities from a preschool program to an inclusive kindergarten with special education support or the transition of an adolescent with emotional or behavioral disabilities from a residential hospital facility back to the public schools, certain actions must occur to achieve the desired results. Implement-

ing transitions frequently suffers from two potential threats: (1) the plan is not executed as it was designed; and (2) certain key aspects of the plan are not carried out because the needs assessment and/or the planning phase were completed inadequately or inappropriately.

The last key element of a successful transition is *coordination and communication* with the various persons at the various settings or agencies involved in the transition itself. Such coordination requires ongoing communication and collaboration. For example, Kevin's transition from high school to community college will be facilitated by coordination between his special education teacher who coordinates his special education services and key individuals at the community college such as admissions officers, advisors, and professionals associated with the office that works with students with disabilities.

When these three key elements are absent, transitions from one setting to another are likely to result only in physical relocation and not the more meaningful outcomes associated with favorable transitions.

Federal Mandate

The Individuals with Disabilities Education Act (IDEA) is the guiding source with regard to transitions for youth with disabilities. The 1997 amendments of IDEA define transition services as:

> A coordinated set of activities for a student with a disability that (1) is designed within an outcome-oriented process, that promotes movement from school to post-school activities, including postsecondary education, vocational training, integrated employment (including supported employment), continuing and adult education, adult services, independent living, or community participation; (2) is based on the individual student's needs, taking into account the student's preferences and interests; and (3) includes—(i) instruction; (ii) related services; (iii) community experiences; (iv) development of employment and other post-school adult living objectives; and (v) if appropriate, acquisition of daily living skills and functional vocational evaluation (*Federal Register,* 1999, s300.29(a)).

The IDEA mandate requires that the individualized education program (IEP) include the following information for each student:

— A statement of the transition services needs beginning at age 14 and updated annually (focus is on student's courses of study)
— A statement of needed transition services— beginning at age 16 (focus on needed services, linkages, and interagency responsibilities)

Using the federal definition as a starting point, the Division on Career Development and Transition (DCDT) of the Council for Exceptional Children developed a definition that reflects the contemporary thinking on this topic. The definition underscores the realities associated with students leaving school and assuming a variety of adult roles in the community. It also stresses the proactive nature of transition education and the importance of actively involving students in this process whenever possible.

> *Transition* refers to a change in status from behaving primarily as a student to assuming emergent adult roles in the community. These roles include employment, participating in post-secondary education, maintaining a home, becoming appropriately involved in the community, and experiencing satisfactory personal and social relationships. The process of enhancing transitions involves the participation and coordination of school programs, adult agency services, and natural supports within the community. The foundations for transition should be laid during the elementary and middle school years, guided by the broad concept of career development. Transition planning should begin no later than age 14, and students should be encouraged, to the full extent of their capabilities, to assume a maximum amount of responsibility for such planning (Halpern, 1994, p. 117)

Overriding Themes of Transition

Certain critical themes should guide the transition process for all youths with disabilities, whether transition planning results from mandate (IDEA) or is part of an ongoing set of services provided to all students in a school (career counseling). The following nine themes reflect best and promising practices (Patton and Dunn, 1998):

— Transition education efforts should (i.e., they can begin at the pr*alize on* *ne obvious*
— Transition planning mu looking at adulthood functioning (i.e. focus).
— Transition a stud

focus on areas of transition need. The process should be strength based.

— Student participation is crucial.

— Family involvement is not only desired but needed.

— Transition activities must be sensitive to cultural, family, community, and gender issues.

— The use of supports—particularly natural supports—is desirable and a part of everyday life.

— Timing is critical if a seamless transition to certain services is to be achieved.

— It may be necessary to prioritize transition needs if there are many to address and there is limited time to do so.

These themes provide a backdrop for the delivery of quality transition services to youth with disabilities. To date, too few transition programs demonstrate all of these themes, and, as a result, too many students are not being served well. A recent study, published by the National Council on Disability (2000), confirmed this point. The study found across the United States significant shortcomings in certain transition practices (notice to parents, statements of needed services, and meeting participants).

LIFE SKILLS OR TRANSITION EDUCATION

~f the themes highlighted in the previous sec-
a~s the importance of beginning the transi-
14), ~v. What is notable about the transition
tion. A ~ ~at it tends to be mostly a retroac-
tive process
successful ad~nsition needs are identified
ementary years a~ool career (e.g., at age
real-life topics. Life~ ~about the situa-
ered broadly, accomplis~ ~more proac-
~d with

The problem with the term *life skills instruction* is that is often is interpreted to mean the program of study provided to students with developmental disabilities or mental retardation. While this might be the case, the notion of life skills instruction used in this chapter is an expansive one that includes a broad array of real-life topics that are likely to be meaningful to all students with disabilities. In fact, life skills are important to all students, with or without disabilities.

The term *transition education* although not widely used in schools, is a refreshing way to refer to life skill–related issues in the context of transition practices. In this chapter, transition education refers to all education-related activities, particularly in the areas of curriculum and instruction, that correspond to and prepare students for the demands of adulthood. The term implies that many transition-related activities can occur prior to the mandated transition process that should formally begin by age 14.

Life Skill Domains

A number of conceptual models can be used as a framework for organizing the real-life content that should be addressed prior to the beginning of the transition planning process. Sitlington (1996) summarized many of the most commonly cited models. Two models serve as good examples of the adult domains that teachers should keep in mind when considering coverage of real-life content. The two models are the Demands of Adulthood (Cronin and Patton, 1993) and the Life-Centered Career Education (LCCE) (Brolin, 1997). The general features of both of these models are presented in Table 10.1.

Adults need to have some degree of at least minimal competence and independence in each of the six adult domains of the Cronin and Patton model. These domains, along with the 23 subdomains and the 147 major life demands, serve as a useful organizational framework from which one can identify important real-life content. Similarly, the Brolin model can also serve as a guide for organizing areas of adult competence. It focuses on three major curricular areas under which 22 competencies and 97 subcompetencies are organized.

■ **TABLE 10.1** *Models of Adult Functioning*

Model	Adult Domain/ Curriculum Area	Subdomains/Competency Areas
Domains of Adulthood (Cronin and Patton, 1993)	Employment/Education	General Job Skills General Education/Training Considerations Employment Setting Career Refinement and Reevaluation
	Home and Family	Home Management Financial Management Family Life Child Rearing
	Leisure Pursuits	Indoor Activities Outdoor Activities Community/Neighborhood Activities Travel Entertainment
	Community Involvement	Citizenship Community Awareness Services/Resources
	Physical/Emotional Health	Physical Health Emotional Health
	Personal Responsibility and Relationships	Personal Confidence/Understanding Goal Setting Self-Improvement Relationships Personal Expression
Life Centered Career Education (Brolin, 1997)	Daily Living Skills	Managing Personal Finances Selecting and Managing a Household Caring for Personal Needs Raising Children and Meeting Marriage Responsibilities Buying, Preparing, and Consuming Food Buying and Caring for Clothing Exhibiting Responsible Citizenship Utilizing Recreational Facilities and Engaging in Leisure Getting Around the Community
	Personal-Social Skills	Achieving Self-Awareness Acquiring Self-Confidence Achieving Socially Responsible Behavior Maintaining Good Interpersonal Skills Achieving Independence Making Adequate Decisions Communicating with Others
	Occupational Guidance and Preparation	Knowing and Exploring Occupational Possibilities Selecting and Planning Occupational Choices Exhibiting Appropriate Work Habits and Behavior

(continued)

TABLE 10.1 *Continued*

Model	Adult Domain/ Curriculum Area	Subdomains/Competency Areas
Life Centered Career Education (Brolin, 1997)	Occupational Guidance and Preparation	Seeking, Securing, and Maintaining Employment Exhibiting Sufficient Physical-Manual Skills Obtaining Specific Occupational Skills

Source: J. R. Patton, M. E. Cronin, and S. Wood, *Infusing Real-Life Topics into Curricula at the Elementary, Middle, and High School Levels: Recommended Procedures and Instructional Examples* (Austin, TX: PRO-ED, 1999), p. 3. Reprinted with permission.

Relationship of Real-Life Topics to Academic or Social Skills Development

The ability to read, write, converse, compute, and problem solve are skills that educators strive to instill in students prior to their exit from school. These skills and others such as the social skills, study skills, and learning strategies discussed in Chapters Seven and Nine are considered by parents and school professionals to be the primary exit skills of all students, and their incorporation into instructional programs is critical. Figure 10.2 illustrates how critical life skills relate to key academic and social skills development at the secondary level.

Integrating a transition education (i.e., life skills) perspective provides a rational method for applying relevant real-life situations to important skill areas associated with the general education curriculum. The sample activities presented in the matrix are only a sampling of everyday functional applications; many others exist. Furthermore, each situation and community setting may demand slightly different types of real-life activities depending on the expectations for adult success in that community.

While most secondary-level students with learning and behavior problems are taking general education classes, they may also still require basic skills instruction in reading or mathematics. These situations, however, do not have to preclude the teaching of other important real-life concepts. Integrating life skills and real-life situations with basic skills instruction often becomes a motivating factor for success in learning the basic skills. For example, mathe-

matical word problems should incorporate instructional activities that relate to the student's current experiences.

Program Options

There are various ways to cover real-life topics in an education program. For students with disabilities who are included in general education classes, finding significant blocks of instructional time to cover these topics can be difficult. However, with careful coordination between general and special educators and the use of coteaching, as discussed in Chapter Eleven, instructional activities that use real-life topics can be provided to students, regardless of their educational placement. Patton, Cronin, and Jairrels (1997) suggest that the life skills needs of students can be addressed through various types of coursework that are life skills or transition education oriented, or through the integration of real-life topics into existing content. These options are depicted in Figure 10.3.

Life Skills Coursework

The first three options on the continuum (from the left) in Figure 10.3 are examples of different types of coursework that are possible. The first option represents a comprehensive approach to covering real-life topics. With this option, a series or set of specific life skills courses, with titles such as "Personal Finance," "Health and Hygiene," and "Practical Communications," is available to students. This particular option is most likely to occur when great curricular freedoms are present. The second option usually results in the creation of a single course that covers a

■ **FIGURE 10.2**   *Secondary Matrix: Relationship of Scholastic/Social Skills to Adult Domains*

	Employment/ Education	*Home and Family*	*Leisure Pursuits*	*Community Involvement*	*Emotional/ Physical Health*	*Personal Responsibility/ Relationships*
Reading	Reading classified ads for jobs	Interpreting bills	Locating and understanding movie information in newspaper	Following directions on tax forms	Comprehending directions on medication	Reading letters from friends
Writing	Writing a letter of application for a job	Writing checks	Writing for information on a city to visit	Filling in a voter registration form	Filling in your medical history on forms	Sending thank-you notes
Listening	Understanding oral directions of a procedure change	Comprehending oral directions about making dinner	Listening for forecast to plan outdoor activity	Understanding campaign ads	Attending lectures for stress	Taking turns in a conversation
Speaking	Asking your boss for a raise	Discussing morning routines with family	Inquiring about tickets for a concert	Stating your opinion at the school board meeting	Describing symptoms to a doctor	Giving feedback to a friend about the purchase of a compact disk
Math Applications	Understanding difference between net and gross pay	Computing the cost of doing laundry in a laundromat versus at home	Calculating the cost of a dinner out versus eating at home	Obtaining informations for a building permit	Using a thermometer	Planning the costs of a date
Problem Solving	Settling a dispute with a coworker	Deciding how much to budget for rent	Role-playing appropriate behaviors for various places	Knowing what to do if you are the victim of fraud	Selecting a doctor	Deciding how to ask someone for a date
Survival Skills	Using a prepared career planning packet	Listing emergency phone numbers	Using a shopping center directory	Marking a calendar for important dates (e.g., recycling, garbage collection)	Using a system to remember to take vitamins	Developing a system to remember birthdays
Personal/ Social	Applying appropriate interview skills	Helping a child with homework	Knowing the rules of a neighborhood pool	Locating self-improvement classes	Getting a yearly physical exam	Discussing how to negotiate a price at a flea market

Source: M. E. Cronin and J. R. Patton, *Life Skills Instruction for All Students with Special Needs: A Practical Guide for Integrating Real-Life Content into the Curriculum* (Austin, TX: PRO-ED, 1993), p. 33. Reprinted by permission.

■ **FIGURE 10.3** *Options for Organizing Life-Skills Content for Formal Instruction*

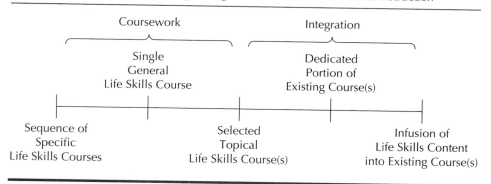

Source: M. E. Cronin and J. R. Patton, *Life Skills Instruction for All Students with Special Needs: A Practical Guide for Integrating Real-Life Content into the Curriculum* (Austin: TX: PRO-ED, 1993) p. 25. Reprinted by permission.

wide variety of real-life topics. Such a course could be entitled "Life 101," "Skills for Life," or "Introduction to Adulthood" and could be offered to all students in the school on an elective basis. The last option usually entails the development a single course that might focus on a single subject area such as "Life Skills" or "Consumer Math" or one of the courses in the comprehensive curriculum just described (e.g., "Personal Finance"). These courses can vary according to local educational or community needs. One example is the "Science for Living" course developed by the Dubuque Iowa Community Schools (Helmke, Havekost, Patton, and Polloway, 1994).

Integration of Real-Life Topics into Existing Curricular Content

Another method of covering life skills topics is to extend the coverage of existing courses into additional meaningful, life-related areas. Figure 10.3 highlights two ways to do this: (1) dedicating a portion of an existing course to relevant topics; and (2) infusing real-life topics/activities into the scope and sequence of existing courses.

The first integration technique, also called *augmentation,* requires that additional instructional time be available to focus on life skills topics. If thoughtfully planned, such allocation of instructional time can be accomplished without sacrificing time needed

to cover the topics that are explicitly stated in the course sequence (Cronin and Patton, 1993; Patton, Cronin, and Jairrels, 1997). For example, it might be appropriate to include additional lessons (i.e., augment) within a consumer math course that address the real-life topics associated with moving into an apartment. Knowing how to do these real-life tasks will be particularly important for many students, like Kevin, when they exit school, and its one that is not typically covered in existing instructional materials presented at the secondary level.

The second integration technique, the infusion approach, uses actual existing course content as the basis for exploring real-life topics. The primary goal is to infuse real-life topics directly into information being covered. With this approach, the course content is closely examined to determine how important life skills that students will need as adults can be woven into instruction.

For example, life skills related to personal relationships could be integrated into a reading lesson in which the topic of the story is a family who is experiencing the realities of divorce (see Figure 10.4). Using the infusion approach, the teacher would read the passage prior to teaching and identify the passage content that relates to various real-life topics and then decide which life skills topics to infuse into the lesson. The amount of time devoted to such coverage

■ **FIGURE 10.4** *Infusing Real-Life Topics into Existing Curricula*

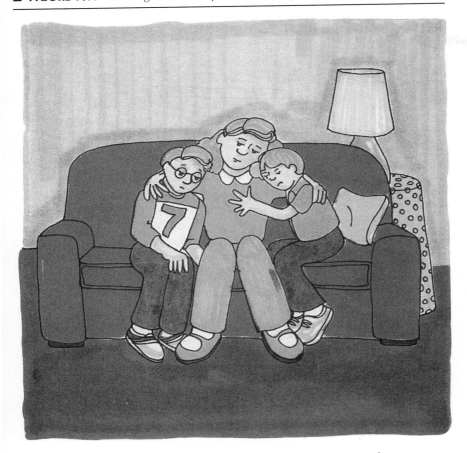

The children did not like to hear arguing. The boys asked Jenny, "What is wrong? Why are Mom and Dad fighting?"

Jenny could not answer the question. She hugged Ian and Bruce. Then Mom and Dad came into the room. They looked very unhappy. Bruce, Ian, and Jenny did not laugh. They all felt very sad, and they were scared. Everyone in the family was worried.

Source: S. P. Quigley, C. M. King, P. L. McAnally, and S. Rose, *Reading Milestones: An Alternative Reading Program*, Level 5, Brown Reader 1, 2nd ed. (Austin, TX: PRO-ED, 1991), p. 22. Copyright 1991 by PRO-ED, Inc. Reprinted by permission.

does not have to be substantial—often a quick "hit" works best. On other occasions, more time might be devoted to a very important topic. In this case, a discussion could ensue on the following issues: describe how it makes you feel when two people in your family argue; identify some ways that you could convey your feelings and concerns, and so on.

This infusion approach provides relevance to course content taught on a daily basis in addition to the importance of covering life skills topics—no matter what the subject of the class might be. In addition, this approach may be the only one available when students are in inclusive settings and the life skills coursework option is not available or does not exist. A valuable point is that this technique gives relevance to the content being taught not only to students identified as disabled but also to other students who are not disabled and who are in the same instructional setting.

Additional examples of these two techniques (augmentation and infusion) for integrating real-life topics into existing math materials are illustrated in Table 10.2. The table shows examples of both augmentation and infusion ideas for a variety of math topics for elementary and secondary levels.

TRANSITION PLANNING PROCESS

The actual process of planning for the transition of students from school to life after school is complex, and, to be done in a supportive manner, it requires that important people are actively involved, certain critical elements of the process are implemented, and specific activities are carried out as highlighted at the beginning of the chapter, An understanding has to be reached whereby all players involved with this transition process must share the responsibility for seeing that it transpires successfully.

Ultimately, the primary objective of this process is the seamless transition to postschool living conditions characterized by being able to deal successfully with the demands of adulthood. The vehicle for documenting that this will happen to the best extent possible is the transition plan. In this section of the chapter,

we will identify best and recommended practices that contribute to this primary objective and that comply with federal mandate.

Key Elements of the Transition Process

The key elements of the transition process are illustrated in Figure 10.5. The first box, identified as "Proactive Transition Education," refers to the life skills or transition curriculum provided in the first part of this chapter. Essentially, it refers to coverage of adult-referenced topics across levels of schooling.

The initial formal phase of the transition planning process involves the comprehensive assessment of a student's transition needs. The general areas on which a transition needs assessment should focus includes a range of transition planning areas. The key transition areas that are identified by different states vary greatly. However, a listing of the more common planning areas (Clark and Patton, 1997) includes:

- Community participation
- Daily living
- Employment
- Financial and income management
- Health
- Independent living (includes living arrangements)
- Leisure and recreation
- Postsecondary education
- Relationships and social skills
- Transportation and mobility
- Vocational training

It is important that a comprehensive transition needs assessment consider all of these areas. If a needs assessment is conducted effectively, the results should lead to the recognition that more in-depth information is needed in some areas and/or the development of transition-related goals.

The transition planning process should illuminate two different types of goals and a number of activities that are needed to accomplish the goals. One type of goal that will be generated is instructional in nature. In other words, these goals focus on knowledge and skills needs in academic, social, and behav-

■ **TABLE 10.2** *Augmentation and Infusion Examples*

Source	Topic Covered	A/I	Sample Activities
Practical math textbook (Secondary level)	"Budgeting for Recreation"	A	Add coverage on the "economics" of dating
		I	Identify best time and cost for going to a movie
	"Credit Card Math"	A	Add coverage of how to get the best deal on a credit card (e.g., low APR, no annual fee)
		I	Present ways to get lower APR or waiver of annual fee
	"Maintaining a Vehicle"	A	Add coverage of the realities of being involved in an accident and what one needs to do
		I	Discuss the importance of keeping tires inflated at the proper levels
Basal math textbook (Elementary level)	"Using Decimals: Adding and Subtracting Money" —buying a sleeping bag	A	Add coverage of costs of purchasing or renting camping gear
		I	Discuss where one can buy or rent a sleeping bag
	"Using Tables to Solve Problems"	A	Add coverage on how to use the weather map from the newspaper
		I	Identify other tables that have numbers

Note: A = augmentation; I = infusion

Source: J. R. Patton, M. E. Cronin, D. S. Bassett, and A. E. Koppel, "A Life Skills Approach to Mathematics Instruction: Preparing Students with Learning Disabilities for the Real-Life Math Demands of Instruction," *Journal of Learning Disabilities, 30* (1997): 185. Reprinted by permission.

ioral areas. Since these goals are instructional goals they should be written into the IEP. The other type of goal emphasizes linkage to needed services and supports. These goals help to ensure that certain services and supports are in place for those students who will benefit from them in adulthood. It is important to note that it is unlikely that both types of goals will be required for every transition area assessed.

In the case study of Kevin, introduced at the beginning of this chapter, we can see that his transition needs will involve both types of goals. Clearly, he has instructional needs in a variety of areas such as writing and study skills. Kevin's transition needs also indicate that he has linkage needs, related to the demands of the community college he is likely to attend.

■ **FIGURE 10.5**   *Transition Planning Process*

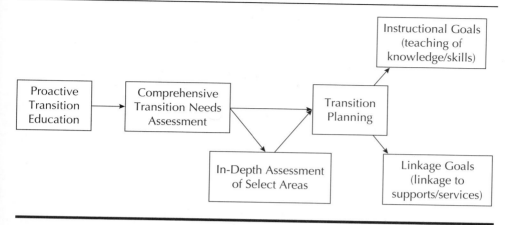

Source: G. M. Clark and J. R. Patton, *Transition Planning Inventory* (Austin, TX: PRO-ED, 1997), p. 26.
Reprinted with permission.

Aside from the implications that are stated in the federal definition of transition services, certain principles should guide the transition planning process. Apply the Concept 10.1 highlights the four key guiding principles, the first two of which are adapted from Patton and Dunn (1998, p. 21).

Assessing Transition Needs

The collection of information about a student's transition needs requires a methodology that school-based personnel who have transition responsibilities find acceptable. In general, they want techniques that are not complicated, are not time-consuming, and deliver useful information for generating transition plans.

A variety of assessment techniques along with a number of existing sources of information are available as a way to generate a comprehensive picture of a student's transition needs. Two useful resources that provide information on transition assessment are *Assess for Success: Handbook on Transition Assessment* (Sitlington, Neubert, Begun, Lombard, and Leconte, 1996) and *Assessment for Transitions Planning* (Clark, 1998). Table 10.3 provides a sampling of select commercially available instruments for acquiring transition planning information. A thorough

discussion of these instruments and other nonstandardized procedures can be found in Clark (1998).

Transition personnel need a systematic way to obtain comprehensive transition-related information on students. Whichever system is ultimately chosen, it must be one that possesses the following features:

— Gathers information effectively, efficiently, and on students who are not known well by the school-based transition person
— Leads logically and quickly to the planning phase
— Can be used with large numbers of students

Case Study: Kevin

Kevin's situation serves as a good example of how a transition-needs assessment works. Kevin was administered the *Transition Planning Inventory* (TPI) (Clark and Patton, 1997), one of the instruments listed in Table 10.3. The TPI requests information from three sources (student, parents, school-based personnel) about 46 competencies (organized along nine transition planning areas). Although the TPI administration identified a number of areas for which transition planning should be done, we will focus only on one of the areas: success in postsecondary education.

APPLY THE CONCEPT 10.1

GUIDING PRINCIPLES FOR THE TRANSITION PLANNING PROCESS

- The more that is known about the receiving settings and about the student's levels of competence to deal with these settings, the more likely a seamless transition can be achieved.
- The more comprehensive the transition needs assessment is, the easier it is to develop useful and meaningful transition plans.
- Effective transition assessment and plans can be achieved only when school-based transition

personnel know the students or have ways to acquire this information.
- Student involvement in the transition planning process is not only highly desirable but also required by law (i.e., based on the student's preferences and interests).

As noted in Figure 10.6, all three sources (the transition coordinator at school, Kevin's parents, and Kevin himself) rated Kevin low on item 10, "Can succeed in a postsecondary program." In essence, the three sources perceived Kevin as likely to have certain problems at the college level, but more detailed information was needed. As a result, another part of the TPI (Clark, Patton, and Moulton, 2001) was used by school personnel to provide a more in-depth analysis of the "succeeding in college" concern. Figure 10.7 on page 448 shows the results of this additional assessment, indicating the areas for which goals need to be written.

Another informal instrument, the *Study Skills Inventory* (Hoover and Patton, 1995) was also completed to further specify the nature of the study skills difficulties. The results of this assessment yielded the following information: "Most [study skill] areas need attention—particular emphasis needs to be given to note taking, test taking, and time management." A discussion of the transition goals that will need to be developed based on the results of this is presented in the next section.

Developing Transition Goals

A thorough assessment of a student's transition needs should lead to the development of sound transition goals that will serve as a guide for the student, the family, and the school in terms of preparing the stu-

dent for postschool life. As noted in Figure 10.5, two types of goal statements can emerge from a transition needs assessment: those related to instructional activities and those related to linkage activities.

Instructional goals relate to knowledge and skills needs and should be written in the IEP as academic or social goals. Linkage goals—the types of goals typically associated with transition planning—focus on making connections to the supports and services that will be needed in postschool situations and are written in the Individual Transition Plan (ITP) or the section of the IEP that deals with transition services.

ITPs versus IEPs

Some states require an ITP, which is a separate document from the IEP, as the principal vehicle for guiding transition activities. Other states simply include transition goals within the existing IEP under a section typically called "Statement of Transition Services." Both of these documents tend to focus on linkage-type goals. The critical issue is that both knowledge/skills and linkage goal statements need to be generated for all required areas.

Essential Components of an Individual Transition Plan

The actual format of ITPs varies greatly. Fortunately, the format is not important, as long as the proper information is listed (i.e., goals are generated for all areas of transition need). Every goal statement within

■ **TABLE 10.3** *Commercially Available Tests and Procedures for Assessing Transition Needs*

General Category	Selected Types of Measures	Specific Example(s)
Nonspecific to transition	Achievement tests	*Adult Basic Learning Examination—Second Edition* (Karlsen and Gardner, 1986)
	Adaptive behavior measures	*AAMR Adaptive Behavior Scales—School, Second Edition* (Lambert, Nihira, and Leland, 1993)
	Aptitude tests	*Differential Aptitude Test, Fifth Edition* (Bennett, Seashore, and Wesman, 1990)
	Communication tests	*Communicative Abilities in Daily Living* (Holland, 1980)
	Learning styles	*Learning Styles Inventory* (Dunn, Dunn, and Price, 1985)
	Manual dexterity	*Crawford Small Parts Dexterity Test* (Crawford, 1981)
	Occupational interest	*Occupational Aptitude Survey and Interest Schedule—2* (Parker, 1991)
	Personality/social skills	*Basic Personality Inventory* (Jackson, 1995)
Specific to transition	Needs assessment	*Transition Planning Inventory* (Clark and Patton, 1997) *Enderle—Severson Transition Rating Scale–Revised* (Brolin, 1992)
	Life skills	*BRIGANCE Life Skills Inventory* (Brigance, 1995) *LCCE Knowledge and Performance Battery* (Brolin, 1992) *Tests for Everyday Living* (Halpern, Irvin, and Landman, 1979)
	Self-determination	*Arc's Self-Determination Scale*
	Quality of life	*Quality of Life Questionnaire* (Schalock and Keith, 1993) *Quality of Student Life Questionnaire* (Keith and Schalock, 1995)
	Work-related behavior	*Transition Behavior Scale* (2nd ed.) (McCarney, 2000)
	Social	*Social and Prevocational Information Battery—Revised* (Halpern, Irvin, and Munkres, 1986)

Source: Adapted form J. R. Patton and C. Dunn, *Transition from School to Young Adulthood: Basic Concepts and Recommended Practices* (Austin, TX: PRO-ED, 1998), p. 24. Reprinted with permission.

the ITP should be accompanied by the following components:

▬ Present level of performance
▬ Specific activities to be performed to accomplish the goal
▬ Anticipated date of completion of activities
▬ Person(s) responsible

All of these components contribute to making the ITP an important plan of action. Depending on the state, ITPs may contain additional sections. Some ITPs use a checklist format to facilitate ease of completion. As you would imagine, a section that lists the persons who will participate in the ITP meeting is required. A sample ITP is provided as an appendix to the chapter (see Appendix 10.1).

Case Study: Kevin

Kevin's situation provides a clear-cut example of why two different types of goals often need to be developed. As can be observed from Figure 10.7 and the

■ FIGURE 10.6 *Portion of Kevin's Transition Planning Inventory*

Section V. Profile

KEVIN

Planning Areas	*School Rating*	*Home Rating*	*Student Rating*	*Knowledge/Skills Goals*	*Linkage Goals*
	Strongly Disagree ⟶ Strongly Agree	Strongly Disagree ⟶ Strongly Agree	Strongly Disagree ⟶ Strongly Agree		
Employment					
1. Knows job requirements and demands	NA 0 1 2 (3) 4 5 DK	NA 0 1 2 3 (4) 5 DK	NA 0 1 (2) 3 4 5 DK		
2. Makes informed choices	NA 0 1 2 (3) 4 5 DK	NA 0 1 2 (3) 4 5 DK	NA 0 1 2 3 (4) 5 DK		
3. Knows how to get a job	NA 0 1 2 3 (4) 5 DK	NA 0 1 2 (3) 4 5 DK	NA 0 1 2 3 (4) 5 DK		
4. Demonstrates general job skills and work attitude	NA 0 1 2 (3) 4 5 DK	NA 0 1 2 (3) 4 5 DK	NA 0 1 2 3 4 (5) DK		
5. Has specific job skills	(NA) 0 1 2 3 4 5 DK	(NA) 0 1 2 3 4 5 (DK)	(NA) 0 1 2 3 4 5 DK		
Further Education/Training					
6. Knows how to gain entry into community employment training	(NA) 0 1 2 3 4 5 DK	(NA) 0 1 2 3 4 5 DK	(NA) 0 1 2 3 4 5 DK		
7. Knows how to gain entry into GED program	(NA) 0 1 2 3 4 5 DK	(NA) 0 1 2 3 4 5 DK	(NA) 0 1 2 3 4 5 DK		
8. Knows how to gain entry into vocational/technical school program	(NA) 0 1 2 3 4 5 DK	(NA) 0 1 2 3 4 5 DK	(NA) 0 1 2 3 4 5 DK		
9. Knows how to gain entry into college or university	NA 0 1 2 3 (4) 5 DK	NA 0 1 (2) 3 4 5 DK	NA 0 1 2 (3) 4 5 DK		
10. Can succeed in a postsecondary program	NA 0 (1) 2 3 4 5 DK	NA 0 1 (2) 3 4 5 DK	NA 0 (1) 2 3 4 5 DK		

Source: G. M. Clark, J. R. Patton, and R. Moulton, *Informal Assessments in Transition Planning* (Austin, TX: PRO-ED, 2001), p. 156. Reprinted with permission.

■ **FIGURE 10.7** *Another Portion of Kevin's* Transition Planning Inventory

KEVIN

Goals/Objectives Needed	Further Assessments Needed	Further Education/Training	Notes
☑	☑	**10.** Can succeed in an appropriate postsecondary program	
☐	☐	Can use the academic support skills (e.g., organizational skills, time management, and other study skills) necessary to succeed in a given postsecondary setting	*Study Skills Inventory*
☑	☐	Can perform reading skills required in the program	
☐	☐	Can perform writing skills required in the program	
☐	☐	Can perform math skills required in the program	
☐	☐	Can analyze information and draw conclusions	
☐	☐	Can manage finances	
☑	☐	Knows how to balance priorities between classes, work, home duties, and leisure time	
☐	☐	Knows how to use disability support services	
☐	☐	Knows how to develop a social support system	
☐	☐	Knows how to assess (with others) what types of support/modifications are needed	
☐	☐	Knows how to appropriately meet with instructor (or professor) to discuss and advocate for reasonable accommodations (e.g., manner of presentation, timeliness, knowledge of necessary reasonable accommodations)	
☐	☐	Knows how to develop and implement a plan and a time line for completion of postsecondary training program	

Source: G. M. Clark, J. R. Patton, and R. Moulton, *Informal Assessments in Transition Planning* (Austin, TX: PRO-ED, 2001), p. 156. Reprinted with permission.

results of the Study Skills Inventory, certain areas were identified as needing attention. The following goals need to be written for Kevin in relation only to item 10 from the TPI assessment.

IEP Goals (i.e., Instructional Goals)
— Improve note-taking skills.
— Improve test-taking skills.
— Develop time management skills.
— Improve various types of writing skills needed in college courses.

*ITP/Transition Services Goals
(i.e., Linkage Goals)*
— Make Kevin aware of the Services for Students with Disabilities office, its services, and how to qualify.
— Identify resources that may be needed to obtain a comprehensive evaluation to document that he has a learning disability if he chooses to disclose and use specialized services.
— Make Kevin aware of the general services (courses, workshops, personal assistance) provided to all students at the community college to improve study skills.
— Connect Kevin with a contact person at the community college to whom he can go if he runs into problems with school, managing time, etc.
— Develop a list of names and phone numbers of private tutors that might be contracted to assist with study skill needs.

Curricular Implications

Although curricular issues were addressed earlier in this chapter, two additional curricular issues are worthy of discussion. Both are intricately involved with preparing students to better engage the transition planning process on their terms. The first issue, primarily one related to skills, involves including students in the transition process. The second, more of a knowledge issue and in many ways related to the first, centers on the need to prepare students for the assessment phase by discussing transition-related topics prior to conducting the assessment.

Student Involvement

Most professionals and researchers interested in transition issues and practice place student involvement/student self-determination high on the list of critical topics (Bassett et al., 1997). The idea of getting students actively involved in their own transition planning makes sense, as it is their lives about which key decisions are being made. However, assuming that students will know how to participate or feel comfortable being actively involved in their transition planning is erroneous. Many students, and especially those with disabilities for whom decision-making, self-determination, and communication may be areas of significant challenge, need to experience involvement and develop skills to be actively involved at an early age. Bassett and Lehman (in press) stress the need to teach students the skills necessary for a variety of student-directed roles during the elementary school years.

Curricular materials are now available that teach students with disabilities how they can direct their own IEP meetings and transition planning process. Table 10.4 describes several commercially available programs that have demonstrated effectiveness with students who have learning and behavior problems.

Preassessment Preparation

The other important curricular issue that must be addressed results from the fact that students really do not know how to respond to many of the adult issues with which they are being confronted if they are being involved in the transition process at all. The stereotypic adolescent response of "I don't know" may well be a valid answer when these transition topics have never been raised before.

Providing students with the opportunity to engage the many topics on which their transition planning will be based and about which we would like to have their input makes perfect sense. How to do this is not so easily recognized. Now that middle school personnel are to be involved with the transition planning process in ways they were not prior to the reauthorization of IDEA in 1997, it is easier to provide opportunities for students to discuss these topics. Some instructional time should be dedicated to introducing

■ **TABLE 10.4**   *Student-Directed IEP Programs*

Program	Description
ChoiceMaker Self-Determination Transition Curriculum (Martin and Marshall, 1995)	Teaches self-determination through student self-management of the IEP process and includes three components: choosing goals, expressing goals, and taking action. Students lead their IEP meetings to the greatest extent possible, based on their strengths.
Whose Future Is It Anyway? (Wehmeyer and Kelchner, 1995)	Introduces the student to the concept of transition planning and teaches them to take an active role in the planning process by focusing on the constructs involved in self-determination. A *Coach's Guide* (Weymeyer and Lawrence, 1995a) is available to assist the person that the student has identified as the coach.
Next S.T.E.P.: Student Transition and Education Planning (Halpern, et al., 1997)	Teaches and engages students in the skills involved in successful transition planning through four instructional modules (getting started, self-exploration and self-evaluation, developing goals and activities, and putting a plan into place). Videos and printed materials for teachers, students, and their families are included.
Self-Advocacy Strategy for Education and Transition Planning (VanReusen, Bos, Schumaker, and Deshler, 1994)	Teaches both student-directed transition planning and self-advocacy skills. The program emphasizes the importance of self-advocacy in increasing student motivation and empowerment using the I-PLAN strategy (inventory your strengths, needs, goals, and needed accommodations; provide your inventory information; listen and respond; ask questions; and name your goals). (See Chapter 1 for a more detailed description.)
TAKE CHARGE for the Future (Powers, 1996)	Promotes student involvement in education and transition planning through: skill facilitation (i.e., achievement, partnership, and coping skills), mentoring with same-gender adults who have had similar experiences, peer support activities, and parent support in promoting their child's active involvement. The model was adapted from a validated approach (TAKE CHARGE) used to increase self-determination skills in students both with and without disabilities.

Source: Adapted from M. L. Wehmeyer, M. Agran, & C. Hughes, *Teaching Self-Determined Students with Disabilites: Basic Skills for Successful Transition* (Baltimore: Paul H. Brookes, 1998); and R. W. Flexer, T. J. Simmons, P. Luft, and R. M. Baer, *Transition Planning for Secondary Students with Disabilities* (Upper Saddle River, NJ: Merrill/Prentice-Hall, 2001).

students to the topics from which transition goals will be developed (e.g., employment, further education, living arrangements).

Ways to address transition topics prior to asking students for their perspective must be developed. Some materials, such as the Next S.T.E.P program (Halpern et al., 2000), that accomplish this task are available. This type of material provides a curricular sequence that exposes students to an array of lessons that help them take charge of their own transition planning process. At very least, it is critical to de-

velop activities or lessons related to a set of major transition areas.

Recommendations

The transition planning process requires that certain key elements—assessment, individual planning, follow-through, and coordination—be implemented effectively and efficiently. As mentioned earlier in this chapter, this process requires the active involvement of several key players: the student; the family,

APPLY THE CONCEPT 10.2

HOW DIFFERENT ENTITIES CAN CONTRIBUTE TO THE TRANSITION PLANNING PROCESS

How Students Can Contribute to the Transition Effort
- Identify their own preferences and interests.
- Take an interest in this process.
- Participate as a contributing member of their transition team.
- Follow through on designated activities.
- Know where and how to access support and services.

How Families Can Ensure Successful Transition
- Become informed about the demands of adulthood and the transition planning process.
- Participate actively in the transition process.
- Follow through on designated linkage activities.
- Seek assistance when needed.
- Advocate for their children.

How Adult Service Providers Can Facilitate Successful Transition
- Identify the demands and requisite skills needed in their particular settings or programs.

- Provide information about their settings or programs to school-based personnel.
- Participate in the transition process when feasible.
- Offer accessibility and assistance to families.

How Schools Can Best Prepare Students for Adulthood
- Address proactively the important life skills within the curriculum.
- Develop self-determination and self-advocacy skills in students.
- Assess and plan comprehensively for transitional needs.
- Provide community-based experiences.
- Assist families in dealing with the adult service arena.

Source: J. R. Patton and C. Dunn, *Transition from School to Young Adulthood: Basic Concepts and Recommended Practices* (Austin, TX: PRO-ED, 1998), pp. 59–60. Reprinted with permission.

who in many situations will become the "service coordinator" for their adult child; a variety of adult service providers; and a combination of school-based personnel whose duties include transition services. Apply the Concept 10.2 presents the four key entities that can best contribute to the transition planning process as was identified originally by a group of professionals connected to the Hawaii Transition Project (1987) and restated by Patton and Dunn (1998).

SUMMARY

This chapter focused on the topic of transition services. The overriding theme of the chapter is that this process should begin during the elementary years and culminate in a series of sound practices that lead to a seamless transition from school to any number and types of postschool settings.

The first major section of the chapter highlighted the fact that all of us move through a relatively large number of transitions throughout our lives. Some of these transitions are predictable and common to all, and others are idiosyncratic. IDEA requires that certain activities occur for two of the transitions that children and youth with disabilities move through.

The discussion stressed how important it is to have certain elements in place when making a transition. Attention was also directed to a set of principles or themes that should guide transition practices. The second section of the chapter focused primarily on how it is possible to teach real-life topics to students with special needs. The concept of transition education was introduced as a way of thinking about the instruction of life skills to all students with disabilities. Major life demands were identified and the relationship of important life skills to academic and social skills was established. Two approaches for covering real-life content were presented.

The last section of the chapter described the key elements of the more formal transition planning process. Emphasis was given to ways to assess transition needs and develop transition goals. The final part of the chapter discussed the importance of student involvement in this process and identified critical curricular issues that must be considered if effective transition planning is to be achieved. Reference is made throughout the chapter to the situation of Kevin, a student with learning disabilities who is preparing to go to college. Examples of Kevin's transition assessment and the goals that resulted from this assessment are provided. Appendix 10.1 shows how the linkage goals were incorporated into his individual transition plan.

WEBSITES AS RESOURCES FOR TRANSITION PLANNING AND LIFE SKILLS/TRANSITION EDUCATION

http://www.nichcy.org/pubs/transum/ts7.pdf
This Website is from the National Information Center for Children and Youth with Disabilities (NICHCY) and provides links to a series of publications on preparing youth with disabilities to make the transition from high school to the adult world.

http://www1.stw.ed.gov
This Website provides basic information about the School-to-Work (STW) Act and resulting initiatives.

http://www.ldonline.org/ld_indepth/ieppub.html#defined
This Website from LD Online provides information about the content of the IEP, transition services as defined by IDEA, and a host of other key transition-related topics.

http://www.dssc.org/summit
This Website provides information related to a national summit on transition that was held in June 2000.

http://www.aafcs.org/resources/ideas.html
This Website provides innovative life skills classroom projects and ideas from family and consumer teachers-of-the-year.

http://www.dssc.org/nta/index.html
This Website provides information about the National Transition Alliance for Youth with Disabilities (NTA).

http://janweb.icdi.wvu.edu
>   This Website provides information about the Job Accommodation Network, a service that shares information about job accommodations and the employability of persons with disabilities.

http://www.ed.gov/databases/ERIC_Digests/ed389879
>   This Website provides basic overview information on the Secretary's Commission on Achieving Necessary Skills (SCANS).

http://www.ed.uiuc.edu/sped/tri/projwebsites.html
>   This Website provides information about model transition projects.

http://www.acenet.edu/about/programs/Access&Equity/HEATH/home.html
>   This Website provides information and resources, related to persons with disabilities who are in higher education settings.

http://www.ahead.org
>   This Website provides information from the Association on Higher Education and Disability (AHEAD), an organization composed of higher education professionals who provide a variety of supports to students with disabilities.

http://www.ed.uiuc.edu/sped.dcdt
>   This Website from the Division on Career Development and Transition of the Council for Exceptional Children provides information and links on a variety of transition topics.

THINK AND APPLY

- Is going to college a realistic goal for Kevin?
- What are some "horizontal" transitions, other than those shown in Figure 10.1, that students with disabilities might experience?
- What themes should guide the preparation of students with disabilities for postschool life?
- How do diversity issues affect the transition planning process?
- What are some other ways that the domains of adulthood could be organized?
- How might you entitle possible life skills courses other than the ones suggested in this chapter?
- What are the differences between instructional goals and linkage goals, as discussed in this chapter?
- What basic components should be part of any individual transition plan?
- Why should the transition process be considered a shared set of activities?
- Why are transition services valuable for all students in school?

APPENDIX 10.1

Individual Transition Plan

Student's Name *Kevin* *J.* *Smith*
First M.I. Last

Birthdate *3/17/85* School *Valley High School*

Student's ID No. *0213* ITP Conference Date *10/7/00*

Participants

Name	Position
Kevin	*student*
Linda	*mother*
John	*father*
Scott	*transition coordinator*
Erica	*diagnostician*

I. Career and Economic Self-Sufficiency

1. Employment Goal	
Level of present performance	
Steps needed to accomplish goal	
Date of completion	
Person(s) responsible for implementation	
2. Vocational Education/Training Goal	
Level of present performance	

Steps needed to accomplish goal	
Date of completion	
Person(s) responsible for implementation	
3. Postsecondary Education Goal #1	*Kevin needs to apply to Central Community College for Fall 2001 admission.*
Level of present performance	*Kevin and his parents know procedures and have appropriate forms.*
Steps needed to accomplish this goal	*complete forms* *send by due date*
Date of completion	*April 1, 2001*
Person(s) responsible for implementation	*Kevin* *parents*
Postsecondary Education Goal #2	*Make Kevin aware of the Services for Students with Disabilities Office.*
Level of present performance	*Kevin and his parents are not aware of this office*
Steps needed to accomplish this goal	*provide documents on services* *provide name and contact information* *of office*
Date of completion	*December 1, 2000*
Person(s) responsible for implementation	*transition coordinator*
Postsecondary Education Goal #3	*Identify resources that may be needed to obtain a comprehensive evaluation.*

(continued)

APPENDIX 10.1 *Continued*

Level of present performance	*Kevin and his parents do not have any information*
Steps needed to accomplish this goal	*Provide a list of professionals who provide evaluations.* *Obtain recommendations from community college staff.*
Date of completion	*April 1, 2001*
Person(s) responsible for implementation	*transition coordinator*
Postsecondary Education Goal #4	*Make Kevin aware of general support services available at the community college.*
Level of present performance	*Kevin and his parents are not aware of these services (i.e., Learning Assistance Center).*
Steps needed to accomplish this goal	*Obtain documents from community college* *Obtain name and contact information for Learning Assistance Center.*
Date of completion	*December 1, 2000*
Person(s) responsible for implementation	*Kevin* *parents*
Postsecondary Education Goal #5	*Connect Kevin with a contact person at Central C.C.*
Level of present performance	*Kevin and his parents do not know any faculty or staff at CCC.*
Steps needed to accomplish this goal	*provide name of a faculty member (Prof. Miller)* *Contact Prof. Miller to alert that she may be contacted.*
Date of completion	*April 1, 2001*

Person(s) responsible for implementation	*transition coordinator*
Postsecondary Education Goal #6	*Develop a list of private tutors.*
Level of present performance	*Kevin and his parents do not have this information*
Steps needed to accomplish this goal	*Contact staff at CCC.* *Combine with current list.* *Provide list to Kevin/parents.*
Date of completion	*April 1, 2001*
Person(s) responsible for implementation	*transition coordinator*

Source: Adapted from P. Wehman, *Individual Transition Plans: The Teacher's Curriculum Guide for Helping Youth with Special Needs* (Austin, TX: PRO-ED, 1995). Copyright © 1995 by PRO-ED, Inc.

11

Coordinating Instruction, Collaborating, and Coteaching

KEY TOPICS FOR MASTERY

- *Arranging the instructional environment of the special education classroom for large-group instruction, small-group instruction, one-to-one instruction, independent learning, collaborative/cooperative learning, and peer teaching*
- *Arranging the physical environment of the special education classroom*
- *Selecting, developing, and organizing instructional materials and equipment*
- *Scheduling considerations: meeting the needs of special education students and their regular classroom teachers*
- *Classroom management practices that help create an environment in which instruction and learning can occur*
- *Mainstreaming special education students: some of the problems and solutions*
- *Working with regular education teachers to ensure the success of mainstreamed special education students*
- *Three models for consultation and collaboration: Coteaching; Teacher Assistance Teams; Collaboration in the Schools*

 BRIGHT IDEA

Turn to page 495 and read Think and Apply.

*W*hen I first decided to be a special education teacher it was because I wanted to help the kids. I felt that I could make a difference in their lives, both educationally and social-emotionally, and I can honestly say I have. Recently, though, I was beginning to feel frustrated as a special education resource room teacher. I was spending 90 percent of my time in my special education classroom working with fairly large, heterogeneous groups of children. While I felt I was still making a difference, I was concerned that there was lots more I should be doing, particularly in the general education classroom where my students spent more than 50 percent of their day. Another one of my concerns was whether my students were receiving adequate instruction that was systematic enough to meet their needs. I was certain that, as the groups in my resource room were getting

larger, the quality of instruction I was able to offer my students was reduced. There were some students who I know would learn to read only if I could work with them one-to one or in very small groups for 30 minutes a day. I was unable to do it consistently.

I met with my principal and assistant principal and proposed that we redesign the role and function of the special education resource room. I suggested that we have three levels of service delivery. (1) Selected students would be placed in the general education classroom for the full day. I would work closely with their general education teacher to monitor their progress. I would work with them in small groups in the classroom several times a week. This level would be for my most independent students who I felt were ready to "phase out" of special education. (2) The second level would *be for students who need intensive instruction in one area—reading, for example—but who were functioning relatively well in the general education classroom in all other areas. These students would be seen by my aide every day for 30 minutes of direct instruction designed by me. I would work with the student and the aide at least once a week. (3) The third level would be for students who the teacher and I felt worked best when they were able to leave the general education classroom for a period of time, one to two hours. For the most part, these were students who demonstrated both learning and behavior disorders. Last year was the first year I implemented the new three-level service-delivery model and while there are still some "kinks" I need to work out, overall we (my students and I) had the best year ever.*

The role of the special education teacher is being redefined at the school district, state, and national level. Largely the movement is toward even more involvement with general education and general education teachers. The skills special education teachers need to be successful in their new roles go beyond sound instructional practices.

If you ask people in business to list the critical elements for a successful business, they will undoubtedly include *communication* and *sound management.* Although the product, service, and marketing are important, communication and management of the business are the cornerstone. It is the ability of the manager or the management team to make sound decisions regarding product development and research, marketing, service, fiscal policies, and personnel that makes the difference between success and failure. It is also the ability to communicate effectively when making and disseminating decisions that determines how effectively and efficiently the business operates.

In the same way that management and communication are the cornerstone of business, so are they the cornerstone of effective teaching. Whether working in a coteaching setting, as a consultant, resource, or self-contained teacher, the special education teacher makes thousands of management decisions each day regarding the teaching-learning process and the instructional cycle. It is the ability of the teacher to develop a teaching-learning context that facilitates communication and learning; to set learning and instructional goals and market those goals to others, including the students; and to establish sound classroom and instructional policies, routines, and procedures that makes the difference between success and failure. Management and communication are central to the task of teaching (Berliner, 1983; Doyle, 1979, 1986). This chapter deals with the issue of the special education teacher as a manager, communicator, and collaborator.

GETTING STARTED

"I'm really looking forward to next year," commented Ms. Downing as she completed her first year of teaching as a junior high special education teacher. "The first year of teaching has to be the hardest. There is so much to get organized at the beginning of the year, so many decisions to be made, and so many new routines and procedures to learn. You have to figure out what your resources are as well as the students' needs. You also have to decide what type of instructional program you want. Based on this, you need to determine how to arrange the room to facilitate learning, what materials to select or develop, and how to organize the materials so that the students can find them easily. You must decide how to group the students and how to schedule the students into the room. In comparison to this year, next year should be a breeze. I'll be able to spend much more time refining my teaching skills, focusing on the students, and strengthening the program."

In many ways, Ms. Downing is a manager. At the beginning of the year, management decisions are required at a fast and furious pace. We will explore some of the decisions that teachers have to consider in getting started and look at some options they might consider in making those decisions.

Arranging the Environment

In Chapter One, we discussed how the teaching–learning process takes place within a context. Making this context or environment pleasant and conducive to learning can facilitate the teaching–learning process. As teachers, we want to consider both the instructional arrangement and the physical arrangement of that context.

Instructional Arrangement

Instructional arrangement refers to the manner in which the teacher groups the students and selects the format for learning. When students are in inclusive settings, this requires arranging grouping instruction with the general education teacher. Generally, there are six instructional arrangements: (1) large-group instruction, (2) small-group instruction, (3) one-to-one instruction, (4) independent learning, (5) collaborative learning, and (6) peer teaching (Mercer and Mercer, 1989). Most teachers want to have the flexibility to provide for several different instructional arrangements within their classrooms.

Large-Group Instruction. Large-group instruction usually consists of the teacher lecturing or engaging in discussions with a group of six or more students. It is appropriate to use when the content of instruction is similar for all students. Teachers often employ this type of instructional arrangement when teaching social skills and content area subjects such as social studies, science, health, and career education. This arrangement can be used both for didactic instruction (i.e., instruction where one person, usually the teacher, is providing information) and for interactive instruction (i.e., where the students and teachers are discussing and sharing information). In large-group instruction students usually get less opportunity to receive feedback concerning their performance and less opportunity to receive corrective feedback. Since large-group instruction is the most frequently used arrangement in general education classrooms, particularly in secondary settings, it is helpful to provide students with experiences in large groups as they make the transition to general education classrooms.

Small-Group Instruction. Small-group instruction usually consists of groups of two to five students and is employed when the teacher wants to be in closer proximity to the students and provide more feedback.

Teachers form small groups of students who are either at different ability levels (heterogeneous groups) or have similar ability in a particular curriculum area (homogeneous groups). One benefit of small groups is that the teacher can individualize instruction to meet each group's specific needs. For example, during a cooperative learning activity where students are grouped heterogeneously, the teacher may need to give a mini-lesson to one group that is having difficulty working together.

Same ability groups or homogeneous groups are often used for teaching specific academic skills, since students are often grouped by skill level when learning basic skills in reading, writing, oral language, and math. When a teacher is using small-group instruction, he or she usually involves one group of students while the remaining students participate in independent learning, cooperative learning, or peer tutoring. Sometimes teachers who work in resource rooms schedule students so that only two to five students come at one time, so that all the students can participate in small-group instruction at once. Many teachers prefer using a horseshoe table for small-group instruction, since it allows them to reach the materials in front of each student in the group easily.

See the section on coteaching at the end of this chapter for more ideas about how a special education and general education teacher can work together to manage a variety of instructional grouping arrangements in one classroom.

One-to-One Instruction. One-to-one instruction is when the teacher works individually with a student. This instructional arrangement allows the teacher to provide intensive instruction, closely monitoring student progress and modifying and adapting procedures to match the student's learning patterns. The Fernald (VAKT) method of teaching word identification and Reading Recovery, as discussed in Chapter Four, are examples where one-to-one instruction is the recommended instructional arrangement. At least some one-to-one instruction is recommended for students with learning and behavior problems, since it provides the students with some time each day to ask questions and receive assistance from the teacher (Archer and Edgar, 1976). The major drawback of one-to-one instruction is that while one student is working with the teacher, the remaining students need to be actively engaged in learning. To accomplish this, independent learning, collaborative learning, or peer tutoring is frequently used.

Independent Learning. Independent learning is one format for providing students practice with a skill for which they have already received instruction and have acquired some proficiency (Stephens, 1977; Wallace and Kauffman, 1986). We frequently associate independent learning with individual worksheets, but computer activities, various audiovisual assignments such as listening to a taped book, writing a story, reading a library book, or making a map for a social studies unit can also be independent learning activities.

The key to effective use of independent learning activities is selecting activities that the student can complete with minimal assistance. For example, when Samantha selects library books, Ms. Martino asks Samantha to read approximately the first hundred words to her and then she asks Samantha several questions. If Samantha misses five words or less and can answer the questions easily, then Ms. Martino encourages her to read the book on her own. If Samantha misses five to ten words, then Ms. Martino arranges for her to read the book using collaborative learning or peer tutoring. If Samantha misses more than ten words and struggles to answer the questions, then Ms. Martino may encourage her to select another book. In fact, Ms. Martino has even taught Samantha and the rest of the students in her self-contained classroom for students with behavior disorders the "Five-Finger Rule."

Five-Finger Rule   If in reading the first couple of pages of a book, you know the words except for about five and you can ask yourself and answer five questions about what you have read, then this book is probably a good book for you to read.

Cooperative Learning. Cooperative learning is when students work together and use each other as a source for learning. Four basic elements need to be included for small-group learning to be cooperative: interdependence, individual accountability, collaborative skills, and group processing (Johnson and Johnson, 1986; Johnson, Johnson, and Holubec, 1993; Slavin, 1987, 1991). Interdependence is facilitated by creating a learning environment where the students perceive that the goal of the group is that *all* members learn, that rewards are based on group performance, that materials needed to complete the task are distributed across the members of the group, and that students are given complementary roles that foster the division of labor.

Individual accountability ensures that each student is responsible for learning the required material and contributing to the group. Teacher evaluations (i.e., quizzes, individual products) can help determine whether each student has learned the material. Students can also use progress monitoring forms to track their own behavior and progress. Progress monitoring forms might include the following questions: (1) How did I contribute to the learning of the group today? and (2) In what way did I help or not help my group complete our work? Collaborative skills are required if a group is to run effectively. Teachers should teach collaborative skills explicitly by defining skills and their importance, modeling how the skills are used, allowing students to practice skills in cooperative groups, and providing students with corrective feedback (Putnam, 1998). *Group processing* refers to giving the students the opportunity to discuss how well they are achieving their goals and working together (Johnson and Johnson, 1984a). Apply the Concept 11.1 provides additional guidelines for including students with disabilities in cooperative learning groups.

Two basic formats for cooperative learning are often used in general or special education classrooms. In a *group project* students pool their knowledge and skills to create a project or complete an assignment. The students in the group are included in all the decisions and tasks that ensure completion of the project. Using the *jigsaw format,* each student in a group is assigned a task that must be completed for the group to reach its goal. For example, in completing a fact-finding sheet on fossils, each student might be assigned to read a different source to obtain information for the different facts required on the sheet.

APPLY THE CONCEPT 11.1

GUIDELINES FOR INCLUDING STUDENTS WITH SPECIAL NEEDS IN COOPERATIVE LEARNING ACTIVITIES

When students with disabilities are included into a cooperative group lesson in the general education classroom, teachers may consider the following during planning (Johnson, Johnson, and Holubec, 1993; Stevens and Slavin, 1995):

- Adjust group size and create heterogeneous groups of students who are likely to work well together. Would some students benefit from three students in a group instead of four or five?
- Consider each student's IEP goals and academic strengths and weaknesses when assigning roles. For example, modifications in materials may be necessary if a student with below-grade level reading skills is assigned the role of reading directions.
- Arrange the room to ensure face-to-face interaction between students and to make groups easily accessible to the teacher. Round tables work well, but chairs clustered together or open floor areas can also be used.
- Inform students of criteria for both academic and interpersonal success. Some teachers hand

out a grading rubric with an outline of specific criteria for grading in each area of evaluation (e.g., creativity, neatness, group work, correct information, quiz).

- Provide mini-lessons before and/or during the cooperative group activity to teach academic or cooperative skills. Students need to know what group work "looks like," and many teachers conduct several lessons on how to work in cooperative groups prior to beginning the learning activities. Teachers can also provide give small doses of instruction to individual groups during the activity as needed.
- Monitor and evaluate both individual achievement and group work. Many teachers carry a clipboard with students' names and lesson objectives so they can record student progress as they monitor groups.
- Reflect on the cooperative learning activity and note changes for future lessons. Did the lesson go as well as you would have liked? Did students learn the required material?

Johnson and Johnson (1975) suggest the following guidelines for working cooperatively:

1. Each group produces one product.
2. Group members assist each other.
3. Group members seek assistance from other group members.
4. Group members will change their ideas only when logically persuaded to do so by the other members.
5. Group members take responsibility for the product.

Collaborative learning can be used to complete group projects in content area subjects. In Chapter Six, the process approach to teaching writing employed aspects of collaborative learning. For example, students shared their written pieces with each other to get ideas and feedback about their writing, and in some cases they wrote pieces together. Slavin and his colleagues (Slavin, Stevens, and Madden, 1988) have developed *Cooperative Integrated Reading and Composition,* which uses cooperative learning with a process approach for teaching composition and basal-related activities and direct instruction in reading comprehension. They have also designed a mathematics curriculum using cooperative learning, Team-Assisted Individualization (Slavin, 1984). Using heterogeneous cooperative learning groups in general elementary classrooms, the researchers found that these types of programs paired with cooperative learning facilitate the learning of most mainstreamed special education and remedial students.

Providing opportunities to participate in cooperative learning experiences is particularly important for students with behavior and learning problems because it assists these students in developing social skills as well as the targeted academic skill. It assists them in developing positive interactions with peers and in developing strategies for supporting others. These skills are particularly important when students are being included into general classrooms where cooperative learning is employed (Johnson and Johnson, 1984b, 1986; Nevin, 1998).

In orchestrating cooperative learning, it is important to provide the students with enough directions that they know the purpose of the activity and the general rules for working in groups. Initially, the teacher may want to participate as a collaborator, modeling such collaborative behaviors as: (1) asking what the other people think, (2) not ridiculing other collaborators for what they think, and (3) helping other collaborators and accepting help from others. As the students become comfortable in collaborating, they can work in teams without the teacher's input.

Peer Teaching. In this instructional arrangement, one student who has learned the skills assists another student in learning the skills. This teaching takes place under the supervision of the teacher. One advantage of peer teaching is that it increases opportunity for the student learning the skills to respond (Delquadri, Greenwood, Whorton, Carta, and Hall, 1986). Peer teaching achieves this by allowing peers to supervise their classmates' responses. When using peer teaching the teacher needs to plan the instruction and demonstrate the task to the pair. The tutor then works with the learner, providing assistance and feedback.

One important aspect of peer teaching is training the students to serve as peer tutors (Fowler, 1986). They need to learn basic instructional procedures for providing reinforcement and corrective feedback and for knowing when to ask the teacher for assistance.

Remember that poor readers show academic and social gains in both the tutor and tutee role (Elbaum et al., 1999). Therefore, it is important to alternate roles so students get the chance to benefit from serving as both the tutor and the tutee. Research focusing on peer tutoring with special education students has most frequently been used to teach or monitor basic skills such as oral reading, answering reading comprehension questions, and practicing spelling words, math facts, and new sight word vocabulary (Gerber and Kauffman, 1981; Scruggs and Richter, 1985).

Another important aspect of peer teaching is cross-age tutoring. In this situation older students instruct younger students. Cross-age tutoring has many advantages including the fact that older students are supposed to know more than younger students; thus there is less of a stigma from being tutored. Also, both the tutor and the tutee enjoy the opportunity to meet someone of a different age. Another aspect of cross-age tutoring that can be effective is the use of students with learning disabilities or behavior disorders to serve as the tutor for younger students who also demonstrate learning or behavior disorders.

Thus peer teaching can serve many roles:

1. Peers teaching peers within the same classroom
2. Peers teaching peers across classrooms but within the same grade level
3. Peers who are older teaching students who are younger
4. Peers with learning and behavior disorders teaching younger nondisabled students
5. Peers with learning and behavior disorders teaching younger students who have learning and behavior disorders

Classwide Peer Tutoring. Classwide peer tutoring (CWPT) is a structured technique for improving students' reading abilities. Students of different reading levels are paired (e.g., a high or average reader paired with a low reader) and work together on a sequence of organized activities such as oral reading, story retelling, and summarization. The reading material may be a basal reader, trade book or magazine, or other appropriate material. The criterion is that the least able reader in each pair be able to easily read the materials assigned to his/her dyad. The extensive research on CWPT (e.g., Mathes et al., 1994; see for a review Topping and Ely, 1998) indicates that when the procedure is implemented consistently (e.g., 30-minute sessions conducted three times per week for at least 16 weeks), students of all ability levels demonstrate improved reading fluency and comprehension.

Physical Arrangement

The room arrangement should be flexible enough so that different instructional arrangements can be employed. For example, the individual learning area can be reorganized into a large group instructional area by rearranging the desks. The small group instructional area can also be used for a cooperative learning project.

Several ideas to keep in mind when developing the room arrangement are:

1. To the extent possible, place the recreational and audiovisual/computer areas away from the teaching area. These areas will naturally be somewhat noisier than the other areas.
2. Place student materials in an area where students can easily get to the materials without bothering other students or the teacher.
3. Place your teaching materials directly behind where you teach so that you can reach materials without having to leave the instructional area.
4. If used, place the time-out area out of the direct line of traffic. Also, use partitions that keep a student in the area from having visual contact with other students. (See Chapter Two for principles governing the use of time-out.)
5. Make the recreational area comfortable with a carpet, comfortable reading chairs, pillows, and a small game table if possible.
6. Place all the materials needed for a learning center in the learning center area. In this way students will not be moving around the room to collect needed materials.
7. Instruct several students as to where materials and supplies are kept so that when students cannot find something they do not ask you but ask other students.
8. Establish procedures and settings for students who have completed tasks and/or are waiting for the teacher.

Instructional Materials and Equipment

Selecting, developing, and organizing the instructional materials and equipment is an important aspect of getting a program organized. The instructional materials and the equipment used by the teacher have a major influence on what and how information and skills are taught (Wallace and Kauffman, 1986; Wilson, 1982).

One decision a teacher has to make is whether to purchase materials already available or develop the materials. Some teachers tend to select published materials for their main instructional materials (e.g., sets of literature books based on different themes or units, several reading programs each representing a different approach to reading such as linguistic and phonic approaches). Then they develop instructional aids and games to supplement the program (e.g., flash cards, sentence strips, tape recordings of the stories, board games).

Whether selecting or developing materials, there are several factors to consider:

1. What evidence is there that these materials or curricula have been effective with students with learning and behavior problems?
2. What curricular areas (e.g., reading, English, math, social skills) will I be responsible for teaching?
3. What are the academic levels of the students I will be teaching?
4. In what instructional arrangement(s) do I plan to teach each curricular area?
5. How can the materials be used across the stages of learning (i.e., acquisition, proficiency, maintenance, generalization, and application)?
6. Will the materials provide a means for measuring learning?
7. Are the materials designed for teacher-directed learning, student-to-student learning, or individual learning?

Selecting Published Materials

Besides considering the factors just mentioned, it is also important to think of the cost, durability, consumability, and quality of the published materials. Before purchasing materials it is advantageous to evaluate them. Sample materials can generally be obtained from the publisher or found at educational conferences or district-wide instructional centers. Read research reports that provide information about the effectiveness of the materials. When research is not available, talk with other teachers who use the materials to determine when and with whom they are effective. Borrow the materials and have the students try them and evaluate them. Chapter Appendix 11.1 presents a form a teacher can use to evaluate published materials. It focuses not only on general information but on how the material will fit into the teacher's program. Chapter Appendix 11.2 presents a form the students can use to evaluate the materials.

Most teachers have restricted budgets for purchasing instructional materials. Once the instructional materials are selected, it is helpful to prioritize them according to need. Before eliminating materials from that list, determine if they can be obtained through means other than the teaching budget. For example, school districts often have an instructional materials library that allows teachers in the district to check out materials for a relatively long period of time. You may be able to borrow the materials from the library rather than purchase them. Librarians are often interested in additional materials to order; it might be possible to request that they order the materials for the library. Publishers are often interested in how their materials work with low-achieving students and students with learning and behavior problems. They may be willing to provide a set of materials if the teacher is willing to evaluate the materials and provide feedback regarding how they work with the students.

Selecting and Using Instructional Equipment

In addition to selecting instructional materials, the teacher will also want to choose some equipment to facilitate learning. Chapter Ten specifically deals with computers, including the selection of computers, peripherals, and computer software. This equipment, along with various software programs, is becoming an increasingly important part of the tools a teacher has available. In addition to a computer in the class-

room and/or the use of a computer lab in the school, there is other equipment that will facilitate learning.

Tape Recorder. Tape recorders are relatively inexpensive and can be used in a variety of ways in the classroom. In selecting a tape recorder, select one of good quality that is easy to operate. Also select a recorder that has a counter. This allows a student to quickly find a particular section in a tape rather than having to hunt for it. Headphones to accompany the tape recorder allow students to listen to the tape recorder without disturbing others. Following are some instructional applications for the tape recorder:

1. Tape record reading books so that students can follow along during recreational reading or for using with repeated reading or the pattern language approach. Apply the Concept 5.2 (page 176) provides guidelines for tape recording books and stories.
2. One way to adapt textbooks is to tape record them. Tech Talk 7.1 (page 303) presents some suggestions for tape recording textbooks.
3. For some students it is helpful for them to record what they want to write before they write their first drafts. They can tape record their ideas and then listen to them as they write the first drafts.
4. So that the students can hear their progress in reading, have them tape record their reading every two to four weeks. Each student should have his or her own tape that serves as a record of progress. After a student records his or her reading, it is important that the teacher and the student discuss the reading, identifying strengths and areas that need improvement. This tape recording can also be shared with parents to demonstrate progress and continuing needs.
5. Spelling tests can be tape recorded so that students can take them independently. First, record the words to be tested, allowing time for the students to spell the words. After the test is recorded, spell each word so the student can self-check.
6. At the secondary level, class lectures can be taped and then listened to so that the student can review the material and complete unfinished notes.

7. Have students practice taking notes by listening to tape recordings of lectures. By using tape recordings, students can regulate the rate at which the material is presented.

8. Oral directions for independent learning activities can be tape recorded so that students can listen to them. This may prove to be particularly helpful if the teacher is trying to conduct small-group or one-to-one instruction while these students are working on independent learning activities.

9. When working on specific social or pragmatic language skills (e.g., answering the telephone, asking for directions, introducing someone), tape record the students so that they can listen to and evaluate themselves.

10. Many instructional materials contain prerecorded tapes.

Overhead Projector.   The overhead projector is an excellent teaching tool. It allows the user to display on a screen or blank wall the images from a transparency. Transparencies are generally teacher-made, although some are available with published instructional materials. The overhead projector allows the teacher to model a skill and to highlight, write, color in, and/or point to important information. For example, a teacher may use an overhead projector to demonstrate how to add quotation marks to a story, or a student may use it to demonstrate how he or she worked a long division problem.

In preparing transparencies, write in large, bold writing. Two types of markers are available for making transparencies—permanent markers and non-permanent markers. Transparencies are also available that can be used in copying machines so that the original is copied onto a transparency rather than a piece of paper.

When using an overhead projector keep the following suggestions in mind:

1. Using an overhead can be easier than a chalkboard for presenting a lecture or leading a discussion since it does not require the teacher to turn around to write.

2. Keep the amount of information presented on the overhead relatively limited.

3. Use a different colored pen to highlight important points.

4. Keep extra markers available when using the overhead.

5. By laying a piece of paper over the transparency, each part of a transparency can be revealed as it is being discussed, thereby helping to focus the students' attention.

6. Use the overhead projector to develop language experience stories.

7. Use the overhead projector to demonstrate editing and revisions in writing.

8. Use the overhead projector along with a "think aloud" procedure to demonstrate math procedures such as how to work long division.

9. Allow students to develop transparencies summarizing individual or group work that they can share with the class as a whole.

Other Small Equipment.   Several other pieces of small equipment should be considered when selecting equipment for either a resource room or a self-contained classroom.

A *stopwatch* can serve as an instructional tool and a motivator. For some tasks it is important that students learn to respond at an automatic level (e.g., sight words, math facts). Students can use a stopwatch to time themselves or their classmates. These times can then be easily recorded on a time chart (see Figure 11.1). Using these charts, students can set goals, record their times, and try to beat previous times.

An *individual writing board* is an excellent tool for obtaining individual written responses during small group and large group discussions. Mr. Howell uses these boards during review sessions in his resource high school history class. During the review sessions he asks students questions and they write their answers on the writing boards. He then asks them to display their boards. In this way each student responds to each question in writing instead of one student orally responding to one question. Mr. Howell and the students feel that this is a better way to review since it requires them to think about and answer every question and to write the answers. Writing is important since it is generally required when

■ **FIGURE 11.1** *Timing Chart*

Student Name: __Hector__

Task: __x facts, 50 facts__

Minutes

5:00
4:45
4:30
4:15
4:00
3:45
3:30
3:15
3:00
2:45
2:30
2:15
2:00
1:45
1:30
1:15
1:00
:45
:30
:15
:00

2/16 2/18 2/19 2/23

Dates

be used in teaching and learning centers for such activities as depicting stories, spelling words, and working simple math problems.

As discussed in the math chapter, Chapter Eight, *calculators* are an invaluable tool for students when learning and for teachers when completing many of the routine activities associated with assessment and evaluation.

Ms. Luciani uses spelling masters to reinforce known spelling words and teach new ones. While she does not feel it serves as a substitute for sound spelling instruction, she allows students to use them for practice when they have finished assigned tasks, or when they are waiting for assistance from her.

Developing Instructional Materials

In addition to published materials and equipment, most teachers find the need to develop their own instructional materials. Many of these materials can be used to supplement commercial materials. For example, sentence strips containing the sentences from each story in beginning readers can be made. Many teachers develop materials to provide students with additional practice in skills they are learning. Therefore, developing self-correcting materials and/or materials in a game format can be advantageous.

Self-Correcting Materials.   Self-correcting materials provide students with immediate feedback. Students with learning and behavior problems frequently have a history of failure and are reluctant to take risks when others are watching or listening. Self-correcting materials allow them to check themselves without sharing the information with others. Many computer programs and electronic learning games incorporate self-correction into their programs. Figure 11.2 presents an example of a self-correcting activity that teachers can easily make.

One key to self-correcting materials is immediate feedback (Mercer, Mercer, and Bott, 1984). The materials should be simple enough so that students can learn to use the materials easily and to check their answers quickly. The materials should be varied so that the interest and novelty level remain relatively high.

the students take tests. Although small chalkboards can be used as individual writing boards, boards with a white erasable writing surface and special felt markers are now available.

A *flannel board* and a *magnetic board* are particularly useful in elementary classrooms. These can

■ **FIGURE 11.2**   *Self-Correcting Activity*

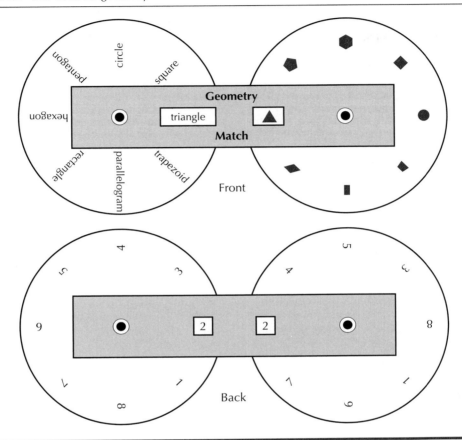

Another key to developing self-correcting materials is to make them durable so that they can be used and reused. Laminating and covering the materials with clear contact paper are good ways to make materials more durable. Special marking pens or grease pencils can then be used. Using heavy cardboard can also increase the durability of materials.

Instructional Games.   Students with learning and behavior problems frequently require numerous opportunities to practice an academic skill. Instructional games can provide this practice in a format that is interesting to the students.

The first step in designing an instructional game is to determine the purpose of the game. For example, the purpose might be to provide practice in:

1. Forming word families (e.g., *-at: fat, sat, cat, rat*)
2. Identifying sight words associated with a specific piece of reading material being used in the classroom
3. Using semantic and syntactic clues by using the cloze procedure (e.g., For dessert Brian wanted an ice _____ cone.)
4. Recalling multiplication facts
5. Reviewing information (e.g., identifying the parts of a flower)

The second step is to select and adapt a game in which to practice a skill or review knowledge. For example, commercial games such as Monopoly, Chutes and Ladders, Candyland, Clue, Sorry, and Parcheesi can be adapted. A generic game board can also be used (see Figure 11.3). Generic game boards can be purchased from some publishing companies. The key in selecting and adapting a game is to require the students to complete the instructional task as part of the turn-taking procedure. For example, when adapting Candyland to practice sight words, students would select a sight word card and a Candyland card. If they can correctly read the sight word then they can use their Candyland card to move as indicated. When adapting Monopoly for math facts, students would have to first select and answer the math fact. If answered correctly, they earn the opportunity to throw the dice and take a turn. When the same skills are practiced by many students in the class, the teacher may want to develop a specific game for the skill. Math Marathon is a specific game in which students move forward on a game board, depicting a marathon race by answering math word problems. Different sets of math word problem game cards can be developed, depending on the math problem-solving levels of the students.

The third step is to write the directions and develop the materials. MacWilliams (1978) recommends making a rough draft of the game and testing it. Posterboard glued to cardboard or manila folders makes a good game board. With manila folders the name of the game can be written on the tab and the board can be stored so that the students can scan the tabs to find the game. The materials for the game can be kept in an envelope inside the folder. The directions for the game and a list of materials that should be found inside may be written on the envelope.

The fourth step is to demonstrate the game to the students so that they can learn to play the games independently.

Organizing and Managing Materials

Selecting and developing materials is only one part of effective materials management. These materials need to be organized in the classroom in such a manner that the teacher and students have easy access to the materials without bothering other students.

Ms. Wilcox coteaches in a language arts classroom for one hour each day, during which the class is divided into either mixed or same ability groups, depending on the lesson. Ms. Wilcox has several suggestions regarding managing materials in the general education classroom.

The first thing Ms. Casey [general education teacher] and I did was expand the student library. We purchased books that represent a wider range of reading levels. We also began to purchase small sets of books to use in reading groups. Finally, we worked together to organize a closet and file cabinet with adapted materials and manipulatives that we both use. I find that these materials are beneficial with children of all ability levels. I didn't realize that we would benefit so much from sharing materials!

Scheduling

When teachers talk about the most difficult aspects of their jobs, they often mention scheduling. Special education teachers generally work with between five and ten general education teachers to coordinate pull-out, in-class, and consultation services. Special education teachers also work closely with counselors and teachers at the secondary level to see that students are placed in classes that will help them reach the goals and objectives developed on the individual education program (IEP) as well as meet graduation requirements. Even special education teachers who work in self-contained classrooms schedule students for integration into general education classroom activities for part of the day. It is essential that teachers work together to find time in the general education schedule that will be beneficial for the inclusion of students with more severe disabilities. In addition to adapting instruction, you will need to consider whether the student will have to be accompanied on his or her way to the general education classroom (by a student or a paraprofessional), and whether you or a paraprofessional will assist the student during the general education class. When students spend most of their day in a self-contained classroom, special education teachers are responsible for their entire curriculum.

Special education teachers make decisions regarding how to provide instruction in the various curricular areas (e.g., reading, math, writing, English,

■ **FIGURE 11.3** *Generic Board Game*

1. You are on a safari, trying to get to the Wild Game Reserve Station.
2. Begin at Start.
3. Each player rolls a die. The player with the highest number goes first.
4. Roll the die and draw a Game Card. If you answer the Game Card correctly, move the number shown on the die. If you do not answer the Game Card correctly, do not take a turn.
5. The first player to get to the Wild Card Reserve Station wins.

social studies, science, art, music), while still providing the students with adequate one-to-one and small group instruction so that the students might reach the educational goals targeted in the academic areas of concern.

Many teachers describe scheduling as the worst aspect of their job. The next section provides some points to consider.

Scheduling within the Classroom

Whether teaching in an inclusion, resource, or self-contained classroom, it is important to use the time students spend in the classroom efficiently.

There are no easy answers to scheduling. However, the following list presents some guidelines to use when developing a schedule.

— Schedule time to communicate with general education classroom teachers. The amount of time you schedule depends on the time your students spend in the general education classroom. Generally speaking, coteachers should schedule more time than resource teachers, and resource teachers schedule more time than self-contained teachers. This time will prove invaluable in assisting students to be successful in regular classrooms.

— Schedule time to observe in the classrooms in which your students are placed or are going to be placed. This alerts you to the class demands and schedules of the classroom and will help you in planning for your students' learning in that classroom.

— Schedule time to meet with other professionals (e.g., speech/language pathologist, school psychologist).

— Schedule so that you alternate instructional arrangements. For example, do not schedule a student to participate in independent learning activities for more than thirty minutes at a time.

— Plan for time to provide the students with advance organizers, feedback and evaluation. In this way students will know what is going to happen, and they will have the opportunity to think about what they have accomplished.

— Plan time for explicit instruction. Sometimes we have students spend the majority of their time in independent learning activities, which results in little time for them to receive direct instruction from the teacher, aide, or tutor.

— Students who are included in general education classrooms still require specialized instruction. Organize time so students with disabilities in general education classrooms receive the explicit instruction they need to be successful.

— Alternate preferred and less preferred activities or make preferred activities contingent upon less preferred activities.

— Let students know when the time for an activity is just about over. This gives them time to reach closure on the one activity and get ready for the next activity or to ask for a time extension.

— Be consistent in scheduling yet flexible and ready for change.

— Provide a session with each student in which you review his or her schedule in your room and in other teachers' classrooms. Be sure students know what is expected of them.

— Plan time to meet with and talk to members of your student's family, including parents.

Figures 11.4 and 11.5 present sample schedules for a resource and special education classrooms. For the resource room, the schedule for one group of students is presented, whereas the entire day's schedule is presented for the special education program.

Developing an Overall Schedule for a Resource Consultant Program

Scheduling students' time while in the special education classroom is one issue, but the overall schedule for teaching in a resource or inclusion setting presents other issues and requires that the teacher work closely with teachers and other professionals in the school. Teachers who assume roles as resource teachers must first clarify and decide what their job responsibilities will be. Generally these responsibilities can be divided into four general areas:

1. Directly provide instruction to the students, either in the general education classroom or in a separate classroom.

■ **FIGURE 11.4**   *Schedule for Fourth- through Sixth-Grade Students*

Date: 4/15

Time	José	Amelia	Scott	Todd	Carmen	Frank
10:00	Small-Group Instruction Reading ↓	Comprehension Computer Activity	Small-Group Instruction Reading ↓	Social Studies Text Using Request Pro- cedure with Carmen ↓	Social Studies Text Using Request Procedure with Todd ↓	Small-Group Instruction Reading ↓
10:20	Inferential Comprehension Activity on Computer	Small-Group Instruction Reading ↓	Social Studies Text with Self- Questioning ↓	Small-Group Instruction Reading ↓	Small-Group Instruction Reading ↓	Word Drill Social Studies Text with Self- Questioning
10:40	Writing Process ↓ Spelling	Writing Process ↓ Spelling	Writing Process (Computer) Spelling	Writing Process ↓ Spelling	Writing Process ↓ Spelling	Writing Process Computer Spelling
11:15	Practice Computer	Practice Game	Practice Game	Practice Tape Recorder Test	Practice Game	Practice Game

2. Indirectly provide instruction to the students by consulting with general classroom teachers and parents
3. Assess current and referred students
4. Serve as an instructional resource for other teachers and professionals within the school

The time a teacher spends in each one of these roles will directly influence the schedule the teacher develops. For example, if the major roles of the teacher are to provide instructional services indirectly to students, to assess current and referred students, and to serve as an instructional resource, then little time will be spent scheduling groups of students into the resource room. Instead, the teacher will serve primarily in the role of a consultant to others. A sample schedule for a teacher who provides direct and indirect support is presented in Figure 11.6.

On the other hand, Ms. Wilcox provides explicit instruction to most of the students she teaches for an average of 60 minutes per day, four days per week. Since she serves 22 students, she has developed a schedule that allows her some time to consult with general classroom teachers, but she has also allocated time to teach and assess current and referred students. To facilitate her scheduling, she grouped students according to grade level for the most part, with the older students attending in the morning and the younger students in the afternoon.

■ **FIGURE 11.5**   *Sample Schedule for Intermediate Level Special Education Program*

	ACTIVITY			
Time	*Group 1*	*Group 2*	*Group 3*	*Group 4*
8:15	Writing Process — Students working on reports			
9:15	Reading: Small-group instruction (teacher)	Reading: Independent learning activities	Learning center: Map reading	Reading: Small-group instruction (aide)
9:45	Reading: Independent learning activities	Reading: Small-group Instruction (aide)	Reading: Small-group instruction (teacher)	Learning center: Map reading
10:15	Announcements			
10:20	Recess			
10:45	Math: Group instruction (teacher)		Computer lab for Math practice (aide)	
11:15	Computer lab (aide)		Group instruction (teacher)	
11:50	Lunch			
12:40	Recreational Reading/Writing			
1:00	Social Studies: Large-group instruction			
1:45	Science: Cooperative learning activities			
2:15	Recess			
2:40	Health—Mon./Art—Tues./P.E.—Wed./Special Activity—Thurs., Fri. (Current: Producing a play)			
3:10	Earned "fun time" or time to complete work			
3:30	Dismissal			

She explains her schedule as follows:

I have arranged for the older students to come in the morning because I feel that I can take over the responsibility for teaching these students reading and writing—the content that is usually taught in the morning in many general education classrooms. I have developed a strong program in teaching reading comprehension, and I am using a process approach to teaching writing [see Figure 11.7]. Currently I am using content area textbooks, trade books, and literature for teaching reading comprehension, and the students are working on writing reports, literature critiques, and short stories on topics of their choice. Since I am responsible for these students' reading and writing, I am accountable for grading these students in these areas. Using this schedule, these students for the most part are in

the general education classroom for content area subjects and math. I feel that this is important. When they go to junior high, they will probably be taking general math, science, social studies, and other content area classes. If they have been missing these classes in the general education classroom during the fourth through sixth grades, they will really have trouble catching up. It's hard enough for these students—we want to give them every advantage possible.

I often provide their reading instruction in content areas such as social studies and science. Thus, while the emphasis is on reading rather than knowledge acquisition, I feel I am extending their background knowledge of concepts they will be taught in social studies and science.

I have the younger students come after lunch, because I feel many of these students need two doses of reading, writing, and math. These

■ **FIGURE 11.6**   *Coteaching Teacher Schedule*

Week of: <u>April 15</u>

Time	Monday	Tuesday	Wednesday	Thursday	Friday
7:30	IEP meeting	Instructional Review Meeting (2nd grade)	Child Study Team Meeting	IEP Meeting	Instructional Review Meeting (4th grade)
8:15	Work with 5th grade low reading group →——————————————————————————————————→				
9:00	Observe and assist LD/EH students in classroom (1st grade)	Assessment	Observe and assist (2nd grade, kindergarten)	3rd grade 4th grade	5th grade 6th grade
11:30	Meet with individual teachers	Planning and material development →———————→		Meet with individual teachers	Planning and material development
12:30	Lunch →——→				
1:00	Work with 2nd grade low reading group →——————————————————————————→				
1:30	Conduct study skills classes for selected 4th–6th graders	Conduct social skills class for group of EH students	Conduct study skills class	Conduct social skills class	Conduct study skills class
2:00	Work with Ms. Jones on implementing writing process →———————————→			Work with Mr. Peterson on using semantic feature analysis for teaching vocabulary	Assessment
2:30	Provide direct instruction in reading to 5 students with learning disabilities →—————————————————————————→				
3:30	Dismissal (check with teachers as needed) →——————————————————————————→				
3:45	End of day				

■ **FIGURE 11.7** *Unit Planning Form*

	Date: _____ Class Period: _____
	Unit Title: _____
What some students will learn.	*Materials/Resources:* _____
What most students will learn.	*Instructional Strategies/Adaptations:*
What ALL students should learn.	*Evaluation/Products:*

students get instruction in these areas in the morning in the general education classroom and then I give them additional instruction in the afternoon. With this arrangement it is important that I communicate with the general education classroom teachers so we each know what the other is doing. We don't want to confuse the students by giving them conflicting information or approaches to reading.

I also have one day a week that I use for assessment, consulting with classroom teachers, checking on the students in the general education classroom, and meeting and planning with my teaching assistant. I feel that this time is very important. All of my students spend most of the school day in the regular classroom. If they are really struggling in those settings, I need to know so that I can provide additional support.

There are always some exceptions to the general guidelines I use for scheduling. I have three students whom I only monitor in the general classroom. These students see me as a group on my assessment/consulting day. We talk about how it is going and discuss what is working for them and what frustrates them. I feel this time is critical for their successful inclusion. I also have two fifth-grade students who have good oral language skills but are reading on the first-grade level. They come for an additional 30 minutes late in the day, and we use the Fernald (VAKT) method to learn sight words.

I also developed a special schedule for my teachers' aide. She works directly with students to supplement and enhance skills they have initiated with me.

Special Considerations for Scheduling in Secondary Settings

Scheduling in resource and consultant programs in secondary settings generally is less flexible than in elementary-level programs. Teachers must work within the confines of the instructional periods and the curricular units that students must complete for high school graduation. One of the major responsibilities for resource/consultant teachers in secondary settings is to determine subject areas in which the students need special classes, and subjects in which they can succeed in general education classes without instructional support. These decisions about scheduling must be made on an individual basis and should be made with the involvement and commitment of the student as well as the teachers involved.

With the greater use of "learning and study strategies" curriculums in secondary special education programs, secondary special education teachers may want to consider their role as that of learning specialists (Schumaker and Deshler, 1988). For the most part, they teach classes in learning and study strategies that provide students with the necessary skills and strategies to function in general content classes. These learning specialists may also spend part of their day consulting with the content area teachers/specialists and in some cases may coteach.

CHALLENGES TO SUCCESSFUL INCLUSION AND COTEACHING

Challenges to General Education Teachers

There has probably never been a time in history when educators have faced greater challenges than those we face in the United States today. Classroom teachers are required to provide instruction for increasingly diverse student populations and are still held accountable for covering the prescribed curriculum in a manner that ensures that most of the students learn that content. Classroom teachers sometimes feel that they must choose between covering the full content of the curriculum or spending sufficient instructional time on the components of that curriculum to ensure that their slower students learn what they are supposed to learn. Many teachers make the choice to "go on," even when students with disabilities and other low-achieving students have not learned very much. Research has shown, however, that high-achieving students *want* teachers to take extra time and to try differing instructional approaches that help ensure that the lower-achieving students also learn the content (Vaughn et al., 1991). Teachers doubt that their curriculum supervisors, fellow teachers, and the parents of the high-achievers are as flexible about content coverage.

Many special education students need more time to master new concepts and skills, and they master those concepts and skills only if instruction is presented to them in a manner that enables them to "grasp" the new material. Students with learning disabilities, for example, have great difficulty with the learning process. Once they learn a new concept or skill, however, they "have" it and tend not to forget it. Unfortunately, an instructional strategy that works for one student may not work for another. Thus, a teacher must know and use a variety of instructional strategies to ensure that all of the students have an opportunity to learn. This effort takes time and planning, and it may result in less content coverage within a given time frame. Teachers need assurance from their supervisors that when there are several special-needs students in their classroom, they will not be held accountable for covering the full content of the curriculum. The first priority must be to ensure that the students succeed in learning the content that is covered.

When a general education teacher is asked to accept a mainstreamed special education student in his or her class, that teacher is, in effect, being asked to become the special education teacher for that student. If general education teachers are to assume the additional role of special educators, they need to receive the appropriate education for that very important job. The need for special training is accentuated by the fact that for every identified special education student in the classroom, there are usually several other students who have undiagnosed learning or behavior problems. Today's students have many needs and their classroom teachers require very specialized training to help them meet those needs.

In general, the regular education teachers at the middle and high school levels indicate that it is not feasible for them to plan specifically for students with special needs (Schumm and Vaughn, 1992; Schumm et al., 1995). They are willing to make accommodations for these students as they teach, and they are willing to help students with special needs as their need for help becomes clear, but they generally resist the idea of making special plans for individual students. They cite large classes made up of nonspecial education students with diverse needs of their own. For example, some students in their general education classes presented serious behavior problems, and some were learning English as a second language and had difficulty understanding and communicating in English (McIntosh et al., 1993).

Challenges to Special Education Teachers

If students with learning and behavior problems are to be successful in general education classrooms, then special education and general education teachers need to work together so that the students can make both academic and social progress. The strategies that follow may be incorporated into an instructional program whose objective is to assist students in the general education classroom:

— Work closely with the regular classroom teacher.
— Observe in the general education classroom to determine the academic and social demands.
— Simulate the academic and social demands of the general education classroom in the special education classroom.
— Assist the classroom teacher in adapting materials, instruction, and the instructional environment to facilitate the student's needs.
— Monitor the student once he or she is in general education classes.
— Meet regularly with the student to discuss progress and concerns.
— At first, communicate frequently with the general education teacher to discuss progress and concerns.

— Suggest that the regular classroom teacher use a "buddy" system in which the student with special needs is paired with a "veteran" to help the student learn the rules, procedures, and routines of the classroom.
— Coteach in the general education classroom to support the integration of students with disabilities.

Ms. Peress demonstrates many of these strategies as she mainstreams the intermediate-level students with learning disabilities from her self-contained classroom to general classrooms. Ms. Peress describes her mainstreaming strategy as follows: "I am convinced that these students need to be in general education classrooms if at all possible. However, I've learned that we need to prepare them both socially and academically. Much of what we do in special education classrooms does not prepare them for general education. They are used to individual and small group instruction, receiving lots of feedback, lots of reinforcement, and being relatively free to ask and receive assistance. This does not reflect what happens in the general education classrooms in this school. Although the teachers are great, they have 28 to 32 students in each class. Large-group instruction and cooperative and independent learning are the most frequently used instructional arrangements." Ms. Peress continues:

The first key to making inclusion work is to cooperate with the general classroom teacher and to observe that classroom to determine the learning and social demands.

The second key is to gain a commitment from the student. He or she has to want to work toward the goal. I always describe the classroom demands to the student and sometimes he or she goes to observe. Then we plan how we're going to get ready for "going to Mrs. Fetter's class for math."

The third key is to begin simulating those learning and social demands in my classroom. I start gradually. Usually I start by decreasing the feedback and reinforcement. Next I focus on the academic demands. I get the lessons and textbooks from the classroom teacher and

I begin to assign the lessons. At first the rate of learning is matched to the student's learning rate. But once the student is succeeding with the assignments, I begin to increase the rate until it matches that of the general education classroom. As this procedure continues, I continue to reduce the amount of reinforcement and feedback and to work with the student to become a more independent learner.

The fourth key is to monitor the student and to continue to work with the classroom teacher to modify and adapt materials, methods, and the teaching–learning environment as needed.

I have developed this strategy through experience. Many times I have found that my test scores, informal assessments, and student progress data indicate that the student is reading at grade level. In the past I would jump to the conclusion that the student was ready to perform without assistance in the general education classroom. Yet too often I would find the student with difficulties within three weeks, after failing. I was really setting the students up for failure. I had only attended to their reading level, not to the social and academic demands.

I've been very successful with this strategy. I have all but 4 of my 14 students included for most of the school day.

Ms. Peress's discussion of how she mainstreams her students into the general education classroom demonstrates that she has a philosophy that places importance on communication, collaboration, and consultation with the general education classroom teachers. A number of models for consultation and collaboration between general educators and special educators have been developed.

What Special Education Students Can Expect in General Education Classrooms

Special education teachers need to understand what students with special needs can reasonably expect in general education classrooms so that they can provide the support and skills necessary for success. While expectations vary considerably between elementary and secondary teachers (Schumm et al., 1992) and obviously from teacher to teacher, there are some common expectations.

— General education teachers are willing to make adaptations and accommodations that they can do with little preplanning. These adaptations and accommodations are more likely to occur if they can be done during the instructional process. See Apply the Concept 11.2 for a list of feasible adaptations.

— Students with special needs are treated by teachers much like other students (McIntosh, Vaughn, Schumm, Haager, and Lee, 1993). This is, of course, both good and bad news. Teachers treat students with special needs with the same respect and consideration provided other students. They provide few accommodations (particularly at the middle and high school level) to meet the individual learning needs of the students.

— Students with special needs participate infrequently in class activities, ask fewer questions, and respond rarely to teachers' questions (Baker and Zigmond, 1990; McIntosh et al., 1993). Students with special needs display a passive learning style that does little to increase the likelihood general education teachers will meet their learning needs.

— Whole-class activities is by far the primary mode of instruction at the middle and high school level and for social studies and science at the elementary level (McIntosh et al., 1993; Schumm et al., 1995). Thus, students with special needs who are accustomed to working in small groups and receiving extensive teacher direction are unlikely to receive these same considerations in the general education classroom.

— Undifferentiated large-group instruction is representative of what occurs in general education classrooms (Baker and Zigmond, 1990; McIntosh et al., 1993). Teachers largely follow the sequence of activities provided in the teacher's manual and do not consider the learning needs of groups or individual students.

APPLY THE CONCEPT 11.2

*ADAPTATIONS GENERAL EDUCATION TEACHERS
ARE WILLING TO MAKE*

Teachers identified the following as *highly* feasible
to implement:

1. Provide reinforcement and encouragement to
   assist students with learning.
2. Establish a personal relationship with the mainstreamed student.
3. Involve the mainstreamed student in whole
   class activities.
4. Establish routines that are appropriate for mainstreamed students.
5. Establish expectations for learning and
   behavior.

Teachers identified the following as *not* likely to be
implemented:

1. Adapt long-range plans to meet the needs of
   mainstreamed students.
2. Adjust the physical arrangement of the room to
   meet the needs of mainstreamed students.
3. Use alternative materials or adapt current materials for students with special needs.
4. Adapt scoring and grading criteria for students
   with special needs.
5. Provide individualizing instruction to meet students' special needs.

Source: Adapted from J. S. Schumm and S. Vaughn, "Making Adaptations for Mainstreamed Students:
General Classroom Teachers' Perspectives," *Remedial and Special Education, 12*(4) (1991): 18–27.

Students' Perceptions
of Teachers' Adaptations

If students are to be held responsible for their own
learning and education, then the perceptions of students should be assessed and considered. A recent
series of studies has investigated students' perceptions
of general classroom teachers' adaptations to meet
the needs of students with special needs (Vaughn,
Schumm, and Kouzekanani, 1993; Vaughn, Schumm,
Niarhos, and Daugherty, 1993; Vaughn, Schumm,
Niarhos, and Gordon, 1993). The perceptions of students are particularly significant with respect to general education teachers' adaptations because students'
perceptions are likely to influence teachers' behavior
and teachers are unlikely to make adaptations for students with special needs that they feel would "take
away" from nondisabled students. A summary of
the findings and their implications for instruction
follow:

— Elementary, middle, and high school students
  overwhelmingly prefer the teacher who makes
  adaptations to meet the special needs of students.
  There are three exceptions and these include

adaptations in tests, homework, and textbooks.
Consistent findings reveal that all students appreciate using the same textbooks and having
the same homework. Interviews with students
reveal that having the same homework is particularly important because homework serves as the
rationale for multiple telephone calls to friends
after school. Students who do not have the same
homework run the risk of being left out of the
social circle.

— Across all grade groupings, high-achieving students are more likely to prefer the teacher who
  makes adaptations than are low-achieving students. This seems surprising at first because it
  would seem that high-achieving students would
  have the least to gain from adaptations the
  teacher makes to meet the needs of students.
  The interest in adaptations on the part of high-
  achieving students seems altruistic.

— Students with special needs placed in the general
  education classroom for more than 50 percent of
  the school day had perceptions of teachers similar to those of the high-achieving students with
  two exceptions. The students with special needs
  did not demonstrate significant preferences for

no adaptations in tests and textbooks. Since students with special needs are accustomed to having tests and textbooks modified they did not find these procedures unusual on the part of the regular classroom teacher.

— All students want to be taught learning strategies to assist them in acquiring information on their own (Vaughn, Schumm, Klingner, and Saumell, 1995).

CONSULTATION AND COLLABORATION

How to Collaborate

Although both terms, *consultation* and *collaboration,* are often used to describe the role of many special education teachers, teachers prefer *collaboration* (Arguelles, Vaughn, and Schumm, 1996; Morrison, Walker, Wakefield, and Solberg, 1994). Why? Teachers indicate that they prefer collaborative modes of working on student problems rather than giving the problem to experts or working on it independently (Morrison et al., 1994). Teachers perceive that collaboration more accurately describes the nature of their relationship. One special education teacher said, "We actually work together to solve problems. It's not like I have all of the answers or she has all of the problems. We really help each other come up with ideas that work." We have found that general education teachers feel much the same way.

What is collaboration? According to Friend and Cook (1992) "Interpersonal collaboration is a style for direct interaction between at least two coequal parties voluntarily engaged in shared decision making as they work toward a common goal" (p. 5). Collaboration refers to the interaction that occurs between two professionals, often between the special education teacher and the general education teacher, and the roles that they play as equal partners in a problem solving endeavor.

As a special education teacher, what are some of the ways you might expect to collaborate with other professionals? As described in the next chapter, a significant part of your role will be to collaborate with parents and any other specialist who is associated with the students with special needs with whom you work. Whether you are working as a resource room teacher, self-contained special education teacher, or coteacher you will also have considerable opportunities to collaborate with general education teachers. You may also work in a program in which most of your work day involves collaboration with other teachers. At the elementary, middle, and secondary school levels, teachers are increasingly working in more collaborative ways with other professionals (Idol, Nevin, and Paolucci-Whitcomb, 2000; Pugach and Johnson, 1995).

One important way you will collaborate with general education professionals is in developing ways to make the curriculum more accessible to students with special needs (Dettmer, Dyck, and Thurston, 1999; Warger and Pugach, 1996). Curriculum planning can address such important issues as identifying changes in curriculum that are forecasted by national boards and professional groups; identify the ways in which these new trends will affect the curriculum and students with special needs; examine the scope and sequence of your present curriculum and determine where changes best fit; identify new goals and discuss the prerequisite skills needed for students with special needs; and identify areas of mismatch or where new curriculum is inappropriate for target students.

Additional ways in which special education teachers collaborate with general education teachers are as follows:

— *Coteaching.* The special educator and classroom teacher provide instruction together in the general education classroom.
— *Consultant teaching.* The special educator works with the classroom teacher to problem solve for students with disabilities who will receive instruction in the general education classroom. The special education teacher may observe, assess, and help plan for instruction but does not provide direct instruction in the general education classroom.
— *Coordinating paraprofessionals.* A paraprofessional assists students with disabilities in the general education classroom and is supported and supervised by the special education teacher

and/or the general education teacher. Both teachers work together to coordinate the paraprofessional's activities.

- *Teacher assistance teams.* A school-based team (including support professionals, classroom teachers, and administrators) assists the classroom teacher in meeting the instructional and behavior needs of individual students.

Procedures for Collaboration

When you work collaboratively with another professional it is helpful to have a common list of procedures that you follow to resolve the dilemma or solve the problem. Most procedures for peer collaboration include the following five steps:

1. *Initiator and facilitator.* Usually one member of the team has a problem or issue that needs to be resolved. That person is referred to as the initiator. The person(s) who is assisting with the problem is referred to as the facilitator. They serve as guides to assist in the resolution of the issue.
2. *Clarifying questions.* The initiator describes the problem or dilemma. The facilitator attempts to clarify the problem by asking questions.
3. *Summarization.* The problem is summarized by the team. The following format can be used to assist in summarizing the problem: (a) establishing the pattern of behavior, (b) acknowledging the teacher's feelings about the problem, and (c) identifying aspects of classroom and school environments that the teacher can modify (Pugach and Johnson, 1995).
4. *Interventions and predictions.* The team generates at least three interventions that address the problem. They consider the likely outcomes of each of the interventions identified.
5. *Evaluation.* The team develops an evaluation plan that includes strategies for keeping track of the intervention, recording the student's progress, and meeting again to review progress.

Resources Needed for Collaboration

No resource impedes successful collaboration more than time. Special and general education teachers confirm the difficulties of finding adequate time to

effectively collaborate during the work day (Voltz, Elliott, and Cobb, 1994). If time is not built into teachers' schedules, collaboration is simply unlikely to occur on a general basis. Furthermore, if it is not part of the schedule, then teachers come to resent having to collaborate because it means taking time from their personal schedules. Another critical aspect of time management for special education teachers is finding a mutual time in which they can collaborate with the many teachers with whom they work. This can be especially challenging at the secondary level. What are some ways in which collaborative time can be arranged (Vaughn, Bos, and Schumm, 1997)?

- Administrators designate a common time for collaborating professionals to work together (e.g., all fifth-grade team members).
- School boards pay professionals for one extra time period each week that can be used to collaborate or meet with parents.
- School districts provide early dismissal for students one day a week so that team members have a common planning time.
- Teachers schedule brief but focused planning periods with each other on a generally scheduled basis.
- Make use of resources such as parents, volunteers, and university students to help cover classes. For example, schedule short planning sessions during recess when larger groups of students can be monitored by a teacher and a parent volunteer.

Space for meeting is another needed resource. Often special education teachers feel fortunate if they have an office or a small classroom for their materials. Finding a quiet place to meet is particularly challenging in many schools where overcrowding is the norm.

Additionally, participants in collaborative models need to be familiar with procedures for successful collaboration. An orientation that addresses basic questions about their roles and responsibilities is helpful to all personnel involved in collaboration.

School Collaboration

Collaboration in the Schools (West, Idol, and Cannon, 1989) is one of a number of consultation models that focus on the special education teacher working directly with classroom teachers to assist them in the successful mainstreaming of students with learning and behavior problems. This consultation model is based on the concept of collaborative consultation which Idol and West and their colleagues define as "an interactive process that enables people with diverse expertise to generate creative solutions to mutually defined problems. . . . The major outcome of collaborative consultation is to provide comprehensive and effective programs for students with special needs within the most appropriate context, thereby enabling them to achieve maximum constructive interaction with their nonhandicapped peers" (Idol, Paolucci-Whitcomb, and Nevin, 1986, p. 1).

This model grew out of a need to provide more effective and coordinated services for students with special needs. West and Idol (1990) cite three reasons for using collaborative consultation models for special-needs students within the schools. One reason is the expense of assessing and placing students with learning and behavior problems in special education. They suggest that collaborative problem solving can serve as a preventative model. The second reason is evidence from research on effective schools (see Purkey and Smith, 1985, for a review), which indicates that collaborative planning and collegial relationships are two key process variables that are present in effective schools. A third reason is based on a professional development needs survey of the members of the Council for Exceptional Children, the major professional organization for special educators. The results indicate that the three top-ranked items focused on collaboration, communication, and consultation between special and general educators.

The purposes for collaborative consultation are to prevent learning and behavior problems, provide appropriate instruction for students with learning and behavior problems, and coordinate instructional programs (West et al., 1989). The model is based on a set of 47 collaborative consultation skills which were validated by experts in the field (West and Cannon, 1988) and are grouped into the following areas:

— Consultation theory/models
— Research on consultation theory, training, and practice

— Personal characteristics
— Interactive communication
— Collaborative problem solving
— Systems change
— Equity issues and value/belief systems
— Evaluation of consultation effectiveness

— **PROCEDURES:** The model is based on a six-stage collaborative consultation process completed by a collaborative team:

Stage 1: Goal/Entry. Roles, objectives, responsibilities, and expectations are negotiated.

Stage 2: Problem Identification. Nature and parameters of the presenting problem are defined.

Stage 3: Intervention of Recommendations. Potential interventions are generated and effects predicted. Recommendations are prioritized and selected. Objectives are developed to specify the intervention details, the procedures, and the means for determining if the problem has been solved.

Stage 4: Implementation of Recommendations. Procedures and plan of action are implemented.

Stage 5: Evaluation. Evaluation of the intervention is completed, including its impact on the child, the consultant and consultee, and the system or context in which the intervention is occurring.

Stage 6: Redesign. Intervention is continued, redesigned, or discontinued based on the evaluation (West and Idol, 1990).

Collaborative consultation may occur at varying levels of teacher and school involvement. For example, special and general education teachers in a middle school or high school may use collaborative consultation to assist students with learning disabilities who are included into general education English classes. Or an intermediate special education teacher and the speech/language pathologist may work with the intermediate teachers in an elementary school to develop strategies for facilitating concept and language development in the content areas. Or an elementary school may adopt collaborative consultation at the building level with the consultation used in the prereferral process as well as for a means of coordinating the special and general education programs for students with special needs.

— COMMENTS: Collaborative consultation has been used in a number of schools and districts throughout the United States and Canada. West and Idol (1990) suggest that a number of factors need to be considered in implementing collaborative consultation including systematic and ongoing staff development, administrative support, and scheduling.

Like other educational approaches, consultation and collaboration models have the potential for benefit as well as misuse and misunderstanding. Apply the Concept 11.3 provides a description of potential benefits and misuses.

Collaboration: Issues and Dilemmas

Since all special education teachers will be working in some collaborative way with general education teachers and many special education teachers will be working with general education teachers at least 50 percent of the time, several issues and dilemmas need to be recognized if special education teachers are to perform their job role effectively.

1. *Student "ownership."* One of the issues is the "ownership" of the student with problems. Traditionally, special education students have been the responsibility of the special education teacher, even if they were placed in the general education classroom for part of the day. This perspective is no longer feasible or desirable. The new perspective is one of shared ownership whereby all educators feel responsible for the success of the student with special needs.

2. *Individual versus class focus.* In a recent year long case study of the planning and adaptations for students with special needs, 12 effective general education teachers (4 elementary, 4 middle school, and 4 high school) (Schumm, Vaughn, Haager, McDowell, Rothlein and Saumell, 1992), the general education teachers did not plan or make adaptations for individual students but considered the class as a whole. This focus contrasts with that of special education teachers whose planning and instruction is aimed at the needs of the individual student. Neither of these perspectives is inherently better than the other (Glatthorn, 1990), but differing perspectives often promote conflict. Mrs. Vermillion put it this way: "I am a special education teacher and so the direction of my interest is always with the individual students and how the educational setting can be altered to meet his or her needs. During the last few years I realize that I've needed to adjust my perspective if I am to work effectively with classroom teachers. When they think about planning for students, they think about the class as a whole."

3. *Content versus accommodation.* When classroom teachers discuss their planning and instruction, one of the most consistent themes is content coverage (Schumm et al., 1992; Vaughn and Schumm, 1994). Classroom teachers feel that many guidelines at the state, local, and school level pressure them to cover more content. Often this need to cover content conflicts with knowledge acquisition. According to Vanessa, a ninth-grade science teacher, "If I waited until the students 'got it' we would never be able to cover all the material" (Vaughn and Schumm, 1994).

This notion of "content coverage" as the horse leading the instructional wagon is a consistent and pervasive problem in general education and now directly influences the instruction of students with special needs. There is some consensus that "less is more" and that reduced focus on content coverage would enhance the quality of instruction for all learners.

You can imagine the difficulty for classroom teachers who feel extreme pressures to cover extensive amounts of content when special education teachers make suggestions that slow down the pace or require them to make adaptations for students' special learning needs. This issue is not insolvable. In a year-long research project designed to increase the planning and adaptations of classroom teachers (social studies and

APPLY THE CONCEPT 11.3

Huefner (1988) has identified several potential benefits and misuses of consultation and collaboration models.

Potential Benefits

1. Reduction of stigma
2. Better understanding across education disciplines
3. On-the-job training for general education teachers in skills for effectively meeting the needs of special education students
4. Reduced mislabeling of students as disabled
5. The model may be more suitable to meeting the needs of secondary school students
6. Spillover benefits to general education students from working cooperatively with special education teacher

Potential Misuses

1. Excessive caseload management for special education teachers
2. Unrealistic expectations from viewing the consulting model as a panacea and/or undertraining and overloading the special education
3. Inadequate support and cooperation from classroom teachers
4. Converting the model to a tutoring or aide approach
5. Providing inadequate funding
6. Faulty assumptions regarding cost savings
7. Faulty assumptions regarding program effectiveness

---

science), teachers are willing to make adaptations and accommodations they feel will help students, and do not require extensive amounts of preparation (Schumm et al., 1992).

4. *Real world versus student's world.* Another dilemma between general and special education teachers is the purpose of education. Classroom teachers feel they are preparing students for the "real world." From their perspective, persons in the real world do not make accommodations for different learning styles. Fundamentally, they view the real world as expecting the same thing from everybody and therefore to best prepare youngsters, their role as teachers is to expect the same thing from every student. This position is more reflective of middle and high school teachers (who feel increased pressures to prepare students for the real world) than elementary teachers (Schumm et al., 1992).

Ms. McDowell, a secondary special education teacher, handles the problem this way: "When classroom teachers talk to me about the real world I'm prepared. First, I present them with the idea that students are never going to be successful in the real world if they do not have an opportunity to learn and experience success in their present world. Their present world is that teacher's classroom. Second, I present them with the fact that employers are required by law to make reasonable accommodations for individuals with disabilities. Also, I never ask general education teachers to make adaptations or accommodations that aren't useful to most students in the classroom." In fact, instructional interventions used to increase learning for students with disabilities are as least- or more effective for students without disabilities (Vaughn, Gersten, and Chard, 2000).

Teacher Assistance Teams

Teacher Assistance Teams (TAT) (Chalfant and Pysh, 1989, 1992; Chalfant, Pysh, and Moultrie, 1979) is a within-building problem-solving model designed to provide a teacher support system for classroom teachers. Chalfant and Pysh identified five reasons schools may struggle with meeting the needs of all students including students with disabilities in the general education classroom. First, with more special needs students remaining in the classroom and the general school population growing in terms of the number of at-risk students, the demands on classroom teachers have increased. Second, sufficient funds are not available to provide direct supportive services to all the children who need individualized assistance within our schools. Third, the classroom teacher may lack the time or preparation to plan and individualize instruction for these students. Fourth, because of the necessary assessment and placement safeguards built into the special education support system, this system is oftentimes not responsive to the immediate needs of teachers. Fifth, in some cases the teachers' perceived need for help has led to the overreferral of students for special education assessment and placement (Chalfant, 1987; 1989; Chalfant, Pysh, and Moultrie, 1979).

The Teacher Assistance Team is a school-based problem-solving unit designed to assist teachers in generating intervention strategies. The TAT model provides a forum whereby classroom teachers can meet and engage in a collaborative problem-solving process. The model is based on four assumptions related to teacher empowerment:

1. Considerable knowledge and talent exists among classroom teachers.
2. Classroom teachers can and do help many students with learning and behavior problems. Every effort should be made in the general classroom before a referral for special education services is made.
3. Teachers can resolve more problems by working together than by working alone.
4. Teachers learn best by doing; the best way to increase teachers' knowledge and skills is by helping them solve immediate classroom problems (Chalfant and Pysh, 1989; Chalfant, Pysh, and Moultrie, 1979).

▬ PROCEDURES: The core team is generally composed of three elected members (primarily classroom rather than special education teachers) with the requesting teacher also participating as a team member. The team may ask other teachers, specialists, or the principal to join the team as they deem necessary or to serve as permanent members. One person serves as coordinator and is charged with such responsibilities as alerting the team members to the time and place for the meetings and distributing

information prior to the meeting so that the members have read the information prior to the problem-solving meeting.

When teachers refer classroom problems to the team, they complete a request for assistance in which they address four areas:

1. Describe what you would like the student *to be able to do* that he/she does not presently do.
2. Describe what the student *does (assets)* and what he/she *does not do (deficits).*
3. Describe what you have done to help the student cope with his or her problems.
4. Provide background information and/or previous assessment data relevant to the problem (Chalfant and Pysh, 1981; Chalfant, Pysh and Moultrie, 1979).

Once a request for assistance is received, the person on the team responsible for that case reviews the information obtained from the request for assistance, observes in the classroom if necessary, interviews the teacher to clarify information, and constructs a problem-interaction diagram that visually represents and summarizes the concerns (Chalfant and Pysh, 1992). This information is distributed to the team members prior to the meeting.

At the TAT meeting, the team members complete a 30-minute problem-solving process for each request consisting of:

1. Reviewing the summary information, providing the opportunity for the teacher to clarify or provide additional information, and reaching consensus on what the problem is
2. Identifying the primary concern and establishing an objective for solving the problem
3. Brainstorming ideas for solving the problem and reaching the objective
4. Having the teacher requesting assistance select intervention strategies, which the teacher and team refine into a classroom intervention plan
5. Developing a means of measuring the success of the intervention plan
6. Establishing a date and time for a fifteen-minute follow-up meeting

APPLY THE CONCEPT 11.4

THE MAINSTREAM ASSISTANCE TEAM

Because consultation is increasingly used in schools and districts throughout the United States, Fuchs and colleagues (Fuchs, Fuchs, and Bahr, 1990) designed a prescriptive approach to problem solving in which the specialist (e.g., the special education teacher or school psychologist) serves in the role of the consultant and the classroom teacher as the consultee. The mainstream assistance team follows four common problem-solving steps:

1. Problem identification
2. Problem analysis
3. Plan implementation
4. Problem evaluation

One of the unique aspects of the mainstream assistance team is that the team uses a list of preidentified potential interventions to facilitate the process, assist on generating ideas, and saving time. Research indicates that both special and general education teachers were satisfied with the idea, the process, and the outcomes from implementing the program.

Using this type of format, a teacher assistance team generally handles two new requests during a one-hour meeting or one new request and two follow-ups.

— COMMENTS: The TAT model has been used widely throughout the United States and Canada. This model has been shown to be effective in assisting teachers in coping with the learning and behavior problems of students in the general school population. It is also particularly effective in reducing the number of students inappropriately referred for special education (Chalfant and Pysh, 1989). Its success in reducing the number of inappropriate referrals to special education has resulted in the TAT model being identified in the literature as a prereferral intervention. However, the original intent of the process was to serve as a resource for all students at a school. This process has also been used with students already identified as handicapped with the children's special education and general education teachers serving as team members and participating in the problem-solving process.

Several factors seem particularly relevant to the success of this model within a school. First, it is important that the school administration support such a program by providing teachers with the time for meetings and some type of support or incentive for serving as team members. Second, school-wide training in effective and efficient problem-solving strategies and the TAT process facilitates the success of the model (Chalfant and Pysh, 1989).

How do you maintain a continuum of services at your school (inclusion, pull-out, or combination)? Keeping in mind that it is necessary to offer a range of services (e.g., Council for Exceptional Children, 1993; Fuchs and Fuchs, 1995; Kauffman, 1995; Roberts and Mather, 1995), decisions should consider what is best for the students you serve and should be made on an individual case-by-case basis. What works for one student will not necessarily work for another. It is recommended that teachers and administrators work with their school districts to develop a plan that can effectively use resources (e.g., time, funding, staff) to implement appropriate services to your population of students (Idol, 1997). See Apply the Concept 11.4 for a description of the mainstream assistance team.

Coteaching

Coteaching or cooperative teaching is when general and special education teachers work in a coordinated way to jointly teach groups of students in the general education setting (Bauwens, Hourcade, and Friend,

1989). Coteaching works well within a collaborative consultation program.

— Special and general education teachers broadly plan their overall goals and desired outcomes for the class and specific students in the class.
— Both special and general classroom teachers preside during the same instruction period.
— While one teacher may provide some instruction to the group as a whole, most of the instructional time involves teachers working with small groups or individual students.
— Since students are frequently heterogeneously grouped, the special education teacher works with many students including those identified as benefitting from special education.
— Complementary instruction and supportive learning activities are part of teachers' coplanning and instruction.
— Tech Talk presents a CD-ROM based program for learning about coteaching.

Coteaching Models

Teachers can implement a variety of models for coteaching. Many teachers select a coteaching model based on the instructional goals as well as the individual needs of students in the classroom. Before choosing a coteaching model, the general and special education teachers need to decide what lesson or unit will be taught, being careful to consider general education curriculum requirements as well as the individual needs of students with disabilities as they are specified on the IEP. Most teachers find that they use more than one model during a week and even during a day. Following are several coteaching models that teachers have found useful (Vaughn, Schumm, and Arguelles, 1997).

Model A: One Group

One Lead Teacher, One Teacher "Teaching on Purpose": "Teaching on purpose" is giving short lessons to individuals, pairs, or small groups of students during or as a follow up to whole-group instruction. In one or two minutes, the teacher who is "teaching on purpose" might approach a student after instruction to follow up on key ideas and concepts, en-

courage participation, answer questions, or review directions. In about five minutes, the teacher can review concepts and vocabulary or check for understanding. If further instruction is needed, the teacher can take a bit longer to provide a mini-lesson that is related to the main lesson (e.g., how to find the main idea). Many teachers in coteaching situations end up spending their time *grazing,* going from student to student to make sure they are following along. Teaching on purpose is a method of checking for understanding and providing short installments of explicit instruction that are related to key ideas, concepts, or vocabulary from the main lesson.

Model B: Two Mixed-Ability Groups

Two Teachers Teach Same Content: In Model B, the class is divided into two mixed-ability groups with each teacher instructing one group. The purpose of this coteaching model is to provide a large number of opportunities for students to participate and interact with one another and to have their responses and knowledge monitored by a teacher. This format is often used during the discussion of a book that has been read as a whole group.

Model C: Two Same Ability Groups

Teachers Teach Different Content: Students are divided into two groups, based on their skill level in the topic area. One teacher reteaches while the other teacher provides alternative information or extension activities to the second group. For example, during a unit on fractions, one teacher can lead a reteach activity on dividing the parts of a whole while the other teacher facilitates an activity on creating story problems using fractions. In effective coteaching, the general education teacher does not always assume the role as lead teacher, nor does the special education teacher always reteach. Teachers share responsibilities and alter roles from one lesson to the next.

Model D: Multiple Groups

Teachers Monitor/Teach: Model D is often used during cooperative learning activities, reading groups, and learning centers. One option for Model D is to have several heterogeneous groups and one or two homogeneous, skill level groups. One or both teach-

TECH TALK 11.1

LEARNING ABOUT COTEACHING

Inclusion of students with disabilities has resulted in collaboration and coteaching between general education and special education teachers. Teachers combine their professional knowledge and skills to achieve success in school for both students with and without disabilities (Ripley, 1997). For a collaborative or coteaching approach to be effective in classrooms, teachers need to learn how to develop and implement this approach.

CD-ROM based training has the advantage that teachers can spend their extra time in their own schedule learning the coteaching approach, rather than scheduling time for workshops. *The Co-Teaching and Co-Planning* CD-ROM (produced by Western Instructional Support Center) is a computer-based training program for teachers. In this program, teachers learn: (1) the benefits of coteaching and co-planning for both students with disabilities and without disabilities; (2) the roles and responsibilities of coteaching and how they are shared by successful coteachers; and (3) strategies for planning and implementing collaboration and coteaching through interactive activities. In addition, teachers will receive forms and worksheets that will guide successful coteaching implementation. More information on this program is available online at http://www.wisc.org/New.CoTeaching/index.html.

---

ers work with individual groups for the entire period. Another possibility is to have students move in small groups through four or five centers. Two centers are teacher assisted and the remaining ones have activities that can be done independently by groups. Students might also work in cooperative groups or pairs while both teachers provide mini-lessons and monitor progress.

Model E: Whole Class

Two Teachers Teach Together: In this model, teachers work cooperatively to teach a lesson. One teacher may lead the whole class lesson while the other teacher interjects to clarify the material. Often the general education teacher provides curriculum material while the special education teacher adds strategies to help students with disabilities remember key ideas and organize information. For example, teachers might spend 10 minutes modeling problem-solving techniques and explaining directions for a science lesson on observation in which students will work cooperatively to record observations and make predictions about "mystery matter."

Coplanning. As a special education teacher, you will often be coplanning with general education teachers for the students with special needs who are in their classrooms. Sometimes you will also be coteaching in those classrooms, other times you will be assisting the teacher in planning lessons and making adaptations for the students with special needs that will be taught without your assistance. Apply the Concept 11.5 presents guidelines for effective coteaching.

With long-range coplanning, the special education and general education teachers broadly plan their overall goals and outcomes for the class and the specific students with disabilities who are in the class. This coplanning of broad goals occurs quarterly or more frequently as needed. This planning fits in with the IEP of the student with disabilities.

In coplanning units or lessons, the special education and general education teachers plan specific lessons and outcomes for a unit of study or for a designated period of time (e.g., weekly). The Planning Pyramid (Schumm, Vaughn, and Harris, 1997; Schumm, Vaughn, and Leavell, 1994) provides an instructional process for coplanning between special and general education teachers to meet the needs of students with disabilities in general education classrooms. As can be seen in Figure 11.7, a form for unit planning, and in Figure 11.8 and 11.9, forms

APPLY THE CONCEPT 11.5

GUIDELINES FOR EFFECTIVE COTEACHING

Effective coteaching involves:

1. *Voluntary participants.* Teachers should choose to work together and should not be forced into a collaborative teaching situation (Vaughn, 1995). Ms. Andrews is a special education teacher who has been coteaching in three fourth-grade classrooms for several years. She began collaborating after attending a workshop on coteaching with the fourth grade team from her school. She says the reason she and her team are successful is because "we enjoy working together, have compatible teaching styles, and feel comfortable discussing differences."

2. *Shared responsibility.* Teachers combine their knowledge and resources to plan instruction. Therefore, they also share the accountability of the outcomes of those decisions.

3. *Reciprocity of Ideas.* While the amount and nature of input will vary by teacher, both teachers must accept each others contributions as integral to the collaboration process.

4. *Problem solving.* Not only must teachers collaborate to identify and find solutions to meet student needs, they also must accept that problems will arise when two professionals work together to coordinate instruction. Dealing with problems that arise during collaboration is not so different from finding solutions to student problems. To solve a problem it is helpful to: (1) identify concerns; (2) share information regarding the problem; (3) brainstorm possible solutions; (4) evaluate the ideas and create a solution plan; (5) try the solution; and (6) evaluate its success (Snell and Janney, 2000).

5. *Interactive communication.* Effective communication occurs when teachers trust each other and are not afraid to voice either their agreement or disagreement, when they communicate accurately and directly, and when they remain sensitive to differences (Snell and Janney, 2000).

6. *Conflict Resolution.* Disagreements and even arguments are inevitable in any collaborative process. Implementing a plan to resolve conflicts can lead to better solutions than if the problem had been ignored (Idol, Nevin, and Paolucci-Whitcomb, 2000).

for lesson planning, forms can be used to facilitate the process. Working together, teachers complete the forms to identify their objectives, materials needed, and their roles and responsibilities in delivering the instruction. Essential to the success of the planning pyramid is the identification of core ideas, concepts, vocabulary, and/or principles that the teachers determine as essential for all students to learn. This information is entered at the base of the pyramid. Information that the teacher deems important for most students to learn is written at the middle of the pyramid. Information for a few students to learn is written at the top of the pyramid. Teachers who implement the planning pyramid find that it facilitates not just the organization of the material they intend to teach, but provides guidelines for instruction (Schumm, Vaughn, and Harris, 1997).

Coteaching. Joyce Duryea is an elementary special education teacher who has worked as a resource room teacher for nine years. Recently she was asked to work collaboratively with three general education teachers who had approximately five students with disabilities in each of their classrooms. Joyce said, "When I was preparing to be a special education teacher it never occurred to me that I would need to know how to coteach in a general education classroom. I always thought I would have my group of stu-

■ **FIGURE 11.8** *Weekly Coplanning Form*

Time Period: _____   Week Of: _____

Content Area: _____

Goals:	GE	SE

_____   _____

_____   _____

Activities:	GE	SE

Monday _____   _____

Tuesday _____   _____

Wednesday _____   _____

Thursday _____   _____

Friday _____   _____

Material(s):	GE	SE

Monday _____   _____

Tuesday _____   _____

Wednesday _____   _____

Thursday _____   _____

Friday _____   _____

Groups/Students:	GE	SE

Monday _____   _____

Tuesday _____   _____

Wednesday _____   _____

Thursday _____   _____

Friday _____   _____

Evaluation:

_____

_____

Other:

_____

_____

■ **FIGURE 11.9** *Example Elementary Coteaching Lesson Plan*

General Educator Ms. Marco   Special Educator Ms. Sanders   Grade 5

Date	Coteaching Technique	Specific Teacher Tasks	Materials	Evaluation	Individual Student Needs
2/8	Model B: Two mixed-ability groups	Literary Discussion: Both teachers lead discussions on the class reading of *The Cay*. In each group, teacher and students write coprehension questions. Students call on volunteers to respond to their questions. Teacher interjects throughout the discussion, making sure all students have a chance to ask and answer questions.	Student copies of *The Cay* Discussion journals	Evaluate discussion journals Monitor participation	Assist Roger in formulating a response to share with the class; remind Sam to pause first to organize thoughts before responding; Joe completes journal on computer
2/9	Model D: Five same-ability groups	Literacy Groups: Teachers each work with one of the two lower groups to provide explicit instruction in word analysis. The other three student groups work independently to complete reading and literacy assignments.	Student books Reading Log	Chart number of words decoded correctly Evaluate reading logs	Ms. M: mini-lesson on *r* controlled vowels Ms. S: reteach syllabication strategy for decoding
2/10	Model D: Six mixed-ability groups	Survival centers: Ms. S works at the Vocabulary center with Roger's group. She then follows his group to the Survival Word Game station and provides a word building mini-lesson. Ms. S remains at the word building station and provides a building words mini-lesson to Sandy's group. Ms. M monitors the remaining groups.	Center activities	Monitor group work Evaluate student work in word building	Roger works in a pair instead of in a foursome; Sandy brings behavior contract to stations

Date	Coteaching Technique	Specific Teacher Tasks	Materials	Evaluation	Individual Student Needs
2/11	Model A: One group: teaching on purpose	Research Reports: Ms. S gives directions for research report. Ms. M monitors work while Ms. S sees three small skill level groups (10–12 minutes each) to work on fluency/decoding.	Step-by-step research planners	Record fluency progress on student charts Evaluate planners	Roger uses modified research planner; Joe and Pedro complete work on computer
2/12	Model C: Two groups: one reteach	Research Reports: Ms. S works with students who are ready to begin research while Ms. M reteaches students who need assistance to develop a plan for their individual research projects.	Step-by-step research planners Research materials	Evaluate planners	Julie and Sam paraphrase steps before writing; Joe and Pedro complete work on computer

dents with special needs and that is the way it would be." However, she has found her new role exciting and challenging. Joyce puts it this way, "I think I'm a better teacher now and I definitely have a much better understanding of what goes on in the general education classroom and what kinds of expectations I need to have for my students."

Based on extended observations and interviews with more than seventy general education/special education teacher teams, we have identified several core issues that must be addressed if coteaching partnerships are likely to be successful (Vaughn and Schumm, 1996).

— Who gives grades and how do we grade? Perhaps the issue that warrants the most discussion prior to coteaching is grading. Special education teachers are accustomed to grading based on the effort, motivation, and abilities of their students. General education teachers consider grades from the perspective of a uniform set of expectations. Communicating about grading procedures for in-class assignments, tests, and homework will reduce the friction frequently associated with grading students with disabilities in the general education classroom.

— Whose classroom management rules do we use and who enforces them? Most general and special education teachers know the types of academic and social behaviors they find acceptable and unacceptable. Rarely is there disagreement between teachers about the more extreme behaviors; however, the subtle classroom management difficulties that are part of the ongoing routines of running a classroom can cause concerns for teachers. It is beneficial for teachers to discuss their classroom management styles and the roles they expect of each other in maintaining a smooth running classroom. Critical to success is determining when and with whom the special education teacher should intervene for discipline purposes.

— What space do I get? When a special education teacher spends part of his/her day instructing in another teacher's classroom, it is extremely useful to have a designated area for him or her to keep materials. Special education teachers who coteach for part of the school day in a teacher's classroom feel more at home and are better accepted by the students when they have a legitimate claim on space including a designated desk and chair.

— What do we tell the students? Teachers often wonder if students should be told they have two teachers or whether they should reveal that one of the teachers is a special teacher? We think it is a good idea to inform the students that they will be having two teachers and to introduce the special teacher as a "learning abilities" specialist. Students both accept and like the idea of having two teachers. In interviews with elementary students who had two teachers (special education and general education) the students revealed that they very much liked having two teachers in the classroom (Klingner et al., 1998).

— How can we get time to coplan and coordinate? The most pervasive concern of both general and special education teachers who coteach is obtaining sufficient time during the school day to plan and discuss their instruction and the learning of their students. This is of particular concern for special education teachers who are working with more than one general education teacher. Teachers need a minimum of forty-five minutes of uninterrupted planning time each week if they are likely to have a successful coteaching experience. One suggestion made by several of the teacher teams with whom we have worked is to designate a day or a half-day every six to eight weeks when teachers meet extensively to plan and discuss the progress of students as well as changes in their instructional practices.

— How do we know if it's working? Many teachers work so hard to make coteaching work that they overlook the most important goal—ensuring that students learn. Teachers must collect and evaluate student data in order to determine if instruction is effective. A general rule to follow if students are not making adequate progress is to increase the intensity of instruction and decrease the teacher–student ratio.

SUMMARY

Effective and efficient management and communication are key aspects of "good" teaching, particularly when designing and implementing educational programs for students with learning and behavior problems. This chapter provided information concerning the management and communication responsibilities of special education teachers. Specifically it focused on strategies and ideas for setting up different types of special education programs, utilizing equipment, designing and arranging instructional materials, scheduling, and consulting and collaborating with general education classroom teachers.

This chapter also addressed issues related to collaborating with other professionals. Collaboration involves shared decision making among coequals who have a common interest. Because working collaboratively takes time, issues arise related to planning time and resources, and developing skills. These skills are needed not just by the special education teacher, but by other professionals in the school as well. This chapter provided suggestions and considerations to make coteaching more successful.

Because management and communication vary depending on the setting, we encourage you to arrange to visit several special education programs and speak with the teachers if you are not familiar with different programs and settings for students with learning and behavior problems. This should help you envision how the information presented in this chapter can be used in school settings.

WEBSITES AS RESOURCES TO ASSIST IN COLLABORATION

http://www.ldonline.org/ld_indepth/teaching_techniques/tec_coteaching.html
This Website provides an overview of coteaching.

http://www.ldonline.org/ld_indepth/teaching_techniques/dld_ecologies.html
This Website describes a variety of issues and provides resources on inclusion.

http://www.libertycornercomputing.com/sri/Inclusion.html
This Website provides a variety of sources for inclusion.

http://www.uni.edu/coe/inclusion/index.html
This Website provides a variety of sources on inclusion (e.g., philosophy, legal requirements, teaching strategies, etc.).

http://www.sherm.com/
This Website introduces consulting and training for successful inclusion.

http://www.quasar.ualberta.ca/ddc/incl/resource.htm
This Website provides useful resources for inclusion (e.g., strategies, curriculum suggestions, etc.).

http://www.quasar.ualberta.ca/ddc/incl/b1a.htm
This Website provides information on collaborative teams.

http://www.weac.org/resource/june96/speced.htm
This Website provides an overview of inclusion (definition, legal issues, etc.).

http://www.uni.edu/coe/inclusion/
This Website provides a brief definition of coteaching and relevant citations.

http://www.usoe.k12.ut.us/sars/Upi/collaboration.htm
This Website contains several useful links related to collaboration (e.g., professional supporting team, inclusion supporting team, etc.).

http://www.projectchoices.org/faq.htm
This Website contains answers to FAQs (frequently asked questions) on inclusion.

http://www.usoe.k12.ut.s/sars/Upi/supports.htm
This Website introduces team-collaborating support for successful inclusion.

THINK AND APPLY

— Why is effective management and communication important for success as a special education teacher?
— What variables should you keep in mind when making decisions regarding the instruction and physical arrangement of the educational environment?
— What special considerations should a special education teacher keep in mind when planning a schedule for a secondary-level program
— Compare and contrast the models of Teacher Assistance Teams and Collaboration in the Schools.
— What is collaboration and what are some ways professionals can collaborate effectively?
— What are some of the resources professionals need in order to collaborate? How might these be obtained?
— What is the Mainstream Assistance Team and how might it resolve problems?
— What are some of the issues and dilemmas that occur when teachers coteach? How might they be resolved?

APPENDIX 11.1

Materials Evaluation Form

General Information

Name: <u>Schoolhouse: A Word Attack Skills Kit</u>
Author(s): <u>M. Clarke and F. Marsden</u>
Publisher: Science Research Associates

Copyright Date: <u>1973</u>
Cost: <u>$220</u>

Description of the Materials

Purpose of Materials: Provide practice with phonic and structural word analysis skills
Instructional Level(s) of Materials: first–third grades
Content of Materials: Plastic overlays and markers, 170 exercise cards (2 copies) and answer keys represent 10 color-coded areas (e.g., initial consonants, vowels), progress sheets
Target Age: Could be used with students ages 6–12
Theoretical Approach to Learning: Behavior approach in that it assumes skills can be taught in isolation
Type of Instructional Arrangement (Individual, Cooperative Learning, etc.): Individual
Teacher Involvement Requirements: Demonstrating mechanics of programs. Checking student understanding of directions and pictures. Spot checking of student self-checks. Evaluating progress.
Time Requirements: 10–15 minutes per exercise card.
Space Requirements: Materials come in 12" × 12" × 24" box.
Equipment Requirements: None

Evaluation

	Poor	Fair	Good
1. Is there any evidence that *these materials are effective?*	1	②	3
2. *Materials sequentially organized* Progress from easy to hard Use pictures in early exercises	1	2	③
3. *Materials organized for easy retrieval* Students should be able to find exercise card without assistance	1	2	③
4. *Directions clear* Yes and written with a low readability level	1	2	③
5. *Provides adequate examples* Most of the time	1	②	3
6. *Provides for adequate practice* Would like to see more cards covering each phonic or structural element	①	2	3
7. *Conducive to providing feedback* Student can self-check and could plot progress	1	2	③
8. *Allows for checking/self-checking*	1	2	③

Evaluation	*Poor*	*Fair*	*Good*
9. *Provides suggestions for adapting the materials*	①	2	3
No			
10. *Provides suggestions for generalization*	①	2	3
No, this is a major concern.			
11. *Interest Level*	1	②	3
Although pictures are fairly easy to interpret, there is a limited number. Format repetitive.			

Description of Role in Instructional Program

How would this material fit into my instructional program?

Only as a reinforcement activity. Need to discuss with students how this practice will help them when they read (generalization).

APPENDIX 11.2 ━━━━━━━

Student Materials Evaluation Form

Student Name: <u>Jason</u>
Date of Evaluation: <u>March 15</u>
Name of Materials: <u>Criminal Justice (textbook)</u>

Evaluation	*Poor*	*Fair*	*Good*

1. *Directions are clear.*
    I understand the activities at the end of the
    chapter.
	1	2	③

2. *Materials are interesting.* Yes. I like the personal stories.	1	2	③
3. *There are enough examples so that I know what* *to do.* Pretty much	1	②	3
4. *I get enough practice so that I learn the informa-* *tion or the skill.* Only if we discuss it in class	1	②	3
5. *It is easy to determine if I am doing the tasks* *correctly.* Not really	①	2	3
6. *I like using these materials.*	1	2	③

7. *I think that these materials teach:*
    About how our government works
8. *The thing(s) I like best about these materials is:*
    They're interesting
9. *The thing(s) I don't like about these materials is:*
    Sometimes it doesn't tell enough and I have to
    read other places
10. *I would recommend using these materials for:*
    Government classes

12 Communicating with Parents and Professionals

O U T L I N E

KEY TOPICS FOR MASTERY

- — *Principles of good communication: mutual respect and trust, acceptance, effective listening, plain language, effective questioning, providing encouragement, keeping the focus of the conversation directed, and developing a working alliance*
- — *Effective interviewing skills for special education teachers*
- — *Why special education teachers need to be sensitive to parents' concerns and to speak honestly about the child's problems*
- — *How special education teachers can work productively with parents and fellow professionals to provide effective help for the special education student*
- — *The role of the special education teacher in an effective mainstreaming program*
- — *Guarding against the potential barriers to successful mainstreaming*
- — *How to gain the building principal's interest and involvement in developing a model special education program*

 BRIGHT IDEA

> *Turn to page 524 and read Think and Apply.*

Mrs. Babson works in a hospital emergency room, so she is accustomed to talking to people who are grieving. Mrs. Babson states:

> *I often speak to parents about the recovery of their children. Fortunately, most of the children have injuries or illnesses in which they will recover completely. I've been trained in the importance of telling the parents as quickly and completely as possible all we know about their child's condition. The only reason I'm telling you this is that I want you to understand that I am accustomed to dealing with difficulties. But I was unprepared for the inconsistent information I would receive about our son.*
>
> *When our third child, Chad, was born, my husband and I couldn't have been happier. Our first two children were girls, who we enjoy immensely, but both of us were hoping for a boy. Chad walked and talked later than the girls, but I knew boys are often developmentally slower*

than girls so we were not concerned. Even when he was a preschooler, we knew Chad was different. He often had difficulty thinking of the right word for an object and he was clumsier than other children his age. When we spoke with his pediatrician he informed us that this was not uncommon.

> *When Chad entered kindergarten he did not know all of his colors and showed little ability to remember the names of the letters in the alphabet. His kindergarten teacher said she had seen a number of students like Chad, often boys, and suggested we keep Chad in kindergarten another year. Our neighbor, who is a teacher, thought this might not be a good idea since Chad was already large for his age. We spoke with the principal, who seemed very busy and thought we should take the advice of the kindergarten teacher. We retained Chad. Spending another year in kindergarten seemed to do little good, however. Chad was still unable to identify let-*

ters, though he was very popular because of his size and knowledge of the kindergarten routine.

First grade was worse yet. Chad showed no signs of reading and was confusing letters. His writing resembled that of a much younger child. By now we were very concerned and made several appointments with his first-grade teacher. She was very responsive and suggested that we have Chad tutored during the summer. The tutor said Chad had an attention problem and was having trouble with letter and word reversals. She suggested we have him tested for learning disabilities. The school psychologist agreed to do the testing and it was late in the fall before we were called and given the results.

Though both my husband and I are professionals, we felt somewhat intimidated by the number of school personnel at the meeting. On our way home, as we tried to reconstruct what we heard, we realized that we had misunderstood and missed a lot of information. I heard the school personnel say Chad's intelligence was normal, but my husband thought that it couldn't be normal because his verbal intelligence was low. We decided to make a list of questions to ask at our next meeting. We felt we had made a major stride forward since Chad would now be receiving special instruction one hour each day from a learning disabilities specialist; however, we still felt we understood very little about his problems. I only wish we had been told more completely and quickly about Chad's problem.

Many parents have had similar experiences. They have noticed that their child is different in some areas from other children the child's age. These parents seek advice from friends, medical professionals, and school professionals, and often feel confused and frustrated. When the child is identified as having learning disabilities or emotional disorders many parents feel relieved at first, hoping this identification will lead to solutions that will eliminate the child's learning or behavior problem. The difficult adjustments are that the child will probably always have learning or behavior problems and the special educa-

tion teacher will be unable to provide any magic cures and certainly no quick solutions.

Learning disabilities and emotional disorders are complex phenomena and knowledge of all the factors they involve is incomplete. Special education teachers must be sensitive to parental concerns about identification and intervention, and yet speak honestly about what they know and do not know. Teachers must provide parents with encouragement without giving false hopes. Parents need to know what educators' best knowledge of their child's learning and behavior problem is, and also to be informed of what educators are less sure of.

This chapter focuses on the teacher as a communicator. This communication occurs between teacher and parent and between special education teacher and other school-related professionals. The first part of the chapter focuses on principles of communication that can be used with parents and professionals. Effective communication skills are the basic needs in working effectively with parents and other professionals. The second part of the chapter focuses on teachers' roles with parents, on parental needs, and on how to facilitate an interactive relationship between school and home that will allow parents and professionals to exchange information. The third part of the chapter discusses special education teachers' roles with other professionals.

COMMUNICATION SKILLS

In addition to assessment, intervention, curriculum development, and classroom management, a major role for the teacher of students with learning and behavior problems is communication. Effective special education teachers communicate regularly with parents, other special and regular education teachers, school administrators, and other educational and psychological professionals such as the school psychologist, speech and language therapist, and so on. Ability to communicate effectively is a skill that significantly affects an exceptional educator's job success. Despite the importance of this skill, most teachers finish school with no formal training in communication.

Principles of Communication

Having parents as partners in the educational process is important to achieve success in education. Many researchers found that the amount and quality of teacher communication encourages parent involvement and influences the success of the partnerships (RMC Research Corp., 1995; Watkins, 1997). In other words, parents become involved based on communications they receive from their children's teachers.

Some teachers communicate effectively with parents and other teachers with little effort. They seem to be naturals at making other people feel at ease and willing to disclose information. However, most teachers can benefit from specific skills training that teaches them effective communication. The following are some basic principles designed to facilitate the communication process with parents, teachers, and other professionals.

Mutual Respect and Trust

Building mutual respect and trust is essential for successful communication (RMC Research Corp., 1995). Several researchers have been interested in studying ways of building mutual respect and trust. Simpson (1990) suggested that parents trust professionals when they feel professionals advocate for their children. Also, he emphasized a positive outlook, sensitivity to needs, and honesty. Stewart (1986) mentioned the importance of safe sharing situations. He suggested that being able to express feeling of anger or frustration facilitates trust and effective communication. In summary, both parents and professional need to perceive that there is a cooperative relationship between them (Berry and Hardman, 1998).

Acceptance

People know if you do not accept them or do not value what they have to say. Parents are aware when teachers do not really want to see them during conferences but are merely fulfilling a responsibility. Lack of acceptance interferes with parental and professional participation in a child's program. Some teachers seem to know how to extend and project their acceptance and interest. Ms. Skruggs has been teaching special education for 12 years. She has worked with a range of parents and professionals during her career—some easier to work with than others. Despite expected frustrations and disappointments, she communicates her care and concern to the parents and professionals with whom she interacts and always manages to find the few minutes necessary to meet with them. Ms. Skruggs claims, "Parents have a great deal to teach me. They have spent a lot of time with their child and have seen patterns of behavior that can assist me in teaching."

Pointers for communicating acceptance include:

1. Demonstrate respect for the parents' knowledge and understanding of their child.
2. Demonstrate respect for the diverse languages and cultures parents and their children represent.
3. Introduce parents to other members of the education team in a way that "sets the tone" for acceptance.
4. Give parents and guardians an opportunity to speak and be heard.
5. Represent the parents to other professionals and ensure that a language of acceptance is used by all professionals and parents.

Listening

Effective listening is more than waiting politely for the person to finish. It requires hearing the message the person is sending. Often this requires restating the message to assure understanding. Effective listeners listen for the "real content" of the message as well as listen for the "feelings" in the message. Without using phony or overused statements or parroting what was said, they restate the message and allow the speaker an opportunity to confirm and/or correct. In summary, effective listening involves:

1. Listening for the "real content" in the message
2. Listening for the "feelings" in the message
3. Restating or summarizing content and feelings (but not after every statement!)
4. Allowing the speaker to confirm or correct the perception

Mrs. Garcia, the mother of 12-year-old Felipe, telephoned his special education resource room teacher, Mr. Sanchez.

Mrs. Garcia:　Felipe has been complaining for the past couple of weeks that he has too much work to do in his biology and math classes and that he is falling behind. He says he is flunking biology.

Mr. Sanchez:　How much would you say he is studying each night?

Mrs. Garcia:　Tell it's hard to say. He stays out with his friends until dinner and then after dinner he starts talking about all his homework. Sometimes he sits in front of the TV with his books and sometimes he goes to his room.

Mr. Sanchez:　He has mentioned how much work he has to do in my class. I wonder if he is feeling a lot of pressure from different teachers, including me?

Mrs. Garcia:　Well, he has said he thinks you are working him too hard. I know sometimes he is lazy but maybe you could talk to him.

Mr. Sanchez:　Felipe works very hard in my class and I expect a great deal from him. I will talk with him after school and arrange a meeting with his other teachers as well.

Mrs. Garcia:　Thank you, and please do not tell Felipe I called. He would be very upset with me.

Plain Language

Teachers often use academic language or jargon when they communicate with parents. Many parents feel intimidated by the academic language or jargon (Skinner, 1991). Plain, straightforward talk by teachers is the most effective with parents. *Plain language* is language that expresses information in a straightforward, simple manner so as to make communication efficient and quick (RMC Research Corp., 1995). Using plain language makes parents understand information better, reduces intimidation, and helps parents whose native language is not English (RMC Research Corp., 1995).

Questioning

Knowing what type of question to ask will often help individuals in obtaining the information they need. Questions can be *open* or *closed*. An *open question* is a question that allows the respondent a full range of responses and discourages the respondent from short, yes or no answers. Open questions may begin with *How, What, Tell me about,* and so forth. Following are several open questions.

— What do you think might be happening?
— What do you know about _____?
— How do you interpret it?
— What do you suggest?
— How might you describe it?
— How does this relate to his behavior at home?
— Tell me your opinion about _____.

Mrs. Gilmore suspected that Matt, one of her students, was staying up very late at night. He was coming to school very tired and seemed to drag all day. He was also resting his head in the afternoon on his desk. She decided to call Matt's father to discuss the problem. She started the conversation by giving Matt's father some information about a meeting of parents that was going to be held in the school district that she thought would be of particular interest to him. She then proceeded to describe Matt's behavior in class. Finally, Mrs. Gilmore asked, "What do you think might be happening?" Matt's father began to confide that he was not paying much attention to Matt's bedtime and that Matt was staying up late watching movies on the new VCR. Mrs. Gilmore's question gave Matt's father the opportunity to explain what he thought was happening. Rather than posing several possibilities, or telling Matt's father that Matt was staying up too late at night, Mrs. Gilmore asked an open question, which allowed Matt's father to interpret the situation. Matt's father suggested that he would establish a firm bedtime. In this situation, asking an open question both allowed Matt's father to indicate how he felt and to offer a solution.

APPLY THE CONCEPT 12.1

*RECOMMENDATIONS FOR ACTIVE COMMUNICATION BETWEEN
TEACHERS AND PARENTS ABOUT HOMEWORK*

General and Special Educators

- Attend IEP meetings and all other conferences between schools and parents.
- Require students to keep a daily assignment book, and remind them of due dates.
- Provide parents with a list of suggestions about assisting with homework, and a list of major assignments at the beginning of the school year.
- Mail important information about homework procedures to the home.

Parents

- Monitor their child's homework daily.
- Attend parent–teacher conferences.
- Sign a daily assignment book.
- Inform teachers of their telephone numbers and reachable time.
- Share their expectations about home–school communication with teachers.

Schools

- Provide teachers with release time to engage in regular communication with parents.
- Encourage frequent written communication about homework with parents.
- Schedule parent–teacher conference in the evenings.
- Provide incentives for teachers engaging in specific activities to improve home–school communication.

- Assign one person in the school for communication with parents about the homework.
- Provide parents with teachers' telephone numbers and reachable times.
- Establish telephone homework hotlines to allow parents to call about homework.
- Provide parents with computerized student progress reports.
- Establish systems that enable teachers to place homework assignments on audiotapes so that parents can access to it by phone.
- Use answering machines so that parents can leave messages at any time.
- Provide mail services so that teachers can send assignments to home electronically.
- Schedule after-school sessions for students to get help on their homework.
- Provide peer tutoring programs.
- Use community volunteers to assist with homework assignment.
- Provide sufficient study hall time during school hours.

Students

- Keep a daily assignment book.
- Make sure they understand what the assignment is.
- Learn how to manage their time effectively.
- Attend parent–teacher conferences.

Source: Adapted from W. D. Bursuck, M. K. Harniss, M. H. Epstein, E. A. Polloway, M. Jayanthi, and L. M. Wissinger, "Solving Communication Problems About Homework: Recommendations of Special Education Teachers," *Learning Disabilities Research and Practice, 14*(3) (1999): 149–158. Reprinted by permission.

Involving people in identifying the problem increases the likelihood that they will not feel threatened by you, and they will be willing to make the necessary changes. Apply the Concept 12.1 provides recommendations for communication between parents and teachers.

Encouragement

Begin and end with something positive but genuine. With every student, even ones who have serious learning and behavior problems, teachers can find something positive to say. Perhaps the child is improving in some area, perhaps he or she contributed some interesting information to a class discussion, perhaps he or she said or did something that was humorous. In addition to hearing positive reports about their children, parents and professionals need encouragement about what they are doing. Since special education teachers often have meetings with parents and professionals to discuss problems, it is important to begin and end these meetings on a positive note. If possible, give genuine, positive feedback to the parents and professionals with whom you work regarding their assistance with a student.

Staying Directed

Follow the lead of parents and professionals whenever they are talking about a student. A skillful consultant is able to respond to others and still keep the discussion focused. It is not uncommon that parents, when speaking about their child, will mention other related home factors that may be influencing their child's progress in school. These may include marital difficulties, financial problems, or other personal problems. When others begin discussing serious problems that are beyond our reach as educators, we need to assist them in finding other resources to help them with their problems.

Listening, summarizing, and responding to the dialogue of parents and professionals often places the teacher in the role of those to whom others divulge confidences. In these situations we need to decide quickly whether the information is within our bounds as educators or we need to refer the parent or professional to someone else. Figure 12.1 provides a list of tips for effective communication with parents and professionals.

■ **FIGURE 12.1**   *Facilitating Effective Communication with Parents and Professionals*

1. Indicate respect for parents' knowledge and understanding of their child.
2. Demonstrate respect for the diverse languages and cultures parents and their children represent.
3. Introduce parents to other members of the education team in a way that sets the tone for acceptance.
4. Give parents an opportunity to speak and be heard.
5. Represent the parents to other professionals and ensure that a language of acceptance is used by all professionals and parents.
6. Even when you are busy, take the time to let parents and professionals know that you value them, and that you are just unable to meet with them at *this* time.
7. Avoid giving advice unless it is requested. This does not mean that you can never give suggestions; however, the suggestions should be given with the expectation that the person may or may not choose to implement them.
8. Avoid providing false reassurances to colleagues or parents. Reassurances may make them and

you feel better in the short run but in the long run are harmful. When things do not work out as you predicted, everyone can become disappointed and potentially lose trust.
9. Ask specific questions. Using unfocused questions makes it difficult to conduct a consistent, purposeful conversation.
10. Avoid changing topics too often; this requires that you monitor the topic and direct others to return to the topic.
11. Avoid interrupting others or being interrupted, which disturbs the conversation and makes effective collaboration difficult.
12. Avoid using cliches. A cliche as a response to a problem situation makes the other person feel as though you are trivializing the problem.
13. Respond to colleagues and parents in ways that attend to both the content of their message and their feelings.
14. Avoid jumping too quickly to a solution. Listening carefully and fully to the message will help you get at the root of the problem.

Source: S. Vaughn, C. S. Bos, and J. S. Schumm, *Teaching Mainstreamed, Diverse, and At-Risk Students in the General Education Classroom* (Boston: Allyn and Bacon, 1997). Reprinted with permission.

Developing a Working Alliance

It is important that, in every way possible, teachers communicate to parents and professionals that all of you share a common goal—developing the best program for the child. Whenever possible share information about changes in a child that would be of interest. Let parents know when the student is making exceptional progress. Let other professionals know when their intervention is paying off. Set up a team spirit in which all members feel they are working together to enhance the education and social development of the student.

Developing Interviewing Skills

Special education teachers often work as consultants to regular classroom teachers, to other educational and psychological specialists, and to parents. Consultants need interviewing skills in order to identify problems fully and to implement appropriate interventions. These interviewing skills help meet the need to ask questions that inform and to follow up appropriately on information provided. There are five steps to good communication:

1. *Ask open questions.* As discussed in the previous section, an open question permits respondents a full range of answers, which allows them to bring up a topic or problem they have on their mind. Open questions are generally followed by questions that require more specificity. Mr. Schwab, the special education resource room teacher, began his interview with Mrs. Francosa, the fourth-grade teacher, by asking an open question: "How is John's behavior lately?"

2. *Obtain specificity.* This requires asking questions or making restatements that identify or document the problem. After Mrs. Francosa describes John's behavior in the regular classroom, Mr. Schwab attempts to identify key points and to obtain specificity in describing the behavior: "You said John's behavior is better in the classroom but worse on the playground. Can you identify which behaviors in the classroom are better and which behaviors on the playground are worse?" Without drilling the interviewee, an attempt is made to identify the problem and provide documentation for its occurrence so that an appropriate intervention can be constructed.

3. *Identify the problem.* Problem identification can be based on information obtained, or it can be decided by the person being interviewed, often in the process of answering questions: "It seems like there is good progress in terms of completing classroom work. Let's figure out a way of reinforcing that behavior. There's a problem with his responding to teasing on the playground. His response has been to fight, which is getting him in more trouble. Any thoughts about how we might change that behavior?"

   After listening to suggestions from the teacher, Mr. Schwab might add, "Let me provide some suggestions that have been effective in the past with other students."

4. *Problem solve.* Suggestions for solving identified problems and implementing the solutions are generated. Both the professional being interviewed as well as the consultant contribute suggestions to solving the problem. Often other professionals are included in the suggestions: "Perhaps we could discuss John's problem with his counselor and ask her to teach him some strategies for coping with teasing. It's also possible to identify the students who are teasing him and reinforce them for not teasing."

   The tone for problem solving should be one of flexibility. There are often many possible solutions, few that work with all students. The goal is to find a solution the teacher is willing to implement that is effective for the student.

5. *Summary and feedback.* Summarize the problem and the plan of action. Be sure to indicate who is responsible for what. Whenever possible, establish a timeline for completing the tasks: "You will send home notes to his parents, informing them of his progress in seatwork in the classroom. I will meet with the counselor regarding his problem on the playground, and you will talk with his peers and arrange a system for reinforcing them for not teasing. I'll check back with you during lunch this week to see how things are going. I'm very pleased with this progress and I

■ **FIGURE 12.2** *Steps to a Successful Interview*

Step 1: Open Question or Statement:
"Tell me about John's behavior."

Step 2: Obtain Specificity:
"How do the other children respond when John gets angry?"

Step 3: Identify the Problem:
"Sounds like fighting is occurring during noon recess most frequently after John is teased."

Step 4: Problem Solving:
"Let's start by seeing how John perceives the problem and developing an intervention that includes his peers. What might be reinforcing to John and/or his peers?"

Step 5: Summary and Feedback:
"You'll meet with John and his peers tomorrow. I'll speak with the counselor and we'll schedule a team meeting for Wednesday."

am sure much of it is due to your hard work and follow-up." Figure 12.2 provides a summary of the interview process.

Effective consultants listen openly without a defensive posture. They stay focused and remember the needs of the student. They note that solutions effective with previous students and teachers may not be effective in current cases. They look for alternatives that can be implemented and they seek the advice of other professionals. When plans for solving problems are developed, they determine who is responsible for what tasks and provide feedback on performance. Interviews are the key to open communication and effective intervention.

Three Forms of Communication between Teachers and Parents

Three forms of communication are commonly used by schools: (1) in-person contact; (2) phone calls; and (3) written information. Each is important and has a different purpose. In-person contact involves scheduled parent–teacher conferences, informal school meetings, home visits, or parent information/training

seminars. Phone calls can be used to provide parents regular reports on the progress of their children, follow up after the conferences, or deal with an immediate crisis. Written information includes progress reports, daily interactive journals, or notification of events (Berry and Hardman, 1998).

WORKING WITH PARENTS

This section of the chapter will highlight the teacher's role with parents. Family adjustment to a child with learning and behavior problems is discussed first. Within this section, parent adjustment, sibling adjustment, and the problems of constructing an effective summer program will be described. Parents' involvement with the schools and their role in the planning of the child's educational program will be presented.

Family Adjustment

A great deal has been written on parental response to having a child with disabilities. Most of what is written focuses on parents of the mentally retarded and physically handicapped. This literature may provide little insight into the adjustment of parents who have children identified by the schools as learning- or behavior-disordered. Most parents of children with learning and behavior problems do not receive a "diagnosis" until the child is in school. Though they may have identified the child's behavior as different from their other children and peers, most parents are unsure of what the problem is. Often they seek advice from their family physician who either makes referrals to other professionals or suggests they wait until the child enters school. Although many parents are aware their child is different long before diagnosis, they still continue to hope that their observations are incorrect and that the child will outgrow the problem.

From a systems perspective, the family is an important force in the child's learning and development. For this reason, many mental health professionals recommend an integrated approach to working with students with learning disabilities and behavior disorders who are troubled. This integrated approach typically involves all or part of the family in the program. This may include an initial meeting with the entire family, involvement of selected family members, or ongoing clinical help that may involve the family at certain times. Not all families who have children with learning and behavior problems need therapeutic assistance.

Because of concern for their child, mothers of children with learning disabilities often expect less of them than the children expect of themselves (Margalit, Raviv, and Ankonina, 1992). Teachers need to realize when parents are expecting too little of their children and assist them in readjusting their expectations. The misconceptions about children under which many parents and teachers function often tell children that they are unable, and as a result, many children act as though they are unable. Many children with learning disabilities leave school unprepared for work, postsecondary education, and life expectations. Often they leave school with fewer skills than the mentally retarded (Cummings and Maddux, 1985). Teachers can help parents by reminding them to communicate the importance of education to their child; for example, sharing their successes and failures when they were in school, and emphasizing that even when they did not do well they continued to do the best they could.

Simpson (1982) suggests that the needs of parents of exceptional children fall into five general categories:

1. *Information exchange.* Parents need conferences, program and classroom information, progress reports, interpretations of their child's academic and social needs, and informal feedback about their child.
2. *Consumer and advocacy training.* Parents need information about their rights and responsibilities, procedures for interacting during conferences, resources available through the school and community, and assertiveness training.
3. *Home/community program implementation.* Parents need procedures for assisting their child academically and behaviorally at home, including procedures for tutoring and behavior management.

4. *Counseling, therapy, and consultation.* Parents need support groups, consultation, referrals for conflict resolution, problem solving, and therapy.
5. *Parent-coordinated service programs.* Parents need to be in a position to provide services to and receive services from other parents through advisory councils, parent-to-parent participation, advocacy, and other options.

In a study reported by Simpson (1988), the most widely requested services by parents of children with learning and behavior problems were program information and informal feedback.

Adjusting to a child with learning and behavior disorders is difficult (Simeonsson and Simeonsson, 1993). Understanding how parents are adjusting and interacting with the child based on their interpretation of the child's needs is an important role for the special education teacher.

Family-Centered Practice

Because family-centered practice is so integral to effective special education, it is important to ensure that there is a common understanding of what is meant by family centered practice. "Family-centered service delivery, across disciplines and settings, views the family as the unit of attention. This model organizes assistance in a collaborative fashion and in accordance with each individual family's wishes, strengths, and needs" (Allen and Petr, 1996, p. 64).

What would this mean to you as a teacher? How could you design each student's program with consideration of the family with strengths and needs? There are two essential things teachers can do implement family-centered practice: (1) family choice and (2) the adoption of strengths. The family should be viewed as the "director" of the service delivery process and as the ultimate decision-maker. And teachers focus on family strengths, not the deficiencies in the family-centered services. The following is a list of the important components of the family-centered practice that you want to keep in mind:

— The concept of family as the unit of attention or concern

— The importance of a collaboration between parents and professionals

— The needs of the family, the strengths or capabilities of families

— Family choice or decision making, and the uniqueness or culture of families

— The provision of specific types of services

— Maintenance of children in their own homes

— Empowerment of families

— Principles of normalization (Allen and Petr, 1996)

Wrap-Around Services

As society has become more aware of individuals with disabilities, many professionals have sought improved services for them. Wrap-around services are a result of new ways of thinking about individualized services. Wrap-around services refer to adding or deleting any services and supports to tailor a program to meet the child's or family's specific needs in order to meet specific goals (Karp, 1996; Katz-Leavy, Lourie, Stroul, and Ziegler-Dendy, 1992). Components of wrap-around services include:

— Community-based and unconditional services that never reject a child or family from appropriate services and make a change based on the needs of the child or family

— Coordinated, custom-made services in three or more life domains of a child and family (i.e., family life, residential, social, educational, medical, recreational, etc.)

— Services developed by a team of interdisciplinary service providers, including family, an advocate, systems' representatives, other people who are important in child's and family's life (Karp, 1996; Katz-Leavy et al., 1992)

What conditions are needed in order to be eligible for individualized and wrap-around services? The following is a list of eligibility criteria for the services: (1) having serious emotional or behavior disorder; (2) having functional impairments; (3) needing multi-agency services; (4) being placed, or at risk for placement, in restrictive residential treatment setting; and

(5) having difficult and complex needs that are not being met within the framework of the existing service system (Katz-Leavy et al., 1992).

Siblings

In addition to how parents respond to a child with learning or behavior problems, the response by other siblings is also important. Having a brother or sister with disabilities provides siblings with special experiences (Lian and Aloia, 1994). On the positive side, siblings develop greater empathy, understanding, and tolerance of individual differences (McLoughlin and Senn, 1994). On the negative side, they may develop inappropriate behaviors, emotional problems related to the experience (i.e., resentment, jealousy, guilt, fear, shame, embarrassment, etc.), or damaged self-esteem (McLoughlin, and Senn, 1994). Lardieri, Blacher, and Swanson (2000) conducted a study to determine whether the presence of a child with learning disabilities, with or without reported behavior problems, impacts upon the psychological well-being and self-concept of his or her siblings. Although sibling relationships in families of children with and without learning disabilities differed in their perception of the quality of their sibling relationships and self-reports of their own behavior, it was not potent enough to render a clinical diagnosis of sibling maladjustment. Not surprisingly, some siblings appear to be affected very little and others more significantly. Many siblings also report many positive aspects of having a brother or sister with disabilities.

Many parents are concerned because their child with learning disabilities or behavior disorders takes more time and consideration than do their other children. Siblings may feel as though the child with special needs is getting all of the attention and special privileges. It is important for parents to develop schedules so they will have assigned special time for all of their children. A sibling of a child with learning disabilities commented:

> *Everything always seems to center around Scott. He always seems to be the focus of the conversation and whom my parents are concerned about. I do pretty well in school and don't seem to have many problems, so*

sometimes I feel left out. It really meant a lot to me when my mother and father both scheduled time during the week for me to be alone with them. Usually my dad and I would go to the park and sometimes we would go on an errand. Often my mom and I would work together in the kitchen, making my favorite dessert, chocolate chip cookies. The best part was that it was just me and them. I really think it helped me be more understanding of Scott. Somehow, I just didn't resent him so much anymore.

Powell and Olge (1985) suggested strategies for parents to respond to siblings, including:

— Be open and honest.
— Value each child individually.
— Limit care-giving responsibilities.
— Use respite care and other supportive services.
— Be fair.
— Accept disability.
— Put together a library of children's books on disabilities.
— Schedule special time with each sibling.
— Let siblings settle their own differences.
— Praise siblings.
— Listen to siblings.
— Involve the siblings.
— Provide opportunities for the child with a disability to be as independent as possible.
— Recognize each child's unique qualities and family contribution.
— Encourage the development of special sibling programs.
— Help establish a sibling support group.
— Recognize special stress times for siblings and plan to minimize negative effects.

Summers

Summers seem to be particularly difficult for children with learning and behavior problems. They often have too much unstructured time and too many opportunities to discover trouble. The summer is an extended time without exposure to structured learning experiences, and often what was done during the school year is undone during the three months without school. Parents often have a very difficult time with summers because of the additional pressure to find an appropriate educational or social experience. Billy's mother describes it this way:

> My son, Billy, needs a special summer program so he can learn to play with other kids. . . . My ex-husband, Arthur, thinks I bug Billy too much and that we should leave him alone. That's what happened last summer, and it didn't work. I don't know how to convince him or where to begin to find a good camp. I'm exhausted. I'm doing all I can manage. Last week, the school people reminded me that it was time to plan for the summer. And then they told me how much trouble Billy was having playing with the other children. Maybe I misinterpreted it, but I felt they were saying I should be helping him even more. (*Exceptional Parent*, 1984, p. 43)

Teachers can assist parents during the summer by developing a list of community resources that provide structured programs for children and adolescents. Each community has a range of such programs, some of which include:

1. *Public library.* The public library offers many programs that focus on literacy, including authors reading their books, books on tapes and records, and other special programs.
2. *Children's museums.* Many towns and cities have developed children's museums that offer a range of special programs for children.
3. *Theater groups.* Often local theater groups offer summer programs on acting, cinema, and stage design.
4. *Museums.* Check with local art museums, historic museums, and science museums to determine what types of programs they will be offering during the summer.
5. *Parks and recreation.* Parks offer arts and crafts as well as organized recreational activities during the summer that are often free or very inexpensive.
6. *YMCA, YWCA.* These organizations offer many special summer programs, including day camps, swimming lessons, and arts and crafts.
7. *Universities, colleges, and community colleges.* Often these organizations offer special programs for children in the summer.

APPLY THE CONCEPT 12. 2

TIPS FOR PARENTS ABOUT SUMMER READING

Summer should not mean taking a break from learning. For reading, this is even more true. Many students lose reading skills over the summer breaks. At the same time, students also need fun time in the summer. So summer reading should be fun. The following is a list of tips for summer reading:

- Read aloud with your children. Do not make this activity formal. Make it fun.
- Show them your enjoyment of reading. Keep lots of reading materials in house.
- Let them choose the books they want to read.
- Provide your children books on tapes. Listen to books often.

- Connect daily events to reading (e.g., let them read sentences on the items at the grocery, let them read traffic signs, play books on tape while in the car).
- Let your children join in summer reading club activities.
- Encourage your children to become pen pals with their friends over summer vacation.
- Encourage your children to make a summer scrapbook where they can put pictures, postcards or photos. They can also write notes under these cards or on the back.

Source: Adapted from Coordinated Campaign for Learning Disabilities, "Summer Reading Tips for Parents," *LDA Newsbriefs, 34*(4) (1999): 1–24.

Preparing a list of activities available in the community as well as a list of tutors available during the summer helps parents and children with a smooth transition from school to summer, and may help teachers with the transition next fall from summer to school. Perhaps the most important thing is to provide a structured activity each day, without demanding that the entire day be structured (Apply the Concept 12.2).

Parents as Tutors

Parental responsibility is to "insure that the home is a relaxed and pleasant place, a source of strength to the child" (Kronik, 1977, p. 327). Often parents want so much to help that they get overly involved in the child's homework or tutoring. Although spending time with their child in relaxing activities such as reading to the child, going for walks, sitting and talking, going to the zoo, and so on, are recommended by all educational and psychological specialists, few recommend direct instructional tutoring in the home. Home tutoring by the parent usually creates more problems than it solves. Often children need help with homework assignments; this is not the equivalent of

home tutoring. Home tutoring is the supplementing of the child's educational program by the parent in the home. Parental teaching improves the cognitive and social skills of their children (Alper, Schloss, and Schloss, 1994). If parents insist on home tutoring, ask them to comply with the following suggestions adapted from Cummings and Maddux (1985).

1. Have specific, realistic goals developed with the special education or classroom teacher.
2. Begin and end each tutoring session with a fun activity in which the child is successful.
3. Keep the tutoring session brief—not more than 15 minutes for children up to grade 6 and not more than 30 minutes for older students.
4. Work on small segments of material at a time.
5. Use creative and novel ways of reviewing and teaching new material.
6. Prevent the student from making mistakes. If the student does not know the answer, give it.
7. Keep a tutoring log in which you record a couple of sentences about what you did and how the child performed.
8. Provide encouragement and support.

APPLY THE CONCEPT 12.3

PARENT INVOLVEMENT IN READING AND WRITING INSTRUCTION FOR THEIR CHILDREN

Hughes, Schumm, and Vaughn (1999) conducted a study of Hispanic parents of children with learning disabilities to determine the type of involvement they value in their child's reading and writing acquisition. Parents were asked to provide information on the types of reading and writing activities that they practiced in the home and the extent to which they thought various reading and writing activities were feasible to implement.

Hispanic parents who participated in the study reported that a wide variety of reading and writing activities were used in the home. Reading to each other was the activity most frequently reported. Parents implemented reading activities more frequently than writing activities. Parents identified the following activities as helpful:

- More communication with teacher about reading and writing activities they could do at home
- Further information about how to do the reading and writing activities with their children since the children had difficulties with reading and writing
- More information about appropriate home reading activities in the parents' language (Spanish)

---

9. Practice the activities in ways that reduce boredom.
10. Work should be challenging but not too difficult.
11. Tutor at the same time and in the same place so the child has an expectation set for what will happen.
12. If you are getting frustrated or your interactions with your child are strained or stressful during the tutoring, stop. Your relationship with your child is much more important than what you can teach him or her during the tutoring session.

Apply the Concept 12.3 provides an overview of a study that examined parental involvement in literacy development.

Parents as Service Providers

Many significant developments in the field of special education have been accomplished by parents, rather than professionals (Turnbull & Turnbull, 1990). Parents of students with disabilities organized with other parents on local and state levels to obtain appropriate services for their children. Some parents conducted fund-raising campaigns, and others even started their own schools. The efforts resulted in today's national organizations formed primarily by parents of students with disabilities. These organizations play multiple roles related to appropriate services for their children with disabilities, including advocacy, political lobbying, raising funds, and providing services (Alper, Schloss, and Schloss, 1994; Roos, 1977).

Parent Involvement with Schools

By the time children reach school, parents have already spent five years observing them. Many parents are aware from the day their child enters school that the child is different from other children. Often the child spends two to three difficult years in school before the child is referred for learning disabilities or behavior disorders. During this time, many parents have spent hours communicating with school counselors, psychologists, and teachers. In a study in which parents of students with learning disabilities were interviewed following the initial placement of their child, parents reported having an average of six contacts with the school before their child was identified (Vaughn, Bos, Harrell, and Laskey, 1988). Some of these contacts were initiated by the parent. Often

APPLY THE CONCEPT 12.4

WHAT PARENTS OF STUDENTS WITH LEARNING DISABILITIES WANT FROM PROFESSIONALS

In a survey of over 200 parents of children with learning disabilities, parents indicated what they really wanted from professionals (Dembinski and Mauser, 1977). A summary of the findings follows:

1. Parents want professionals to communicate without the use of jargon. When technical terms are necessary, they would like to have them explained so they can understand.
2. Whenever possible, they would like conferences to be held so both parents can attend.

3. They would like to receive written materials that provide information that will assist them in understanding their child's problem.
4. They would like to receive a copy of a written report about their child.
5. Parents would like specific advice on how to manage specific behavior problems of their children or how to teach them needed skills.
6. Parents would like information on their child's social as well as academic behavior.

---

parents feel frustrated and alone. They are unsure what to do and, because of the complexity of their child's condition, professionals are often unable to provide the precise answers parents need. See Apply the Concept 12.4. See Tech Talk for ideas about using technology to build partnerships.

Parental Involvement in Planning and Placement Conferences

Turnbull, Turnbull, and Wheat (1982) consider the provisions of PL 94-142 radical because of the extent of parent participation guaranteed. Parents provide consent for evaluation, participate in the program and educational plan, and are kept involved in all decisions regarding the child's educational program.

The rationale for extensive parent involvement is twofold. First, it assures a cooperative role between home and school. Parents can provide information about the child the schools may not have access to, and parents can follow up on educational goals in the home. Second, it assures that parents will have access to information regarding student evaluations and records and can better monitor appropriate placement and programming by the school. One of the greatest potential benefits to the child and family is to involve the parents in the planning and placement conference

for the child. The information obtained about the child's learning and behavior problems can increase parental understanding, which leads to changes in parent behavior toward the child. In addition, parents learn about the focus of the child's program at school and can follow up on those learning and behavior programs in the home. Unfortunately, this is more often a description of the ideal than the real. Despite the best intentions of school personnel and parents, cooperative and extensive involvement in the placement and planning process is minimal.

There are many explanations for lack of parent involvement in the educational planning. One is that school personnel do not have adequate time to meet with parents and fully explain the child's program, or do not understand how to take advantage of parents' knowledge and preferences (Harry, 1992; Harry, Allen, and McLaughlin, 1995). Often parent meetings must be held early in the morning before parents go to work, or late at night on their way home. These times usually conflict with school personnel schedules and require school personnel to meet with parents outside of their required work time. Because of their dedication and interest in the child, professionals are often willing to meet at these times, but they are not motivated to meet for extended periods of time.

TECH TALK 12.1

BUILDING PARTNERSHIPS WITH PARENTS THROUGH TECHNOLOGY

Strong partnerships between parents and school can result in increases in students' achievement and parental involvement. In addition, such partnerships are related to a decrease in student absenteeism (Adams and Christenson, 1998).

SchoolCall provides parents and schools with the opportunity to build partnership easily. SchoolCall is an interactive voice response system, designed to facilitate the communication between parents, students, and schools. There are five types of systems: (1) Admin Messaging; (2) Auto Attendance; (3) MemoCall; (4) Homework Hotline; and (5) Bulletin Board.

Admin Messaging is designed for superintendents, principals, and administrative staff. Personnel can deliver a voice message to the entire school or send a message to a particular grade level, class, or student. They can also receive responses to their messages, thus keeping the entire school informed of important school announcements such as test date reminders, emergency notification, and dates when report cards are coming home, and can collect immediate responses to these notifications.

Auto Attendance is a communication system that informs parents by phone of their children's attendance violations. It lets parents know when their children are absent and also prompt parents to record the reason automatically.

MemoCall is a voice response system that allows teachers or administrators, coaches, and club leaders to record and send voice messages to parents, team members, organizations, clubs, and PTA members. MemoCall is an easy way to keep them informed about important events or students' schedules.

Homework Hotline is an interactive communication link between teachers, parents, and students. It allows parents and students to keep up with class assignments, test dates, deadlines, and much more. It reduces reasons for missed homework assignments and eliminates the excuse of not being aware of upcoming tests.

Bulletin Board is a direct communication link between school administrators and parents and students. It allows parents and students to access a wide variety of school announcements 24 hours a day from any touch-tone phone.

More information on SchoolCall is available online at http://www.schoolcall.com/.

A second explanation is that many parents feel professionals will make the best decisions in their child's interest and do not want to be coparticipants in their child's educational program. This may not indicate a lack of interest in the child's program but merely less confidence in participating in this way. To assume that all parents want to be actively involved in planning their child's educational program may not be accurate. Winton and Turnbull (1981) found that when they interviewed parents of preschool children

with disabilities, 65 percent of the parents identified informal contact with teachers as the activity they most preferred, followed by 13 percent who chose parent training opportunities, and 10 percent identified opportunities to help others understand the child. It is interesting to note that a common theme in studies evaluating parent satisfaction with the placement and IEP conference is that parents state that they feel satisfied with the conference even though data indicate they played relatively passive roles (Lynch and Stein, 1982; Vaughn, Bos, Harrell, and Laskey, 1988). Some 25 percent of the parents of students with learning disabilities who participated in placement and planning conferences did not recall the IEP document itself, and of those who did recall it, few had any knowledge of its content (McKinney and Hocutt, 1982).

It could be that parents would like to be more involved but feel intimidated by the number of professionals and the uncommon terminology.

> No matter how well we might know our own children, we are not prepared to talk to teachers, principals, psychologists, or counselors, much less participate in the educational decision making process. Although parents do have a lot of information, it is not the "right" kind. When we go to speak to administrators at school we hear about IEP's, MA's, criteria, auditory processing, regulations, and sometimes, due process. At first, there seems to be no correspondence between what we know and what the people in schools are talking about (*Exceptional Parent,* 1984, p. 41).

During conferences, special education teachers need to be sensitive to parents' feelings and needs and serve as advocates for the parents. Often the teacher can "act as if" he or she is the parent and ask questions of the classroom teacher or other professionals that he or she feels the parent may have wanted to ask but did not.

Parent Conferences: Planned and Unplanned

Planned conferences with parents occur frequently and include: multidisciplinary team meetings, annual parent-student meetings, or regularly scheduled meetings to report on academic and behavioral progress. Conferences provide teachers with the opportunity to:

— Review the student's materials, grades, and work progress.
— Meeting with other professionals to provide an overall review and report on student progress.
— Review the student's portfolio, assessment information, and progress reports.
— Provide samples of the student's most recent work.
— Establish and review goals and criteria for academic and behavioral work.

Often conferences with parents are unplanned (Turnbull and Turnbull, 1990). Parents may phone, stop by the school, or schedule a conference with little notice. When this occurs, there are several procedures to remember: listen carefully until the parents have expressed the purpose of their visit, paraphrase what you understand to be their question or issues, and respond to the question and issue as completely as possible. Often parents stop by with a simple question or concern that is a disguise for a larger issue. That is why it's important to listen carefully and wait until parents are finished. Apply the Concept 12.5 provides considerations for working with parents from culturally and linguistically diverse groups.

Individuals with Disabilities Education Act (IDEA) and Parent Involvement

The Individuals with Disabilities Education Act (IDEA) was passed in 1990 and was amended 1997. This law assures that all youngsters with disabilities receive a free, appropriate public education, which emphasizes special education and related services designed to meet their unique needs. All students between the ages of 3 and 21 are eligible for a program of special education and related services under Part B; children with disabilities from birth through age three are eligible for special education and related services under Part C. Part C, which is a subchapter of the IDEA, is about infants and toddlers with disabilities.

The law provides for early intervention services that meet the developmental needs of the youngster and his or her family including: physical development, cognition, language, social, and self-help skills. The parents and family play an important role, and an individualized program plan must be designed to meet their needs. This program plan, called the Individualized Family Service Plan (IFSP), should provide a coordinated array of services, including:

— Screening and assessment
— Psychological assessment and intervention
— Occupational and physical therapy
— Speech, language, and audiology
— Family involvement, training, and home visits

APPLY THE CONCEPT 12.5

CONSIDERATIONS FOR CULTURALLY AND LINGUISTICALLY DIVERSE PARENTS

1. Assume that parents want to help their children.
2. Provide materials in a range of formats including orally, in writing (parents' language), through videotape, and through formal and informal presentations.
3. Provide opportunities for parents to learn the skills and activities the students are learning so they can reinforce them in the home.
4. Provide opportunities for parents to influence their children's educational program.
5. Provide workshops that include role-playing and rehearsing situations between parents and

school personnel to increase parents' confidence in working with school personnel.
6. Involve parents from the community who are familiar with the culture of the families and speak the home language of the parents to work at the school.
7. Provide an informal meeting with parents so they can exchange experiences and learn tips from each other.
8. Invite parents to school and ask them to share their backgrounds or activities with other students and parents.

Source: Adapted from T. W. Sileo, A. P. Sileo, and M. A. Prater, "Parent and Professional Partnerships in Special Education: Multicultural Considerations," *Intervention in School and Clinic, 31*(3) (1996): 145–153; and A. Misra, "Partnership with Multicultural Families," in S. K. Alper, P. J. Schloss, and C. N. Schloss, *Families of Students with Disabilities* (Needham Heights, MA: Allyn and Bacon, 1994): pp. 143–176.

— Specialized instruction for parents and the target youngster
— Case management
— Health services that may be needed to allow the child to benefit from the intervention service

See Apply the Concept 12.6 for an overview of parent involvement in special education.

What Are the Criteria for Establishing an IFSP?

The IFSP is a family-oriented approach to designing an effective management plan for the youngster with disabilities. The IFSP must be developed by a multidisciplinary team and should include:

— A description of the child's level of functioning across the developmental areas: physical, cognitive, communication, social or emotional, and adaptive
— An assessment of the family, including a description of the family's strengths and needs as they

relate to enhancing the development of the child with disabilities
— A description of the major goals or outcomes expected for the child with disabilities and the family (as they relate to providing opportunities for the child)
— Procedures for measuring progress, including time line, objectives, and evaluation procedures
— A description of natural environments in which the early intervention services will be provided
— A description of the early intervention services needed to provide appropriate help for the child and family
— Specifically when the specialized intervention will begin and how long it will last
— An appointed case manager
— A specific transition plan from the birth-to-three program into the preschool program

Parent Education Programs

In a review of parent involvement programs for parents of children with learning disabilities, the

APPLY THE CONCEPT 12.6

PARENT INVOLVEMENT IN THE SPECIAL EDUCATION PROCESS

The chart presents an overview of the special education process for parents. It covers issues from the time a child is referred for evaluation through the development of the IEP for the child. It shows how to share information between schools and families or how parents can participate in the process.

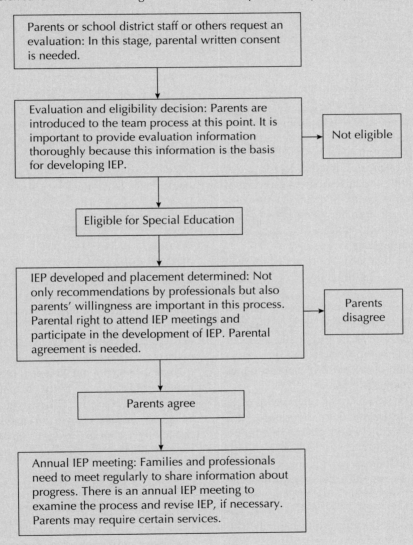

Parents or school district staff or others request an evaluation: In this stage, parental written consent is needed.

Evaluation and eligibility decision: Parents are introduced to the team process at this point. It is important to provide evaluation information thoroughly because this information is the basis for developing IEP.

Not eligible

Eligible for Special Education

IEP developed and placement determined: Not only recommendations by professionals but also parents' willingness are important in this process. Parental right to attend IEP meetings and participate in the development of IEP. Parental agreement is needed.

Parents disagree

Parents agree

Annual IEP meeting: Families and professionals need to meet regularly to share information about progress. There is an annual IEP meeting to examine the process and revise IEP, if necessary. Parents may require certain services.

APPLY THE CONCEPT 12.7

PAIRING TEACHER PRAISE NOTES WITH PARENT PRAISE

Imber, Imber, and Rothstein (1979) found that pairing teacher praise notes with parent praise regarding the note was effective in producing improvement in the academic performance of their children. After praise notes from the teacher were sent home, parents were asked to:

1. Read the note and praise the child as soon as possible.
2. Praise the child in front of others in the family.
3. Place the note where others can see it.
4. Express to the child that they hope the child will receive another one.

two types of programs most frequently provided for parents were counseling and tutoring (Shapero and Forbes, 1981). Overall findings indicated parent involvement programs can have positive effects on the academic performance of children with learning disabilities. Providing organized parental programs may be helpful to some parents of children with learning and behavior problems. These programs need to be interactive and take advantage of the knowledge and needs of the participants.

One procedure that involves parents in their child's education is described in Apply the Concept 12.7.

A number of variables influence the success of adults with learning disabilities, including parental factors. The educational and economic levels of the parents significantly influence the likelihood that children with learning disabilities will have good jobs that pay well (O'Connor and Spreen, 1988).

Waggoner and Wilgosh (1990) interviewed eight different families regarding their experiences and concerns of having a child with learning disabilities. The results of these interviews elucidated several common themes including: parent involvement in the child's education, parents' relationship with the school, support for the parents, social concerns for the child, concerns about the child's future, emotional strains of parenting, and the effects on the family. The interviews indicated that parents needed to be willing to help the child at home with school work and to interact frequently with the school to serve as an advocate for their child. While all of the parents reported at least one positive experience with teachers

and the schools, seven out of eight of the parents also reported negative experiences. These negative experiences revolved around teachers feeling not only that the child did not have a "real" problem but also that the child was just not performing as well as he or she could.

WORKING WITH PROFESSIONALS

Consulting and communicating with professionals is an important task for teachers of students with learning and behavior problems. Teachers need to develop and maintain contact with the school psychologist, counselor, speech and language therapist, physical therapist, occupational therapist, principal, and other related professionals. Since 90 percent of all students with learning and behavior disorders are mainstreamed for all or part of the day, a positive, cooperative working relationship with the general classroom teacher may be most important of all.

Communication with General Education Teachers

Peters and Austin (1985) describe the characteristics of a leader and a nonleader. Many of these characteristics are important for special education teachers as they often serve as team leaders looking to develop the best programs for students with special needs. Table 12.1 lists these characteristics.

■ **TABLE 12.1**   *Characteristics of a Leader and a Nonleader*

Leader	Nonleader
Appeals to the best in each person.	Gives orders to staff—expects them to be carried out.
Thinks of ways to make people more successful. Looks for ways to reinforce them.	Thinks of personal rewards or how she or he looks to others.
Schedules frequent, short meetings to "touch base."	Meets infrequently with coworkers.
Good listener.	Good talker.
Notices what's going well and improving.	Only notices what's going wrong.
Available.	Hard to reach.
Persistent.	Gives up.
Gives credit to others.	Takes credit.
Consistent and credible.	Unpredictable.
Never divulges a confidence.	Cannot be trusted with confidences.
Makes tough decisions.	Avoids difficult decisions.
Treats teachers and students with respect.	Treats others as if they don't matter.

Source: Adapted from T. Peters and N. Austin, *A Passion for Excellence* (New York: Random House, 1985).

When a student with special needs is placed in the regular classroom, there are several steps the special education teacher can take to communicate effectively with the general education teacher. These steps include:

1. Describe the type of learning or behavior problem the child has and some general guidelines for how to deal with it in the regular classroom.
2. Provide a copy of the child's IEP to the classroom teacher and discuss the goals, objectives, special materials, and procedures needed.
3. Describe the progress reports you will be providing to the home and putting in your files.
4. Develop a schedule for regular meetings and discuss other times that both the classroom teacher and special teacher are available for meetings.
5. Ask the classroom teacher how you can help, and describe the special accommodations that are needed.

In addition to communicating with teachers, there are a number of other services that the special education teacher can provide to facilitate mainstreaming. These services include providing inservice education on special education procedures or methods, bringing in guest speakers to discuss relevant topics, writing newsletters, and developing Teacher Assistance Teams. The special education teacher's role in the Teacher Assistance Team was discussed in Chapter Eleven.

Even when special education teachers develop and maintain an effective communication program with regular education teachers, there are still a number of potential barriers to successful inclusion.

1. *The general education teacher may feel unable to meet the needs of the included student with disabilities.* Ms. Clements has been teaching second grade for two years. When she was informed that Samuel, a student identified as

having emotional disorders, was going to be included in her general education classroom for several hours each morning, she panicked. She explained to the principal that she had not taken any coursework in special education and was unable to meet the needs of the new student. The special education teacher met with Ms. Clements. She described Samuel's behavior and explained the progress he was making. She assured Ms. Clements that Samuel would be carefully monitored and that she would check with Samuel and her daily and then less frequently as he adapted to the new setting and schedule. She asked Ms. Clements to explain what types of activities usually occurred during the time Samuel would be in her room, and she identified ways for Ms. Clements to be successful with Samuel. The special education teacher took careful notes and asked many questions about Ms. Clements' expectations so she could prepare Samuel before his transition to the regular classroom. In this situation, communication that provides specific information about the student's learning problems and what the classroom teacher can do to assure a successful learning environment is most helpful. In addition, the special education teacher obtained expectations about the general education classroom so she could best prepare the student for the transition.

2. *The general education classroom teacher may not want to work with the included student with disabilities.* Mr. Caruffe, a seventh-grade science teacher, expected all students to perform the same work at the same time, with no exceptions. He was particularly opposed to having special education students included into his classroom because he felt they needed modifications from his core program. His philosophy was, "If students need modifications they don't belong in the general education classroom, they belong in special education." Teachers like Mr. Caruffe can be particularly challenging for the special education teacher. Despite continuous attempts to work out a collaborative effort, educational philosophies can be sufficiently different that the special education teacher feels it is hopeless to attempt including in certain classrooms. Problems arise when alternative classrooms are not available without reducing the content areas available to special students. If there are multiple teachers for each content area, students may be included into classes where teachers are more accepting. Principals can be helpful by setting school policy that rewards teachers for working appropriately with pupils who have learning and behavior problems.

In a survey of elementary, middle, and high school students (Schumm and Vaughn, 1992) the majority of teachers indicated that they felt unprepared to meet the needs of special education students but were willing to have them in their classrooms. This suggests that special education teachers will need to work closely with other teachers to facilitate their knowledge, skills, and confidence.

3. *Finding time to meet regularly with all classroom teachers is difficult.* At the elementary level the special education teacher meets regularly with all classroom teachers who have students included for all or part of the day. This consultation includes discussing student progress, planning the student's program, adapting instruction in the general classroom, and solving immediate academic and social problems with the student. It is better to meet weekly with classroom teachers for a short period of time (10 to 15 minutes) than to meet less often for longer periods of time. When classroom teachers and their students perceive the special education room as a resource, rather than a closed room for special students, they have positive perceptions of the teacher and the students who attend (Vaughn and Bos, 1987).

At the secondary level, continued involvement with all classroom teachers is a challenge. In large schools the exceptional students' general education classroom teachers vary within content area and by year. It is possible for exceptional education teachers to have over 25 teachers with whom they consult. Special education teachers manage this by meeting with teachers in small groups. Sometimes they organize these groups by content area to discuss successful adaptations made within a common content. Sometimes meetings are organized to focus on the needs of a particular student, and all teachers who work with this student meet at the same time. Finding time and maintaining contact with regular education teachers requires creativity and persistence.

4. *Students may not be accepted socially by peers in the general education classroom.* This problem occurs not just with students who have behavior problems but also with students who have learning disabilities. Placing students in classrooms where their peers are displaying appropriate social behaviors does not mean that students with learning and behavior disorders will model these appropriate behaviors (Gresham, 1982). According to both general education and special classroom teachers, the skills most essential to success in the general education classroom are interacting positively with others, following class rules, and exhibiting proper work habits (Salend and Lutz, 1984). Following is a list of behaviors considered important by both general education and special educators for success in the general education classrooms.

— Follows directions
— Asks for help when it's appropriate
— Begins an assignment after teacher gives assignment to the class
— Demonstrates adequate attention
— Obeys class rules
— Tries to complete task before giving up
— Doesn't speak when others are talking
— Works well with others
— Respects feelings of others
— Refrains from cursing and swearing
— Avoids getting in fights with other students
— Plays cooperatively with others
— Respects property of others
— Shares materials and property with others
— Refrains from stealing property of others
— Tells the truth*

Special education teachers may want to focus on teaching these behaviors before and during their transition to inclusion.

Working with Paraprofessionals

Many exceptional education specialists work closely with paraprofessionals as teaching assistants. Although teaching assistants never have complete responsibility for planning, implementing, or evaluating a student's program, they often participate in all of these roles. It is important for paraprofessionals not to be assigned to students who the teacher then spends little time seeing. Paraprofessionals need to have their teaching responsibilities rotated among many students so that the teacher spends frequent intervals teaching and evaluating all students. Since paraprofessionals are often responsible for implementing class rules, they need to be completely familiar with class and school rules and their consequences. Many paraprofessionals comment that they are successful in their roles when they have confidence in understanding what is expected of them.

Working with Administrators

The principal is the instructional and administrative leader of the school. The principal's perceptions and interactions with special education will be conveyed to classroom teachers and will be reflected in the procedures established to handle students with special needs. A supportive principal is the key to a supportive staff. When building principals find special education nothing but a headache or more paper work, this message is conveyed to the staff. When principals find special education an opportunity to provide

*Source: From "Mainstreaming or Mainlining: A Competency Based Approach to Mainstreaming" by S. J. Salend and G. Lutz, 1984, *Journal of Learning Disabilities, 17,* pp. 27–29. Copyright 1984 by PRO-ED, Inc. Reprinted by permission.

necessary services to students with special needs, this message is also conveyed. An effective relationship between the principal and the special education teacher will promote better programs for students and overall job satisfaction (Cheek and Lindsey, 1986).

Often the principal serves as the leader and coordinator of services between regular and special education. There are five activities principals can perform to facilitate the role of special education in the school (Chalfant and Pysh, 1979, 1986).

1. *Set the tone.* The principal sets a tone that establishes the importance of developing effective and responsive programs for students with learning and behavior problems. Too few teachers view administrators as support personnel. Many special education teachers feel they have to do as much as they can for students with little administrative support. In fact, many teachers state they just wish administrators wouldn't get in the way—they have long since given up on support. Many special education teachers have found that a positive tone about special education can be obtained from building-level principals through informing and involving principals in special education achievements, not just problems; providing feedback about how special education is demonstrating child gains; soliciting parent and community support; and developing good intervention programs that get school and district recognition.

2. *Reinforce teachers for developing programs that respond to the individual needs of students.* Principals can be effective agents for encouraging classroom teachers to develop programs that respond to the individual needs of the special students in their classrooms.

3. *Provide consultation time.* Principals can arrange schedules of their support staff to serve as consultants to regular classroom teachers, providing programs for students with learning and behavior problems. The services of the school psychologist, speech and language therapist, physical therapist, counselor, special education teacher, and other support staff can be made available to regular classroom teachers.

4. *Provide inservice activities to staff.* This includes the provision of workshops, consultants, or lectures, focusing on the needs of staff to provide adequate service to students with learning and behavior disorders.

5. *Organize school-based assistance teams.* School-based assistance teams focus on the development of teams to assist classroom teachers with all students having learning and behavior problems, not just students identified to receive special education services. In fact, the school-based assistance teams (Chalfant and Pysh, 1979, 1983) were originally developed to assist in reducing unnecessary referrals for special education. The next section describes the role of school-based assistance teams.

School-Based Teacher Assistance Teams

The purpose of school-based assistance teams is to develop a team of professionals to work cooperatively with classroom teachers to develop successful programs and strategies in the regular classroom for students with learning and behavior problems. Often these teams are established to eliminate unnecessary testing and referral for special education. Whereas the original purpose was to work with students who have learning and behavior problems who were currently not placed in special education, it is possible to establish teams that focus on students already identified as special-needs students.

Who serves on the team? The membership can include the building principal, two regular classroom teachers, the teacher seeking assistance, and other persons as needed, such as a parent, the student, or a member of the special education staff. Team members can be selected by the staff or appointed by the principal.

How is the team contacted for assistance? When a classroom teacher seeks assistance in solving a student's learning or behavior problems in the classroom, the teacher seeks help from the school-based assistance team. Chalfant and Pysh (1979, 1983) suggest assistance be requested by answering four questions:

1. What do you want the student to do that he or she is not presently doing?
2. What does the student do (assets) and not do (deficits)?
3. What have you done to help the student cope with his or her problem?
4. What other background information and/or test data are relevant to the problem?

What does the team do? The team often responds to a problem identified by the classroom teacher. Frequently the teacher identifies the problem and selects a member of the team to observe the student and/or the teacher. In addition, informal assessment may be conducted. The team generates instructional alternatives and may assist in the implementation of these alternatives. It also establishes policies for monitoring progress and providing feedback.

School-based assistance teams have successfully decreased the number of referrals for special education. They also provide the necessary support needed by classroom teachers to cope effectively with students who have learning and behavior disorders.

SUMMARY

This chapter focuses on an important role for the special education teacher: communicating with parents and professionals. Although most of the chapters in this book discuss strategies for increasing teachers' skills in working directly with students who have learning and behavior disorders, this chapter is about communicating with the key people who interact with the student.

The first part of the chapter discusses the communication skills necessary for interacting with parents and professionals. These skills include mutual respect, trust, acceptance, effective listening, plain language, effective questioning, providing encouragement, keeping the focus of the conversation directed, and developing a working alliance. In addition to these communication skills, acquiring interviewing skills such as asking open questions, obtaining specificity, identifying the problem, solving the problem, and providing feedback are discussed.

The second part of the chapter centers on understanding the needs of parents and communicating with them. Parents play a critical role in the successful delivery of services to students with special needs. They are involved in the identification, assessment, and educational planning of their child. Parents who are aware of academic and social goals for the child are more likely to follow up on these goals at home. Unlike youngsters with other disabilities (e.g., mental retardation and sensory impairment), learning and behavior disorders are often not identified until the student begins school. Although parents may be aware their child is different from peers, they often receive the identification of the learning or behavior disorder only from the school. Special education teachers play a critical role in communicating assessment and educational planning information to parents. They are also the professionals who communicate most frequently with parents regarding the daily progress of their child. This section presents suggestions for facilitating family adjustment as well as procedures for facilitating parent involvement in the placement and programming for their child.

The third part of the chapter presents the special education teacher's role in working with other professionals. Working with professionals is particularly important for teachers of students with learning and behavior problems, as their students are frequently included in general education classrooms for all or part of the school day. Often the special education teacher serves as the primary consultant for the regular classroom teacher, who may have few skills in effectively teaching students with special needs. Barriers that may interfere with successful inclusion were discussed. Establishing effective working relationships with the school principal is an important role for the special education teacher. The school principal sets the tone in the building for the acceptance of students with special needs.

Although teachers may be effective in providing the academic and social instruction their students require, unless they are equally effective in communicating with parents and professionals, they will be unsuccessful. The special education teacher spends relatively little time with the student, compared to the time the child spends with others. When all persons who interact with the student are working cooperatively to advance educational and social goals, the child's progress is assured.

WEBSITES AS RESOURCES TO ASSIST IN FACILITATING COMMUNICATION WITH PARENTS AND PROFESSIONALS

http://www.ncld.org/tips/tips14.html
  This Website provides several tips for teacher–parent communication.

http://www.ldonline.org/ld_indepth/add_adhd/tec_home_school_collab.html
  This Website introduces home–school collaboration.

http://specialed.about.com/education/specialed/library/weekly/blswchwaub2.htm?terms=collaboration
  This Website provides information on collaboration between home and school.

http://www.urbanext.uiuc.edu/succeed/09-communication.html
  This Website provides a brief tip to facilitate parent–teacher communication.

http://nde4.nde.state.ne.us/SPED/parent/parentrights.html
  This Website provides the information of parental rights in special education.

http://aperc.asu.edu/pages/pepspeced.html
  This Website provides several resources to facilitate parent involvement in special education.

http://www.ed.gov/legislation/ESEA/Title_I/parinv.html
  This Website contains policy guidance for parent involvement in a state level, LEA level, and school level.

http://www.quasar.ualberta.ca/ddc/incl/rainfor.htm
  This Website provides guidance for communicating with parents.

THINK AND APPLY

— What are the principles of communication that facilitate the communication process with parents, teachers, and other professionals?
— What are the steps for conducting an effective interview?

— What are some of the needs of parents of children with learning disabilities and behavior problems? How might these needs be met?
— How do the parents of children with learning disabilities, particularly mothers, sometimes contribute unwittingly to their child's low self-expectation?
— Why are summers a particularly difficult time for children with learning and behavior problems? What are some possible solutions to the problem of long, unproductive summers?
— What skills are most essential to a student's success in the regular classroom?

APPENDIX

Educational Materials and Software Publishers

ABC School Supply, Inc.
3312 N. Berkeley Lake Road
P.O. Box 100019
Duluth, GA 30136
www.abcschoolsupply.com
(770) 497-0001

Academic Communication
 Associates
Publication Center, Dept. 206
4149 Avenida de la Plata
P.O. Box 586249
Oceanside, CA 92056-6249
www.acadcom.com
(760) 758-9593

Academic Press, Inc.
525 B Street, Suite 1900
San Diego, CA 92101
www.apnet.com
(619) 230-1840

Academic Therapy Publications
20 Commercial Boulevard
Novato, CA 94949
www.atpub.com
(415) 883-3314

A.D.D. Warehouse
300 Northwest 70th Avenue, Suite
 102
Plantation, FL 33317
(954) 792-8944

Addison-Wesley Publishing
 Company
1 Jacob Way
Reading, MA 01867

www.awonline.com/aw
(800) 282-0693

AGS American Guidance Service
4201 Woodland Road, #1
P.O. Box 99
Circle Pines, MN 55014-1796
(763) 786-4343

Allyn & Bacon
160 Gould Street
Needham Heights, MA 02494
www.ablongman.com
(800) 666-9433

The American Education Corp.
7506 N. Broadway Extension
Oklahoma City, OK 73116-9016
www.amered.com
(800) 222-2811

American Speech–
 Language–Hearing Association
10801 Rockville Pike
Rockville, MD 20852
www.asha.org
(888) 321-ASHA

A-Plus Computing
P.O. Box 26496
Prescott Valley, AZ 86312
www.a-plus-computing.com
(800) 878-1354

Association for Supervision and
 Curriculum Development
1250 N. Pitt Street
Alexandria, VA 22314

www.ascd.org
(800) 933-2723

Barron's Educational Series, Inc.
250 Wireless Boulevard
Hauppauge, NY 11788
www.barronseduc.com
(800) 645-3476

Bell & Howell Information
 and Learning
300 North Zeeb Road
P.O. Box 1346
Ann Arbor, MI 48106-1346
www.umi.com
(800) 521-0600

Benefic Press
10300 West Roosevelt Road
Westchester, IL 60153

Boys Town Press
Father Flanagan's Boy's Home
14100 Crawford Street
Boys Town, NE 68010
www.boystown.org
(800) 282-6657

Carson-Dellosa Instructional
 Materials
P.O. Box 35665
Greensboro, NC 27425-5665
(800) 321-0943

Chariot Software Group
123 Camino De la Reina
San Diego, CA 92108

www.chariot.com
(619) 298-0202

Childcraft Education Corp.
P.O. Box 3239
Lancaster, PA 17604
www.childcrafteducation.com
(800) 631-5652

Child Development Media, Inc.
5632 Van Nuys Boulevard, Suite 286
Van Nuys, CA 91401
www.childdevmedia.com
(800) 405-8942

Children's Book Press
246 First Street, Suite 101
San Francisco, CA 94105

Claris Corporation
5201 Patrick Henry Drive
Santa Clara, CA 95052-8168
(800) 325-2747

Closing the Gap
526 Main Street
P.O. Box 68
Henderson, MN 56044
www.closingthegap.com
(507) 248-3294

Communication Skill Builders
A Harcourt Health Sciences
    Company
P.O. Box 839954
San Antonio, TX 78283-3954
www.psychcorp.com
(800) 872-1726

Continental Press
520 E. Bainbridge Street
Elizabethtown, PA 17022
www.continentalpress.com
(800) 233-0759

Council for Exceptional Children
1920 Association Drive
Reston, VA 20191-1589
www.cec.sped.org
(888) CEC-SPED

Creative Publications
5623 W. 115th Street
Alsip, IL 60803
www.creativepublications.com
(800) 624-0822

Critical Thinking Press and Software
P.O. Box 448
Pacific Grove, CA 93950
www.criticalthinking.com
(800) 458-4849

Curriculum Associates
P.O. Box 2001
North Billerica, MA 01862-0901
www.curriculumassociates.com
(800) 225-0248

Dale Seymour Publications
An Imprint of Pearson Learning
299 Jefferson Road
P.O. Box 480
Parsippany, NJ 07054
www.pearsonlearning.com/dsp-
    publications
(800) 526-9907

Delacorte Press
An Imprint of Random House, Inc.
1540 Broadway
New York, NY 10036
www.randomhouse.com
(800) 733-3000

Devereux Foundation
444 Devereux Drive
P.O. Box 638
Villanova, PA 19085
www.devereux.org
(800) 935-6789

Disney Books
114 Fifth Avenue
New York, NY 10011
www.disney.go.com

Dominie Press
1949 Kellogg Avenue
Carlsbad, CA 92008
www.dominie.com
(800) 232-4570

Don Johnston
26799 W. Commerce Drive
Volo, IL 60073
www.donjohnston.com
(800) 999-4660

EBSCO Curriculum Materials
10 Estes Street
Box 682

Ipswich, MA 01938
www.epnet.com
(800) 653-2726

ECS Learning Systems
P.O. Box 791439
San Antonio, TX 78279-1439
www.educyberstore.com
(800) 688-3224

Edmark Corporation
P.O. Box 97021
Redmond, WA 98073-9721
www.edmark.com
(800) 691-2686

Educational Activities, Inc.
P.O. Box 392
Freeport, NY 11520
www.edact.com
(800) 950-4949

Educational Productions, Inc.
9000 SW Gemini Drive
Beaverton, OR 97008-7151
www.edpro.com
(800) 950-4949

Educators Publishing Service, Inc.
31 Smith Place
Cambridge, MA 02138-1000
www.epsbooks.com
(800) 435-7728

ETA/Cuisenaire
500 Greenview Court
Vernon Hills, IL 60061
www.etacuisenaire.com
(800) 445-5985

Fanlight Productions
4196 Washington Street, Suite 2
Boston, MA 02131
www.fanlight.com
(800) 937-4113

Flyleaf Publishing
P.O. Box 185
Lyme, NH 03768
www.flyleafpublishing.com
(603) 795-2875

Flaghouse
601 Flaghouse Drive
Hasbrouck Heights, NJ 07604-3116

www.flaghouse.com
(800) 793-7922

Focused Learning
P.O. Box 684765
Austin, TX 78768-4765
www.focusedlearning.com
(877) 708-9370

Frog Publications
P.O. Box 280096
Tampa, FL 33682-0096
www.frog.com
(800) 777-FROG

Gardner's Book Service
16461 N. 25th Avenue
Phoenix, AZ 85023
www.gsbooks.com
(800) 851-6001

Garrard Publishing Company
1607 North Market Street
Champaign, IL 61820

George F. Cram Co., Inc.
P.O. Box 426
Indianapolis, IN 46206
www.georgefcram.com
(800) 227-4199

Globe Fearon Educational Publisher
4350 Equity Drive
P.O. Box 2649
Columbus, OH 43216-2649
www.globefearon.com
(800) 848-9500

Greenwillow Books
An Imprint of HarperCollins
10 East 53rd Street
New York, NY 10022
www.harpercollins.com
(212) 207-7000

Guidance Associates
100 South Bedford Road
Mount Kisco, NY 10549
www.guidanceassociates.com
(914) 666-4100

D. C. Heath and Company
An Imprint of Houghton Mifflin
222 Berkeley Street
Boston, MA 02116

www.hmco.com
(800) 225-1464

Heinemann
361 Hanover Street
Portsmouth, NH 03801-3959
www.heinemann.com
(800) 793-2154

Holt, Rinehart and Winston
1120 S. Capital of Texas Hwy.
Austin, TX 78746-6487
www.hrw.com
(800) 225-5425

Houghton Mifflin
222 Berkeley Street
Boston, MA 02116
www.hmco.com
(800) 225-1464

Incentive Publications
3835 Cleghorn Avenue
Nashville, TN 37215
www.incentivepublications.com
(800) 421-2830

Instructional Materials Laboratory
University of Missouri Columbia
2316 Industrial Drive
Columbia, MO 65211-8120
http://iml.coe.missouri.edu
(800) 669-2465

The International Dyslexia
  Association
8600 La Salle Road
Chester Building, Suite 382
Baltimore, MD 21286-2044
www.interdys.org
(800) ABCD123

International Reading Association
800 Barksdale Road
P.O. Box 8139
Newark, DE 19714-8139
www.reading.org
(302) 731-1600

Janus Books
P.O. Box 40787
Tuscon, AZ 85717
www.janusbooks.com
(520) 881-8192

Lakeshore Learning Materials
2695 E. Dominguez Street
P.O. Box 6261
Carason, CA 90749
www.lakeshorelearning.com
(800) 428-4414

The Learning Company/School
  Division
500 Redwood Boulevard
Novato, CA 94947
www.learningcompanyschool.com
(800) 825-4420

Learning Skills, Inc.
10020 Canoga Avenue
Chatsworth, CA 91311
http://member.aol.com/rybett/lsi.htm
(818) 341-3624

Learning Well
111 Kane Street
Baltimore, MD 21224-1728
(800) 645-6564

LinguiSystem, Inc.
3100 Fourth Avenue
P.O. Box 747
East Moline, IL 61224-0747
www.linbuistystems.com
(800) PRO-IDEA

Love Publishing Co.
9101 E. Kenyon Avenue, Suite 2200
Denver, CO 80237
(303) 221-7333

Mattel Interactive
Customer Service
2850 Earhart Court
Hebron, KY 41048
www.mattelinteractive.com
(800) 395-0277

Merrill
An Imprint of Prentice Hall
445 Hutchinson Avenue
Columbus, OH 43235-5677
www.merrilleducation.com
(800) 526-0485

Milton Bradley Co.
443 Shaker Road
East Longmeadow, MA 01028
www.mbcreative.com

Mind Ware
121 5th Avenue NW
New Brighton, MN 55112
www.mindwareonline.com
(800) 999-0398

Modern Curriculum Press
An Imprint of Pearson Learning
4350 Equity Drive
P.O. Box 2649
Columbus, OH 43216
www.mcschool.com
(800) 321-3106

National Council of Teachers of
  English
1111 Kenyon Road
Urbana, IL 61801-1096
www.ncte.org
(800) 369-6283

National Education Association
  Publications
1201 16th Street NW
Washington, DC 20036
www.nea.org
(202) 833-4000

National Geographic Society
1145 17th Street NW
Washington, DC 20036-4688
www.nationalgeographic.com
(800) NGS-LINE

New Readers Press
P.O. Box 35888
Syracuse, NY 13235-5888
www.newreaderspress.com
(800) 448-8878

NTC/Contemporary Publishing
  Group
4255 W. Touhy Avenue
Lincolnwood, IL 60646-1975
www.ntc-cb.com
(800) 323-4900

PBS Video
1320 Braddock Place
Alexandria, VA 22314-1698
www.pbs.org
(877) PBS-SHOP

PCI
P.O. Box 34270
San Antonio, TX 78265-4270

www.pcicatalog.com
(800) 594-4263

Penguin USA
375 Hudson Street
New York, NY 10014
www.penguin.com
(800) 788-6262

Perfection Learning Corporation
1000 N. Second Avenue
P.O. Box 500
Logan, IA 51546-0500
www.perfectionlearning.com
(800) 831-4190

Perma-Bound Books
617 E. Vandalia Road
Jacksonville, IL 62650
www.perma-bound.com
(800) 637-6581

Phoenix Learning Resources
2349 Chaffee Drive
Street Louis, MO 63146
(800) 221-1274

PRO-ED, Inc.
8700 Shoal Creek Boulevard
Austin, TX 78757-6897
www.proedinc.com
(800) 897-3202

The Psychological Corp.
555 Academic Court
P.O. Box 9954
San Antonio, Tx 78204-2498
www.psychcorp.com
(800) 211-8378

Reader's Digest Services
Educational Division
P.O. Box 235
Pleasantville, NJ 10570-0235
www.readersdigeStreetcom
(800) 310-6261

Recording for the Blind and Dislexic
20 Roszel Road
Princeton, NJ 08540
www.rfbd.org
(800) 803-7201

Remedia Publications
10135 E Via Linda #D124
Scotsdale, AZ 85258-5312

www.rempub.com
(800) 826-4740

Rigby
500 Coventry Lane
Crystal Lake, IL 60014
www.rigby.com
(800) 822-8661

Riverside Publishing Company
A Houghton Mifflin Company
425 Spring Lake Drive
Itasca, IL 60143-2079
www.riverpub.com
(800) 323-9540

Saddleback Educational, Inc.
3 Watson
Irvine, CA 92618-2767
www.sdlback.com
(888) SDL-BACK

Scholastic, Inc.
P.O. Box 7502
Jefferson City, MO 65102-9968
www.scholastic.com
(800) SCHOLASTIC

Scott, Foresman and Company
A Division of Addison-Wesley
  Educational Publishers, Inc.
1900 East Lake Avenue
Glenview, IL 60025
www.scottforesman.com
(800) 552-2259

Shortland Publications, Inc.
50 S. Steele Street, Suite 755
Denver, CO 80209
www.shortland.com
(800) 775-9995

Slosson Educational
  Publications
P.O. Box 280
East Aurora, NY 14052-0280
www.slosson.com
(888) SLOSSON

Sopris West
4093 Specialty Place
Longmont, CO 80504
www.soprisweStreetcom
(800) 547-6747

Spalding Educational Foundation News
2814 W. Bell Road, Suite 1405
Glendale, AZ 85306
www.spalding.org
(602) 866-7801

The Speech Bin, Inc.
1965 25th Avenue
Vero Beach, FL 32960
www.speechbin.com
(800) 4SPEECH

SRA
A Division of McGraw-Hill
220 East Danieldale Road
DeSoto, TX 75115-2490
www.sraforkids.com
(800) SRA-4543

Startwrite
A Product of Idea Makers, Inc.
80 South Redwood Road, Suite 212
North Salt Lake, UT 84054
www.startwrite.com
(801) 936-7779

Steck-Vaughn Company
A Harcourt Company
P.O. Box 690789
Austin, TX 78755

www.steck-vaughn.com
(800) 531-5015

Sundance Publishing
234 Taylor Street
P.O. Box 1326
Littleton, MA 01460
www.sundancepub.com
(800) 343-8204

Super Duper Publications
P.O. Box 24997
Greenville, SC 29616-2497
www.superduperinc.com
(800) 277-8737

Thinking Publications
424 Galloway Street
P.O. Box 163
Eau Claire, WI 54702-0163
www.thinkingpublications.com
(800) 225-GROW

Charles C. Thomas Publisher
2600 S. 1st Street
Springfield, IL 62704
www.ccthomas.com
(800) 258-8980

Troll Associates
100 Corporation Drive
Mahwah, NJ 07430
www.troll.com
(800) 99-TROLL

Western Psychological Services
12031 Wilshire Boulevard
Los Angeles, CA 90025-1251
www.wpspublish.com
(800) 648-8857

Webster
A Division of McGraw-Hill Book Co.
1221 Avenue of the Americas
New York, NY 10020
www.mmhschool.com

The Wright Group
19201 120th Avenue NE
Bothell, WA 98011
www.wrightgroup.com
(800) 523-2371

Xerox Adaptive Technologies
9 Centennial Drive
Peabody, MA 01960
www.fkpi.com/xeroxfile2.html

Zaner-Bloser Company
2200 W. Fifth Avenue
Columbus, OH 43215
www.zaner-bloser.com

Zephyr Press Learning Materials
3316 N. Chapel Avenue
P.O. Box 66006-C2
Tucson, AZ 85716-1416
www.zephyrpress.com
(800) 232-2187

References

Adams, A., Carnine, D., and Gersten, R. (1982). Instructional strategies for studying context area texts in the intermediate grades. *Reading Research Quarterly, 18*(1), 27–55.

Adams, K. S., and Christenson, S. L. (1998). Differences in parent and teacher trust levels: Implications for creating collaborative family-school relationships. *Special Services in the Schools, 14,* 1–22.

Adams, M. J. (1990). *Beginning to read: Thinking and learning about print.* Cambridge, MA: MIT Press.

Adams, M. J., and Brunk, M. (1995). Resolving the "great debate." *American Educator, 19*(2), 7, 10–20.

Alber, S. R., Heward, W. L., and Hippler, B. J. (1999). Teaching middle school students with learning disabilities to recruit positive teacher attention. *Exceptional Children, 65,* 253–270.

Allen, R. I., and Peter, C. G. (1996). Toward developing standards and measurements for family-centered practice in family support programs. In G. H. S. Singer, L. E. Powers, and A. L. Olson. (Eds.), *Redefining Family Support* (pp. 57–86). Baltimore, MD: Paul H. Brookes Publishing.

Allen, R. V. (1976). *Language experiences in communication.* Boston: Houghton Mifflin.

Allen, R. V., and Allen, C. (1966–68). *Language experiences in reading* (Levels I, II, and III). Chicago: Encyclopedia Britannica.

Allen, R. V., and Allen, C. (1982), *Language experience activities* (2nd ed.). Boston: Houghton Mifflin.

Alley, G. R., and Deshler, D. D. (1979). *Teaching the learning disabled adolescent: Strategies and methods.* Denver: Love Publishing.

Allington, R. L. (1983). Fluency: The neglected reading goal. *The Reading Teacher, 36,* 556–561.

Allington, R. L. (1983). The reading instruction provided readers of differing reading abilities. *The Elementary School Journal, 83,* 548–559.

Alper, S. K., Schloss, P. J., and Schloss, C. N. (1994). *Families of students with disabilities.* Needham Heights, MA: Allyn and Bacon.

Alsup, R. (1982). *WH-questions.* Allen, TX: DLM.

Altwerger, B., and Ivener, B. L. (1994). Self-esteem: Access to literacy in multicultural and multilingual classrooms. In K. Spangenberg-Urbschat and R. Pritchard (Eds.), *Kids come in all languages: Reading instruction for ESL students* (pp. 65–81). Newark, DE: International Reading Association.

Alvermann, D., Bridge, C., Schmidt, R., Seafoss, L., Winograd, P., Paris, S., Priestly, C., and Santeusanio, N. (1989). *Heath reading.* Lexington, MA: D.C. Heath.

Alvermann, D. E., and Moore, D. W. (1991). Secondary school reading. In R. Barr, M. L. Kamil, P. B. Mosenthal, and P. D. Pearson (Eds.), *Handbook of reading research* (Vol. 2, pp. 951–983). New York: Longman.

Alvermann, D. E., and Phelps, S. (1994). *Content area reading and literacy: Succeeding in today's diverse classrooms.* Boston: Allyn and Bacon.

Alvermann, D. E., and Phelps, S. (1998). *Content reading and literacy: Succeeding in today's diverse classrooms.* Boston: Allyn and Bacon.

American Psychiatric Association. (1994). *Diagnostic and statistical manual of mental disorders* (4th ed.). Washington, DC.

Amish, P. L., Gesten, E. L., Smith, J. K., Clark, H. B., and Stark, C. (1988). Social problem-solving training for severely emotionally and behaviorally disturbed children. *Behavioral Disorders, 13*(3), 175–186.

Anders, P. L., and Bos, C. S. (1984). In the beginning: Vocabulary instruction in content classroom. *Topics in Learning and Learning Disabilities, 3*(4), 53–65.

Anders, P. L., and Bos, C. S. (1986). Semantic feature analysis: An interactive strategy for vocabulary development and text comprehension. *Journal of Reading, 29*(7), 610–616.

Anders, P. L., and Guzzetti, B. J. (1996). *Literacy instruction in the content areas.* Fort Worth, TX: Harcourt Brace College Publishers.

Anderson, J. R. (1990). *Cognitive psychology and its implications* (3rd ed.). San Francisco: W. H. Freeman.

Anderson, J. R. (1994). *Learning and memory: An integrated approach.* New York: Wiley.

Anderson, L., Brubaker, N., Alleman-Brooks, J., and Duffy, G. (1986). A qualitative study of seatwork in first-grade classrooms. *Elementary School Journal, 86,* 123–140.

Anderson, L. M., Raphael, T. E., Englert, C. S., and Stevens, D. D. (April 1991). *Teaching writing with a new instructional model: Variations in teachers' practices and student performance.* Paper presented at the annual meeting of the American Education Research Association, Chicago.

Anderson, R. C. (1977). The notion of schemata and the educational enterprise. In R. C. Anderson, R. J. Spiro, and W. E. Montague (Eds.), *Schooling and the acquisition of knowledge* (pp. 415–431). Hillsdale, N.J.: Erlbaum.

Anderson, R. C., and Freebody, P. (1981). Vocabulary knowledge. In J. T. Guthrie (Ed.), *Comprehension and reading: Research reviews.* Newark, NJ: International Reading Association.

Anderson, R. C., Hiebert, E., Scott, J., and Wilkinson, I. (1985). *Becoming a nation of readers: The Report on the Commission on Reading.* Washington, DC: National Institute of Education.

Anderson, R. C., and Pearson, P. D. (1984). A schema-theoretic view of basic processes in reading. In P. D. Pearson (Ed.), *Handbook of reading research* (pp. 255–201). New York: Longman.

Anderson, R. C., Reynolds, R. E., Schallert, D. L., and Goetz, E. T. (1977). Frameworks for comprehending discourse. *American Educational Research Journal, 14,* 367–382.

Anglin, J. (1970). *The growth of meaning.* Cambridge, MA: MIT Press.

Archer, A., and Edgar, E. (1976). Teaching academic skills to mildly handicapped children. In S. Lowenbraun and J. Q. Afflect (Eds.), *Teaching mildly handicapped children in regular classes.* Columbus, OH: Merrill.

Arguelles, M. E., Vaughn, S., and Schumm, J. S. (1996). *Executive summaries of 69 schools throughout the state of Florida participating in the ESE/FEFP 1995–1996 pilot program.* Manuscript in preparation.

Armbruster, B. B., and Anderson, T. H. (1988). On selecting "considerate" content area textbooks. *Remedial and Special Education, 9*(1), 47–52.

Ashbaker, M. H., and Swanson, H. L. (1996). Short-term memory and working memory operations and their contribution to reading in adolescents with and without learning disabilities. *Learning Disabilities Research and Practice, 11,* 206–213.

Ashby, J. S., Kottman, T., and Schoen, E. (1998). Perfectionism and eating disorders. *Journal of Mental Health Counseling, 20*(3), 261–271.

Asher, S. R., Gabriel, S. W., and Hopmeyer, A. (1993, April). *Children's loneliness in different school contexts.* Paper presented at the biennial meeting of the Society for Research in Child Development, New Orleans, LA.

Ashton-Warner, S. (1958). *Spinster.* New York: Simon and Schuster.

Ashton-Warner, S. (1963). *Teacher.* New York: Simon and Schuster.

Ashton-Warner, S. (1972). *Spearpoint.* New York: Alfred A. Knopf.

Atkinson, J. W., and Shiffrin, R. M. (1968). Human memory: A proposed system and its control processes. In K. W. Spence and J. T. Spence (Eds.), *The psychology of learning and motivation: Advances in research and theory* (Vol. 2). New York: Academic Press.

Atwell, N. (1984). Writing and reading literature from the inside out. *Language Arts, 61,* 240–252.

Atwell, N. (1985). Writing and reading from the inside out. In J. Hansen, T. Newkirk, and D. Graves (Eds.), *Breaking ground: Teachers relate reading and writing in the elementary school* (pp. 147–168). Portsmouth, NH: Heinemann.

Atwell, N. (1987). *In the middle: Writing, reading, and learning with adolescents.* Portsmouth, NH: Heinemann.

Atwell, N. (Ed.) (1991). *Side by side: Essays on teaching to learn.* Portsmouth, NH: Heinemann.

Ausubel, D. P. (1963). *The psychology of meaningful verbal learning.* New York: Grune and Stratton.

Axline, V. (1947). *Play therapy.* Boston: Houghton Mifflin.

Badian, N. A., and Ghublikian, M. (1983). The personal-social characteristics of children with poor mathematical computation skills. *Journal of Learning Disabilities, 16*(3), 154–157.

Bahr, C., Nelson, N., and Van Meter, A. (1996). The effects of text-based and graphics-based software tools on planning and organizing of stories. *Journal of Learning Disabilities, 29*(4), 366–370.

Bahr, C. M., Nelson, N. W., Van Meter, A., and Yanna, J. V. (1996). Children's use of desktop publishing features: Process and product. *Journal of Computing in Childhood Education, 7*(3–4), 149–177.

Baker, C. (1993). *Foundations of bilingual education and bilingualism.* Clevedon, England: Multilingual Matters.

Baker, G. A. (1977). *A comparison of traditional spelling with phonemic spelling of fifth and sixth grade students.* Unpublished doctoral dissertation, Wayne State University, Detroit.

Ball, E., and Blachman, B. (1991). Does phoneme segmentation training in kindergarten make a difference in early word recognition and developmental spelling? *Reading Research Quarterly, 26,* 49–86.

Bandura, A. (1977). *Social learning theory.* Englewood Cliffs, NJ: Prentice-Hall.

Barker, T. A., and Torgesen, J. K. (1995). An evaluation of computer-assisted instruction in phonological awareness with below average readers. *Journal of Educational Computing Research, 13*(1), 89–103.

Barney, L. (1973). The first and third R's. *Today's Education, 62,* 57–58.

Barrett, T. (1976). Taxonomy of reading comprehension. In R. Smith and T. Barrett (Eds.), *Teaching reading in the middle grades.* Reading, MA: Addison-Wesley.

Barron, R. (1969). The use of vocabulary as an advanced organizer. In H. L. Herber and P. L. Sanders (Eds.), *Research in reading in the content areas: First reports.* Syracuse, NY: Syracuse University Reading and Language Arts Center.

Barrouillet, P., Fayol, M., and Lathuliere, E. (1997). Selecting between competitors in multiplication tasks: An explanation of the errors produced by adolescents with learning difficulties. *International Journal of Behavioral Development, 21*(2), 253–275.

Bartek, M. M. (1997). Hands-on addition and subtraction with the three pigs. *Teaching Children Mathematics, 4*(2), 68–71.

Bartlett, R. C. (1932). *Remembering.* Cambridge: Cambridge University Press.

Bashir, A. S., and Scavuzzo, A. (1992). Children with language disorders: Natural history and academic success. *Journal of Learning Disabilities, 25,* 53–65.

Bassett, D. S., and Lehman, J. (in press). *Student involvement.* Austin, TX: PRO-ED.

Bassett, D. S., Patton, J. R., White, W., Blalock, G., and Smith, T. E. C. (1997). Research issues in career development and transition: An exploratory survey of professionals in the field. *Career Development for Exceptional Individuals, 20,* 81–100.

Battle, J., and Blowers, T. (1982). A longitudinal comparative study of the self-esteem of students in regular and special education classes. *Journal of Learning Disabilities, 15*(2), 100–102.

Bauer, R. H. (1987). Control processes as a way of understanding, diagnosing, and remediating learning disabilities. In H. L. Swanson (Ed.), *Advances in learning and behavioral disabilities* (Supplement 2, pp. 41–81). Greenwich, CT: JAI Press.

Baumann, J. F., Hooten, H., and White, P. (1999). Teaching comprehension through literature: A teacher-research project to develop fifth graders' reading strategies and motivation. *The Reading Teacher, 53*, 38–51.

Baumann, J. F., and Serra, J. K. (1984). The frequency and placement of main ideas in children's social studies textbooks: A modified replication of Braddock's research on topic sentences. *Journal of Reading Behavior, 16*, 27–40.

Bear, D. R., Invernizzi, M., Templeton, S., and Johnston, F. (2000). *Words their way: Word study for phonics, vocabularly, and spelling instruction* (2nd ed.). Columbus, OH: Merrill.

Bear, G. C., Clever, A., and Proctor, W. A. (1991). Self-perceptions of nonhandicapped children and children with learning disabilities in integrated classes. *Journal of Special Education, 24*, 409–426.

Beck, J., and McKeown, M. G. (1981). Developing questions that promote comprehension: The story map. *Language Arts, 58*, 913–918.

Becker, W. C. (1977). Teaching reading and language to the disadvantaged—What we have learned from field research. *Harvard Educational Review, 44*(4), 518–543.

Berninger, V. W., Abbott, R. D., Whitaker, D., Sylvester, L., and Nolen, S. B. (1995). Integrating low- and high-level skills in instructional protocols for writing disabilities. *Learning Disability Quarterly, 18*, 293–310.

Berres, F., and Eyer, J. T. (1970). In A. J. Harris (Ed.), *Casebook on reading disability* (pp. 25–47). New York: David McKay.

Berry, J. O., and Hardman, M. L. (1998). *Lifespan perspectives on the family and disability.* Needham Heights, MA: Allyn and Bacon.

Betts, E. A. (1946). *Foundations of reading instruction.* New York: American Book.

Bickett, L. G., and Milich, R. (April 1987). *First impressions of learning disabled and attention deficit disordered boys.* Paper presented at the Biennial Meeting of the Society for Research in Child Development, Baltimore, MD.

Bierman, K. L., and Furman, W. (1984). The effects of social skills training and peer involvement on the social adjustment of preadolescents. *Child Development, 55*, 151–162.

Billingsley, B. S., and Wildman, T. M. (1990). Facilitating reading comprehension in learning disabled students: Metacognitive goals and instructional strategies. *Remedial and Special Education, 11*(2), 18–31.

Bitter, G. G., and Pierson, M. E. (1999). *Using technology in the classroom* (4th ed.). Boston: Allyn and Bacon.

Blachman, B. A. (2000). Phonological awareness. In M. L. Kamil, P. B. Mosenthal, P. D. Pearson, and R. Barr (Eds.), *Handbook of reading research* (pp. 251–284). Mahwah, NJ: Erlbaum.

Blachman, B. A. (ed.). (1997). *Foundations of reading acquisition and dyslexia implications for early intervention.* Mahwah, NJ: Erlbaum Associates.

Black, F. (1974). Self-concept as related to achievement and age in learning disabled children. *Child Development, 45*, 1137–1140.

Blackman, S., and Goldman, K. M. (1982). Cognitive styles and learning disabilities. *Journal of Learning Disabilities, 15*, 106–115.

Blair, K. S. (1996). *Context-based functional assessment and intervention for preschool age children with problem behaviors in childcare.* Unpublished dissertation, University of Arizona, Tucson.

Blankenship, C. S. (1984). Curriculum and instruction: An examination of models in special and regular education. In J. F. Cawley (Ed.), *Developmental teaching of mathematics for the learning disabled.* Rockville, MD: Aspen.

Blankenship, C. S., and Lovitt, T. C. (1976). Story problems: Merely confusing or downright befuddling. *Journal for Research in Mathematics Education, 7*, 290–298.

Blanton, W. E., and Moorman, G. B. (1990). The presentation of reading lessons. *Reading Research and Instruction, 29*, 35–55.

Bley, N. S., and Thornton, C. A. (1981). *Teaching mathematics to the learning disabled.* Rockville, MD: Aspen.

Blischak, D. M. (1999). Increases in natural speech production following experience with synthetic speech. *Journal of Special Education Technology, 14*(2), 44–53.

Bloodgood, J. (1991). A new approach to spelling instruction in language arts programs. *Elementary School Journal, 92*, 203–211.

Bloom, B. S. (1976). *Human characteristics and school learning.* New York: McGraw-Hill.

Bloom, L., and Lahey, M. (1978). *Language development and language disorders.* New York: Wiley.

Bloomfield, L., and Barnhart, C. L. (1961). *Let's read: A linguistic approach.* Detroit: Wayne State University Press.

Boatner, M. T., Gates, J. E., and Makkai, A. (1975). *A dictionary of American idioms* (rev. ed.). Woodbury, NJ: Barron's.

Borkowski, J. G., Weyhing, R. S., and Carr, M. (1988). Effects of attributional retraining on strategy-based reading comprehension in learning-disabled students. *Journal of Educational Psychology, 80*(1), 46–53.

Borkowski, J. G., Weyhing, R. S., and Turner, L. A. (1986). Attributional retraining and the teaching of strategies. *Exceptional Children, 53*(2), 130–137.

Bos, C. S. (1979). *Inferential operations in the reading comprehension of educable mentally retarded and average students.* Doctoral dissertation, University of Arizona, Tucson.

Bos, C. S. (1982). Getting past decoding: Using modeled and repeated readings as a remedial method for learning disabled students. *Topics in Learning and Learning Disabilities, 1*, 51–57.

Bos, C. S. (October 1987). *Promoting story comprehension using a story retelling strategy.* Paper presented at the Teachers Applying Whole Language Conference, Tucson, AZ.

Bos, C. S. (1988). Academic interventions for learning disabilities. In K. A. Kavale (Ed.), *Learning disabilities: State of the art* and practice (pp. 98–122). Boston: Little, Brown–College Hill.

Bos, C. S. (1999). Informed, flexible teaching: Promoting student advocacy and action. In P. Westwood, and W. Scott, (Eds.), *Learning Disabilities: Advocacy and action* (pp. 9–19). Melbourne: Australian Resource Educators Association.

Bos, C. S., Allen, A. A., and Scanlon, D. J. (1989). Vocabulary instruction and reading comprehension with bilingual learning disabled students. In S. McCormick and J. Zutell (Eds.), *Cognitive and social perspectives for literacy research and instruction* (Thirty-eighth yearbook, pp. 173–180). Chicago: National Reading Conference.

Bos, C. S., and Anders, P. L. (1990a). Effects of interactive vocabulary instruction on the vocabulary learning and reading comprehension of junior-high learning disabled students. *Learning Disability Quarterly, 13*, 31–42.

Bos, C. S., and Anders, P. L. (1990b). Toward an interactive model: Teaching text-based concepts to learning disabled students. In H. L. Swanson and B. Keogh (Eds.), *Learning disabilities: Theoretical and research issues* (pp. 247–261). Hillsdale, NJ: Erlbaum.

Bos, C. S., and Anders, P. L. (1990c). Interactive teaching and learning: Instructional practices for teaching content and strategic knowledge. In T. E. Scruggs and B. Y. L. Wong (Eds.), *Intervention research in learning disabilities* (pp. 166–185). New York: Springer-Verlag.

Bos, C. S., and Anders, P. L. (1992). A theory-driven interactive instructional model for text comprehension and content learning. In B. Y. L. Wong (Ed.), *Contemporary intervention research in learning disabilities: An international perspective* (pp. 81–95). New York: Springer-Verlag.

Bos, C. S., Anders, P. L., Jaffe, L. E., and Filip, D. (1985). Semantic feature analysis and long-term learning. In J. A. Niles (Ed.), *Issues in literacy: A research perspective* (Thirty-fourth yearbook, pp. 42–46). Rochester, NY: National Reading Conference.

Bos, C. S., and Duffy, M. L. (1991). Facilitating content learning and text comprehension for students with learning disabilities. *Exceptionality Education Canada, 1*(3), 1–13.

Bos, C. S., and Filip, D. (1984). Comprehension monitoring in learning disabled and average students. *Journal of Learning Disabilities, 17*(4), 229–233.

Bos, C. S., and Reyes, E. I. (1996). Conversations with a Latina teacher about education for language-minority students with special needs. *Elementary School Journal, 96*, 343–352.

Bos, C. S., and Van Reusen, A. K. (1986). *Effects of teaching a strategy for facilitating student and parent participation in the IEP process* (Partner Project Final Report G008400643). Tucson: University of Arizona, Department of Special Education.

Boyle, J. R. (1996). The effects of a cognitive mapping strategy on the literal and inferential comprehension of students with mild disabilities. *Learning Disability Quarterly, 19*, 86–98.

Bradley, J. M. (1975). Sight word association procedure. Unpublished manuscript, College of Education, University of Arizona, Tucson.

Bradley, L. (1981). The organization of motor patterns for spelling: An effective remedial strategy for backward readers. *Developmental Medicine and Child Neurology, 23*, 83–91.

Bradley, L., and Bryant, P. (1983). Categorizing sounds and learning to read: A causal connection. *Nature, 39*, 419–421.

Bragstad, B. J., and Stumpf, S. M. (1982). *A guidebook for teaching: Study skills and motivation*. Boston: Allyn and Bacon.

Brainerd, C. J., and Reyna, V. F. (1991). Acquisition and forgetting processes in normal and learning-disabled children: A disintegration/reintegration theory. In J. E. Obrzut and G. W. Hynd (Eds.), *Neuropsychological foundations of learning disabilities* (pp. 147–178). San Diego: Academic Press.

Bransford, J. D., and Johnson, M. D. (1972). Contextual prerequisites for understanding: Some investigations of comprehension and recall. *Journal of Verbal Learning and Verbal Behavior, 11*, 717–726.

Brewer, W. R., and Nakamura, G. V. (1984). *The nature and functions of schemas* (Tech. Rep. 325). Champaign: University of Illinois, Center for the Study of Reading.

Brice, A., and Montgomery, J. (1996). Adolescent pragmatic skills: A comparison of Latino students in English as a second language and speech and language programs. *Language, Speech, and Hearing Services in Schools, 27*, 68–81.

Briggs, A., Austin, R., and Underwood, G. (1984). Phonological coding in good and poor readers. *Reading Research Quarterly, 20*, 54–66.

Brigman, G., and Molina, B. (1999). Developing social interest and enhancing school success skills: A service learning approach. *Journal of Individual Psychology, 55*(3), 342–354.

Brinckerhoff, L. C., Shaw, S. F., and McGuire, J. M. (1992). Promoting access, accommodations, and independence for college students with learning disabilities. *Journal of Learning Disabilities, 25*, 417–429.

Brinton, B., and Fujiki, M. (1999). Social interactional behaviors of children with specific language impairment. *Topics in Language Disorders, 18*(2), 49–69.

Brinton, B., Fujiki, M., and McKee, L. (1998). Negotiation skills of children with specific language impairment. *Journal of Speech, Language, and Hearing Research, 41*, 927–940.

Brolin, D. E. (1997). *Life centered career education: A competency-based approach* (5th ed.). Reston, VA: The Council for Exceptional Children.

Brophy, J. (1988). Educating teachers about managing classrooms and students. *Teacher and Teacher Education, 4*, 1–18.

Brophy, J. (1998). Classroom management as socializing students into clearly articulated roles. *Journal of Classroom Interaction, 33*(1), 1–4.

Brown, A. L. (1980). Metacognitive development and reading. In R. J. Spiro, B. C. Bruce, and W. F. Brewer (Eds.), *Theoretical issues in reading comprehension* (pp. 453–482). Hillsdale, NJ: Erlbaum.

Brown, A. L., and Day, J. D. (1983). Macrorules for summarizing texts: The development of expertise. *Journal of Verbal Learning and Verbal Behavior, 22*, 1–14.

Brown, A. L., and Palincsar, A. S. (1982). Including strategic learning from texts by means of informed, self-control training. *Topics in Learning and Learning Disabilities, 2*(1), 1–17.

Brown, A. L., Palincsar, A. S., and Armbruster, B. B. (1984). Instructing comprehension-fostering activities in interactive learning situations. In H. Mandl, N. L. Stein, and T. Trabasso

(Eds.), *Learning and comprehension of text* (pp. 255–286). Hillsdale, NJ: Erlbaum.

Brown, K. J. (1999/2000). What kind of text—For whom and when? Textual scaffolding for beginning readers. *The Reading Teacher, 53*(4), 292–307.

Brown, R. (1973). *A first language: The early stages.* Cambridge, MA: Harvard University Press.

Bruck, M., and Treiman, R. (1992). Learning to pronounce words: The limitations of analogies. *Reading Research Quarterly, 27*, 375–388.

Bryan, J. H., Bryan, T. H., and Sonnefeld, L. J. (1982). Being known by the company we keep! The contagion of first impressions. *Learning Disability Quarterly, 5*(3), 228–293.

Bryan, J. H., and Perlmutter, B. (1979). Immediate impressions of LD children by female adults. *Learning Disability Quarterly, 2*, 80–88.

Bryan, J. H., and Sherman, R. (1980). Immediate impressions of nonverbal ingratiation attempts by learning disabled boys. *Learning Disabilities Quarterly, 3*, 19–29.

Bryan, T., Pearl, R., and Fallon, P. (1989). Conformity to peer pressure by students with learning disabilities: A replication. *Journal of Learning Disabilities, 22*(7), 458–459.

Bryan, T. H. (1986). Self-concept and attributions of the learning disabled. *Learning Disabilities Focus, 1*(2), 82–89.

Bryan, T. H., and Pflaum, S. (1978). Social interactions of learning disability children: A linguistic, social, and cognitive analysis. *Learning Disability Quarterly, 1*, 70–78.

Bryan, T. S. (1974). An observational analysis of classroom behaviors of children with learning disabilities. *Journal of Learning Disabilities, 7*(1), 35–43.

Bryant, B. R., and Rivera, D. P. (1997). Educational assessment of mathematics skills and abilities. *Journal of Learning Disabilities, 30*(1), 57–68.

Bryant, D., Vaughn S., Linan-Thompson, S., Ugel, N., Hamff, A., and Hougen, M. (2000). Reading outcomes for students with and without reading disabilities in general education middle school content area classes. *Learning Disability Quarterly, 23*, 238–252.

Bryant, J. (1998). K-W-W-L: Questioning the known. *The Reading Teacher, 51*, 618–620.

Bryant, N. D., Drabin, I. R., and Gettinger, M. (1981). Effects of varying unit size on spelling achievement in learning disabled children. *Journal of Learning Disabilities, 14*(4), 200–203.

Buchanan, C. O. (1968). *Sullivan Associates programmed reading.* New York: Sullivan Press, Webster Division—McGraw-Hill.

Bulgren J., and Lenz, K. (1996). Strategic instruction in the content areas. In D. D. Deshler, E. S. Ellis, and B. K. Lenz (Authors), *Teaching adolescents with learning disabilities: Strategies and methods* (2nd ed., pp. 409–473). Denver: Love.

Bulgren, J., Schumaker, J. B., and Deshler, D. D. (1988). Effectiveness of a concept teaching routine in enhancing the performance of LD students in secondary-level mainstream classes. *Learning Disability Quarterly, 11*, 3–17.

Bulgren, J., Schumaker, J. B., and Deshler, D. D. (1996). *The content enhancement series: The concept mastery routine.* Lawrence, KS: Edge Enterprises.

Bulgren, J. A., Hock, M. F., Schumaker, J. B., and Deshler, D. D. (1995). The effects of instruction in a paired associates strategy on the information mastery performance of students with learning disabilities. *Learning Disabilities Research and Practice, 10*(1), 22–37.

Bulgren, J. A., and Scanlon, D. (1997). Instructional routines and learning strategies that promote understanding of content area concepts. *Journal of Adolescent and Adult Literacy, 41,* 292–302.

Bullock, J. (1991). *Touchmath.* Colorado Springs, CO: Innovative Learning Concepts.

Bullock, J. (1996). *Touchmath resource center set.* Colorado Springs, CO: Innovative Learning Concepts.

Bullock, J., Pierce, S., Strand, L., and Branine, K. (1981). *Touchmath teachers manual.* Colorado Springs, CO: Innovative Learning Concepts.

Bunce, B. H. (1993). Language of the classroom. In A. Gerber (Ed.), *Language related learning disabilities: Their nature and treatment* (pp. 135–159). Baltimore, MD: Brookes Publishing.

Burns, J. P., and Allen, J. D. (1998). Managing inclusive classrooms, *Kappa Delta Pi Record, 35*(1), 28–30.

Bursuck, W. D., Harniss, M. K., Epstein, M. H., Polloway, E. A., Jayanthi, M., and Wissinger, L. M. (1999). Solving communication problems about homework: Recommendations of special education teachers, *Learning Disabilities Research & Practice, 14*(3), 149–158.

Button, E. (1993). *Eating disorders: Personal construct therapy and change.* New York: Wiley.

Byrnes, J. P. (1996). *Cognitive development and learning in instructional contexts.* Boston: Allyn and Bacon.

Cambourne, B., and Turnbull, J. (1987). *Coping with chaos.* Portsmouth, NH: Heinemann.

Camp, B. W., and Bash, M. A. S. (1981). *The think aloud series: Increasing social and cognitive skills.* Champaign, IL: Research Press.

Camp, B. W., Blom, G. E., Herbert, F., and Van Doorninck, W. J. (1977). "Think around": A program for developing self-control in young aggressive boys. *Journal of Abnormal Child Psychology, 5*, 157–169.

Carbo, M. (1978). Teaching reading with talking books. *The Reading Teacher, 32*, 267–273.

Carbo, M. (1997). *Continuum of modeling methods: Release your students' learning power.* Syosset, NY: National Reading Styles Institute.

Carnine, D. (1989). Teaching complex content to learning disabled students: The role of technology. *Exceptional Children, 55*, 524–533.

Carnine, D. (1991). Curricular interventions for teaching higher order thinking to all students: Introduction to the special series. *Journal of Learning Disabilities, 24*, 261–269.

Carnine, D. (1997). Instructional design in mathematics for students with learning disabilities. *Journal of Learning Disabilities, 30*(2), 130–141.

Carnine, D., Silbert, J., and Kameenui, E. J. (1997). *Direct instruction reading* (3rd ed.). Columbus, OH: Merrill.

Carpenter, D., and Miller, L. J. (1982). Spelling ability of reading disabled LD students and able readers. *Learning Disability Quarterly, 5*(1), 65–70.

Carpenter, R. L. (1985). Mathematics instruction in resource rooms: Instruction time and teacher competence. *Learning Disability Quarterly, 8,* 95–100.

Carr, E., and Ogle, D. (1987). K-W-L plus: A strategy for comprehension and summarization. *Journal of Reading, 30,* 626–631.

Carr, E. G., and Durand, V. M. (1985). Reducing behavior problems through functional communication training. *Journal of Applied Behavior Analysis, 18,* 111–126.

Carr, S. C., and Thompson, B. (1996). The effects of prior knowledge and schema activation strategies on the inferential reading comprehension of children with and without learning disabilities. *Learning Disability Quarterly, 19,* 48–61.

Carrekar, S. (1999). Teaching spelling. In J. R. Birsh (Ed.) *Multisensory teaching of basic language skills* (pp. 217–256). Baltimore, MD: Paul H. Brookes.

Carrier, C. A. (1983). Notetaking research: Implications for the classroom. *Journal of Instructional Development, 6*(3), 19–25.

Carrier, C. A., and Newell, K. (1983). *What dental hygiene undergraduates think about notetaking in lecture classes: Report of a survey.* Unpublished manuscript, University of Minnesota, Minneapolis.

Carroll, J. (1964). *Language and thought.* Englewood Cliffs, NJ: Prentice-Hall.

Carrow, E. (1973). *Test of auditory comprehension of language.* Austin, TX: Urban Research Group.

Casby, M. (1992). An intervention approach for naming problems in children. *American Journal of Speech-Language Pathology, 1*(3), 35–42.

Catts, H. W., and Kamhi, A. G., (Eds.). (1999). *Language and reading disabilities.* Boston: Allyn and Bacon.

Cawley, J. F. (1984). An integrative approach to needs of learning disabled children: Expanded use of mathematics. In J. F. Cawley (Ed.), *Developmental teaching of mathematics for the learning disabled.* Rockville, MD: Aspen.

Cawley, J. F. and Miller, J. H. (1986). Selected views on metacognition, arithmetic problem solving, and learning disabilities. *Learning Disabilities Focus, 2*(1), 36–48.

Cawley, J. F., and Miller, J. H. (1989). Cross-sectional comparisons of the mathematical performance of children with learning disabilities: Are we on the right track toward comprehensive programming? *Journal of Learning Disabilities, 22,* 250–254, 259.

Cawley, J. F., Parmar, R. S., Yan, W., and Miller, J. H. (1998). Arithmetic computation performance of students with learning disabilities: Implications for curriculum. *Learning Disabilities Research & Practice, 13*(2), 68–74.

Ceci, S. (1985). A developmental study of learning disabilities and memory. *Journal of Experimental Child Psychology, 39,* 202–221.

Chalfant, J. C. (1987). Providing services to all students with learning problems: Implications for policy and programs. In S. Vaughn and C. Bos (Eds.), *Research in learning disabilities: Issues and future trends* (pp. 239–251). Boston: College-Hill, Little Brown.

Chalfant, J. C. (1989). Learning disabilities: Policy issues and promising approaches. *American Psychologist, 44,* 392–398.

Chalfant, J. C., and Pysh, M. V. (1989). Teacher assistance teams: Five descriptive studies on 96 teams. *Remedial and Special Education, 10*(6), 49–58.

Chalfant, J. C., and Pysh, M. V. (1993). Teacher assistance teams: Implications for the gifted. In C. J. Maker (Ed.), *Critical issues in gifted education: Vol III—Gifted students in the regular classroom* (pp. 32–48). Austin, TX: PRO-ED.

Chalfant, J. C., Pysh, M. V., and Moultrie, R. (1979). Teacher assistance teams: A model for within-building problem solving. *Learning Disability Quarterly, 2,* 85–96.

Chall, J. S. (1983). *Learning to read: The great debate* (2nd ed.), New York: McGraw-Hill.

Chall, J. S., and Popp, H. M. (1996). *Teaching and assessing phonics: Why, what, when, how.* Cambridge, MA: Educators Publishing Service.

Chambers, D. L., and Kepner, H. S. (1985). Applied mathematics: A three-year program for non-college-bound students. In C. R. Hirsch and M. J. Zweng (Eds.), *The secondary school mathematics curriculum* (pp. 211–229). Reston, VA: National Council of Teachers of Mathematics.

Chamot, A. (1998). Effective instruction for high school English language learners. In R. M. Gersten and R. T. Jimenez (Eds.), *Promoting learning for culturally and linguistically diverse students* (pp. 187–209). Belmont, CA: Wadsworth Publishing.

Chamot, A., and O'Malley, J. M. (1994). The CALLA Handbook: How to implement the cognitive academic language learning approach. In K. Spangenberg-Urbschat and R. Pritchard (Eds.), *Kids come in all languages: Reading instruction for ESL students* (pp. 82–103). Newark, DE: International Reading Association.

Chamot, A., and O'Malley, J. M. (1994). *The CALLA handbook: Implementing the cognitive academic language learning approach.* Reading, MA: Addison-Wesley.

Chan, L. K. S. (1991). Promoting strategy generalization through self-instructional training in students with reading disabilities. *Journal of Learning Disabilities, 24,* 427–433.

Chapman, J. W., and Boersman, F. J. (1980). *Affective correlates of learning disabilities.* Lisse: Swets & Zeitlinger.

Chard, D. J., and Dickson, S. V. (1999). Phonological awareness: Instructional and assessment guidelines. *Intervention in Clinic and School, 34*(5), 261–270.

Chard, D., Elliott, B., Morris, P. B., Smith, M., and Vaughn, S. (2000). *First grade teacher reading academy.* Austin, TX: Texas Education Agency.

Chase, C. H., and Tallal, P. (1991). Cognitive models of developmental reading disorders. In J. E. Obrzut and G. W. Hynd (Eds.), *Neuropsychological foundations of learning disabilities.* San Diego: Academic Press, pp. 199–240.

Chen, H. C., and Graves, M. F. (1996). Effects of previewing and providing background knowledge on Taiwanese college students' comprehension of American short stories. *TESOL Quarterly, 29,* 663–686.

Cherkes-Julkowski, M. (1985). Metacognitive considerations in mathematics for the learning disabled. In J. Cawley (Ed.), *Cognitive strategies and mathematics for the learning disabled.* Rockville, MD: Aspen.

Chiang, B. (1986). Initial learning and transfer effects of microcomputer drills on LD students' multiplication skills. *Learning Disability Quarterly, 9,* 118–123.

Chomsky, C. (1969). *The acquisition of syntax in children from 5 to 10.* Cambridge, MA: MIT Press.

Chomsky, C. (1976). After decoding: What? *Language Arts, 53,* 288–296.

Christian, B. T. (1983). A practical reinforcement hierarchy for classroom behavior modification. *Psychology in the Schools, 20,* 83–84.

Ciborowski, J. (1992). *Textbooks and the students who can't read them: A guide to teaching content.* Boston: Brookline.

Clark, D. B., and Uhry, J. K. (1995). *Dyslexia: Theory and practice of remedial instruction.* Baltimore, MD: York Press.

Clark, F. L., Deshler, D. D., Schumaker, J. B., Alley, G. R., and Warner, M. M. (1984). Visual imagery and self-questioning: Strategies to improve comprehension of written materials. *Journal of Learning Disabilities, 17*(3), 145–149.

Clark, G. M. (1998). *Assessment for transitions planning.* Austin, TX: PRO-ED.

Clark, G. M., and Patton, J. R. (1997). *Transition planning inventory.* Austin, TX: PRO-ED.

Clark, G. M., Patton, J. R., and Moulton, R. (2001). *Informal assessments in transition planning.* Austin, TX: PRO-ED.

Clark, J., and Klecan-Aker, J. S. (1992). Therapeutic strategies for language disordered children: The impact of visual imagery on verbal encoding in vocabulary instruction. *Journal of Childhood Communication Disorders, 14*(2), 129–145.

Clark, J. O. (1990). *Harrup's dictionary of English idioms.* London: Harrup.

Cline, B. V., and Billingsley, B. S. (1991). Teachers' and supervisors' perceptions of secondary learning disabilities programs: A multi-state survey. *Learning Disabilities Research and Practice, 6,* 158–165.

Coffland, J. A., and Baldwin, R. S. (1985). *Wordmath.* St. Louis: Milliken.

Cohen, V. B. (January 1983). Criteria for the evaluation of microcomputer courseware. *Educational Technology,* 9–14.

Coie, J. D., Dodge, K. A., and Coppotelli, H. (1982). Dimensions and types of social status: A cross-age perspective. *Developmental Psychology, 18,* 557–570.

Coldwell, J., (1997). *Introducing word families through literature.* Greensboro, NC: Carson-Dellosa.

Cole, J. (1989). *Anna Banana: 101 jump rope rhymes.* New York: Morrow Junior Books.

Cole, J., and Calmenson, S. (1990). *Miss Mary Mack and other children's street rhymes.* New York: Morrow Junior Books.

Collis, B., and Heeren, E. (1993). Tele-collaboration and groupware. *The Computing Teacher, 8,* 36–39.

Connolly, A. J. (1985). *Key math teach and practice.* Circle Pines, MN: American Guidance Service.

Conte, R., and Humphreys, R. (1989). Repeated readings using audiotaped material enhances oral reading in children with reading difficulties. *Journal of Communication Disorders, 22,* 65–79.

Cooley, E. J., and Ayres, R. R. (1988). Self-concept and success-failure attributions of nonhandicapped students and students with learning disabilities. *Journal of Learning Disabilities, 21*(3), 174–178.

Corkill, A. J. (1992). Advance organizers: Facilitators of recall. *Educational Psychology Review, 4,* 33–67.

Cornwall, A. (1992). The relationship of phonological awareness, rapid naming, and verbal memory to severe reading and spelling disability. *Journal of Learning Disabilities, 25,* 532–538.

Cosden, M. A., Gerber, M. M., Semmel, D. S., Goldman, S. R., and Semmel, M. I., (1987). Microcomputer use within micro-educational environments. *Exceptional Children, 53,* 399–409.

Coterell, G. (1972). A case of severe learning disability. *Remedial Education, 7,* 5–9.

Council for Children with Behavior Disorders, 1990.

Council for Exceptional Children (1993). *CEC Statement on Inclusion.* Reston, VA: Author.

Cox, A. R. (1992). *Foundations for literacy: Structures and techniques for multisensory teaching of basic written English language skills (Alphabetic Phonics).* Cambridge, MA: Educators Publishing Service.

Cox, C., and Many, J. E. (1992). Towards an understanding of the aesthetic stance towards literature. *Language Arts, 66,* 287–294.

Cronbach, L., and Snow, R. (1977). *Aptitudes and instructional methods.* New York: Irvington Press.

Cronin, M. E., and Patton, J. R. (1993). *Life skills instruction for all students with special needs: A practical guide for integrating real-life content into the curriculum.* Austin, TX: PRO-ED.

Cuevas, G., and Driscoll, M. (Eds.). (1993). *Reaching all students with mathematics.* Reston, VA: National Council of Teachers of Mathematics.

Cullinan, B. E. (Ed.) (1992). *Invitation to read: More children's literature in the reading program.* Newark, DE: International Reading Association.

Culp, A. M., Clyman, M. M., and Culp, R. E. (1995). Adolescent depressed mood, reports of suicide attempts, and asking for help. *Adolescence, 30,* 827–837.

Cummings, R. W., and Maddux, C. D. (1985). *Parenting the learning disabled: A realistic approach.* Springfield, IL: Charles C. Thomas.

Cummins, J. (1981). *Bilingualism and minority language children.* Ontario: Ontario Institute for Students in Education.

Cummins, J. (1984). *Bilingualism and special education: Issues in assessment and pedagogy.* San Diego, CA: College Hill.

Cummins, J. (1989). A theoretical framework for bilingual special education. *Exceptional Children, 56,* 111–119.

Cummins, J. (1991). Interdependence of first- and second-language proficiency in bilingual children. In E. Bialystok (Ed.), *Language processing in bilingual children.* Cambridge, England: Cambridge University Press.

Cummins, J. (1994). The acquisition of English as a second language. In K. Spangenberg-Urbschat and R. Pritchard (Eds.), *Kids come in all languages: Reading instruction for ESL students* (pp. 36–62). Newark, DE: International Reading Association.

Cunningham, P. (1979). Beginning reading without readiness: Structured language experience. *Reading Horizons, 11,* 222–227.

Cunningham, P. M. (1991). *Phonics they use: Words for reading and writing.* New York: HarperCollins.

Cunningham, P. M. (1995). *Phonics they use: Words for reading and writing* (2nd ed.). New York: HarperCollins.

Cunningham, P. M. (2000). *Phonics they use: Words for reading and writing* (3rd ed.). New York: Longman.

Cunningham, P. M., and Allington, R. L. (1994). *Classrooms that work: They can ALL read and write.* New York: Harper-Collins.

Cunningham, P. M., and Cunningham, J. W. (1992). Making words: Enhancing the invented spelling-decoding connection. *The Reading Teacher, 46,* 106–116.

Cunningham, P. M., and Hall, D. P. (1994a). *Making words.* Parsippany, NJ: Good Apple.

Cunningham, P. M., and Hall, D. P. (1994b). *Making big words.* Parsippany, NJ: Good Apple.

Deshler, D. D., Ellis, E. S., and Lenz, B. K. (1996). *Teaching adolescents with learning disabilities: Strategies and methods* (2nd ed.). Denver: Love.

de Villiers, J., and de Villiers, P. (1978). *Language acquisition.* Cambridge, MA: Harvard University Press.

Devine, T. G. (1987). *Teaching study skills: A guide for teachers* (2nd ed.). Boston: Allyn and Bacon.

Diaz, S., Moll., L. C., and Mehan, H. (1986). Sociocultural resources in instruction: A context-specific approach. In *Beyond language: Social and cultural factors in schooling language minority students* (pp. 187–229). Sacramento, CA: Bilingual Education Office, California State Department of Education.

Dole, J. A., Brown, K. J., and Trathen, W. (1996). The effects of strategy instruction on the comprehension performance of at-risk students. *Reading Research Quarterly, 31,* 62–88.

Dole, J. A., Valencia, S. W., Greer, E. A., and Wardrop, J. L. (1991). Effects of two types of reading instruction on the comprehension of narrative and expository text. *Reading Research Quarterly, 26,* 142–159.

Donahue, M., Pearl, R., and Bryan, T. (1980). Learning disabled children's conversational competence: Responses in inadequate messages. *Applied Psycholinguistics, 1,* 387–403.

Dorval, B., McKinney, J. D., and Feagans, L. (1982). Teacher interaction with learning disabled children and average achievers. *Journal of Pediatric Psychology, 7*(3), 317–330.

Dowhower, S. L. (1987). Effects of repeated reading on second-grade transitional readers' fluency and comprehension. *Reading Research Quarterly, 22,* 389–406.

Dowhower, S. L. (1994). Repeated reading revisited: Research into practice. *Reading and Writing Quarterly, 10,* 343–358.

Doyle, W. (1979). Making managerial decisions in classrooms. In D. L. Duke (Ed.), *Classroom management.* Seventy-eighth yearbook of the National Society for the Study of Education, Part 2. Chicago: University of Chicago Press.

Doyle, W. (1986). Classroom organization and management. In M. C. Wittrock (Ed.), *Handbook of research on teaching* (3rd ed, pp. 392–431). New York: Macmillan.

Dreher, M. J., and Singer, H. (1980). Story grammar instruction is unnecessary for intermediate grade students. *The Reading Teacher, 34,* 261–268.

Drum, R. L., and Petty, W. G., Jr. (1999). Teaching the values of coins. *Teaching Children Mathematics, 5*(5), 264–268.

Duffy, G., Lanier, J. E., and Roehler, L. R. (1980). *On the need to consider instructional practice when looking for instruction implications.* Paper presented at the Reading Expository Materials. University of Wisconsin–Madison.

Duffy, G. G., and McIntyre, L. D. (1982). A naturalistic study of instructional assistance in primary-grade reading. *Elementary School Journal, 83*(1), 15–23.

Duke, D. L., and Meckel, A. M. (1980). *Managing student behavior problems.* New York: Teachers College Press, Columbia University.

Duling, W. P. (1999). Literacy development of second language learners with technology and LEA. In O. G. Nelson and W. M. Linek (Eds.), *Practical classroom applications of language experience: Looking back, looking forward* (pp. 248–256). Boston: Allyn and Bacon.

Duran, R. P. (1989). Assessment and instruction of at-risk Hispanic students. *Exceptional Children, 56,* 154–159.

Durkin, D. D. (1978–79). What classroom observations reveal about reading comprehension instruction. *Reading Research Quarterly, 14*(4), 481–533.

Dweck, C. S., and Kamins, M. L. (1999). Person versus process praise and criticism: Implications for contingent self-worth and coping. *Developmental Psychology, 35*(3), 835–47.

D'Zurilla, T., and Goldfired, M. (1971). Problem solving and behavior modification. *Journal of Applied Psychology, 78,* 107–129.

Echevarria, J., and Graves, A. (1998). *Sheltered content instruction: Teaching English-Language Learners with diverse abilities.* Boston: Allyn and Bacon.

Echevarria, J., and McDonough, R. (1996). An alternative reading approach: Instructional conversations in a bilingual special education setting. *Learning Disabilities Research and Practice, 10,* 108–119.

Eckert, P. (1990). Cooperative competition in adolescent "girl talk." *Discourse Processes, 13,* 91–122.

Eggen, P. D., and Kauchak, D. (1992). *Educational psychology: Classroom connections.* New York: Macmillan.

Ehri, L. C. (1989). The development of spelling knowledge and its role in reading acquisition and reading disability. *Journal of Learning Disabilities, 22*(6), 356–365.

Ehri, L. C. (1998). Grapheme-phoneme knowledge is essential for learning to read words in English. In J. Methsala and L. Ehri (Eds.). *Word recognition in beginning literacy* (pp. 3–40). Mahwah, NJ: Erlbaum Associates.

Ehri, L. C., and Robbins, C. (1992). Beginners need some decoding skill to read words by analogy. *Reading Research Quarterly, 27,* 13–26.

Ehri, L. C., and Wilce, L. S. (1983). Development of word identification speed in skilled and less skilled beginning readers. *Journal of Education Psychology, 75,* 3–18.

Elam, S. M., and Gallup. A. M. (1989). The 21st annual Gallup poll of the public's attitudes toward the public schools. *Phi Delta Kappan, 71,* 41–54.

Elbaum, B., Vaughn, S., Hughs, M., and Moody, S. W. (1999). Grouping practices and reading outcomes for students with disabilities. *Exceptional Children, 65*(3), 399–415.

Elbaum, B. E., Schumm, J. S., and Vaughn, S. (1997). Urban middle-elementary students' perceptions of grouping formats for reading instruction. *Elementary School Journal, 97*(5), 475–500.

Eldredge, J. L. (1990). Increasing the performance of poor readers in the third grade with a group-assisted strategy. *Journal of Educational Research, 84,* 69–77.

Eldredge, J. L. (1995). *Teaching decoding in holistic classrooms.* Boston: Allyn and Bacon.

Eldredge, J. L., and Quinn, D. W. (1988). Increasing reading performance of low-achieving second graders with dyad reading groups. *Journal of Educational Research, 82*(1), 40–46.

Elias, M. J., and Clabby, J. F. (1989). *Social decision-making skills: A curriculum guide for the elementary grades.* Rockville, MD: Aspen.

Elkind, J. (1998a). *A study of the efficacy of the Kurzweil 3000 Reading Machine in enhancing poor reading performance.* Portola Valley, CA: Lexia Institute.

Elkind, J. (1998b). Computer reading machines for poor readers. *Perspectives, 24*(2), 4–6.

Elkind, J., Black, M., and Murray, C. (1996). Computer-based comprehension of adult reading disabilities. *Annals of Dyslexia, 46,* 159–186.

Elkonin, D. B. (1973). U.S.S.R. In J. Downing (Ed.), *Comparative reading* (pp. 551–579). New York: Macmillan.

Ellis, E. (1991). *SLANT: A starter strategy for participation.* Lawrence, KS: Edge Enterprises.

Ellis, E. S. (1996). Reading strategy instruction. In D. D. Deshler, E. S. Ellis, and B. K. Lenz (Authors.), *Teaching adolescents with learning disabilities: Strategies and methods* (2nd ed., pp. 61–126). Denver: Love.

Ellis, E. S., Deshler, D. D., Schumaker, J. B., Lenz, B. K., and Clark, R. L. (1991). An instructional model for teaching learning strategies. *Focus on Exceptional Children, 23*(1), 1–22.

Elster, C. (1994). Patterns within preschoolers' emergent readings. *Reading Research Quarterly, 29,* 402–418.

Emery, D. W. (1996). Helping readers comprehend stories from the characters' perspectives. *The Reading Teacher, 49,* 534–541.

Emmer, E., Evertson, C., and Anderson, L. (1980). Effective classroom management at the beginning of the school year. *Elementary School Journal, 80*(5), 219–231.

Emmer, E. T., Evertson, C. M., Sanford, J. P., Clements, B. S., and Worsham, M. E. (1989). *Classroom management for secondary teachers* (2nd ed.). Englewood Cliffs, NJ: Prentice-Hall.

Enfield, M. L., and Greene, V. (1997). *Project read.* Bloomington, MN: Language Circle Enterprise.

Engelhardt, Ashlock, and Wiebe (1984). *Helping children understand and use numerals* (pp. 89–149). Boston: Allyn and Bacon.

Englemann, S., Bruner, E. C., Hanner, S., Osborn, J., Osborn, S., and Zoref, L. (1995). *Reading mastery: Rainbow edition.* Columbus, OH: SRA/McGraw-Hill.

Engelmann, S., and Carnine, D. (1972). *DISTAR arithmetic level I.* Chicago: Science Research Associates.

Engelmann, S., and Carnine, D. (1975). *DISTAR arithmetic level I.* Chicago: Science Research Associates.

Engelmann, S., and Carnine, D. (1976). *DISTAR arithmetic level II.* Chicago, Science Research Associates.

Engelmann, S., and Carnine, D. (1982). *Corrective mathematics program.* Chicago: Science Research Associates.

Engelmann, S., Carnine, D. and Steely, D. G. (1991) Making connections in mathematics. *Journal of Learning Disabilities, 24*(5), 292–303.

Engelmann, S., Meyer, L., Carnine, L., Becker, W., Eisele, J., and Johnson, G. (1999). *Corrective reading program.* Columbus, OH: SRA/McGraw-Hill.

Engelmann, S., and Osborn, J. (1999). *Language for Learning.* DeSoto, TX: SRA/McGraw-Hill.

Englert, C. S. (1992). Writing instruction from a sociocultural perspective: The holistic, dialogic, and social enterprise of writing. *Journal of Learning Disabilities, 25,* 153–172.

Englert, C. S., Garmon, A., Mariage, T., Rozendal, M., Tarrant, K., and Urba, J. (1995). The early literacy project: Connecting across the literacy curriculum. *Learning Disability Quarterly, 18,* 253–277.

Englert, C. S., and Mariage, T. (1990). Send for the POSSE: Structuring the comprehension dialogue. *Academic Therapy, 25,* 473–487.

Englert, C. S., and Mariage, T. V. (1991). Making students partners in the comprehension process: Organizing the reading "POSSE." *Learning Disability Quarterly, 14,* 123–138.

Englert, C. S., and Raphael, T. E. (1988). Constructive well-formed prose: Process, structure, and metacognitive knowledge. *Exceptional Children, 54,* 513–520.

Englert, C. S., Raphael, T. E., Anderson, L. M., Anthony, H. M., and Stevens, D. D. (1991). Making strategies and self-talk visible: Writing instruction in regular and special education classrooms. *American Educational Research Journal, 23,* 337–372.

Englert, C. S., Raphael, T. E., Fear, K. L., and Anderson, L. M. (1988). Students' metacognitive knowledge about how to write informational texts. *Learning Disability Quarterly, 11,* 18–46.

Englert, C. S., Rozendal, M. S., and Mariage, M. (1994). Fostering the search for understanding: A teacher's strategies for leading cognitive development in "zones of proximal development." *Learning Disability Quarterly, 17,* 187–204.

Ericcson, K. A., and Kintsch, W. (1995). Long-term working memory. *Psychological Review, 102,* 211–245.

Erickson, R., and Schultz, J. (1981). When is a context? Some issues and methods in the analysis of social competence. In J. L. Green and C. Wallat (Eds.), *Ethnography and language in educational settings.* Norwood, NJ: Ablex.

Estes, T. J., and Vaughn, J. L. (1978). *Reading and learning in the content classroom: Diagnostic and instructional strategies.* Boston: Allyn and Bacon.

Exceptional Parent. (1984, March). *Parent advocacy.* Exceptional Parent, 14 (2), 41–45.

Farmer, T. W., Pearl, R., and Van Acker, R. M. (1996). Expanding the social skills deficit framework: A developmental synthesis perspective, classroom social networks, and implications for the social growth of students with disabilities. *Journal of Special Education, 30*(3), 232–256.

Fauke, J., Burnett, J., Powers, M., and Sulzer-Azaroff, B. (1973). Improvement of handwriting and letter recognition skills: A behavior modification procedure. *Journal of Learning Disabilities, 6,* 25–29.

Fearn, L., and Farnan, N. (1998). Writing effectively: Helping children master the conventions of writing. Needham Heights, MA: Allyn and Bacon.

Feldmann, S. C., and Fish, M. D. (1991). The use of computer-mediated reading supports to enhance reading comprehension. *Journal of Educational Computing Research, 7*(1), 25–36.

Fernald, G. M. (1943). *Remedial techniques in basic school subjects.* New York: McGraw-Hill.

Fernald, G. M. (1988). *Remedial techniques in basic school subjects.* (L. Idol, Ed.). Austin, TX: PRO-ED (original edition 1943).

Fettler, F., and Tokar, E. (1982). Getting a handle on teacher stress. *Educational Leadership, 39,* 456–457.

Fielding, L., and Roller, C. (1992). Making difficult books accessible and easy books acceptable. *The Reading Teacher, 45,* 678–682.

Finn, J. D. (1989). Withdrawing from school. *Review of Educational Research, 59,* 117–142.

Fisher, J. L., and Harris, M. B. (1973). Effect of notetaking and review on recall. *Journal of Educational Psychology, 65*(3), 321–325.

Fitzsimmons, R. J., and Loomer, B. M. (1978). *Spelling: Learning and instruction.* (Report No. CS 205 117). Des Moines: Iowa State Department of Public Instruction. (ERIC Document Reproduction Service No. ED 176 285).

Flavell, J. H. (1976). Metacognitive aspects of problem solving. In L. B. Resnick (Ed.), *The nature of intelligence.* Hillsdale, NJ: Erlbaum.

Fleischner, J. E., Nuzum, M. G., and Marzola, E. S. (1987). Devising an instructional program to teach arithmetic problem-solving skills to students with learning disabilities. *Journal of Learning Disabilities, 20*(4), 214–217.

Fletcher, J. M. (1989). Nonverbal learning disabilities and suicide: Classification leads to prevention. *Journal of Learning Disabilities, 22,* 176–179.

Fletcher, R. J., and Rosenberger, N. (1987). Beware of tapping pencils. *Arithmetic Teacher, 34*(5), 6–10.

Flexer, R. W., Simmons, T. J., Luft, P., and Baer, R. M. (2001). *Transition planning for secondary students with disabilities.* Upper Saddle River, NJ: Merrill/Prentice-Hall.

Foorman, B. R., Fletcher, J. M., Francis, D. J., and Schatschneider, C. (1998). The role of instruction in learning to read: Preventing reading failure in at-risk children. *Journal of Education Psychology, 90,* 37–55.

Foorman, B. R., Francis, D. J., and Fletcher, J. M. (in press). Early intervention for children with reading disabilities and at risk for developmental reading disabilities. *Scientific studies of reading.*

Forness, S. R. (1973). The reinforcement hierarchy. *Psychology in the Schools, 19,* 168–177.

Foster, K. C., Erickson, G. C., Foster, D. F., Brinkman, D., and Torgesen, J. K. (1994). Computer administered instruction in phonological awareness: Evaluation of the DaisyQuest program. *Journal of Research and Development in Education, 27,* 126–137.

Foster, S. L., and Ritchey, W. C. (1979). Issues in the assessment of social competence in children. *Journal of Applied Behavior Analysis, 12,* 625–631.

Fountas, I. C., and Pinnell, G. S. (1999). *Matching books to readers: Using leveled books in guided reading, K–3.* Portsmouth, NH: Heinemann.

Fowler, G. L., and Davis, M. (1985). The story frame approach: A tool for improving reading comprehension of EMR children. *Teaching Exceptional Children, 17*(4), 296–298.

Fowler, S. A. (1986). Peer-monitoring and self-monitoring: Alternatives to traditional teacher management. *Exceptional Children, 52*(6), 573–582.

Fox, C. (1989). Peer acceptance of learning disabled children in the regular classroom. *Exceptional Children, 56*(1), 50–57.

Frayer, D. A., Frederick, W. C., and Klausmeier, H. J. (1969). *A schema for testing the level of concept mastery* (Working Paper No. 16). Madison: University of Wisconsin, Wisconsin Research and Development Center for Cognitive Learning.

Freeman, E. B., and Person, D. G. (1992). *Using nonfiction trade books in the elementary classroom from ants to zeppelins.* Urbana, IL: National Council of Teachers of English.

Freppon, P. A., and Dahl, K. L. (1998). Theory and research into practice: Balanced instruction: Insights and considerations. *Reading Research Quarterly, 33,* 240–251.

Friend, M., and Cook, L. (1992). *Interactions: Collaboration skills for school professionals.* White Plains, NY: Longman.

Fries, C. C. (1963). *Linguistics and reading.* New York: Holt, Rinehart and Winston.

Frith, G. H., and Armstong, W. W. (1986). Self-monitoring for behavior disordered students. *Teaching Exceptional Children, 18*(2), 144–148.

Frith, U. (1980). *Cognitive processes in spelling.* London: Academic Press.

Fromkin, V., and Rodman, R. (1993). *Introduction to language.* New York: Holt, Rinehart.

Fromkin, V., and Rodman, R. (1998). *An instruction to language* (6th ed.). Orlando, FL: Harcourt Brace & Co.

Fry, E. B. (1977). Fry's readability graph: Clarifications, validity, and extension to level 17. *Journal of Reading, 21,* 242–252.

Fry, E. B., Fountoukidis, D. L., and Polk, J. K. (1985). *The new reading teacher's book of lists.* Englewood Cliffs, NJ: Prentice-Hall.

Fry, E. B., Kress, J. E., and Fountoukidis, D. L. (1993). *The reading teacher's book of lists.* New York: The Center for Applied Research in Education.

Fuchs, D., and Fuchs, L. S. (1994). Inclusive school movement and radicalization of special education reform. *Exceptional Children, 60,* 294–309.

Fuchs, D., and Fuchs, L. S. (1995). What's "special" about special education? *Phi Delta Kappan, 76,* 522–530.

Fuchs, D., Fuchs, L. S., and Bahr, M. W. (1990). Mainstream assistance teams: A scientific basis for the art of consultation. *Exceptional Children, 57,* 128–139.

Fuchs, D., Fuchs, L. S., and Burish, P. (2000). Peer-assisted learning strategies: An evidence-based practice to promote reading achievement. *Learning Disabilities Research and Practice, 25,* 85–91.

Fuchs, D., Fuchs, L. S., Mathes, P. G., and Simmons, D. C. (1997). Peer-assisted learning strategies: Making classrooms more responsive to diversity. *American Educational Research Journal, 34,* 174–206.

Fuchs, L., Deno, S., and Mirkin, P. (1984). The effects of frequent curriculum-based measurement and evaluation on pedagogy, student achievement, and student awareness of learning. *American Educational Research Journal, 21,* 449–460.

Fuchs, L. S., Bahr, C. M., and Rieth, H. J. (1989). Effects of goal structures and performance contingencies on the math performance of adolescents with learning disabilities. *Journal of Learning Disabilities, 22,* 554–560.

Fuchs, L. S., and Deno, S. L. (1991). Paradigmatic distinctions between instructionally relevant measurement models. *Exceptional Children, 57,* 488–500.

Fuchs, L. S., Fuchs, D., and Hamlett, C. L. (1989). Effects of instructional use of curriculum-based measurement to enhance instruction programs. *Remedial and Special education 10*(2), 43–52.

Fuchs, L. S., Fuchs, D., Hamlett, C. L., and Allinder, R. M. (1991). The contribution of skills analysis to curriculum-based measurement in spelling. *Exceptional Children, 57,* 443–452.

Fuchs, L. S., Fuchs, D., Hamlett, C. L., Phillips, N. B., and Karns, K. (1995). General educators' specialized adaptation for students with learning disabilities. *Exceptional Children, 61*(5), 440–459.

Fuchs, L. S., Fuchs, D., Hamlett, C. L., Walz, L., and Germann, G. (1993). Formative evaluation of academic progress: How much growth can we expect? *School Psychology Review, 22*(1), 27–48.

Fuchs, L. S., Hamlett, C., and Fuchs, D. (1990). *Monitoring basic skills progress: Basic math.* Austin, TX: PRO-ED.

Fujiki, M., Brinton, B., and Todd, C. M. (1996). Social skills of children with specific language impairment. *Language, Speech, and Hearing Services in Schools, 27,* 195–202.

Fulk, B. J. M., Mastropieri, M. A., and Scruggs, T. E. (1992). Mnemonic generalization training with learning disabled adolescents. *Learning Disabilities Research and Practice, 7,* 2–10.

Fulk, B. M., and Stormont-Spurgin, M. (1995). Spelling interventions for students with disabilities: A review. *Journal of Special Education, 28,* 488–513.

Furner, B. (1969). The perceptual-motor nature of learning in handwriting. *Elementary English, 46,* 886–894.

Furner, B. (1969). Recommended instructional procedures in a method emphasizing the perceptual-motor nature of learning in handwriting. *Elementary English, 46,* 1021–1030.

Furner, B. (1970). An analysis of the effectiveness of a program of instruction emphasizing the perceptual-motor nature of learning in handwriting. *Elementary English, 47,* 61–69.

Gaffney, J. S., and Anderson, R. C. (2000). Trends in reading research in the United States: Changing intellectual currents over three decades. In M. L. Kamil, P. B. Mosenthal, P. D. Pearson, and R. Barr (Eds.), *Handbook of reading research,* (Vol. III, pp. 53–76). Mawah, NJ: Erlbaum Associates.

Gajria, M., and Salend, S. J. (1995). Homework practices of students with and without learning disabilities: A comparison. *Journal of Learning Disabilities, 28,* 291–296.

Gajria, M., and Salvia, J. (1992). The effects of summarization instruction on text comprehension of students with learning disabilities. *Exceptional Children, 58,* 508–516.

Galambos, S., and Goldin-Meadow, S. (1990). The effects of learning two languages on metalinguistic development. *Cognition, 34,* 1–56.

Garcia, E. E. (1991). Effective instruction for language minority students: The teacher. *Journal of Education, 173,* 130–141.

García, G. E., Pearson, P. D., and Jiménez, R. T. (1994). *The at-risk situation: A synthesis of reding research.* Champaign: University of Illinois, Center for the Study of Reading.

Gaskins, I. W. with Cress, C., O'Hara, C., and Donnelly, K. (1998). *Word detectives: Benchmark extended word identification program for beginning readers.* Media, PA: Benchmark Press.

Gaskins, I. W., Anderson, R. C., Pressley, M., Cunicelli, E. A., and Satlow, E. (1993). Six teachers' dialogue during cognitive process instruction. *Elementary School Journal, 93,* 277–304.

Gast, D., Ault, M., Wolery, M., Doyle, P., and Belanger, S. (1988). Comparison of constant time delay and the system of least prompts in teaching sight word reading to students with moderate retardation. *Education and Training in Mental Retardation, 23,* 117–128.

Gerber, A. (1993). *Language related learning disabilities: Their nature and treatment.* Baltimore, MD: Brookes Publishing.

Gerber, M., and Kauffman, J. (1981). Peer tutoring in academic settings. In P. Strain (Ed.), *Utilization of classroom peers as behavior change agents* (pp. 155–187). New York: Plenum Press.

Gerber, M. M., and Hall, R. J. (1989). Cognitive-behavioral training in spelling for learning handicapped students. *Learning Disabilities Quarterly, 12,* 159–171.

German, D. J. (1987). Spontaneous language profiles of children with word-finding problems. *Language, Speech, and Hearing Services in Schools, 18,* 217–230.

German, D. J. (1992). Word-finding intervention for children and adolescents. *Topics in Language Disorders, 13*(1), 33–50.

Gertsen, B., and Baker, S. (2000). What we know about effective instructional practices for English-language learners. *Exceptional Children, 66,* 454–470.

Gersten, R., and Baker, S. (in press). Teaching expressive writing to students with learning disabilities: A meta-analysis. *The Journal of Special Education.*

Gersten, R., Becker, W. C., Heiry, T. J., and White, W. A. T. (1984). Entry IQ and yearly academic growth of children in Direct Instruction programs: A longitudinal study of low SES children. *Education Evaluation and Policy Analysis, 6,* 109–121.

Gersten, R., Carnine, D., and Woodward, J. (1987). Direct Instruction research: The third decade. *Remedial and Special Education, 8*(6), 48–56.

Gersten, R., Schiller, E. P., and Vaughn, S. (2000). *Contemporary special education research: Syntheses of knowledge bases in critical instructional issues.* Mahwah, NJ: Erlbaum.

Gersten, R., Williams, J. P., Fuchs, L. S., and Baker, S. (in press). Teaching reading comprehension strategies to students with learning disabilities: A review of research. *Review of Educational Research.*

Gettinger, M. (1984). Applying learning principles to remedial spelling instruction. *Academic Therapy, 20*(1), 41–48.

Gettinger, M., Bryant, M. D., and Fayne, H. R. (1982). Designing spelling instruction for learning disabled children: An emphasis on unit size, distributed practice, and training for transfer. *Journal of Special Education, 16*(4), 439–448.

Gibbons, P. (1993). *Learning to learn in a second language.* NSW, Australia: Heinemann.

Gibbs, R. W. (1987). Linguistic factors in children's understanding of idioms. *Journal of Speech and Hearing Research, 54,* 613–620.

Giddan, J. J., Bade, K. M., Rickenberg, C., and Ryley, A. T. (1995). Teaching the language of feelings to students with severe emotional and behavioral handicaps. *Language, Speech, and Hearing Services in Schools, 26,* 3–10.

Gillingham, A., and Stillman, B. W. (1973). *Remedial training for children with specific disability in reading, spelling, and penmanship.* Cambridge, MA: Educators Publishing Service.

Ginsburg, H. P. (1997). Mathematics learning disabilities: A view from developmental psychology. *Journal of Learning Disabilities, 30*(1), 20–33.

Glass, G., and Glass, E. (1976). *The Glass-analysis for decoding only.* Garden City, NY: Easier to Learn.

Glatthorn, A. A. (1990). Cooperative professional development: Facilitating the growth of the special education teacher and the classroom teacher. *Remedial and Special Education, 11*(3), 29–35.

Gold, V. (1976). *The effect of an experimental program involving acquisition of phoneme-grapheme relationships incorporating criterion referenced tests with evaluative feedback upon spelling performance of third grade pupils.* Unpublished doctoral dissertation, University of Southern California, Los Angeles.

Goldenberg, C. (1992). Instructional conversations: Promoting comprehension through discussion. *The Reading Teacher, 46,* 316–326.

Goldenberg, C., and Gallimore, R. (1991). Changing teaching takes more than a one-shot workshop. *Educational Leadership, 49*(3), 69–72.

Goldman, S. R., Hasselbring, T. S., and the Cognition and Technology Group at Vanderbilt (1997). Achieving meaningful mathematics literacy for students with learning disabilities. *Journal of Learning Disabilities, 30*(2), 198–208.

Goldstein, A. P., Sprafkin, R. P., Gershaw, N. J., and Klein, P. (1980). *Skillstreaming the adolescent.* Champaign, IL: Research Press.

Goldstein, S. (1995). *Understanding and managing children's classroom behavior.* New York: Wiley.

Good, T. L., and Brophy, J. E. (1997). *Looking in classrooms* (7th ed.). New York: Addison-Wesley, Longman.

Goodman, K. (1986). *What's whole in whole language?* Portsmouth, NH: Heinemann.

Goodman, K. (1993). *Phonics phacts.* Portsmouth, NH: Heinemann.

Goodman, K. S. (1984). Unity in reading. In A. C. Purves and O. Niles (Eds.), *Becoming readers in a complex society* (pp. 79–114). Eighty-third yearbook of the National Society for the Study of Education. Chicago: University of Chicago Press.

Goodman, K. S. (1996). *On reading.* Portsmouth, NH: Heinemann.

Goodman, Y. M. (1996). Revaluing readers while readers revalue themselves: Retrospective miscue analysis. *The Reading Teacher, 49,* 600–609.

Goodman, Y. M. and Goodman, K. S. (1990). Vygotsky in the whole-language perspective. In L. C. Moll (Ed.), *Vygotsky and education: Instructional implications and applications of sociohistorical psychology* (pp. 223–250). Cambridge: Cambridge University Press.

Goodman, Y. M., Watson, D. J., and Burke, C. L. (1996). *Reading strategies: Focus on comprehension* (2nd ed.). Katonah, NY: Richard C. Owens.

Goodstein, H. A. (1981). Are the errors we see the true errors? Error analysis in verbal problem solving. *Topics in Learning and Learning Disabilities, 1*(3), 31–45.

Gordon, J., Vaughn, S., and Schumm, J. S. (1993). Spelling intervention: A review of literature and implications for instruction for students with learning disabilities. *Learning Disabilities Research and Practice, 8,* 175–181.

Gorman-Gard, K. A. (1992). *Figurative language: A comprehensive program.* Eau Claire, WI: Thinking Publications.

Gough, P. B. (1996). How children learn to read and why they fail. *Annals of Dyslexia, 46,* 3–19.

Goss, J. L., and Harste, J. C. (1985). *It didn't frighten me!* Worthington, OH: Willow Press.

Goswami, U. (1998). Rime-based coding in early reading development in English: Orthographic analogies and rime neighborhoods. In D. Hulme, and R. M. Joshi, (Eds.), *Reading and spelling: Development and disorders* (pp. 69–86). Mahwah, NJ: Erlbaum Associates.

Goswami, U., and Bryant, P. E. (1990). *Phonological skills and learning to read.* Mahwah, NJ: Erlbaum Associates.

Graham, S. (1983). The effect of self-instructional procedures on LD students' handwriting performance. *Learning Disability Quarterly, 6*(2), 231–244.

Graham, S. (1999). Handwriting and spelling instruction for students with learning disabilities: A review. *Learning Disability Quarterly, 22*(2), 78–98.

Graham, S., Berninger, V., and Weintraub, N. (1998). The relationship between handwriting style and speed and legibility. *Journal of Educational Research, 91,* 290–297.

Graham, S., and Freeman, S. (1986). Strategy training and teacher- vs. student-controlled study conditions: Effects on LD students' spelling performance. *Learning Disability Quarterly, 9,* 15–22.

Graham, S., Harris, K., and Troia, G. (1998). Writing and self-regulation: Cases from the self-regulated strategy development model. In D. Schunk and B. Zimmerman (Eds.), *Self-regulated learning: From teaching to self-reflective practice* (pp. 20–41). New York: Guilford.

Graham, S., and Harris, K. R. (1988). Instructional recommendations for teaching writing to exceptional students. *Exceptional Children, 54,* 506–512.

Graham, S., and Harris, K. R. (1989a). Components analysis of cognitive strategy instruction: Effects on learning disabled students' compositions and self-efficacy. *Journal of Educational Psychology, 81,* 353–361.

Graham, S., and Harris, K. R. (1989b). Improving learning disabled students' skills at composing essays: Self-instructional strategy training. *Exceptional Children, 56,* 201–214.

Graham, S., and Harris, K. R. (1993). Teaching writing strategies to students with learning disabilities: Issues and recommendations. In L. Meltzer (Ed.), *Strategy assessment and instruction for students with learning disabilities: From theory to practice* (pp. 271–292). Austin, TX: PRO-ED.

Graham, S., and Harris, K. R. (1994). Implications of constructivism for teaching writing to students with special needs. *Journal of Special Education, 28,* 275–289.

Graham, S., Harris, K. R., and Loynachan, C. (1996). The directed spelling thinking activity: Application with high-frequency words. *Learning Disabilities Research & Practice,* *1,* 34–40.

Graham, S., Harris, K. R., and MacArthur, C. A. (1995). Introduction to special issue: Research on writing and literacy. *Learning Disability Quarterly, 18,* 250–252.

Graham, S., MacArthur, C., and Schwartz, S. (1995). Effects of goal setting and procedural facilitation on the revising behavior and writing performance of students with writing and learning problems. *Journal of Educational Psychology, 87,* 230–240.

Graham, S., MacArthur, C., Schwartz, S., and Page-Voth, V. (1992). Improving the compositions of students with learning disabilities using a strategy involving product and process goal setting. *Exceptional Children, 58,* 322–334.

Graham, S., and Miller, L. (1979). Spelling research and practice: A unified approach. *Focus on Exceptional Children, 12*(2), 1–16.

Graham, S., and Miller, L. (1980). Handwriting research and practice: A unified approach. *Focus on Exceptional Children, 13*(2), 1–16.

Graham, S., and Voth, V. (1990). Spelling instruction: Making modifications for students with learning disabilities. *Academic Therapy, 25,* 447–457.

Grasser, A., Golding, J. M., and Long, D. L. (1991). Narrative representation and comprehension. In R. Barr, M. L. Kamil, P. Mosenthal, and P. D. Pearson (Eds.), *Handbook of reading research,* (Vol. II, pp. 171–205). New York: Longman.

Graves, A. W. (1986). Effects of direct instruction and metacomprehension training on finding main ideas. *Learning Disabilities Research, 1*(2), 90–100.

Graves, A. W. (1995). Teaching students who are culturally and linguistically diverse. *Teacher Educator's Journal, 15*(3), 32–40.

Graves, A. W., Valles, E. C., and Rueda, R. (2000). Variations in interactive writing instruction: A study in four bilingual special education settings. *Learning Disabilities Research & Practice, 15*(3), 1–9.

Graves, D. (1985). Personal correspondence.

Graves, D. H. (1983). *Writing: Teachers and children at work.* Portsmouth, NH: Heinemann.

Graves, D. H. (1985). All children can write. *Learning Disability Focus, 1*(1), 36–43.

Graves, D. H., and Hansen, J. (1983). The author's chair. *Language Arts, 60,* 176–183.

Graves, M. F., Juel, C., and Graves, B. B. (2001). *Teaching reading in the 21st century* (2nd ed.). Boston: Allyn and Bacon.

Greaney, U. K. T., Tunmer, W. E., and Chapman, J. W. (1997). Effects of rime-based orthographic analogy training on the word recognition skills of children with reading disability. *Journal of Education Psychology, 89,* 645–651.

Greene, J. R. (1995). *Language: A curriculum for at-risk and ESL students.* Longmont, CO: Sopris West.

Greene, J. R. (1996). Language: The effects of an individualized structured language curriculum for middle and high school students. *Annals of Dyslexia, 38,* 258–275.

Greenwood, C. R., Delquardri, J. C., and Hall, R. V. (1989). Longitudinal effects of classwide peer tutoring. *Journal of Educational Psychology, 81,* 371–383.

Gregory, R. P., Hackney, C., and Gregory, N. M. (1982). Corrective reading programme: An evaluation. *British Journal of Educational Psychology, 52,* 33–50.

Gresham, F. M. (1982). Misguided mainstreaming: The case for social skills training with handicapped children. *Exceptional Children, 48,* 422–433.

Griffiths, D. (1991). An analysis of social competence training with persons with developmental handicaps. Unpublished doctoral dissertation, University of Toronto.

Grimm, J. A., Bijou, S. W., and Parsons, J. A. (1973). A problem solving model for teaching remedial arithmetic to handicapped children. *Journal of Abnormal Child Psychology, 1,* 26–39.

Grossen, B. (1999). *The research base for corrective reading.* Columbus, OH: SRA/McGraw-Hill.

Grossen, B., and Carnine, D. (1992). Phonics instruction: Comparing research and practice. *Teaching Exceptional Children, 25*(2), 22–25.

Grossman, H. (1995). *Special education in a diverse society.* Boston: Allyn and Bacon.

Grottenthaler, J. A. (1970). *A comparison of the effectiveness of three programs of elementary school spelling.* Unpublished doctoral dissertation, University of Pittsburgh.

Guetzloe, E. C. (1989). *Youth suicide: What the educator should know.* Reston, VA: The Council for Exceptional Children.

Gulland, D. M. and Hinds-Howell, D. G. (1986). *The Penguin dictionary of English idioms.* London: Penguin.

Gunning, T. G. (1988). *Teaching phonics and other word attack skills.* Springfield, IL: Charles C. Thomas.

Gunning, T. G. (1998). *Assessing and correcting reading and writing difficulties.* Boston: Allyn and Bacon.

Gunning, T. G. (2000). *Creating literacy instruction for all children* (3rd ed.). Boston: Allyn and Bacon.

Gunning, T. G. (2001). *Building words: A resource manual for teaching owrd analysis and spelling patterns.* Boston: Allyn and Bacon.

Gurney, D., Gersten, R., Dimino, J., and Carnine, D. (1990). Story grammar: Effective literature instruction for high school students with learning disabilities. *Journal of Learning Disabilities, 23,* 335–342.

Guszak, F. J. (1972). *Diagnostic reading instruction in the elementary school.* New York: Harper & Row.

Hacker, D. J., Dunlosky, J., and Graesser, A. C. (1998). *Metacognition in educational theory and practice.* Mahwah, NJ: Erlbaum Associates.

Hagin, R. A. (1983). Write right or left: A practical approach to handwriting. *Journal of Learning Disabilities, 16*(5), 266–271.

Hall, R. V. (1975). *Behavior modification: Basic principles, managing behavior (Part 2)* (Rev. ed.). Lawrence, KS: H & H Enterprises.

Hall, R. V., and Hall, M. L. (1998). *How to use planned ignoring (Extinction)* (2nd ed.). Austin, TX: PRO-ED.

Hallahan, D. P., Keller, C. E., McKinney, J. D., Lloyd, J. W., and Bryan, T. (1988). Examining the research base of the regular education initiative: Efficacy studies and the adaptive learning environments model. *Journal of Learning Disabilities, 21,* 29–35, 55.

Hallahan, D. P., Lloyd, J., Kosiewicz, M. M., Kauffman, J. M., and Graves, A. W. (1979). Self-monitoring of attention as a treatment for learning disabled boy's off-task behavior. *Learning Disability Quarterly, 2*, 24–32.

Halliday, M. A. K., and Hassan, R. (1976). *Cohesion in English.* London: Longman.

Hallowell, E. M., and Ratey, J. J. (1995). *Driven to distraction: Recognizing and coping with attention deficit disorder from childhood through adulthood.* New York: Touchstone.

Halperin, M. S. (1974). Developmental changes in the recall and recognition of categorized word lists. *Child Development, 45*, 144–151.

Halpern, A. S. (1994). The transition of youth with disabilities to adult life: A position statement of the Division on Career Development and Transition, The Council for Exceptional Children. *Career Development for Exceptional Individuals, 17*, 115–124.

Halpern, A. S., Herr, C. M., Doren, B., and Wolf, N. K. (2000). *Next S. T. E. P.: Student transition and evaluation planning* (2nd ed.). Austin, TX: PRO-ED.

Halpern, N. (1981). Mathematics for the learning disabled. *Journal of Learning Disabilities, 14*(9), 505–506.

Hamayan, E. V., and Damico, J. S. (Eds.), (1991). *Limiting bias in the assessment of bilingual students.* Austin, TX: PRO-ED.

Hamstra-Bletz, L., and Blote, A. W. (1993). A longitudinal study on dysgraphic handwriting in primary school. *Journal of Learning Disabilities, 26*, 689–699.

Hanover, S. (1983). Handwriting comes naturally? *Academic Therapy, 18*, 407–412.

Hansen, J. (1981). The effect of inference training and practice on young children's reading comprehension. *Reading Research Quarterly, 16*(3), 391–417.

Hansen, J. (1985). Skills. In J. Hansen, T. Newkirk, and D. Graves (Eds.), *Breaking ground: Teachers relate reading and writing in the elementary school* (pp. 147–168). Portsmouth, NH: Heinemann.

Hansen, J. (1992). Students' evaluations bring reading and writing together. *The Reading Teacher, 46*, 100–105.

Hansen, J., and Hubbard, R. (1984). Poor readers can draw inferences. *The Reading Teacher, 37*(7), 586–590.

Hansen, J., Newkirk, T., and Graves, D. (Eds.). (1985). *Breaking ground: Teachers relate reading and writing in the elementary school.* Portsmouth, NH: Heinemann.

Hansen, J., and Pearson, P. D. (1983). An instructional study: Improving the inferential comprehension of good and poor fourth grade readers. *Journal of Educational Psychology, 75*(6), 821–829.

Harper, G. F., Mallete, B. and Moore, J. (1991). Peer-mediated instruction: Teaching spelling to primary school children with mild disabilities. *Reading, Writing, and Learning Disabilities, 7*, 137–151.

Harris, K. R. (1982). Cognitive-behavior modification: Application with exceptional students. *Focus on Exceptional Children, 15*(2), 1–16.

Harris, K. R., (1985). Conceptual, methodological, and clinical issues in cognitive behavior assessment. *Journal of Abnormal Child Psychology, 13*, 373–390.

Harris, K. R., and Graham, S. (1985). Improving learning disabled students' composition skills: Self-control strategy training. *Learning Disability Quarterly, 8*, 27–36.

Harris, K. R., and Graham, S. (1992). *Helping young writers master the craft.* Cambridge, MA: Brookline Press.

Harris, K. R., and Pressley, M. E. (1991). The nature of cognitive strategy instruction: Interactive strategy construction. *Exceptional Children, 57*, 392–404.

Harry, B. (1992). *Cultural diversity, families, and the special education system.* New York: Teachers College Press.

Harry, B., Allen, N., and McLaughlin, M. (1995). Communication versus compliance: African-American parents' involvement in special education. *Exceptional Children, 6*(4), 364–377.

Harste, J. C., Short, K. G., with Burke, C. (1988). *Creating classrooms for authors: The reading-writing connection.* Portsmouth, NH: Heinemann.

Hartas, D., and Donahue, L. M. (1997). Conversational and social problem-solving skills in adolescents with learning disabilities. *Learning Disabilities Research and Practice, 12*(4), 213–220.

Hasbrouck, J. E., Ihnot, C., and Rogers, G. H. (1999). "Read naturally": A strategy to increase oral reading fluency. *Reading Research and Instruction, 39*(1), 27–38.

Hasbrouck, J. E., and Tindal, G. (1992). Curriculum-based oral reading fluency norms for students in Grades 2 through 5. *Teaching Exceptional Children, 24*(3), 41–44.

Hasselbring, T. S., and Goin, L. I. (1989). Making knowledge meaningful: Applications of hypermedia. *Journal of Special Education Technology, 10*(2), 61–72.

Hasselbring, T. S., and Goin, L. I. (1993). Integrated technology and media. In E. A. Polloway and J. R. Patton (Eds.), *Strategies for teaching learners with special needs* (5th ed., pp. 145–162). New York: Merrill/Macmillan.

Hasselbring, T., Goin, L, and Bransford, J. (1987). Developing automaticity. *Teaching Exceptional Children, 19*, 30–33.

Hawaii Transition Project. (1987). Honolulu: Department of Special Education, University of Hawaii.

Hazel, J. S., Schumaker, J. B., Sherman, J. A., and Sheldon, J. (1982). Application of a group training program in social skills and problem solving to learning disabled and non-learning disabled youth. *Learning Disability Quarterly, 5*, 398–409.

Hazel, J. S., Schumaker, J. B., Sherman, J. A., and Sheldon-Wildgen, J. (1981). *ASSET: A social skills program for adolescents.* Champaign, IL: Research Press.

Helmke, L. M., Havekost, D. M., Patton, J. R., and Polloway, E. A. (1994). Life skills programming: Development of a high school science course. *Teaching Exceptional Children, 26*(2), 49–53.

Hembree, R. (1986). Research gives calculators a green light. *Arithmetic Teacher, 34*(1), 18–21.

Henderson, E. H. (1990). *Teaching spelling* (2nd ed.). Boston: Houghton Mifflin.

Henry, C. S., Stephenson, A. L., Hanson, M. F., and Hargett, W. (1993). Adolescent suicide and families: An ecological approach. *Adolescence, 28*, 291–308.

Henry, M. (1997). The decoding/spelling curriculum: Integrated decoding and spelling instruction from pre-school to early secondary school. *Dyslexia, 3,* 178–189.

Herman, P. A. (1985). The effect of repeated readings on reading rate, speech pauses, and word recognition memory. *Reading Research Quarterly, 20,* 553–574.

Herman, P. A., Anderson, R. C., Pearson, P. D., and Nagy, W. E. (1987). Incidental acquisition of word meaning from expositions with varied text features. *Reading Research Quarterly, 22,* 263–284.

Herman, R. D. (1993). *The Herman method for reversing reading failure.* Sherman Oaks, CA: The Herman Method Institute.

Horton, S. V., Lovitt, T. C., and Bergerud, D. (1990). The effectiveness of graphic organizers for three classifications of secondary students in content area classes. *Journal of Learning Disabilities, 23,* 12–22, 29.

Hoskins, B. (1987). *Conversations: Language intervention for adolescents.* Allen, TX: Developmental Learning Materials.

Hoskins, B. (1990). Language and literacy: Participating in the conversation. *Topics in Language and Language Disorders, 10*(2), 46–62.

Hoskisson, K., and Krohm, B. (1974). Reading by immersion: Assisted reading. *Elementary English, 5,* 831–836.

Howe, M. L., Brainerd, C. J., and Kingma, J. (1985). Storage-retrieval process of normal and learning disabled children: A stages-of-learning analysis of picture-word effects. *Child Development, 56,* 1120–1133.

Howe, M. L., O'Sullivan, J. T., Brainerd, C. J., and Kingma, J. (1989). Localizing the development of ability differences in organized memory. *Contemporary Education Psychology, 14,* 336–356.

Hudson, F., Ormsbee, C. K., and Myles, B. S. (1994). Study guides: An instructional tool for equalizing student achievement. *Intervention in School and Clinic, 30*(20), 99–102.

Hudson, P., Lignugaris-Kraft, B., and Miller, T. (1993). Using content enhancements to improve the performance of adolescents with learning disabilities in content classes. *Learning Disabilities Research and Practice, 8,* 106–126.

Hudson, P. J. (1987). *The pause procedure: A technique to help mildly handicapped students learn lecture content.* Unpublished doctoral dissertation, University of Florida, Gainesville.

Huefner, D. S. (1988). The consulting teacher model: Risks and Opportunities. *Exceptional Children, 54,* 403–414.

Hughes, C. A. (1996). Memory and test-taking strategies. In D. D. Deshler, E. S. Ellis, and B. K. Lenz, *Teaching adolescents with learning disabilities: Strategies and methods* (2nd ed., pp. 209–266). Denver: Love.

Hughes, C. A., Ruhl, K. L., Deshler, D. D., and Schumaker, J. B. (1995). *The assignment completion strategy.* Lawrence, KS: Edge Enterprises.

Hughes, C. A., and Schumaker, J. B. (1991). Test-taking strategy instruction for adolescents with learning disabilities. *Exceptionality, 2,* 205–221.

Hughes, C. A., Schumaker, J. B., Deshler, D. D., and Mercer, C. D. (1993). *The test-taking strategy* (rev. ed.). Lawrence, KS: Edge Enterprises.

Hughes, C. A., Schumaker, J. B., and Deshler, D. D. (in preparation). *The essay test-taking strategy.* Lawrence, KS: Edge Enterprises.

Hughes, M. E. T. (1995). *Parental involvement in literacy instruction: Perceptions and practices of Hispanic parents of children with learning disabilities.* Unpublished doctoral dissertation, University of Miami, Coral Gables.

Hughes, M. T., Schumm, J. S., and Vaughn, S. (1999). Home literacy activities: Perceptions and practices of Hispanic parents of children with learning disabilities. *Learning Disabilities Quarterly, 22,* 224–235.

Hutton, J. B., and Palo, L. (1976). A sociometric study of learning disability children and type of teaching strategy. *Group Psychotherapy, Psychodrama and Sociometry, 29,* 113–121.

Hynd, G. W., Obrzut, J. E., and Bowen, S. M. (1987). Neuropsychological basis of attention and memory in learning disabilities. In H. L. Swanson (Ed.), *Advances in learning and behavior disabilities: Memory and learning disabilities* (pp. 175–201). Greenwich, CT: JAI Press.

Idol, L. (1987a). A critical thinking map to improve content area comprehension of poor readers. *Remedial and Special Education, 8*(4), 28–40.

Idol, L. (1987b). Group story mapping: A comprehension strategy for both skilled and unskilled readers. *Journal of Learning Disabilities, 20*(4), 196–205.

Idol, L. (1997). Key questions related to building collaborative and inclusive schools. *Journal of Learning Disabilities, 30*(4), 384–394.

Idol, L., Nevin, A., and Paolucci-Whitcomb, P. (2000). *Collaborative Consultation* (3rd ed.). Austin, TX: PRO-ED.

Idol, L., Paolucci-Whitcomb, P., and Nevin, A. (1986). *Collaborative consultation.* Austin, TX: PRO-ED.

Imber, S. C., Imber, S. C., and Rothstein, C. (1979). Modifying independent work habits: An effective teacher-parent communication program. *Exceptional Children, 46,* 218–221.

Institute for Research in Learning Disabilities (1990a). *Planning for a strategic environment.* Lawrence: University of Kansas.

Institute for Research in Learning Disabilities (1990b). *Ensuring strategic instruction.* Lawrence: University of Kansas.

Irvine, J. J. (1991). *Black students and school failure: Policies, practice, and prescriptions.* New York: Praeger.

Isaacson, S. (1988). Assessing the writing product: Qualitative and quantitative measures. *Exceptional Children, 54,* 528–534.

Isaacson, S., and Gleason, M. M. (1997). Mechanical obstacles to writing: What can teachers do to help students with learning problems? *Learning Disabilities Research & Practice, 12*(3), 188–194.

Ives, J. P., Bursuk, L. Z., and Ives, S. A. (1979). *Word identification techniques.* Chicago: Rand McNally College Publishing.

Jackson, H. J., and Boag, P. G. (1981). The efficacy of self control procedures as motivational strategies with mentally retarded persons: A review of the literature and guidelines for future research. *Australian Journal of Developmental Disabilities, 7,* 65–79.

Janney, R., and Snell, M. E. (2000). *Behavioral support.* Baltimore, Maryland: Paul H. Brookes.

Jay, T. B. (January 1983). The cognitive approach to computer courseware design and evaluation. *Educational Technology*, 22–26.

Jayanthi, M., Epstein, M. H., Polloway, E. A., and Bursuck, W. D. (1996). Testing adaptations: A national survey of the testing practices of general education teachers. *Journal of Special Education, 30*, 99–115.

Jewell, T. A., and Pratt, D. (1999). Literature discussions in the primary grades: Children's thoughtful discourse about books and what teachers can do to make it happen. *The Reading Teacher, 52*, 842–850.

Jiménez, R. T., García, G. E., and Pearson, P. D. (1996). The reading strategies of bilingual Latina/o students who are successful English readers: Opportunities and obstacles. *Reading Research Quarterly, 31*, 90–112.

Jimenez, R. T., and Gersten, R. (1999). Lessons and dilemmas derived from the literacy instruction of two Latina/o teachers. *American Educational Research Journal, 36*, 265–301.

Jitendra, A. K., Hoff, K., and Beck, M. M. (1999). Teaching middle school students with learning disabilities to solve word problems using a schema-based approach. *Remedial and Special Education, 20*(1), 50–64.

Johnson, C. J., Beitchman, J. H., Young, A., Escobar, M., Atkinson, L., Wilson, B. Brownlie, E. B., Douglas, L., Taback, N., Lam, I., and Wang, M. (1999). Fourteen-year follow-up of children with and without speech/language impairments: Speech/language stability and outcomes. *Journal of Speech, Language, and Hearing Research, 42*, 744–760.

Johnson, D., Johnson, R., and Holubec, E. (1993). *Cooperation in the classroom.* Edina, MN: Interaction Book Company.

Johnson, D. D., and Pearson, P. D. (1984). *Teaching reading vocabulary* (2nd ed.). New York: Holt, Rinehart and Winston.

Johnson, D. D., Pittelman, S. D., and Heimlich, J. E. (1986). Semantic mapping. *The Reading Teacher, 39*(8), 778–783.

Johnson, D. J., and Myklebust, H. R. (1967). *Learning disabilities: Educational principles and practices.* New York: Grune and Stratton.

Johnson, D. W., and Johnson, R. T. (1975). *Learning together and alone.* Engelwood Cliffs, NJ: Prentice-Hall.

Johnson, D. W., and Johnson, R. T. (1984a). Classroom learning structure and attitudes toward handicapped students in mainstream settings: A theoretical model and research evidence. In R. Jones (Ed.), *Special education in transition: Attitudes toward the handicapped.* Reston, Va.: ERIC Clearinghouse on Handicapped and Gifted Children, The Council for Exceptional Children.

Johnson, D. W., and Johnson, R. T. (1984b). Building acceptance of differences between handicapped and nonhandicapped students: The effects of cooperative and individualistic problems. *Journal of Social Psychology, 122*, 257–267.

Johnson Santamaria, L., Fletcher, T. V., and Bos, C. S. (in press). Scaffolded instruction: Promoting biliteracy for second language learners with language/learning disabilities. In A. Artilles and A. Ortiz (Eds.),

Jones, D. J., Fox, M. M., Haroutun-Babigian, H. M., and Hutton, H. E. (1980). Epidemiology of anorexia nervosa in Monroe County, New York: 1960–1976. *Psychosomatic Medicine, 42*(6), 551–558.

Juel, C. (1983). The development and use of mediated word identification. *Reading Research Quarterly, 18*, 306–327.

Juel, C. (1994). *Learning to read and write in one elementary school.* New York: Springer-Verlag.

Juvonen, J., and Bear, G. (1992). Social adjustment of children with and without learning disabilities in integrated classrooms. *Journal of Educational Psychology, 84*(3), 322–330.

Kail, R., and Leonard, L. B. (1986). Word-finding abilities in language-impaired children. *ASHA Monograph Number 25.* Rockville, MD: American Speech-Language-Hearing Association.

Kalafat, J. (1990). Adolescent suicide and the implications for school response programs. *The School Counselor, 37*, 359–39.

Kameenui, E. J., and Carnine, D. W. (1998). *Effective teaching strategies that accommodate diverse learners.* Upper Saddle River, NJ: Prentice-Hall.

Kameenui, E. J., Simmons, D. C., Baker, S., Chard, D., Dickson, S., Gunn, B., Smith, S., Sprick, M., and Lin, S. (1998). Effective strategies for teaching beginning reading. In E. J. Kameenui and D. W. Carnine (Eds.), *Effective teaching strategies that accommodate diverse learners* (pp. 45–70). Columbus, OH: Merrill.

Kamhi, A. G. (1999). To use or not to use: Factors that invluence the selection of new treatment approaches. *Language, Speech, and Hearing Services in Schools, 30*, 92–98.

Kamhi, A. G., and Catts, H. W. (1989). Language and reading: Convergences, divergences, and development. In A. G. Kamhi and H. W. Catts (Eds.), *Reading disabilities: A developmental language perspective* (pp. 1–34). Boston: Allyn and Bacon.

Kaplan, P., Kohfeldt, J., and Sturla, K. (1974). *It's positively fun: Techniques for managing learning environment.* Denver: Love.

Karlin, R. (1980). *Teaching elementary reading* (3rd ed.). New York: Harcourt Brace Jovanovich.

Karp, N. (1996). Individualized wrap-around services for children with emotional, behavior, and mental disorders. In G. H. S. Singer, L. E. Powers, and A. L. Olson (1996). *Redefining Family Support* (pp. 291–312). Baltimore, MD: Paul H. Brookes Publishing Co., Inc.

Katz-Leavy, J. W., Lourie, I. S., Stroul, B. A., and Ziegler-Dendy, C. (1992, July). *Individualized services in a system of care.* Washington, DC: CASSP Technical Assistance Center, Center for Child Health and Mental Health Policy, Georgetown University Child Development Center.

Kauffman, J., Hallahan, D., Haas, K., Brame, T., and Boren, R. (1978). Imitating children's errors to improve spelling performance. *Journal of Learning Disabilities, 11*, 33–38.

Kauffman, J. M. (1995). Why we must celebrate diversity of restrictive environments. *Learning Disabilities Research and Practice, 10*, 225–232.

Kauffman, J. M. (2001). *Characteristics of children's behavior disorders* (7th ed.). Columbus, OH: Merrill.

Kavale, K., and Forness, S. R. (1996). Social skill deficits and learning disabilities: A meta-analysis. *Journal of Learning Disabilities, 29*(3), 226–37.

Kavanagh, J. F., and Truss, T. J., Jr. (1988). *Learning disabilities: Proceedings of the national conference.* Parkton, MD: York Press.

Kazdin, A. E. (1982). *Single-case research designs*. New York: Oxford University Press.

Kazdin, A. E. (1989). *Behavior modification in applied settings* (4th ed.). Pacific Grove, CA: Brooks/Cole.

Kelly, B., Carnine, D., Gersten, R., and Grossen, B. (1987). The effectiveness of videodisc instruction in teaching fractions to learning handicapped and remedial high school students. *Journal of Special Education Technology, 8*(2), 5–17.

King-Sears, M. E., Mercer, C. D., and Sindelar, P. T. (1992). Toward independence with key word mnemonics: A strategy for science vocabulary instruction. *Remedial and Special Education, 13*(5), 22–33.

Kirk, S. A., Kirk, W. D., and Minskoff, E. H. (1985). *Phonic remedial reading lessons*. Novato, CA: Academic Therapy Publications.

Kirkpatrick, E. M., and Schwarz, C. M. (Eds.). (1982). *Chambers idioms*. Edinburgh, Scotland: Chambers.

Klausmeier, J. H., and Sipple, T. S. (1980). *Learning and teaching process concepts: A strategy for testing applications for theory*. New York: Academic Press.

Klingner, J. K., and Vaughn, S. (1996). Reciprocal teaching of reading comprehension strategies for students with learning disabilities who use English as a second language. *Elementary School Journal, 96*, 275–293.

Klingner, J. K., and Vaughn, S. (1998). Using collaborative strategic reading. *Teaching Exceptional Children, 30*(6), 32–37.

Klingner, J. K., and Vaughn, S. (1999a). Promoting reading comprehension, content learning, and English acquisition through collaborative strategic reading (CSR). *The Reading Teacher, 52*(7), 738–747.

Klingner, J. K., and Vaughn, S. (1999b). Students' perceptions of instructional practice. *Exceptional Children, 66*, 23–37.

Klingner, J. K., and Vaughn, S. (2000). The helping behaviors of fifth graders while using collaborative strategic reading during ESL content classes. *TESOL Quarterly, 34*(1), 69–98.

Klingner, J. K., Vaughn, J. S., and Schumm, J. S. (1996). *Collaborative Strategic Reading*. Miami: University of Miami, School-Based Reseach.

Klingner, J. K., Vaughn, S., and Schumm, J. S. (1998). Collaborative strategic reading during social studies in heterogeneous fourth-grade classrooms. *Elementary School Journal, 99*, 3–22.

Klingner, J. K., Vaughn, S., Schumm, J. S., Cohen, P., and Forgan, J. W. (1998). Inclusion or pull-out: Which do students prefer? *Journal of Learning Disabilities, 32*(2), 148–158.

Kloomok, S., and Cosden, M. (1994). Self-concept in children with learning disabilities: The relationship between global self-concept, academic discounting, nonacademic self-concept, and perceived social support. *Learning Disability Quarterly, 17*(2), 140–153.

Knight-Arest, I. (1984). Communicative effectiveness of learning disabled and normally achieving 10- to 13-year-old boys. *Learning Disability Quarterly, 7*, 237–245.

Knowlton, E. K. (1982). *Secondary teacher's expectations of learning disabled students* (Research Report No. 75.). Lawrence: University of Kansas, Center for Research on Learning.

Korbin, B. (1988). *Eyeopeners! How to choose and use children's books about real people, places, and things*. New York: Penguin.

Kosc, L. (1981). Neuropsychological implications of diagnosis and treatment of mathematical learning disabilities. *Topics in Learning and Learning Disabilities, 1*(3), 19–30.

Kosiewicz, M. M., Hallahan, D. P., Lloyd. J. W., and Graves, A. W. (1982). Effects of self-instruction and self-correction procedures on handwriting performance. *Learning Disability Quarterly, 5*(1), 71–78.

Koskinen, P. A., and Blum, I. H. (1984). Paired repeated reading: A classroom strategy for developing fluent reading. *The Reading Teacher, 40*, 70–75.

Koskinen, P. S., Blum, I. H., Bisson, S. A., Phillips, S. M., Creamer, T. S., and Baker, T. K. (1999). Shared reading, books, and audiotapes: Supporting diverse students in school and at home. *The Reading Teacher, 52*, 430–444.

Koziol, S. (1973). The development of noun plural rules during the primary grades. *Research in the Teaching of English, 7*, 30–50.

Kozulin, A., and Presseisen, B. Z. (1995). Mediated learning experience and psychological tools: Vygotsky's and Feuerstein's perspectives in a study of student learning. *Educational Psychologists, 30*, 67–75.

Krashen, S. (1985). *The input hypothesis: Issues and implications*. London: Longman.

Krauss, R., and Glucksberg, S. (1967). The development of communication competence as a function of age. *Child Development, 40*, 255–260.

Kress, R. A., and Johnson, M. S. (1970). Martin. In A. J. Harris (Ed.), *Casebook on reading disability* (pp. 1–24). New York: David McKay.

Kreviski, J., and Linfield, J. L. (1974). *Bad speller's dictionary*. New York: Random House.

Kronik, D. (1977). A parent's thought for parents and teachers. In N. Haring and B. Bateman (Eds.), *Teaching the learning disabled child*. Englewood Cliffs, NJ: Prentice-Hall.

Krug, R. S. (1983). Substance abuse. In C. E. Walker and McRoberts (Eds.), *Handbook of clinical child psychology* (pp. 853–879). New York: Wiley.

Kucer, S. B. (1986). Helping writers get the "big picture." *Journal of Reading, 30*(1), 18–25.

Kuder, S. J. (1997). *Teaching students with language and communication disabilities*. Boston: Allyn and Bacon.

LaBerge, D., and Samuels, S. J. (1974). Toward a theory of automatic information processing in reading. *Cognitive Psychology, 6*, 293–323.

Ladas, H. S. (1980). Notetaking on lectures: An information processing approach. *Educational Psychologist, 15*(1), 44–53.

Ladson-Billings, G. (1995). Toward a theory of culturally relevant pedagogy. *American Educational Research Journal, 32*, 465–491.

LaGreca, A. M. (November 1982). Issues in the assessment of social skills with learning disabled children. In *Children's social skills: Future directions*, S. Beck (Chair). Paper presented at the annual meeting of the Association for the Advancement of Behavior Therapy, Los Angeles.

LaGreca, A. M., and Stone, W. L. (1990). Children with learning disabilities: The role of achievement in their social, personal and behavioral functioning. In H. L. Swanson and B. Keogh

(Eds.), *Learning disabilities: Theoretical and research issues* (pp. 333–352). Hillsdale, NJ: Erlbaum.

Lahey, M., and Edwards, J. (1999). Naming errors of children with specific language impairment. *Journal of Speech, Language, and Hearing Research, 42,* 196–202.

Lambert, N. M., and Sandoval, J. (1980). The prevalence of learning disabilities in a sample of children considered hyperactive. *Journal of Abnormal Child Psychology, 8*(1), 33–50.

Lancelotta, G. X., and Vaughn, S. R. (1989). Relation between types of aggression and sociometric status: Peer and teacher perceptions. *Journal of Educational Psychology, 81*(1), 86–90. Reprinted by permission in W. R. Borg, *Applying educational research,* (1993), New York: Longman.

Langan, J. (1982). *Reading and study skills* (2nd ed.). New York: McGraw-Hill.

Langdon, H. W. (1992). Speech and language assessment of LEP/bilingual Hispanic students. In H. W. Langdon and L. L. Cheng (Eds.), *Hispanic children and adults with communication disorders* (pp. 201–271). Gaithersburg, MD: Aspen Publishers.

Langer, J. A. (1981). From theory to practice: A prereading plan. *Journal of Reading, 25*(2), 152–156.

Langer, J. A., and Nicolich, M. (1981). Prior knowledge and its effects on comprehension. *Journal of Reading Behavior, 13,* 375–378.

Lankford, F. G. (1974). *Some computational strategies in seventh grade pupils.* Unpublished manuscript, University of Virginia.

Lardieri, L. A., Blacher, J., and Swanson, H. L. (2000). Sibling relationships and parent stress in families of children with and without learning disabilities, *Learning Disability Quarterly, 23*(2), 105–116.

Larkin, M. J., and Ellis, E. S. (1998). Adolescents with learning disabilities. In B. Y. L. Wong (Ed.). *Learning about learning disabilities* (2nd ed., pp. 557–584). San Diego: Academic Press.

Larsen, S. (1995). What is "quality" in the use of technology for children with learning disabilities? *Learning Disability Quarterly, 18,* 118–130.

Larsen, S. C., Parker, R., and Trenholme, B. (1978). The effects of syntactic complexity upon arithmetic performance. *Learning Disability Quarterly, 1*(4), 80–85.

Lazar, Warr-Leeper, Nicholson, and Johnson, (1989). Use of figurative language in classrooms. *ELT Journal, 50,* 43–51.

Leadholm, B., and Miller, J. (1992). *Language sample analysis: The Wisconsin guide.* Madison, WI: Bureau for Exceptional Children, Wisconsin Department of Public Education.

Lederer, J. M. (2000). Reciprocal teaching of social studies in inclusive elementary classrooms. *Journal of Learning Disabilities, 33,* 51–106.

Lee, C. P. (1992). *Taxonomic and frequency associations in memory in learning disabled and non-disabled children.* Unpublished doctoral dissertation, University of Arizona, Tucson.

Legenza, A. (1974). *Questioning behavior of kindergarten children.* Paper presented at the 19th Annual Convention, International Reading Association.

Leinhardt, G., Zigmond, N., and Cooley, W. W. (1981). Reading instruction and its effects. *American Education Research Journal, 18,* 343–366.

Lennox, C., and Siegel, L. S. (1996). The development of phonological rules and visual strategies in average and poor spellers. *Journal of Experimental Child Psychology, 62,* 60–83.

Lennox, C., and Siegel, L. S. (1998). Phonological and orthographic processes in good and poor spellers. In C. Hulme and R. M. Joshi (Eds.), *Reading and spelling development and disorders* (pp. 395–404). Mahwah, NJ: Erlbaum Associates.

Lenz, B. K. (1983). Promoting active learning through effective instruction: Using advance organizers. *Pointer, 27*(2), 11–13.

Lenz, B. K., Alley, G. R., and Schumaker, J. B. (1987). Activating the inactive learner: Advance organizers in the secondary content classroom. *Learning Disability Quarterly, 10*(10), 53–67.

Lenz, B. K., and Bulgren, J. A. (1995). Promoting learning in content classes. In P. A. Cegleka and W. H. Berdine (Eds.), *Effective instruction for students with learning problems* (pp. 385–417). Boston: Allyn and Bacon.

Lenz, B. K., Ehren, B. J., and Smiley, L. R. (1991). A goal attainment approach to improve completion of project-type assignments by adolescents with learning disabilities. *Learning Disabilities Research and Practice, 6,* 165–176.

Lenz, B. K., Ellis, E. S., and Scanlon, D. (1996). *Teaching learning strategies to adolescents and adults with learning disabilities.* Austin, TX: PRO-ED.

Lenz, B. K., and Hughes, C. A. (1990). A word identification strategy for adolescents with learning disabilities. *Journal of Learning Disabilities, 23*(3), 149–158, 163.

Leon, J. A., and Pepe, H. J. (1983). Self-instructional training: Cognitive behavior modification for remediating arithmetic deficits. *Exceptional Children, 50*(1), 54–60.

Leong, C. K. (1995). Effects of on-line reading and simultaneous DECtalk auding in helping below-average and poor readers comprehend and summarize text. *Learning Disability Quarterly, 18,* 101–117.

Lerner, J. W. (2000). *Learning disabilities: Theories, diagnosis, and teaching strategies* (8th ed.). Boston: Houghton Mifflin.

Levine, M. P. (1987). *Student eating disorders: Anorexia nervosa and bulimia.* Washington, DC: National Education Association.

Levy, B. A., and Lysynchuk, L. (1997). Beginning word recognition: Benefits of training by segmentation and whole word methods. *Scientific Studies of Reading, 1,* 359–387.

Lewis, S. K., and Lawrence-Patterson, E. (1989). Locus of control of children with learning disabilities and perceived locus of control by significant others. *Journal of Learning Disabilities, 22,* 255–257.

Lian M. J., and Aloia, G. F. (1994). Parental responses, roles, and responsibilities. In S. K. Alper, P. J. Schloss, and C. N. Schloss, *Families of students with disabilities* (pp. 51–94). Needham Heights, MA: Allyn and Bacon.

Liberman, I., and Shankweiler, D. (1979). Speech, the alphabet, and teaching of reading. In L. Resnick and P. Weavers (Eds.), *Theory and practice in early reading* (vol. 2, pp. 109–132). Hillsdale, NJ: Erlbaum.

Liberman, I. Y., and Shankweiler, D. (1987). Phonology and the problems of learning to read and write. In H. L. Swanson (Ed.), *Advances in learning and behavioral disabilities* (Supplement 2, pp. 203–224). Greenwich, CT: JAI Press.

Licht, B. G. (1983). Cognitive-motivational factors that contribute to the achievement of learning disabled children. *Journal of Learning Disabilities, 16*, 483–489.

Lindamood, P. A., and Lindamood, P. (1998). *The Lindamood phoneme sequencing program for reading, spelling, and speech: The LiPS program.* Austin, TX: PRO-ED.

Lindsay, E. R. (1979). This is your life: An applied mathematics curriculum for young adults. In S. Sharron and R. E. Reys (Eds.), *Applications in school mathematics* (1979 Yearbook). Reston, VA: National Council of Teachers of Mathematics.

Link, D. (1980). *Essential learning skills and the low achieving student at the secondary level: A rating of the importance of 24 academic abilities.* Unpublished master's thesis, University of Kansas, Lawrence.

Lloyd, J. W. (1980). Academic instruction and cognitive behavior modification: The need for attack strategy training. *Exceptional Educational Quarterly, 1*(1), 53–64.

Loban, W. (1976). *Language development: Kindergarten through grade twelve* (Res. Report #18). Urbana, IL: National Council of Teachers of English.

Lock, C. (1981). *Study skills.* West Lafayette, IN: Kappa Delta Pi.

Loftus, G., and Loftus, E. R. (1976). *Human memory.* Hillsdale, NJ: Erlbaum.

Lovett, M. W., Borden, S. L., Warren-Chaplin, P. M., Lacerenza, L., DeLuca, T., and Giovinazzo, R. (1996). Text comprehension training for disabled readers: An evaluation of reciprocal teaching and text analysis training programs. *Brain and Language, 54*, 477–480.

Lovitt, T. C., and Horton, S. V. (1994). Strategies for adapting science textbooks for youth with learning disabilities. *Remedial and Special Education, 15*, 105–116.

Lucangeli, D., Galderisi, D., and Cornoldi, C. (1995). Specific and general transfer effects following metamemory training. *Learning Disabilities Research and Practice, 10*, 11–21.

Lyerla, K. D., Schumaker, J. B., and Deshler, D. D. (1994). *The paragraph writing strategy* (rev. ed.). Lawrence, KS: Edge Enterprises.

Lynch, E. W., and Stein, R. (1982). Perspectives on parent participation in special education. *Exceptional Education Quarterly, 3*(2), 56–63.

Lynch, P. (1986). *Big books and predictable books.* New York: Scholastic.

Lyon, G. R. (1985). Identification and remediation of learning disability subtypes: Preliminary findings. *Learning Disabilities Focus, 1*, 21–35.

Lyon, G. R. (1995). Research initiatives in learning disabilities: Contributions from scientists supported by the National Institute of Child Health and Human Development. *Journal of Child Neurology, 10*, S121–S126.

Lyon, G. R. (1998). *Congressional testimony: Reading Research.* Committee on Labor and Human Resources Washington, DC.

MacArthur, C. (1994). Peers + word processing + strategies: A powerful strategy for revising student writing. *Teaching Exceptional Children, 27*(l), 24–29.

MacArthur, C. (1996). Using technology to enhance the writing processes of students with learning disabilities. *Journal of Learning Disabilities, 29*, 344–354.

MacArthur, C., Graham, S., Haynes, J., and DeLaPaz, S. (1996). Spelling checkers and students with learning disabilities: Performance comparisons and impact on spelling. *Journal of Special Education, 30*, 35–57.

MacArthur, C., Graham, S., and Schwartz, S. (1991). Knowledge of revision and revising behavior among learning disabled students. *Learning Disability Quarterly, 14*, 61–73.

MacArthur, C., Graham, S., and Schwartz, S. (1993). Integrating word processing and strategy instruction into a process approach to writing. *School Psychology Review, 22*, 671–681.

MacArthur, C., Graham, S., Schwartz, S., and Schafer, W. D. (1995). Evaluation of a writing instruction model that integrated a process approach, strategy instruction, and word processing. *Learning Disability Quarterly, 18*, 278–291.

MacArthur, C. A., and Schwartz, S. S. (1990). *Preliminary evaluation of the Computers and Writing Instruction Project,* (Technical Report 301). College Park: University of Maryland, Institute for the Study of Exceptional Children and Youth.

MacArthur, C. A., Schwartz, S. S., and Graham, S. (1991). A model for writing instruction: Integrating word processing and strategy instruction into a process approach to writing. *Learning Disabilities Research and Practice, 6*(4), 230–236.

MacArthur, C. A., Schwartz, S. S., Graham, S., Molloy, D., and Harris, K. (1996). Integration of strategy instruction into a whole-language classroom: A case study. *Learning Disabilities Research and Practice, 11*, 168–176.

Maccini, P., and Hughes, C. A. (1997). Mathematics interventions for adolescents with learning disabilities. *Learning Disabilities Research & Practice, 12*(3), 168–176.

MacWilliams, L. J. (1978). Mobility board games: Not only for rainy days. *Teaching Exceptional Children, 11*(1), 22–25.

Maheady, L., Harper, G. F., and Sacca, M. K. (1988). Peer mediated instruction: A promising approach to meeting the needs of learning disabled adolescents. *Learning Disability Quarterly, 11*, 108–113.

Majsterek, D. J. (1990). Writing disabilities: Is word processing the answer? *Intervention in School and Clinic, 26*, 93–97.

Majsterek, D. J., and Wilson, R. (1989). Computer-assisted instruction for students with learning disabilities: Considerations for practitioners. *Learning Disabilities Focus, 5*(1), 18–27.

Malone, L. D., and Mastropieri, M. A. (1992). Reading comprehension instruction: Summarization and self-monitoring training for students with learning disabilities. *Exceptional Children, 58*, 270–279.

Mandler, J. M., and Johnson, N. S. (1977). Rememberance of things passed: Story structure and recall. *Cognitive Psychology, 9*, 111–151.

Mandoli, M., Mandoli, P., and McLaughlin, T. F. (1982). Effects of same-age peer tutoring on the spelling performance of a mainstreamed elementary learning disabled student. *Learning Disability Quarterly, 5*(2), 185–189.

Mann, V. (1991). Language problems: A key to early reading problems. In B. Y. L. Wong (Ed.), *Learning about learning disabilities* (pp. 129–162). San Diego, CA: Academic Press.

Manzo, A. V. (1969). The request procedure. *Journal of Reading, 13*, 123–126.

Manzo, A., and Manzo, U. (1990). *Content area reading: A heuristic approach.* Columbus, OH: Merrill.

Manzo, A. V., and Manzo, U. C. (1993). *Literacy disorders: Holistic diagnosis and remediation.* Fort Worth: Harcourt Brace Jovanovich.

Margalit, M., Raviv, A., and Ankonina, D. B. (1992). Coping and coherence among parents with disabled children. *Journal of Clinical Child Psychology, 21*(3), 202–209.

Maria, K. (1989). Developing disadvantaged children's background knowledge interactively. *The Reading Teacher, 42,* 296–300.

Mariage, T. V. (2000). Constructing educational possibilities: A sociolinguistic examination of meaning-making in "sharing chair." *Learning Disability Quarterly, 23,* 79–103.

Markham, L. (1976). Influence of handwriting quality on teacher evaluation of written work. *American Educational Research Journal, 13,* 277–283.

Marsh, L. G., and Cooke, N. L. (1996). The effects of using manipulatives in teaching math problem solving to students with learning disabilities. *Learning Disabilities Research and Practice, 11,* 58–65.

Martin, B., Jr. (1983). *Brown bear, brown bear, what do you see?* New York: Holt.

Martin, J. E., and Marshall, L. H. (1995). Choicemaker: A comprehensive self-determination transition program. *Intervention in School and Clinic, 30,* 147–156.

Martinez-Roldan, C. M., and Lopez-Robertson, J. M. (2000). Initiating literature circles in a first-grade bilingual classroom. *The Reading Teacher, 53,* 270–281.

Massaro, D. W., and Cowan, N. (1993). Information processing models: Microscopes of the mind. *Annual Review of Psychology, 44,* 383–425.

Mastropieri, M. A., Leinart, A., and Scruggs, T. E. (1999). Strategies to increase reading fluency. *Intervention in School and Clinic, 34*(5), 278–283.

Mastropieri, M. A., and Scruggs, T. E. (1989). Reconstructive elaborations: Strategies that facilitate content learning. *Learning Disabilities Focus, 4,* 73–77.

Mastropieri, M. A., and Scruggs, T. E. (1997). Best practices in promoting reading comprehension in students with learning disabilities: 1976–1996. *Remedial and Special Education, 18,* 197–213.

Mastropieri, M. A., and Scruggs, T. E. (1998). Constructing more meaningful relationships in the classroom: Mnemonic research into practice. *Learning Disabilities Research and Practice, 13*(3), 138–145.

Mastropieri, M. A., Scruggs, T. E., Hamilton, S. L., Wolfe, S., Whedon, C., and Canevaro, A. (1996). Promoting thinking skills of students with learning disabilities: Effects on recall and comprehension of expository prose. *Exceptionality, 6,* 1–11.

Mastropieri, M. A., Scruggs, T. E., and Shiah, S. (1991). Mathematics instruction for learning disabled students: A review of research. *Learning Disabilities Research and Practice, 6,* 89–98.

Mastropieri, M. A., Sweda, J., and Scruggs, T. E. (2000). Putting mnemonic strategies to work in an inclusive classroom. *Learning Disabilities Research and Practice, 15*(2), 69–74.

Mather, N. (1992). Whole language reading instruction for students with learning disabilities: Caught in the crossfire. *Learning Disabilities Research and Practice, 7,* 87–95.

Mathes, P. A., and Fuchs, L. S. (1994). The efficacy of peer tutoring in reading for students with mild disabilities: A best-evidence synthesis. *School Psychology Review, 23,* 59–80.

Mathes, P. G., Grek, M. L., Howard, J. K., Babyak, A. E., and Allen, S. H. (1999). Peer-assisted learning strategies for first-grade readers: A tool for preventing early reading failure. *Learning Disabilities Research and Practice, 14,* 50–60.

Maxwell, J. C., and Liu, L. Y. (1998). Texas school survey of substance use among students: Grades 7–12. (ERIC Document Reproduction No. 429256). Austin, TX: Texas commission on alcohol and drug abuse.

Mayer, R. E. (1979). Twenty years of research on advance organizers: Assimilation theory is still the best predictor of results. *Instructional Science, 8,* 133–167.

McCauley, J. K., and McCauley, D. S. (1992). Using choral reading to promote language learning for ESL students. *The Reading Teacher, 45,* 526–533.

McCormick, S. (1992). Disable readers' erroneous responses to inferential comprehension questions: Description and analysis. *Reading Research Quarterly, 27,* 54–77.

McCormick, S., and Cooper, J. O. (1991). Can SQ3R facilitate secondary learning disabled students' literal comprehension of expository text? Three experiments. *Reading Psychology, 12,* 239–271.

McDonough, K. M. (1989). Analysis of the expressive language characteristics of emotionally handicapped students in social interactions. *Behavior Disorders, 14,* 127–139.

McGregor, K. K., and Leonard, L. B. (1989). Facilitating word-finding skills of language-impaired children. *Journal of Speech and Hearing Disorders, 54,* 141–147.

McIntosh, R., Vaughn, S., and Bennerson, D. (1995). FAST social skills training for students with learning disabilities. *Teaching Exceptional Children, 28,* 37–41.

McIntosh, R., Vaughn, S., Schumm, J., Haager, D., and Lee, O. (1993). Observations of students with learning disabilities in general education classrooms: You don't bother me and I won't bother you. *Exceptional Children, 60,* 249–261.

McIntosh, R., Vaughn, S., and Zaragoza, N. (1991). A review of social interventions for students with learning disabilities. *Journal of Learning Disabilities, 24*(8), 451–458.

McIntyre, C. W., and Pickering, J. S. (1995). *Clinical studies of multisensory structured language education for students with dyslexia and related disorders.* Poughkeepsie, NY: Hamco Corporation.

McKenzie, R. G. (1991). Content area instruction delivered by secondary learning disabilities teachers: A national survey. *Learning Disability Quarterly, 14,* 115–122.

McKeown, M. G., and Beck, I. L. (1988). Learning vocabulary: Different ways for different goals. *Remedial and Special Education, 9*(1), 42–52.

McKeown, M. G., Beck, I. S., Sinatra, G. M., and Loxterman, J. A. (1992). The contribution of prior knowledge and coherent text to comprehension. *Reading Research Quarterly, 27,* 78–93.

McKinley, N., and Larson, V. L. (1991, November). *Seven, eighth, and ninth graders' conversations in two experimental condi-*

tions. Paper presented at the annual convention of the American Speech-Language-Hearing Association, Atlanta.

McKinney, J. D., and Hocutt, A. M. (1982). Public school involvement of parents of learning disabled and average achievers. *Exceptional Education Quarterly, 3*(2), 64–73.

McKinney, J. D., and Hocutt, A. M. (1988). Policy issues in the evaluation of the regular education initiative. *Learning Disabilities Focus, 4,* 15–23.

McKinney, J. D., McClure, S., and Feagans, L. (1982). Classroom behavior of learning disabled children. *Learning Disabilities Quarterly, 5,* 45–52.

McKinney, J., Montague, M., and Hocutt, A. (1993). Educational assessment of students with attention deficit disorder. *Exceptional Children, 60,* 125–131.

McLoughlin, J. A., and Senn, C. (1994). Siblings of children with disabilities. In Alper, S. K., Schloss, P. J., and Schloss, C. N. (1994). *Families of students with disabilities* (pp. 95–122). Needham Heights, MA: Allyn and Bacon.

McNaughton, D., Hughes, C., and Ofiesh, N. (1997). Proofreading for students with learning disabilities: Integrating computer and strategy use. *Learning Disabilities Research and Practice, 12*(1), 16–28.

Meichenbaum, D. (1977). *Cognitive-behavior modification: An integrative approach.* New York: Plenum.

Meichenbaum, D. (1983). Teaching thinking: A cognitive-behavioral approach. In *Interdisciplinary voices in learning disabilities and remedial education.* Austin, TX: PRO-ED.

Meichenbaum, D. (1985). *Stress inoculation training: A clinical guidebook.* Elmsford, NY: Pergamon Press.

Menke, P. J., and Pressley, M. (1994). Elaborative interrogation: Using "why" questions to enhance the learning from text. *Journal of Reading, 37,* 642–645.

Menyuk, P. (1971). *The acquisition and development of language.* Englewood Cliffs, NJ: Prentice-Hall.

Mercer, C. D., and Mercer, A. R. (1989). *Teaching students with learning problems* (3rd ed.). Columbus, OH: Merrill.

Mercer, C. D., and Mercer, A. R. (1993). *Teaching students with learning problems* (4th ed.). New York: Merrill/ Macmillan.

Mercer, C. D., Mercer, A. R., and Bott, D. A. (1984). *Self-correcting learning materials for the classroom.* Columbus, OH: Merrill.

Merrel, K. W., and Stein, S. (1992). Behavior problems of learning-disabled, low-achieving, and average boys: A comparative study with the Conners Teacher Ratings Scales-28. *Journal of Psychoeducational Assessment, 10,* 76–82.

Merritt, D. D., and Culatta, B. (1998). *Language intervention in the classroom.* San Diego: Singular Press.

Mesmer, H. A. E., (1999). Scaffolding a crucial transition using text with some decodability. *The Reading Teacher, 53*(2), 130–142.

Meyer, C. A. (1978). Reviewing the literature on Fernald's technique of remedial reading. *The Reading Teacher, 31,* 614–619.

Meyer, M. S., and Felton, R. H. (1999). Repeated reading to enhance fluency: Old approaches and new directions. *Annals of Dyslexia, 49,* 283–306.

Michenbaum, D., and Biemiller, A. (1998). *Nurturing independent learners: Helping students take change of their learning.* Cambridge, MA: Brookline Books.

Miller, D. E. (1992), Math across America. *Teaching Exceptional Children, 24*(2), 47–49.

Mills, H., O'Keefe, T., and Stephens, D. (1992). *Looking closely: Exploring the role of phonics in one whole language classroom.* Urbana, IL: National Council of Teachers of English.

Misra, A. (1994). Partnership with Multicultural Families. In Alper, S. K., Schloss, P. J., and Schloss, C. N. (1994). *Families of students with disabilities* (pp. 143–176). Needham Heights, MA: Allyn and Bacon.

Misspeller's Dictionary. (1983). New York: Simon and Schuster.

Moats, L. C. (1995). *Spelling: Development, disability, and instruction.* Baltimore, MD: York Press.

Moats, L. C. (2000). *Speech to print: Language essentials for teachers.* Baltimore, MD: Paul H. Brookes.

Moll, L. C. (1990). Introduction. In L. C., Moll (Ed.), *Vygotsky and education: Instructional implications and applications of sociohistorical psychology* (pp. 1–27). Cambridge: Cambridge University Press.

Moll, L. C. (1994). Literacy research in community and classrooms: A sociocultural approach. In R. B. Ruddell, M. R. Ruddell, and H. Singer (Eds.), *Theoretical models and processes of reading* (pp. 179–207). Newark, DE: International Reading Association.

Montague, M., and Bos, C. S. (1990). Cognitive and metacognitive characteristics of eighth grade students' mathematical problem solving. *Learning and Individual Differences, 2,* 371–388.

Moody, S. W., Vaughn, S., and Schumm, J. S. (1997). Instructional grouping for reading: Teachers' views. *Remedial and Special Education 18*(6), 347–356.

Moore, J., and Fine, M. J. (1978). Regular and special class teachers' perceptions of normal and exceptional children and their attitudes toward mainstreaming. *Psychology in the Schools, 15*(2), 253–259.

Moran, M. (1980). *An investigation of the demands on oral language skills of learning disabled students in secondary classrooms* (Res. Rep. 1). Lawrence: University of Kansas, Institute for Research in Learning Disabilities.

Morgan, H. (1980). How schools fail black children. *Social Policy, 10*(4), 49–54.

Morgan, S. R. (1986). Locus of control in children labeled learning disabled, behaviorally disordered, and learning disabled/ behaviorally disordered. *Learning Disabilities Research, 2,* 10–13.

Morocco, C. C., Dalton, B., and Tivnan, T. (1992). The impact of computer-supported writing instruction on 4th grade students with and without learning disabilities. *Reading and Writing Quarterly: Overcoming Learning Disabilities, 8,* 87–113.

Morrison, G. M., Walker, D., Wakefield, P., and Solberg, S. (1994). Teacher preferences for collaborative relationships: Relationship to efficacy for teaching in prevention-related domains. *Psychology in the Schools, 31,* 221–231.

Morrow, L. M. (1992). The impact of a literature-based program on literacy achievement, use of literature, and attitudes of children from minority backgrounds. *Reading Research Quarterly, 25,* 251–275.

Mosberg, L., and Johns, D. (1994). Reading and listening comprehension in college students with developmental dyslexia. *Learning Disabilities Research and Practice, 9,* 130–135.

Moss, J. F. (1984). *Focus units in literature: A handbook for elementary school teacher.* Urbana, IL: National Council of Teachers of English.

Muma, J. (1986). *Language acquisition: A functional perspective.* Austin, TX: PRO-ED.

Murphy, J., Hern, C., Williams, R., and McLaughlin, T. (1990). The effects of the copy, cover, compare approach in increasing spelling accuracy with learning disabled students. *Contemporary Educational Psychology, 15,* 378–386.

Murphy, S., and Walsh, J. (1989). Economics and the real life connections. *Social Studies and Young Learner, 2,* 6–8.

Murray, D. (1984). *Write to learn.* New York: Holt, Rinehart and Winston.

Murray, D. (1985). *A writer teaches writing.* Boston: Houghton Mifflin.

Muter, V., and Snowling, M. (1998). Concurrent and longitudinal predictors of reading: The role of metalinguistic and short-term memory skills. *Reading Research Quarterly, 33,* 320–337.

Muth, K. D. (1987). Teachers' connection questions: Prompting student to organize text idea. *Journal of Reading, 31,* 254–259.

Nagel, B. R., Schumaker, J. B., and Deshler, D. D. (1994). *The FIRST-letter mnemonic strategy* (rev. ed.). Lawrence, KS: Edge Enterprises.

National Council of Supervisors of Mathematics. (1977). *Position paper on basic mathematical skills.* Minneapolis, MN: National Council of Supervisors of Mathematics.

National Council of Teachers of Mathematics. (2000). Principles and Standards for School Mathematics [On-line]. Available: http://www.nctm.org/standards/

National Council on Disability. (2000). *Back to school on civil rights: Advancing the federal commitment to leave no child behind.* Washington, DC: Author.

National Reading Panel. (2000). *Teaching children to read: An evidence-based assessment of the scientific research literature on reading and its implications for reading instruction.* Bethesda, MD: National Institute of Child Health and Human Development, National Institutes of Health.

National Research Council. (1989). *Everybody counts: A report to the nation on the future of mathematics education.* Washington, DC: National Academy Press.

NCTM. (December 1974). NCTM board approves policy statement of the use of minicalculators in the mathematics classroom. *NCTM Newsletter,* p. 3.

Neisser, U. (1967). *Cognitive psychology.* New York: Appleton.

Neisser, U. (1976). *Cognition and reality: Principles and implications of cognitive psychology.* San Francisco: Freeman.

Nelson, A. (1998). *A long hard day on the ranch.* Buffalo, NY: Firefly Books Limited.

Nelson, J. R., Smith, D. J., Young, R. K., and Dodd, J. M. (1991). A review of self-management outcome research conducted with students who exhibit behavioral disorders. *Behavioral Disorders, 16,* 169–179.

Nelson, N. W. (1998). *Childhood language disorders in context: Infancy through adolescence* (2nd ed.). Boston: Allyn and Bacon.

Nelson, O. G., and Linek, W. M. (Eds.) (1999). *Practical classroom applications of language experience: Looking back, looking forward.* Boston: Allyn and Bacon.

Nevin, A. (1998). Curricular and instructional adaptations for including students with disabilities in cooperative groups. In J. W. Putnam (Ed.), *Cooperative Learning and strategies for inclusion* (pp. 49–66). Baltimore, MD: Paul H. Brookes Publishing.

Newland, E. (1932). An analytic study of the development of illegibilities in handwriting from the lower grades to adulthood. *Journal of Educational Research, 26,* 249–258.

Nippold, M. A. (1992). The nature of normal and disordered word finding in children and adolescents. *Topics in Language Disorders, 13*(1), 1–14.

Nippold, M. A. (1993). Adolescents language developmental markers in adolescent language: Syntax, semantics, and pragmatics. *Language, Speech, and Hearing Services in Schools, 24,* 21–28.

Nippold, M. A. (1998). *Later language development: The school-age and adolescent years.* Austin, TX: PRO-ED.

Nolet, V., and Tindal, G. (1993). Special education in content area classes: Development of a model and practical procedures. *Remedial and Special Education, 14*(1), 36–48.

Norton, D. E. (1987). *Through the eyes of a child: An introduction to children's literature* (2nd ed.). Columbus, OH: Merrill.

Nulman, J. H., and Gerber, M. M. (1984). Improving spelling performance by imitating a child's errors. *Journal of Learning Disabilities, 17,* 328–333.

O'Brien, C. A. (1973). *Teaching the language-different child to read.* Columbus, OH: Merrill.

O'Brien, D. G., Stewart, R. A., and Moje, E. B. (1995). Why content literacy is difficult to infuse into the secondary school: Complexities of curriculum, pedagogy, and school culture. *Reading Research Quarterly, 30,* 442–465.

O'Connor, R. (2000). Increasing the intensity of intervention in kindergarten and first grade. *Learning Disabilities Research and Practice, 15,* 43–54.

O'Connor, R. E., and Jenkins, J. R. (1995). Improving the generalization of sound/symbol knowledge: Teaching spelling to kindergarten children with disabilities. *Journal of Special Education, 29,* 255–275.

O'Connor, R. E., Notari-Syverson, A., and Vadasy, P. F. (1998). *Ladders to literacy: A kindergarten activity book.* Baltimore, MD: Brookes.

O'Connor, S. C., and Spreen, O. (1988). The relationship between parents' socioeconomic status and education level, and adult occupational and educational achievement of children with learning disabilities. *Journal of Learning Disabilities 21*(3), 148–153.

Ogle, D. M. (1986). K-W-L: A teaching model that develops active reading of expository text. *The Reading Teacher, 39,* 564–570.

Ogle, D. M. (1989). The know, want to know, learn strategy. In K. D. Muth (Ed.), *Children's comprehension of text: Re-*

search into practice (pp. 205–233). Newark, DE: International Reading Association.

Okolo, C. M. (1992). The effects of computer-based attribution retraining on the attributions, persistence, and mathematics computation of students with learning disabilities. *Journal of Learning Disabilities, 25,* 327–334.

Okolo, C. M., Cavalier, A. R., Reffetti, R. P., and MacArthur, C. A. (2000). Technology, literacy, and disabilities: A review of the research. In R. Gersten, E. Schiller, and S. Vaughn (Eds.), *Contemporary special education research: Syntheses of the knowledge based on critical instructional issues* (pp. 179–250). Mawah, NJ: Erlbaum.

Olson, R. K., and Wise, B. W. (1992). Reading on the computer with orthographic and speech feedback: An overview of the Colorado remediation project. *Reading and Writing, 4*(2), 107–144.

Oppenheim, J., Brenner, B., and Doegenhold, B. D. (1986). *Choosing books for kids: Choosing the right book for the right child at the right time.* New York: Ballantine Books.

Orton, S. T. (1937). *Reading, writing, and speech problems in children.* New York: W. W. Norton.

O'Shea, D. J., Williams, A., and Sattler, R. O. (1999). Collaboration across special education and general education: Preservice teacher's views. *Journal of Teacher Education, 50*(2), 147–158.

O'Shea, L. J., Sindelar, P. T., and O'Shea, D. J. (1987). The effects of repeated readings and attentioned cues on the reading fluency and comprehension of learning disabled readers. *Learning Disabilities Research, 2,* 103–109.

Ovander, C. J., and Collier, V. P. (1998). Bilingual and ESL classrooms: Teaching in multicultural contexts. Boston: McGraw Hill.

Owens, Jr., R. E. (1999). *Language disorders: A functional approach to assessment and intervention* (3rd ed.). New York: Merrill/Macmillan.

Owens, Jr., R. E. (2001). *Language development: An introduction* (5th ed.). Boston: Allyn and Bacon.

Paddock, C. (1992). Ice cream stick math. *Teaching Exceptional Children, 24*(2), 50–51.

Palincsar, A. S. (1982). Improving the reading comprehension of junior high students through the reciprocal teaching of comprehension-monitoring. Unpublished doctoral dissertation, University of Illinois, Urbana.

Palincsar, A. S. (1986). The role of dialogue in providing scaffolded instruction. *Educational Psychologist, 21*(1–2), 73–98.

Palincsar, A. S. (1988). *Reciprocal teaching instructional materials packet.* East Lansing: Michigan State University.

Palincsar, A. S., and Brown, A. L. (1984). Reciprocal teaching of comprehension fostering and comprehension monitoring activities. *Cognition and Instruction, 1*(2), 117–175.

Palincsar, A. S., and Brown, A. L. (1986). Interactive teaching to promote independent learning from text. *The Reading Teacher, 39*(8), 771–777.

Palincsar, A. S., and Brown, D. A. (1987). Enhancing instructional time through attention to metacognition. *Journal of Learning Disabilities, 20*(2), 66–75.

Palmatier, R. A. (1973). A note-taking system for learning. *Journal of Reading, 17,* 36–39.

Palmatier, R. A., and Ray, H. L. (1989). *Sports talk: A dictionary of sports metaphors.* New York: Greenwood.

Parmar, R. S., and Cawley, J. F. (1997). Preparing teachers to teach mathematics to students with learning disabilities. *Journal of Learning Disabilities, 30*(2), 188–197.

Parsons, J. A. (1972). The reciprocal modification of arithmetic behavior and program development. In G. Semb (Ed.), *Behavior analysis and education.* Lawrence: University of Kansas, Department of Human Development.

Partington, G. (1998, April). *Power, discipline and minority students in high school.* Paper presented at the 1998 annual meeting of the American Educational Research Association, San Diego, CA.

Paterson, K. (1978). *The great Gilly Hopkins.* New York: Crowell.

Patterson, J. H., and Smith, M. S. (1986). The role of computers in higher-order thinking. In J. A. Culbertson and L. L. Cunningham (Eds.), *Microcomputers and education.* Eighty-fifth Yearbook of the National Society for the Study of Education (pp. 81–108). Chicago: University of Chicago Press.

Patton, J. R., Cronin, M. E., Bassett, D. S., and Koppel, A. E. (1997). A life skills approach to mathematics instruction: Preparing students with learning disabilities for the real-life math demands of adulthood. *Journal of Learning Disabilities, 30*(2), 178–187.

Patton, J. R., Cronin, M. E., and Jairrels, V. (1997). Curricular implications of transition: Life skills instruction as an integral part of transition education. *Remedial and Special Education, 18,* 294–306.

Patton, J. R., Cronin, M. E., and Wood, S. (1999). *Infusing real-life topics into existing curricula at the elementary, middle, and high school levels: Recommended procedures and instructional examples.* Austin, TX: PRO-ED.

Patton, J. R., and Dunn, C. (1998). *Transition from school to young adulthood: Basic concepts and recommended practices.* Austin, TX: PRO-ED.

Pauk, W. (1974). *How to study in college* (2nd ed.). Boston: Houghton Mifflin.

Pauk, W. (2001). *Essential study strategies.* Columbus, OH: Prentice Hall.

Paulson, F. L., Paulson, P. R., and Meyer, C. A. (1991). What makes a portfolio a portfolio? *Educational Leadership, 48*(5), 60–63.

Pavri, S., and Monda-Amaya, L. (2000). Loneliness and students with learning disabilities in inclusive classrooms: Self-perceptions, coping strategies, and preferred interventions. *Learning Disabilities Research and Practice,15*(1), 22–33.

Pea, R. D., Kurland, M., and Hawkins, J. (1987). Logo and the development of thinking skills. In R. D. Pea, and K. Sheingold (Eds.), *Mirrors of minds: Patterns of experience in educational computing* (pp. 178–197). Norwood, NJ: Ablex.

Pea, R. D., and Sheingold, K. (Eds.). (1987). *Mirrors of minds: Patterns of experience in educational computing.* Norwood, NJ: Ablex.

Pearl, R., Bryan, T., Fallon, P., and Herzog, A. (1991). Learning disabled students' detection of deception. *Learning Disabilities Research and Practice, 6,* 12–16.

Pearson, P. D. (1984). Direct explicit teaching of reading comprehension. In G. G. Duffy, L. R. Roehler, and J. Mason

(Eds.), *Comprehension instruction: Perspectives and suggestions* (pp. 222–233). New York: Longman.

Pearson, P. D., and Camperell, K. (1994). Comprehension of text structures. In R. B. Ruddell, M. R. Ruddell, and H. Singer (Eds.), *Theoretical models and process of reading* (4th ed., pp. 448–568). Newark, DE: International Reading Association.

Pearson, P. D., and Johnson, D. D. (1978). *Teaching reading comprehension.* New York: Holt, Rinehart and Winston.

Pecyna-Rhyner, P., Lehr, D., and Pudlas, K. (1990). An analysis of teacher responsiveness to communicative initiations of children with handicaps. *Language, Speech, and Hearing Services in Schools, 21,* 91–97.

Peetoom, A. (1986). *Shared reading: Safe risks with whole books.* Richmond Hill, Ontario, CA: Scholastic-TAB Publications.

Pehrsson, R. S., and Robinson, H. A. (1985). *The semantic organizer approach to writing and reading instruction.* Rockville, MD: Aspen.

Perez, B., and Torres-Guzman, M. E. (1992). *Learning in two worlds.* New York: Longman.

Perfect, K. A. (2000). Rhyme and reason: Poetry for the heart and head. *The Reading Teacher, 52,* 728–737.

Perlmutter, B. F. (1986). Personality variables and peer relations of children and adolescents with learning disabilities. In S. J. Ceci (Ed.), *Handbook of cognitive, social, and neuropsychological aspects of learning disabilities* (pp. 339–359). Hillsdale, NJ: Erlbaum.

Perry, R. P. (1999). Teaching for success: Assisting helpless students in their academic development. *Education Canada, 39*(1), 16–19.

Personkee, C., and Yee, A. (1971). *Comprehensive spelling instruction: Theory, research, and application.* Scranton, PA: Intext Educational.

Peters, T., and Austin, N. (1985). *A passion for excellence.* New York: Random House.

Pfeffer, C. R. (1986). *The suicidal child.* New York: Guilford Press.

Phillips, M. (1996). Beyond the best CDs list. *Electronic Learning, 15*(6), 16.

Pickard, S. (1990). Integrating math skills into vocational education curricula. *Journal for Vocational Special Needs Education, 13,* 9–13.

Pinel, J. P. J. (1993). *Biopsychology* (2nd ed.). Boston: Allyn and Bacon.

Pinnell, G. S., and Fountas, I. C. (1998). *Word matters: Teaching phonics and spelling in the reading/writing classroom.* Portsmouth, NH: Heinemann.

Platt, J. J., and Spivack, G. (1972). Social competence and effective problem solving thinking in psychiatric patients. *Journal of Clinical Psychiatry, 28,* 3–5.

Podhajski, B. (1999). *Time for teachers: What teachers need to know about what children need to know to learn to read.* Williston, VT: Stern Center for Language and Learning.

Polloway, E., Epstein, M., Polloway, C., Patton, J., and Ball, D. (1986). Corrective reading program: An analysis of effectiveness with learning disabled and mentally retarded students. *Remedial and Special Education, 7,* 41–47.

Pompa, D. (1998, March). *Testimony for the House Appropriations Subcommittee on Labor, Health & Human Services and Education on the fiscal year 1999 budget request.* Washington, DC: Office of Bilingual Education and Minority Languages Affairs.

Popenhagen, M. P., and Qualley, R. M. (1998). Adolescent suicide: Detection, intervention, and prevention. *Professional School Counseling, 1*(4), 30–35.

Powers, L. E. (1996). *TAKE CHARGE transition planning project.* (Grant No. HH158U50001 from the U. S. Department of Education and Oregon Health Sciences). Portland: Oregon Health Sciences University.

Premack, D. (1959). Toward empirical behavior laws. *Psychological Review, 66*(4), 219–233.

Pressley, M. (1998). *Reading instruction that works: The case for balanced teaching.* New York: Guilford.

Pressley, M. (2000). What should comprehension instruction be the instruction of? In M. L. Kamil, P. B. Mosenthal, P. D. Pearson, and R. Barr (Eds.), *Handbook of reading research,* (vol. III, pp. 545–561). Mahwah, NJ: Erlbaum Associates.

Pressley, M., Brown, R., El-Dinary, P. B., and Afflerbach, P. (1995). The comprehension instruction that students need: Instruction fostering constructively responsive reading. *Learning Disabilities Research and Practice, 10,* 215–224.

Pressley, M., El-Dinary, P. B., Gaskins, I., Schuder, T., Bergman, J., Almasi, L., and Brown, R. (1992). Beyond direct explanation: Transactional instruction of reading comprehension strategies. *Elementary School Journal, 92,* 511–554.

Pressley, M., and Rankin, J. (1994). More about whole language methods of reading instruction for students at risk for early reading failure. *Learning Disabilities Research and Practice, 9,* 156–167.

Prickett, E., Higgins, K., and Boone, R. (1994). Technology for learning . . . Not learning about technology. *Teaching Exceptional Children, 26*(4), 56–60.

Prillaman, D. (1981). Acceptance of learning disabled students in the mainstream environment: A failure to replicate. *Journal of Learning Disabilities, 14,* 344–346.

Prutting, C. (1982). Pragmatics as social competence. *Journal of Speech and Hearing Disorders, 47,* 123–124.

Pugach, M. C., and Johnson, L. J. (1995). *Collaborative practitioners, collaborative schools.* Denver, CO: Love.

Purkey, S. C., and Smith, M. S. (1985). School reform: The district policy implications of the effective schools literature. *Elementary School Journal, 85,* 353–389.

Putnam, M. L. (1992a). The testing practices of mainstream secondary classroom teachers. *Remedial and Special Education, 13*(5), 11–21.

Putnam, M. L. (1992b). Characteristics of questions on tests administered by mainstream secondary classrooms teachers. *Learning Disabilities Research and Practice, 7,* 129–136.

Putnam, M. L., Deshler, D. D., and Schumaker, J. S. (1993). The investigation of setting demands: A missing link in learning strategy instruction. In L. S. Meltzer (Ed.), *Strategy assessment and instruction for students with learning disabilities* (pp. 325–354). Austin, TX: PRO-ED.

Quigley, S. P., King, C. M., McAnally, P. L., and Rose, S. (1991). *Reading milestones: An alternative reading program.* Austin, TX: PRO-ED.

Radencich, M. C., Beers, P. C., and Schumm, J. S. (1993). *A handbook for the K–12 reading resource specialist.* Boston: Allyn and Bacon.

Raines, S. C., and Canady, R. J. (1991). *More story stretchers: More activities to expand children's favorite books.* Mt. Rainier, MD: Gryphon House.

Raphael, T. E. (1982). Question-answering strategies for children. *The Reading Teacher, 36,* 188.

Raphael, T. E. (1984). Teaching learners about sources of information for answering comprehension questions. *Journal of Reading, 27,* 303–311.

Raphael, T. E. (1986). Teaching question-answer relationships revisited. *The Reading Teacher, 39*(6), 516–523.

Raphael, T. E. (2000). Balancing literature and instruction: Lessons from the book club project. In B. M. Taylor, M. F. Graves, and P. Van den Broek (Eds.), *Reading for meaning: Fostering comprehension in the middle grades* (pp. 70–94). Newark, DE: International Reading Association.

Raphael, T. E., and Pearson, P. D. (1982). *The effect of metacognitive awareness training on children's question-answering behavior* (Tech. Rep. No. 238). Urbana: University of Illinois, Center for Study of Reading.

Rashotte, C. A., and Torgesen, J. K. (1985). Repeated reading and reading fluency in learning disabled children. *Reading Research Quarterly, 20*(2), 180–188.

Rasinski, T. V. (1990a). Effects of repeated reading and listening-while-reading on reading fluency. *Journal of Education Research, 83,* 147–150.

Rasinski, T. V. (1990b). Investigating measures of reading fluency. *Educational Research Quarterly, 14*(3), 37–44.

Raskind, M. (1993). Assistive technology and adults with learning disabilities: A blueprint for exploration and advancement. *Learning Disability Quarterly, 16,* 185–196.

Raskind, M. H., and Higgins, E. L. (1999). Speaking to read: The effects of speech recognition technology on the reading and spelling performance of children with learning disabilities. *Annals of Dyslexia, 49,* 251–281.

Read, C. (1975). *Children's categorization of speech sounds in English.* Research Report No. 17. Urbana, IL: National Council of Teacher of English.

Readence, J. E., Bean, T. W., and Baldwin, R. S. (1995). *Content area reading: An integrated approach* (5th ed.). Dubuque, IA: Kendall/Hunt.

Reed, A. J. S. (1994a). *Comics to classics: A parent's guide to books for teens and preteens.* Newark, DE: International Reading Association.

Reed, V. A. (1994b). *An introduction to children with language disorders* (2nd ed.). New York: Macmillan.

Reinking, D. (1988). Computer-mediated text and comprehension differences: The role of reading time, reader preference, and estimation of learning. *Reading Research Quarterly, 23,* 484–498.

Reinking, D., and Schreiner, R. (1985). The effects of computer-mediated text on measures of reading comprehension and reading behavior. *Reading Research Quarterly, 20,* 536–551.

Renik, M. J. (April 1987). *Measuring the relationship between academic self-perceptions and global self-worth: The self-perception profile for learning disabled students.* Presented at the Society for Research in Child Development, Baltimore, MD.

Reutzel, D. R., and Hollingsworth, P. M. (1993). Effects of fluency training on second graders' reading comprehension. *Journal of Educational Research, 86,* 325–331.

Reutzel, D. R., Hollingsworth, P. M., and Eldredge, J. L. (1994). Oral reading instruction: The impact on student reading development. *Reading Research Quarterly, 29,* 40–59.

Reyes, E. I., and Bos, C. S. (1998). Interactive semantic mapping and charting: Enhancing content area learning for language minority students. In R. Gersten and R. Jimenez (Eds.), *Innovative practices for language minority students* (pp. 133–150). Pacific Grove, CA: Brooks/Cole.

Reyes, E. I., Duran, G. Z., and Bos, C. S. (1989). Language as a resource for mediating comprehension. In S. McCormick and J. Zutell (Eds.), *Cognitive and social perspectives for literacy research and instruction* (Thirty-eighth yearbook of the National Reading Conference, pp. 253–260). Chicago, IL: National Reading Conference.

Reynolds, M. E., and Fucci, D. (1998). Synthetic speech comprehension: A comparison of children with normal and impaired language skills. *Journal of Speech, Language, and Hearing Research, 41,* 458–466.

Rhodes, L. K. (1981). I can read! Predictable books as resources for reading and writing instruction. *The Reading Teacher, 34,* 511–518.

Rhodes, L. K., and Dudley-Marling, C. (1996). *Readers and writers with a difference* (2nd ed.). Portsmouth, NH: Heinemann.

Richards, G. P., Samuels, S. J., Turnuree, J., and Ysseldyke, J. (1990). Sustained and selective attention in children with learning disabilities. *Journal of Learning Disabilities, 23,* 129–136.

Richards, M. (2000). Be a good detective: Solve the case of oral reading fluency. *The Reading Teacher, 53,* 534–539.

Richardson, J. E. (1971). *The linguistic readers.* New York: Benziger.

Richgels, D. J., Poremba, K. J., and McGee, L. M. (1996). Kindergartners talk about print: Phonemic awareness in meaningful contexts. *The Reading Teacher, 49,* 632–642.

Ridley, C. A., and Vaughn, S. R. (1982). Interpersonal problem solving: An intervention program for preschool children. *Journal of Applied Developmental Psychology, 3,* 177–190.

Ripley, S. (1997). *Collaboration between general and special education teachers.* (ERIC Document Reproduction Service No. ED 409 317).

Rivera, D. P., and Smith, D. D. (1997). *Teaching students with learning and behavior problems* (3rd ed.). Boston: Allyn and Bacon.

Rivera, D. P., Smith, R. G., Goodwin, M. W., and Bryant, D. P. (1998). Mathematical word problem solving: A synthesis of intervention research for students with learning disabilities. In T. E. Scruggs and M. A. *Mastropieri, Advances in learning and behavioral disabilities* (vol. 12, pp. 245–285). Greenwich, CT: JAI Press.

RMC Research Corp. (1995). *Communicating with parents. Training guides for the Head Start Learning Community.* (ERIC Document Reproduction Service No. ED 407 138).

Robb, L. (1996). *Reading strategies that work: Teaching your students to become better readers.* New York: Scholastic.

Roberts, G. H. (1968). The failure strategies of third grade arithmetic pupils. *The Arithmetic Teacher, 15,* 442–446.

Roberts, J., and Crais, E. (1989). Assessing communication skills. In D. Bailey and M. Wolery (Eds.), *Assessing infants and preschoolers with handicaps* (pp. 337–389). New York: Macmillan.

Roberts, J. M. (1999). *Effective study skills: Maximizing your academic potential.* Columbus, OH: Prentice-Hall.

Roberts, R., and Mather, N. (1995). The return of students with learning disabilities to regular classrooms: A sellout. *Learning Disabilities Research & Practice, 10,* 46–58.

Robertson, H. M. (1999). LEA and students with special needs. In O. G. Nelson and W. M. Linek (Eds.), *Practical classroom applications of language experience: Looking back, looking forward* (pp. 221–223). Boston: Allyn and Bacon.

Robinett, R. F., Bell, P. W., and Rojas, P. M. (1970). *Miami linguistic readers.* Lexington, MA: D. C. Heath.

Robinson, F. P. (1946). *Effective study.* New York: Harper and Brothers.

Rogoff, B. (1990). *Apprenticeship in thinking.* New York: Oxford University Press.

Rooney, K. J., and Hallahan, D. P. (1985). Future directions for cognitive behavior modification research: The quest for cognitive change. *Remedial and Special Education, 6*(2), 46–51.

Rooney, K. J., and Hallahan, D. P. (1988). The effects of self-monitoring on adult behavior and student independence. *Learning Disabilities Research, 3,* 88–93.

Roos, P. (1985). Parents of mentally retarded children: Misunderstood and mistreated. In H. R. Thurnbull and A. P. Turnbull (Eds.) *Parents speak out: Then and now* (pp. 245–257). Columbus, OH: Merrill Publishing Co.

Rose, T. L. (1984). The effect of two prepractice procedures on oral reading. *Journal of Learning Disabilities, 17,* 544–548.

Rose, T. L., and Beattie, J. R. (1986). Relative effects of teacher-directed and taped previewing on oral reading. *Learning Disability Quarterly, 9,* 193–199.

Rosenshine, B. (1997). Advances in research in instruction. In J. W. Lloyd, E. J. Kameenui, and D. Chard (Eds.), *Issues in educating students with disabilities.* Mahwah, NJ: Erlbaum.

Rosenshine, B., and Meister, C. (1994). Reciprocal teaching: A review of the research. *Review of Education Research, 64,* 479–530.

Roser, N. L., Hoffman, J. V., and Farest, C. (1990). Language, literature, and at-risk children. *The Reading Teacher, 43,* 554–559.

Rothman, H. R., and Casden, M. (1995). The relationship between self-perception of a learning disability and achievement, self-concept and social support. *Learning Disability Quarterly, 18,* 203–212.

Rothman, T. R., and Cross, D. R. (1990). Using informed strategies for learning to enhance the reading and thinking skills of children with learning disabilities. *Journal of Learning Disabilities, 23,* 270–278.

Rourke, B. P., and Fuerst, D. R. (1992). Psychological dimensions of learning disability subtypes: Neuropsychological studies in the Windsor Laboratory. *School Psychology Review, 21*(3), 361–74.

Rourke, B. P., Young, G. C., and Leenaars, A. A. (1989). A childhood learning disability that predisposes those afflicted to adolescent and adult depression and suicide risk. *Journal of Learning Disabilities, 22*(3), 169–175.

Routh, D. K. (1979). Activity, attention, and aggression in learning disabled children. *Journal of Clinical Child Psychology, 8,* 183–187.

Rubin, H. (1988). Morphological knowledge and early writing ability. *Language and Speech, 31,* 337–355.

Rubin, H., Patterson, P. A., and Kantor, M. (1991). Morphological development and writing ability in children and adults. *Language, Speech, and Hearing Services in School, 22,* 228–235.

Rude, R. T., and Oehlkers, W. J. (1984). *Helping students with reading problems.* Englewood Cliffs, NJ: Prentice-Hall.

Rudolph, S., and Luckner, J. L. (1991). Social skills training for students with learning disabilities. *Journal of Humanistic Education and Development, 29*(4), 163–71.

Ruedy, L. R. (1983). Handwriting instruction: It can be part of the high school curriculum. *Academic Therapy, 18*(4), 421–429.

Ruhl, K. L., Hughes, C. A., and Gajar, A. H. (1990). Efficacy of the pause procedure for enhancing learning disabled and nondisabled college students' long- and short-term recall of facts presented through lecture. *Learning Disability Quarterly, 13,* 55–64.

Ruhl, K. L., Hughes, C. A., and Schlos, P. J. (1987). Using the pause procedure to enhance lecture recall. *Teacher Education and Special Education, 10,* 14–18.

Ruiz, N. T. (1989). An optimal learning environment for Rosemary. *Exceptional Children, 56,* 130–144.

Ruiz, N. T., and Figueroa, R. A. (1995). Learning-handicapped classrooms with Latino students: The optimal learning environment (OLE) project. *Education and Urban Society, 27,* 463–483.

Ruiz, N. T, Figueroa, R. A., and Boothroyd, M. (1995). Bilingual special education teacher's shifting paradigms: Complex responses to educational reform. *Journal of Learning Disabilities, 28,* 622–635.

Ruiz, N. T., Garcia, E., and Figueroa, R. A. (1996). *The OLE curriculum guide: Creating optimal learning environments for students from diverse backgrounds in special and general education.* Sacramento, CA: Specialized Program Branch, California Department of Education.

Rumelhart, D. E. (1977). *Introduction to human information processing.* New York: John Wiley.

Rumelhart, D. E. (1980). Schemata: The building blocks of cognition. In R. J. Spiro, B. C. Bruce, and W. F. Brewer (Eds.), *Theoretical issues in reading comprehension* (pp. 33–58). Hillsdale, NJ: Erlbaum.

Rumelhart, D. E. (1985). Toward an interactive model of reading. In H. Singer and R. B. Ruddell (Eds.), *Theoretical models and processes of reading* (3rd ed.). Newark, DE: International Reading Association.

Salend, S. J. (1995). Modifying tests for diverse learners. *Intervention in School and Clinic, 31*(2), 84–90.

Salend, S. J. (2000). *Effective mainstreaming: Creating inclusive classrooms* (3rd ed). New York: Macmillan.

Salend, S. J., Jantzen, N. R., and Giek, K. (1992). Using a peer confrontation system in a group setting. *Behavioral Disorders, 17*, 211–218.

Salend, S. J., and Lutz, J. G. (1984). Mainstreaming or mainlining: A competency based approach to mainstreaming. *Journal of Learning Disabilities, 17*(1), 27–29.

Salend, S. J., and Nowak, M. R. (1988). Effects of peer-previewing on LD students' oral reading skills. *Learning Disability Quarterly, 11*, 47–53.

Samuels, S. J. (1979). The method of repeated readings. *The Reading Teacher, 32*, 403–408.

Samuels, S. J. (1987). Information processing abilities and reading. *Journal of Learning Disabilities, 20*(1), 18–22.

Samuels, S. J. (1997). The method of repeated reading. *The Reading Teacher, 50*, 376–381. Originally published in *The Reading Teacher* in January 1979, (vol. 32).

Sanger, D., Maag, J. W., and Shapera, N. R. (1994). Language problems among students with emotional and behavioral disorders. *Intervention in School and Clinic, 30*, 103–108.

Saunders, W., Goldenberg, C., and Hamann, J. (1992). Instructional conversation begets instructional conversation. *Teaching and Teacher Education, 8*, 199–218.

Sawyer, V., Nelson, J. S., Jayanthi, M., Bursuck, W., and Epstein, M. H. (1996). Views of students with learning disabilities of their homework in general education classes: Student interviews. *Learning Disability Quarterly, 19*, 70–85.

Scanlon, D. J., and Anders, P. L. (December, 1988). *Conceptual complexity and considerateness of vocation textbooks.* Paper presented at the annual meeting of the National Reading Conference, Tucson, Ariz.

Scanlon, D., Deshler, D. D., and Schumaker, J. B. (1996). Can a strategy be taught and learned in secondary inclusive classrooms? *Learning Disabilities Research and Practice, 11*, 41–57.

Scanlon, D. J., Duran, G. Z., Reyes, E. I., and Gallego, M. A. (1992). Interactive semantic mapping: An interactive approach to enhancing LD students' content area comprehension. *Learning Disabilities Research and Practice, 7*, 142–146.

Schank, R. C., and Abelson, R. (1977). *Scripts, plans, goals, and understanding.* Hillsdale, NJ: Erlbaum.

Scheuermann, B., Jacobs, W. R., McCall, C., and Knies, W. C. (1994). The personal spelling dictionary: An adaptive approach to reducing the spelling hurdle in written language. *Intervention in School and Clinic, 29*, 292–299.

Schloss, P. J., Smith, M. A., and Schloss, C. N. (2001). *Instructional methods for adolescents with learning and behavior problems* (3rd ed.). Boston: Allyn and Bacon.

Schmidt, P. R. (1999). KWLQ: Inquiry and literacy learning in science. *The Reading Teacher, 52*, 789–792.

Schultz, J. B., and Turnbull, A. P. (1984). *Mainstreaming handicapped students: A guide for classroom teachers* (2nd ed.). Boston: Allyn and Bacon.

Schultz, T. (1974). Development of the appreciation of riddles. *Child Development, 45*, 100–105.

Schumaker, J. B., Denton, P. H., and Deshler, D. D. (1993). *The paraphrasing strategy (rev. ed.) (Learning Strategies Curriculum).* Lawrence: University of Kansas.

Schumaker, J. B., and Deshler, D. D. (1988). Implementing the regular education initiative in secondary schools: A different ball game. *Journal of Learning Disabilities, 21*, 36–42.

Schumaker, J. B., Deshler, D. D., Alley, G. R., and Warner, M. M. (1983). Toward the development of an intervention model for learning disabled adolescents: University of Kansas Institute. *Exceptional Education Quarterly, 4*(1), 45–74.

Schumaker, J. B., Deshler, D. D., Alley, G. R., Warner, M. M., and Denton, P. H. (1982). Multipass: A learning strategy for improving reading comprehension. *Learning Disability Quarterly, 5*(3), 295–304.

Schumaker, J. B., Nolan, S. M., and Deshler, D. D. (1994). *The error monitoring strategy* (rev. ed.). Lawrence: Center for Research on Learning Disabilities, University of Kansas.

Schumaker, J. D., Wildgen, J. S., and Sherman, J. A. (1982). Social interaction of learning disabled junior high school students in their regular classrooms: An observational analysis. *Journal of Learning Disabilities, 11*, 98–102.

Schumm, J. S., and Mangrum, C. T. (1991). FLIP: A framework for textbook thinking. *Journal of Reading, 35*, 120–124.

Schumm, J. S., and Post, S. A. (1997). *Executive learning: successful strategies for college reading and studying.* Columbus, OH: Prentice-Hall.

Schumm, J. S., and Strickler, K. (1991). Guidelines for adapting content area textbooks: Keeping teachers and students content. *Intervention in School and Clinic, 27*, 79–84.

Schumm, J. S. and Vaughn, S. (1991). Making adaptations for mainstreamed students: General classroom teachers' perspectives. *Remedial and Special Education, 12*(4), 18–27.

Schumm, J. S., and Vaughn, S. (1992a). Planning for mainstreamed special education students: Perceptions of general classroom teachers. *Exceptionality, 3*, 81–98.

Schumm, J. S., and Vaughn, S. (1992b). Reflections on planning for mainstreamed special education students. *Exceptionality, 3*, 121–126.

Schumm, J. S., and Vaughn, S. (1995). *Using Making Words in heterogeneous classrooms.* Miami: School Based Research, University of Miami, unpublished manuscript.

Schumm, J. S, Vaughn, S., Haager, D., McDowell, J., Rothlein, L., and Saumell, L. (1995a). General education teacher planning: What can students with learning disabilities expect? *Exceptional Children, 61*(4), 335–352.

Schumm, J. S., Vaughn, S., Haager, D., McDowell, J., Rothlein, L., and Saumell, L. (1995b). Teacher planning for individual student needs: What can mainstreamed special education students expect? *Exceptional Children, 61*, 335–352.

Schumm, J. S., Vaughn, S., and Harris, J. (1997). Pyramid power for collaborative planning. *Teaching Exceptional Children, 29*(6), 62–66.

Schumm, J. S., Vaughn, S., and Leavell, A. G. (1994). Planning pyramid: A framework for planning for diverse student needs during content area instruction. *The Reading Teacher, 47*, 608–615.

Schumm, J. S., Vaughn, S., and Saumell, L. (1992). What teachers do when the textbook is tough: Students speak out. *Journal of Reading Behavior, 24,* 481–503.

Schunk, D. H. (1989). Self-efficacy and cognitive achievement: Implications for students with learning problems. *Journal of Learning Disabilities, 22,* 14–22.

Schunk, D. H. (1996). Goal and self-evaluative influences during children's cognitive skill learning. *American Education Research Journal, 33,* 359–382.

Schuster, J. W., Stevens, K. B., and Doak, P. K. (1990). Using constant time delay to teach word definitions. *Journal of Special Education, 24,* 306–318.

Schwartz, N. H., Ellsworth, L. S., Graham, L., and Knight, B. (1998). Assessing prior knowledge to remember text: A comparison of advance organizers and maps. *Contemporary Educational Psychology, 23*(1), 65–89.

Schwartz, S., and Doehring, D. (1977). A developmental study of children's ability to acquire knowledge of spelling patterns. *Developmental Psychology, 13,* 419–420.

Schwartz, S. E., and Budd, D. (1981). Mathematics for handicapped learners: A functional approach for adolescents. *Focus on Exceptional Children, 13*(7), 1–12.

Scott, C. M., and Stokes, S. L. (1995). Measures of syntax in school-age children and adolescents. *Language, Speech, and Hearing Services in Schools, 26,* 309–319.

Scruggs, T. E., and Mastropieri, M. A. (1988). Are learning disabled students "test-wise"?: A review of recent research. *Learning Disabilities Focus, 3,* 87–97.

Scruggs, T. E., and Mastropieri, M. A. (1989a). Mnemonic instruction of LD students: A field-based evaluation. *Learning Disability Quarterly, 12,* 119–125.

Scruggs, T. E., and Mastropieri, M. A. (1989b). Reconstructive elaborations: A model for content area learning. *American Educational Research Journal, 26,* 311–327.

Scruggs, T. E., and Richter, L. (1985). Tutoring learning disabled students: A critical review. *Learning Disability Quarterly, 8*(4), 286–298.

Seidel, J. F., and Vaughn, S. (1991). Social alienation and the LD school dropout. *Learning Disabilities Research and Practice, 6*(3), 152–157.

Seligman, M. E. P. (1975). *Helplessness: On depression, development, and death.* San Francisco: W. H. Freeman.

Seuss, Dr. (1974). *There's a wocket in my pocket.* New York: Random House.

Sexton, M., Harris, K. R., and Graham, S. (1998). Self-regulated strategy development and the writing process: Effects on essay writing and attributions. *Exceptional Children, 64*(3), 290–291.

Shannon, P., Kameenui, E., and Baumann, J. (1988). An investigation of children's ability to comprehend character motives. *American Educational Research Journal, 25,* 441–462.

Shany, M. T., and Biemiller, A. (1995). Assisted reading practice: Effects on performance for poor readers in grades 3 and 4. *Reading Research Quarterly, 30,* 382–395.

Shapero, S., and Forbes, C. R. (1981). A review of involvement programs for parents of learning disabled children. *Journal of Learning Disabilities, 14*(9), 499–504.

Shapiro, E. G., Lipton, M. E., and Krivit, W. (1992). White matter dysfunction and its neuropsychological correlates: A longitudinal study of a case of metachromatic leukodystrophy. *Journal of Clinical and Experimental Neuropsychology, 14*(4), 610–624.

Share, D. L., and Stanovich, K. E. (1995). Cognitive processes in early reading development: A model of acquisition and individual differences. *Issues in Education: Contributions from Education Psychology, 1,* 1–57.

Sharma, M. C. (1984). Mathematics in the real world. In J. F. Cawley (Ed.), *Developmental teaching of mathematics for learning disabled.* Rockville, MD: Aspen.

Shaywitz, S., and Shaywitz, B. (1996, November). *State of the art: Functional MRI of the brain during reading.* Paper presented at the annual meeting of the Orton Dyslexia Society, Boston.

Sheras, P. L. (1983). Suicide in adolescence. In E. Walker and M. Roberts (Eds.), *Handbook of clinical child psychology.* New York: Wiley.

Shiah, R. L., Mastropieri, M. A., Scruggs, T. E., and Fulk, B. J. (1994). The effects of computer-assisted instruction on the mathematical problem solving of students with learning disabilities. *Exceptionality, 5,* 131–161.

Shipley, E., Maddox, M., and Driver, J. (1991). Children's development of irregular past tense verb forms. *Language, Speech, and Hearing Services in Schools, 22,* 115–122.

Shipley, K. B., and Banis, C. J. (1981). *Teaching morphology developmentally.* Tucson, AZ: Communication Skill Builders.

Shondrick, D. D., Serafica, F. C., Clark, P., and Miller, K. G. (1992). *Learning Disability Quarterly, 15*(2), 95–102.

Short, K. (1997). *Literature as a way of knowing.* York, ME: Stenhouse.

Short, K. G., Harste, J. C., with Burke, C. (1995). *Creating classrooms for authors and inquirers.* Portsmouth, NH: Heinemann.

Short, K. G., and Pierce, K. M. (Eds.). (1990). *Talking about books.* Portsmouth, NH: Heinemann.

Shure, M. B., and Spivack, G. (1978). *Problem solving techniques in child-rearing.* San Francisco: Jossey-Bass.

Shure, M. B., and Spivack, G. (1979). Interpersonal cognitive problem solving and primary prevention: Programming for preschool and kindergarten children. *Journal of Clinical Child Psychology, 8,* 89–94.

Shure, M. B., and Spivack, G. (1980). Interpersonal problem solving as a mediator of behavioral adjustment in preschool and kindergarten children. *Journal of Applied Developmental Psychology, 1,* 29–44.

Sileo, T. W., Sileo, A. P., and Prater, M. A. (1996). Parent and professional partnerships in special education: Multicultural considerations. *Intervention in School and Clinic, 31*(3), 145–153.

Simeonsson, R. J., and Simeonsson, N. E. (1993). Children, families and disability: Psychological dimensions. In J. L. Paul and R. J. Simeonsson (Eds.), *Children with special needs* (pp. 25–50). Orlando, Fla.: Harcourt, Brace, Jovanovich.

Simmonds, E. P. M. (1992). The effects of teacher training and implementation of two methods for improving the comprehension skills of students with learning disabilities. *Learning Disabilities Research and Practice, 7,* 194–198.

Simmons, D., Fuchs, D., Fuchs, L. S. Hodge, J. P., and Mathes, P. G. (1994). Importance of instructional complexity and role reciprocity to classwide peer tutoring. *Learning Disabilities Research and Practice, 9,* 203–212.

Simon, C. S. (Ed.) (1985). *Communication skills and classroom success: Assessment of language-learning disabled students.* San Diego, CA: College-Hill.

Simpson, R. (1990). *Conferencing parents of exceptional children* (2nd ed.). Austin, TX: PRO-ED.

Simpson, R. L. (1982). *Conferencing parents of exceptional children.* Rockville, MD: Aspen.

Simpson, R. L. (1988). Needs of parents and families whose children have learning and behavior problems. *Behavioral Disorders, 14*(1), 40–47.

Singer, H., and Donlan, D. (1989). *Reading and learning from text* (2nd ed.). Hillsdale, NJ: Erlbaum.

Siperstein, G. N., Bopp, M. J., and Bak, J. J. (1978). Social status of learning disabled children. *Journal of Learning Disabilities, 11,* 217–228.

Siperstein, G. N., and Goding, M. J. (1985). Teachers' behavior toward learning disabled and non–learning disabled children: A strategy for change. *Journal of Learning Disabilities, 18,* 139–144.

Sitlington, P. L. (1996). Transition to living: The neglected components of transition programming for individuals with learning disabilities. *Journal of Learning Disabilities, 29,* 31–39, 52.

Sitlington, P. L., Neubert, D. A., Begun, W., Lombard, R. C., and Leconte, P. J. (1996). *Assess for success: Handbook on transition assessment.* Reston, VA: Division on Career Development and Transition, Council for Exceptional Children.

Skinner, M. E. (1991). Facilitating parental participation during individualized education program conferences. *Journal of Educational and Psychological Consultation, 2,* 285–289.

Skutnabb-Kangas, T. (1981, February). *Linguistic genocide and bilingual education.* Paper presented at the California Association for Bilingual Education, Anaheim, CA.

Slavin, R. E. (1984). Team assisted individualization: Cooperative learning and individualized instruction in the mainstreamed classroom. *Remedial and Special Education, 5*(6), 33–42.

Slavin, R. E. (1987). Cooperative learning: Where behavioral and humanistic approaches to classroom motivation meet. *Elementary School Journal, 88,* 29–37.

Slavin, R. E. (1991). Synthesis of research on cooperative learning. *Educational Leadership, 48*(5), 71–82.

Slavin, R. E. (2000). *Educational psychology: Theory and practice.* Boston: Allyn and Bacon.

Slavin, R. E., Stevens, R. J., and Madden, N. A. (1988). Accommodating student diversity in reading and writing instruction: A cooperative learning approach. *Remedial and Special Education, 9*(1), 60–66.

Slingerland, B. H., and Aho, M. (1994–96). *Multi-sensory approach to language arts for specific language disability children* (vols. 1–3, rev. ed.). Cambridge, MA: Educators Publishing Service.

Sloan, G. D. (1984). *The child as critic* (2nd ed.). New York: Teachers College Press.

Smith, C. R. (1998). From gibberish to phonemic awareness: Effective decoding instruction. *Teaching Exceptional Children, 30*(6), 20–25.

Smith, D. D., and Lovitt, T. C. (1982). *The computational arithmetic program.* Austin, TX: PRO-ED.

Smith, E. M., and Alley, G. R. (1981). *The effect of teaching sixth graders with learning difficulties a strategy for solving verbal math problems* (Research Report No. 39). Institute for Research in Learning Disabilities.

Smith, F., and Goodman, K. S. (1971). On the psycholinguistic method of teaching reading. *Elementary School Journal, 71,* 177–181.

Snell, M. E., and Janney, R. J. (2000). *Collaborative teaming.* Baltimore, MD: Paul H. Brooks Publishing.

Snow, C. E., Burns, M. S., and Griffin, P. (Eds.) (1998). *Preventing reading difficulties in young children.* Washington, DC: National Academy Press.

Sobol, M. P., Earn, B. M., Bennett, D., and Humphries, T. (1983). A categorical analysis of the social attributions of learning disabled children. *Journal of Abnormal Child Psychology, 11*(2), 217–228.

Sonnabend, T. (1985). Noncareer mathematics: The mathematics we all need. In C. R. Hirsch and M. J. Zweng (Eds.), *The secondary school mathematics curriculum* (pp. 107–118). Reston, VA: National Council of Teachers of Mathematics.

Spalding, R. B., and Spalding, W. T. (1990). *The writing road to reading* (4th ed.). New York: Quill.

Spangenberg-Urbschat, K., and Pritchard, R. (1994). *Kids come in all languages: Reading instruction for ESL students.* Newark, DE: International Reading Association.

Spargo, E., Williston, G. R., and Browning, L. (1980). *Time readings: Book one.* Providence, RI: Jamestown Publishers.

Special Education Report. (1997). *More IDEA students receiving mainstream instruction, 23*(26), p. 3. Alexandria, VA: Capitol Publications Inc.

Spector, J. E. (1995). Phonemic awareness training: Applications of principles of direct instruction. *Reading and Writing Quarterly: Overcoming Learning Difficulties, 11,* 37–51.

Speece, D. L., MacDonald, V., Kilsheimer, L., and Krist, J. (1997). Research to practice: Preservice teachers reflect on reciprocal teaching. *Learning Disabilities Research and Practice, 12,* 177–187.

Spiro, R. J. (1980). Constructive processes in prose comprehension and recall. In R. J. Spiro, B. C. Bruce, and W. F. Brewer (Eds.), *Theoretical issues in reading comprehension* (pp. 245–276). Hillsdale, NJ: Erlbaum.

Spivack, G., Platt, J. J., and Shure, M. B. (1976). *The problem solving approach to adjustment: A guide to research and intervention.* San Francisco: Jossey-Bass.

Sridhar, D., and Vaughn, S. (2000). Bibliotherapy for all. *Teaching Exceptional Children, 33* (2), 74–82.

Stahl, S. A., Hare, V. C., Sinatra, R., and Gregory, J. F. (1991). Defining the role of prior knowledge and vocabulary in reading comprehension: The retiring of number 41. *Journal of Reading Behavior, 23,* 487–508.

Stahl, S. A., and Miller, P. D. (1989). Whole language and language experience approaches for beginning reading: A quantitative research synthesis. *Review of Educational Research, 59,* 87–116.

Stahl, S. A., Pagnucco, J. R., and Suttles, C. W. (1996). First graders' reading and writing instruction in traditional and process-oriented classes. *The Journal of Educational Research, 89,* 131–144.

Stainback, S., and Stainback, W. (1992). *Curriculum consideration in inclusive classrooms: Facilitating learning for all students.* Baltimore, MD: Brooks.

Stallings, J. (1975). Relationships between classroom instructional practices and child development (Rep. No. PLEDE-C-75). Menlo Park, CA: Stanford Research Institute. ERIC Document Reproduction Service No. ED 110 200.

Stallings, J. S., and Kaskowitz, D. H. (1974). *Follow through classroom observation evaluation.* Menlo Park, CA: Stanford Research Institute.

Stanovich, K. (1986). Cognitive processes and the reading problems of learning-disabled children: Evaluating the assumption of specificity. In J. K. Torgesen and B. Y. L. Wong (Eds.), *Psychological and educational perspectives on learning disabilities* (pp. 85–131). Orlando, FL: Academic Press.

Stanovich, K. I. (1992). Speculations on the causes and consequences of individual differences in early reading acquisition. In P. B. Gough, L. D. Ehri, and R. Treiman (Eds.). *Reading acquisition* (pp. 307–342). Mahwah, NJ: Erlbaum Associates.

Stauffer, R. G. (1969). *Directing reading maturity as a cognitive process.* New York: Harper and Row.

Stauffer, R. G. (1970). *The language-experience approach to the teaching of reading.* New York: Harper and Row.

Stauffer, R. G. (1976). *Teaching reading as a thinking process.* New York: Harper and Row.

Stein, N. L., and Glenn, C. G. (1979). An analysis of story comprehension in elementary school children. In R. O. Freedle (Ed.), *New directions in discourse processing* (vol. II, pp. 53–120). Norwood, NJ: Ablex.

Stephens, T. (1977). *Teaching skills to children with learning and behavior problems.* Columbus, OH: Merrill.

Stern, C. (1965). *Structural arithmetic.* Boston: Houghton Mifflin.

Stevens, K. B., and Schuster, J. W. (1987). Effects of a constant time delay procedure on the written spelling performance of a learning disabled student. *Learning Disability Quarterly, 10,* 9–16.

Stevens, K. B., and Schuster, J. W. (1988). Time delay: Systematic instruction for academic tasks. *Remedial and Special Education, 9*(5), 16–21.

Stevens, R. J., and Slavin, R. E. (1995). Effects of cooperative learning approach in reading and writing on academically handicapped and nonhandicapped students. *Elementary School Journal, 95*(3), 1–25.

Stewart, J. C. (1986). *Counseling parents of exceptional children* (2nd ed.). Columbus, OH: Merrill.

Stires, S. (Ed.) (1991). *With promise: Redefining reading and writing for "special students."* Portsmouth, NH: Heinemann.

Stokes, S. M. (1989). LD students and language experience. *Journal of Language Experience, 10*(2), 19–23.

Stone, W. C., and LaGreca, A. M. (1984). Comprehension of nonverbal communication: A reexamination of the social competencies of learning disabled children. *Journal of Abnormal Child Psychology, 12*(4), 505–518.

Stone, W. L., and LaGreca, A. M. (1990). The social status of children with learning disabilities: A reexamination. *Journal of Learning Disabilities, 23* (1), 32–37.

Stratton, B. D., Grindler, M. C., and Postell, C. M. (1992). Discovering oneself. *Middle School Journal, 24,* 42–43.

Strecker, S., Roser, N., and Martinez. N. (1998). Toward understanding oral reading fluency. In T. Shanahan and F. Rodriquez-Brown (Eds.), *Forty-seventh yearbook of the National Reading Conference* (pp. 295–310). Chicago, IL: The National Reading Conference.

Strichart, S. S., Mangrum II, C. T., and Iannuzzi, P. (1998). *Teaching study skills and strategies to students with learning disabilities, attention deficit disorders, or spcial needs* (2nd ed.). Boston: Allyn and Bacon.

Strickland, B. B., and Turnbull, A. P. (1990). *Developing and implementing individual education programs* (3rd ed.). Columbus, OH: Merrill.

Sullivan, P., (1992). *ESL in context.* New York: Corwin Press.

Sulzby, E., and Teale, W. H. (1991). Emergent literacy. In R. Barr, M. L. Kamil, P. B. Mosenthal, and P. D. Pearson (Eds.), *Handbook of reading research* (2nd ed., pp. 727–757). New York: Longman.

Sulzer-Azaroff, B., and Mayer, G. R. (1991). *Behavior analysis for lasting change.* Fort Worth, TX: Holt, Rinehart and Winston.

Sundbye, N. (1987). Text explicitness and inferential questioning: Effects on story understanding and recall. *Reading Research Quarterly, 22,* 82–98.

Suritsky, S. K., and Hughes, C. A. (1996). Notetaking strategy instruction. In D. D. Deshler, E. S. Ellis, and B. K. Lenz (Authors), *Teaching adolescents with learning disabilities* (2nd ed., pp. 267–312). Denver: Love.

Suydam, M. N. (1982). *The use of calculators in precollege education: Fifth annual state-of-the-art review.* Columbus, OH: Calculator Information Center. (ERIC Document Reproduction Service no. ED206454.).

Suydam, M. N., and Weaver, J. F. (1977). Research on problem solving: Implications for elementary-school classrooms. *Arithmetic Teacher, 25,* 40–42.

Swafford, K. M., and Reed, V. A. (1986). Language and learning-disabled children. In V. A. Reed (Ed.), *An introduction to children with language disorders* (pp. 105–128). New York: Macmillan.

Swank, L. K., and Catts, H. W. (1994). Phonological awareness and written word decoding. *Language, Speech, and Hearing Services in Schools, 25,* 9–14.

Swanson, H. L. (1985). Verbal coding deficits in learning disabled readers. In S. J. Ceci (Ed.), *Handbook of cognitive, social and neuropsychological aspects of learning disabilities* (vol. 1, pp. 203–228). Hillsdale, NJ: Erlbaum.

Swanson, H. L. (1987). Information processing theory and learning disabilities: An overview. *Journal of Learning Disabilities, 20*(1), 3–7.

Swanson, H. L. (1991). Learning disabilities, distinctive encoding, and hemispheric resources: An information-processing perspective. In J. E. Obrzut and G. W. Hynd (Eds.), *Neuropsychological foundations of learning disabilities* (pp. 241–280). San Diego, CA: Academic Press.

Swanson, H. L. (1996). Information processing: An introduction. In D. K. Reid, W. P. Hresko, and H. L. Swanson (Eds.), *Cognitive approaches to learning disabilities* (3rd ed., pp. 251–286). Austin, TX: PRO-ED.

Swanson, H. L. (1999a). Reading research for students with LD: A meta-analysis of intervention outcomes. *Journal of Learning Disabilities, 32,* 504–532.

Swanson, H. L. (1999b). Instructional components that predict treatment outcomes for students with learning disabilities: Support for a combined strategy and direct instruction model. *Learning Disabilities Research and Practice, 14*(3), 129–140.

Swanson, H. L., and Cooney, J. B. (1996). Learning disabilities and memory. In D. K. Reid, W. P. Hresko, and H. L. Swanson (Eds.), *Cognitive approaches to learning disabilities* (3rd ed., pp. 287–315). Austin, TX: PRO-ED.

Swanson, H. L., with, Hoskyn, M., and Lee, C. (1999). *Intervention for students with learning disabilities: A meta-analysis of treatment outcomes.* New York: Guilford Press.

Swanson, H. L., and Trahan, M. F. (1992). Learning disabled readers' comprehension of computer-mediated text: The influence of working memory, metacognition, and attribution. *Learning Disabilities Research and Practice, 7,* 75–86.

Swanson, M., McBurnett, K., Wigal, T., Pfiffner, L., Lerner, M., Williams, L., Christian, D., Tamm. L., Willcutt, E., Crowley, K., Clevenger, W., Khouzam, N., Woo, C., Crinella, F., and Fisher, T. (1993). Effect of stimulant medication on children with attention deficit disorder: A "review of reviews." *Exceptional Children, 60,* 154–162.

Tangel, D. M., and Blachman, B. A. (1992). Effect of phoneme awareness instruction on kindergarten children's invented spelling. *Journal of Reading Behavior, 24,* 233–261.

Tangel, D. M. and Blachman, B. A. (1995). Effect of phoneme awareness instruction on the invented spelling of first-grade children: A one-year follow-up. *Journal of Reading Behavior, 27,* 153–185.

Tarver, S. G., Hallahan, D. P., Kauffman, J. M., and Ball, D. W. (1976). Verbal rehearsal and selective attention in children with learning disabilities: A development lag. *Journal of Experimental Child Psychology, 22,* 375–385.

Taylor, R. (1980). *The computer in the school: Tutor, tool, tutee.* New York: Teachers College Press.

Teicher, J. D. (1973). A solution to the chronic problem of living: Adolescent attempted suicide. In J. C. Schoolar (Ed.), *Current issues in adolescent psychiatry* (pp. 129–147). New York: Brunner/Mazel.

Tharp, R., Estrada, P., Dalton, S. S., and Yamauchi, L. (1999). *Teaching transformed: Achieving Excellence, Fairness, Inclusion, and Harmony.* Boulder, CO: Westview Press.

Tharp, R. G., and Gallimore, R. (1988). *Rousing minds to life: Teaching, learning, and schooling in social context.* New York: Cambridge University Press.

Thomas, A. (1979). Learned helplessness and expectancy factors: Implications for research in learning disabilities. *Review of Education Research, 49*(2), 208–221.

Thomas, K. (1978). The directed inquiry activity: An instructional procedure for content reading. *Reading Improvement, 15,* 138–140.

Thomkins, G. E., and Friend, M. (1986). On your mark, get set, write! *Teaching Exceptional Children, 18*(2), 82–89.

Thompson, M. (1977). *The effects of spelling pattern training on the spelling behavior of primary elementary students.* Unpublished doctoral dissertation, University of Pittsburgh.

Thorne, M. T. (1978). "Payment for reading": The use of the *Corrective Reading* scheme" with junior high maladjusted boys. *Remedial Education, 13*(2), 87–90.

Thornton, C. A. (1978). Emphasizing thinking strategies in basic fact instruction. *Journal for Research in Mathematics Education,* 215–227.

Thornton, C. A., and Toohey, M. A. (1985). Basic math facts: Guidelines for teaching and learning. *Learning Disabilities Focus, 1*(1), 44–57.

Thornton, C. A., Tucker, B. F., Dossey, J. A., and Bazik, E. F. (1983). *Teaching mathematics to children with special needs.* Menlo Park, CA: Addison-Wesley.

Thorpe, H. W., and Borden, K. F. (1985). The effect of multisensory instruction upon the on-task behavior and word reading accuracy of learning disabled students. *Journal of Learning Disabilities, 18,* 279–286.

Tierney, R. J., Carter, M. A., and Desai, L. E. (1991). *Portfolio assessment in the reading-writing classroom.* Norwood, MA: Christopher-Gordon.

Tierney, R. J., Readence, J. E., and Dishner, E. K. (1980). *Reading strategies and practices: Guide for improving instruction.* Boston: Allyn and Bacon.

Tierney, R. J., Readence, J. E., and Dishner, E. K. (1995). *Reading strategies and practices: A compendium* (4th ed.). Boston: Allyn and Bacon.

Tikunoff, W. J. (1983). *Compatibility of the SBIF features with other research instruction of LEP students.* San Francisco: Far West Laboratory.

Tindal, G., and Nolet, V. (1996). Serving students in middle school content classes: A heuristic study of critical variables linking instruction and assessment. *Journal of Special Education, 29,* 414–432.

Tindal, G. A., and Marston, D. B. (1990). *Classroom-based assessment: Evaluating instructional outcomes.* New York: Merrill/Macmillan.

Tobias, S. (1978). Achievement treatment interactions. *Review of Educational Research, 46,* 61–74.

Tollefson, N., Tracy, D. B., Johnen, E. P. Buenning, M., and Farmer, A. (1981). *Implementing goal setting activities with LD adolescents* (Res. Rep. No. 48). Lawrence: The University of Kansas Institute for Research in Learning Disabilities.

Tompkins, G. E., and McGee, L. M. (1993). *Teaching reading with literature: Case studies to action plans.* New York: Merrill/Macmillan.

Toolan, J. M. (1981). Depression and suicide in children: An overview. *American Journal of Psychotherapy, 35*(3), 311–323.

Topping, K., and Eli, S. (1998). *Peer-assisted learning.* Mahwah, NJ: Erlbaum.

Torgesen, J. K. (1978). Performance of reading disabled children on serial memory tasks: A review. *Reading Research Quarterly, 19,* 57–87.

Torgesen, J. K. (1982). The learning disabled child as an inactive learner: Educational implications. *Topics in Learning and Learning Disabilities, 2*(1), 45–52.

Torgesen, J. K. (1985). Memory processes in reading disabled children. *Journal of Learning Disabilities, 18*(6), 350–357.

Torgesen, J. K. (1997). The prevention and remediation of reading: Evaluating what we know from research. *Journal of Academic Language Therapy, 1,* 10–52.

Torgesen, J. K. (1999). Assessment and instruction for phonemic awareness and word recognition skills. In H. W. Catts and A. G. Kamhi (Eds.), *Language and reading disabilities* (pp. 128–153). Boston: Allyn and Bacon.

Torgesen, J. K. (2000). Individual differences in response to early interventions in reading: The lingering problem of treatment resisters. *Learning Disabilities Research and Practice, 15,* 55–64.

Torgesen, J. K., and Barker, T. A. (1995). Computers as aids in the prevention and remediation of reading disabilities. *Learning Disability Quarterly, 18,* 76–88.

Torgesen, J. K., and Burgess, S. R. (1998). Consistency of reading-related phonological processes throughout early childhood: Evidence from longitudinal, correlational and instructional studies. In J. Metsala and L. Ehri (Eds.). *Word recognition in beginning literacy* (pp. 161–188). Mahwah, NJ: Erlbaum Associates.

Torgesen, J. K., and Davis, C. (1996). Individual difference variables that predict response to training in phonological awareness. *Journal of Experimental Child Psychology, 63,* 1–21.

Torgesen, J. K., and Horen, N. M. (1992). Using computers to assist in reading instruction for children with learning disabilities. In S. A. Vogel (Ed.), *Educational alternative for students with learning disabilities* (pp. 159–181). New York: Springer-Verlag.

Torgesen, J. K., and Licht, B. G. (1983). The learning disabled child as an inactive learner: Retrospect and prospects. In J. D. McKinney and L. Feagans (Eds.), *Current topics in learning disabilities.* Norwood, NJ: Ablex.

Torgesen, J. K., and Mathes, P. G. (2000). *A basic guide to understanding, assessing, and teaching phonological awareness.* Austin, TX: PRO-ED.

Torgesen, J. K., Rashotte, C. A., Greenstein, J., Houck, G., and Portes, P. (1987). Academic difficulties of learning disabled children who perform poorly on memory span tasks. In H. L. Swanson (Ed.), *Advances in learning and behavioral disabilities* (Supplement 2, pp. 305–333). Greenwich, CT: JAI Press.

Torgesen, J. K., Wagner, R. K., and Rashotte, C. A. (1994). Longitudinal studies of phonological processing and reading. *Journal of Learning Disabilities 19,* 623–630.

Torgesen, J. K., Wagner, R. K., and Rashotte, C. A. (1997). Approaches to the prevention and remediation of phonologically based reading disabilities. In B. Blachman (Ed.), *Foundations of reading acquisition and dyslexia: Implications for early intervention.* Mahwah, NJ: Erlbaum Associates.

Torgesen, J. K., Wagner, R. K., Rashotte, C. A., Alexander, A. W., and Conway, T. (1997). Preventive and remedial interventions for children with severe reading disabilities. *Learning Disabilities: A Multidisciplinary Journal, 8*(1), 51–61.

Towell, J., and Wink, J. (1993). *Strategies for monolingual teachers in multilingual classrooms.* Turlock, CA: California State University, Stanislaus. (ERIC Document Reproduction Service No. ED 359 797)

Townsend, M. A. R., and Clarihew, A. (1989). Facilitating children's comprehension through the use of advance organizers. *Journal of Reading Behavior, 21,* 15–36.

Tralli, R., Colombo, B., Deshler, D., and Schumaker, J. B. (1996). The strategies intervention model: A model for supported inclusion at the secondary level. *Remedial and Special Education, 17,* 204–216.

Traub, N. (2000). *Recipe for reading: A structured approach to linguistics.* Cambridge, MA: Educators Publishing Service.

Trelease, J. (1989). Jim Trelease speaks on reading aloud to children. *The Reading Teacher, 43,* 200–206.

Trelease, J. (1995). *The new read-aloud handbook* (3rd ed.). New York: Penguin.

Tremt, S., Artilles, A. J., and Englert, C. S. (1998). From deficit thinking to social constructivism: A review of theory, research, and practice in special education. In P. D. Pearson and A. Iran-Nejad (Eds.), *Review of research in education* (pp. 277–307). Washington, DC: American Educational Research Association.

Troia, G. A., Harris, K. R., and Graham, S. (1999). Teaching students with learning disabilities to mindfully plan when writing. *Exceptional Children, 65*(2), 235–252.

Tulving, E. (1993). What is episodic memory: *Current Directions in Psychological Science, 2,* 67–70.

Tunnell, M. O., and Jacobs, J. S. (1989). Using "real" books: Research findings on literature based reading instruction. *The Reading Teacher, 42,* 470–477.

Tur-Kaspa, H., and Bryan, T. (1994). Social information-processing skills of students with learning disabilities. *Learning Disabilities Research and Practice, 9*(1), 12–23.

Turnbull, A. P., Blue-Banning, M. J., Anderson, E. L., Turnbull, H. R., Seaton, K. A., and Dinas, P. A. (1996). Enhancing self-determination through Group Action Planning: A holistic emphasis. In D. J. Sands and M. L. Wehmeyer (Ed.), *Self-determination across the life span: Independence and choice for people with disabilities* (pp. 237–256). Baltimore, MD: Paul H. Brookes Publishing Co.

Turnbull, A. P., and Turnbull, H. R. (1990). *Families, professionals, and exceptionality: A special partnership* (2nd ed.). Columbus, OH: Merrill.

Turnbull, H. R., Turnbull, A. P., and Wheat, M. J. (1982). Assumptions about parental participation: A legislative history. *Exceptional Education Quarterly, 3*(2), 1–8.

Tylka, T. L., and Subich, L. M. (1999). Exploring the construct validity of the eating disorder continuum. *Journal of Counseling Psychology, 46*(2), 268–76.

Utley, B. L., Zigmond, M., and Strain, P. S. (1987). How various forms of data affect teacher analysis of student performance. *Exceptional Children 53*(5), 411–422.

Vacca, R. T., and Vacca, J. A. (1999). *Content area reading: Literacy and learning across the curriculum.* New York: Longman.

Vandergrift, K. (1980). *Child and story.* New York: Neal-Schuman.

Van Luit, J. E. H., and Naglieri, J. A. (1999). Effectiveness of the MASTER program for teaching special children multiplication and division. *Journal of Learning Disabilities, 32*(2), 98–107.

Van Reusen, A. K., and Bos, C. S. (1990). I PLAN: Helping students communicate in planning conferences. *Teaching Exceptional Children, 22,* 30–32.

Van Reusen, A. K., Bos, C. S., Schumaker, J. B., and Deshler, D. D. (1994). *The self-advocacy strategy for education and transition planning.* Lawrence, KS: Edge Enterprises.

VanWagenen, M. A., Williams, R. L., and McLaughlin, T. F. (1994). Use of assisted reading to improve reading rate, word accuracy, and comprehension with ESL Spanish-speaking students. *Perceptual and Motor Skills, 79,* 227–230.

Vatter, T. (1994). Civic mathematics: A real-life general mathematics course. *The Mathematics Teacher, 87,* 396–401.

Vaughn, S., Bos, C. S., and Lund, K. A. (1986). . . . But they can do it in my room: Strategies for promoting generalization. *Teaching Exceptional Children, 18,* 176–180.

Vaughn, S., Bos, C. S., and Schumm, J. S. (1997). *Teaching mainstreamed, diverse, and at-risk students in the general education classroom.* Boston: Allyn and Bacon.

Vaughn, S., Cohen, J., Fournier, L., Gervasi, J., Levasseur, T., and Newton, S. (1984). *Teaching interpersonal problem solving to behavior disordered adolescents.* Paper presented at Council for Exceptional Children, Washington, DC.

Vaughn, S., Elbaum, B. E., Schumm, J. S., and Hughes, M. T. (1998). Social outcomes for students with and without learning disabilities in inclusive classrooms. *Journal of Learning Disabilities, 31*(5), 428–436.

Vaughn, S., Gersten, R., and Chard, D. J. (2000). The underlying message in LD intervention research: Findings from research syntheses. *Exceptional Children, 67*(1), 99–114.

Vaughn, S., Haager, D., Hogan, A., and Kouzekanani, K. (1992). Self-concept and peer acceptance in students with learning disabilities: A four to five year prospective study. *Journal of Educational Psychology, 84,* 43–50.

Vaughn, S., and Hogan, A. (1990). Social competence and learning disabilities: A prospective study. In H. L. Swanson and B. K. Keogh (Eds.), *Learning Disabilities: Theoretical and research issues* (pp. 175–191). Hillsdale, NJ: Erlbaum.

Vaughn, S., Hogan, A., Kouzekanani, K., and Shapiro, S. (1990). Peer acceptance, self-perceptions, and social skills of LD students prior to identification. *Journal of Educational Psychology, 82*(1), 1–6.

Vaughn, S., and Klingner, J. (1999). Teaching reading comprehension through collaborative strategic reading. *Intervention in School and Clinic, 34*(5), 284–292.

Vaughn, S., Klingner, J. K., and Schumm, J. S. (1996). *Collaborative strategic reading.* Miami: School-Based Research, University of Miami.

Vaughn, S., and LaGreca, A. M. (1992). Beyond greetings and making friends: Social skills from a broader perspective. In B. Y. L. Wong (Ed.), *Contemporary intervention research in learning disabilities: An international perspective* (pp. 96–114). New York: Springer-Verlag.

Vaughn, S., and Lancelotta, G. X. (1990). Teaching interpersonal skills to poorly accepted students: Peer-pairing versus non-peer-pairing. *Journal of School Psychology, 28,* 181–188.

Vaughn, S., Lancelotta, G. X., and Minnis, S. (1988). Social strategy training and peer involvement: Increasing peer acceptance of a female, LD student. *Learning Disabilities Focus, 4*(1), 32–37.

Vaughn, S., McIntosh, R., Schumm, J. S., Haager, D., and Callwood, D. (1993). Social status and peer acceptance revisited. *Learning Disabilities Research and Practice, 8,* 82–88.

Vaughn, S., McIntosh, R., and Spencer-Rowe, J. (1991). Peer rejection is a stubborn thing: Increasing peer acceptance of rejected students with learning disabilities. *Learning Disabilities Research and Practice, 6*(2), 83–88, 152–157.

Vaughn, S. and Schumm, J. S. (1994). Middle school teachers' planning for students with learning disabilities. *Remedial and Special Education, 15,* 152–161.

Vaughn, S., and Schumm, J. S. (1995). Responsible inclusion for students with learning disabilities. *Journal of Learning Disabilities 28*(5), 264–70.

Vaughn, S., and Schumm, J. S. (1996). Classroom ecologies: Classroom interactions and implications for inclusion of students with learning disabilities. In D. L. Speece and B. Keogh (Eds.), *Research on classroom ecologies: Implications for inclusion of children with learning disabilities* (pp. 107–124). Mahwah, NJ: Lawrence Erlbaum.

Vaughn, S., Schumm, J. S., and Arguelles, M. E., (1997). The ABCDE's of co-teaching. *Teaching Exceptional Children, 30*(2), 4–10.

Vaughn, S., Schumm, J. S., and Forgan, J. W. (1995). Instructing students with high-incidence disabilities in the general education classroom. In J. A. Welter (Ed.), *Communicating students learning* (pp. 12.269–12.307). Alexandria, VA: Association for Supervision and Curriculum Development.

Vaughn, S., Schumm, J. S., Jallad, B., Slusher, J., and Saumell, L. (1996). Teachers' views of inclusion. *Learning Disabilities Research and Practice, 11*(2), 96–106.

Vaughn, S., Schumm, J. S., Klingner, J., and Saumell, L. (1995). Students' views of instructional practices: Implications for inclusion. *Learning Disability Quarterly, 18,* 236–248.

Vaughn, S., Schumm, J. S., and Kouzekanani, K. (1993). What do students with learning disabilities think when their general education teachers make adaptations? *Journal of Learning Disabilities, 26,* 545–555.

Vaughn, S., Schumm, J. S., Niarhos, F. J., and Gordon, J. (1993). Students' perceptions of two hypothetical teachers' instructional adaptations for low achievers. *Elementary School Journal, 94,* 87–102.

Vaughn, S., Schumm, J. S., Niarhos, F., and Daugherty, T. (1993). What do students think when teachers make adaptations? *Teaching and Teacher Education, 9,* 107–118.

Vaughn, S., Zaragoza, N., Hogan, A., and Walker (1993). A four year longitudinal investigation of the social skills and behavior problems of students with learning disabilities. *Journal of Learning Disabilities, 26,* 353–424.

Vaughn, S. R. (1985). Why teach social skills to learning disabled students? *Journal of Learning Disabilities, 18*(10), 588–591.

Vaughn, S. R. (1987). TLC—Teaching, learning, and caring: Teaching interpersonal problem solving skills to emotionally disturbed adolescents. *Pointer, 31,* 25–30.

Vaughn, S. R., and Bos, C. S. (1987). Knowledge and perception of the resource room. The students' perspective. *Journal of Learning Disabilities, 20,* 218–223.

Vaughn, S. R., Bos, C. S., Harrell, J., and Lasky, B. (1988). Parent participation in the initial placement/IEP conference ten years after mandated involvement. *Journal of Learning Disabilities, 21,* 82–89.

Vaughn, S. R., Levine, L., and Ridley, C. A. (1986). *PALS: Problem solving and affective learning strategies.* Chicago: Science Research Associates.

Vaughn, S. R., Ridley, C. A., and Bullock, D. D. (1984). Interpersonal problem solving skills training with aggressive young children. *Journal of Applied Developmental Psychology, 5,* 213–223.

Vaughn, S. R., Ridley, C. A., and Cox, J. (1983). Evaluating the efficacy of an interpersonal skills training program with children who are mentally retarded. *Education and Training of the Mentally Retarded, 18*(3), 191–196.

Veatch, J. (1991). *Whole language and its predecessors: Commentary.* Paper presented at the annual meeting of the College Reading Association. ERIC Document 341–035.

Vellutino, F. R., and Scanlon, D. M. (1987). Phonological coding, phonological awareness, and reading ability: Evidence from a longitudinal and experimental study. *Merrill-Palmer Quarterly, 33,* 321–363.

Vitale, M., Medland, M., Romance, N., and Weaver, H. P. (1993). Accelerating reading and thinking skills of low-achieving elementary students: Implications for curricular change. *Effective School Practices, 12*(1), 26–31.

Vogel, S. (1983). A qualitative analysis of morphological ability in learning disabled and achieving children. *Journal of Learning Disabilities, 16,* 416–420.

Voltz, D. L., Elliott, R. N., and Cobb, H. B. (1994). Collaborative teacher roles: Special and general educators. *Journal of Learning Disabilities, 27,* 527–535.

Vygotsky, L. S. (1962). *Thought and language* (E. Hanfmann and G. Vakar, eds. and trans.). Cambridge, MA: MIT Press.

Vygotsky, L. S. (1978). *Mind in society: The development of higher psychological processes.* Cambridge, MA: Harvard University Press.

Wagner, R. K., Torgesen, J. K., and Rashotte, C. A. (1994). The development of reading-related phonological processing abilities: New evidence of bi-directional causality from a latent variable longitudinal study. *Developmental Psychology, 30,* 73–87.

Walker, D., and Williamson, R. (1995). Computers and adolescents with emotional/behavior disorders. *Closing the Gap, 14*(2), 10–11, 16–17, 29.

Wallace, G., and Kauffman, J. M. (1986). *Teaching students with learning and behavior problems* (3rd ed.). Columbus, OH: Merrill.

Wallach, G. P. (1984). Later language learning: Syntactic structures and strategies. In G. P. Wallach and K. G. Butler (Eds.), *Language learning disabilities in school-age children* (pp. 82–102). Baltimore: Williams and Wilkins.

Wallach, G. P., and Miller, L. (1988). *Language intervention and academic success.* Boston: Little, Brown—College-Hill.

Walther-Thomas, C., and Brownell, M. (2000). An interview with Dr. Janice Bulgren. *Intervention in School and Clinic, 35,* 232–236.

Wannan, G., and Fombonne, E. (1998). Gender differences in rates and correlates of suicidal behavior amongst child psychiatric outpatients. *Journal of Adolescence, 21*(4), 371–81.

Warger, C. L., and Pugach, M. C. (1996). Forming partnerships around curriculum. *Educational Leadership, 53*(5), 62–65.

Warren, J. (1970). *Phonetic generalizations to aid spelling instruction at the fifth-grade level.* Unpublished doctoral dissertation, Boston University.

Warren, R. M., and Warren, R. P. (1970). Auditory illusions and confusions. *Scientific American, 223,* 30–36.

Watkins, M. W., and Webb, C. (1981). Computer-assisted instruction with learning disabled students. *Educational Computer Magazine, 1*(3), 24–27.

Watkins, T. J. (1997). Teacher communications, child achievement, and parent traits in parent involvement models, *Journal of Educational Research, 91*(1), 3–14.

Watson, D. (1997). Beyond decodable texts: Supportable and workable literature. *Language Arts, 74,* 635–643.

Watson, D., and Crowley, P. (1988). How can we implement a whole-language approach? In C. Weaver (Ed.), *Reading process and practice.* Portsmouth, NH: Heinemann.

Weaver, C. (1990). *Understanding whole language: Principles and practices.* Portsmouth, NH: Heinemann.

Weaver, C. (Ed.) (1998). *Reconsidering a balanced approach to reading.* Urbana, IL: National Council of Teachers of English.

Wehmeyer, M. L., Agran, M., and Hughes, C. (1997). *Teaching self-determination to students with disabilities: Basic skills for successful transition.* Baltimore, MD: Paul H. Brookes Publishing.

Wehmeyer, M. L., and Kelchner, K. (1995). *Whose future is it anyway? A student-directed transition planning program.* Arlington, TX: The Arc National Headquarters.

Weinstein, G., and Cooke, N. L. (1992). The effects of two repeated reading interventions on generalizations of fluency. *Learning Disability Quarterly, 15,* 21–28.

Weintraub, N., and Graham, S. (1998). Writing legibly and quickly: A study of children's ability to adjust their handwriting to meet common classroom demands. *Learning Disability Research & Practice, 13*(3), 146–152.

Welch, M. (November/December 1983). Social skills in the resource room. *ACLD Newsbriefs* (No. 152).

Welch, M. (1992). The PLEASE strategy: A metacognitive learning strategy for improving the paragraph writing of students with mild learning disabilities. *Learning Disability Quarterly, 15,* 119–128.

Wells, G. (1973). *Coding manual of the description of child speech.* Bristol, England: University of Bristol School of Education.

Wepner, S. B., and Feeley, J. T. (1993). *Moving forward with literature: Basals, books, and beyond.* New York: Merrill/Macmillan.

West, G. F. (1978). *Teaching reading skills in content areas: A practical guide to the construction of student exercises.* Oviedo, FL: Sandpiper Press.

West, J. F., and Cannon, G. S. (1988). Essential collaborative consultation competencies for regular and special educators. *Journal of Learning Disabilities, 21,* 56–63, 28.

West, J. F., and Idol, L. (1990). Collaborative consultation in the education of mildly handicapped and at-risk students. *Remedial and Special Education, 11*(1), 22–31.

West, J. F., Idol, L., and Cannon, G. (1989). *Collaboration in the schools: An inservice and preservice curriculum for teachers, support staff, and administrators.* Austin, TX: PRO-ED.

Whinnery, K. W. (1995). Perceptions of students with learning disabilities: Inclusion versus pull-out services. *Preventing School Failure, 40*(1), 5–9.

White, B. (1975). Critical influences in the origins of competence. *Merrill-Palmer Quarterly, 2,* 243–266.

Wicks-Nelson, R., and Israel, A. L. (1984). *Behavior disorders of childhood.* Englewood Cliffs, NJ: Prentice-Hall.

Widomski, C. L. (1983). Building foundations for reading comprehension. *Reading World, 22,* 306–313.

Wiener, H., Harris, P. J., and Shirer, C. (1990). Achievement and social-behavioral correlates of peer status in learning disabled children. *Learning Disability Quarterly, 13,* 114–127.

Wiener, J., and Harris, P. J. (1997). Evaluation of an individualized, context-based social skills training program for children with learning disabilities. *Learning Disabilities Research & Practice, 12*(1), 40–53.

Wiig, E. H. (1982). *Let's talk: Developing prosocial communication skills.* Columbus, OH: Merrill.

Wiig, E. H. (1992). Strategy training for people with language-learning disabilities. In L. Meltzer (Ed.), *Strategy assessment and training for students with learning disabilities: From theory to practice* (pp. 167–194). Austin, TX: PRO-ED.

Wiig, E. H., and Bray, C. M. (1983). *Let's talk for children.* Columbus, OH: Merrill.

Wiig, E. H., Freedman, E., and Secord, W. A. (1992). Developing words and concepts in the classroom: A holistic-thematic approach. *Intervention in School and Clinic, 27,* 278–285.

Wiig, E. H., and Secord, W. A. (1998). Language disabilities in school-age children and youth. In G. H. Shames, E. H. Wiig, and W. A. Secord (Eds.), *Human communication disorders* (5th ed., pp. 212–247). New York: Merrill.

Wiig, E. H., and Semel, E. M. (1984). *Language assessment and intervention for the learning disabled* (2nd ed.). Columbus, OH: Merrill.

Wiig, E. H., and Wilson, C. C. (1994). Is a question a question? Passage understanding by preadolescents with learning disabilities. *Language, Speech, and Hearing Services in Schools, 25,* 241–249.

Wilkinson, I. A. G., and Anderson, R. C. (1995). Sociocognitive processes in guided silent reading: A microanalysis of small-group lessons. *Reading Research Quarterly, 30*(4), 710–740.

Will, M. (1984). *OSERS programming for the transition of youth with disabilities: Bridges from school to working life.* Washington, DC: Office of Special Education and Rehabilitative Services.

Williams, F., and Williams, V. (1984). *Microcomputers in elementary education: Perspectives on implementation.* Belmont, CA: Wadsworth.

Williams, J. P. (1998). Improving the comprehension of disabled readers. *Annals of Dyslexia, 48,* 213–238.

Williams, J. P., Brown, L. G., Silverstein, A. K., and deCani, J. S. (1994). An instructional program in comprehension of narrative themes for adolescents with learning disabilities. *Learning Disability Quarterly, 17,* 205–221.

Williams, P. L., Reese, C. M., Campbell, J. R., Mazzeo, J., and Phillips, G. W. (1995). *1994 NAEP reading: A first look.* Washington, DC: Office of Educational Research and Improvement, U.S. Department of Education.

Williams, S. (1990). *I went walking.* New York: Harcourt.

Willig, A. C., and Ortiz, A. A. (1991). The nonbiased individualized educational program: Linking assessment to instruction. In E. V. Hamayan and J. S. Damico (Eds.), *Limiting bias in the assessment of bilingual students* (pp. 281–302). Austin, TX: PRO-ED.

Willman, A. T. (1999). "Hello, Mrs. Willman, it's me!" Keep kids reading over the summer by using voice mail. *The Reading Teacher, 52,* 788–789.

Wilson, B. A. (1996). *Wilson Reading System.* Millbury, MA: Wilson Language Training Corporation.

Wilson, C. L., and Sindelar, P. T. (1991). Direct instruction in math word problems: Students with learning disabilities. *Journal of Learning Disabilities, 23*(1), 23–29.

Wilson, D. R., and David, W. J. (1994). Academic intrinsic motivation and attitudes toward school and learning of learning disabled students. *Learning Disabilities Research and Practice, 9,* 148–156.

Wilson, R., Majsterek, D., and Simmons, D. (1996). The effects of computer-assisted versus teacher-directed instruction on the multiplication performance of elementary students with learning disabilities. *Journal of Learning Disabilities, 29*(4), 382–390.

Wilson, R. M. (2001). *Phonemic awareness and word analysis for teachers: A computerized tutorial* (CD-ROM Format). Upper Saddle River, NJ: Prentice-Hall.

Winton, P. J., and Turnbull, A. P. (1981). Parent involvement as viewed by parents of preschool handicapped children.

Wise, B. W., and Olson, R. K. (1998). Studies of computer-aided remediation of reading disabilities. In C. Hulme and R. Malatesha Joshi (Eds.), *Reading and spelling: Development and disorders* (pp. 473–488). Mahwah, NJ: Erlbaum.

Wolery, M., Cybriwsky, C. A., Gast, D. L., and Boyle-Gast, K. (1991). Use of constant time delay and attentional responses with adolescents. *Exceptional Children, 57,* 462–474.

Wong, B. Y. L. (1979). Increasing retention of main ideas through questioning strategies. *Learning Disability Quarterly, 2*(2), 42–47.

Wong, B. Y. L. (1986). A cognitive approach to teaching spelling. *Exceptional Children, 53,* 169–173.

Wong, B. Y. L. (1987). Directions in future research on metacognition in learning disabilities. In H. L. Swanson (Ed.), *Memory and learning disabilities: Advances in learning and behavioral disabilities* (Supplement 2, pp. 335–356). Greenwich, CT: JAI Press.

Wong, B. Y. L. (1996). *The ABCs of learning disabilities.* San Diego, CA: Academic Press.

Wong, B. Y. L., Butler, D. L., Ficzere, S. A., and Kuperis, S. (1997). Teaching adolescents with learning disabilities and low achievers to plan, write, and revise compare-and-contrast essays. *Learning Disabilities Research & Practice, 12*(1), 2–15.

Wong, B. Y. L., and Jones, W. (1982). Increasing metacomprehension in learning disabled and normally achieving students through self-questioning training. *Learning Disability Quarterly, 5,* 228–240.

Wong, B. Y. L., and Wilson, M. (1984). Investigating awareness of and teaching passage organization in learning disabled children. *Journal of Learning Disabilities, 17*(8), 447–482.

Wong, B. Y. L., and Wong, R. (1980). Role taking skills in normal achieving and learning disabled children. *Learning Disability Quarterly, 3,* 11–18.

Wong, B. Y. L., and Wong, R. (1988). Cognitive interventions for learning disabilities. In K. A. Kavale (Ed.), *Learning disabilities: State of the art and practice* (pp. 141–160). Boston: Little, Brown–College Hill.

Wong, B. Y. L., Wong, R., and Blenkinsop, J. (1989). Cognitive and metacognitive aspects of learning disabled adolescents' composing problems. *Learning Disability Quarterly, 12,* 300–322.

Wong, B. Y. L., Wong, R., Perry, N., and Sawatsky, D. (1986). The efficacy of a self-questioning summarization strategy for use by underachievers and learning disabled adolescents in social studies. *Learning Disabilities Focus, 2*(1), 20–35.

Wood, J. W., and Wooley, J. A. (1986). Adapting textbooks. *The Clearing House, 59,* 332–335.

Wood, K. D., Lapp, D., and Flood, J. (1992). *Guiding readers through the text: A review of study guides.* Newark, DE: International Reading Association.

Woodcock, R. W., Clark, C. R., and Davies, C. O. (1969). *The Peabody rebus reading program.* Circle Pines, MN: American Guidance Service.

Woodward, A., and Elliott, D. L. (1990). Textbook use and teacher professionalism. In D. L. Elliott and A. Woodward (Eds.), *Textbooks and schooling in the United States* (Eighty-ninth yearbook of the National Society for the Study of Education, Part I, pp. 178–193). Chicago: University of Chicago Press.

Woodward, J. (1995). Technology-based research in mathematics for special education. *Focus on Learning Problems in Mathematics, 17*(2), 3–23.

Woodward, J., and Carnine, D. (1993). Uses of technology for mathematics assessment and instruction: Reflection on a decade of innovations. *Journal of Special Education Technology, 12,* 38–48.

Woodward, J., and Gersten, R. (1992). Innovative technology for secondary students with learning disabilities. *Exceptional Children, 58,* 407–421.

Worthy, J. (1996). A matter of interest: Literature that hooks reluctant readers and keeps them reading. *The Reading Teacher, 50,* 204–212

Worthy, J., and Broaddus, K. (in press). Fluency beyond the primary grades: From group performance to silent, independent reading. *The Reading Teacher.*

Wylie, R. E., and Durrell, D. D. (1970). Teaching vowels through phonograms. *Elementary English, 47,* 787–791.

Wysocki, K., and Jenkins, J. R. (1987). Deriving word meanings through morphological generalization. *Reading Research Quarterly, 22,* 66–81.

Xin, Y. P, and Jitendra, A. K. (1999). The effects of instruction in solving mathematical word problems for students with learning problems: A meta-analysis. *The Journal of Special Education, 32*(4), 207–225.

Yauman, B. E. (1980). Special education placement and the self-concepts of elementary school age children. *Learning Disability Quarterly, 3,* 30–35.

Yee, A. (1969). Is the phonetic generalization hypothesis in spelling valid? *Journal of Experimental Education, 37,* 82–91.

Yell, M. L. (1998). *The Law and Special Education.* Upper Saddle River, NJ: Prentice-Hall, Inc.

Yopp, H. K. (1992). Developing phonemic awareness in young children. *The Reading Teacher, 45,* 696–703.

Zaragoza, N., and Vaughn, S. (1992). The effects of process instruction on three second-grade students with different achievement profiles. *Learning Disabilities Research and Practice, 7*(4), 184–193.

Zeno, S. M., Ivens, S. H., Millard, R. T., and Duvvuri, R. (1995). *The educator's word frequency guide.* Brewster, NY: Touchstone Applied Science Associates.

Zinberg, N. E. (1984). *Drug, set, and setting.* New Haven, CT: Yale University Press.

Zorfass, J., Corley, P., and Remz, A. (1994). Helping students with disabilities become writers. *Educational Leadership, 51*(5), 62–66.

Zutell, J. (1993). *Directed spelling thinking activity: A developmental, conceptual approach to advance spelling word knowledge.* Paper presented at the First International and 19th National Conference of the Australian Reading Association, Melbourne, Australia.

Zutell, J., and Rasinski, T. (1989). Reading and spelling connections in third and fifth grade students. *Reading Psychology, 10,* 137–155.

Zutell, J., and Rasinski, T. V. (1991). Training teachers to attend to their students' oral reading fluency. *Theory Into Practice, 30,* 211–217.

Index